AMERICAN GENERATIONS

AMERICAN
GENERATIONS

Who They Are and How They Live

BY THE EDITORS OF NEW STRATEGIST PUBLICATIONS

New Strategist Publications, Inc.

Ithaca, New York

New Strategist Publications, Inc.
P.O. Box 242, Ithaca, New York 14851
800/848-0842; 607/273-0913
www.newstrategist.com

ISBN 978-1-933588-95-7
ISBN 1-933588-95-0

Printed in the United States of America

Table of Contents

List of Tables

Chapter 11. Time Use

Chapter 12. Wealth

List of Charts

Chapter 5. Housing

Chapter 6. Income

Chapter 7. Labor Force

Chapter 8. Living Arrangements

Chapter 9. Population

Chapter 10. Spending

Chapter 11. Time Use

Chapter 12. Wealth

Introduction

In the past, when the pace of change was slow, the concept of generations had little importance for society, public policy, or commerce. But today the world changes rapidly, and people who are as little as ten years apart in age may have very different experiences growing up—which makes them unlike one another in significant ways. *American Generations* reveals the differences and similarities among the generations of Americans.

The population is now fragmented by generation as much as by race and sex, *American Generations* is an important tool for understanding the nation today and tomorrow. The generational profiles contained in this book are of value not only to marketers, but also to social scientists and policy makers. Each generation, after all, makes its demands on public policy just as it does on business. And those seeking to understand societal or consumer change must address how attitudes and values, wants and needs, evolve with generational replacement.

The sixth edition of *American Generations* examines both generations and age groups. Age groups are static, never changing; generations pass through age groups. People aged 40 today are members of Generation X, but in another decade the Millennial generation will occupy the age group. Since each generation has a distinct character, the policy issues, products, services, advertising, and media that resonate with people aged 40 today may not work for 40-year-olds a decade from now.

Explaining generational differences

Several factors account for generational differences. One is education, which greatly influences people's attitudes and values, wants and needs. The generations born after World War II are much better educated than older Americans. This fact alone means that middle-aged and younger generations will think and behave differently from the way their parents did at the same age. Another important difference is the greater degree of diversity among younger generations. Accustomed to a wide variety of cultures, younger generations are more likely to view the nation as a "salad bowl" rather than a melting pot. Technology also divides the generations. The Internet and cell phones are an integral part of the lives of younger generations, setting them apart from their elders.

Differences in attitudes and behavior are not the only factors that make each generation unique. The relative size of the generations affects the age distribution of the population. When generations are of uneven size, as they are today, the social and economic effects can be far-reaching. In the 1950s, for example, schools that had been adequate for educating the relatively small Swing generation suddenly were flooded with students as Boomers arrived. As the last classes of Boomers graduated from high school, public schools had to adapt to the smaller Generation X. Many of them sold their school buildings in the belief that the crush was over. Wrong. Behind Generation X came the much larger Millennial generation, rivaling the Baby Boom in size and straining school budgets and facilities all over again.

This expansion and contraction can catch business and public policy off guard. But it is possible to look down the road and know what is coming. That is what *American Generations* is all about—preparing businesses and policymakers for what lies ahead, helping them plan for the population booms and busts to come as the generations move through the age structure and change our society.

Much of the social change of the past half-century has been caused by "generational replacement." As older generations die and are replaced by new generations, society adopts the attitudes and values of the living generations. From the expanding roles of women to the increased acceptance of cohabitation and casual dress in the workplace, attitudes are changing because new generations are taking over.

Using age group data

Differences among generations are too often buried in statistics that look only at the population as a whole, or divide it by a characteristic such as sex, but not age. Overall, 28 percent of Americans aged 25 or older have a bachelor's degree, but this single statistic fails to tell an important part of the story—there is a distinct generational difference in education. Only 17 percent of the World War II generation has a college degree compared with 32 percent of Generation X. The incomes, labor force participation, living arrangements, spending patterns, and even time use all vary by generation.

Because generations do not always fit easily into the age group data collected by the Census Bureau and other organizations, much of the statistical information presented in this book approximates the generations. Baby Boomers, for example, were aged 43 to 61 in 2007. They do not fit into the standard five- or ten-year age groups, such as 45-to-54-year-olds, for which researchers typically collect data. When generations are split by age groupings, the text of this book discusses the generation that accounts for the majority of the age group's members. In many of the book's tables, New Strategist's editors have estimated the size of each generation, allowing readers to see at a glance the differing educational attainment, household income, living arrangements, and labor force status of the generations.

New to this edition of *American Generations* is a chapter that reveals the major attitudinal differences among the generations, based on 2006 General Social Survey data. The book also contains the latest income, spending, housing, and labor force statistics as well as an updated look at time use based on unpublished 2006 data from the American Time Use Survey.

How to use this book

American Generations is divided into 12 chapters: The Generations, Attitudes, Education, Health, Housing, Income, Labor Force, Living Arrangements, Population, Spending, Time Use, and Wealth. Each chapter includes tables and text describing the most important trends, including what to expect in the future.

Most of the tables in *American Generations* are based on data collected by the federal government, in particular the Census Bureau, the Bureau of Labor Statistics, the National Center for Education Statistics, the National Center for Health Statistics, and the Federal Reserve Board. The federal government continues to be the best source of up-to-date, reliable information on the changing characteristics of Americans.

Several government surveys are of particular importance to *American Generations.* One is the Census Bureau's Current Population Survey. The CPS is a nationally representative survey of the civilian noninstitutional population aged 15 or older. The Census Bureau takes it monthly, collecting information on employment and unemployment from more than 50,000 households. Each year, the March survey includes a demographic supplement that is the source of most national data on the characteristics of Americans, such as their educational attainment, living arrangements, and incomes. CPS data appear in many tables of this book.

The American Community Survey is another important source of data for *American Generations.* The ACS, an ongoing nationwide survey of 250,000 households per month, provides detailed demographic data at the community level. Designed to replace the census long-form questionnaire, the ACS includes more than 60 questions that formerly appeared on the long form, such as language spoken at home, income, and education. ACS data are available for the nation, regions, states, counties, metropolitan areas, and smaller geographic units.

The Consumer Expenditure Survey is the data source for the Spending chapter. Sponsored by the Bureau of Labor Statistics, the CEX is an ongoing study of the day-to-day spending of American households. The data collected by the survey are used to update prices for the consumer price index. The CEX includes an interview survey and a diary survey administered to two separate, nationally representative samples. The average spending figures shown in the Spending chapters of this book are the integrated data from both the diary and interview components of the survey. For the interview survey, about 7,500 consumer units are interviewed on a rotating panel basis each quarter for five consecutive quarters. For the diary survey, another 7,500 consumer units keep weekly diaries of spending for two consecutive weeks.

The Bureau of Labor Statistics' American Time Use Survey is the source of data for the Time Use chapter. Through telephone interviews with a nationally representative sample of noninstitutionalized Americans aged 15 or older, ATUS collects information in minute detail about what survey respondents did during the previous 24 hours—or diary day. Time use data allow social scientists to better understand our economy and lifestyle and how policy decisions affect our lives.

The data in the Wealth chapter come from the Survey of Consumer Finances, a triennial survey taken by the Federal Reserve Board. The SCF collects data on the assets, debt, and net worth of American households. The latest data available are from the 2004 survey, for which the Federal Reserve Board interviewed a representative sample of 4,522 households.

To explore changes in attitudes, New Strategist extracted data from the nationally representative General Social Survey of the University of Chicago's National Opinion Research Center. NORC conducts the biennial survey through face-to-face interviews with an independently drawn, representative sample of to 3,000 to 4,000 noninstitutionalized people aged 18 or older who live in the United States. The GSS is one of the best sources of attitudinal data on Americans available today. As the University of California—Berkeley has put the dataset online, this valuable resource has become more accessible than ever before. The results are available in the Attitudes chapter.

Value added

While the government collected the data presented in *American Generations*, the tables published here are not reprints from government reports—as is the case in many reference books. Instead, New Strategist's editors spent hundreds of hours scouring web sites, compiling numbers into meaningful statistics, and creating tables with calculations that reveal the trends.

Government web sites are useful for obtaining summary data and for tapping into complex databases. But too often summary data are not enough, and those complex data bases usually require analysis by statistical program. With this volume, New Strategist has done the work for you, delving into the data and providing analysis and comparisons, placing the important information about the generations at your fingertips. The text and chart accompanying most of the tables tell a story about the generations, explaining past and future trends. Researchers who want even more can use the source listed at the bottom of each table to explore the original data. The book contains a comprehensive table list to help readers locate the information they need. For a more detailed search, use the index at the back of the book. Also in the back of the book is the glossary, which defines most of the terms commonly used in tables and text.

With *American Generations* in hand, you will discover the many ways in which the five generations of living Americans differ. Those who know the differences will better understand the change in store for the decades ahead.

1

The Generations

The five generations of American adults are, from youngest to oldest, the Millennial generation, Generation X, the Baby Boom, the Swing generation, and the World War II generation. Below is a brief overview of the generations, followed by a more detailed look at their demographics.

• **Millennial Generation** Like the Baby Boom, this generation, which was born between 1977 and 1994, is marked by its large size. Unlike Boomers, however, Millennials do not face a generation gap. They share many of the values and interests of their parents.

The world in which Millennials are growing up is very different from that of their parents' childhood, however. Racial and ethnic diversity is much greater among Millennials than among older generations. Global boundaries are becoming more transparent, as travel, migration, and the Internet connect members of the generation across the globe. Millennials also face a harsher world, one in which economic anxiety is palpable as their parents cope with a fragile economy, falling housing prices, soaring health care costs, and uncertain retirement prospects.

Millennials are likely to continue trends that are hallmarks of Boomers and Generation Xers. On civil liberties issues, the generation seems even more liberal than Generation X. Millennial girls and women will further the gains made by their elders. They are already moving into the remaining male-dominated arenas, such as sports. Young women greatly outnumber young men in the nation's colleges.

The Millennials are the first generation born into the high-tech world. They are growing up with the Internet and cell phones. Unlike older generations, which have had to struggle to adapt, most Millennials are proficient in using these technologies. The future belongs to them.

• **Generation X** Born between 1965 and 1976, this well-educated, media-savvy generation now makes up the largest share of the nation's parents with children under age 18. The small size of Generation X has made it relatively easy to overlook—and it is painfully aware of this fact. When Gen Xers were teenagers, attention was focused on the Baby Boom. Businesses retailored youth-oriented offerings to suit the tastes of Boomer families. Now that Generation X has children, businesses are focusing on teens and young adults to capture the spending of the large Millennial generation.

As parents, Gen Xers face the same problems that confronted Boomers—a conflict between work and family roles. With the workplace demanding ever more from employees, and children demanding ever more from parents, Gen Xers find themselves with little time or money to spend on themselves. Some Gen Xers lack health insurance, and others have problems keeping up with their mortgage payments. With Boomers clogging the promotional pipeline at work, the housing market shaky, and health insurance costs rising, many Gen Xers wonder when their day will come.

• **Baby-Boom Generation** Born between 1946 and 1964, this is still the largest generation of Americans. Because of their numbers, Boomers have been the focus of attention since their birth. Businesses that sold diapers, baby food, and grade-school books rejoiced at their arrival. But as Boomers matured into successive stages of life, the businesses they left behind had to choose between tracking them or shifting their loyalties to a new generation.

Boomers were raised by young, stay-at-home mothers who followed Dr. Spock's every word. They were taught to be independent and to believe they could control their own destinies. During the 1960s, this upbringing manifested itself in the anti-authoritarian counterculture movement. In the 1980s, it translated into see-how-fast-I-can-get-rich materialism. In the 21st century, Boomers are reaching the empty-nest stage of life. Instead of breathing a sigh of relief, however, Boomers are confronted with a fragile economy, housing market woes, health insurance and college expenses that are rising much faster than their incomes, and a retirement postponed by years as defined-benefit pension plans disappear. While the greatly anticipated empty-nest lifestage could be an opportunity for self-expression and personal growth, it may turn out to be more work than play as Boomers put their children through college, pay off their mortgage, and save for retirement.

Baby Boomers have been affected by their generation's immense size throughout their lives. In turn, the massive generation has had an enormous influence on the American economy and culture. This influence will continue for at least two more decades.

• **Swing Generation** Born between 1933 and 1945, this small generation of Americans was caught between two powerful forces—the Boomers and the World War II generation. Consequently, the generation swings between the attitudes and lifestyles of the generations on either side, which accounts for its name. Some members adopted the more casual lifestyle commonly associated with Boomers. Many leaders of the civil rights, women's, and antiwar movements in the 1960s were members of the Swing generation. Other Swing generation members are as conservative as their World War II elders. Many of the nation's politicians and CEOs are members of the Swing generation.

The Swing generation came of age during a period of quiet prosperity. Its relatively small size benefited its members—companies needed entry-level workers when they were young adults and managers as they reached middle age. They benefited from an expanding economy and skyrocketing real estate prices. This is the most affluent group of older Americans in history—and likely will remain so, a footnote in the history books.

• **World War II Generation** Born before 1933, these are the oldest living Americans. Many members of the generation fought in the war that gave the generation its name. The Great Depression and World War II shaped their attitudes and values more than anything else. Sometimes called the GI Generation, they were once a major force in the United States. Their size and power has diminished greatly with age, but they still wield some political influence because they vote at a much higher rate than young adults. The World War II generation is less educated than younger Americans because a high school education was once sufficient to get a good-paying, secure job. This generation's lower level of education is one reason why its members see things differently from younger Americans.

The Millennial Generation: Another Baby Boom

The current youth generation numbers a powerful 76 million.

In 1977, a new birth boom began when 3.3 million babies were born—159,000 more than in the previous year. This large rise in the number of births followed the 12-year lull that is commonly called Generation X. By 1980, annual births were up to 3.6 million. By 1989, they topped 4 million. Altogether, nearly 68 million babies were born between 1977 and 1994—when births once again dropped below the 4 million mark.

The large Millennial generation—the name for those born between 1977 and 1994—spanned the ages from 14 to 31 in 2008. Because of their numbers, Millennials command the nation's attention. Today, there are 76 million Millennials as immigrants boost their ranks. Millennials account for 25.0 percent of the total population, virtually equal to Boomers' 25.4 percent. Millennials aged 18 or older account for a substantial 26 percent of the nation's adults—a substantially greater share than Generation X's 22 percent.

Like Boomers before them, Millennials have already had an enormous impact on the nation's public schools. Now the generation is inflating the entry-level workforce and is about to enter the housing market—perhaps helping to stabilize declining housing values.

Millennials have strength in numbers—and they know it. Like their Boomer parents, their voices are heard when they take up a cause. And they have their parents' political and economic clout to help them find their place in American society.

■ The Millennial generation has diversified the youth market. Asians, blacks, and Hispanics account for a large share of Millennials—affecting everything from fashion to politics.

■ The first generation to be raised on cell phones and the Internet, Millennials are always connected.

■ Millennials must compete against their many peers for colleges, jobs, and houses. This competitive crush shapes the attitudes and lifestyles of Millennials and is one of the factors that distinguishes them from Generation X.

Table 1.1 Birth of the Millennial Generation, 1977 to 1994

(annual number of births, 1977 to 1994; numbers in thousands)

	number
Total births	**67,949**
1977	3,327
1978	3,333
1979	3,494
1980	3,612
1981	3,629
1982	3,681
1983	3,639
1984	3,669
1985	3,761
1986	3,757
1987	3,809
1988	3,910
1989	4,041
1990	4,158
1991	4,111
1992	4,065
1993	4,000
1994	3,953

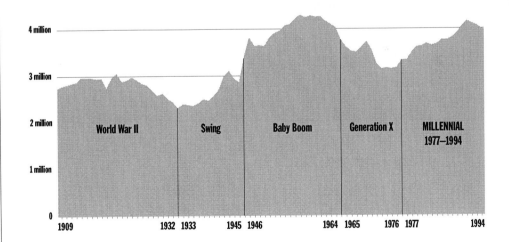

Source: National Center for Health Statistics, Report of Final Natility Statistics, Monthly Vital Statistics Report, Vol. 45, No. 11 Supplement, 1997

Table 1.2 Size of the Millennial and Post-Millennial Generations, 2008

(number of people in the Millennial and Post-Millennial generations by single year of age, 2008)

	number
Post-Millennial, under age 14	**57,022,017**
Under age 1	4,266,450
Aged 1	4,232,060
Aged 2	4,201,064
Aged 3	4,170,106
Aged 4	4,140,234
Aged 5	4,116,284
Aged 6	4,097,526
Aged 7	4,101,310
Aged 8	3,941,919
Aged 9	3,898,535
Aged 10	3,881,888
Aged 11	3,911,686
Aged 12	4,000,262
Aged 13	4,062,693
Millennial, aged 14 to 31	**75,955,712**
Aged 14	4,124,736
Aged 15	4,224,441
Aged 16	4,307,814
Aged 17	4,403,060
Aged 18	4,444,982
Aged 19	4,337,285
Aged 20	4,275,120
Aged 21	4,218,301
Aged 22	4,230,682
Aged 23	4,215,145
Aged 24	4,173,940
Aged 25	4,217,782
Aged 26	4,240,622
Aged 27	4,300,205
Aged 28	4,261,853
Aged 29	4,089,671
Aged 30	3,984,903
Aged 31	3,905,170

Source: Bureau of the Census, Internet site http://www.census.gov/ipc/www/usinterimproj/; calculations by New Strategist

Table 1.3 Millennial Generation by Age, 2000 to 2020

(age range of the Millennial generation, 2000 to 2020)

	age range
2000	6–23
2001	7–24
2002	8–25
2003	9–26
2004	10–27
2005	11–28
2006	12–29
2007	13–30
2008	14–31
2009	15–32
2010	16–33
2011	17–34
2012	18–35
2013	19–36
2014	20–37
2015	21–38
2016	22–39
2017	23–40
2018	24–41
2019	25–42
2020	26–43

Source: Calculations by New Strategist

Table 1.4 Millennial Share of Population, 2008

(number and percent distribution of the total population and the population aged 18 or older by generation, 2008)

	number	share of total population	share of adult* population
Total people	**303,597,646**	**100.0%**	–
Post-Millennial (under age 14)	57,022,017	18.8	0.0%
MILLENNIAL (aged 14 to 31)	**75,955,712**	**25.0**	**25.7**
Generation X (aged 32 to 43)	49,347,057	16.3	21.5
Baby Boom (aged 44 to 62)	77,263,383	25.4	33.7
Swing (aged 63 to 75)	26,903,025	8.9	11.7
World War II (aged 76 or older)	17,106,452	5.6	7.5

* Population aged 18 or older, projected to be 229,515,578 in 2008.
Source: Bureau of the Census, Internet site http://www.census.gov/ipc/www/usinterimproj/; calculations by New Strategist

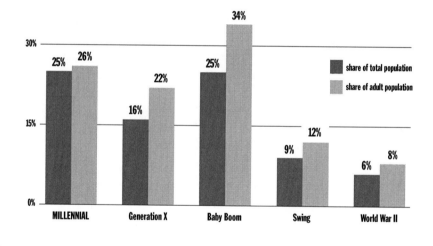

Generation X: The Baby-Bust Generation

Though small, Generation X is a powerhouse in the marketplace.

It is the fate of Generation X, born between 1965 and 1976, to be overshadowed by the large generations on either side of it—the Millennial and Baby Boom generations. The reason is simple arithmetic.

After the 19-year birth fest that created the Baby Boom, the annual number of births declined. In 1964, the last year of the Baby Boom, more than 4 million babies were born. In 1965, there were only 3.8 million births. The annual number of births continued to slide in a generally downward direction through 1976 before beginning to rise again. This period of fewer births resulted in a numerically small generation sandwiched between two much larger ones.

In 2008, there were 49 million Generation Xers, aged 32 to 43. The generation accounts for only 16 percent of the population, well below the 25 percent share accounted for by Boomers and Millennials. Generation X makes up 22 percent of the adult population compared with Boomers' 34 percent and Millennials' 26 percent.

Although the media often overlook Generation Xers, businesses cannot afford to ignore them. That is because Generation X now dominates family life, heading the largest share (45 percent) of households with children.

■ Generation Xers are now the nation's parents, and they are entering their peak earning and spending years.

■ Generation X is well-educated. The women of Generation X have a higher level of educational attainment than any other group of Americans.

■ The falling incomes of Generation X may affect many businesses that market products and services for families with children.

Table 1.5 Birth of Generation X, 1965 to 1976

(annual number of births, 1965 to 1976; numbers in thousands)

	number
Total births	**41,143**
1965	3,760
1966	3,606
1967	3,521
1968	3,502
1969	3,600
1970	3,731
1971	3,556
1972	3,258
1973	3,137
1974	3,160
1975	3,144
1976	3,168

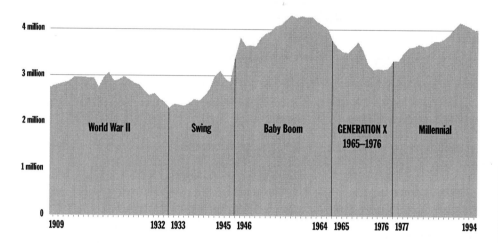

Source: National Center for Health Statistics, Report of Final Natality Statistics, Monthly Vital Statistics Report, Vol. 45, No. 11 Supplement, 1997

Table 1.6 Size of Generation X, 2008

(number of people in Generation X by single year of age, 2008)

	number
Total, aged 32 to 43	**49,347,057**
Aged 32	3,856,270
Aged 33	3,914,681
Aged 34	3,832,045
Aged 35	3,911,864
Aged 36	4,083,651
Aged 37	4,308,430
Aged 38	4,392,479
Aged 39	4,179,191
Aged 40	4,085,970
Aged 41	4,093,624
Aged 42	4,209,370
Aged 43	4,479,482

Source: Bureau of the Census, Internet site http://www.census.gov/ipc/www/usinterimproj/; calculations by New Strategist

Table 1.7   Generation X by Age, 2000 to 2020

(age range of Generation X, 2000 to 2020)

	age range
2000	24–35
2001	25–36
2002	26–37
2003	27–38
2004	28–39
2005	29–40
2006	30–41
2007	31–42
2008	32–43
2009	33–44
2010	34–45
2011	35–46
2012	36–47
2013	37–48
2014	38–49
2015	39–50
2016	40–51
2017	41–52
2018	42–53
2019	43–54
2020	44–55

Source: Calculations by New Strategist

Table 1.8 Generation X Share of Population, 2008

(number and percent distribution of the total population and the population aged 18 or older by generation, 2008)

	number	share of total population	share of adult* population
Total people	**303,597,646**	**100.0%**	–
Post-Millennial (under age 14)	57,022,017	18.8	0.0%
Millennial (aged 14 to 31)	75,955,712	25.0	25.7
GENERATION X (aged 32 to 43)	**49,347,057**	**16.3**	**21.5**
Baby Boom (aged 44 to 62)	77,263,383	25.4	33.7
Swing (aged 63 to 75)	26,903,025	8.9	11.7
World War II (aged 76 or older)	17,106,452	5.6	7.5

* Population aged 18 or older, projected to be 229,515,578 in 2008.
Source: Bureau of the Census, Internet site http://www.census.gov/ipc/www/usinterimproj/; calculations by New Strategist

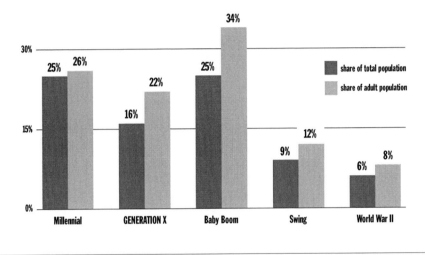

The Baby-Boom Generation: Still Center Stage

In middle age, Boomers dominate the nation's politics and economy.

Nine months after the end of World War II the nation's maternity wards filled with babies—and no one so much as blinked, for this is the sort of thing demographers expect following the end of a war. But no one anticipated that the boom in births would last an astonishing 19 years. In 1957, the peak birth year, 4.3 million babies were born.

The Baby Boom numbers 77 million people. Having grown up declaring they would never trust anyone over 30, the youngest members of the generation are now in their mid-forties. The oldest turn 62 in 2008 and become eligible to draw Social Security benefits. Retirement is on the minds of many Boomers, although most will not be able to afford to retire before they become eligible for Medicare at age 65.

Because of its size, the Baby-Boom generation has been the focus of business and media attention for the past half-century. It is hard to ignore a generation that accounts for 25 percent of the total population and 34 percent of adults—a larger share of adults than any other generation. In turn, Boomers have transformed American culture and the economy.

Boomers finally have some competition, however, with the arrival of the 76-million-strong Millennial generation. The younger cohort accounts for another 25 percent of the population and is drawing the spotlight away from Boomers. But this does not make Boomers resentful, since most Millennials are their beloved children. And besides, the economic clout of the Baby-Boom generation guarantees it will remain a force to be reckoned with for decades to come.

■ Boomers are becoming demanding customers of the health care industry, which will increasingly cater to Boomer wants and needs.

■ Most Boomers are now in the empty-nest lifestage, when free time and discretionary income are supposed to increase. But the sharply rising cost of a middle-class lifestyle is curtailing their dreams.

■ Even as empty-nesters, the primary focus of many Boomers is the well-being of their adult children. Look for Boomer spending to be directed toward the needs of the extended family.

Table 1.9 Birth of the Baby-Boom Generation, 1946 to 1964

(annual number of births, 1946 to 1964; numbers in thousands)

	number
Total births	**75,862**
1946	3,411
1947	3,817
1948	3,637
1949	3,649
1950	3,632
1951	3,820
1952	3,909
1953	3,959
1954	4,071
1955	4,097
1956	4,210
1957	4,300
1958	4,246
1959	4,286
1960	4,258
1961	4,268
1962	4,167
1963	4,098
1964	4,027

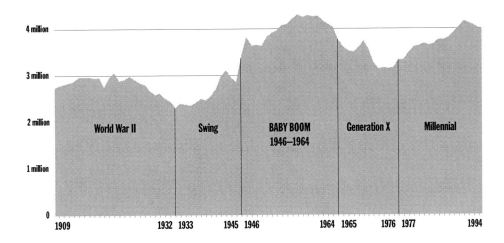

Source: Bureau of the Census, Historical Statistics of the United States—Colonial Times to 1970, Part 1, 1975

Table 1.10 Size of the Baby-Boom Generation, 2008

(number of people in the Baby-Boom generation by single year of age, 2008)

	number
Total, aged 44 to 62	**77,263,383**
Aged 44	4,546,700
Aged 45	4,537,915
Aged 46	4,554,845
Aged 47	4,592,337
Aged 48	4,668,783
Aged 49	4,499,945
Aged 50	4,487,073
Aged 51	4,389,640
Aged 52	4,268,968
Aged 53	4,254,730
Aged 54	4,061,850
Aged 55	3,937,094
Aged 56	3,806,969
Aged 57	3,667,311
Aged 58	3,655,987
Aged 59	3,513,404
Aged 60	3,515,558
Aged 61	3,466,203
Aged 62	2,838,071

Source: Bureau of the Census, Internet site http://www.census.gov/ipc/www/usinterimproj/; calculations by New Strategist

Table 1.11 Baby-Boom Generation by Age, 2000 to 2020

(age range of the Baby-Boom generation, 2000 to 2020)

	age range
2000	36–54
2001	37–55
2002	38–56
2003	39–57
2004	40–58
2005	41–59
2006	42–60
2007	43–61
2008	44–62
2009	45–63
2010	46–64
2011	47–65
2012	48–66
2013	49–67
2014	50–68
2015	51–69
2016	52–70
2017	53–71
2018	54–72
2019	55–73
2020	56–74

Source: Calculations by New Strategist

Table 1.12 Baby Boom Share of Population, 2008

(number and percent distribution of the total population and the population aged 18 or older by generation, 2008)

	number	share of total population	share of adult* population
Total people	303,597,646	100.0%	–
Post-Millennial (under age 14)	57,022,017	18.8	0.0%
Millennial (aged 14 to 31)	75,955,712	25.0	25.7
Generation X (aged 32 to 43)	49,347,057	16.3	21.5
BABY BOOM (aged 44 to 62)	**77,263,383**	**25.4**	**33.7**
Swing (aged 63 to 75)	26,903,025	8.9	11.7
World War II (aged 76 or older)	17,106,452	5.6	7.5

* Population aged 18 or older, projected to be 229,515,578 in 2008.
Source: Bureau of the Census, Internet site http://www.census.gov/ipc/www/usinterimproj/; calculations by New Strategist

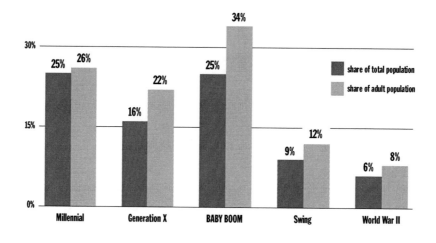

The Swing Generation: Quiet Pioneers

Although small in number, this generation has produced its share of notable figures.

Like Generation X, the Swing generation is smaller than the generations that surround it—the older World War II generation and the younger Baby-Boom generation. And like its younger counterpart, the generation generally has been overlooked. But the members of the generation pioneered many of the changes in American society during the last half of the 20th century.

As the stock market fell in the 1930s, so too did the annual number of births, dropping to 2.3 million in 1933. The number of births remained below 2.5 million from 1933 until 1940 when it began to climb again, although only slightly. It wasn't until the early 1940s that the annual number of births again matched the level of the early years of the 20th century. Altogether, 34 million babies were born between 1933 and 1945.

The Swing generation now numbers 27 million. It accounts for 9 percent of the total population and 12 percent of adults. But its small size belies the influence it wields on American society. The women of the Swing generation were the first to move into the workforce in substantial proportions. Many leaders of the social movements of the 1960s and 1970s were members of the generation, including Gloria Steinem, Jesse Jackson, and Abbie Hoffman. Much of the popular culture credited to the Baby Boom was actually created by the Swing generation. Bob Dylan, for example, is a member of the Swing generation. In 2008, the Swing generation is aged 63 to 75, an age group that continues to hold power and influence.

■ The political power of the Swing generation is much greater than its small size would suggest because the voting rate peaks among people in their sixties and seventies.

■ Although most members of the Swing generation are retired, many still hold powerful positions in government and business.

■ The Swing generation will probably go down in history as the most affluent cohort of older Americans, thanks to generous government and corporate retirement benefits.

Table 1.13 Birth of the Swing Generation, 1933 to 1945

(annual number of births, 1933 to 1945; numbers in thousands)

	number
Total births	**33,962**
1933	2,307
1934	2,396
1935	2,377
1936	2,355
1937	2,413
1938	2,496
1939	2,466
1940	2,559
1941	2,703
1942	2,989
1943	3,104
1944	2,939
1945	2,858

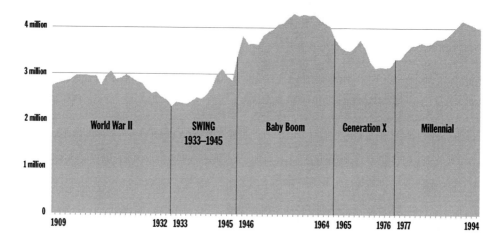

Source: Bureau of the Census, Historical Statistics of the United States—Colonial Times to 1970, Part 1, 1975

Table 1.14 Size of the Swing Generation, 2008

(number of people in the Swing generation by single year of age, 2008)

	number
Total, aged 63 to 75	**26,903,025**
Aged 63	2,670,600
Aged 64	2,648,708
Aged 65	2,640,747
Aged 66	2,398,153
Aged 67	2,193,606
Aged 68	2,095,841
Aged 69	1,993,516
Aged 70	1,914,049
Aged 71	1,800,933
Aged 72	1,742,209
Aged 73	1,705,649
Aged 74	1,569,509
Aged 75	1,529,505

Source: Bureau of the Census, Internet site http://www.census.gov/ipc/www/usinterimproj/; calculations by New Strategist

Table 1.15 Swing Generation by Age, 2000 to 2020

(age range of the Swing generation, 2000 to 2020)

	age range
2000	55–67
2001	56–68
2002	57–69
2003	58–70
2004	59–71
2005	60–72
2006	61–73
2007	62–74
2008	63–75
2009	64–76
2010	65–77
2011	66–78
2012	67–79
2013	68–80
2014	69–81
2015	70–82
2016	71–83
2017	72–84
2018	73–85
2019	74–86
2020	75–87

Source: Calculations by New Strategist

Table 1.16 Swing Share of Population, 2008

(number and percent distribution of the total population and the population aged 18 or older by generation, 2008)

	number	share of total population	share of adult* population
Total people	**303,597,646**	**100.0%**	–
Post-Millennial (under age 14)	57,022,017	18.8	0.0%
Millennial (aged 14 to 31)	75,955,712	25.0	25.7
Generation X (aged 32 to 43)	49,347,057	16.3	21.5
Baby Boom (aged 44 to 62)	77,263,383	25.4	33.7
SWING (aged 63 to 75)	**26,903,025**	**8.9**	**11.7**
World War II (aged 76 or older)	17,106,452	5.6	7.5

* Population aged 18 or older, projected to be 229,515,578 in 2008.
Source: Bureau of the Census, Internet site http://www.census.gov/ipc/www/usinterimproj/; calculations by New Strategist

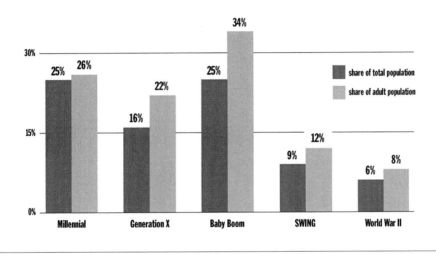

The World War II Generation: Going Out in Style

This is the Greatest Generation, and perhaps also the luckiest.

During the early part of the 20th century, the annual number of births varied only slightly, ranging between 2.7 million and 3.0 million per year. In the late 1920s, the number of births began to fall, coinciding with the Great Depression.

The World War II generation, whose members were born in the years prior to 1933, is aged 76 or older in 2008. Because mortality rates among Americans have fallen sharply over the last century, a substantial portion of the generation is living to a ripe old age. Today there are more than 17 million Americans aged 76 or older. Although the World War II generation suffered through the Great Depression and World War II, it prospered in the aftermath. The lifestyles of the nation's oldest Americans were improved by generous government benefits and private-sector retirement plans.

The financial security and relative good health of the World War II generation has enabled it to enjoy life after retirement. Popular culture may have turned its back on them, but they are, nonetheless, still finding ways to amuse themselves. Their influence is waning, however. Members of the World War II generation account for only 6 percent of the total population and 7 percent of adults.

■ The World War II generation has redefined what it means to be old. In contrast to the stereotype of frail, impoverished old people, most still feel good and live comfortably.

Table 1.17 Birth of the World War II Generation, 1909 to 1932

(annual number of births, 1909 to 1932; numbers in thousands)

	number
Total births	**67,686**
1909	2,718
1910	2,777
1911	2,809
1912	2,840
1913	2,869
1914	2,966
1915	2,965
1916	2,964
1917	2,944
1918	2,948
1919	2,740
1920	2,950
1921	3,055
1922	2,882
1923	2,910
1924	2,979
1925	2,909
1926	2,839
1927	2,802
1928	2,674
1929	2,582
1930	2,618
1931	2,506
1932	2,440

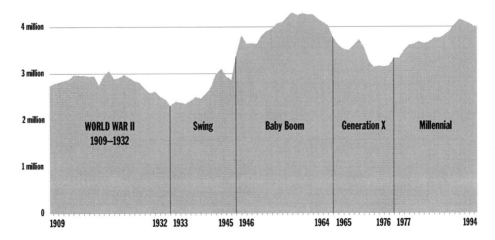

Source: Bureau of the Census, Historical Statistics of the United States—Colonial Times to 1970, Part 1, 1975

Table 1.18 Size of the World War II Generation, 2008

(number of people in the World War II generation by single year of age, 2008)

	number
Total, aged 76 or older	**17,106,452**
Aged 76	1,486,286
Aged 77	1,456,781
Aged 78	1,420,634
Aged 79	1,333,487
Aged 80	1,281,126
Aged 81	1,206,939
Aged 82	1,131,424
Aged 83	1,069,250
Aged 84	976,966
Aged 85	877,236
Aged 86	809,648
Aged 87	716,611
Aged 88	621,519
Aged 89	522,738
Aged 90	443,516
Aged 91	372,430
Aged 92	311,527
Aged 93	260,027
Aged 94	208,278
Aged 95	164,960
Aged 96	125,170
Aged 97	95,418
Aged 98	69,651
Aged 99	49,522
Aged 100 or older	95,308

Source: Bureau of the Census, Internet site http://www.census.gov/ipc/www/usinterimproj/; calculations by New Strategist

Table 1.19 World War II Generation by Age, 2000 to 2020

(age range of the World War II generation, 2000 to 2020)

	age range
2000	68+
2001	69+
2002	70+
2003	71+
2004	72+
2005	73+
2006	74+
2007	75+
2008	76+
2009	77+
2010	78+
2011	79+
2012	80+
2013	81+
2014	82+
2015	83+
2016	84+
2017	85+
2018	86+
2019	87+
2020	88+

Source: Calculations by New Strategist

Table 1.20   World War II Share of Population, 2008

(number and percent distribution of the total population and the population aged 18 or older by generation, 2008)

	number	share of total population	share of adult* population
Total people	**303,597,646**	**100.0%**	–
Post-Millennial (under age 14)	57,022,017	18.8	0.0%
Millennial (aged 14 to 31)	75,955,712	25.0	25.7
Generation X (aged 32 to 43)	49,347,057	16.3	21.5
Baby Boom (aged 44 to 62)	77,263,383	25.4	33.7
Swing (aged 63 to 75)	26,903,025	8.9	11.7
WORLD WAR II (aged 76 or older)	**17,106,452**	**5.6**	**7.5**

* Population aged 18 or older, projected to be 229,515,578 in 2008.
Source: Bureau of the Census, Internet site http://www.census.gov/ipc/www/usinterimproj/; calculations by New Strategist

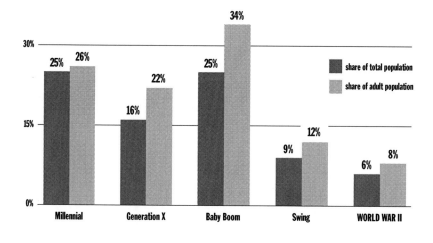

2

Attitudes

The Baby-Boom generation has long been credited with rebelling against its elders. But over the years the National Opinion Research Center's General Social Survey has consistently shown that the rebels were a small portion of Boomers, and that the majority of the Baby-Boom generation held middle-of-the-road or even conservative positions on many issues. Interestingly, the latest results from the General Social Survey suggest that the Baby Boom's children—the Millennial generation—may turn out to be the real rebels.

Whether the topic is the Bible in the public schools, premarital sex, or political leanings, Millennial attitudes are distinctly more liberal than those of older generations. Will they retain these distinct attitudes as they age? Chances are, the answer is yes. Boomer attitudes on most issues have barely shifted over the years, nor have the attitudes of each succeeding older generation changed much with age. If the attitudes of Millennials continue into middle and old age, then American society will become more scientifically oriented, politically liberal, and socially tolerant in the years ahead.

What to expect in the future

■ Sweeping change in media consumption is underway as Millennials adopt the Internet as their primary source of scientific and other news.

■ Americans will become increasingly tolerant of homosexuality as a growing share of the population sees nothing wrong with it.

■ Politics will be redefined as the most liberal generation in modern history becomes a political powerhouse.

Printed Newspapers Have Lost the Youngest Generation

For adults under age 30, the Internet is a more important source for news.

When asked where they get most of their information about current news events, 27 percent of Millennials say the Internet and only 13 percent say (printed) newspapers, according to the 2006 General Social Survey.

Every generation names television as the number-one medium for news about current events, although Millennials are least likely to say so (43 percent). The middle aged are most dependent on television for news, with more than half of Gen Xers, Boomers, and the Swing generations saying TV is most important.

The Internet is the number-two choice only for Millennials. Gen X and older generations are more likely to say newspapers rank second as a source of information about current events. For the oldest generation, newspapers rival television as the most important source for news.

Among Millennials, only 16 percent say they read a newspaper every day. Among the World War II generation, the figure is 72 percent.

■ The media preferences of the Millennial generation suggest that major change lies ahead for the newspaper industry.

Media use varies sharply by generation

(percentage naming medium as most important source of information about current events, by generation, 2006)

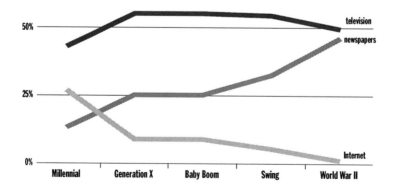

Table 2.1 Main Source of News, 2006

"Where do you get most of your information about current news events?"

(percent of people aged 18 or older responding by generation, 2006)

	television	newspapers	Internet
Total people	**49.5%**	**23.6%**	**14.2%**
Millennial (18 to 29)	43.0	13.2	26.9
Generation X (30 to 41)	55.1	25.2	8.9
Baby Boom (42 to 60)	55.1	25.2	8.9
Swing (61 to 73)	54.4	32.5	5.4
World War II (74 or older)	49.5	46.2	1.1

Source: Survey Documentation and Analysis, Computer-assisted Survey Methods Program, University of California, Berkeley, General Social Surveys, 1972–2006 Cumulative Data Files, Internet site http://sda.berkeley.edu/cgi-bin32/hsda?harcsda+gss06; calculations by New Strategist

Table 2.2 Newspaper Readership, 2006

"How often do you read the newspaper?"

(percent of people aged 18 or older responding by generation, 2006)

	everyday	few times a week	once a week	less than once a week	never
Total people	**34.2%**	**22.1%**	**15.8%**	**15.8%**	**12.1%**
Millennial (18 to 29)	16.3	26.8	17.9	24.4	14.6
Generation X (30 to 41)	24.6	23.9	19.0	20.0	12.4
Baby Boom (42 to 60)	36.2	24.1	15.2	12.9	11.7
Swing (61 to 73)	56.9	12.1	12.9	7.7	10.4
World War II (74 or older)	71.7	8.6	6.3	4.2	9.2

Source: Survey Documentation and Analysis, Computer-assisted Survey Methods Program, University of California, Berkeley, General Social Surveys, 1972–2006 Cumulative Data Files, Internet site http://sda.berkeley.edu/cgi-bin32/hsda?harcsda+gss06; calculations by New Strategist

The Internet Is an Important Source of Science News

Television is number one, but not among Millennials.

When asked where they get most of their information about science and technology, the largest share of Millennials (39 percent) say the Internet. A smaller 33 percent of Millennials name television as their primary source of information about science and technology, according to the 2006 General Social Survey. Among Gen Xers and Boomers, television is the number one source of science news, and the Internet is number two. For the Swing and WW II generations, television is in first place, but newspapers rather than the Internet rank second.

Most Millennials disagree with the notion that science makes our way of life change too fast (nearly 60 percent disagree). Most Gen Xers and Boomers also disagree, although the share is slightly smaller than among Millennials. In contrast, the majority of the Swing and World War II generations agree that science makes things change too fast.

■ Not only do Millennials depend on the Internet for most of their science and technology news, but they are most welcoming of the changes brought about by scientific progress.

Millennials welcome the change brought about by scientific progress

(percentage disagreeing with the statement, "Science makes our way of life change too fast," by generation, 2006)

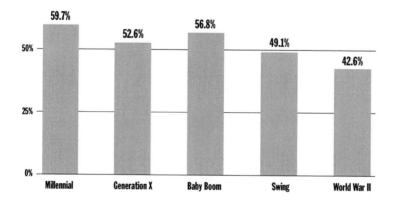

Table 2.3 Main Source of Information about Science and Technology, 2006

"Where do you get most of your information about science and technology?"

(percent of people aged 18 or older responding by generation, 2006)

	television	Internet	newspapers	magazines	books
Total people	**35.7%**	**28.0%**	**11.3%**	**10.7%**	**6.3%**
Millennial (18 to 29)	33.0	39.3	3.3	3.8	7.7
Generation X (30 to 41)	35.7	28.0	11.3	10.7	6.3
Baby Boom (42 to 60)	42.6	19.3	10.9	14.0	6.5
Swing (61 to 73)	44.9	11.4	19.0	10.6	9.6
World War II (74 or older)	50.8	3.2	21.3	13.6	7.8

Source: Survey Documentation and Analysis, Computer-assisted Survey Methods Program, University of California, Berkeley, General Social Surveys, 1972–2006 Cumulative Data Files, Internet site http://sda.berkeley.edu/cgi-bin32/hsda?harcsda+gss06; calculations by New Strategist

Table 2.4 Science Makes Our Way of Life Change Too Fast, 2006

"Science makes our way of life change too fast."

(percent of people aged 18 or older responding by generation, 2006)

	agree	disagree
Total people	**45.5%**	**54.6%**
Millennial (18 to 29)	40.3	59.7
Generation X (30 to 41)	47.4	52.6
Baby Boom (42 to 60)	43.1	56.8
Swing (61 to 73)	50.9	49.1
World War II (74 or older)	57.4	42.6

Source: Survey Documentation and Analysis, Computer-assisted Survey Methods Program, University of California, Berkeley, General Social Surveys, 1972–2006 Cumulative Data Files, Internet site http://sda.berkeley.edu/cgi-bin32/hsda?harcsda+gss06; calculations by New Strategist

Religious Beliefs Shape the Perspectives of Older Americans

Younger generations are more secular in their outlook.

Most Americans heartily disagree with the decades-old Supreme Court decision banning the Bible from public schools. Overall, only 44 percent of Americans approve of the Supreme Court's decision. Attitudes toward this issue do not vary much by generation—with one exception. Most Millennials agree with the Supreme Court's decision. Fully 58 percent of Millennials approve of the Bible ban compared with a much smaller 43 percent of Gen Xers and Boomers and even smaller shares of the Swing and WW II generations.

Millennials are also the ones most likely to believe in evolution. When asked whether it is true or false that human beings developed from earlier species of animals, 58 percent of Millennials say it is true. The majority of Gen Xers also believe that, but most Boomers and older generations do not support the theory of evolution.

■ Belief in evolution is linked to education. Because younger generations are better educated than older generations, support for the theory of evolution grows with each succeeding generation.

Most Millennials and Generation Xers believe in evolution

(percentage agreeing with the statement, "It is true that human beings, as we know them today, developed from earlier species of animals," by generation, 2006)

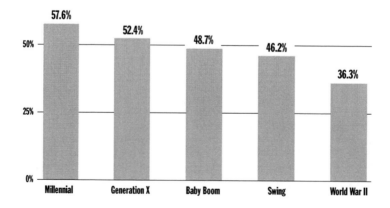

Millennial	Generation X	Baby Boom	Swing	World War II
57.6%	52.4%	48.7%	46.2%	36.3%

Table 2.5 Bible in Public Schools, 2006

"The United States Supreme Court has ruled that no state or local government may require the reading of the Lord's Prayer or Bible verses in public schools. Do you approve or disapprove of the court ruling?"

(percent of people aged 18 or older responding by generation, 2006)

	approve	disapprove
Total people	**43.9%**	**56.1%**
Millennial (18 to 29)	58.1	41.9
Generation X (30 to 41)	43.1	56.9
Baby Boom (42 to 60)	42.7	57.3
Swing (61 to 73)	33.5	66.5
World War II (74 or older)	28.2	71.8

Source: Survey Documentation and Analysis, Computer-assisted Survey Methods Program, University of California, Berkeley, General Social Surveys, 1972–2006 Cumulative Data Files, Internet site http://sda.berkeley.edu/cgi-bin32/hsda?harcsda+gss06; calculations by New Strategist

Table 2.6 Human Evolution, 2006

"Human beings, as we know them today, developed from earlier species of animals. Is this true or false?"

(percent of people aged 18 or older responding by generation, 2006)

	true	false
Total people	**50.3%**	**49.7%**
Millennial (18 to 29)	57.6	42.4
Generation X (30 to 41)	52.4	47.6
Baby Boom (42 to 60)	48.7	51.3
Swing (61 to 73)	46.2	53.8
World War II (74 or older)	36.3	63.7

Source: Survey Documentation and Analysis, Computer-assisted Survey Methods Program, University of California, Berkeley, General Social Surveys, 1972–2006 Cumulative Data Files, Internet site http://sda.berkeley.edu/cgi-bin32/hsda?harcsda+gss06; calculations by New Strategist

Younger Generations Spurn Traditional Sex Roles

The percentage who see nothing wrong with homosexuality grows with each succeeding younger generation.

There is no longer any controversy about working women in our society. That is because most Americans disagree that traditional sex roles—where men go to work and women stay home—are best. More than three out of four Millennials disagree that traditional sex roles are best versus two out of three Gen Xers and Boomers, 53 percent of the Swing generation, and just 34 percent of the World War II generation.

Tolerance of premarital sex is also lower in the older age groups. The Millennial generation is the only one in which the majority says premarital sex is not wrong at all. The percentage falls with age to just over 30 percent among the World War II generation. Americans are far more ambivalent about homosexuality. But again the Millennial generation is far more tolerant than older Americans. Forty-one percent of Millennials say homosexuality is not wrong at all, a figure that falls with age to just 13 percent of World War IIers.

■ As Millennials age and replace older generations, Americans' attitude toward homosexuality will become increasingly tolerant.

The young do not think traditional sex roles are best

(percentage disagreeing with the statement, "It is much better for everyone involved if the man is the achiever outside the home and the woman takes care of the home and family," by generation, 2006)

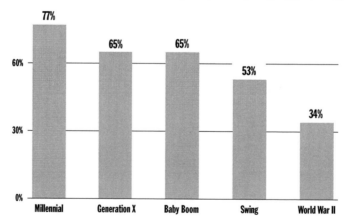

Table 2.7 Sex Roles, 2006

"It is much better for everyone involved if the man is the achiever outside the home and the woman takes care of the home and family."

(percent of people aged 18 or older responding by generation, 2006)

	strongly agree	agree	disagree	strongly disagree
Total people	**9.1%**	**26.2%**	**47.4%**	**17.3%**
Millennial (18 to 29)	9.3	13.9	57.0	19.8
Generation X (30 to 41)	6.8	28.2	45.7	19.3
Baby Boom (42 to 60)	8.2	24.9	47.6	19.3
Swing (61 to 73)	12.6	34.3	43.0	10.1
World War II (74 or older)	14.3	52.1	28.4	5.3

Source: Survey Documentation and Analysis, Computer-assisted Survey Methods Program, University of California, Berkeley, General Social Surveys, 1972-2006 Cumulative Data Files, Internet site http://sda.berkeley.edu/cgi-bin32/hsda?harcsda+gss06; calculations by New Strategist"

Table 2.8 Premarital Sex, 2006

"If a man and a woman have sex relations before marriage, do you think it is always wrong, almost always wrong, sometimes wrong, or not wrong at all?"

(percent of people aged 18 or older responding by generation, 2006)

	always wrong	almost always wrong	sometimes wrong	not wrong at all
Total people	**25.6%**	**8.9%**	**19.8%**	**45.7%**
Millennial (18 to 29)	16.6	6.0	23.7	53.6
Generation X (30 to 41)	28.6	8.1	17.2	46.1
Baby Boom (42 to 60)	24.5	9.8	17.6	48.0
Swing (61 to 73)	36.5	10.4	20.8	32.3
World War II (74 or older)	29.1	14.2	26.2	30.5

Source: Survey Documentation and Analysis, Computer-assisted Survey Methods Program, University of California, Berkeley, General Social Surveys, 1972–2006 Cumulative Data Files, Internet site http://sda.berkeley.edu/cgi-bin32/hsda?harcsda+gss06; calculations by New Strategist

Table 2.9 Homosexuality, 2006

"What about sexual relations between two adults of the same sex? Is it always wrong, almost always wrong, sometimes wrong, or not wrong at all?"

(percent of people aged 18 or older responding by generation, 2006)

	always wrong	almost always wrong	sometimes wrong	not wrong at all
Total people	**56.2%**	**4.9%**	**6.7%**	**32.3%**
Millennial (18 to 29)	45.1	5.5	8.6	40.8
Generation X (30 to 41)	51.7	5.1	6.1	37.2
Baby Boom (42 to 60)	57.3	4.4	6.3	32.0
Swing (61 to 73)	68.9	4.3	6.7	20.1
World War II (74 or older)	76.9	5.7	4.6	12.8

Source: Survey Documentation and Analysis, Computer-assisted Survey Methods Program, University of California, Berkeley, General Social Surveys, 1972–2006 Cumulative Data Files, Internet site http://sda.berkeley.edu/cgi-bin32/ hsda?harcsda+gss06; calculations by New Strategist

Most Americans Do Not Trust Others

Younger generations are less trusting than older ones.

When Americans are asked whether most people can be trusted, the 62 percent majority says no. The percentage of people who say others cannot be trusted is highest among the young, ranging from 71 percent among Millennials to 52 percent among the World War II generation.

Perhaps because they have so little trust, most Millennials do not think the government should have the power to detain people indefinitely without a trial. In fact, Millennials are the only generation in which the majority upholds the writ of habeas corpus—or a defendant's right to a trial. The other generations waffle on this issue, the majority saying the government should be able to hold people indefinitely without a trial.

■ With so many Americans iffy on the rule of law in the United States, expect the debate over the government's power to continue for many years.

Millennials are the only ones who uphold the principle of habeas corpus

(percentage agreeing that the government has the right to detain people without trial, by generation, 2006)

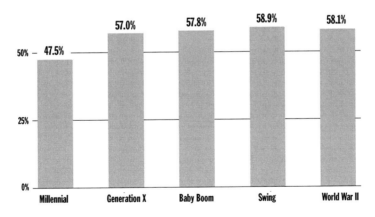

Table 2.10 Trust in Others, 2006

"Generally speaking, would you say that most people can
be trusted or that you can't be too careful in life?"

(percent of people aged 18 or older responding by generation, 2006)

	can trust	cannot trust	depends
Total people	**32.3%**	**62.4%**	**5.2%**
Millennial (18 to 29)	22.3	71.0	6.7
Generation X (30 to 41)	24.5	68.9	6.6
Baby Boom (42 to 60)	38.7	57.7	3.6
Swing (61 to 73)	40.1	54.9	4.9
World War II (74 or older)	42.8	51.7	5.4

Source: Survey Documentation and Analysis, Computer-assisted Survey Methods Program, University of California, Berkeley, General Social Surveys, 1972–2006 Cumulative Data Files, Internet site http://sda.berkeley.edu/cgi-bin32/hsda?harcsda+gss06; calculations by New Strategist

Taable 2.11 Detaining People without a Trial, 2006

"Suppose the government suspected that a terrorist act was about to happen.
Do you think the authorities should have the right to detain people
for as long as they want without putting them on trial?"

(percent of people aged 18 or older responding by generation, 2006)

	definitely should	probably should	probably should not	definitely should not
Total people	**24.8%**	**30.9%**	**22.2%**	**22.1%**
Millennial (18 to 29)	15.9	31.6	26.3	26.2
Generation X (30 to 41)	24.1	32.9	20.7	22.4
Baby Boom (42 to 60)	28.5	29.3	23.4	18.9
Swing (61 to 73)	26.1	32.8	17.2	23.8
World War II (74 or older)	28.9	29.2	15.6	26.3

Source: Survey Documentation and Analysis, Computer-assisted Survey Methods Program, University of California, Berkeley, General Social Surveys, 1972-2006 Cumulative Data Files, Internet site http://sda.berkeley.edu/cgi-bin32/hsda?harcsda+gss06; calculations by New Strategist"

Among the Generations, Millennials Are the Most Liberal

The Swing and World War II generations are the most conservative.

There is a common misconception that people become increasingly conservative with age. In fact, political outlook develops in early adulthood and tends to remain stable throughout life. Although the Baby-Boom generation is known for having been liberal in its youth, they were no more liberal as young adults than they are today. In fact, conservatives have always outnumbered liberals among Boomers, and the political leanings of Boomers have barely changed over the decades.

The stability in political leanings over the life course makes the current findings from the General Social Survey especially interesting. The 2006 results show Millennials to be the most liberal generation and the only one in which liberals outnumber conservatives. In 2006, 34 percent of Millennials identified themselves as liberals compared with a smaller 30 percent who identified themselves as conservatives. Among Gen Xers and older generations, the balance tips the other way. The Swing and World War II generations are the most conservative, with twice as many self-identified conservatives as liberals.

■ If Millennials are like the preceding generations, their political perspective will not change significantly as they get older.

Baby Boomers have not become more conservative with age

(percent distribution of people born between 1946 and 1964 by political leanings, 1986, 1996, and 2006)

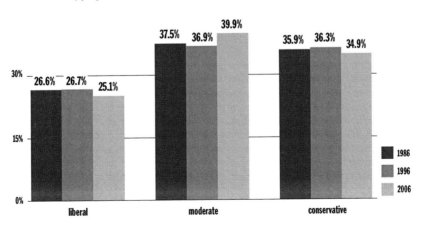

Table 2.12 Political Leanings, 2006

"We hear a lot of talk these days about liberals and conservatives. Where would you place yourself on a seven-point scale from extremely liberal (1) to extremely conservative (7)?"

(percent of people aged 18 or older responding by generation, 2006)

	liberal (1 to 3)	moderate (4)	conservative (5 to 7)
Total people	**26.2%**	**39.0%**	**34.7%**
Millennial (18 to 29)	34.3	36.2	29.6
Generation X (30 to 41)	26.0	40.7	33.3
Baby Boom (42 to 60)	25.1	39.9	34.9
Swing (61 to 73)	20.8	37.7	41.6
World War II (74 or older)	18.5	39.9	41.7

Source: Survey Documentation and Analysis, Computer-assisted Survey Methods Program, University of California, Berkeley, General Social Surveys, 1972–2006 Cumulative Data Files, Internet site http://sda.berkeley.edu/cgi-bin32/ hsda?harcsda+gss06; calculations by New Strategist

3

Education

Increasingly, job success depends upon being able to research, understand, and manage information. In today's complex, information-rich world, having a college degree is rapidly becoming a minimum requirement for obtaining jobs that provide a middle-class lifestyle. As a result, education no longer ends with a high school diploma for most young people. The majority attends college, and almost one-third eventually obtains a bachelor's or higher degree.

The higher educational attainment of younger generations is a factor in many of the changes in our economy and society during the past half-century. This is because education influences a person's attitudes, lifestyle, expectations, and consumer behavior. As a growing number of Baby Boomers celebrate their 60th birthdays over the next few years, the educational differences between older and younger generations will disappear. This will greatly diminish the generation gap in attitudes and lifestyles that has characterized relations among the generations for the past few decades.

What to expect in the future

■ Success in the information age depends on continually updating skills. Consequently, middle-aged and older adults are becoming increasingly important consumers of education.

■ As Americans become better educated, they are less willing to leave decision making to experts. This hands-on attitude is reshaping institutions in fields ranging from education to finance and medicine.

Generation X Is the Best Educated

By age group, 35-to-44-year-olds are most likely to be college graduates.

The educational attainment of the Swing and World War II generations is considerably lower than that of younger generations. Because education influences attitudes, this difference is the key element in the enduring generation gap between older and younger Americans.

A substantial 28 percent of the World War II generation never graduated from high school. Among the Swing generation, the proportion is 19 percent. Among Boomers and Generation Xers, only 11 to 12 percent did not graduate from high school.

Generation X now is the best-educated generation, 32 percent of its members having completed college. This compares with a slightly smaller 30 percent of Baby Boomers who are college graduates. In contrast, only 18 to 23 percent of the members of the Swing and World War generations are college graduates. Most Millennials are not old enough to have completed their education yet, which is why only 13 percent are college graduates—a figure that will climb as Millennials age into their late twenties and beyond.

■ Although a college degree almost guarantees higher lifetime earnings, many young adults cannot afford the cost of college.

The Swing and World War II generations are the least educated

(percent of people with a bachelor's degree or more, by generation, 2006)

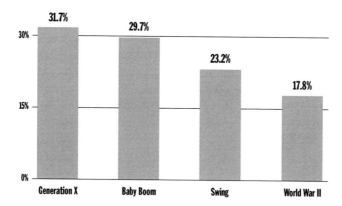

Table 3.1 Educational Attainment by Age, 2006

(number and percent distribution of people aged 25 or older by educational attainment and age, 2006; numbers in thousands)

	total	25 to 34	35 to 44	45 to 54	55 to 64	65 or older
Total people	**191,884**	**39,481**	**43,120**	**42,797**	**30,980**	**35,505**
Not a high school graduate	27,896	5,142	5,116	4,891	3,936	8,810
High school graduate only	60,898	11,302	13,136	13,500	9,925	13,035
Some college, no degree	32,611	7,543	7,247	7,445	5,449	4,926
Associate's degree	16,759	3,687	4,234	4,392	2,636	1,810
Bachelor's degree	35,153	8,617	9,089	8,112	5,182	4,152
Master's degree	13,053	2,407	3,013	3,131	2,721	1,780
Professional degree	3,050	466	757	767	521	538
Doctoral degree	2,464	316	528	559	610	450
High school graduate or more	163,988	34,338	38,004	37,906	27,044	26,691
Some college or more	103,090	23,036	24,868	24,406	17,119	13,656
Bachelor's degree or more	53,720	11,806	13,387	12,569	9,034	6,920
Total people	**100.0%**	**100.0%**	**100.0%**	**100.0%**	**100.0%**	**100.0%**
Not a high school graduate	14.5	13.0	11.9	11.4	12.7	24.8
High school graduate only	31.7	28.6	30.5	31.5	32.0	36.7
Some college, no degree	17.0	19.1	16.8	17.4	17.6	13.9
Associate's degree	8.7	9.3	9.8	10.3	8.5	5.1
Bachelor's degree	18.3	21.8	21.1	19.0	16.7	11.7
Master's degree	6.8	6.1	7.0	7.3	8.8	5.0
Professional degree	1.6	1.2	1.8	1.8	1.7	1.5
Doctoral degree	1.3	0.8	1.2	1.3	2.0	1.3
High school graduate or more	85.5	87.0	88.1	88.6	87.3	75.2
Some college or more	53.7	58.3	57.7	57.0	55.3	38.5
Bachelor's degree or more	28.0	29.9	31.0	29.4	29.2	19.5

Source: Bureau of the Census, 2006 Current Population Survey Annual Social and Economic Supplement, Educational Attainment in the United States: 2006, detailed tables, Internet site http://www.census.gov/population/www/socdemo/education/cps2006.html; calculations by New Strategist

Table 3.2 Educational Attainment by Generation, 2006

(number and percent distribution of people aged 15 or older by educational attainment and generation, 2006; numbers in thousands)

	total	Millennials (15 to 29)	Generation X (30 to 41)	Baby Boom (42 to 60)	Swing (61 to 73)	World War II (74 or older)
TOTAL PEOPLE	**233,194**	**61,448**	**48,984**	**76,853**	**27,420**	**18,488**
Not a high school graduate	46,963	21,801	5,921	8,836	5,174	5,239
High school graduate only	69,548	14,421	14,402	24,062	9,945	6,718
Some college, no degree	42,464	13,920	8,487	13,445	4,196	2,412
Associate's degree	18,151	3,242	4,669	7,660	1,757	827
Bachelor's degree	37,334	6,610	10,525	14,539	3,620	2,038
Master's degree	13,184	1,120	3,603	5,824	1,809	830
Professional degree	3,061	198	818	1,349	477	224
Doctoral degree	2,489	141	561	1,140	444	201
High school graduate or more	186,231	39,652	43,065	68,019	22,248	13,250
Some college or more	116,683	25,231	28,663	43,957	12,303	6,532
Bachelor's degree or more	56,068	8,069	15,507	22,852	6,350	3,293
Total people	**100.0%**	**100.0%**	**100.0%**	**100.0%**	**100.0%**	**100.0%**
Not a high school graduate	20.1	35.5	12.1	11.5	18.9	28.3
High school graduate only	29.8	23.5	29.4	31.3	36.3	36.3
Some college, no degree	18.2	22.7	17.3	17.5	15.3	13.0
Associate's degree	7.8	5.3	9.5	10.0	6.4	4.5
Bachelor's degree	16.0	10.8	21.5	18.9	13.2	11.0
Master's degree	5.7	1.8	7.4	7.6	6.6	4.5
Professional degree	1.3	0.3	1.7	1.8	1.7	1.2
Doctoral degree	1.1	0.2	1.1	1.5	1.6	1.1
High school graduate or more	79.9	64.5	87.9	88.5	81.1	71.7
Some college or more	50.0	41.1	58.5	57.2	44.9	35.3
Bachelor's degree or more	24.0	13.1	31.7	29.7	23.2	17.8

Note: Numbers by generation are estimates by New Strategist.
Source: Bureau of the Census, 2006 Current Population Survey Annual Social and Economic Supplement, Educational Attainment in the United States: 2006, detailed tables, Internet site http://www.census.gov/population/www/socdemo/education/cps2006.html; calculations by New Strategist

Young Women Are Better Educated than Young Men

Among Gen Xers, women are more likely than men to be college graduates.

Among both men and women, middle-aged and younger adults are better educated than their elders. But college graduation rates differ for men and women in interesting ways.

The women of Generation X are better educated than the women of any other generation. Thirty-four percent have a college degree, more than double the percentage among women in the World War II generation. Among men, the Baby-Boom generation has the highest level of education, with 31 percent of Boomer men having a college degree.

For Boomers and older generations of Americans, men are better educated than women. Among Generation Xers and Millennials, women are better educated than men. Generation X women have a higher level of education than anyone else. With 34 percent having a college degree, they are far more educated than their male counterparts, only 30 percent of whom graduated from college.

■ With young women better educated than young men, the earnings gap between men and women should continue to shrink.

Boomer men are better educated than their female counterparts

(percent of people aged 25 or older with a bachelor's degree or more, by generation and sex, 2006)

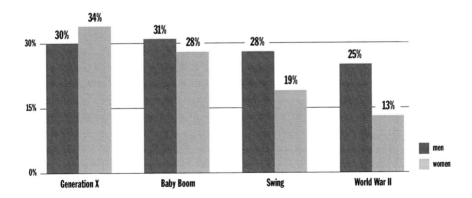

Table 3.3 Educational Attainment of Men by Age, 2006

(number and percent distribution of men aged 25 or older by educational attainment and age, 2006; numbers in thousands)

	total	25 to 34	35 to 44	45 to 54	55 to 64	65 or older
Total men	**92,233**	**19,827**	**21,371**	**20,973**	**14,876**	**15,185**
Not a high school graduate	13,807	2,887	2,860	2,517	1,886	3,657
High school graduate only	29,380	6,233	6,922	6,738	4,489	4,999
Some college, no degree	15,001	3,638	3,398	3,461	2,480	2,023
Associate's degree	7,135	1,698	1,852	1,897	1,073	616
Bachelor's degree	17,082	4,000	4,220	3,970	2,782	2,109
Master's degree	6,205	989	1,366	1,506	1,360	983
Professional degree	1,937	215	421	498	372	431
Doctoral degree	1,686	167	334	386	435	364
High school graduate or more	78,426	16,940	18,513	18,456	12,991	11,525
Some college or more	49,046	10,707	11,591	11,718	8,502	6,526
Bachelor's degree or more	26,910	5,371	6,341	6,360	4,949	3,887
Total men	**100.0%**	**100.0%**	**100.0%**	**100.0%**	**100.0%**	**100.0%**
Not a high school graduate	15.0	14.6	13.4	12.0	12.7	24.1
High school graduate only	31.9	31.4	32.4	32.1	30.2	32.9
Some college, no degree	16.3	18.3	15.9	16.5	16.7	13.3
Associate's degree	7.7	8.6	8.7	9.0	7.2	4.1
Bachelor's degree	18.5	20.2	19.7	18.9	18.7	13.9
Master's degree	6.7	5.0	6.4	7.2	9.1	6.5
Professional degree	2.1	1.1	2.0	2.4	2.5	2.8
Doctoral degree	1.8	0.8	1.6	1.8	2.9	2.4
High school graduate or more	85.0	85.4	86.6	88.0	87.3	75.9
Some college or more	53.2	54.0	54.2	55.9	57.2	43.0
Bachelor's degree or more	29.2	27.1	29.7	30.3	33.3	25.6

Source: Bureau of the Census, 2006 Current Population Survey Annual Social and Economic Supplement, Educational Attainment in the United States: 2006, detailed tables, Internet site http://www.census.gov/population/www/socdemo/education/cps2006.html; calculations by New Strategist

Table 3.4 Educational Attainment of Men by Generation, 2006

(number and percent distribution of men aged 15 or older by educational attainment and generation, 2006; numbers in thousands)

	total	Millennials (15 to 29)	Generation X (30 to 41)	Baby Boom (42 to 60)	Swing (61 to 73)	World War II (74 or older)
Total men	**113,163**	**31,116**	**24,437**	**37,472**	**12,788**	**7,347**
Not a high school graduate	23,870	11,653	3,273	4,512	2,389	2,049
High school graduate only	33,957	7,742	7,819	11,810	4,260	2,325
Some college, no degree	19,709	6,702	4,019	6,201	1,860	934
Associate's degree	7,789	1,519	2,100	3,251	694	224
Bachelor's degree	17,945	2,921	4,875	7,240	1,901	1,013
Master's degree	6,244	421	1,590	2,806	983	444
Professional degree	1,943	84	433	869	374	184
Doctoral degree	1,704	76	338	792	326	174
High school graduate or more	89,291	19,465	21,174	32,969	10,398	5,298
Some college or more	55,334	11,723	13,355	21,159	6,138	2,973
Bachelor's degree or more	27,836	3,502	7,236	11,707	3,584	1,815
Total men	**100.0%**	**100.0%**	**100.0%**	**100.0%**	**100.0%**	**100.0%**
Not a high school graduate	21.1	37.5	13.4	12.0	18.7	27.9
High school graduate only	30.0	24.9	32.0	31.5	33.3	31.6
Some college, no degree	17.4	21.5	16.4	16.5	14.5	12.7
Associate's degree	6.9	4.9	8.6	8.7	5.4	3.0
Bachelor's degree	15.9	9.4	19.9	19.3	14.9	13.8
Master's degree	5.5	1.4	6.5	7.5	7.7	6.0
Professional degree	1.7	0.3	1.8	2.3	2.9	2.5
Doctoral degree	1.5	0.2	1.4	2.1	2.5	2.4
High school graduate or more	78.9	62.6	86.6	88.0	81.3	72.1
Some college or more	48.9	37.7	54.7	56.5	48.0	40.5
Bachelor's degree or more	24.6	11.3	29.6	31.2	28.0	24.7

Note: Numbers by generation are estimates by New Strategist.
Source: Bureau of the Census, 2006 Current Population Survey Annual Social and Economic Supplement, Educational Attainment in the United States: 2006, detailed tables, Internet site http://www.census.gov/population/www/socdemo/education/cps2006.html; calculations by New Strategist

Table 3.5 Educational Attainment of Women by Age, 2006

(number and percent distribution of women aged 25 or older by educational attainment and age, 2006; numbers in thousands)

	total	25 to 34	35 to 44	45 to 54	55 to 64	65 or older
Total women	**99,651**	**19,654**	**21,749**	**21,824**	**16,104**	**20,320**
Not a high school graduate	14,089	2,255	2,256	2,374	2,050	5,153
High school graduate only	31,518	5,069	6,214	6,762	5,436	8,036
Some college, no degree	17,610	3,905	3,849	3,984	2,969	2,903
Associate's degree	9,624	1,989	2,382	2,495	1,563	1,194
Bachelor's degree	18,071	4,617	4,869	4,142	2,400	2,043
Master's degree	6,848	1,418	1,647	1,625	1,361	797
Professional degree	1,113	251	336	269	149	107
Doctoral degree	778	149	194	173	175	86
High school graduate or more	85,562	17,398	19,491	19,450	14,053	15,166
Some college or more	54,044	12,329	13,277	12,688	8,617	7,130
Bachelor's degree or more	26,810	6,435	7,046	6,209	4,085	3,033
Total women	**100.0%**	**100.0%**	**100.0%**	**100.0%**	**100.0%**	**100.0%**
Not a high school graduate	14.1	11.5	10.4	10.9	12.7	25.4
High school graduate only	31.6	25.8	28.6	31.0	33.8	39.5
Some college, no degree	17.7	19.9	17.7	18.3	18.4	14.3
Associate's degree	9.7	10.1	11.0	11.4	9.7	5.9
Bachelor's degree	18.1	23.5	22.4	19.0	14.9	10.1
Master's degree	6.9	7.2	7.6	7.4	8.5	3.9
Professional degree	1.1	1.3	1.5	1.2	0.9	0.5
Doctoral degree	0.8	0.8	0.9	0.8	1.1	0.4
High school graduate or more	85.9	88.5	89.6	89.1	87.3	74.6
Some college or more	54.2	62.7	61.0	58.1	53.5	35.1
Bachelor's degree or more	26.9	32.7	32.4	28.5	25.4	14.9

Source: Bureau of the Census, 2006 Current Population Survey Annual Social and Economic Supplement, Educational Attainment in the United States: 2006, detailed tables, Internet site http://www.census.gov/population/www/socdemo/education/cps2006.html; calculations by New Strategist

Table 3.6 Educational Attainment of Women by Generation, 2006

(number and percent distribution of women aged 15 or older by educational attainment and generation, 2006; numbers in thousands)

	total	Millennials (15 to 29)	Generation X (30 to 41)	Baby Boom (42 to 60)	Swing (61 to 73)	World War II (74 or older)
Total women	**120,031**	**30,332**	**24,546**	**39,378**	**14,633**	**11,141**
Not a high school graduate	23,091	10,146	2,645	4,320	2,782	3,190
High school graduate only	35,591	6,675	6,584	12,252	5,686	4,393
Some college, no degree	22,754	7,219	4,471	7,249	2,334	1,478
Associate's degree	10,361	1,721	2,570	4,411	1,056	601
Bachelor's degree	19,390	3,690	5,651	7,304	1,720	1,025
Master's degree	6,940	699	2,010	3,016	828	386
Professional degree	1,119	116	385	479	102	41
Doctoral degree	784	66	227	348	120	26
High school graduate or more	96,939	20,186	21,898	35,059	11,846	7,950
Some college or more	61,348	13,511	15,314	22,807	6,160	3,557
Bachelor's degree or more	28,233	4,571	8,273	11,147	2,770	1,478
Total women	**100.0%**	**100.0%**	**100.0%**	**100.0%**	**100.0%**	**100.0%**
Not a high school graduate	19.2	33.4	10.8	11.0	19.0	28.6
High school graduate only	29.7	22.0	26.8	31.1	38.9	39.4
Some college, no degree	19.0	23.8	18.2	18.4	16.0	13.3
Associate's degree	8.6	5.7	10.5	11.2	7.2	5.4
Bachelor's degree	16.2	12.2	23.0	18.5	11.8	9.2
Master's degree	5.8	2.3	8.2	7.7	5.7	3.5
Professional degree	0.9	0.4	1.6	1.2	0.7	0.4
Doctoral degree	0.7	0.2	0.9	0.9	0.8	0.2
High school graduate or more	80.8	66.6	89.2	89.0	81.0	71.4
Some college or more	51.1	44.5	62.4	57.9	42.1	31.9
Bachelor's degree or more	23.5	15.1	33.7	28.3	18.9	13.3

Note: Numbers by generation are estimates by New Strategist.
Source: Bureau of the Census, 2006 Current Population Survey Annual Social and Economic Supplement, Educational Attainment in the United States: 2006, detailed tables, Internet site http://www.census.gov/population/www/socdemo/education/cps2006.html; calculations by New Strategist

Asians Are Well Educated

Many Hispanics have not even graduated from high school.

The educational attainment of Hispanics lags far behind that of Asians, blacks, or non-Hispanic whites. Overall, only 59 percent of Hispanics aged 25 or older have a high school diploma, and just 12 percent are college graduates. Younger Hispanics are better educated than older ones, but even among young adults fewer than two out of three have a high school diploma. One reason for the low level of educational attainment among Hispanics is that many are recent immigrants with little formal schooling.

More than 80 percent of blacks have a high school diploma, a figure that ranges from a low of 55 percent among the oldest blacks to a high of 89 percent among blacks aged 35 to 39. Nearly one in five blacks has a college degree, the proportion peaking at 27 percent among black women aged 35 to 39.

Asians are by far the best-educated Americans. More than half of Asian men—51 percent—have a bachelor's degree. Among women, the proportion is 47 percent. Asians are far better educated than non-Hispanic whites, only 31 percent of whom are college graduates.

■ With tuition expenses rising rapidly, young blacks and Hispanics—many from low-income families—face a particularly difficult time paying for college.

Among 30-to-34-year-olds, educational attainment varies by race and Hispanic origin

(percent of 30-to-34-year-olds who are college graduates, by race and Hispanic origin, 2006)

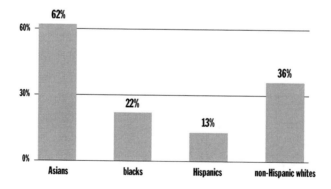

Table 3.7 High School and College Graduates by Age, Race, and Hispanic Origin, 2006: Total People

(percent of total people aged 25 or older with at least a high school diploma and percent with at least a college degree, by age, race, and Hispanic origin, 2006; numbers in thousands)

	total	Asian	black	Hispanic	non-Hispanic white
High school diploma or more					
Total people	**85.5%**	**87.6%**	**80.8%**	**59.3%**	**90.5%**
Aged 25 to 29	86.4	96.0	85.6	63.2	93.4
Aged 30 to 34	87.5	95.1	87.3	63.5	94.3
Aged 35 to 39	88.0	93.4	88.6	60.6	94.3
Aged 40 to 44	88.3	89.5	86.9	62.2	93.6
Aged 45 to 49	88.8	88.8	86.5	61.3	93.3
Aged 50 to 54	88.3	83.2	83.2	58.1	93.3
Aged 55 to 59	88.8	81.3	80.6	60.9	93.2
Aged 60 to 64	85.3	85.0	72.4	54.3	90.0
Aged 65 or older	75.2	70.5	55.4	39.8	80.4
Bachelor's degree or more					
Total people	**28.0**	**49.0**	**18.7**	**12.4**	**31.0**
Aged 25 to 29	28.4	59.4	19.0	9.5	34.3
Aged 30 to 34	31.5	62.1	21.8	13.0	36.4
Aged 35 to 39	32.6	57.8	22.5	13.8	37.3
Aged 40 to 44	29.6	47.4	21.5	13.9	33.2
Aged 45 to 49	28.5	47.5	19.0	14.1	31.4
Aged 50 to 54	30.3	41.0	18.6	12.9	33.9
Aged 55 to 59	30.9	39.4	20.2	15.9	33.5
Aged 60 to 64	26.8	46.3	13.9	10.0	29.2
Aged 65 or older	19.5	30.8	10.8	9.0	20.9

Note: Asians and blacks are those who identify themselves as being of the race alone and those who identify themselves as being of the race in combination with other races. Hispanics may be of any race. Non-Hispanic whites are those who identify themselves as being white alone and not Hispanic.
Source: Bureau of the Census, 2006 Current Population Survey Annual Social and Economic Supplement, Educational Attainment in the United States: 2006, detailed tables, Internet site http://www.census.gov/population/www/socdemo/education/cps2006.html; calculations by New Strategist

Table 3.8 High School and College Graduates by Age, Race, and Hispanic Origin, 2006: Men

(percent of men aged 25 or older with at least a high school diploma and percent with at least a college degree, by age, race, and Hispanic origin, 2006; numbers in thousands)

	total	Asian	black	Hispanic	non-Hispanic white
High school diploma or more					
Total men	**85.0%**	**89.6%**	**80.3%**	**58.5**	**90.2%**
Aged 25 to 29	84.4	96.4	83.2	60.5	92.3
Aged 30 to 34	86.5	95.8	88.9	61.2	93.5
Aged 35 to 39	86.2	92.6	86.7	56.3	93.4
Aged 40 to 44	87.1	87.9	85.1	62.2	92.5
Aged 45 to 49	88.1	91.4	85.5	60.2	92.5
Aged 50 to 54	87.9	83.4	83.0	58.6	92.7
Aged 55 to 59	88.8	84.3	82.5	60.7	92.8
Aged 60 to 64	85.2	87.4	69.2	55.9	89.7
Aged 65 or older	75.9	80.8	53.0	44.4	80.5
Bachelor's degree or more					
Total men	**29.2**	**51.4**	**17.4**	**11.9**	**32.8**
Aged 25 to 29	25.3	58.4	15.0	6.9	31.4
Aged 30 to 34	29.0	62.5	20.5	12.2	33.1
Aged 35 to 39	30.7	57.3	17.6	12.0	35.8
Aged 40 to 44	28.7	47.0	21.1	13.4	32.0
Aged 45 to 49	29.5	51.2	16.5	14.6	32.8
Aged 50 to 54	31.2	41.1	18.6	12.5	35.0
Aged 55 to 59	34.7	43.5	23.0	18.6	37.6
Aged 60 to 64	31.3	53.0	13.8	13.4	34.2
Aged 65 or older	25.6	41.3	10.4	11.1	27.7

Note: Asians and blacks are those who identify themselves as being of the race alone and those who identify themselves as being of the race in combination with other races. Hispanics may be of any race. Non-Hispanic whites are those who identify themselves as being white alone and not Hispanic.
Source: Bureau of the Census, 2006 Current Population Survey Annual Social and Economic Supplement, Educational Attainment in the United States: 2006, detailed tables, Internet site http://www.census.gov/population/www/socdemo/education/cps2006.html; calculations by New Strategist

Table 3.9 High School and College Graduates by Age, Race, and Hispanic Origin, 2006: Women

(percent of women aged 25 or older with at least a high school diploma and percent with at least a college degree, by age, race, Hispanic origin, 2006; numbers in thousands)

	total	Asian	black	Hispanic	non-Hispanic white
High school diploma or more					
Total women	**85.9%**	**85.8%**	**81.2%**	**60.1%**	**90.8%**
Aged 25 to 29	88.5	95.7	87.7	66.6	94.6
Aged 30 to 34	88.5	94.5	86.1	66.1	95.1
Aged 35 to 39	89.8	94.1	90.1	65.3	95.2
Aged 40 to 44	89.5	91.1	88.4	62.3	94.6
Aged 45 to 49	89.5	86.6	87.3	62.4	94.1
Aged 50 to 54	88.8	83.0	83.3	57.6	93.9
Aged 55 to 59	88.8	78.8	79.1	61.2	93.5
Aged 60 to 64	85.3	82.8	74.7	53.0	90.3
Aged 65 or older	74.6	63.1	56.9	36.3	80.3
Bachelor's degree or more					
Total women	**26.9**	**46.8**	**19.7**	**12.9**	**29.3**
Aged 25 to 29	31.6	60.5	22.4	12.8	37.2
Aged 30 to 34	33.9	61.6	22.9	14.0	39.7
Aged 35 to 39	34.4	58.3	26.6	15.7	38.7
Aged 40 to 44	30.5	47.9	21.8	14.3	34.5
Aged 45 to 49	27.5	44.3	21.2	13.6	29.9
Aged 50 to 54	29.5	40.9	18.5	13.3	32.9
Aged 55 to 59	27.4	36.1	18.0	13.3	29.6
Aged 60 to 64	22.7	40.3	14.0	7.0	24.6
Aged 65 or older	14.9	23.3	11.0	7.5	15.7

Note: Asians and blacks are those who identify themselves as being of the race alone and those who identify themselves as being of the race in combination with other races. Hispanics may be of any race. Non-Hispanic whites are those who identify themselves as being white alone and not Hispanic.
Source: Bureau of the Census, 2006 Current Population Survey Annual Social and Economic Supplement, Educational Attainment in the United States: 2006, detailed tables, Internet site http://www.census.gov/population/www/socdemo/education/cps2006.html; calculations by New Strategist

Young Adults in the Northeast Are Most Likely to Be College Graduates

Those living in the South are least likely to have a college degree

The Northeast has the best-educated population, particularly among younger adults. Thirty-eight percent of 25-to-34-year-olds in the Northeast are college graduates—a substantially higher share than in any other region. In the South, only 27 percent of people aged 25 to 34 are college graduates. In the West the figure is 28 percent.

The regional story is reversed for older adults. Among people aged 65 or older, the best educated live in the West. Twenty-four percent of Western residents aged 65 or older have a college degree. This compares with a smaller 20 percent of their counterparts in the Northeast, 19 percent in the South, and just 16 percent in the Midwest.

■ Differences in educational attainment by region can lead to differences in regional economies as business locates in areas with well-educated workers.

The best-educated young adults are in the Northeast

(percent of people aged 25 to 34 with a college degree, by region, 2006)

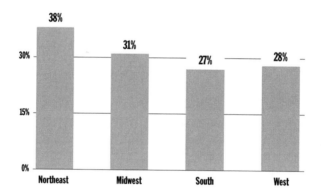

Table 3.10 High School and College Graduates by Age and Region, 2006

(percent of people aged 25 or older with at least a high school diploma and percent with at least a college degree, by age and region of residence, 2006)

	total	Northeast	Midwest	South	West
High school degree or more					
Total people	**85.5%**	**87.0%**	**89.1%**	**83.1%**	**84.3%**
Aged 25 to 34	87.0	90.5	91.5	84.9	83.5
Aged 35 to 44	88.1	90.2	92.2	86.8	84.8
Aged 45 to 54	88.6	90.4	92.7	85.7	87.3
Aged 55 to 64	87.3	88.8	90.5	84.4	87.3
Aged 65 or older	75.2	74.6	77.0	72.6	78.3
Bachelor's degree or more					
Total people	**28.0**	**32.5**	**26.7**	**25.7**	**29.1**
Aged 25 to 34	29.9	37.7	30.7	26.9	28.1
Aged 35 to 44	31.0	35.4	30.5	29.0	31.2
Aged 45 to 54	29.4	34.8	28.3	26.5	30.3
Aged 55 to 64	29.2	33.9	26.1	26.8	32.0
Aged 65 or older	19.5	20.3	16.2	18.6	23.6

Source: Bureau of the Census, 2006 Current Population Survey Annual Social and Economic Supplement, Educational Attainment in the United States: 2006, detailed tables, Internet site http://www.census.gov/population/www/socdemo/education/cps2006.html; calculations by New Strategist

More Preschoolers Attend School

Young adults are also more likely to be in school.

The percentage of preschoolers enrolled in school continues to grow, rising from 52 to 54 percent between 2000 and 2005. Working mothers are behind the increase, with the majority of mothers with preschoolers now in the labor force.

The percentage of young adults enrolled in school grew sharply between 2000 and 2005. Among those aged 18 to 19, the share rose by 6 percentage points. The gain was 5 percentage points among those aged 20 to 21. Although college costs are rising rapidly, a growing share of young adults are determined to earn their educational credentials in an effort to keep up with the changing economy.

■ Rising college costs are becoming a hardship for many young adults, and they may limit school enrollment in the coming years.

The growing majority of 18- and 19-year-olds are in school

(percent of people aged 18 to 19 who are enrolled in school, 2000 and 2005)

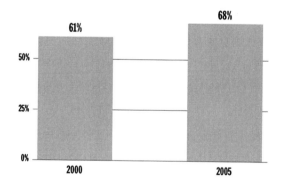

Table 3.11 School Enrollment by Age, 2000 and 2005

(percent of people aged 3 or older enrolled in school, by age, 2000 and 2005; percentage point change, 2000–05)

	2005	2000	percentage point change 2000–05
Total, aged 3 or older	**27.1%**	**27.5%**	**–0.4**
Aged 3 to 4	53.6	52.1	1.5
Aged 5 to 6	95.4	95.6	–0.2
Aged 7 to 9	98.6	98.1	0.5
Aged 10 to 13	98.6	98.3	0.3
Aged 14 to 15	98.0	98.7	–0.7
Aged 16 to 17	95.1	92.8	2.3
Aged 18 to 19	67.6	61.2	6.4
Aged 20 to 21	48.7	44.1	4.6
Aged 22 to 24	27.3	24.6	2.7
Aged 25 to 29	11.9	11.4	0.5
Aged 30 to 34	6.9	6.7	0.2
Aged 35 or older	2.0	1.9	0.1

Source: Bureau of the Census, School Enrollment, Historical Table A-2, Internet site http://www.census.gov/population/www/socdemo/school.html; calculations by New Strategist

More than One in Four Americans Attend School

The majority of 5-to-19-year-olds are in school.

Twenty-seven percent of Americans aged 3 or older are enrolled in school. Not surprisingly, enrollment peaks among school-aged children. More than 95 percent of 5-to-17-year-olds are in school.

Enrollment drops to 68 percent among 18-to-19-year-olds, most of whom are in college. Although about two out of three young adults enroll in college, many will not graduate as evidenced by lower school enrollment among people aged 20 to 21.

Women are more likely than men to go to school as adults. Overall, 51 percent of people enrolled in school are female. The figure rises to a peak of 64 percent among 35-to-44-year-olds.

■ Because education is strongly linked to higher incomes, many of those who do not complete high school or college eventually return to school to get their degree.

Many young adults attend school

(percent of people aged 18 or older who are enrolled in school, by age, 2005)

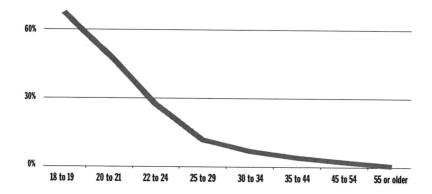

Table 3.12 School Enrollment by Age and Sex, 2005

(number and percent of people aged 3 or older enrolled in school, and females as a percent of total, by age and sex, 2005; numbers in thousands)

	total		female		male		female share of total
	number	percent	number	percent	number	percent	
Total people	**75,780**	**27.1%**	**38,394**	**26.8%**	**37,386**	**27.4%**	**50.7%**
Aged 3 to 4	4,383	53.6	2,187	54.4	2,196	52.8	49.9
Aged 5 to 6	7,486	95.4	3,636	96.1	3,850	94.8	48.6
Aged 7 to 9	11,628	98.6	5,743	99.0	5,886	98.2	49.4
Aged 10 to 13	16,308	98.6	7,965	98.9	8,343	98.4	48.8
Aged 14 to 15	8,375	98.0	4,130	98.4	4,245	97.5	49.3
Aged 16 to 17	8,472	95.1	4,220	95.1	4,252	95.1	49.8
Aged 18 to 19	5,109	67.6	2,530	68.8	2,580	66.5	49.5
Aged 20 to 21	4,069	48.7	2,120	52.3	1,949	45.3	52.1
Aged 22 to 24	3,254	27.3	1,767	29.2	1,487	25.2	54.3
Aged 25 to 29	2,340	11.9	1,396	14.2	944	9.6	59.7
Aged 30 to 34	1,344	6.9	778	7.9	565	5.9	57.9
Aged 35 to 44	1,762	4.1	1,135	5.2	627	3.0	64.4
Aged 45 to 54	913	2.2	577	2.7	336	1.6	63.2
Aged 55 or older	336	0.5	211	0.6	126	0.4	62.8

Source: Bureau of the Census, School Enrollment—Social and Economic Characteristics of Students: October 2005, Detailed Tables, Internet site http://www.census.gov/population/www/socdemo/school/cps2005.html; calculations by New Strategist

Millennials Are Boosting College Enrollment

The number of students on the nation's college campuses grew by 14 percent between 2000 and 2005.

College enrollment has been expanding steadily since 1950, when only 2 million people were in enrolled in an institution of higher education. By 2005, college enrollment exceeded 17 million. Three factors are behind the increase: the large size of the Millennial generation, which is now in the age group most likely to be in college; rising college enrollment rates for both men and women; and a growing number of older students. On college campuses today, students aged 22 or older outnumber those aged 18 to 21, which is the traditional age of college enrollment.

Women account for the 57 percent majority of college students. The female share is even greater among students aged 35 or older, at 64 percent.

■ As the Millennial generation ages into its thirties and forties, campuses across the nation are likely to see a continuing increase in older students.

Most students on college campuses are aged 22 or older

(percent distribution of college students by age, 2005)

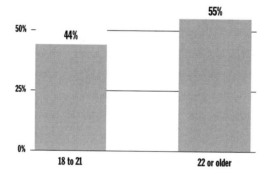

Table 3.13 College Students by Age, 2000 and 2005

(number and percent distribution of people aged 14 or older enrolled in institutions of higher education, by age, 2000 and 2005; percent and percentage point change, 2000–05; numbers in thousands)

	2005	2000	percent change 2000–05
Total students	**17,472**	**15,314**	**14.1%**
Aged 14 to 17	181	149	21.5
Aged 18 to 19	3,727	3,599	3.6
Aged 20 to 21	3,945	3,169	24.5
Aged 22 to 24	3,162	2,683	17.9
Aged 25 to 29	2,291	1,962	16.8
Aged 30 to 34	1,309	1,244	5.2
Aged 35 or older	2,857	2,507	14.0

			percentage point change 2000–05
Total students	**100.0%**	**100.0%**	–
Aged 14 to 17	1.0	1.0	0.1
Aged 18 to 19	21.3	23.5	–2.2
Aged 20 to 21	22.6	20.7	1.9
Aged 22 to 24	18.1	17.5	0.6
Aged 25 to 29	13.1	12.8	0.3
Aged 30 to 34	7.5	8.1	–0.6
Aged 35 or older	16.4	16.4	0.0

Note: "–" means not applicable.
Source: Bureau of the Census, School Enrollment, Historical Table A-6, Internet site http://www.census.gov/population/www/socdemo/school.html; calculations by New Strategist

Table 3.14 College Students by Age and Sex, 2005

(number of people aged 14 or older enrolled in institutions of higher education, by age and sex, and female share of total, 2005; numbers in thousands)

	total	female	male	female share of total
Total students	**17,472**	**9,934**	**7,539**	**56.9%**
Aged 14 to 17	181	119	62	65.7
Aged 18 to 19	3,727	2,052	1,675	55.1
Aged 20 to 21	3,945	2,067	1,878	52.4
Aged 22 to 24	3,162	1,742	1,420	55.1
Aged 25 to 29	2,291	1,368	923	59.7
Aged 30 to 34	1,309	747	562	57.1
Aged 35 or older	2,857	1,838	1,019	64.3

Source: Bureau of the Census, School Enrollment, Historical Table A-6, Internet site http://www.census.gov/population/www/socdemo/school.html; calculations by New Strategist

Part-Time Study Is the Norm for Older Students

With families to support, older students cannot afford full-time study.

Among students at four-year institutions of higher education, 81 percent attend full-time. The proportion going to school full-time is a smaller 61 percent among students attending two-year schools. Part-time study becomes the norm at two-year schools in the 25-to-29 age group. It becomes the norm at four-year schools in the 35-to-39 age group. Most graduate students attend school part-time.

The atmosphere of a college campus is largely determined by the age and attendance status of its student body. Four-year schools are much more likely to provide the stereotypical college experience, with the 70 percent majority of the student body composed of full-time students under age 25. At two-year schools, in contrast, only 46 percent of students are full-timers under age 25.

■ Rising college costs require many students to attend college part-time as they juggle work and school.

Full-time attendance falls with age

(percent of college students at four-year institutions who attend school full-time, by age, 2005)

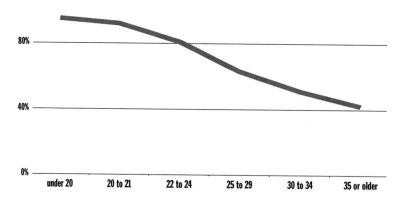

Table 3.15 College Students by Type of School, Age, and Attendance Status, 2005

(number, percent, and percent distribution of people aged 15 or older enrolled in institutions of higher education, by age and attendance status, 2005; numbers in thousands)

		full-time	
	total	number	share of total
Two-year undergraduate			
Total students	**4,327**	**2,632**	**60.8%**
Aged 15 to 17	62	34	54.8
Aged 18 to 19	1,197	997	83.3
Aged 20 to 21	833	605	72.6
Aged 22 to 24	603	373	61.9
Aged 25 to 29	544	234	43.0
Aged 30 to 34	337	158	46.9
Aged 35 to 39	266	87	32.7
Aged 40 to 44	191	62	32.5
Aged 45 to 49	143	47	32.9
Aged 50 to 54	88	21	23.9
Aged 55 to 59	25	10	40.0
Aged 60 or older	37	4	10.8
Four-year undergraduate			
Total students	**9,841**	**8,018**	**81.5**
Aged 15 to 17	116	110	94.8
Aged 18 to 19	2,527	2,400	95.0
Aged 20 to 21	3,014	2,764	91.7
Aged 22 to 24	1,986	1,605	80.8
Aged 25 to 29	849	537	63.3
Aged 30 to 34	412	209	50.7
Aged 35 to 39	313	139	44.4
Aged 40 to 44	241	104	43.2
Aged 45 to 49	173	85	49.1
Aged 50 to 54	113	29	25.7
Aged 55 to 59	72	26	36.1
Aged 60 or older	27	11	40.7
Graduate school			
Total students	**3,304**	**1,587**	**48.0**
Under age 20	7	4	57.1
Aged 20 to 21	98	98	100.0
Aged 22 to 24	573	423	73.8
Aged 25 to 29	898	520	57.9
Aged 30 to 34	560	247	44.1
Aged 35 to 39	369	107	29.0
Aged 40 to 44	277	57	20.6
Aged 45 to 49	199	55	27.6
Aged 50 to 54	167	40	24.0
Aged 55 to 59	103	26	25.2
Aged 60 or older	54	10	18.5

Source: Bureau of the Census, School Enrollment—Social and Economic Characteristics of Students: October 2005, Detailed Tables, Internet site http://www.census.gov/population/www/socdemo/school/cps2005.html; calculations by New Strategist

Few High School Students Have Jobs

But most college students are employed.

Among the nation's 14 million high school students, a surprisingly small 21 percent have jobs. Even among 18-to-19-year-olds in high school, only 30 percent are employed. But employment is the norm for college students.

Among full-time college student, half have jobs. Thirty-five percent of full-time college students work part-time, while a busy 15 percent work full-time on top of their studies. The proportion of full-time students with full-time jobs increases with age to more than one-third of students aged 30 or older.

Among part-time college students, nearly 87 percent have jobs. The 67 percent majority works full-time, while just 19 percent work part-time. The percentage of part-time students who work full-time rises with age from 34 percent of those aged 18 to 19 to nearly two-thirds of those aged 22 or older.

■ The distractions of work may explain why about half of students who enroll in college do not finish their degree.

The proportion of college students who work rises with age

(percent of full-time college students who are employed, by age, 2005)

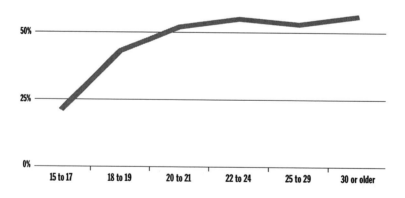

Table 3.16 High School Students by Age and Employment Status, 2005

(number and percent distribution of high school students by age and employment status, 2005)

		employed			
	total	total	full-time	part-time	not employed
Total high school students	**14,060**	**2,952**	**274**	**2,678**	**11,108**
Aged 15	4,014	300	4	296	3,714
Aged 16 to 17	8,272	2,081	82	1,999	6,191
Aged 18 to 19	1,372	418	74	344	954
Aged 20 or older	402	153	114	39	249
Total high school students	**100.0%**	**21.0%**	**1.9%**	**19.0%**	**79.0%**
Aged 15	100.0	7.5	0.1	7.4	92.5
Aged 16 to 17	100.0	25.2	1.0	24.2	74.8
Aged 18 to 19	100.0	30.5	5.4	25.1	69.5
Aged 20 or older	100.0	38.1	28.4	9.7	61.9

Source: Bureau of the Census, School Enrollment—Social and Economic Characteristics of Students: October 2005, Detailed Tables, Internet site http://www.census.gov/population/www/socdemo/school/cps2005.html; calculations by New Strategist

Table 3.17 College Students by Age and Employment Status, 2005

(number and percent distribution of college students by age, attendance status, and employment status, 2005)

| | full-time students | | | | |
| | | employed | | | |
	total	total	full-time	part-time	not employed
Total college students	**12,237**	**6,162**	**1,847**	**4,315**	**6,075**
Aged 15 to 17	147	31	0	31	117
Aged 18 to 19	3,397	1,470	201	1,269	1,926
Aged 20 to 21	3,466	1,799	403	1,396	1,667
Aged 22 to 24	2,401	1,315	371	944	1,086
Aged 25 to 29	1,292	684	325	359	608
Aged 30 to 34	615	346	209	137	269
Aged 35 or older	919	517	338	179	402
Total college students	**100.0%**	**50.4%**	**15.1%**	**35.3%**	**49.6%**
Aged 15 to 17	100.0	21.1	0.0	21.1	79.6
Aged 18 to 19	100.0	43.3	5.9	37.4	56.7
Aged 20 to 21	100.0	51.9	11.6	40.3	48.1
Aged 22 to 24	100.0	54.8	15.5	39.3	45.2
Aged 25 to 29	100.0	52.9	25.2	27.8	47.1
Aged 30 to 34	100.0	56.3	34.0	22.3	43.7
Aged 35 or older	100.0	56.3	36.8	19.5	43.7

| | part-time students | | | | |
| | | employed | | | |
	total	total	full-time	part-time	not employed
Total college students	**5,234**	**4,530**	**3,520**	**1,010**	**705**
Aged 15 to 17	33	17	9	8	16
Aged 18 to 19	330	249	113	136	81
Aged 20 to 21	479	425	246	179	53
Aged 22 to 24	761	672	493	179	90
Aged 25 to 29	999	863	691	172	137
Aged 30 to 34	694	622	519	103	72
Aged 35 or older	1,938	1,682	1,449	233	256
Total college students	**100.0%**	**86.5%**	**67.3%**	**19.3%**	**13.5%**
Aged 15 to 17	100.0	51.5	27.3	24.2	48.5
Aged 18 to 19	100.0	75.5	34.2	41.2	24.5
Aged 20 to 21	100.0	88.7	51.4	37.4	11.1
Aged 22 to 24	100.0	88.3	64.8	23.5	11.8
Aged 25 to 29	100.0	86.4	69.2	17.2	13.7
Aged 30 to 34	100.0	89.6	74.8	14.8	10.4
Aged 35 or older	100.0	86.8	74.8	12.0	13.2

Source: Bureau of the Census, School Enrollment—Social and Economic Characteristics of Students: October 2005, Detailed Tables, Internet site http://www.census.gov/population/www/socdemo/school/cps2005.html; calculations by New Strategist

Millennials Will Boost the Number of College Students Aged 25 to 34

The number of students aged 35 or older is projected to grow more slowly.

According to projections by the National Center for Education Statistics (NCES), the number of college students will grow by 13 percent between 2006 and 2015. The number of women on campus will expand more rapidly than the number of men—up 15 and 9 percent, respectively, during those years.

The most rapid growth in college students will occur among 25-to-34-year-olds as the large Millennial generation replaces the smaller Generation X in the age group. The NCES projects that the number of college students aged 25 to 34 will expand by 26 percent between 2006 and 2015. The number of students aged 35 or older is projected to rise by a smaller 6 percent, a consequence of Generation X moving into the older age group.

■ Distance learning may change the look of college campuses as older students opt for online classes rather than trekking to classrooms on campus.

The number of college students will increase in every age group

(percent change in number of college students by age, 2006 to 2015)

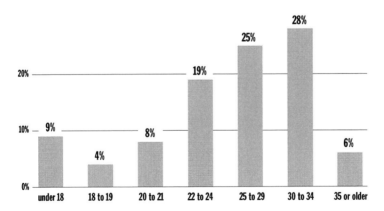

Table 3.18 Projections of College Students by Sex and Age, 2006 and 2015

(number and percent distribution of people aged 14 or older enrolled in institutions of higher education, by sex and age, 2006 and 2015; percent change in number, 2006–15; numbers in thousands)

	2006 number	2006 percent distribution	2015 number	2015 percent distribution	percent change in number 2006–15
Total students	**17,648**	**100.0%**	**19,874**	**100.0%**	**12.6%**
Aged 14 to 17	181	1.0	197	1.0	9.0
Aged 18 to 19	3,700	21.0	3,853	19.4	4.1
Aged 20 to 21	3,780	21.4	4,075	20.5	7.8
Aged 22 to 24	3,049	17.3	3,631	18.3	19.1
Aged 25 to 29	2,538	14.4	3,164	15.9	24.7
Aged 30 to 34	1,294	7.3	1,658	8.3	28.1
Aged 35 or older	3,105	17.6	3,294	16.6	6.1
Female students	**10,190**	**100.0**	**11,712**	**100.0**	**14.9**
Aged 14 to 17	101	1.0	117	1.0	15.6
Aged 18 to 19	2,114	20.7	2,208	18.8	4.4
Aged 20 to 21	2,009	19.7	2,183	18.6	8.7
Aged 22 to 24	1,683	16.5	2,073	17.7	23.2
Aged 25 to 29	1,448	14.2	1,875	16.0	29.5
Aged 30 to 34	797	7.8	1,051	9.0	31.9
Aged 35 or older	2,038	20.0	2,206	18.8	8.2
Male students	**7,458**	**100.0**	**8,161**	**100.0**	**9.4**
Aged 14 to 17	80	1.1	81	1.0	0.8
Aged 18 to 19	1,587	21.3	1,646	20.2	3.7
Aged 20 to 21	1,771	23.7	1,892	23.2	6.8
Aged 22 to 24	1,366	18.3	1,558	19.1	14.1
Aged 25 to 29	1,090	14.6	1,289	15.8	18.2
Aged 30 to 34	497	6.7	608	7.4	22.2
Aged 35 or older	1,067	14.3	1,088	13.3	2.0

Source: National Center for Education Statistics, Projections of Education Statistics to 2015, Internet site http://nces.ed.gov/programs/projections/tables.asp; calculations by New Strategist

Adult Education Is Popular

Professional advancement is the primary reason why adults take courses.

Forty-four percent of adults took some type of adult education course in 2004–05, up from 32 percent in 1991. About half of adults under age 55 participate in some form of adult education during a year's time.

Work-related courses are the most popular type of adult education activity. Twenty-seven percent of those who participate in adult education in 2004–05 took a work-related course. This type of course is particularly important for the middle-aged, with more than one in three 35-to-54-year-olds taking a work-related course. Personal interest courses rank second in popularity, with 21 percent of adult education participants taking this type of course.

■ Adult education is getting a boost from technology as the Internet brings courses of every description to homes and offices across the nation.

Younger adults are most likely to participate in adult education

(percent of people aged 16 or older who participated in an adult education activity in the past 12 months, by age, 2004–05)

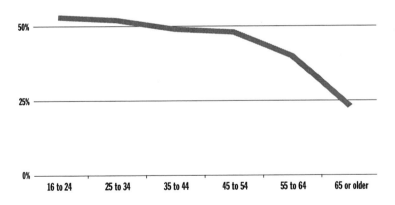

Table 3.19 Participation in Adult Education, 2004–05

(total number of people aged 16 or older and percent participating in adult education, by type of educational activity and age, 2004–05; numbers in thousands)

	total	16 to 24	25 to 34	35 to 44	45 to 54	55 to 64	65 or older
Total people, number	211,607	25,104	38,784	42,890	41,840	29,068	33,922
Total people, percent	100%	100%	100%	100%	100%	100%	100%
Any formal adult education	**44%**	**53%**	**52%**	**49%**	**48%**	**40%**	**23%**
English-as-a-second-language classes	1	2	2	1	0	0	0
GED classes	1	6	2	1	0	0	0
Part-time college degree program	4	9	7	4	3	1	0
Part-time vocational degree program	1	2	2	1	1	1	0
Apprenticeships	1	3	3	1	1	0	0
Work-related courses	27	21	32	34	37	27	5
Personal interest courses	21	27	22	22	20	21	19

Source: National Center for Education Statistics, Adult Education Participation in 2004–05; National Household Education Surveys Program, Internet site http://nces.ed.gov/pubs2006/adulted/tables.asp; calculations by New Strategist

4

Health

In many ways, Americans are healthier than ever, thanks to lifestyle changes spearheaded by well-educated and health-conscious younger generations. Far fewer Americans smoke today, for example, than did in the 1960s. Fewer people have high cholesterol, although the percentage of Americans with high blood pressure is up.

Some things have not changed, however. The young are still most likely to die from accidents, the old from cancer and heart disease. And in spite of millions of dollars spent on diet products, health clubs, and exercise equipment, Americans of all ages are losing the battle of the bulge. Sedentary jobs, fast food, and labor-saving appliances all conspire to keep everyone running a calorie surplus.

One trend that is particularly troubling is the growing number of people without health insurance. Although the nation's leaders have periodically examined this problem, they have yet to come up with a solution.

What to expect in the future

■ Obesity has become a major health issue as Americans put on the pounds. Problems with weight affect many people, making it certain that eating less and exercising more will be top priorities for all age groups in the coming years.

■ The debate over the future of the nation's health care delivery and payment systems is just beginning. As aging Boomers face more health problems, costs will soar. So will demand for changes in the health care system.

Most Americans Feel Very Good or Excellent

But adults under age 55 are less likely than they once were to rate their health highly

Overall, 55 percent of adults say their health is very good or excellent, ranging from a high of 62 percent among people aged 25 to 34 to a low of 37 percent among people aged 65 or older. The percentage of adults under age 55 who rate their health highly has fallen over the past decade for unknown reasons. The decline was particularly steep among adults aged 25 to 34, down more than 6 percentage points.

The 54 percent majority of parents say their children's health is excellent—a figure that does not vary much by age of child. Interestingly, however, while 52 percent of parents with children aged 12 to 17 say their children's health status is excellent, a much smaller 24 percent of 18-to-24-year-olds say they are in excellent health.

■ Among the oldest Americans, the number of those who rate their health as very good or excellent surpasses the number of those who say their health is only fair or poor.

Adults of prime working age do not feel as good as they did

(percent of people aged 25 to 54 who say their health is very good or excellent, by age, 1996 and 2006)

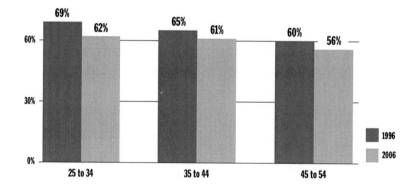

Table 4.1 Health Status of Adults by Age, 2006

"How is your general health?"

(percent of people aged 18 or older responding by age, 2006)

	excellent	very good	good	fair	poor
Total people	**20.7%**	**34.4%**	**30.2%**	**10.9%**	**3.7%**
Aged 18 to 24	24.1	36.1	29.6	7.2	0.9
Aged 25 to 34	25.1	37.2	28.5	6.6	1.3
Aged 35 to 44	24.0	37.1	28.4	8.5	2.2
Aged 45 to 54	21.1	34.4	29.6	10.4	4.0
Aged 55 to 64	17.6	31.9	30.6	13.2	5.9
Aged 65 or older	10.9	26.5	33.8	18.7	8.1

Source: Centers for Disease Control and Prevention, Behavioral Risk Factor Surveillance System, Prevalence Data, Internet site http://apps.nccd.cdc.gov/brfss/; calculations by New Strategist

Table 4.2 Health Status of Children by Age, 2006

(percent distribution of children under age 18 by parent-reported health status, by age, 2006)

	excellent	very good	good	fair/poor
Total children	**53.7%**	**28.1%**	**16.2%**	**1.9%**
Aged 0 to 4	56.0	26.7	15.4	1.8
Aged 5 to 11	54.0	28.7	15.4	1.9
Aged 12 to 17	51.7	28.5	17.8	2.0

Source: National Center for Health Statistics, Summary Health Statistics for U.S. Children: National Health Interview Survey, 2006, Series 10, No. 234, 2007, Internet site http://www.cdc.gov/nchs/nhis.htm

Table 4.3 Health Status by Age, 1996 and 2006

"How is your general health?"

(percent of people aged 18 or older responding "excellent" or "very good," by age, 1996 and 2006; percentage point change, 1996–2006)

	2006	1996	percentage point change, 1996 to 2006
Total people	**55.1%**	**58.2%**	**–3.1**
Aged 18 to 24	60.2	62.4	–2.2
Aged 25 to 34	62.3	68.6	–6.3
Aged 35 to 44	61.1	65.2	–4.1
Aged 45 to 54	55.5	59.6	–4.1
Aged 55 to 64	49.5	49.2	0.3
Aged 65 or older	37.4	37.1	0.3

Source: Centers for Disease Control and Prevention, Behavioral Risk Factor Surveillance System, Prevalence Data, Internet site http://apps.nccd.cdc.gov/brfss/; calculations by New Strategist

The Birth Rate Has Increased Since 2000

The biggest increase has been among women aged 30 or older.

Between 2000 and 2006, the birth rate (the number of live births per 1,000 women aged 15 to 44) rose from 65.9 to 68.5. The rise is almost entirely due to increased childbearing among women aged 30 or older. The birth rate among women aged 30 to 34 climbed 7 percent between 2000 and 2006, while the rate among women aged 35 to 39 rose 19 percent.

The birth rate among women aged 25 to 29 grew by 3 percent between 2000 and 2006. The rate for women under age 25 fell during those years. Although the birth rate of 15-to-19-year-olds was higher in 2006 than in 2004, the 2006 rate is still a substantial 12 percent below the teen birth rate in 2000.

■ The birth rate among older women is rising because of postponed childbearing.

The birth rate is higher today than it was in 2000

(number of births per 1,000 women aged 15 to 44, 2000 to 2006)

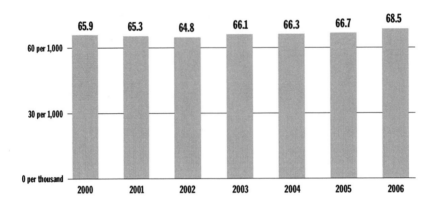

Table 4.4 Birth Rates by Age, 2000 to 2006

(number of live births per 1,000 women in age group and percent change in rate, 2000 to 2006)

	total*	15 to 19	20 to 24	25 to 29	30 to 34	35 to 39	40 to 44	45 to 54
2006	68.5	41.9	105.9	116.8	97.7	47.3	9.4	0.6
2005	66.7	40.5	102.2	115.5	95.8	46.3	9.1	0.6
2004	66.3	41.1	101.7	115.5	95.3	45.4	8.9	0.5
2003	66.1	41.6	102.6	115.6	95.1	43.8	8.7	0.5
2002	64.8	43.0	103.6	113.6	91.5	41.4	8.3	0.5
2001	65.3	45.3	106.2	113.4	91.9	40.6	8.1	0.5
2000	65.9	47.7	109.7	113.5	91.2	39.7	8.0	0.5
Percent change								
2000 to 2006	**3.9%**	**–12.2%**	**–3.5%**	**2.9%**	**7.1%**	**19.1%**	**17.5%**	**20.0%**

* Total is the number of births per 1,000 women aged 15 to 44.
Source: National Center for Health Statistics, Births: Preliminary Data for 2006, National Vital Statistics Reports, Vol. 56, No. 7, 2007; and Births: Final Data for 2004, National Vital Statistics Reports, Vol. 55, No. 1, 2006, Internet site http://www.cdc .gov/nchs/births.htm; calculations by New Strategist

Blacks and Hispanics Have Children at a Younger Age

Asian and non-Hispanic white women are more likely to delay childbearing.

Among all women giving birth in 2006, the 53 percent majority were in their twenties. But there is great variation in the age of childbearing by race and Hispanic origin. Asian and non-Hispanic white women have children at an older age than American Indian, black, or Hispanic women.

Among Asian women who gave birth in 2006, most (56 percent) were aged 30 or older. Among non-Hispanic whites, the figure was a smaller but still substantial 41 percent. In contrast, only 26 percent of black women and 30 percent of Hispanic women who gave birth in 2006 were aged 30 or older.

Nearly half—49 percent—of black women who gave birth in 2006 were younger than age 25, as were 43 percent of Hispanics. In contrast, just 16 percent of Asian women giving birth in that year were under age 25.

■ Variation in the timing of childbearing creates lifestyle differences by race and Hispanic origin.

Most Asian women delay childbearing until their thirties

(percent of births to women aged 30 or older, by race and Hispanic origin, 2006)

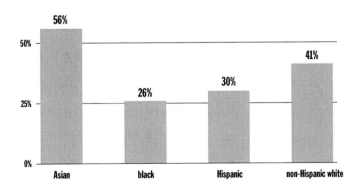

Table 4.5 Births by Age, Race, and Hispanic Origin, 2006

(number and percent distribution of births by age, race, and Hispanic origin of mother, 2006)

	total	American Indian	Asian	black	Hispanic	non-Hispanic white
Total births	**4,265,996**	**47,494**	**239,829**	**617,220**	**1,039,051**	**2,309,833**
Under age 15	6,405	122	71	2,470	2,455	1,270
Aged 15 to 17	138,920	2,795	2,396	36,331	51,982	45,307
Aged 18 to 19	296,507	5,427	5,276	67,361	93,669	124,530
Aged 20 to 24	1,080,507	16,388	31,535	198,718	303,443	528,596
Aged 25 to 29	1,182,187	12,127	66,562	153,639	280,630	665,889
Aged 30 to 34	950,472	6,752	82,614	95,804	194,590	567,103
Aged 35 to 39	498,566	3,120	42,290	49,893	91,562	309,130
Aged 40 to 44	105,476	722	8,525	12,270	19,697	63,546
Aged 45 or older	6,956	41	560	733	1,022	4,461

Percent distribution by race and Hispanic origin

Total births	**100.0%**	**1.1%**	**5.6%**	**14.5%**	**24.4%**	**54.1%**
Under age 15	100.0	1.9	1.1	38.6	38.3	19.8
Aged 15 to 17	100.0	2.0	1.7	26.2	37.4	32.6
Aged 18 to 19	100.0	1.8	1.8	22.7	31.6	42.0
Aged 20 to 24	100.0	1.5	2.9	18.4	28.1	48.9
Aged 25 to 29	100.0	1.0	5.6	13.0	23.7	56.3
Aged 30 to 34	100.0	0.7	8.7	10.1	20.5	59.7
Aged 35 to 39	100.0	0.6	8.5	10.0	18.4	62.0
Aged 40 to 44	100.0	0.7	8.1	11.6	18.7	60.2
Aged 45 or older	100.0	0.6	8.1	10.5	14.7	64.1

Percent distribution by age

Total births	**100.0%**	**100.0%**	**100.0%**	**100.0%**	**100.0%**	**100.0%**
Under age 15	0.2	0.3	0.0	0.4	0.2	0.1
Aged 15 to 17	3.3	5.9	1.0	5.9	5.0	2.0
Aged 18 to 19	7.0	11.4	2.2	10.9	9.0	5.4
Aged 20 to 24	25.3	34.5	13.1	32.2	29.2	22.9
Aged 25 to 29	27.7	25.5	27.8	24.9	27.0	28.8
Aged 30 to 34	22.3	14.2	34.4	15.5	18.7	24.6
Aged 35 to 39	11.7	6.6	17.6	8.1	8.8	13.4
Aged 40 to 44	2.5	1.5	3.6	2.0	1.9	2.8
Aged 45 or older	0.2	0.1	0.2	0.1	0.1	0.2

Note: Births by race and Hispanic origin will not add to total because Hispanics may be of any race and "not stated" is not shown.
Source: National Center for Health Statistics, Births: Preliminary Data for 2006, National Vital Statistics Reports, Vol. 56, No. 7, 2007, Internet site http://www.cdc.gov/nchs/births.htm; calculations by New Strategist

More than One-Third of New Mothers Are Not Married

The proportion of babies born out-of-wedlock bottoms out among women in their thirties.

In 2006, a substantial 38 percent of the nation's births were to unmarried women, up from just 11 percent in 1970. More than 1.6 million single women gave birth in 2006.

Among new mothers under age 20, fully 84 percent were unmarried. The proportion is well above 50 percent in the 20-to-24 age group as well. The share falls below 50 percent in the 25-to-29 age group and bottoms out at 16 percent among women aged 35 to 39.

■ Unmarried women now account for a substantial segment of mothers. Their wants and needs differ significantly from those of married mothers.

Women in their late thirties are most likely to be married when they give birth

(percent of births to unmarried women, by age, 2006)

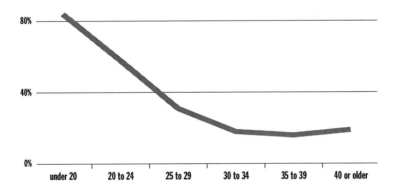

Table 4.6 Births to Unmarried Women by Age, 2006

(total number of births and number and percent to unmarried women, by age, 2006)

		births to unmarried women	
	total	number	share of total
Total births	**4,265,996**	**1,641,700**	**38.5%**
Under age 20	441,832	372,826	84.4
Under age 15	6,405	6,297	98.3
Aged 15 to 17	138,920	127,718	91.9
Aged 18 to 19	296,507	238,811	80.5
Aged 20 to 24	1,080,507	625,701	57.9
Aged 25 to 29	1,182,187	366,056	31.0
Aged 30 to 34	950,472	173,538	18.3
Aged 35 to 39	498,566	81,786	16.4
Aged 40 or older	112,432	21,792	19.4

Source: National Center for Health Statistics, Births: Preliminary Data for 2006, National Vital Statistics Reports, Vol. 56, No. 7, 2007, Internet site http://www.cdc.gov/nchs/births.htm; calculations by New Strategist

Most First-Time Mothers Are Young

Few first children are born to mothers aged 30 or older.

Among the 4.3 million babies born in 2006, 40 percent were first births. Thirty-two percent were second births, 17 percent were third births, and 11 percent were fourth or higher-order births.

    Older mothers make interesting media stories, but in reality the great majority of women who are having their first child are under age 30—76 percent in 2006. Among women having their second child, 61 percent are under age 30. Even among women having their third child, most are younger than age 30. Among women having their fourth or later child, however, the 60 percent majority is aged 30 or older.

■ Although women are delaying childbearing, few wait until their thirties to start families.

Three out of four first-borns have mothers under age 30

(percent of babies born to mothers under age 30, by birth order, 2006)

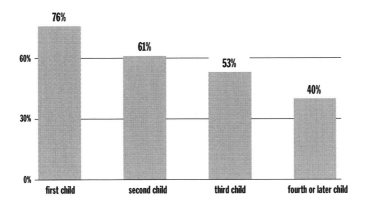

Table 4.7 Births by Age and Birth Order, 2006

(number and percent distribution of births by age and birth order, 2006)

	total	first child	second child	third child	fourth or later child
Total births	**4,265,996**	**1,697,281**	**1,354,637**	**716,756**	**473,685**
Under age 15	6,405	6,253	101	5	0
Aged 15 to 19	435,427	348,469	72,537	10,921	1,430
Aged 20 to 24	1,080,507	518,608	359,749	143,515	53,014
Aged 25 to 29	1,182,187	419,023	394,403	225,457	136,931
Aged 30 to 34	950,472	267,253	332,794	198,189	146,715
Aged 35 to 39	498,566	113,390	163,456	115,339	103,182
Aged 40 to 44	105,476	22,557	29,855	22,147	30,161
Aged 45 to 54	6,956	1,727	1,741	1,183	2,252
Percent distribution by birth order					
Total births	**100.0%**	**39.8%**	**31.8%**	**16.8%**	**11.1%**
Under age 15	100.0	97.6	1.6	0.1	0.0
Aged 15 to 19	100.0	80.0	16.7	2.5	0.3
Aged 20 to 24	100.0	48.0	33.3	13.3	4.9
Aged 25 to 29	100.0	35.4	33.4	19.1	11.6
Aged 30 to 34	100.0	28.1	35.0	20.9	15.4
Aged 35 to 39	100.0	22.7	32.8	23.1	20.7
Aged 40 to 44	100.0	21.4	28.3	21.0	28.6
Aged 45 to 54	100.0	24.8	25.0	17.0	32.4
Percent distribution by age					
Total births	**100.0%**	**100.0%**	**100.0%**	**100.0%**	**100.0%**
Under age 15	0.2	0.4	0.0	0.0	0.0
Aged 15 to 19	10.2	20.5	5.4	1.5	0.3
Aged 20 to 24	25.3	30.6	26.6	20.0	11.2
Aged 25 to 29	27.7	24.7	29.1	31.5	28.9
Aged 30 to 34	22.3	15.7	24.6	27.7	31.0
Aged 35 to 39	11.7	6.7	12.1	16.1	21.8
Aged 40 to 44	2.5	1.3	2.2	3.1	6.4
Aged 45 to 54	0.2	0.1	0.1	0.2	0.5

Note: Numbers by order will not add to total because "not stated" is not shown.
Source: National Center for Health Statistics, Births: Preliminary Data for 2006, National Vital Statistics Reports, Vol. 56, No. 7, 2007, Internet site http://www.cdc.gov/nchs/births.htm; calculations by New Strategist

Many Women Have Not Had Children

Postponing pregnancy sometimes results in no pregnancy.

A growing proportion of older women are childless. Among women aged 25 or older, a larger share are childless today than a generation ago in 1980. Among women aged 25 to 29, the childless proportion climbed from 37 percent in 1980 to 45 percent in 2004. Most of the childless in this age group will eventually have children.

More significant are the increases in childlessness among women in their thirties and forties. Twenty-eight percent of women aged 30 to 34 in 2004 had no children, up from 20 percent in 1980. Among women aged 35 to 39, the childless proportion grew from 12 to 20 percent.

In the 40-to-44 age group, 19 percent of women are childless today, nearly double the rate in 1980. Most of these women will never have children.

Some of the increase in childlessness among older women is the result of fertility problems associated with delayed childbearing, but changing attitudes toward parenthood also play a role.

■ The higher fertility of Hispanic women may lower rates of childlessness in the younger age groups in the years ahead.

More women aged 40 to 44 are childless

(percent of women aged 40 to 44 who have had no children, 1980 and 2004)

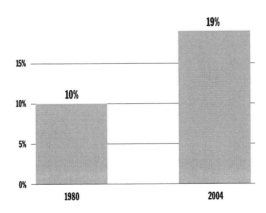

Table 4.8   Childless Women by Age, 1980 to 2004

(percent of women aged 15 to 44 who have not had a live birth, by age, 1980 to 2004)

	total	15–19	20–24	25–29	30–34	35–39	40–44
2004	44.6%	93.3%	68.9%	44.2%	27.6%	19.6%	19.3%
2002	43.5	91.2	67.0	45.2	27.6	20.2	17.9
2000	42.8	90.5	63.6	44.2	28.1	20.1	19.0
1990	41.6	91.9	64.6	42.1	25.7	17.7	16.0
1980	36.7	–	70.0	36.8	19.8	12.1	10.1

Note: "–" means data are not available.
Source: Bureau of the Census, Fertility of American Women, Historical Time Series Tables, Internet site http://www.census
.gov/population/www/socdemo/fertility.html

Most Adults Are Overweight

No one is immune from weight problems, regardless of age.

Americans are losing the battle of the bulge. Desk jobs and fast food are taking their toll. Regardless of age, Americans weigh much more than they did a generation ago. The average man, in fact, weighs 17 pounds more than his counterpart did in 1976–80. The average woman weighs 19 pounds more.

In 2001–04, nearly 71 percent of men and 61 percent of women were overweight, up from 53 and 42 percent, respectively in 1976–80. Thirty percent of men and 34 percent of women are now obese, more than double the 13 and 17 percent, respectively, of 1976–80.

■ With many restaurants competing to offer ever-larger portions to a population that appears to have little will power, it will be an uphill battle to reduce the nation's collective girth.

Men are more likely than women to be overweight

(percent of people aged 20 to 74 who are overweight, by sex, 2001–04)

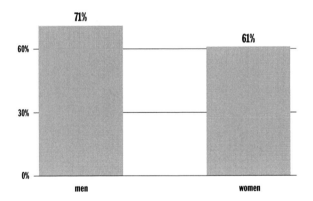

Table 4.9 Average Measured Weight by Sex and Age, 1976–80 to 1999–2002

(average weight in pounds of people aged 20 to 74, by sex and age, 1976–80 and 1999–2002; change in pounds 1976–80 to 1999–2002)

	1999–2002	1976–80	change in pounds
Men aged 20 to 74	**191.0**	**173.8**	**17.2**
Aged 20 to 29	183.4	167.9	15.5
Aged 30 to 39	189.1	175.5	13.6
Aged 40 to 49	196.0	179.7	16.3
Aged 50 to 59	195.4	176.0	19.4
Aged 60 to 74	191.5	167.5	24.0
Women aged 20 to 74	**164.3**	**145.4**	**18.9**
Aged 20 to 29	156.5	135.7	20.8
Aged 30 to 39	163.0	145.5	17.5
Aged 40 to 49	168.2	148.8	19.4
Aged 50 to 59	169.2	150.4	18.8
Aged 60 to 74	164.7	146.9	17.8

Note: Data are based on measured weight of a sample of the civilian noninstitutionalized population.
Source: National Center for Health Statistics, Mean Body Weight, Height, and Body Mass Index, United States 1960–2002, Advance Data, No. 347, 2004, Internet site http://www.cdc.gov/nchs/pressroom/04news/americans.htm; calculations by New Strategist

Table 4.10 Adults Measured as Overweight and Obese by Sex and Age, 1976–80 to 2001–04

(percent of people aged 20 to 74 who are overweight or obese, by sex and age, 1976–80 and 2001–04; percentage point change, 1976–80 to 2001–04)

	overweight			obese		
	2001–04	1976–80	percentage point change	2001–04	1976–80	percentage point change
TOTAL AGED 20 TO 74	**66.0%**	**47.4%**	**18.6**	**32.1%**	**15.1%**	**17.0**
Men aged 20 to 74	**70.7**	**52.9**	**17.8**	**30.2**	**12.8**	**17.4**
Aged 20 to 34	59.0	41.2	17.8	23.2	8.9	14.3
Aged 35 to 44	72.9	57.2	15.7	33.8	13.5	20.3
Aged 45 to 54	78.5	60.2	18.3	31.8	16.7	15.1
Aged 55 to 64	77.3	60.2	17.1	36.0	14.1	21.9
Aged 65 to 74	76.1	54.2	21.9	32.1	13.2	18.9
Women aged 20 to 74	**61.4**	**42.0**	**19.4**	**34.0**	**17.1**	**16.9**
Aged 20 to 34	51.6	27.9	23.7	28.6	11.0	17.6
Aged 35 to 44	60.1	40.7	19.4	33.3	17.8	15.5
Aged 45 to 54	67.4	48.7	18.7	38.0	19.6	18.4
Aged 55 to 64	69.9	53.7	16.2	39.0	22.9	16.1
Aged 65 to 74	71.5	59.5	12.0	37.9	21.5	16.4

Note: Overweight is defined as a body mass index of 25 or higher. Obesity is defined as a body mass index of 30 or higher. Body mass index is calculated by dividing weight in kilograms by height in meters squared. Data are based on measured height and weight of a sample of the civilian noninstitutionalized population.
Source: National Center for Health Statistics, Health United States, 2007, Internet site http://www.cdc.gov/nchs/hus.htm; calculations by New Strategist

Weight Problems Start Young

Many teenagers are trying to lose weight.

The weight problems of adults could become even worse as today's children grow up. A significant proportion of the nation's school children are already overweight. According to measurements taken by the National Center for Health Statistics, 17 percent of children aged 12 to 19 are overweight—up from just 5 percent in 1976–80.

Among high school students, one in four is either overweight or at risk for becoming overweight, according to the Centers for Disease Control and Prevention. Although high school boys are more likely than girls to be overweight, girls are much more likely to think they are overweight and to try to lose weight. Thirty-eight percent of high school girls think they are overweight, and 62 percent are trying to lose weight. Among boys, 25 percent think they are overweight and 30 percent are trying to shed pounds.

■ Ready access to soft drinks and fast food, as well as a couch-potato lifestyle, are putting the pounds on the nation's children.

Boys are more likely than girls to be overweight

(percent of high school students who are overweight or at risk of becoming overweight, by sex, 2005)

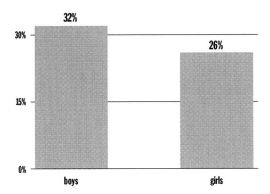

Table 4.11 Children Measured as Overweight by Age, 1976–80 to 2003–04

(percent of people aged 2 to 19 who are overweight, 1976–80 to 2003–04)

	2 to 5	6 to 11	12 to 19
2003–2004	13.9%	18.8%	17.4%
2001–2002	10.6	16.3	16.7
1999–2000	10.3	15.1	14.8
1988–1994	7.2	11.3	10.5
1976–1980	–	6.5	5.0

Note: Overweight is defined as a body mass index of 25 or higher. Body mass index is calculated by dividing weight in kilograms by height in meters squared. Data are based on measured height and weight of a sample of the civilian noninstitutionalized population. "–" means data are not available.

Source: National Center for Health Statistics, Health United States, 2007, Internet site http://www.cdc.gov/nchs/hus.htm

Table 4.12 Weight Problems and Dieting Behavior of 9th to 12th Graders by Sex, 2005

(percent of 9th to 12th graders by weight status and dieting behavior, by sex and grade, 2005)

	total	9th grade	10th grade	11th grade	12th grade
Females					
At risk for becoming overweight*	15.5%	15.9%	15.4%	15.2%	15.6%
Overweight**	10.0	10.4	10.6	9.4	9.7
Described themselves as overweight	38.1	36.2	36.2	39.1	41.8
Were trying to lose weight	61.7	60.1	61.5	61.7	64.0
Ate less food, fewer calories, or foods low in fat to lose weight or to avoid gaining weight in past 30 days	54.8	50.8	55.3	55.6	58.4
Exercised to lose weight or to avoid gaining weight in past 30 days	67.4	68.3	69.0	66.3	65.5
Went without eating for at least 24 hours to lose weight or to avoid gaining weight in past 30 days	17.0	18.4	16.2	17.2	16.0
Took diet pills, powders, or liquids without a doctor's advice to lose weight or avoid gaining weight in past 30 days	8.1	6.0	7.7	9.2	10.2
Vomited or took a laxative to lose weight or to avoid gaining weight in past 30 days	6.2	5.5	7.2	6.1	5.9
Males					
At risk for becoming overweight*	15.8	18.3	14.5	15.9	14.1
Overweight**	16.0	15.0	16.5	17.2	15.5
Described themselves as overweight	25.1	24.3	24.5	26.0	25.6
Were trying to lose weight	29.9	31.9	28.2	30.5	28.7
Ate less food, fewer calories, or foods low in fat to lose weight or to avoid gaining weight in past 30 days	26.8	27.1	25.7	26.8	27.6
Exercised to lose weight or to avoid gaining weight in past 30 days	52.9	57.7	52.1	49.4	51.2
Went without eating for at least 24 hours to lose weight or to avoid gaining weight in past 30 days	7.6	8.1	7.4	6.8	7.8
Took diet pills, powders, or liquids without a doctor's advice to lose weight or avoid gaining weight in past 30 days	4.6	4.3	4.4	4.8	4.4
Vomited or took a laxative to lose weight or to avoid gaining weight in past 30 days	2.8	2.7	3.0	2.5	2.6

* Students at risk of becoming overweight were between the 85th and 95th percentile for body mass index, by age and sex.
** Students who were overweight were at or above the 95th percentile for body mass index, by age and sex.
Source: Centers for Disease Control and Prevention, Youth Risk Behavior Surveillance–United States, 2005, Mortality and Morbidity Weekly Report, Vol. 55/SS-5, June 9, 2006, Internet site http://www.cdc.gov/HealthyYouth/yrbs/index.htm

Most Americans Do Not Get Enough Exercise

Many are physically inactive.

No wonder Americans are gaining weight. Most do not exercise enough—meaning 30 minutes of moderate physical activity at least five times a week or 20 minutes of vigorous physical activity at least three times a week. Only 48 percent of adults get the right amount of exercise, while the 52 percent majority does not.

Among both men and women, young adults are most likely to meet recommended physical activity levels. In the 18-to-29 age group, 59 percent of men and 52 percent of women get enough exercise. Among 30-to-44-year-olds, the proportion is 50 percent. But it is downhill from there. The majority of men and women aged 45 or older do not exercise enough. The percentage of people who are physically inactive peaks in the 75-or-older age group.

■ Government efforts to get people to eat less and exercise more have so far failed to change people's sedentary lifestyles.

Young adults are most likely to get the right amount of exercise

(percent of women who meet recommended physical activity levels, by age, 2005)

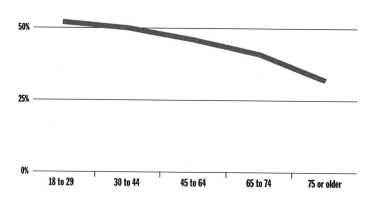

Table 4.13 Participation in Leisure-Time Physical Activity by Age, 2005

(percent of people aged 18 or older who engage in leisure-time physical activity, by sex, age, and level of activity, 2005)

| | people who meet recommended activity | people with insufficient activity | |
		total	physically inactive
TOTAL PEOPLE	**48.3%**	**51.7%**	**25.1%**
Men	**49.9**	**50.1**	**22.9**
Aged 18 to 29	58.5	41.5	18.8
Aged 30 to 44	50.1	49.9	21.0
Aged 45 to 64	46.6	53.4	24.6
Aged 65 to 74	47.7	52.3	26.0
Aged 75 or older	40.3	59.7	32.0
Women	**47.0**	**53.0**	**27.1**
Aged 18 to 29	52.1	47.9	23.2
Aged 30 to 44	50.3	49.7	24.3
Aged 45 to 64	45.8	54.2	27.3
Aged 65 to 74	41.2	58.8	31.7
Aged 75 or older	31.8	68.2	41.8

Note: Recommended activity is physical activity at least five times per week for 30 minutes each time or vigorous physical activity for 20 minutes each time at least three times per week. Insufficient activity is physical activity that does not meet the recommended level. The physically inactive are people with no reported physical activity.
Source: Bureau of the Census, Statistical Abstract of the United States: 2007, Internet site http://www.census.gov/compendia/statab/2007edition.html; calculations by New Strategist

New Drugs Help Lower Cholesterol Levels

Cholesterol levels have declined in most age groups.

Thanks to screening programs, dietary changes, and the development of new medications, high cholesterol is becoming less of a health problem. The proportion of adults with high cholesterol fell 3 percentage points between 1988–94 and 2001–04. Declines occurred in most age groups.

Older women have had the most success in bringing down their cholesterol, although they are still more likely than men to have high cholesterol. Among women aged 65 to 74, the percentage with high cholesterol fell 15 percentage points between 1988–94 and 2001–04. The decline was 14 percentage points among women aged 75 or older.

For some younger adults, cholesterol levels are up. Twenty-one percent of men aged 35 to 44 have high cholesterol, about 2 percentage points higher than in the late 1980s. Women aged 20 to 34 also saw an increase in the percentage with high cholesterol since 1988–94, the figure rising from 7 to 9 percent.

■ The significant decline in the proportion of the population with high cholesterol could help lower mortality from heart disease in the future.

Older women are most likely to have high cholesterol

(percent of people aged 20 or older with high serum cholesterol, by age and sex, 2001–04)

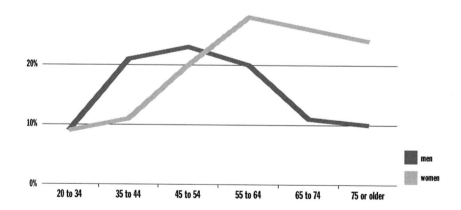

Table 4.14 High Cholesterol by Sex and Age, 1988–94 and 2001–04

(percent of people aged 20 or older who have high serum cholesterol, by sex and age, 1988–94 and 2001–04; percentage point change, 1988–94 to 2001–04)

	2001–04	1988–94	percentage point change
TOTAL PEOPLE	**16.7%**	**19.6%**	**–2.9**
Total men	**16.4**	**17.7**	**–1.3**
Aged 20 to 34	9.0	8.2	0.8
Aged 35 to 44	21.2	19.4	1.8
Aged 45 to 54	23.1	26.6	–3.5
Aged 55 to 64	19.9	28.0	–8.1
Aged 65 to 74	11.0	21.9	–10.9
Aged 75 or older	9.9	20.4	–10.5
Total women	**17.0**	**21.3**	**–4.3**
Aged 20 to 34	9.3	7.3	2.0
Aged 35 to 44	11.4	12.3	–0.9
Aged 45 to 54	20.0	26.7	–6.7
Aged 55 to 64	27.6	40.9	–13.3
Aged 65 to 74	26.3	41.3	–15.0
Aged 75 or older	23.8	38.2	–14.4

Note: High cholesterol is defined as 240 mg/dL or more.
Source: National Center for Health Statistics, Health United States, 2007, Internet site http://www.cdc.gov/nchs/hus.htm; calculations by New Strategist

Blood Pressure Has Risen

The biggest increase has occurred among older women.

Americans are more likely to have high blood pressure today than they were a decade ago. The proportion of adults with high blood pressure rose from 24 to 31 percent between 1988–94 and 2001–04. Behind the rise is a substantial increase in the proportion of older men and women with high blood pressure.

Among women aged 45 to 64, the percentage with high blood pressure rose 11 to 12 percentage points between 1988–94 and 2001–04. The increase was an even greater 17 percentage points for those aged 65 to 74. Most men aged 65 or older and most women aged 55 or older have high blood pressure.

■ As the population ages, the proportion of Americans with high blood pressure is likely to rise, boosting demand for antihypertensive medications.

High blood pressure is more likely with increasing age

(percent of people aged 20 or older who have hypertension, by age and sex, 2001–04)

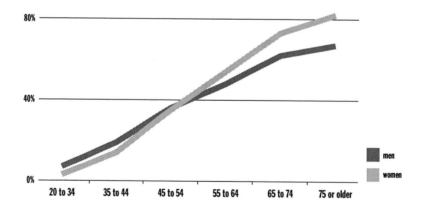

Table 4.15 Hypertension by Sex and Age, 1988–94 and 2001–04

(percent of people aged 20 or older with hypertension or taking antihypertensive medication, by sex and age, 1988–94 and 2001–04; percentage point change, 1988–94 to 2001–04)

	2001–04	1988–94	percentage point change
TOTAL PEOPLE	**30.8%**	**24.1%**	**6.7**
Total men	**29.0**	**23.8**	**5.2**
Aged 20 to 34	7.0	7.1	–0.1
Aged 35 to 44	19.2	17.1	2.1
Aged 45 to 54	35.9	29.2	6.7
Aged 55 to 64	47.5	40.6	6.9
Aged 65 to 74	61.7	54.4	7.3
Aged 75 or older	67.1	60.4	6.7
Total women	**32.5**	**24.4**	**8.1**
Aged 20 to 34	2.7	2.9	–0.2
Aged 35 to 44	14.0	11.2	2.8
Aged 45 to 54	35.2	23.9	11.3
Aged 55 to 64	54.4	42.6	11.8
Aged 65 to 74	72.9	56.2	16.7
Aged 75 or older	82.0	73.6	8.4

Note: People are considered to have hypertension if they have a systolic pressure of at least 140 mmHg or a diastolic pressure of at least 90 mmHg or they take antihypertensive medication.
Source: National Center for Health Statistics, Health United States, 2007, Internet site http://www.cdc.gov/nchs/hus.htm; calculations by New Strategist

Diabetes Is a Growing Problem

Nearly one in four older adults have diabetes.

Diabetes is a growing problem as Americans put on weight. In 2001–04, one in ten adults aged 20 or older had been diagnosed with diabetes or had a fasting blood glucose level that indicated diabetes. The percentage of Americans with diabetes has grown by 2 percentage points since 1988–94.

The percentage of adults with diabetes increased in every age group between 1988–94 and 2001–04. The biggest increase has been among people aged 60 or older, with the proportion rising from 19 to 23 percent during those years.

■ As Americans continue to put on the pounds, the percentage with diabetes will grow.

The percentage of people with diabetes rises with age

(percent of people aged 20 or older with diabetes, by age, 2001–04)

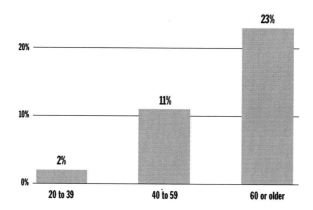

Table 4.16 Diabetes by Selected Characteristics, 1988–94 and 2001–04

(percent of people aged 20 or older with diabetes, by age, 1988–94 and 2001–04, and percentage point change 1988–94 to 2001–04)

	2001–04	1988–94	percentage point change
Total people	**10.0%**	**7.8%**	**2.2**
Aged 20 to 39	2.3	1.6	0.7
Aged 40 to 59	10.9	8.8	2.1
Aged 60 or older	22.5	18.9	3.6

Note: People with diabetes include those diagnosed by a physician and those who have not been diagnosed but who have a fasting blood glucose of at least 126 mg/dL.
Source: National Center for Health Statistics, Health United States, 2007, Internet site http://www.cdc.gov/nchs/hus.htm; calculations by New Strategist

More than One in Five Americans Smoke

Most high school students have tried cigarettes.

Most try smoking cigarettes at some point in their lives—often as teenagers. Among the population aged 12 or older, 25 percent have smoked a cigarette in the past month. Smoking peaks among people in their twenties. More than 40 percent of 22- and 23-year-olds have smoked a cigarette in the past month. Smoking declines with age, in part because some people quit and also because smokers have a higher mortality rate than nonsmokers.

The majority of high school students have tried cigarettes, but only 23 percent have smoked a cigarette in the past month. Evidently, teens have no problem procuring cigarettes, as 19 percent of teen boys and 12 percent of teen girls were able to purchase cigarettes from a store during the past month.

■ Despite extensive antismoking campaigns, most young adults try cigarettes and many adopt the habit.

Many high school students smoke regularly

(percent of high school students who have smoked cigarettes during the past 30 days, by grade, 2005)

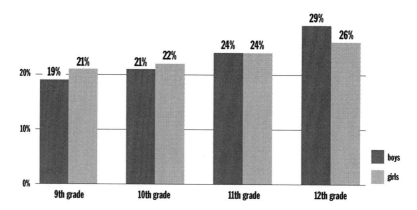

Table 4.17 Cigarette Smoking by Age, 2006

(percent of people aged 12 or older reporting any, past year, or past month use of cigarettes, 2006)

	ever used	used in past year	used in past month
Total people	**66.3%**	**29.1%**	**25.0%**
Aged 12	5.6	3.1	0.7
Aged 13	12.1	6.9	2.6
Aged 14	20.0	12.8	6.7
Aged 15	30.1	18.6	11.3
Aged 16	38.1	26.4	17.0
Aged 17	46.9	32.8	22.9
Aged 18	55.4	42.1	32.4
Aged 19	62.1	46.9	36.9
Aged 20	65.3	47.3	37.9
Aged 21	68.5	49.2	39.9
Aged 22	70.3	49.4	41.3
Aged 23	70.9	49.3	41.6
Aged 24	70.8	46.0	38.5
Aged 25	71.3	46.5	39.9
Aged 26 to 29	71.8	43.2	36.4
Aged 30 to 34	70.4	36.3	32.0
Aged 35 to 39	69.3	31.5	28.0
Aged 40 to 44	72.5	31.9	29.4
Aged 45 to 49	75.7	32.6	29.6
Aged 50 to 54	72.5	29.3	26.7
Aged 55 to 59	74.2	25.3	22.7
Aged 60 to 64	75.3	20.1	18.6
Aged 65 or older	67.5	11.1	9.5

Source: SAMHSA, Office of Applied Studies, National Survey on Drug Use and Health, 2006, Internet site http://oas.samhsa .gov/NSDUH/2k6NSDUH/tabs/Sect2peTabs1to42.htm#Tab2.1A

Table 4.18 Tobacco Use among 9th to 12th Graders by Sex, 2005

(percent of 9th to 12th graders by tobacco use status, by sex and grade, 2005)

	total	9th grade	10th grade	11th grade	12th grade
Females					
Lifetime cigarette use (ever tried a cigarette)	52.7%	47.7%	50.8%	55.3%	58.3%
Lifetime daily cigarette use (ever smoked cigarettes every day for 30 days)	13.5	10.2	11.5	16.0	17.4
Current cigarette use (smoked cigarettes in the past 30 days)	23.0	20.5	21.9	24.3	26.0
Current frequent cigarette use (smoked cigarettes on 20 of the past 30 days)	9.3	7.0	8.4	10.0	12.5
Smoked 10 or more cigarettes a day on the days they smoked in the past 30 days	7.2	4.6	6.5	8.6	9.2
Purchased cigarettes at a store or gas station during the past 30 days	11.7	5.0	7.8	14.8	27.7
Used chewing tobacco, snuff, or dip during the past 30 days	2.2	3.4	1.9	2.1	1.3
Smoked cigars, cigarillos, or little cigars in the past 30 days	8.7	8.7	9.4	7.3	9.4
Used tobacco of any kind in the past 30 days	25.1	22.0	24.6	25.4	29.3
Males					
Lifetime cigarette use (ever tried a cigarette)	55.9	49.8	54.1	59.6	62.2
Lifetime daily cigarette use (ever smoked cigarettes every day for 30 days)	13.3	9.9	11.6	14.5	18.1
Current cigarette use (smoked cigarettes in the past 30 days)	22.9	18.9	21.1	24.2	29.1
Current frequent cigarette use (smoked cigarettes on 20 of the past 30 days)	9.3	6.7	7.0	10.5	13.9
Smoked 10 or more cigarettes a day on the days they smoked in the past 30 days	14.2	12.8	6.7	17.9	16.9
Purchased cigarettes at a store or gas station during the past 30 days	18.8	11.6	13.4	25.8	34.0
Used chewing tobacco, snuff, or dip during the past 30 days	13.6	11.8	12.8	14.8	15.5
Smoked cigars, cigarillos, or little cigars in the past 30 days	19.2	15.5	15.7	21.3	25.8
Used tobacco of any kind in the past 30 days	31.7	26.8	28.2	34.6	39.1

Source: Centers for Disease Control and Prevention, Youth Risk Behavior Surveillance—United States, 2005, Mortality and Morbidity Weekly Report, Vol. 55/SS-5, June 9, 2006, Internet site http://www.cdc.gov/HealthyYouth/yrbs/index.htm

Many Young Adults Are Binge Drinkers

Alcohol use is widespread among teenagers.

Although parents worry that their children will use illegal drugs, alcohol use is a bigger threat. The percentage of teenagers who have had an alcoholic beverage in the past month rises into the double digits by age 14, according to the federal government's National Survey on Drug Use and Health. By age 19, the majority has had a drink in the past month. Nearly half of 21-to-23-year-olds have had a binge-drinking episode in the past month—defined as having five or more drinks on one occasion.

Among 9th graders, 36 percent have had a drink in the past month, according to a survey by the Centers for Disease Control and Prevention. The figure rises to 51 percent among high school seniors. Thirty-three percent of high school seniors have had a binge-drinking episode in the past month.

■ Alcohol is currently the drug of choice on college campuses, sometimes leading to injury or death.

Most young adults do not wait for legal drinking age

(percent of 18-to-20-year-olds who have consumed alcoholic beverages during the past month, 2006)

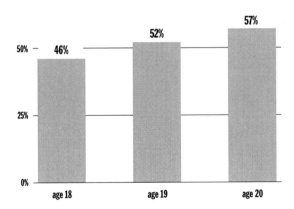

Table 4.19 Alcohol Use by Age, 2006

(percent of people aged 12 or older who drank alcoholic beverages during the past month, by level of alcohol use, 2006)

	any drinking	binge drinking	heavy drinking
Total people	**50.9%**	**23.0%**	**6.9%**
Aged 12	1.9	0.6	–
Aged 13	5.7	2.3	0.5
Aged 14	11.8	6.2	0.7
Aged 15	19.2	11.5	1.7
Aged 16	27.3	18.2	4.5
Aged 17	32.3	22.0	6.7
Aged 18	46.2	32.7	12.8
Aged 19	52.4	37.2	14.4
Aged 20	56.9	39.0	14.0
Aged 21	70.2	49.3	19.5
Aged 22	70.8	48.9	17.3
Aged 23	69.7	47.2	17.2
Aged 24	66.5	43.3	16.1
Aged 25	65.5	41.2	13.2
Aged 26 to 29	63.5	38.3	11.9
Aged 30 to 34	60.3	30.5	8.4
Aged 35 to 39	59.1	27.6	7.3
Aged 40 to 44	56.7	25.4	6.7
Aged 45 to 49	58.9	23.8	7.0
Aged 50 to 54	55.9	22.0	6.7
Aged 55 to 59	53.0	13.8	4.6
Aged 60 to 64	48.0	12.8	2.7
Aged 65 or older	38.4	7.6	1.6

Note: Binge drinking is defined as having five or more drinks on the same occasion on at least one day in the 30 days prior to the survey. Heavy drinking is having five or more drinks on the same occasion on each of five or more days in the 30 days prior to the survey. "–" means sample is too small to make a reliable estimate.
Source: SAMHSA, Office of Applied Studies, National Survey on Drug Use and Health, 2006, Internet site http://oas.samhsa .gov/NSDUH/2k6NSDUH/tabs/Sect2peTabs1to42.htm#Tab2.1A

Table 4.20 Alcohol Use by High School Students, 2005

(percent of 9th to 12th graders who have ever used or currently use acohol, and percent who have drunk heavily in past 30 days, by grade, 2005)

	lifetime use (ever had one or more drinks)	current use (one or more drinks in past 30 days)	episodic heavy drinking (drank five or more drinks in a row in past 30 days)
Total high school students	**74.3%**	**43.3%**	**25.5%**
9th graders	65.0	36.2	19.0
10th graders	74.4	42.0	24.6
11th graders	76.3	46.0	27.6
12th graders	81.7	50.8	32.8

Source: Centers for Disease Control and Prevention, Youth Risk Behavior Surveillance—United States, 2005, Mortality and Morbidity Weekly Report, Vol. 55/SS-5, June 9, 2006, Internet site http://www.cdc.gov/HealthyYouth/yrbs/index.htm

Many Adults Have Used Illicit Drugs

Lifetime illicit drug use surpasses 60 percent among people ranging in age from 21 to 49.

Teens and young adults are most likely to experiment with drugs. More than 20 percent of people aged 18 to 21 used some type of an illicit drug during the past month. (An illicit drug is defined as an illegal drug or the nonmedical use of a prescription drug.) The figure falls below 10 percent among people aged 35 or older.

Marijuana has long been the most popular illicit drug. The percentage of 18-to-25-year-olds who had ever used marijuana exceeded 50 percent for the first time in 1978. Although most young adults still try marijuana, few continue to use it as they age into their thirties. Less than 10 percent of adults aged 30 or older have used marijuana in the past month. Forty-eight percent of high school seniors have tried marijuana, and a smaller 23 percent have used marijuana in the past month.

■ Although most people do not regularly use illicit drugs, the large percentage who have ever tried them attests to the difficulty of winning the war on drugs.

Marijuana use became common among young adults in the 1970s

(percent of people aged 18 to 25 who have ever used marijuana, by age, 1965 to 2006)

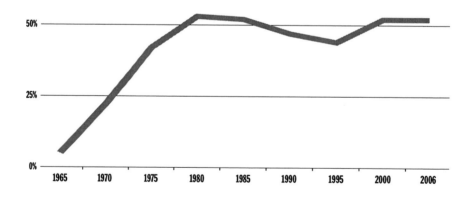

Table 4.21 Illicit Drug Use by Age, 2006

(percent of people aged 12 or older who ever used any illicit drug, who used an illicit drug in the past year, and who used an illicit drug in the past month, by age, 2006)

	ever used	used in past year	used in past month
Total people	**45.4%**	**14.5%**	**8.3%**
Aged 12	12.1	6.9	3.1
Aged 13	16.3	9.9	4.6
Aged 14	23.2	15.8	7.0
Aged 15	31.9	22.8	11.1
Aged 16	37.3	28.3	14.9
Aged 17	43.1	32.2	17.1
Aged 18	50.1	37.6	20.7
Aged 19	54.9	37.2	22.4
Aged 20	59.7	38.2	23.6
Aged 21	61.7	36.0	20.1
Aged 22	62.3	34.3	19.5
Aged 23	61.9	30.9	18.1
Aged 24	62.4	31.4	17.9
Aged 25	60.5	28.3	15.5
Aged 26 to 29	60.4	24.7	14.1
Aged 30 to 34	55.3	17.5	10.0
Aged 35 to 39	56.2	14.2	8.0
Aged 40 to 44	60.9	13.6	8.3
Aged 45 to 49	61.6	11.9	6.7
Aged 50 to 54	54.6	9.1	6.0
Aged 55 to 59	43.4	4.9	2.4
Aged 60 to 64	28.2	3.4	2.1
Aged 65 or older	9.8	1.1	0.7

Note: Illicit drugs include marijuana, hashish, cocaine (including crack), heroin, hallucinogens, inhalants, or any prescription-type psychotherapeutic used nonmedically.
Source: SAMHSA, Office of Applied Studies, National Survey on Drug Use and Health, 2006, Internet site http://oas.samhsa.gov/NSDUH/2k6NSDUH/tabs/Sect1peTabs1to46.htm#Tab1.1A

Table 4.22 Lifetime Marijuana Use by People Aged 12 to 25, 1965 to 2006

(percent of people aged 12 to 25 who have ever used marijuana, 1965 to 2006)

	12 to 17	18 to 25
2006	17.3%	52.4%
2005	17.4	52.4
2004	19.0	52.8
2003	19.6	53.9
2002	20.6	53.8
2001	21.9	53.0
2000	20.4	51.8
1999	19.7	50.3
1998	19.9	47.0
1997	18.6	45.7
1996	17.9	44.3
1995	16.4	44.1
1994	13.9	43.5
1993	12.4	43.4
1992	11.8	44.5
1991	11.5	45.1
1990	11.9	46.6
1989	12.5	47.3
1988	13.2	48.8
1987	14.9	49.7
1986	15.2	50.4
1985	15.4	51.5
1984	15.6	53.2
1983	16.0	53.8
1982	16.9	54.4
1981	17.6	54.3
1980	19.4	53.0
1979	19.6	52.1
1978	18.0	51.0
1977	18.7	48.6
1976	17.9	44.9
1975	15.8	41.6
1974	14.8	39.3
1973	13.2	34.5
1972	11.0	30.8
1971	9.4	27.1
1970	7.4	22.0
1969	5.9	16.0
1968	4.9	10.6
1967	2.8	7.7
1966	1.8	6.1
1965	1.8	5.1

Source: SAMHSA, Office of Applied Studies, National Survey on Drug Use and Health, various years, Internet site http://www .oas.samhsa.gov/WebOnly.htm#NSDUHtabs

Table 4.23 Marijuana Use by Age, 2006

(percent of people aged 12 or older who ever used marijuana, who used marijuana in the past year, and who used marijuana in the past month, by age, 2006)

	ever used	used in past year	used in past month
Total people	**39.8%**	**10.3%**	**6.0%**
Aged 12	1.4	1.0	0.3
Aged 13	4.6	3.3	1.4
Aged 14	10.7	8.5	3.7
Aged 15	20.6	15.9	7.7
Aged 16	29.1	22.5	11.9
Aged 17	35.6	26.6	14.2
Aged 18	43.0	31.2	17.1
Aged 19	47.5	31.3	18.7
Aged 20	53.0	32.1	20.2
Aged 21	55.4	29.9	16.4
Aged 22	55.9	27.7	16.0
Aged 23	56.3	25.4	15.6
Aged 24	55.9	23.8	13.7
Aged 25	53.8	21.4	11.9
Aged 26 to 29	53.0	17.2	10.1
Aged 30 to 34	48.6	11.7	7.0
Aged 35 to 39	50.4	9.4	5.8
Aged 40 to 44	55.5	8.7	5.3
Aged 45 to 49	57.1	7.5	4.8
Aged 50 to 54	50.7	6.4	4.1
Aged 55 to 59	39.6	2.7	1.3
Aged 60 to 64	23.1	2.2	1.5
Aged 65 or older	6.5	0.5	0.2

Source: SAMHSA, Office of Applied Studies, National Survey on Drug Use and Health, 2006, Internet site http://oas.samhsa .gov/NSDUH/2k6NSDUH/tabs/Sect1peTabs1to46.htm#Tab1.1A

Table 4.24 Marijuana Use by High School Students by Sex, 2005

(percent of 9th to 12th graders who have ever used marijuana or have used marijuana in the past 30 days, by grade and sex, 2005)

	lifetime	past month
Total in 9th to 12th grade	**38.4%**	**20.2%**
Female	35.9	18.2
Male	40.9	22.1
Total 9th graders	**29.3**	**17.4**
Female	27.8	16.2
Male	30.9	18.6
Total 10th graders	**37.4**	**20.2**
Female	35.7	18.9
Male	39.0	21.5
Total 11th graders	**42.3**	**21.0**
Female	39.4	18.5
Male	45.1	23.5
Total 12th graders	**47.6**	**22.8**
Female	42.8	19.5
Male	52.4	26.1

Source: Centers for Disease Control and Prevention, Youth Risk Behavior Surveillance—United States, 2005, Mortality and Morbidity Weekly Report, Vol. 55/SS-5, June 9, 2006, Internet site http://www.cdc.gov/HealthyYouth/yrbs/index.htm

Most Women of Childbearing Age Use Contraceptives

The pill and female sterilization are the most popular contraceptives.

Among the nation's women of childbearing age—15 to 44—the 62 percent majority uses contraceptives. The pill is most popular, with 19 percent of women taking it, according to the federal government's National Survey of Family Growth. Female sterilization is the contraceptive choice of 17 percent of women, while condoms rank third at 11 percent. Use of the pill peaks at 32 percent among women aged 20 to 24, while women aged 35 or older are more likely to use female sterilization than the pill.

For most Americans, sexual activity begins in high school. Fully 62 percent of 12th grade girls and 64 percent of 12th grade boys have had sexual intercourse. Most sexually active teens used birth control the last time they had sex.

■ Sexual activity being the norm among high school students, sex education is a necessity.

The pill is popular among young women

(percent of women aged 15 to 44 who are using the contraceptive pill, 2002)

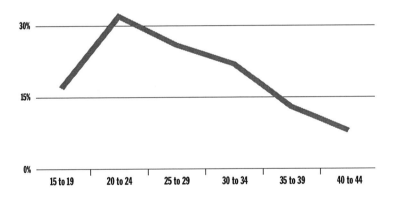

Table 4.25 Contraceptive Use by Age, 2002

(total number of women aged 15 to 44 and percent distribution by contraceptive status and age, 2002; numbers in thousands)

	total	15 to 19	20 to 24	25 to 29	30 to 34	35 to 39	40 to 44
Total women aged 15 to 44 (number)	61,561	9,834	9,840	9,249	10,272	10,853	11,512
Total women aged 15 to 44 (percent)	100.0%	100.0%	100.0%	100.0%	100.0%	100.0%	100.0%
Using contraception	**61.9%**	**31.5%**	**60.7%**	**68.0%**	**69.2%**	**70.8%**	**69.1%**
Female sterilization	16.7	–	2.2	10.3	19.0	29.2	34.7
Male sterilization	5.7	–	0.5	2.8	6.4	10.0	12.7
Pill	18.9	16.7	31.9	25.6	21.8	13.2	7.6
Implant, Lunelle, or Patch	0.8	0.4	0.9	1.7	0.9	0.5	0.2
Three-month injectable (Depo-Provera)	3.3	4.4	6.1	4.4	2.9	1.5	1.1
Intrauterine device (IUD)	1.3	0.1	1.1	2.5	2.2	1.0	0.8
Diaphragm	0.2	–	0.1	0.3	0.1	–	0.4
Condom	11.1	8.5	14.0	14.0	11.8	11.1	8.0
Periodic abstinence—calendar rhythm method	0.7	–	0.8	0.3	0.9	1.1	1.2
Periodic abstinence—natural family planning	0.2	–	–	0.4	0.2	0.3	0.4
Withdrawal	2.5	0.8	3.1	5.3	2.6	2.4	1.0
Other methods	0.6	0.6	0.2	0.4	0.4	0.5	1.1
Not using contraception	**38.1**	**68.5**	**39.3**	**32.0**	**30.8**	**29.2**	**30.9**
Surgically sterile, female (noncontraceptive)	1.5	–	–	0.4	0.9	2.1	4.9
Nonsurgically sterile, male or female	1.6	0.7	0.7	0.9	1.4	1.2	4.4
Pregnant or postpartum	5.3	3.5	9.5	8.4	6.9	3.8	0.8
Seeking pregnancy	4.2	1.2	2.8	5.5	7.0	5.1	3.3
Other nonuse							
Never had intercourse or no intercourse in past three months	18.1	56.2	17.9	8.9	7.6	9.1	10.8
Had intercourse during past three months	7.4	6.9	8.4	8.0	7.0	7.7	6.7

Note: Other methods includes Today sponge, cervical cap, female condom, and other methods. "–" means percentage is less than 0.05 or zero.
Source: National Center for Health Statistics, Use of Contraception and Use of Family Planning Services in the United States: 1982–2002, Advance Data, No. 350, 2004, Internet site http://www.cdc.gov/nchs/nsfg.htm

Table 4.26 Sexual Behavior among High School Students by Sex, 2005

(percent of 9th to 12th graders engaging in selected sexual activities, by sex and grade, 2005)

	total	9th grade	10th grade	11th grade	12th grade
FEMALES					
Ever had sexual intercourse	**45.7%**	**29.3%**	**44.0%**	**52.1%**	**62.4%**
First sexual intercourse before age 13	3.7	5.4	4.1	2.6	2.0
Four or more sex partners during lifetime	12.0	5.7	9.7	14.2	20.2
Currently sexually active*	**34.6**	**19.5**	**31.1**	**40.8**	**51.7**
Condom use during last sexual intercourse	55.9	71.5	57.1	57.8	46.1
Birth control pill use before last sexual intercourse	20.6	8.8	18.0	20.2	28.9
MALES					
Ever had sexual intercourse	**47.9**	**39.3**	**41.5**	**50.6**	**63.8**
First sexual intercourse before age 13	8.8	12.0	7.7	8.0	6.2
Four or more sex partners during lifetime	16.5	13.2	13.2	18.1	22.6
Currently sexually active*	**33.3**	**24.5**	**27.2**	**37.9**	**47.0**
Condom use during last sexual intercourse	70.0	77.1	74.4	66.0	65.8
Birth control pill use before last sexual intercourse	14.6	6.4	10.3	16.6	21.9

* Sexual intercourse during the three months preceding the survey.
Source: Centers for Disease Control and Prevention, Youth Risk Behavior Surveillance—United States, 2005, Mortality and Morbidity Weekly Report, Vol. 55/SS-5, June 9, 2006, Internet site http://www.cdc.gov/HealthyYouth/yrbs/index.htm

Most Teens Avoid Risky Behavior

The Millennial Generation lives neither recklessly nor risk free.

A survey of teen behavior by the Centers for Disease Control and Prevention shows that most 9th through 12th graders do not participate in risky activities—although many do. Most teens wear seat belts, but 13 percent of boys say they rarely or never use them. Most do not drink and drive, but 12 percent of boys say they have done so in the past month. Thirty percent of boys say they have carried a weapon in the past 30 days, and 43 percent have been in a physical fight in the past year.

Teenage boys are more likely than girls to engage in most risk behaviors. Boys are considerably more likely than girls to carry a weapon (30 versus 7 percent) or get in a physical fight (43 versus 28 percent). Girls, on the other hand, are more likely to have contemplated suicide (22 versus 12 percent).

■ Teenagers are notoriously unaware of the risks of reckless behavior. This is why accidents (particularly motor vehicle accidents) are one of the leading causes of death among young people.

Many teens say they rode with a driver who had been drinking

(percent of 9th through 12th graders who rode with a driver who had been drinking in the past 30 days, by sex, 2005)

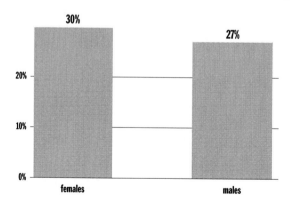

Table 4.27 Risk Behavior among 9th to 12th Graders by Sex, 2005

(percent of 9th to 12th graders engaging in selected risk behaviors, by sex, 2005)

	total	9th grade	10th grade	11th grade	12th grade
Females					
Rarely or never use seat belts when riding in car driven by someone else	7.8%	8.7%	7.7%	7.1%	7.5%
Rode in past 30 days with driver who had been drinking	29.6	30.1	29.5	28.1	30.7
Drove in past 30 days after drinking	8.1	4.5	4.8	9.5	15.0
Carried a weapon (gun, knife, club, etc.) in past 30 days	7.1	8.1	7.8	6.1	6.2
Carried a gun in past 30 days	0.9	1.0	1.0	0.9	0.8
Seriously considered attempting suicide during past 12 months	21.8	23.9	23.0	21.6	18.0
Attempted suicide during past 12 months	10.8	14.1	10.8	11.0	6.5
Was in a physical fight during past 12 months	28.1	37.2	27.6	25.0	20.3
Did no vigorous or moderate physical activity during past 7 days	11.3	8.2	10.3	12.4	15.2
Males					
Rarely or never use seat belts when riding in car driven by someone else	12.5	13.0	9.5	13.2	14.1
Rode with driver who had been drinking in past 30 days	27.2	25.8	26.2	27.7	29.5
Drove after drinking in past 30 days	11.7	6.5	8.3	14.7	19.2
Carried a weapon (gun, knife, club, etc.) in past 30 days	29.8	31.6	30.6	28.6	27.6
Carried a gun in past 30 days	9.9	11.3	9.4	9.1	9.0
Seriously considered attempting suicide during past 12 months	12.0	12.2	11.9	11.9	11.6
Attempted suicide during past 12 months	1.2	2.5	2.1	1.5	1.5
Was in a physical fight during past 12 months	43.4	49.6	45.2	38.2	38.0
Did no vigorous or moderate physical activity during past 7 days	7.9	7.2	7.5	8.4	8.4

Source: Centers for Disease Control and Prevention, Youth Risk Behavior Surveillance—United States, 2005, Mortality and Morbidity Weekly Report, Vol. 55/SS-5, June 9, 2006, Internet site http://www.cdc.gov/HealthyYouth/yrbs/index.htm

Many Older Americans Have Physical Difficulties

The biggest problem is stooping, bending, and kneeling.

A 2006 survey by the National Center for Health Statistics estimated that 32 million Americans—15 percent of people aged 18 or older—have physical difficulties. The difficulties range from walking a quarter-mile to climbing stairs and grasping small objects. Not surprisingly, older Americans are much more likely than younger adults to say they have physical difficulties.

Just 5 percent of people aged 18 to 44 reported having any physical difficulty. The proportion rises to 17 percent among 45-to-64-year-olds, and peaks at 48 percent among people aged 75 or older. The most common problem is difficulty stooping, bending, and kneeling, with 9 percent of people aged 18 or older saying this would be very difficult for them or they cannot do it at all. Almost the same proportion of adults say they would have difficulty standing for two hours.

Among people aged 75 or older, 32 percent say they would have difficulty standing for two hours. Thirty percent say it would be very difficult or impossible for them to walk a quarter of a mile. Twenty-nine percent have difficulty stooping, bending, and kneeling. People aged 75 or older account for one in four Americans with physical difficulties.

■ Although older Americans are most likely to report physical difficulties, adults under age 65 account for the majority of those with physical difficulties.

Physical difficulties rise with age

(percent of people with physical difficulties, by age, 2006)

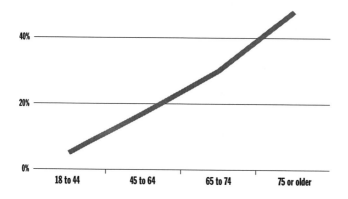

Table 4.28 Difficulties in Physical Functioning among Adults by Age, 2006

(number of people aged 18 or older with difficulties in physical functioning, by type of difficulty and age, 2006; numbers in thousands)

	total	18 to 44	45 to 64	aged 65 or older total	65 to 74	75 or older
TOTAL PEOPLE	220,267	110,391	74,203	35,674	19,081	16,593
Total with any physical difficulty	32,338	6,018	12,567	13,753	5,769	7,984
Walk quarter of a mile	15,739	2,180	5,699	7,860	2,950	4,910
Climb up ten steps without resting	12,018	1,530	4,511	5,977	2,278	3,699
Stand for two hours	18,960	2,924	7,240	8,795	3,418	5,377
Sit for two hours	7,219	1,750	3,455	2,014	909	1,105
Stoop, bend, or kneel	19,328	3,107	7,777	8,444	3,626	4,818
Reach over head	5,864	856	2,333	2,676	1,066	1,610
Grasp or handle small objects	3,997	628	1,649	1,720	607	1,113
Lift or carry ten pounds	9,681	1,501	3,659	4,521	1,699	2,822
Push or pull large objects	14,327	2,439	5,743	6,144	2,347	3,797

Percent with physical difficulty by age

	total	18 to 44	45 to 64	aged 65 or older total	65 to 74	75 or older
TOTAL PEOPLE	100.0%	100.0%	100.0%	100.0%	100.0%	100.0%
Total with any physical difficulty	14.7	5.5	16.9	38.6	30.2	48.1
Walk quarter of a mile	7.1	2.0	7.7	22.0	15.5	29.6
Climb up 10 steps without resting	5.5	1.4	6.1	16.8	11.9	22.3
Stand for two hours	8.6	2.6	9.8	24.7	17.9	32.4
Sit for two hours	3.3	1.6	4.7	5.6	4.8	6.7
Stoop, bend, or kneel	8.8	2.8	10.5	23.7	19.0	29.0
Reach over head	2.7	0.8	3.1	7.5	5.6	9.7
Grasp or handle small objects	1.8	0.6	2.2	4.8	3.2	6.7
Lift or carry ten pounds	4.4	1.4	4.9	12.7	8.9	17.0
Push or pull large objects	6.5	2.2	7.7	17.2	12.3	22.9

Percent distribution of those with physical difficulties by age

	total	18 to 44	45 to 64	aged 65 or older total	65 to 74	75 or older
TOTAL PEOPLE	100.0%	50.1%	33.7%	16.2%	8.7%	7.5%
Total with any physical difficulty	100.0	18.6	38.9	42.5	17.8	24.7
Walk quarter of a mile	100.0	13.9	36.2	49.9	18.7	31.2
Climb up 10 steps without resting	100.0	12.7	37.5	49.7	19.0	30.8
Stand for two hours	100.0	15.4	38.2	46.4	18.0	28.4
Sit for two hours	100.0	24.2	47.9	27.9	12.6	15.3
Stoop, bend, or kneel	100.0	16.1	40.2	43.7	18.8	24.9
Reach over head	100.0	14.6	39.8	45.6	18.2	27.5
Grasp or handle small objects	100.0	15.7	41.3	43.0	15.2	27.8
Lift or carry ten pounds	100.0	15.5	37.8	46.7	17.5	29.1
Push or pull large objects	100.0	17.0	40.1	42.9	16.4	26.5

Note: Respondents were classified as having difficulties if they responded "very difficult" or "can't do at all."
Source: National Center for Health Statistics, Summary Health Statistics for U.S. Adults: National Health Interview Survey, 2006, Series 10, No. 235, 2007, Internet site http://www.cdc.gov/nchs/nhis.htm; calculations by New Strategist

Health Problems Are Common among Older Americans

Lower back pain is the most frequently reported health condition.

Twenty-eight percent of Americans aged 18 or older have experienced lower back pain for at least one full day in the past three months, making it the most frequently reported health problem. Arthritis has been diagnosed in 21 percent of the adult population, and chronic joint symptoms trouble an even larger 26 percent.

Many ailments are more common among older than younger Americans. Fifty-one percent of people aged 75 or older have been diagnosed with arthritis, for example, compared with only 7 percent of 18-to-44-year-olds. Half the oldest Americans have hearing problems. But only 6 percent of people aged 75 or older suffer from migraines or severe headaches compared with a larger 18 percent of people aged 18 to 44.

■ As the Baby-Boom generation ages into its sixties, the number of people with arthritis or hearing problems will soar.

Most people aged 75 or older have arthritis

(percent of people diagnosed with arthritis, by age, 2006)

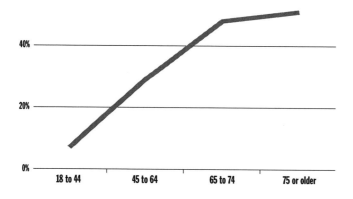

Table 4.29 Number of Adults with Health Condition by Age, 2006

(number of people aged 18 or older with selected health conditions, by type of condition and age, 2006; numbers in thousands)

	total	18 to 44	45 to 64	aged 65 or older total	65 to 74	75 or older
TOTAL PEOPLE	**220,267**	**110,391**	**74,203**	**35,674**	**19,081**	**16,593**
Selected circulatory diseases						
Heart disease, all types	24,107	4,013	9,094	11,000	4,985	6,015
Coronary	14,063	985	5,346	7,732	3,504	4,228
Hypertension	51,562	8,552	24,073	18,937	10,062	8,875
Stroke	5,642	532	1,809	3,300	1,445	1,855
Selected respiratory conditions						
Emphysema	4,069	290	1,765	2,014	945	1,069
Asthma						
Ever	24,256	12,668	7,806	3,782	2,238	1,544
Still	16,057	7,990	5,576	2,491	1,481	1,010
Hay fever	17,579	7,756	7,154	2,668	1,670	998
Sinusitis	30,693	13,254	12,499	4,940	2,987	1,953
Chronic bronchitis	9,463	3,182	4,108	2,173	1,063	1,110
Selected type of cancer						
Any cancer	15,820	2,336	5,956	7,528	3,279	4,249
Breast cancer	2,504	200	1,090	1,214	407	807
Cervical cancer	1,395	770	436	189	97	92
Prostate cancer	1,840	0	330	1,511	644	867
Other selected diseases and conditions						
Diabetes	17,110	2,924	7,752	6,434	3,469	2,965
Ulcers	14,474	4,524	6,125	3,825	1,821	2,004
Kidney disease	3,347	797	1,339	1,211	464	747
Liver disease	3,294	826	1,948	519	288	231
Arthritis diagnosis	46,502	7,646	21,269	17,586	9,121	8,465
Chronic joint symptoms	56,364	15,958	24,981	15,425	8,131	7,294
Migraines, severe headaches	33,099	19,598	10,913	2,588	1,611	977
Pain in neck	32,002	12,934	13,756	5,312	3,010	2,302
Pain in lower back	60,607	26,309	23,036	11,261	5,942	5,319
Pain in face or jaw	9,893	4,913	3,662	1,318	768	550
Selected sensory problems						
Hearing	37,215	8,439	14,360	14,416	6,082	8,334
Vision	21,211	6,007	9,016	6,188	2,596	3,592
Absence of all natural teeth	17,577	2,481	5,920	9,175	4,330	4,845

Note: The conditions shown are those that have ever been diagnosed by a doctor, except as noted. Hay fever, sinusitis, and chronic bronchitis have been diagnosed in the past 12 months. Kidney and liver disease have been diagnosed in the past 12 months and exclude kidney stones, bladder infections, and incontinence. Chronic joint symptoms are shown if respondent had pain, aching, or stiffness in or around a joint (excluding back and neck) and the condition began more than three months ago. Migraines, pain in neck, lower back, face, or jaw are shown only if pain lasted a whole day or more.
Source: National Center for Health Statistics, Summary Health Statistics for U.S. Adults: National Health Interview Survey, 2006, Series 10, No. 235, 2007, Internet site http://www.cdc.gov/nchs/nhis.htm

Table 4.30 Distribution of Health Conditions among Adults by Age, 2006

(percent distribution of people aged 18 or older with selected health conditions, by type of condition and age, 2006)

	total	18 to 44	45 to 64	aged 65 or older total	65 to 74	75 or older
TOTAL PEOPLE	100.0%	50.1%	33.7%	16.2%	8.7%	7.5%
Selected circulatory diseases						
Heart disease, all types	100.0	16.6	37.7	45.6	20.7	25.0
Coronary	100.0	7.0	38.0	55.0	24.9	30.1
Hypertension	100.0	16.6	46.7	36.7	19.5	17.2
Stroke	100.0	9.4	32.1	58.5	25.6	32.9
Selected respiratory conditions						
Emphysema	100.0	7.1	43.4	49.5	23.2	26.3
Asthma						
Ever	100.0	52.2	32.2	15.6	9.2	6.4
Still	100.0	49.8	34.7	15.5	9.2	6.3
Hay fever	100.0	44.1	40.7	15.2	9.5	5.7
Sinusitis	100.0	43.2	40.7	16.1	9.7	6.4
Chronic bronchitis	100.0	33.6	43.4	23.0	11.2	11.7
Selected type of cancer						
Any cancer	100.0	14.8	37.6	47.6	20.7	26.9
Breast cancer	100.0	8.0	43.5	48.5	16.3	32.2
Cervical cancer	100.0	55.2	31.3	13.5	7.0	6.6
Prostate cancer	100.0	0.0	17.9	82.1	35.0	47.1
Other selected diseases and conditions						
Diabetes	100.0	17.1	45.3	37.6	20.3	17.3
Ulcers	100.0	31.3	42.3	26.4	12.6	13.8
Kidney disease	100.0	23.8	40.0	36.2	13.9	22.3
Liver disease	100.0	25.1	59.1	15.8	8.7	7.0
Arthritis diagnosis	100.0	16.4	45.7	37.8	19.6	18.2
Chronic joint symptoms	100.0	28.3	44.3	27.4	14.4	12.9
Migraines, severe headaches	100.0	59.2	33.0	7.8	4.9	3.0
Pain in neck	100.0	40.4	43.0	16.6	9.4	7.2
Pain in lower back	100.0	43.4	38.0	18.6	9.8	8.8
Pain in face or jaw	100.0	49.7	37.0	13.3	7.8	5.6
Selected sensory problems						
Hearing	100.0	22.7	38.6	38.7	16.3	22.4
Vision	100.0	28.3	42.5	29.2	12.2	16.9
Absence of all natural teeth	100.0	14.1	33.7	52.2	24.6	27.6

Note: The conditions shown are those that have ever been diagnosed by a doctor, except as noted. Hay fever, sinusitis, and chronic bronchitis have been diagnosed in the past 12 months. Kidney and liver disease have been diagnosed in the past 12 months and exclude kidney stones, bladder infections, and incontinence. Chronic joint symptoms are shown if respondent had pain, aching, or stiffness in or around a joint (excluding back and neck) and the condition began more than three months ago. Migraines, pain in neck, lower back, face, or jaw are shown only if pain lasted a whole day or more.
Source: National Center for Health Statistics, Summary Health Statistics for U.S. Adults: National Health Interview Survey, 2006, Series 10, No. 235, 2007, Internet site http://www.cdc.gov/nchs/nhis.htm; calculations by New Strategist

Table 4.31 Percent of Adults with Health Conditions by Age, 2006

(percent of people aged 18 or older with selected health conditions, by type of condition and age, 2006)

	total	18 to 44	45 to 64	aged 65 or older total	65 to 74	75 or older
TOTAL PEOPLE	100.0%	100.0%	100.0%	100.0%	100.0%	100.0%
Selected circulatory diseases						
Heart disease, all types	10.9	3.6	12.3	30.8	26.1	36.3
Coronary	6.4	0.9	7.2	21.7	18.4	25.5
Hypertension	23.4	7.7	32.4	53.1	52.7	53.5
Stroke	2.6	0.5	2.4	9.3	7.6	11.2
Selected respiratory conditions						
Emphysema	1.8	0.3	2.4	5.6	5.0	6.4
Asthma						
Ever	11.0	11.5	10.5	10.6	11.7	9.3
Still	7.3	7.2	7.5	7.0	7.8	6.1
Hay fever	8.0	7.0	9.6	7.5	8.8	6.0
Sinusitis	13.9	12.0	16.8	13.8	15.7	11.8
Chronic bronchitis	4.3	2.9	5.5	6.1	5.6	6.7
Selected type of cancer						
Any cancer	7.2	2.1	8.0	21.1	17.2	25.6
Breast cancer	1.1	0.2	1.5	3.4	2.1	4.9
Cervical cancer	0.6	0.7	0.6	0.5	0.5	0.6
Prostate cancer	0.8	0.0	0.4	4.2	3.4	5.2
Other selected diseases and conditions						
Diabetes	7.8	2.6	10.4	18.0	18.2	17.9
Ulcers	6.6	4.1	8.3	10.7	9.5	12.1
Kidney disease	1.5	0.7	1.8	3.4	2.4	4.5
Liver disease	1.5	0.7	2.6	1.5	1.5	1.4
Arthritis diagnosis	21.1	6.9	28.7	49.3	47.8	51.0
Chronic joint symptoms	25.6	14.5	33.7	43.2	42.6	44.0
Migraines, severe headaches	15.0	17.8	14.7	7.3	8.4	5.9
Pain in neck	14.5	11.7	18.5	14.9	15.8	13.9
Pain in lower back	27.5	23.8	31.0	31.6	31.1	32.1
Pain in face or jaw	4.5	4.5	4.9	3.7	4.0	3.3
Selected sensory problems						
Hearing	16.9	7.6	19.4	40.4	31.9	50.2
Vision	9.6	5.4	12.2	17.3	13.6	21.6
Absence of all natural teeth	8.0	2.2	8.0	25.7	22.7	29.2

Note: The conditions shown are those that have ever been diagnosed by a doctor, except as noted. Hay fever, sinusitis, and chronic bronchitis have been diagnosed in the past 12 months. Kidney and liver disease have been diagnosed in the past 12 months and exclude kidney stones, bladder infections, and incontinence. Chronic joint symptoms are shown if respondent had pain, aching, or stiffness in or around a joint (excluding back and neck) and the condition began more than three months ago. Migraines, pain in neck, lower back, face, or jaw are shown only if pain lasted a whole day or more.
Source: National Center for Health Statistics, Summary Health Statistics for U.S. Adults: National Health Interview Survey, 2006, Series 10, No. 235, 2007, Internet site http://www.cdc.gov/nchs/nhis.htm; calculations by New Strategist

Men Aged 25 to 44 Account for Most AIDS Cases

Only 19 percent of those who have been diagnosed with AIDS are women.

Through June 2006, more than 950,000 people had been diagnosed with AIDS. While new drug therapies have been successful in reducing the AIDS mortality rate, the number of AIDS cases continues to climb.

Men accounted for 80 percent of people diagnosed with AIDS through June 2006, and the 58 percent majority were aged 25 to 44 at the time of diagnosis. Men aged 35 to 44 account for the largest share of people diagnosed with AIDS—32 percent of the total through June 2006. Men aged 25 to 34 account for another 26 percent.

Among women who have been diagnosed with AIDS, the 35-to-44 age group accounts for the largest share—7 percent of all AIDS cases through June 2006. Children under age 13 account for less than 1 percent of AIDS victims.

■ Although AIDS mortality has been reduced, the disease is still a devastating diagnosis requiring expensive drug regimens to manage—and drug treatments do not always work.

Men dominate AIDS cases

(percent distribution of people diagnosed with AIDS by age and sex, through 2006)

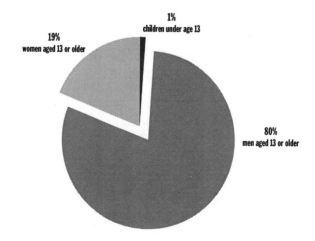

1%
children under age 13

19%
women aged 13 or older

80%
men aged 13 or older

Table 4.32 AIDS Cases by Sex and Age, through June 30, 2006

(cumulative number and percent distribution of AIDS cases by age at diagnosis and sex for those aged 13 or older, through June 30, 2006)

	number	percent distribution
Total cases	**952,629**	**100.0%**
Under age 13	9,101	1.0
Aged 13 to 14	1,062	0.1
Aged 15 to 24	40,084	4.2
Aged 25 to 34	308,067	32.3
Aged 35 to 44	373,201	39.2
Aged 45 to 54	159,681	16.8
Aged 55 to 64	46,917	4.9
Aged 65 or older	14,504	1.5
Men		
Total, aged 13 or older	**761,723**	**80.0**
Aged 13 to 14	615	0.1
Aged 15 to 24	27,413	2.9
Aged 25 to 34	246,054	25.8
Aged 35 to 44	305,376	32.1
Aged 45 to 54	132,339	13.9
Aged 55 to 64	38,713	4.1
Aged 65 or older	11,207	1.2
Women		
Total, aged 13 or older	**181,802**	**19.1**
Aged 13 to 14	447	0.0
Aged 15 to 24	12,671	1.3
Aged 25 to 34	62,013	6.5
Aged 35 to 44	67,825	7.1
Aged 45 to 54	27,342	2.9
Aged 55 to 64	8,204	0.9
Aged 65 or older	3,297	0.3

Note: Numbers will not add to total because of methodology and unknown sex.
Source: National Center for Health Statistics, Health United States 2007, Internet site http://www.cdc.gov/nchs/hus.htm

Asthma and Allergies Affect Many Children

Boys are more likely than girls to have learning disabilities.

Asthma is a growing problem among children. Fully 13 percent of the nation's 73 million children under age 18 have been diagnosed with asthma. Nine percent have had an asthma attack in the past year. Boys are more likely to have asthma than girls (16 versus 11 percent), and blacks more than whites (17 versus 13 percent). Children in single-parent families headed by women are much more likely to have asthma than those from two-parent families (20 versus 11 percent).

Nearly 5 million children (6 percent) have been diagnosed with a learning disability, and about the same number (6 percent) have attention deficit hyperactivity disorder. Boys are far more likely than girls to have these conditions and account for nearly two-thirds of those with learning disabilities and nearly three-fourths of those with attention deficit hyperactivity disorder.

Many children use prescription medications. Nearly 10 million children have taken prescription medications regularly for at least three months during the past year. That's a substantial 13 percent of the nation's children. Among 12-to-17-year-olds, the figure is an even higher 16 percent.

■ Prescription drug use is growing, even among children.

Asthma is a big problem for children in single-parent families

(percent of people under age 18 diagnosed with asthma, by family type, 2006)

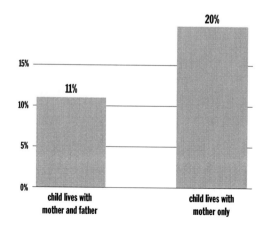

Table 4.33 Health Conditions among Children by Selected Characteristics, 2006

(number of people under age 18 with selected health conditions, by characteristic and type of condition, 2006; numbers in thousands)

| | total children | diagnosed with asthma | experienced in last 12 months | | | | ever told had* | | prescription medication taken regularly for at least 3 months |
			asthma attack	hay fever	respiratory allergies	other allergies	learning disability	attention deficit hyperactivity disorder	
TOTAL CHILDREN	73,493	9,876	6,819	6,785	8,614	9,557	4,748	4,545	9,572
Sex									
Female	35,924	4,001	2,697	3,014	3,732	4,797	1,746	1,193	4,130
Male	37,569	5,875	4,122	3,771	4,882	4,760	3,002	3,352	5,442
Age									
Aged 0 to 4	20,410	1,521	1,178	1,024	1,726	3,117	172	46	1,642
Aged 5 to 11	27,776	4,455	3,191	2,951	3,800	3,376	2,001	2,055	3,947
Aged 12 to 17	25,307	3,900	2,451	2,809	3,088	3,064	2,575	2,443	3,983
Race and Hispanic origin									
Asian	2,835	334	177	277	260	334	54	34	207
Black	11,455	1,921	1,461	796	1,200	1,723	739	705	1,306
Hispanic	14,815	1,901	1,328	1,213	1,364	1,347	753	602	1,170
Non-Hispanic white	42,480	5,428	3,649	4,218	5,451	5,796	3,103	3,059	6,581
Family structure									
Mother and father	51,777	5,829	3,928	4,761	5,729	6,437	2,809	2,489	6,363
Mother, no father	17,083	3,425	2,487	1,599	2,389	2,655	1,457	1,611	2,653
Father, no mother	2,479	294	197	180	187	250	237	226	210
Neither mother nor father	2,154	328	207	245	309	216	245	219	347
Parent's education									
Less than high school diploma	10,103	1,343	961	594	849	976	631	408	786
High school diploma	16,106	2,039	1,457	1,215	1,629	1,879	1,213	1,133	1,900
More than high school	44,356	6,110	4,138	4,723	5,802	6,478	2,640	2,762	6,508
Household income									
Less than $20,000	12,865	2,269	1,711	919	1,656	1,821	1,195	955	1,911
$20,000 to $34,999	10,320	1,397	986	738	1,241	1,284	723	689	1,194
$35,000 to $54,999	10,843	1,640	1,111	1,136	1,262	1,571	688	646	1,302
$55,000 to $74,999	8,071	905	618	847	1,045	1,082	591	599	1,064
$75,000 or more	17,425	2,162	1,347	2,132	2,113	2,355	954	1,045	2,609

* Ever told by a school representative or health professional. Data exclude children under age 3.
Note: Mother and father can include biological, adoptive, step, in-law, or foster relationships. Legal guardians are classified as neither mother nor father. Parent's education is the education level of the parent with the higher level of education. Other allergies include food or digestive allergies, eczema, and other skin allergies.
Source: National Center for Health Statistics, Summary Health Statistics for U.S. Children: National Health Interview Survey, 2006, Series 10, No. 234, 2007, Internet site http://www.cdc.gov/nchs/nhis.htm

Table 4.34 Distribution of Health Conditions by Selected Characteristics of Children, 2006

(percent distribution of people under age 18 with health condition by selected characteristics, 2006)

	total children	diagnosed with asthma	experienced in last 12 months asthma attack	hay fever	respiratory allergies	other allergies	learning disability	ever told had* attention deficit hyperactivity disorder	prescription medication taken regularly for at least 3 months
TOTAL CHILDREN	100.0%	100.0%	100.0%	100.0%	100.0%	100.0%	100.0%	100.0%	100.0%
Sex									
Female	48.9	40.5	39.6	44.4	43.3	50.2	36.8	26.2	43.1
Male	51.1	59.5	60.4	55.6	56.7	49.8	63.2	73.8	56.9
Age									
Aged 0 to 4	27.8	15.4	17.3	15.1	20.0	32.6	3.6	1.0	17.2
Aged 5 to 11	37.8	45.1	46.8	43.5	44.1	35.3	42.1	45.2	41.2
Aged 12 to 17	34.4	39.5	35.9	41.4	35.8	32.1	54.2	53.8	41.6
Race and Hispanic origin									
Asian	3.9	3.4	2.6	4.1	3.0	3.5	1.1	0.7	2.2
Black	15.6	19.5	21.4	11.7	13.9	18.0	15.6	15.5	13.6
Hispanic	20.2	19.2	19.5	17.9	15.8	14.1	15.9	13.2	12.2
Non-Hispanic white	57.8	55.0	53.5	62.2	63.3	60.6	65.4	67.3	68.8
Family structure									
Mother and father	70.5	59.0	57.6	70.2	66.5	67.4	59.2	54.8	66.5
Mother, no father	23.2	34.7	36.5	23.6	27.7	27.8	30.7	35.4	27.7
Father, no mother	3.4	3.0	2.9	2.7	2.2	2.6	5.0	5.0	2.2
Neither mother nor father	2.9	3.3	3.0	3.6	3.6	2.3	5.2	4.8	3.6
Parent's education									
Less than high school diploma	13.7	13.6	14.1	8.8	9.9	10.2	13.3	9.0	8.2
High school diploma	21.9	20.6	21.4	17.9	18.9	19.7	25.5	24.9	19.8
More than high school	60.4	61.9	60.7	69.6	67.4	67.8	55.6	60.8	68.0
Household income									
Less than $20,000	17.5	23.0	25.1	13.5	19.2	19.1	25.2	21.0	20.0
$20,000 to $34,999	14.0	14.1	14.5	10.9	14.4	13.4	15.2	15.2	12.5
$35,000 to $54,999	14.8	16.6	16.3	16.7	14.7	16.4	14.5	14.2	13.6
$55,000 to $74,999	11.0	9.2	9.1	12.5	12.1	11.3	12.4	13.2	11.1
$75,000 or more	23.7	21.9	19.8	31.4	24.5	24.6	20.1	23.0	27.3

* Ever told by a school representative or health professional. Data exclude children under age 3.
Note: Mother and father can include biological, adoptive, step, in-law, or foster relationships. Legal guardians are classified as neither mother nor father. Parent's education is the education level of the parent with the higher level of education. Other allergies include food or digestive allergies, eczema, and other skin allergies.
Source: National Center for Health Statistics, Summary Health Statistics for U.S. Children: National Health Interview Survey, 2006, Series 10, No. 234, 2007, Internet site http://www.cdc.gov/nchs/nhis.htm; calculations by New Strategist

Table 4.35 Percent of Children with Health Conditions by Selected Characteristics, 2006

(percent of people under age 18 with selected health conditions, by type of condition and selected characteristics, 2006)

| | total children | diagnosed with asthma | experienced in last 12 months | | | | ever told had* | | prescription medication taken regularly for at least 3 months |
			asthma attack	hay fever	respiratory allergies	other allergies	learning disability	attention deficit hyperactivity disorder	
TOTAL CHILDREN	100.0%	13.4%	9.3%	9.2%	11.7%	13.0%	6.5%	6.2%	13.0%
Sex									
Female	100.0	11.1	7.5	8.4	10.4	13.4	4.9	3.3	11.5
Male	100.0	15.6	11.0	10.0	13.0	12.7	8.0	8.9	14.5
Age									
Aged 0 to 4	100.0	7.5	5.8	5.0	8.5	15.3	0.8	0.2	8.0
Aged 5 to 11	100.0	16.0	11.5	10.6	13.7	12.2	7.2	7.4	14.2
Aged 12 to 17	100.0	15.4	9.7	11.1	12.2	12.1	10.2	9.7	15.7
Race and Hispanic origin									
Asian	100.0	11.8	6.2	9.8	9.2	11.8	1.9	1.2	7.3
Black	100.0	16.8	12.8	6.9	10.5	15.0	6.5	6.2	11.4
Hispanic	100.0	12.8	9.0	8.2	9.2	9.1	5.1	4.1	7.9
Non-Hispanic white	100.0	12.8	8.6	9.9	12.8	13.6	7.3	7.2	15.5
Family structure									
Mother and father	100.0	11.3	7.6	9.2	11.1	12.4	5.4	4.8	12.3
Mother, no father	100.0	20.0	14.6	9.4	14.0	15.5	8.5	9.4	15.5
Father, no mother	100.0	11.9	7.9	7.3	7.5	10.1	9.6	9.1	8.5
Neither mother nor father	100.0	15.2	9.6	11.4	14.3	10.0	11.4	10.2	16.1
Parent's education									
Less than high school diploma	100.0	13.3	9.5	5.9	8.4	9.7	6.2	4.0	7.8
High school diploma	100.0	12.7	9.0	7.5	10.1	11.7	7.5	7.0	11.8
More than high school	100.0	13.8	9.3	10.6	13.1	14.6	6.0	6.2	14.7
Household income									
Less than $20,000	100.0	17.6	13.3	7.1	12.9	14.2	9.3	7.4	14.9
$20,000 to $34,999	100.0	13.5	9.6	7.2	12.0	12.4	7.0	6.7	11.6
$35,000 to $54,999	100.0	15.1	10.2	10.5	11.6	14.5	6.3	6.0	12.0
$55,000 to $74,999	100.0	11.2	7.7	10.5	12.9	13.4	7.3	7.4	13.2
$75,000 or more	100.0	12.4	7.7	12.2	12.1	13.5	5.5	6.0	15.0

* Ever told by a school representative or health professional. Data exclude children under age 3.
Note: Mother and father can include biological, adoptive, step, in-law, or foster relationships. Legal guardians are classified as neither mother nor father. Parent's education is the education level of the parent with the higher level of education. Other allergies include food or digestive allergies, eczema, and other skin allergies.
Source: National Center for Health Statistics, Summary Health Statistics for U.S. Children: National Health Interview Survey, 2006, Series 10, No. 234, 2007, Internet site http://www.cdc.gov/nchs/nhis.htm; calculations by New Strategist

More People Do Not Have Health Insurance

Thanks to Medicare, older Americans are most likely to be insured.

Eighty-four percent of Americans were covered by public or private health insurance in 2006, leaving 47 million people without insurance. The percentage of people without health insurance rose from 14 to 16 percent between 2000 and 2006. In some age groups the increase was much steeper. The proportion of people aged 25 to 34 without health insurance climbed from 21 to 27 percent between 2000 and 2006. Cost is the number-one reason for not having health insurance, cited by 46 percent of those under age 65 without insurance.

Only 31 percent of Americans are covered by employment-based health insurance through their own employer. Another 28 percent are covered by the employment-based health insurance of a spouse or parent. Only 9 percent can afford to buy their own private health insurance. The government's Medicare program covers 94 percent of Americans aged 65 or older. Medicaid, the health insurance program for the poor, covers 13 percent of all Americans—including 27 percent of children.

■ With so many Americans covered by a spouse's or parent's employment-based health insurance, many people are only a divorce or a birthday away from no coverage at all.

Twenty-nine percent of 18-to-24-year-olds do not have health insurance

(percent of people without health insurance, by age, 2006)

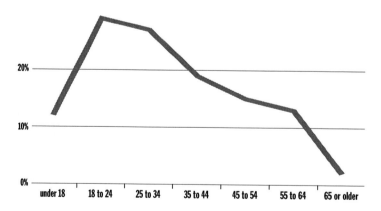

Table 4.36 Health Insurance Coverage by Age, 2006: Private Health Insurance Type

(number and percent distribution of people by age and health insurance coverage status, 2006; numbers in thousands)

		with any health insurance						
			with private health insurance					
				employment-based		direct	government	no
	total	total	total	total	own	purchase	insurance	insurance
Total people	**296,824**	**249,829**	**201,690**	**177,152**	**93,150**	**27,066**	**80,270**	**46,995**
Under age 18	74,101	65,440	47,906	44,257	209	3,890	22,109	8,661
Aged 18 to 24	28,405	20,081	17,030	13,768	5,406	1,736	4,006	8,323
Aged 25 to 34	39,868	29,154	25,814	24,009	18,193	2,160	4,460	10,713
Aged 35 to 44	42,762	34,744	31,531	29,463	21,035	2,788	4,409	8,018
Aged 45 to 54	43,461	36,819	33,250	30,868	22,406	3,297	5,182	6,642
Aged 55 to 64	32,191	28,096	24,255	21,701	15,989	3,276	6,122	4,095
Aged 65 or older	36,035	35,494	21,904	13,086	9,912	9,918	33,982	541
Percent distribution by coverage status								
Total people	**100.0%**	**84.2%**	**67.9%**	**59.7%**	**31.4%**	**9.1%**	**27.0%**	**15.8%**
Under age 18	100.0	88.3	64.6	59.7	0.3	5.2	29.8	11.7
Aged 18 to 24	100.0	70.7	60.0	48.5	19.0	6.1	14.1	29.3
Aged 25 to 34	100.0	73.1	64.7	60.2	45.6	5.4	11.2	26.9
Aged 35 to 44	100.0	81.2	73.7	68.9	49.2	6.5	10.3	18.8
Aged 45 to 54	100.0	84.7	76.5	71.0	51.6	7.6	11.9	15.3
Aged 55 to 64	100.0	87.3	75.3	67.4	49.7	10.2	19.0	12.7
Aged 65 or older	100.0	98.5	60.8	36.3	27.5	27.5	94.3	1.5
Percent distribution by age								
Total people	**100.0%**	**100.0%**	**100.0%**	**100.0%**	**100.0%**	**100.0%**	**100.0%**	**100.0%**
Under age 18	25.0	26.2	23.8	25.0	0.2	14.4	27.5	18.4
Aged 18 to 24	9.6	8.0	8.4	7.8	5.8	6.4	5.0	17.7
Aged 25 to 34	13.4	11.7	12.8	13.6	19.5	8.0	5.6	22.8
Aged 35 to 44	14.4	13.9	15.6	16.6	22.6	10.3	5.5	17.1
Aged 45 to 54	14.6	14.7	16.5	17.4	24.1	12.2	6.5	14.1
Aged 55 to 64	10.8	11.2	12.0	12.2	17.2	12.1	7.6	8.7
Aged 65 or older	12.1	14.2	10.9	7.4	10.6	36.6	42.3	1.2

Note: Numbers may not add to total because some people have more than one type of health insurance coverage.
Source: Bureau of the Census, 2007 Current Population Survey, Internet site http://pubdb3.census.gov/macro/032007/health/toc.htm; calculations by New Strategist

Table 4.37 Health Insurance Coverage by Age, 2006: Government Health Insurance Type

(number and percent distribution of people by age and health insurance status, 2006; numbers in thousands)

	total	total	with any health insurance — with government health insurance — total	Medicaid	Medicare	military	private insurance	no insurance
Total people	**296,824**	**249,829**	**80,270**	**38,281**	**40,343**	**10,547**	**201,690**	**46,995**
Under age 18	74,101	65,440	22,109	20,067	411	2,058	47,906	8,661
Aged 18 to 24	28,405	20,081	4,006	3,252	154	721	17,030	8,323
Aged 25 to 34	39,868	29,154	4,460	3,374	472	890	25,814	10,713
Aged 35 to 44	42,762	34,744	4,409	2,977	806	1,015	31,531	8,018
Aged 45 to 54	43,461	36,819	5,182	2,885	1,739	1,337	33,250	6,642
Aged 55 to 64	32,191	28,096	6,122	2,362	2,956	1,845	24,255	4,095
Aged 65 or older	36,035	35,494	33,982	3,364	33,806	2,682	21,904	541

Percent distribution by coverage status

	total	total	total	Medicaid	Medicare	military	private insurance	no insurance
Total people	**100.0%**	**84.2%**	**27.0%**	**12.9%**	**13.6%**	**3.6%**	**67.9%**	**15.8%**
Under age 18	100.0	88.3	29.8	27.1	0.6	2.8	64.6	11.7
Aged 18 to 24	100.0	70.7	14.1	11.4	0.5	2.5	60.0	29.3
Aged 25 to 34	100.0	73.1	11.2	8.5	1.2	2.2	64.7	26.9
Aged 35 to 44	100.0	81.2	10.3	7.0	1.9	2.4	73.7	18.8
Aged 45 to 54	100.0	84.7	11.9	6.6	4.0	3.1	76.5	15.3
Aged 55 to 64	100.0	87.3	19.0	7.3	9.2	5.7	75.3	12.7
Aged 65 or older	100.0	98.5	94.3	9.3	93.8	7.4	60.8	1.5

Percent distribution by age

	total	total	total	Medicaid	Medicare	military	private insurance	no insurance
Total people	**100.0%**	**100.0%**	**100.0%**	**100.0%**	**100.0%**	**100.0%**	**100.0%**	**100.0%**
Under age 18	25.0	26.2	27.5	52.4	1.0	19.5	23.8	18.4
Aged 18 to 24	9.6	8.0	5.0	8.5	0.4	6.8	8.4	17.7
Aged 25 to 34	13.4	11.7	5.6	8.8	1.2	8.4	12.8	22.8
Aged 35 to 44	14.4	13.9	5.5	7.8	2.0	9.6	15.6	17.1
Aged 45 to 54	14.6	14.7	6.5	7.5	4.3	12.7	16.5	14.1
Aged 55 to 64	10.8	11.2	7.6	6.2	7.3	17.5	12.0	8.7
Aged 65 or older	12.1	14.2	42.3	8.8	83.8	25.4	10.9	1.2

Note: Numbers may not add to total because some people have more than one type of health insurance coverage.
Source: Bureau of the Census, 2007 Current Population Survey, Internet site http://pubdb3.census.gov/macro/032007/health/toc
.htm; calculations by New Strategist

Table 4.38 People without Health Insurance by Age, 2000 and 2006

(number and percent of people without health insurance coverge by age, 2000 and 2006; percent change in number and percentage point change in share, 2000–2006; numbers in thousands)

	2006	2000	percent change 2000–06
Total without coverage	**46,995**	**38,426**	**22.3%**
Under age 18	8,661	8,385	3.3
Aged 18 to 24	8,323	7,203	15.5
Aged 25 to 34	10,713	8,318	28.8
Aged 35 to 44	8,018	6,746	18.9
Aged 45 to 54	6,642	4,492	47.9
Aged 55 to 64	4,095	3,031	35.1
Aged 65 or older	541	251	115.5

	2006	2000	percentage point change 2000–06
Total without coverage	**15.8%**	**13.7%**	**2.1**
Under age 18	11.7	11.6	0.1
Aged 18 to 24	29.3	26.9	2.4
Aged 25 to 34	26.9	21.4	5.5
Aged 35 to 44	18.8	15.1	3.7
Aged 45 to 54	15.3	11.6	3.7
Aged 55 to 64	12.7	12.3	0.4
Aged 65 or older	1.5	0.7	0.8

Source: Bureau of the Census, Current Population Surveys, Internet site http://www.census.gov/hhes/hlthins/historic/index.html; calculations by New Strategist

Table 4.39 Reason for No Health Insurance Coverage by Age, 2006

(number of people under age 65 without health insurance and percent distribution by reason for no coverage, by age, 2006; numbers in thousands)

	total people under age 65 without health insurance		cost	lost job or change in employment	employer didn't offer or company refused	Medicaid stopped	ineligible due to age or left school	change in marital status or death of parent	other
	number	percent							
Total under age 65	**43,420**	**100.0%**	**46.4%**	**21.5%**	**13.4%**	**9.6%**	**7.8%**	**2.7%**	**5.9%**
Under age 12	4,140	100.0	39.3	18.3	6.8	21.9	1.1	2.7	8.4
Aged 12 to 17	2,782	100.0	45.3	18.4	8.1	14.6	2.9	2.6	8.3
Aged 18 to 44	26,803	100.0	46.4	19.4	15.1	8.8	12.0	2.2	5.5
Aged 45 to 64	9,696	100.0	49.6	29.5	12.9	5.2	0.5	4.1	5.2

Note: Numbers may not sum to total because people can report more than one reason. "Other reason" includes moved, self-employed, never had coverage, did not want or need coverage, and other unspecified reasons.
Source: National Center for Health Statistics, Summary Health Statistics for the U.S. Population: National Health Interview Survey, 2006, Vital and Health Statistics, Series 10, No. 236, 2007, Internet site http://www.cdc.gov/nchs/nhis.htm; calculations by New Strategist

More than One Billion Health Care Visits in 2005

Most health care visits are made by people aged 45 or older.

Americans visited a doctor 964 million times in 2005. They visited emergency rooms 115 million times and made 90 million trips to hospital outpatient departments. Older Americans dominate doctor visits. People aged 45 or older accounted for the 55 percent majority of doctor visits in 2005. They accounted for a smaller 41 percent share of visits to hospital outpatient departments and for an even smaller 34 percent of visits to emergency rooms.

The 82 percent majority of health care visits in 2005 were to physician's offices. Only 8 percent were to hospital outpatient departments and 10 percent to emergency rooms. The likelihood of visiting an emergency room rather than a doctor varies by age. Among health care visits by people aged 15 to 24, a substantial 19 percent are to emergency rooms. Among visits by people aged 65 or older, only 6 percent are to emergency rooms.

■ As the population ages, the number of all types of health care visits will continue to rise.

Emergency rooms account for a large share of health care visits by young adults

(emergency room visits as a percentage of total health care visits, by age, 2005)

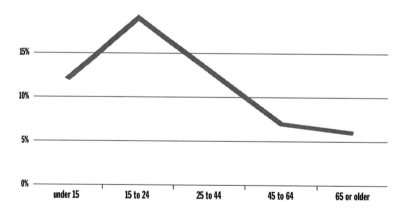

Table 4.40 Health Care Visits by Age, 2005

(total number and percent distribution of health care visits, and number per 100 persons per year, by age and type of visit, 2005; numbers in thousands)

		physician office visits				hospital outpatient departments	hospital emergency rooms
	total visits	total	primary care	surgical specialty	medical specialty		
Number							
Total visits	**1,169,333**	**963,618**	**573,169**	**200,217**	**190,232**	**90,393**	**115,323**
Under age 15	206,158	160,551	139,048	10,444	11,059	21,109	24,497
Aged 15 to 24	99,683	70,583	48,362	10,696	11,525	10,418	18,682
Aged 25 to 44	256,656	201,619	129,253	37,017	35,349	21,805	33,232
Aged 45 to 64	328,564	283,180	148,117	66,919	68,144	23,202	22,182
Aged 65 or older	278,272	247,683	108,389	75,140	64,154	13,859	16,730
Aged 65 to 74	133,334	119,061	52,738	35,448	30,875	7,517	6,756
Aged 75 or older	144,938	128,623	55,651	39,692	33,280	6,341	9,974
Percent distribution by age							
Total visits	**100.0%**	**100.0%**	**100.0%**	**100.0%**	**100.0%**	**100.0%**	**100.0%**
Under age 15	17.6	16.7	24.3	5.2	5.8	23.4	21.2
Aged 15 to 24	8.5	7.3	8.4	5.3	6.1	11.5	16.2
Aged 25 to 44	21.9	20.9	22.6	18.5	18.6	24.1	28.8
Aged 45 to 64	28.1	29.4	25.8	33.4	35.8	25.7	19.2
Aged 65 or older	23.8	25.7	18.9	37.5	33.7	15.3	14.5
Aged 65 to 74	11.4	12.4	9.2	17.7	16.2	8.3	5.9
Aged 75 or older	12.4	13.3	9.7	19.8	17.5	7.0	8.6
Percent distribution by place of care							
Total visits	**100.0%**	**82.4%**	**49.0%**	**17.1%**	**16.3%**	**7.7%**	**9.9%**
Under age 15	100.0	77.9	67.4	5.1	5.4	10.2	11.9
Aged 15 to 24	100.0	70.8	48.5	10.7	11.6	10.5	18.7
Aged 25 to 44	100.0	78.6	50.4	14.4	13.8	8.5	12.9
Aged 45 to 64	100.0	86.2	45.1	20.4	20.7	7.1	6.8
Aged 65 or older	100.0	89.0	39.0	27.0	23.1	5.0	6.0
Aged 65 to 74	100.0	89.3	39.6	26.6	23.2	5.6	5.1
Aged 75 or older	100.0	88.7	38.4	27.4	23.0	4.4	6.9
Visits per 100 persons per year							
Total visits	**401.6**	**331.0**	**196.9**	**68.8**	**65.3**	**31.0**	**39.6**
Under age 15	339.9	264.7	229.3	17.2	18.2	34.8	40.4
Aged 15 to 24	243.0	172.1	117.9	26.1	28.1	25.4	45.5
Aged 25 to 44	313.0	245.8	157.6	45.1	43.1	26.6	40.5
Aged 45 to 64	454.2	391.4	204.7	92.5	94.2	32.1	30.7
Aged 65 or older	791.7	704.7	308.4	213.8	182.5	39.4	47.6
Aged 65 to 74	724.8	647.2	286.7	192.7	167.8	40.9	36.7
Aged 75 or older	865.1	767.7	332.2	236.9	198.6	37.9	59.5

Source: National Center for Health Statistics, Ambulatory Medical Care Utilization Estimates for 2005, Advance Data, No. 388, 2007, Internet site http://www.cdc.gov/nchs/about/major/ahcd/adata.htm#CombinedReports; calculations by New Strategist

One in 12 Americans Had a Hospital Stay in 2006

Older Americans are most likely to be hospitalized.

As health insurance companies try to cut costs, hospitals have changed their strategy. They are less likely to keep patients overnight and more likely to care for them through outpatient services.

In 2006, only 8 percent of people aged 18 or older were hospitalized overnight. People aged 65 or older are most likely to experience a hospital stay, with 17 percent doing so in 2006. This compares with only 2 percent of teenagers—the 12-to-17 age group is least likely to be hospitalized.

■ Children under age 12 are more likely than teens to be hospitalized because of the greater likelihood of health problems in infancy.

Hospitalization is least likely among teenagers

(percent of people who experienced an overnight hospital stay in the past 12 months, by age, 2006)

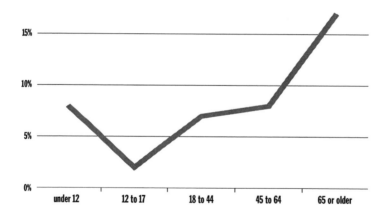

Table 4.41 Number of Overnight Hospital Stays by Age, 2006

(total number of people, and percent distribution by number of overnight hospital stays in past 12 months, by age, 2006; numbers in thousands)

	total		no overnight hospital stays	one or more overnight hospital stays			
	number	percent		total	one	two	three or more
Total people	**293,756**	**100.0%**	**91.2%**	**8.0%**	**6.2%**	**1.1%**	**0.8%**
Under age 12	48,216	100.0	91.4	8.1	7.2	0.6	0.3
Aged 12 to 17	25,276	100.0	97.0	2.2	2.0	0.2	0.1
Aged 18 to 44	110,389	100.0	92.9	6.5	5.4	0.7	0.5
Aged 45 to 64	74,287	100.0	91.2	8.0	5.6	1.3	1.0
Aged 65 or older	35,588	100.0	81.9	16.9	11.7	3.0	2.2

Note: Numbers will not add to total because of unknown hospital stays.
Source: National Center for Health Statistics, Summary Health Statistics for the U.S. Population: National Health Interview Survey, 2006, Vital and Health Statistics, Series 10, No. 236, 2007, Internet site http://www.cdc.gov/nchs/nhis.htm; calculations by New Strategist

Heart Disease Is the Leading Killer of the Oldest Adults

Cancer claims more lives among those under age 75, however.

The majority of deaths in any given year occur among people aged 75 or older. In 2004, fully 84 percent of deaths occurred in the 55-or-older age group, and 57 percent were among people aged 75 or older.

People aged 75 or older account for the majority of deaths for most of the 15 leading causes of death. They account for 66 percent of deaths from heart disease, for example, and 93 percent of deaths from Alzheimer's disease. Only five of the 15 leading causes of death are more likely to claim people under age 75—cancer, accidents, suicide, chronic liver disease, and homicide.

Accidents are the number-one cause of death among people under age 45 (except for infants). Cancer is the leading cause of death among people aged 45 to 74. Although heart disease kills more Americans than cancer, cancer is a more important cause of death in most age groups. Only among people aged 75 or older does heart disease overtake cancer as a cause of death.

■ More effective treatments for heart disease and cancer would extend the lives of older Americans.

The majority of deaths occur to people aged 75 or older

(percent distribution of deaths by age, 2004)

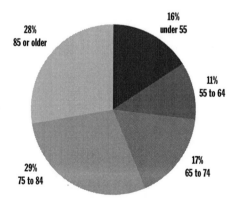

28% 85 or older

16% under 55

11% 55 to 64

17% 65 to 74

29% 75 to 84

Table 4.42 Deaths from the 15 Leading Causes by Age, 2004

(number and percent distribution of deaths from the 15 leading causes, by age, 2004; ranked by total number of deaths)

	total	aged 55 or older				
		total	55 to 64	65 to 74	75 to 84	85+
Total deaths	**2,397,615**	**2,020,366**	**264,697**	**399,666**	**684,230**	**671,773**
Diseases of the heart	652,486	596,915	63,613	99,999	195,379	237,924
Malignant neoplasms (cancer)	553,888	482,803	96,956	139,417	166,085	80,345
Cerebrovascular disease	150,074	140,504	9,966	19,901	50,092	60,545
Chronic lower respiratory disease	121,987	116,951	11,754	28,390	47,568	29,239
Accidents (unintentional injuries)	112,012	44,671	9,651	8,116	13,457	13,447
Diabetes mellitus	73,138	64,736	10,780	16,093	22,945	14,918
Alzheimer's disease	65,965	65,855	542	3,641	21,882	39,790
Influenza and pneumonia	59,664	55,914	3,154	6,382	18,066	28,312
Nephritis, nephrotic syndrome, and nephrosis	42,480	39,068	3,963	7,119	14,058	13,928
Septicemia	33,373	29,389	3,745	5,983	10,586	9,075
Suicide	32,439	9,209	4,011	2,279	2,120	799
Chronic liver disease and cirrhosis	27,013	16,378	6,569	5,119	3,733	957
Essential (primary) hypertension and hypertensive renal disease	23,076	21,458	1,839	3,152	6,819	9,648
Parkinson's disease	17,989	17,913	349	2,214	8,752	6,598
Homicide	17,357	1,718	879	446	289	104
All other causes	414,674	316,884	36,926	51,415	102,399	126,144
Percent distribution by age						
Total deaths	**100.0%**	**84.3%**	**11.0%**	**16.7%**	**28.5%**	**28.0%**
Diseases of the heart	100.0	91.5	9.7	15.3	29.9	36.5
Malignant neoplasms (cancer)	100.0	87.2	17.5	25.2	30.0	14.5
Cerebrovascular disease	100.0	93.6	6.6	13.3	33.4	40.3
Chronic lower respiratory disease	100.0	95.9	9.6	23.3	39.0	24.0
Accidents (unintentional injuries)	100.0	39.9	8.6	7.2	12.0	12.0
Diabetes mellitus	100.0	88.5	14.7	22.0	31.4	20.4
Alzheimer's disease	100.0	99.8	0.8	5.5	33.2	60.3
Influenza and pneumonia	100.0	93.7	5.3	10.7	30.3	47.5
Nephritis, nephrotic syndrome, and nephrosis	100.0	92.0	9.3	16.8	33.1	32.8
Septicemia	100.0	88.1	11.2	17.9	31.7	27.2
Suicide	100.0	28.4	12.4	7.0	6.5	2.5
Chronic liver disease and cirrhosis	100.0	60.6	24.3	19.0	13.8	3.5
Essential (primary) hypertension and hypertensive renal disease	100.0	93.0	8.0	13.7	29.6	41.8
Parkinson's disease	100.0	99.6	1.9	12.3	48.7	36.7
Homicide	100.0	9.9	5.1	2.6	1.7	0.6
All other causes	100.0	76.4	8.9	12.4	24.7	30.4

(continued)

	total	aged 55 or older				
		total	55 to 64	65 to 74	75 to 84	85+
Percent distribution by cause of death						
Total deaths	**100.0%**	**100.0%**	**100.0%**	**100.0%**	**100.0%**	**100.0%**
Diseases of the heart	27.2	29.5	24.0	25.0	28.6	35.4
Malignant neoplasms (cancer)	23.1	23.9	36.6	34.9	24.3	12.0
Cerebrovascular disease	6.3	7.0	3.8	5.0	7.3	9.0
Chronic lower respiratory disease	5.1	5.8	4.4	7.1	7.0	4.4
Accidents (unintentional injuries)	4.7	2.2	3.6	2.0	2.0	2.0
Diabetes mellitus	3.1	3.2	4.1	4.0	3.4	2.2
Alzheimer's disease	2.8	3.3	0.2	0.9	3.2	5.9
Influenza and pneumonia	2.5	2.8	1.2	1.6	2.6	4.2
Nephritis, nephrotic syndrome, and nephrosis	1.8	1.9	1.5	1.8	2.1	2.1
Septicemia	1.4	1.5	1.4	1.5	1.5	1.4
Suicide	1.4	0.5	1.5	0.6	0.3	0.1
Chronic liver disease and cirrhosis	1.1	0.8	2.5	1.3	0.5	0.1
Essential (primary) hypertension and hypertensive renal disease	1.0	1.1	0.7	0.8	1.0	1.4
Parkinson's disease	0.8	0.9	0.1	0.6	1.3	1.0
Homicide	0.7	0.1	0.3	0.1	0.0	0.0
All other causes	17.3	15.7	14.0	12.9	15.0	18.8

Note: Numbers will not add to total because "age not stated" is not shown.
Source: National Center for Health Statistics, Deaths: Final Data for 2004, National Vital Statistics Reports, Vol. 55, No. 19, 2007, Internet site http://www.cdc.gov/nchs/deaths.htm; calculations by New Strategist

Table 4.43 Leading Causes of Death for Infants, 2004

(number and percent distribution of deaths accounted for by the 10 leading causes of death for children under age 1, 2004)

		number	percent distribution
	All causes	**27,936**	**100.0%**
1.	Congenital malformations, deformations, and chromosomal abnormalities	5,622	20.1
2.	Disorders relating to short gestation and low birthweight	4,642	16.6
3.	Sudden infant death syndrome	2,246	8.0
4.	Newborn affected by maternal complications of pregnancy	1,715	6.1
5.	Accidents (5)	1,052	3.8
6.	Newborn affected by complications of placenta, cord, and membranes	1,042	3.7
7.	Respiratory distress syndrome	875	3.1
8.	Bacterial sepsis of newborn	827	3.0
9.	Neonatal hemorrhage	616	2.2
10.	Diseases of the circulatory system	593	2.1
	All other causes	8,706	31.2

Note: Number in parentheses shows rank for all Americans if the cause of death is among top 15.
Source: National Center for Health Statistics, Deaths: Leading Causes for 2004, National Vital Statistics Reports, Vol. 56, No. 5, 2007, Internet site http://www.cdc.gov/nchs/deaths.htm; calculations by New Strategist

Table 4.44 Leading Causes of Death for Children Aged 1 to 4, 2004

(number and percent distribution of deaths accounted for by the 10 leading causes of death for children aged 1 to 4, 2004)

		number	percent distribution
	All causes	**4,785**	**100.0%**
1.	Accidents (5)	1,641	34.3
2.	Congenital malformations, deformations, and chromosomal abnormalities	569	11.9
3.	Malignant neoplasms (cancer) (2)	399	8.3
4.	Homicide (15)	377	7.9
5.	Diseases of the heart (1)	187	3.9
6.	Influenza and pneumonia (8)	119	2.5
7.	Septicemia (10)	84	1.8
8.	Certain conditions originating in perinatal period	61	1.3
9.	In situ neoplasms and benign neoplams	53	1.1
10.	Chronic lower respiratory diseases (4)	48	1.0
	All other causes	1,247	26.1

Note: Number in parentheses shows rank for all Americans if the cause of death is among top 15.
Source: National Center for Health Statistics, Deaths: Leading Causes for 2004, National Vital Statistics Reports, Vol. 56, No. 5, 2007, Internet site http://www.cdc.gov/nchs/deaths.htm; calculations by New Strategist

Table 4.45 Leading Causes of Death for Children Aged 5 to 9, 2004

(number and percent distribution of deaths accounted for by the 10 leading causes of death for children aged 5 to 9, 2004)

		number	percent distribution
	All causes	**2,888**	**100.0%**
1.	Accidents (5)	1,126	39.0
2.	Malignant neoplasms (cancer) (2)	526	18.2
3.	Congenital malformations, deformations	205	7.1
4.	Homicide (15)	122	4.2
5.	Diseases of the heart (1)	83	2.9
6.	Chronic lower respiratory disease (4)	46	1.6
7.	In situ neoplasms and benign neoplams	41	1.4
8.	Septicemia (10)	38	1.3
9.	Cerebrovascular diseases (3)	34	1.2
10.	Influenza and pneumonia (8)	33	1.1
	All other causes	634	22.0

Note: Number in parentheses shows rank for all Americans if the cause of death is among top 15.
Source: National Center for Health Statistics, Deaths: Leading Causes for 2004, National Vital Statistics Reports, Vol. 56, No. 5, 2007, Internet site http://www.cdc.gov/nchs/deaths.htm; calculations by New Strategist

Table 4.46 Leading Causes of Death for Children Aged 10 to 14, 2004

(number and percent distribution of deaths accounted for by the 10 leading causes of death for children aged 10 to 14, 2004)

		number	percent distribution
	All causes	**3,946**	**100.0%**
1.	Accidents (5)	1,540	39.0
2.	Malignant neoplasms (cancer) (2)	493	12.5
3.	Suicide (11)	283	7.2
4.	Homicide (15)	207	5.2
5.	Congenital malformations, deformations	184	4.7
6.	Diseases of the heart (1)	162	4.1
7.	Chronic lower respiratory disease (4)	74	1.9
8.	Influenza and pneumonia (8)	49	1.2
9.	In situ neoplasms and benign neoplams	43	1.1
10.	Cerebrovascular diseases (3)	43	1.1
	All other causes	868	22.0

Note: Number in parentheses shows rank for all Americans if the cause of death is among top 15.
Source: National Center for Health Statistics, Deaths: Leading Causes for 2004, National Vital Statistics Reports, Vol. 56, No. 5, 2007, Internet site http://www.cdc.gov/nchs/deaths.htm; calculations by New Strategist

Table 4.47 Leading Causes of Death for People Aged 15 to 19, 2004

(number and percent distribution of deaths accounted for by the 10 leading causes of death for people aged 15 to 19, 2004)

		number	percent distribution
	All causes	**13,706**	**100.0%**
1.	Accidents (5)	6,825	49.8
2.	Homicide (15)	1,932	14.1
3.	Suicide (11)	1,700	12.4
4.	Malignant neoplasms (cancer) (2)	731	5.3
5.	Diseases of the heart (1)	366	2.7
6.	Congenital malformations, deformations	257	1.9
7.	Chronic lower respiratory disease (4)	85	0.6
8.	Cerebrovascular diseases (3)	69	0.5
9.	Influenza and pneumonia (8)	67	0.5
10.	In situ neoplasms and benign neoplams	50	0.4
10.	Anemias	50	0.4
	All other causes	1,574	11.5

Note: Number in parentheses shows rank for all Americans if the cause of death is among top 15.
Source: National Center for Health Statistics, Deaths: Leading Causes for 2004, National Vital Statistics Reports, Vol. 56, No. 5, 2007, Internet site http://www.cdc.gov/nchs/deaths.htm; calculations by New Strategist

Table 4.48 Leading Causes of Death for People Aged 20 to 24, 2004

(number and percent distribution of deaths accounted for by the 10 leading causes of death for people aged 20 to 24, 2004)

		number	percent distribution
	All causes	**19,715**	**100.0%**
1.	Accidents (5)	8,624	43.7
2.	Homicide (15)	3,153	16.0
3.	Suicide (11)	2,616	13.3
4.	Malignant neoplasms (cancer) (2)	978	5.0
5.	Diseases of the heart (1)	672	3.4
6.	Congenital malformations, deformations	226	1.1
7.	Human immunodeficiency virus infection	160	0.8
8.	Cerebrovascular diseases (3)	142	0.7
9.	Pregnancy, childbirth, and the puerperium	131	0.7
10.	Influenza and pneumonia (8)	118	0.6
	All other causes	2,895	14.7

Note: Number in parentheses shows rank for all Americans if the cause of death is among top 15.
Source: National Center for Health Statistics, Deaths: Leading Causes for 2004, National Vital Statistics Reports, Vol. 56, No. 5, 2007, Internet site http://www.cdc.gov/nchs/deaths.htm; calculations by New Strategist

Table 4.49 Leading Causes of Death for People Aged 25 to 34, 2004

(number and percent distribution of deaths accounted for by the 10 leading causes of death for people aged 25 to 34, 2004)

		number	percent distribution
	All causes	**40,868**	**100.0%**
1.	Accidents (5)	13,032	31.9
2.	Suicide (11)	5,074	12.4
3.	Homicide (15)	4,495	11.0
4.	Malignant neoplasms (cancer) (2)	3,633	8.9
5.	Diseases of the heart (1)	3,163	7.7
6.	Human immunodeficiency virus infection	1,468	3.6
7.	Diabetes mellitus (6)	599	1.5
8.	Cerebrovascular diseases (3)	567	1.4
9.	Congenital malformations, deformations	420	1.0
10.	Septicemia (10)	328	0.8
	All other causes	8,089	19.8

Note: Number in parentheses shows rank for all Americans if the cause of death is among top 15.
Source: National Center for Health Statistics, Deaths: Leading Causes for 2004, National Vital Statistics Reports, Vol. 56, No. 5, 2007, Internet site http://www.cdc.gov/nchs/deaths.htm; calculations by New Strategist

Table 4.50 Leading Causes of Death for People Aged 35 to 44, 2004

(number and percent distribution of deaths accounted for by the 10 leading causes of death for people aged 35 to 44, 2004)

		number	percent distribution
	All causes	**85,362**	**100.0%**
1.	Accidents (5)	16,471	19.3
2.	Malignant neoplasms (cancer) (2)	14,723	17.2
3.	Diseases of the heart (1)	12,925	15.1
4.	Suicide (11)	6,638	7.8
5.	Human immunodeficiency virus infection	4,826	5.7
6.	Homicide (15)	2,984	3.5
7.	Chronic liver disease and cirrhosis (12)	2,799	3.3
8.	Cerebrovascular diseases (3)	2,361	2.8
9.	Diabetes mellitus (6)	2,026	2.4
10.	Influenza and pneumonia (8)	891	1.0
	All other causes	18,718	21.9

Note: Number in parentheses shows rank for all Americans if the cause of death is among top 15.
Source: National Center for Health Statistics, Deaths: Leading Causes for 2004, National Vital Statistics Reports, Vol. 56, No. 5, 2007, Internet site http://www.cdc.gov/nchs/deaths.htm; calculations by New Strategist

Table 4.51 Leading Causes of Death for People Aged 45 to 54, 2004

(number and percent distribution of deaths accounted for by the 10 leading causes of death for people aged 45 to 54, 2004)

		number	percent distribution
	All causes	**177,697**	**100.0%**
1.	Malignant neoplasms (cancer) (2)	49,520	27.9
2.	Diseases of heart (1)	37,556	21.1
3.	Accidents (5)	16,942	9.5
4.	Chronic liver disease and cirrhosis (12)	7,496	4.2
5.	Suicide (11)	6,906	3.9
6.	Cerebrovascular diseases (3)	6,181	3.5
7.	Diabetes mellitus (6)	5,567	3.1
8.	Human immunodeficiency virus infection	4,422	2.5
9.	Chronic lower respiratory disease (4)	3,511	2.0
10.	Septicemia (10)	2,251	1.3
	All other causes	37,345	21.0

Note: Number in parentheses shows rank for all Americans if the cause of death is among top 15.
Source: National Center for Health Statistics, Deaths: Leading Causes for 2004, National Vital Statistics Reports, Vol. 56, No. 5, 2007, Internet site http://www.cdc.gov/nchs/deaths.htm; calculations by New Strategist

Table 4.52 Leading Causes of Death for People Aged 55 to 64, 2004

(number and percent distribution of deaths accounted for by the 10 leading causes of death for people aged 55 to 64, 2004)

		number	percent distribution
	All causes	**264,697**	**100.0%**
1.	Malignant neoplasms (cancer) (2)	96,956	36.6
2.	Diseases of heart (1)	63,613	24.0
3.	Chronic lower respiratory disease (4)	11,754	4.4
4.	Diabetes mellitus (6)	10,780	4.1
5.	Cerebrovascular diseases (3)	9,966	3.8
6.	Accidents (5)	9,651	3.6
7.	Chronic liver disease and cirrhosis (12)	6,569	2.5
8.	Suicide (11)	4,011	1.5
9.	Nephritis, nephrotic syndrome, nephrosis (9)	3,963	1.5
10.	Septicemia (10)	3,745	1.4
	All other causes	43,689	16.5

Note: Number in parentheses shows rank for all Americans if the cause of death is among top 15.
Source: National Center for Health Statistics, Deaths: Leading Causes for 2004, National Vital Statistics Reports, Vol. 56, No. 5, 2007, Internet site http://www.cdc.gov/nchs/deaths.htm; calculations by New Strategist

Table 4.53 Leading Causes of Death for People Aged 65 to 74, 2004

(number and percent distribution of deaths accounted for by the 10 leading causes of death for people aged 65 to 74, 2004)

		number	percent distribution
	All causes	**399,666**	**100.0%**
1.	Malignant neoplasms (cancer) (2)	139,417	34.9
2.	Diseases of the heart (1)	99,999	25.0
3.	Chronic lower respiratory disease (4)	28,390	7.1
4.	Cerebrovascular diseases (3)	19,901	5.0
5.	Diabetes mellitus (6)	16,093	4.0
6.	Accidents (5)	8,116	2.0
7.	Nephritis, nephrotic syndrome, nephrosis (9)	7,119	1.8
8.	Influenza and pneumonia (8)	6,382	1.6
9.	Septicemia (10)	5,983	1.5
10.	Chronic liver disease and cirrhosis (12)	5,119	1.3
	All other causes	63,147	15.8

Note: Number in parentheses shows rank for all Americans if the cause of death is among top 15.
Source: National Center for Health Statistics, Deaths: Leading Causes for 2004, National Vital Statistics Reports, Vol. 56, No. 5, 2007, Internet site http://www.cdc.gov/nchs/deaths.htm; calculations by New Strategist

Table 4.54 Leading Causes of Death for People Aged 75 to 84, 2004

(number and percent distribution of deaths accounted for by the 10 leading causes of death for people aged 75 to 84, 2004)

		number	percent distribution
	All causes	**684,230**	**100.0%**
1.	Diseases of the heart (1)	195,379	28.6
2.	Malignant neoplasms (cancer) (2)	166,085	24.3
3.	Cerebrovascular diseases (3)	50,092	7.3
4.	Chronic lower respiratory disease (4)	47,568	7.0
5.	Diabetes mellitus (6)	22,945	3.4
6.	Alzheimer's disease (7)	21,882	3.2
7.	Influenza and pneumonia (8)	18,066	2.6
8.	Nephritis, nephrotic syndrome, nephrosis (9)	14,058	2.1
9.	Accidents (5)	13,457	2.0
10.	Septicemia (10)	10,586	1.5
	All other causes	124,112	18.1

Note: Number in parentheses shows rank for all Americans if the cause of death is among top 15.
Source: National Center for Health Statistics, Deaths: Leading Causes for 2004, National Vital Statistics Reports, Vol. 56, No. 5, 2007, Internet site http://www.cdc.gov/nchs/deaths.htm; calculations by New Strategist

Table 4.55 Leading Causes of Death for People Aged 85 or Older, 2004

(number and percent distribution of deaths accounted for by the 10 leading causes of death for people aged 85 or older, 2004)

		number	percent distribution
	All causes	**671,773**	**100.0%**
1.	Diseases of the heart (1)	237,924	35.4
2.	Malignant neoplasms (cancer) (2)	80,345	12.0
3.	Cerebrovascular diseases (3)	60,545	9.0
4.	Alzheimer's disease (7)	39,790	5.9
5.	Chronic lower respiratory disease (4)	29,239	4.4
6.	Influenza and pneumonia (8)	28,312	4.2
7.	Diabetes mellitus (6)	14,918	2.2
8.	Nephritis, nephrotic syndrome, nephrosis (9)	13,928	2.1
9.	Accidents (5)	13,447	2.0
10.	Essential (primary) hypertension and hypertensive renal disease (13)	9,648	1.4
	All other causes	143,677	21.4

Note: Number in parentheses shows rank for all Americans if the cause of death is among top 15.
Source: National Center for Health Statistics, Deaths: Leading Causes for 2004, National Vital Statistics Reports, Vol. 56, No. 5, 2007, Internet site http://www.cdc.gov/nchs/deaths.htm; calculations by New Strategist

Americans Are Living Longer

Scientific advances have reduced the number of deaths from many causes.

The longer people live, the longer they can expect to live, on average. Life expectancy increases as people get older because they have managed to live through life's dangers up to that point.

Women aged 20 in 2004 could expect to live to be 81 years old (61.2 years of life remaining), on average. But a 50-year-old woman could expect to live to be 83 (32.7 years remaining.) A woman aged 80 could expect to reach the ripe old age of nearly 90 (9.8 years of life remaining).

Men have a shorter life expectancy than women, but the same pattern holds. At age 20, the average man can expect to live to age 76 (56.2 years remaining). If a man reaches age 50, his life expectancy rises to 79 (28.8 years remaining). By age 80, the life expectancy of men differs little from women—at this age men can expect to live to age 88 (8.2 years remaining).

■ The dramatic increase in life expectancy during the past century is largely the result of a sharp decline in infant and childhood mortality and some reductions in mortality at older ages.

Life expectancy is more than 77 years

(number of years of life remaining at selected ages, 2004)

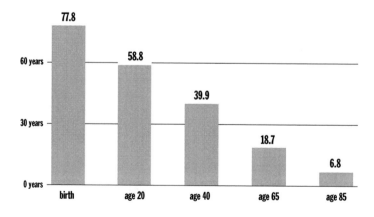

Table 4.56   Life Expectancy by Age and Sex, 2004

(years of life remaining at selected ages, by sex, 2004)

	total	females	males
At birth	77.8 yrs.	80.4 yrs.	75.2 yrs.
Aged 1	77.4	79.9	74.7
Aged 5	73.5	76.0	70.8
Aged 10	68.5	71.0	65.9
Aged 15	63.6	66.1	61.0
Aged 20	58.8	61.2	56.2
Aged 25	54.0	56.3	51.6
Aged 30	49.3	51.5	46.9
Aged 35	44.5	46.6	42.2
Aged 40	39.9	41.9	37.6
Aged 45	35.3	37.2	33.1
Aged 50	30.9	32.7	28.8
Aged 55	26.6	28.3	24.7
Aged 60	22.5	24.0	20.8
Aged 65	18.7	20.0	17.1
Aged 70	15.1	16.2	13.7
Aged 75	11.9	12.8	10.7
Aged 80	9.1	9.8	8.2
Aged 85	6.8	7.2	6.1
Aged 90	5.0	5.2	4.4
Aged 95	3.6	3.7	3.2
Aged 100	2.6	2.6	2.3

Source: National Center for Health Statistics, Deaths: Final Data for 2004, National Vital Statistics Reports, Vol. 55, No. 19, 2007, Internet site http://www.cdc.gov/nchs/deaths.htm; calculations by New Strategist

5

Housing

The nation's homeownership rate peaked in 2004 and has fallen since then. In 2007, the homeownership rate was lower in most age groups than it was in 2000. Still, today's rates are above those of 1990 regardless of age. Young adults and older Americans saw their homeownership rate rise the most between 1990 and 2007, while middle-aged householders saw little gain in homeownership during those years.

The slump in the housing market is affecting the generations differently. Those who entered the housing market when prices were at their peak (Generation X and some Millennials) may lose their homes. Boomers and older Americans who have traditional mortgages and plenty of equity in their homes may wonder what all the fuss is about. As housing prices plunge, buying opportunities will emerge for the majority of Millennials who are not yet homeowners.

What to expect in the future

■ The large Millennial generation will help prop up the housing market as they enter the home-buying age groups.

■ The financial well-being of Boomers in old age will be determined by their mortgage status. Those who have paid off their mortgage will have a much more comfortable retirement than those still paying off the loan.

Young Adults Are Most Likely to Move

But older people move the farthest.

People in their twenties are most likely to move in a given year. Nearly 30 percent of people aged 20 to 29 moved between March 2005 and March 2006. Most of their moves are triggered by life changes such as college graduation, marriage, or new jobs.

The likelihood of moving is much smaller among people aged 30 or older. Nineteen percent of people aged 30 to 34 moved between 2005 and 2006, as did 15 percent of 35-to-39-year-olds. Among people aged 45 or older, fewer than 10 percent move in a given year. One reason for the lower mobility of middle-aged and older Americans is their higher rate of homeownership.

Most movers (62 percent) stay in the same county. Only 20 percent move to a different state. Older people are most likely to cross state lines, and more than 25 percent of movers in most age groups from 62 to 84 settle in a different state. Many are retirees moving to warmer climates or the frail elderly moving closer to family members.

■ The slump in the housing market could push mobility rates even lower because houses have become more difficult to sell.

Older people are least likely to move

(percent of people who moved between March 2005 and March 2006, by age)

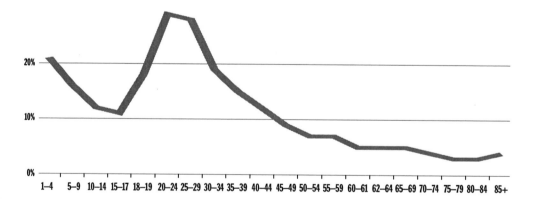

Table 5.1 Geographic Mobility by Age, 2005–06

(total number of people aged 1 or older, number and percent who moved between March 2005 and March 2006, and percent distribution of movers by type of move, by age; numbers in thousands)

	total	same house (nonmovers)	total movers	same county	different county, same state	different state total	different state same region	different state different region	movers from abroad
Total, 1 or older	**289,781**	**249,945**	**39,836**	**24,851**	**8,010**	**5,679**	**2,939**	**2,740**	**1,296**
Aged 1 to 4	16,310	12,885	3,426	2,277	607	434	211	223	108
Aged 5 to 9	19,626	16,527	3,100	2,038	550	435	195	240	77
Aged 10 to 14	20,651	18,106	2,546	1,698	433	355	179	176	60
Aged 15 to 17	13,344	11,814	1,530	1,027	283	166	92	74	54
Aged 18 to 19	7,572	6,187	1,385	895	252	188	101	87	50
Aged 20 to 24	20,393	14,490	5,903	3,566	1,245	881	478	403	211
Aged 25 to 29	20,138	14,592	5,547	3,474	1,104	735	389	346	234
Aged 30 to 34	19,343	15,579	3,764	2,304	723	589	298	291	148
Aged 35 to 39	20,771	17,558	3,213	1,950	648	498	239	259	117
Aged 40 to 44	22,350	19,777	2,572	1,569	569	355	179	176	79
Aged 45 to 49	22,518	20,438	2,080	1,317	441	270	130	140	52
Aged 50 to 54	20,279	18,789	1,491	885	330	238	120	118	38
Aged 55 to 59	17,827	16,659	1,169	675	270	192	117	75	32
Aged 60 to 61	5,470	5,191	280	169	64	44	27	17	3
Aged 62 to 64	7,683	7,290	393	211	99	71	50	21	12
Aged 65 to 69	10,231	9,727	504	278	145	74	45	29	7
Aged 70 to 74	8,323	7,990	333	185	77	61	36	25	10
Aged 75 to 79	7,644	7,394	249	136	77	33	18	15	3
Aged 80 to 84	5,318	5,138	181	95	53	31	24	7	2
Aged 85 or older	3,989	3,815	175	103	40	32	11	21	0

Percent distribution by mobility status

	total	same house (nonmovers)	total movers	same county	different county, same state	different state total	different state same region	different state different region	movers from abroad
Total, 1 or older	**100.0%**	**86.3%**	**13.7%**	**8.6%**	**2.8%**	**2.0%**	**1.0%**	**0.9%**	**0.4%**
Aged 1 to 4	100.0	79.0	21.0	14.0	3.7	2.7	1.3	1.4	0.7
Aged 5 to 9	100.0	84.2	15.8	10.4	2.8	2.2	1.0	1.2	0.4
Aged 10 to 14	100.0	87.7	12.3	8.2	2.1	1.7	0.9	0.9	0.3
Aged 15 to 17	100.0	88.5	11.5	7.7	2.1	1.2	0.7	0.6	0.4
Aged 18 to 19	100.0	81.7	18.3	11.8	3.3	2.5	1.3	1.1	0.7
Aged 20 to 24	100.0	71.1	28.9	17.5	6.1	4.3	2.3	2.0	1.0
Aged 25 to 29	100.0	72.5	27.5	17.3	5.5	3.6	1.9	1.7	1.2
Aged 30 to 34	100.0	80.5	19.5	11.9	3.7	3.0	1.5	1.5	0.8
Aged 35 to 39	100.0	84.5	15.5	9.4	3.1	2.4	1.2	1.2	0.6
Aged 40 to 44	100.0	88.5	11.5	7.0	2.5	1.6	0.8	0.8	0.4
Aged 45 to 49	100.0	90.8	9.2	5.8	2.0	1.2	0.6	0.6	0.2
Aged 50 to 54	100.0	92.7	7.4	4.4	1.6	1.2	0.6	0.6	0.2
Aged 55 to 59	100.0	93.4	6.6	3.8	1.5	1.1	0.7	0.4	0.2
Aged 60 to 61	100.0	94.9	5.1	3.1	1.2	0.8	0.5	0.3	0.1
Aged 62 to 64	100.0	94.9	5.1	2.7	1.3	0.9	0.7	0.3	0.2
Aged 65 to 69	100.0	95.1	4.9	2.7	1.4	0.7	0.4	0.3	0.1
Aged 70 to 74	100.0	96.0	4.0	2.2	0.9	0.7	0.4	0.3	0.1
Aged 75 to 79	100.0	96.7	3.3	1.8	1.0	0.4	0.2	0.2	0.0
Aged 80 to 84	100.0	96.6	3.4	1.8	1.0	0.6	0.5	0.1	0.0
Aged 85 or older	100.0	95.6	4.4	2.6	1.0	0.8	0.3	0.5	0.0

Source: Bureau of the Census, Geographical Mobility: 2005 to 2006, Detailed Tables, Internet site http://www.census.gov/population/www/socdemo/migrate/cps2006.html; calculations by New Strategist

Table 5.2 Movers by Age and Destination, 2005–06

(number of people aged 1 or older who moved and percent distribution by destination of move, March 2005 to March 2006; numbers in thousands)

	total movers	same county	different county, same state	different state — total	different state — same region	different state — different region	movers from abroad
Total, aged 1 or older	39,836	24,851	8,010	5,679	2,939	2,740	1,296
Aged 1 to 4	3,426	2,277	607	434	211	223	108
Aged 5 to 9	3,100	2,038	550	435	195	240	77
Aged 10 to 14	2,546	1,698	433	355	179	176	60
Aged 15 to 17	1,530	1,027	283	166	92	74	54
Aged 18 to 19	1,385	895	252	188	101	87	50
Aged 20 to 24	5,903	3,566	1,245	881	478	403	211
Aged 25 to 29	5,547	3,474	1,104	735	389	346	234
Aged 30 to 34	3,764	2,304	723	589	298	291	148
Aged 35 to 39	3,213	1,950	648	498	239	259	117
Aged 40 to 44	2,572	1,569	569	355	179	176	79
Aged 45 to 49	2,080	1,317	441	270	130	140	52
Aged 50 to 54	1,491	885	330	238	120	118	38
Aged 55 to 59	1,169	675	270	192	117	75	32
Aged 60 to 61	280	169	64	44	27	17	3
Aged 62 to 64	393	211	99	71	50	21	12
Aged 65 to 69	504	278	145	74	45	29	7
Aged 70 to 74	333	185	77	61	36	25	10
Aged 75 to 79	249	136	77	33	18	15	3
Aged 80 to 84	181	95	53	31	24	7	2
Aged 85 or older	175	103	40	32	11	21	0
Total, aged 1 or older	100.0%	62.4%	20.1%	14.3%	7.4%	6.9%	3.3%
Aged 1 to 4	100.0	66.5	17.7	12.7	6.2	6.5	3.2
Aged 5 to 9	100.0	65.7	17.7	14.0	6.3	7.7	2.5
Aged 10 to 14	100.0	66.7	17.0	13.9	7.0	6.9	2.4
Aged 15 to 17	100.0	67.1	18.5	10.8	6.0	4.8	3.5
Aged 18 to 19	100.0	64.6	18.2	13.6	7.3	6.3	3.6
Aged 20 to 24	100.0	60.4	21.1	14.9	8.1	6.8	3.6
Aged 25 to 29	100.0	62.6	19.9	13.3	7.0	6.2	4.2
Aged 30 to 34	100.0	61.2	19.2	15.6	7.9	7.7	3.9
Aged 35 to 39	100.0	60.7	20.2	15.5	7.4	8.1	3.6
Aged 40 to 44	100.0	61.0	22.1	13.8	7.0	6.8	3.1
Aged 45 to 49	100.0	63.3	21.2	13.0	6.3	6.7	2.5
Aged 50 to 54	100.0	59.4	22.1	16.0	8.0	7.9	2.5
Aged 55 to 59	100.0	57.7	23.1	16.4	10.0	6.4	2.7
Aged 60 to 61	100.0	60.4	22.9	15.7	9.6	6.1	1.1
Aged 62 to 64	100.0	53.7	25.2	18.1	12.7	5.3	3.1
Aged 65 to 69	100.0	55.2	28.8	14.7	8.9	5.8	1.4
Aged 70 to 74	100.0	55.6	23.1	18.3	10.8	7.5	3.0
Aged 75 to 79	100.0	54.6	30.9	13.3	7.2	6.0	1.2
Aged 80 to 84	100.0	52.5	29.3	17.1	13.3	3.9	1.1
Aged 85 or older	100.0	58.9	22.9	18.3	6.3	12.0	0.0

Source: Bureau of the Census, Geographical Mobility: 2005 to 2006, Detailed Tables, Internet site http://www.census.gov/ population/www/socdemo/migrate/cps2006.html; calculations by New Strategist

Homeownership Rises with Age

Most householders aged 30 or older are homeowners.

The homeownership rate peaks at more than 80 percent among Americans aged 60 to 74. Predictably, those least likely to own a home are young adults who have not yet accumulated enough savings for a down payment and are not yet earning enough to qualify for a mortgage. Only 25 percent of householders under age 25 own a home.

By age 30 to 34, more than half of householders own their home. In the 60-to-74 age groups, the homeownership rate surpasses 80 percent. Homeownership declines after age 75, however, as some older people sell their homes to move into nursing homes or assisted living facilities. Nevertheless, 79 percent of householders aged 75 or older are homeowners.

■ Exceptionally low interest rates and mortgage terms during the past few years allowed many younger adults to buy homes, and some of those buyers are now in financial trouble.

Homeownership reaches the majority in the 30-to-34 age group

(percent of householders who own a home, by age, 2007)

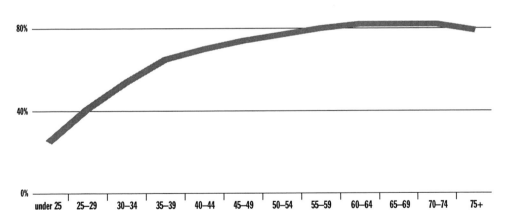

Table 5.3 Owners and Renters by Age of Householder, 2007

(number and percent distribution of householders by homeownership status, by age of householder, 2007; numbers in thousands)

		number		percent	
	total	owner	renter	owner	renter
Total households	**110,306**	**75,159**	**35,147**	**68.1%**	**31.9%**
Under age 25	6,494	1,609	4,885	24.8	75.2
Aged 25 to 29	9,170	3,719	5,451	40.6	59.4
Aged 30 to 34	9,349	5,090	4,259	54.4	45.6
Aged 35 to 39	10,499	6,829	3,670	65.0	35.0
Aged 40 to 44	11,125	7,834	3,291	70.4	29.6
Aged 45 to 49	12,007	8,889	3,118	74.0	26.0
Aged 50 to 54	11,082	8,522	2,560	76.9	23.1
Aged 55 to 59	10,013	7,999	2,014	79.9	20.1
Aged 60 to 64	8,108	6,611	1,497	81.5	18.5
Aged 65 to 69	6,330	5,169	1,161	81.7	18.3
Aged 70 to 74	5,063	4,173	890	82.4	17.6
Aged 75 or older	11,065	8,714	2,351	78.8	21.2

Source: Bureau of the Census, Housing Vacancies and Homeownership Survey, Internet site http://www.census.gov/hhes/www/ housing/hvs/hvs.html; calculations by New Strategist

Married Couples Are Most Likely to Be Homeowners

Two incomes make homes more affordable.

The homeownership rate among all households was 68 percent in 2007. But among married couples, 84 percent owned their home. A much smaller 57 percent of male-headed families and 50 percent of female-headed families were homeowners. The primary reason for the higher homeownership rate of married couples is economic—most are dual earners and can afford to buy a house.

Among the youngest householders (under age 25) male-headed families are slightly more likely than married couples to be homeowners. But among all other age groups, married couples have a higher homeownership rate than other types of households.

Homeownership rates rise with age regardless of household type. The gap in homeownership rates by household type is smallest among older householders.

■ The lax regulatory standards of the past few years allowed many more people to buy a home, but they did not narrow the gap in homeownership between married couples and other household types.

Fifty-nine percent of women who live alone own their home

(percent of households that own a home, by household type, 2007)

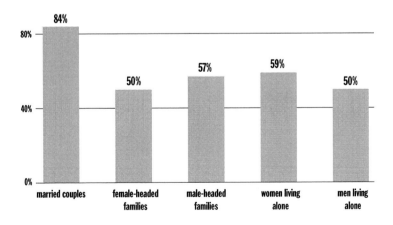

Table 5.4 Homeownership Rate by Age of Householder and Type of Household, 2007

(percent of households that own their home, by age of householder and type of household, 2007)

	total	married couples	female-headed families, no spouse present	male-headed families, no spouse present	women living alone	men living alone
Total households	**68.1%**	**83.8%**	**49.9%**	**57.4%**	**59.1%**	**50.2%**
Under age 25	24.8	38.7	25.6	40.2	13.4	17.9
Aged 25 to 29	40.6	59.8	23.8	43.1	24.6	28.3
Aged 30 to 34	54.4	70.7	32.9	45.2	35.3	36.9
Aged 35 to 39	65.0	79.3	42.8	54.5	47.0	42.6
Aged 40 to 44	70.4	84.9	50.3	58.9	51.6	47.8
Aged 45 to 49	74.0	88.0	59.1	68.2	51.3	51.9
Aged 50 to 54	76.9	89.6	62.0	72.9	56.5	56.3
Aged 55 to 59	79.9	91.2	67.2	72.5	67.2	58.9
Aged 60 to 64	81.5	92.4	70.9	76.2	67.6	62.5
Aged 65 to 69	81.7	93.2	75.4	73.6	68.1	61.5
Aged 70 to 74	82.4	93.0	77.8	77.8	71.8	66.5
Aged 75 or older	78.7	90.9	83.5	85.8	69.9	71.8

Source: Bureau of the Census, Housing Vacancies and Homeownership Survey, Internet site http://www.census.gov/hhes/www/housing/hvs/hvs.html; calculations by New Strategist

Non-Hispanic Whites Are Most Likely to Own a Home

Black and Hispanic households are far less likely to be homeowners.

Regardless of race, homeownership rises with age as people acquire the savings and income needed to become homeowners. But there is considerable difference in homeownership rates by race and Hispanic origin, according to the 2000 census.

Non-Hispanic white households are much more likely than black or Hispanic households to own their home. In 2000, 72 percent of non-Hispanic white households were home owners compared with only 46 percent of black or Hispanic households. A slim majority of Asian householders (53 percent) were homeowners.

More recent data on homeownership by race and age from the 2005 American Housing Survey show the majority of blacks becoming homeowners in the 45-to-54 age group. Among Hispanics, most become homeowners in the 35-to-44 age group.

■ With the housing market in a tailspin and mortgages more difficult to get, minority homeownership rates may fall during the next few years.

Homeownership varies greatly by race and Hispanic origin

(percent of households that own their home, by race and Hispanic origin, 2005)

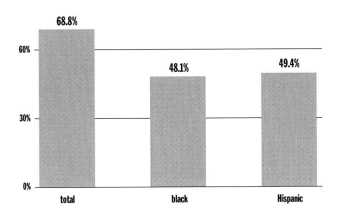

Table 5.5 Homeowners by Age, Race, and Hispanic Origin of Householder, 2000 Census

(percent of households owning their home by age, race, and Hispanic origin of householder, 2000)

	total	Asian	black	Hispanic	non-Hispanic white
Total households	**66.2%**	**52.8%**	**46.0%**	**45.7%**	**72.4%**
Under age 25	17.9	11.3	10.4	15.3	20.5
Aged 25 to 34	45.6	32.1	27.2	32.9	53.0
Aged 35 to 44	66.2	57.8	44.4	48.8	73.2
Aged 45 to 54	74.9	67.9	55.2	56.8	80.3
Aged 55 to 64	79.8	71.2	61.6	61.9	84.1
Aged 65 or older	78.1	62.0	64.3	62.8	80.6

Note: Each racial category includes those who identified themselves as being of the race alone and those who identified themselves as being of the race in combination with one or more other races. Hispanics may be of any race. Non-Hispanic whites include only those who identified themselves as being white alone and not Hispanic.
Source: Bureau of the Census, Census 2000, American Factfinder, Internet site http://factfinder.census.gov/home/saff/main .html?_lang=en

Table 5.6 Homeowners by Age, Race, and Hispanic Origin of Householder, 2005

(percent of households owning their home by age, race, and Hispanic origin of householder, 2005)

	total	black	Hispanic
Total households	**68.8%**	**48.1%**	**49.4%**
Under age 25	23.9	11.0	17.6
Aged 25 to 29	40.2	17.2	32.3
Aged 30 to 34	56.7	34.2	38.2
Aged 35 to 44	68.7	47.8	53.7
Aged 45 to 54	76.7	58.0	60.5
Aged 55 to 64	81.1	61.2	64.1
Aged 65 to 74	82.9	68.4	63.0
Aged 75 or older	77.7	67.5	63.7

Note: Blacks include only those who identify themselves as being of the race alone.
Source: Bureau of the Census, American Housing Survey for the United States: 2005, Internet site http://www.census.gov/hhes/ www/housing/ahs/ahs05/ahs05.html; calculations by New Strategist

The Homeownership Rate Is Falling

The rate of homeownership is falling in almost every age group.

Evidence of the downturn in the housing market can be seen in the latest statistics on homeownership from the Census Bureau. In 2007, for the third year in a row, the nation's homeownership rate fell. The rate peaked in 2004 at 69.0 percent. In 2007, the homeownership rate stood at 68.1 percent. Homeownership has declined in almost every age group since peaking in 2004. Only householders aged 25 to 29 have seen their homeownership rate climb since then, although the gain was just 0.4 percentage points.

Despite the decline in the overall homeownership rate over the past three years, the rate in 2007 was higher than in 2000 or 1990. Every age group was more likely to own a home in 2007 than in 1990. Some age groups—especially the middle aged—were less likely to own a home in 2007 than in 2000, however. The number of homeowners has grown by 25 percent since 1990 with especially big gains among the youngest adults as Millennials entered their twenties, the middle aged (thanks to Baby Boomers), and the oldest Americans.

■ Lax lending standards played a role in boosting homeownership rates over the past few years, but the aging of the population has been the most important reason for the rise of homeownership.

Many age groups are losing ground

(percentage point change in homeownership rate, by age of householder, 2000 to 2007)

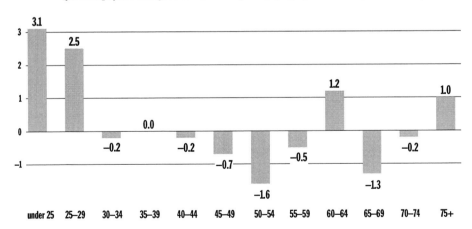

Table 5.7 Homeownership Rate by Age, 2000 to 2007

(percent of householders who own their home by age of householder, 2000 to 2007; percentage point change for selected years)

	2007	2006	2005	2004	2003	2002	2001	2000	percentage point change	
									2006–07	2004–07
Total households	**68.1%**	**68.8%**	**68.9%**	**69.0%**	**68.3%**	**67.9%**	**67.8%**	**67.4%**	**−0.7**	**−0.9**
Under age 25	24.8	24.8	25.7	25.2	22.8	22.9	22.5	21.7	0.0	−0.4
Aged 25 to 29	40.6	41.8	40.9	40.2	39.8	38.8	38.9	38.1	−1.2	0.4
Aged 30 to 34	54.4	55.9	56.8	57.4	56.5	54.9	54.8	54.6	−1.5	−3.0
Aged 35 to 39	65.0	66.4	66.6	66.2	65.1	65.2	65.5	65.0	−1.4	−1.2
Aged 40 to 44	70.4	71.2	71.7	71.9	71.3	71.7	70.8	70.6	−0.8	−1.5
Aged 45 to 49	74.0	74.9	75.0	76.3	75.4	74.8	75.4	74.7	−0.9	−2.3
Aged 50 to 54	76.9	77.7	78.3	78.2	77.9	77.9	78.2	78.5	−0.8	−1.3
Aged 55 to 59	79.9	80.4	80.6	81.2	80.9	80.8	81.0	80.4	−0.5	−1.3
Aged 60 to 64	81.5	81.5	81.9	82.4	81.9	81.6	81.8	80.3	0.0	−0.9
Aged 65 to 69	81.7	82.4	82.8	83.2	82.5	82.9	82.4	83.0	−0.7	−1.5
Aged 70 to 74	82.4	83.0	82.9	83.4	82.0	82.5	82.5	82.6	−0.6	−1.0
Aged 75 or older	78.7	79.1	78.4	78.8	78.7	78.4	78.1	77.7	−0.4	−0.1

Source: Bureau of the Census, Housing Vacancies and Homeownership surveys, Internet site http://www.census.gov/hhes/www/housing/hvs/hvs.html; calculations by New Strategist

Table 5.8 Homeownership Rate by Age, 1990 to 2007

(percent of householders who own their home by age of householder, 1990 to 2007; percentage point change for selected years)

	2007	2000	1990	percentage point change	
				2000–07	1990–07
Total households	**68.1%**	**67.4%**	**63.9%**	**0.7**	**4.2**
Under age 25	24.8	21.7	15.7	3.1	9.1
Aged 25 to 29	40.6	38.1	35.2	2.5	5.4
Aged 30 to 34	54.4	54.6	51.8	−0.2	2.6
Aged 35 to 39	65.0	65.0	63.0	0.0	2.0
Aged 40 to 44	70.4	70.6	69.8	−0.2	0.6
Aged 45 to 49	74.0	74.7	73.9	−0.7	0.1
Aged 50 to 54	76.9	78.5	76.8	−1.6	0.1
Aged 55 to 59	79.9	80.4	78.8	−0.5	1.1
Aged 60 to 64	81.5	80.3	79.8	1.2	1.7
Aged 65 to 69	81.7	83.0	80.0	−1.3	1.7
Aged 70 to 74	82.4	82.6	78.4	−0.2	4.0
Aged 75 or older	78.7	77.7	72.3	1.0	6.4

Source: Bureau of the Census, Housing Vacancies and Homeownership surveys, Internet site http://www.census.gov/hhes/www/housing/hvs/hvs.html; calculations by New Strategist

Table 5.9 Number of Homeowners by Age, 1990 to 2007

(number of householders who own their home by age of householder, 1990 to 2007; percent change for selected years; numbers in thousands)

	2007	2000	1990	percent change 2000–07	1990–07
Total homeowners	**75,159**	**71,249**	**60,248**	**5.5%**	**24.7%**
Under age 25	1,609	1,350	806	19.2	99.6
Aged 25 to 29	3,719	3,228	3,344	15.2	11.2
Aged 30 to 34	5,090	5,583	5,805	–8.8	–12.3
Aged 35 to 39	6,829	7,689	6,880	–11.2	–0.7
Aged 40 to 44	7,834	8,740	6,909	–10.4	13.4
Aged 45 to 49	8,889	8,340	5,941	6.6	49.6
Aged 50 to 54	8,522	7,718	5,016	10.4	69.9
Aged 55 to 59	7,999	6,109	4,870	30.9	64.3
Aged 60 to 64	6,611	4,991	5,141	32.5	28.6
Aged 65 to 69	5,169	4,829	5,128	7.0	0.8
Aged 70 to 74	4,173	4,598	4,230	–9.2	–1.3
Aged 75 or older	8,714	8,074	6,178	7.9	41.0

Source: Bureau of the Census, Housing Vacancies and Homeownership surveys, Internet site http://www.census.gov/hhes/www/ housing/hvs/hvs.html; calculations by New Strategist

Homeownership Is Highest in the Midwest

Most age groups in the Midwest have lost ground since 2000, however.

The homeownership rate stood at 71.9 percent in the Midwest in 2007. This compares with a rate of 70.1 percent in the South, 65.0 percent in the Northeast, and just 63.5 percent in the West. Between 1990 and 2007, the overall homeownership rate increased in every region.

Between 2000 and 2007, homeownership climbed in all but the Midwest. In every region, however, some age groups lost ground during those years. Some of the biggest declines were recorded by the middle aged. Householders aged 45 to 49 in the Midwest saw their homeownership rate fall by 2.8 percentage points between 2000 and 2007. In contrast, the youngest householders in the Northeast and West boosted their homeownership rate by 4 to 5 percentage points.

■ The availability of low-cost mortgages boosted the homeownership of young adults in every region during the past few years. Some young adults may lose their home in the housing downturn.

Young adults made gains in every region, while the middle aged lost ground in most

(percentage point change in homeownership rate for selected age groups, by region, 2000–07)

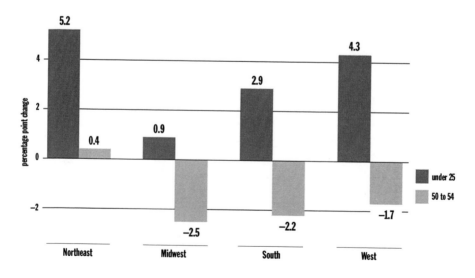

Table 5.10 Homeownership Rate by Age and Region, 1990 to 2007: Northeast

(percent of householders in the Northeast who own their home by age of householder, 1990 to 2007; percentage point change for selected years)

	2007	2000	1990	percentage point change 2000–07	percentage point change 1990–07
Total households in Northeast	**65.0%**	**63.4%**	**62.6%**	**1.6**	**2.4**
Under age 25	23.0	17.8	14.6	5.2	8.4
Aged 25 to 29	34.3	33.0	35.5	1.3	−1.2
Aged 30 to 34	49.9	49.6	53.7	0.3	−3.8
Aged 35 to 39	60.5	60.5	61.8	0.0	−1.3
Aged 40 to 44	67.7	66.6	68.4	1.1	−0.7
Aged 45 to 49	71.1	71.2	71.7	−0.1	−0.6
Aged 50 to 54	73.7	73.3	71.5	0.4	2.2
Aged 55 to 59	75.8	75.0	74.6	0.8	1.2
Aged 60 to 64	76.4	74.2	74.7	2.2	1.7
Aged 65 to 69	74.9	75.0	75.4	−0.1	−0.5
Aged 70 to 74	75.4	74.3	72.1	1.1	3.3
Aged 75 or older	71.9	68.5	64.5	3.4	7.4

Source: Bureau of the Census, Housing Vacancies and Homeownership surveys, Internet site http://www.census.gov/hhes/www/ housing/hvs/hvs.html; calculations by New Strategist

Table 5.11 Homeownership Rate by Age and Region, 1990 to 2007: Midwest

(percent of householders in the Midwest who own their home by age of householder, 1990 to 2007; percentage point change for selected years)

	2007	2000	1990	percentage point change 2000–07	percentage point change 1990–07
Total households in Midwest	**71.9%**	**72.5%**	**67.5%**	**−0.6**	**4.4**
Under age 25	25.7	24.8	16.5	0.9	9.2
Aged 25 to 29	47.3	45.7	38.6	1.6	8.7
Aged 30 to 34	63.0	64.3	57.1	−1.3	5.9
Aged 35 to 39	73.1	72.6	69.6	0.5	3.5
Aged 40 to 44	76.0	76.9	76.1	−0.9	−0.1
Aged 45 to 49	77.6	80.4	78.1	−2.8	−0.5
Aged 50 to 54	80.9	83.4	82.7	−2.5	−1.8
Aged 55 to 59	82.8	83.6	82.8	−0.8	0.0
Aged 60 to 64	83.9	83.2	82.9	0.7	1.0
Aged 65 to 69	83.8	86.6	82.1	−2.8	1.7
Aged 70 to 74	82.9	84.6	79.2	−1.7	3.7
Aged 75 or older	78.2	78.9	71.3	−0.7	6.9

Source: Bureau of the Census, Housing Vacancies and Homeownership surveys, Internet site http://www.census.gov/hhes/www/ housing/hvs/hvs.html; calculations by New Strategist

Table 5.12 Homeownership Rate by Age and Region, 1990 to 2007: South

(percent of householders in the South who own their home by age of householder, 1990 to 2007; percentage point change for selected years)

	2007	2000	1990	percentage point change	
				2000–07	1990–07
Total households in South	**70.1%**	**69.6%**	**65.7%**	**0.5**	**4.4**
Under age 25	26.6	23.7	18.4	2.9	8.2
Aged 25 to 29	41.9	40.1	37.2	1.8	4.7
Aged 30 to 34	55.8	56.6	51.2	−0.8	4.6
Aged 35 to 39	66.6	66.9	63.9	−0.3	2.7
Aged 40 to 44	71.0	72.4	70.4	−1.4	0.6
Aged 45 to 49	75.5	75.7	75.0	−0.2	0.5
Aged 50 to 54	78.5	80.7	78.8	−2.2	−0.3
Aged 55 to 59	82.3	82.8	80.2	−0.5	2.1
Aged 60 to 64	84.2	83.4	82.2	0.8	2.0
Aged 65 to 69	85.1	85.8	82.5	−0.7	2.6
Aged 70 to 74	86.9	86.4	83.0	0.5	3.9
Aged 75 or older	84.8	83.5	78.7	1.3	6.1

Source: Bureau of the Census, Housing Vacancies and Homeownership surveys, Internet site http://www.census.gov/hhes/www/housing/hvs/hvs.html; calculations by New Strategist

Table 5.13 Homeownership Rate by Age and Region, 1990 to 2007: West

(percent of householders in the West who own their home by age of householder, 1990 to 2007; percentage point change for selected years)

	2007	2000	1990	percentage point change	
				2000–07	1990–07
Total households in West	**63.5%**	**61.7%**	**58.0%**	**1.8**	**5.5**
Under age 25	21.7	17.4	11.0	4.3	10.7
Aged 25 to 29	35.7	30.7	27.8	5.0	7.9
Aged 30 to 34	47.7	46.1	44.9	1.6	2.8
Aged 35 to 39	58.9	57.8	55.6	1.1	3.3
Aged 40 to 44	65.9	64.8	63.8	1.1	2.1
Aged 45 to 49	70.4	70.1	69.7	0.3	0.7
Aged 50 to 54	72.7	74.4	71.7	−1.7	1.0
Aged 55 to 59	76.5	77.7	75.7	−1.2	0.8
Aged 60 to 64	78.9	77.7	77.1	1.2	1.8
Aged 65 to 69	79.4	81.6	78.4	−2.2	1.0
Aged 70 to 74	79.8	80	76.3	−0.2	3.5
Aged 75 or older	76.3	76.4	70.7	−0.1	5.6

Source: Bureau of the Census, Housing Vacancies and Homeownership surveys, Internet site http://www.census.gov/hhes/www/housing/hvs/hvs.html; calculations by New Strategist

Most Americans Live in Single-Family Homes

The majority of renters live in apartment buildings, however.

Most American households (64 percent) live in detached, single-family homes. The middle aged are most likely to live in this type of house. Among householders aged 45 to 64, fully 72 percent live in a detached, single-family housing unit.

Among homeowners, 82 percent live in detached, single-family homes. Ownership of duplexes is most common among homeowners aged 25 to 29, at 9 percent. Condo ownership is most common among homeowners under age 25, at 11 percent.

Only 24 percent of renters live in detached, single-family homes. Nearly two out of three live in apartments. Among renters, those most likely to live in the largest apartment buildings, with 50 or more units, are those aged 75 or older. Nearly one-third of renters in the age group reside in the largest apartment buildings.

■ Condo ownership may become more common in the years ahead if housing prices resume their upward climb.

The youngest homeowners are most likely to live in a condo

(percent of homeowners who live in multi-unit buildings, by age of householder, 2005)

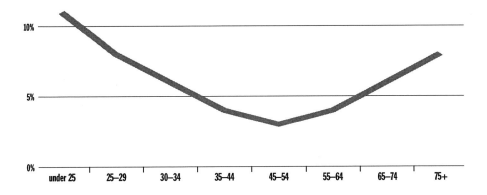

Table 5.14 Type of Structure by Age of Householder, 2005: Total Households

(number and percent distribution of households by age of householder and type of structure, 2005; numbers in thousands)

	total	one, detached	one, attached	multi-unit dwellings total	2 to 4	5 to 9	10 to 19	20 to 49	50 or more	mobile homes
Total households	108,871	69,996	6,158	25,778	8,379	5,109	4,739	3,639	3,912	6,940
Under age 25	6,013	1,840	385	3,401	1,036	792	805	466	301	387
Aged 25 to 29	8,457	3,511	681	3,756	1,166	808	861	584	338	508
Aged 30 to 34	10,186	5,758	676	3,063	985	672	648	468	290	689
Aged 35 to 44	22,456	15,238	1,120	4,771	1,680	1,039	882	604	565	1,327
Aged 45 to 54	22,575	16,233	1,157	3,773	1,332	733	685	535	488	1,412
Aged 55 to 64	16,988	12,271	972	2,587	949	440	394	345	458	1,157
Aged 65 to 74	11,082	7,892	571	1,858	563	309	255	240	491	761
Aged 75 or older	11,115	7,253	595	2,569	668	316	209	397	980	698
Median age	48	50	47	41	41	38	36	40	54	49

Percent distribution by type of structure

	total	one, detached	one, attached	multi-unit dwellings total	2 to 4	5 to 9	10 to 19	20 to 49	50 or more	mobile homes
Total households	100.0%	64.3%	5.7%	23.7%	7.7%	4.7%	4.4%	3.3%	3.6%	6.4%
Under age 25	100.0	30.6	6.4	56.6	17.2	13.2	13.4	7.7	5.0	6.4
Aged 25 to 29	100.0	41.5	8.1	44.4	13.8	9.6	10.2	6.9	4.0	6.0
Aged 30 to 34	100.0	56.5	6.6	30.1	9.7	6.6	6.4	4.6	2.8	6.8
Aged 35 to 44	100.0	67.9	5.0	21.2	7.5	4.6	3.9	2.7	2.5	5.9
Aged 45 to 54	100.0	71.9	5.1	16.7	5.9	3.2	3.0	2.4	2.2	6.3
Aged 55 to 64	100.0	72.2	5.7	15.2	5.6	2.6	2.3	2.0	2.7	6.8
Aged 65 to 74	100.0	71.2	5.2	16.8	5.1	2.8	2.3	2.2	4.4	6.9
Aged 75 or older	100.0	65.3	5.4	23.1	6.0	2.8	1.9	3.6	8.8	6.3

Percent distribution by age of householder

	total	one, detached	one, attached	multi-unit dwellings total	2 to 4	5 to 9	10 to 19	20 to 49	50 or more	mobile homes
Total households	100.0%	100.0%	100.0%	100.0%	100.0%	100.0%	100.0%	100.0%	100.0%	100.0%
Under age 25	5.5	2.6	6.3	13.2	12.4	15.5	17.0	12.8	7.7	5.6
Aged 25 to 29	7.8	5.0	11.1	14.6	13.9	15.8	18.2	16.0	8.6	7.3
Aged 30 to 34	9.4	8.2	11.0	11.9	11.8	13.2	13.7	12.9	7.4	9.9
Aged 35 to 44	20.6	21.8	18.2	18.5	20.1	20.3	18.6	16.6	14.4	19.1
Aged 45 to 54	20.7	23.2	18.8	14.6	15.9	14.3	14.5	14.7	12.5	20.3
Aged 55 to 64	15.6	17.5	15.8	10.0	11.3	8.6	8.3	9.5	11.7	16.7
Aged 65 to 74	10.2	11.3	9.3	7.2	6.7	6.0	5.4	6.6	12.6	11.0
Aged 75 or older	10.2	10.4	9.7	10.0	8.0	6.2	4.4	10.9	25.1	10.1

Source: Bureau of the Census, American Housing Survey for the United States: 2005, Internet site http://www.census.gov/hhes/www/housing/ahs/ahs05/ahs05.html; calculations by New Strategist

Table 5.15 Type of Structure by Age of Householder, 2005: Homeowners

(number and percent distribution of homeowners by age of householder and type of structure, 2005; numbers in thousands)

	total	one, detached	one, attached	multi-unit dwellings total	2 to 4	5 to 9	10 to 19	20 to 49	50 or more	mobile homes
Total owners	**74,931**	**61,699**	**3,976**	**3,740**	**1,550**	**502**	**563**	**436**	**689**	**5,516**
Under age 25	1,436	998	98	163	60	18	37	22	26	177
Aged 25 to 29	3,402	2,502	313	282	95	47	57	30	53	305
Aged 30 to 34	5,777	4,599	349	356	126	51	82	52	46	473
Aged 35 to 44	15,419	13,068	665	604	253	94	106	56	95	1,082
Aged 45 to 54	17,305	14,728	847	577	259	78	84	55	101	1,153
Aged 55 to 64	13,773	11,433	757	578	286	72	51	67	103	1,006
Aged 65 to 74	9,185	7,523	468	529	231	72	95	39	91	665
Aged 75 or older	8,633	6,849	479	651	240	70	51	114	175	655
Median age	52	52	52	53	54	50	45	55	57	51

Percent distribution by type of structure

	total	one, detached	one, attached	multi-unit dwellings total	2 to 4	5 to 9	10 to 19	20 to 49	50 or more	mobile homes
Total owners	**100.0%**	**82.3%**	**5.3%**	**5.0%**	**2.1%**	**0.7%**	**0.8%**	**0.6%**	**0.9%**	**7.4%**
Under age 25	100.0	69.5	6.8	11.4	4.2	1.3	2.6	1.5	1.8	12.3
Aged 25 to 29	100.0	73.5	9.2	8.3	2.8	1.4	1.7	0.9	1.6	9.0
Aged 30 to 34	100.0	79.6	6.0	6.2	2.2	0.9	1.4	0.9	0.8	8.2
Aged 35 to 44	100.0	84.8	4.3	3.9	1.6	0.6	0.7	0.4	0.6	7.0
Aged 45 to 54	100.0	85.1	4.9	3.3	1.5	0.5	0.5	0.3	0.6	6.7
Aged 55 to 64	100.0	83.0	5.5	4.2	2.1	0.5	0.4	0.5	0.7	7.3
Aged 65 to 74	100.0	81.9	5.1	5.8	2.5	0.8	1.0	0.4	1.0	7.2
Aged 75 or older	100.0	79.3	5.5	7.5	2.8	0.8	0.6	1.3	2.0	7.6

Percent distribution by age of householder

	total	one, detached	one, attached	multi-unit dwellings total	2 to 4	5 to 9	10 to 19	20 to 49	50 or more	mobile homes
Total owners	**100.0%**	**100.0%**	**100.0%**	**100.0%**	**100.0%**	**100.0%**	**100.0%**	**100.0%**	**100.0%**	**100.0%**
Under age 25	1.9	1.6	2.5	4.4	3.9	3.6	6.6	5.0	3.8	3.2
Aged 25 to 29	4.5	4.1	7.9	7.5	6.1	9.4	10.1	6.9	7.7	5.5
Aged 30 to 34	7.7	7.5	8.8	9.5	8.1	10.2	14.6	11.9	6.7	8.6
Aged 35 to 44	20.6	21.2	16.7	16.1	16.3	18.7	18.8	12.8	13.8	19.6
Aged 45 to 54	23.1	23.9	21.3	15.4	16.7	15.5	14.9	12.6	14.7	20.9
Aged 55 to 64	18.4	18.5	19.0	15.5	18.5	14.3	9.1	15.4	14.9	18.2
Aged 65 to 74	12.3	12.2	11.8	14.1	14.9	14.3	16.9	8.9	13.2	12.1
Aged 75 or older	11.5	11.1	12.0	17.4	15.5	13.9	9.1	26.1	25.4	11.9

Source: Bureau of the Census, American Housing Survey for the United States: 2005, Internet site http://www.census.gov/hhes/ www/housing/ahs/ahs05/ahs05.html; calculations by New Strategist

Table 5.16 Type of Structure by Age of Householder, 2005: Renters

(number and percent distribution of renters by age of householder and type of structure, 2005; numbers in thousands)

	total	one, detached	one, attached	multi-unit dwellings total	2 to 4	5 to 9	10 to 19	20 to 49	50 or more	mobile homes
Total renters	**33,940**	**8,297**	**2,182**	**22,038**	**6,829**	**4,607**	**4,175**	**3,203**	**3,222**	**1,424**
Under age 25	4,577	842	287	3,238	976	774	768	445	275	211
Aged 25 to 29	5,056	1,010	369	3,474	1,071	761	804	553	285	203
Aged 30 to 34	4,408	1,159	326	2,707	859	622	565	416	244	216
Aged 35 to 44	7,036	2,169	455	4,167	1,428	945	776	548	470	245
Aged 45 to 54	5,270	1,505	310	3,195	1,072	655	601	479	387	259
Aged 55 to 64	3,215	838	216	2,009	664	368	343	279	355	152
Aged 65 to 74	1,897	369	103	1,329	332	236	160	201	400	96
Aged 75 or older	2,482	405	116	1,919	428	246	157	283	805	42
Median age	39	40	37	39	39	37	35	38	54	38

Percent distribution by type of structure

	total	one, detached	one, attached	multi-unit dwellings total	2 to 4	5 to 9	10 to 19	20 to 49	50 or more	mobile homes
Total renters	**100.0%**	**24.4%**	**6.4%**	**64.9%**	**20.1%**	**13.6%**	**12.3%**	**9.4%**	**9.5%**	**4.2%**
Under age 25	100.0	18.4	6.3	70.7	21.3	16.9	16.8	9.7	6.0	4.6
Aged 25 to 29	100.0	20.0	7.3	68.7	21.2	15.1	15.9	10.9	5.6	4.0
Aged 30 to 34	100.0	26.3	7.4	61.4	19.5	14.1	12.8	9.4	5.5	4.9
Aged 35 to 44	100.0	30.8	6.5	59.2	20.3	13.4	11.0	7.8	6.7	3.5
Aged 45 to 54	100.0	28.6	5.9	60.6	20.3	12.4	11.4	9.1	7.3	4.9
Aged 55 to 64	100.0	26.1	6.7	62.5	20.7	11.4	10.7	8.7	11.0	4.7
Aged 65 to 74	100.0	19.5	5.4	70.1	17.5	12.4	8.4	10.6	21.1	5.1
Aged 75 or older	100.0	16.3	4.7	77.3	17.2	9.9	6.3	11.4	32.4	1.7

Percent distribution by age of householder

	total	one, detached	one, attached	multi-unit dwellings total	2 to 4	5 to 9	10 to 19	20 to 49	50 or more	mobile homes
Total renters	**100.0%**	**100.0%**	**100.0%**	**100.0%**	**100.0%**	**100.0%**	**100.0%**	**100.0%**	**100.0%**	**100.0%**
Under age 25	13.5	10.1	13.2	14.7	14.3	16.8	18.4	13.9	8.5	14.8
Aged 25 to 29	14.9	12.2	16.9	15.8	15.7	16.5	19.3	17.3	8.8	14.3
Aged 30 to 34	13.0	14.0	14.9	12.3	12.6	13.5	13.5	13.0	7.6	15.2
Aged 35 to 44	20.7	26.1	20.9	18.9	20.9	20.5	18.6	17.1	14.6	17.2
Aged 45 to 54	15.5	18.1	14.2	14.5	15.7	14.2	14.4	15.0	12.0	18.2
Aged 55 to 64	9.5	10.1	9.9	9.1	9.7	8.0	8.2	8.7	11.0	10.7
Aged 65 to 74	5.6	4.4	4.7	6.0	4.9	5.1	3.8	6.3	12.4	6.7
Aged 75 or older	7.3	4.9	5.3	8.7	6.3	5.3	3.8	8.8	25.0	2.9

Source: Bureau of the Census, American Housing Survey for the United States: 2005, Internet site http://www.census.gov/hhes/www/housing/ahs/ahs05/ahs05.html; calculations by New Strategist

Middle-Aged Married Couples Have the Most Valuable Homes

Dual-earner couples can afford more expensive homes.

The median value of the homes owned by middle-aged married couples stood at more than $195,000 in 2005, according to the biennial American Housing Survey. This is 18 percent greater than the $165,344 median value of all homes. More than 30 percent of couples aged 35 to 64 who own a home live in a house worth $300,000 or more.

A substantial 29 percent of the nation's homeowners own a home worth less than $100,000. Among married couples, fewer than one in four own a home with a value of less than $100,000. But the figure surpasses one-third for other household types. Those most likely to own a home with a value of less than $100,000 are women aged 65 or older who are family heads, at nearly 45 percent.

■ Homes are the most important asset owned by the average American household. The housing market slump will lower the net worth of many households.

Home values are lowest among the youngest homeowners

(median value of homes owned by married couples, by age of householder, 2005)

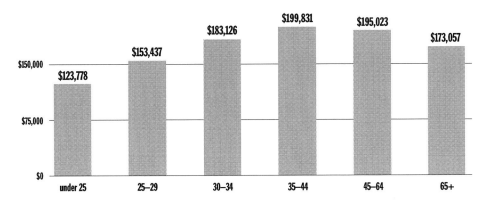

Table 5.17 Home Values by Type of Household and Age of Householder, 2005

(total number and percent distribution of homeowners by type of household, age of householder, and median value of home, 2005; number of homeowners in thousands)

	total number	total percent	less than $100,000	$100,000–$149,999	$150,000–$199,999	$200,000–$249,999	$250,000–$299,999	$300,000 or more	median value
Total homeowners	**74,931**	**100.0%**	**29.3%**	**16.7%**	**13.0%**	**8.9%**	**6.6%**	**25.5%**	**$165,344**
Married couples	**46,000**	**100.0**	**24.0**	**15.8**	**13.6**	**9.3**	**7.8**	**29.5**	**187,518**
Under age 25	536	100.0	37.3	26.5	10.1	8.6	4.3	13.1	123,778
Aged 25 to 29	2,042	100.0	26.1	22.7	18.4	9.3	7.3	16.2	153,437
Aged 30 to 34	3,738	100.0	23.3	17.0	14.7	10.7	8.3	26.0	183,126
Aged 35 to 44	10,494	100.0	20.9	14.9	14.2	9.7	7.8	32.5	199,831
Aged 45 to 64	20,460	100.0	23.2	15.3	12.8	9.0	7.9	31.8	195,023
Aged 65 or older	8,730	100.0	28.4	15.4	13.5	9.2	7.6	25.9	173,057
Female-headed families	**8,023**	**100.0**	**38.7**	**17.6**	**11.2**	**7.7**	**5.0**	**19.8**	**132,159**
Under age 45	3,227	100.0	40.9	18.5	11.7	6.6	5.7	16.6	124,581
Aged 45 to 64	3,208	100.0	33.5	17.0	12.6	9.7	4.1	23.2	148,586
Aged 65 or older	1,589	100.0	44.6	17.0	7.3	6.0	5.5	19.6	115,840
Male-headed families	**4,702**	**100.0**	**32.5**	**18.2**	**12.7**	**9.2**	**4.8**	**22.6**	**148,250**
Under age 45	2,406	100.0	34.3	19.9	11.8	9.9	4.7	19.5	139,367
Aged 45 to 64	1,712	100.0	31.0	15.5	13.4	8.0	5.5	26.7	163,334
Aged 65 or older	585	100.0	29.1	18.8	14.4	10.3	3.6	23.6	156,478
Women living alone	**9,690**	**100.0**	**38.7**	**18.5**	**12.7**	**8.2**	**4.7**	**17.2**	**130,502**
Under age 45	1,394	100.0	30.1	20.0	17.1	7.6	5.7	19.3	149,367
Aged 45 to 64	3,210	100.0	35.9	19.8	13.4	9.3	4.7	17.0	135,588
Aged 65 or older	5,086	100.0	42.8	17.2	11.0	7.6	4.5	16.8	120,821
Men living alone	**6,515**	**100.0**	**39.4**	**18.0**	**11.7**	**7.9**	**4.2**	**18.8**	**129,584**
Under age 45	2,198	100.0	35.2	18.9	13.9	9.1	4.6	18.4	139,250
Aged 45 to 64	2,488	100.0	40.3	18.0	10.5	7.6	4.6	18.9	126,852
Aged 65 or older	1,829	100.0	43.1	16.8	10.7	6.8	3.2	19.4	120,477

Source: Bureau of the Census, American Housing Survey for the United States: 2005, Internet site http://www.census.gov/hhes/ www/housing/ahs/ahs05/ahs05.html; calculations by New Strategist

Housing Costs Are Low for Older Homeowners

Renters do not see their housing costs decline much with age.

Housing costs are lowest for homeowners aged 65 or older regardless of household type. Median monthly housing costs for married homeowners aged 65 or older were just $466 in 2005. For all couples who own a home, the cost is a much higher $949. Behind the lower housing costs for older homeowners is the fact that most have paid off their mortgage, lowering their monthly bills.

Regardless of household type, homeowners typically have higher monthly housing costs than renters—but only until age 65. Among couples aged 65 or older, for example, renters pay a median of $720 per month for housing versus the $466 paid by homeowners. Among women who live alone, homeowners aged 65 or older had a median monthly housing cost of $347 versus $537 for renters.

■ Homeowners who do not pay down their mortgage as they age will face steep housing costs well into old age.

Housing costs are highest for the middle aged

(median monthly housing costs for married couples, by age of householder, 2005)

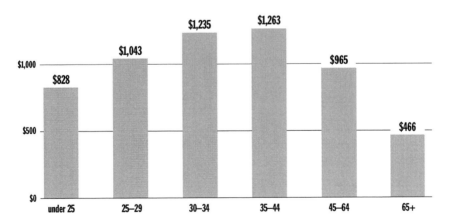

Table 5.18   Median Monthly Housing Costs by Age of Householder, 2005

(median monthly housing costs by type of household, age of householder, and homeownership status, 2005)

	owners	renters
Total households	**$809**	**$694**
Married couples	**949**	**798**
Under age 25	828	666
Aged 25 to 29	1,043	756
Aged 30 to 34	1,235	804
Aged 35 to 44	1,263	889
Aged 45 to 64	965	827
Aged 65 or older	466	720
Female-headed families	**751**	**699**
Under age 45	855	695
Aged 45 to 64	807	717
Aged 65 or older	443	665
Male-headed families	**824**	**773**
Under age 45	914	780
Aged 45 to 64	842	751
Aged 65 or older	476	760
Women living alone	**470**	**596**
Under age 45	881	658
Aged 45 to 64	660	559
Aged 65 or older	347	537
Men living alone	**587**	**601**
Under age 45	848	634
Aged 45 to 64	594	575
Aged 65 or older	360	493

Note: Housing costs include mortgages, rent, utilities, real estate taxes, property insurance, and regime fees.
Source: Bureau of the Census, American Housing Survey for the United States: 2005, Internet site http://www.census.gov/hhes/ www/housing/ahs/ahs05/ahs05.html; calculations by New Strategist

6

Income

The economic ups and downs of the 20th century influenced both the attitudes and financial status of each generation. After enduring the Depression and World War II, today's older generations of Americans (the World War II and Swing generations) prospered in the 1950s and 1960s thanks to a rapidly expanding postwar economy. Since 1980, the incomes of older Americans have grown faster than those of middle-aged or younger adults as they replaced a less affluent elderly cohort.

Many Boomers enjoyed expanding economic fortunes during their youth, but as they reached adulthood the incomes of men fell. Consequently, for Boomers and younger generations, two incomes are now a necessity for a middle-class lifestyle.

As Boomer, Gen X, and Millennial women entered the workforce and committed themselves to full-time jobs, the incomes of women have grown substantially. Their growing incomes have allowed families to stay afloat despite the declining fortunes of men.

What to expect in the future

■ Women's incomes will continue to rise as well-educated, career-oriented younger generations replace older just-a-job women in the labor force.

■ The large Baby-Boom generation is filling the 55-to-64 age group, and labor force participation rates among older Americans are climbing. Look for rising incomes among 55-to-64-year-olds as they postpone retirement.

■ Millennials are entering the labor market in a time of economic uncertainty. Their incomes have taken a hit. Expect them to be cautious and pragmatic spenders as they strive to achieve the American Dream.

Men's Incomes Have Fallen Since 2000

Many men have lower incomes today than they did in 1980.

Men's median income reached a record high in 2000, topping the previous peak set in 1973. Between 2000 and 2006, however, men's median income fell 3 percent after adjusting for inflation. Nevertheless, the 2006 median of $32,265 was 11 percent higher than the 1980 median, after adjusting for inflation.

Men spanning the ages from 25 to 54 had lower median incomes in 2006 than they did in 1980. The drop was particularly pronounced among men aged 25 to 44, whose income declined 8 to 11 percent after adjusting for inflation. In contrast, men aged 65 or older saw their median income climb 38 percent during those years. The median income of men aged 55 to 64 grew 13 percent between 1980 and 2006. Men aged 55 or older were the only ones to make gains since 2000, with median income rising by 3 to 4 percent between 2000 and 2006 thanks to an increase in the labor force participation of older men.

■ The incomes of men aged 55 to 64 will continue to climb as Boomers fill the age group and early retirement becomes less common.

Older men have gained ground since 1980

(percent change in median income of men aged 15 or older, by age, 1980 to 2006; in 2006 dollars)

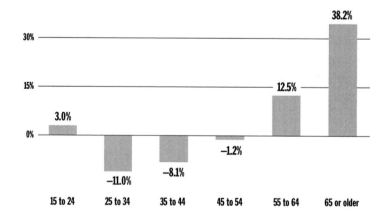

Table 6.1 Median Income of Men by Age, 1980 to 2006

(median income of men aged 15 or older with income, by age, 1980 to 2006; percent change for selected years; in 2006 dollars)

	total	15 to 24	25 to 34	35 to 44	45 to 54	55 to 64	65 or older
2006	$32,265	$10,964	$32,131	$42,637	$45,693	$41,477	$23,500
2005	32,284	10,807	32,166	42,285	45,034	41,965	22,487
2004	32,554	10,755	33,061	43,241	44,661	41,912	22,542
2003	32,788	10,912	33,479	42,936	46,095	42,629	22,307
2002	32,763	10,805	34,375	42,460	45,908	40,650	21,779
2001	33,127	10,588	34,731	43,645	46,791	40,568	22,412
2000	33,165	11,170	35,401	44,374	48,022	40,006	22,714
1999	33,002	10,097	35,522	44,011	49,340	40,489	23,337
1998	32,708	10,112	34,714	43,430	48,054	40,467	22,428
1997	31,565	9,350	32,547	41,129	47,106	39,009	22,246
1996	30,477	8,900	32,197	41,133	46,331	37,756	21,335
1995	29,626	9,078	31,000	41,256	46,727	38,053	21,644
1994	29,213	9,479	30,404	41,300	46,983	36,415	20,511
1993	28,979	8,829	30,112	41,668	45,530	34,523	20,576
1992	28,791	8,863	30,258	41,509	45,295	36,054	20,546
1991	29,533	9,062	31,158	42,276	45,852	36,734	20,714
1990	30,338	9,447	31,982	44,511	46,356	37,082	21,204
1989	31,220	9,908	33,533	46,198	48,590	38,335	20,570
1988	30,948	9,564	34,015	46,721	48,412	37,067	20,412
1987	30,172	9,257	33,803	45,874	48,324	37,121	20,232
1986	30,021	9,268	33,613	45,910	48,689	36,897	20,250
1985	29,134	8,922	33,334	45,294	46,164	36,183	19,469
1984	28,794	8,692	33,395	45,342	45,384	36,041	19,288
1983	28,083	8,223	32,255	43,071	44,366	35,880	18,698
1982	27,887	8,851	32,818	43,279	43,067	35,641	18,368
1981	28,527	6,504	34,073	44,713	44,512	36,769	17,231
1980	29,023	10,648	36,088	46,411	46,265	36,861	16,999

Percent change

	total	15 to 24	25 to 34	35 to 44	45 to 54	55 to 64	65 or older
2000 to 2006	−2.7%	−1.8%	−9.2%	−3.9%	−4.8%	3.7%	3.5%
1980 to 2006	11.2	3.0	−11.0	−8.1	−1.2	12.5	38.2

Source: Bureau of the Census, Current Population Surveys, Internet site http://www.census.gov/hhes/www/income/histinc/inchhtoc.html; calculations by New Strategist

Women's Median Income Is at a Record High

Women's incomes have been growing rapidly for decades.

As better-educated and career-oriented Baby-Boom women entered the labor force, they boosted women's median income. Generation X and Millennial women followed in their footsteps, with a growing percentage of women committed to full-time jobs. As more women work full-time, their median income has increased substantially, climbing 76 percent to $20,014 in 2006, after adjusting for inflation.

Most women experienced large income gains between 1980 and 2006, with women aged 55 to 64 seeing their median income more than double during those years. In contrast, the median income of women under age 25 grew only 20 percent, after adjusting for inflation. The slower growth among the youngest women is due largely to the increasing proportion of women in the age group who are going to college and unavailable for full-time work.

Between 2000 and 2006, the median income of women climbed by 6 percent. Women under age 55 saw little growth in median income, and those aged 25 to 34 saw their median income fall by 2 percent. But women aged 55 or older continued to make gains. The median income of those aged 55 to 64 grew 22 percent between 2000 and 2006 as Boomers filled the age group.

■ The incomes of women aged 55 to 64 will continue to grow rapidly as career-oriented Boomers replace just-a-job women in the age group.

Women's incomes have made big gains since 1980

(percent change in median income of women aged 15 or older, by age, 1980 to 2006; in 2006 dollars)

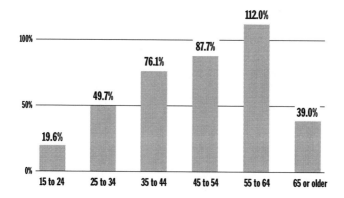

Table 6.2 Median Income of Women by Age, 1980 to 2006

(median income of women aged 15 or older with income, by age, 1980 to 2006; percent change for selected years; in 2006 dollars)

	total	15 to 24	25 to 34	35 to 44	45 to 54	55 to 64	65 or older
2006	$20,014	$8,653	$24,179	$26,368	$27,844	$24,186	$13,603
2005	19,175	8,485	23,551	26,255	27,330	22,836	12,898
2004	18,847	8,218	23,541	26,031	27,983	22,191	12,888
2003	18,907	8,145	24,091	25,713	28,334	22,312	12,975
2002	18,839	8,495	24,259	25,013	28,198	21,475	12,781
2001	18,913	8,501	24,444	25,580	27,475	20,289	12,878
2000	18,796	8,612	24,631	25,833	27,770	19,799	12,898
1999	18,505	8,075	23,347	24,982	27,289	19,277	13,250
1998	17,816	8,067	22,540	25,045	26,653	18,118	12,968
1997	17,156	7,940	22,094	23,420	25,708	17,998	12,598
1996	16,387	7,520	20,951	23,589	24,355	17,028	12,309
1995	15,928	6,973	20,427	22,844	23,271	16,257	12,284
1994	15,421	7,409	20,019	21,773	22,933	14,616	12,037
1993	15,169	7,349	19,209	21,758	22,418	14,872	11,672
1992	15,080	7,277	19,187	21,700	22,312	14,263	11,518
1991	15,115	7,498	18,705	21,823	21,244	14,286	11,815
1990	15,054	7,329	18,821	21,684	21,274	14,053	12,026
1989	15,104	7,437	19,195	21,665	20,627	14,380	12,013
1988	14,541	7,340	18,930	20,535	19,674	13,711	11,626
1987	14,072	7,478	18,624	20,348	19,106	12,793	11,699
1986	13,349	7,094	18,085	19,409	18,208	12,940	11,270
1985	12,891	6,772	17,645	18,354	17,181	12,812	11,276
1984	12,676	6,661	17,335	17,647	16,433	12,619	11,111
1983	12,128	6,635	16,320	17,005	15,748	11,764	10,747
1982	11,769	6,701	15,937	15,695	14,998	11,809	10,725
1981	11,557	4,226	16,088	15,596	14,885	11,381	9,964
1980	11,396	7,236	16,152	14,975	14,831	11,410	9,789

Percent change

	total	15 to 24	25 to 34	35 to 44	45 to 54	55 to 64	65 or older
2000 to 2006	6.5%	0.5%	−1.8%	2.1%	0.3%	22.2%	5.5%
1980 to 2006	75.6	19.6	49.7	76.1	87.7	112.0	39.0

Source: Bureau of the Census, Current Population Surveys, Internet site http://www.census.gov/hhes/www/income/histinc/inchhtoc.html; calculations by New Strategist

Baby-Boom Men Have the Highest Incomes

The median income of Boomer men is 38 percent above average.

Given the stagnation in men's earnings over the past few decades, it is no surprise that the majority of men have modest incomes. Half of men had incomes below $32,265 in 2006. It is only when husbands and wives combine their earnings that most families can achieve a middle-class standard of living.

Incomes are highest for Boomer men, aged 43 to 61 in 2006, because most Boomers are still in their peak earning years. The median income of Boomer men stood at $44,678. More than one in eight Boomer men had an income of $100,000 or more.

Gen X men, aged 31 to 42, had the second highest median income—$40,858 in 2006. Men in the Swing generation had a much lower median income of $30,066 because many are retired. Among men working full-time, median income continues to rise well into old age, peaking in the 65-to-74 age group.

■ Millennial men have the lowest incomes because many are still in school.

Generation X men have the second-highest median income

(median income of men by generation, 2006)

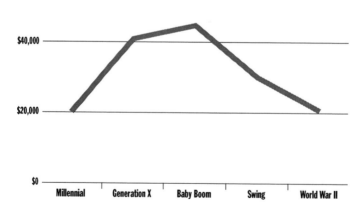

Table 6.3 Income of Men by Age, 2006

(number and percent distribution of men aged 15 or older with income, median income of those with income and of those working full-time year-round, and percent working full-time year-round, by income and age, 2006; men in thousands as of 2007)

	total	15 to 24	25 to 34	35 to 44	45 to 54	55 to 64	aged 65 or older total	65 to 74	75 or older
TOTAL MEN	**114,576**	**21,156**	**20,024**	**21,181**	**21,296**	**15,478**	**15,443**	**8,739**	**6,703**
Without income	**10,667**	**7,063**	**979**	**807**	**869**	**573**	**379**	**222**	**156**
With income	**103,909**	**14,093**	**19,045**	**20,374**	**20,427**	**14,905**	**15,064**	**8,517**	**6,547**
Under $10,000	13,759	6,550	1,644	1,293	1,410	1,297	1,565	829	735
$10,000 to $19,999	17,394	3,517	2,906	2,128	2,145	1,930	4,768	2,342	2,427
$20,000 to $29,999	15,871	2,058	3,727	2,734	2,474	1,844	3,034	1,628	1,406
$30,000 to $39,999	13,851	982	3,447	2,972	2,666	2,009	1,774	1,062	713
$40,000 to $49,999	10,501	470	2,493	2,550	2,376	1,560	1,053	652	402
$50,000 to $59,999	8,078	209	1,623	2,076	2,060	1,395	715	464	250
$60,000 to $69,999	5,912	106	1,053	1,545	1,635	1,076	497	375	123
$70,000 to $79,999	4,253	70	700	1,105	1,239	805	335	228	107
$80,000 to $89,999	2,864	34	425	808	806	536	256	195	61
$90,000 to $99,999	2,128	28	248	541	603	463	247	174	73
$100,000 or more	9,295	70	779	2,622	3,014	1,991	819	569	250
Median income of men with income	$32,265	$10,964	$32,131	$42,637	$45,693	$41,477	$23,500	$26,273	$20,639
Median income of full-time workers	44,958	22,434	36,937	48,607	51,751	52,520	57,974	59,254	50,783
Percent working full-time	55.0%	23.4%	73.0%	78.9%	75.7%	57.1%	11.9%	17.3%	4.8%
TOTAL MEN	**100.0%**	**100.0%**	**100.0%**	**100.0%**	**100.0%**	**100.0%**	**100.0%**	**100.0%**	**100.0%**
Without income	**9.3**	**33.4**	**4.9**	**3.8**	**4.1**	**3.7**	**2.5**	**2.5**	**2.3**
With income	**90.7**	**66.6**	**95.1**	**96.2**	**95.9**	**96.3**	**97.5**	**97.5**	**97.7**
Under $10,000	12.0	31.0	8.2	6.1	6.6	8.4	10.1	9.5	11.0
$10,000 to $19,999	15.2	16.6	14.5	10.0	10.1	12.5	30.9	26.8	36.2
$20,000 to $29,999	13.9	9.7	18.6	12.9	11.6	11.9	19.6	18.6	21.0
$30,000 to $39,999	12.1	4.6	17.2	14.0	12.5	13.0	11.5	12.2	10.6
$40,000 to $49,999	9.2	2.2	12.5	12.0	11.2	10.1	6.8	7.5	6.0
$50,000 to $59,999	7.1	1.0	8.1	9.8	9.7	9.0	4.6	5.3	3.7
$60,000 to $69,999	5.2	0.5	5.3	7.3	7.7	7.0	3.2	4.3	1.8
$70,000 to $79,999	3.7	0.3	3.5	5.2	5.8	5.2	2.2	2.6	1.6
$80,000 to $89,999	2.5	0.2	2.1	3.8	3.8	3.5	1.7	2.2	0.9
$90,000 to $99,999	1.9	0.1	1.2	2.6	2.8	3.0	1.6	2.0	1.1
$100,000 or more	8.1	0.3	3.9	12.4	14.2	12.9	5.3	6.5	3.7

Source: Bureau of the Census, 2007 Current Population Survey, Internet site http://pubdb3.census.gov/macro/032007/perinc/toc.htm; calculations by New Strategist

Table 6.4 Income of Men by Generation, 2006

(number and percent distribution of men aged 15 or older with income, by income and generation, 2006; men in thousands as of 2007)

	total	Millennial (15 to 30)	Generation X (31 to 42)	Baby Boom (43 to 61)	Swing (62 to 74)	World War II (75 or older)
TOTAL MEN	**114,576**	**33,513**	**24,537**	**37,125**	**12,698**	**6,703**
Without income	**10,667**	**7,738**	**945**	**1,463**	**365**	**156**
With income	**103,909**	**25,775**	**23,591**	**35,662**	**12,334**	**6,547**
Under $10,000	13,759	7,675	1,535	2,609	1,204	735
$10,000 to $19,999	17,394	5,467	2,684	3,904	2,912	2,427
$20,000 to $29,999	15,871	4,498	3,480	4,356	2,130	1,406
$30,000 to $39,999	13,851	3,176	3,640	4,730	1,594	713
$40,000 to $49,999	10,501	1,932	3,063	4,088	1,015	402
$50,000 to $59,999	8,078	1,129	2,359	3,525	815	250
$60,000 to $69,999	5,912	675	1,715	2,786	616	123
$70,000 to $79,999	4,253	422	1,210	2,113	405	107
$80,000 to $89,999	2,864	228	865	1,399	310	61
$90,000 to $99,999	2,128	137	561	1,084	274	73
$100,000 or more	9,295	439	2,479	5,068	1,060	250
Median income of men with income	$32,265	$20,159	$40,858	$44,678	$30,066	$20,639
TOTAL MEN	**100.0%**	**100.0%**	**100.0%**	**100.0%**	**100.0%**	**100.0%**
Without income	**9.3**	**23.1**	**3.9**	**3.9**	**2.9**	**2.3**
With income	**90.7**	**76.9**	**96.1**	**96.1**	**97.1**	**97.7**
Under $10,000	12.0	22.9	6.3	7.0	9.5	11.0
$10,000 to $19,999	15.2	16.3	10.9	10.5	22.9	36.2
$20,000 to $29,999	13.9	13.4	14.2	11.7	16.8	21.0
$30,000 to $39,999	12.1	9.5	14.8	12.7	12.6	10.6
$40,000 to $49,999	9.2	5.8	12.5	11.0	8.0	6.0
$50,000 to $59,999	7.1	3.4	9.6	9.5	6.4	3.7
$60,000 to $69,999	5.2	2.0	7.0	7.5	4.9	1.8
$70,000 to $79,999	3.7	1.3	4.9	5.7	3.2	1.6
$80,000 to $89,999	2.5	0.7	3.5	3.8	2.4	0.9
$90,000 to $99,999	1.9	0.4	2.3	2.9	2.2	1.1
$100,000 or more	8.1	1.3	10.1	13.7	8.3	3.7

Note: Number of men and median income by generation are estimates by New Strategist.
Source: Bureau of the Census, 2007 Current Population Survey, Internet site http://pubdb3.census.gov/macro/032007/perinc/ toc.htm; calculations by New Strategist

Baby-Boom Women Have the Highest Incomes

The women of Generation X are close behind, however.

Women's median income was only $20,014 in 2006. The figure is far below the $32,265 median income of men in part because a larger proportion of women work part-time. Although women's incomes are well below men's, they have become a necessity to achieving a middle-class lifestyle because men's incomes are not keeping up with the rising cost of housing, health care, gasoline, and college tuition.

Incomes are highest for Boomer women, aged 43 to 61, who had a median income of $27,095 in 2006. Gen X women are not far behind, with a median income of $26,058. Only 4 percent of Boomer women and 3 percent of Gen X women had an income of $100,000 or more.

Women in the Swing generation have much lower incomes than Gen X or Boomer women, with a median of just $15,961. Most Swing women are retired. Among women who work full-time, incomes vary little by age, being above $36,000 for workers ranging in age from 35 to 74.

■ Millennial women have low incomes because many are still in school.

Swing women have much lower incomes than Boomers or Gen Xers

(median income of women by generation, 2006)

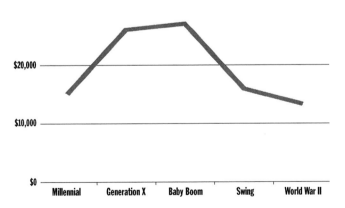

Table 6.5 Income of Women by Age, 2006

(number and percent distribution of women aged 15 or older with income, median income of those with income and of those working full-time year-round, and percent working full-time year-round, by income and age, 2006; women in thousands as of 2007)

	total	15 to 24	25 to 34	35 to 44	45 to 54	55 to 64	aged 65 or older total	65 to 74	75 or older
TOTAL WOMEN	121,443	20,546	19,843	21,582	22,166	16,713	20,593	10,259	10,334
Without income	16,861	7,279	2,692	2,383	2,031	1,640	836	478	359
With income	104,582	13,267	17,151	19,199	20,135	15,073	19,757	9,781	9,975
Under $10,000	28,064	7,205	3,553	3,869	3,517	3,433	6,488	3,272	3,216
$10,000 to $19,999	24,194	3,296	3,446	3,502	3,602	3,006	7,343	3,127	4,216
$20,000 to $29,999	16,820	1,523	3,431	3,182	3,434	2,450	2,800	1,415	1,385
$30,000 to $39,999	11,911	736	2,533	2,753	2,822	1,823	1,244	764	479
$40,000 to $49,999	7,720	293	1,689	1,921	1,995	1,229	594	371	223
$50,000 to $59,999	5,081	107	903	1,213	1,434	974	450	264	184
$60,000 to $69,999	3,335	46	611	762	1,058	621	238	194	43
$70,000 to $79,999	2,262	30	316	607	676	493	142	91	52
$80,000 to $89,999	1,286	10	201	342	397	249	92	61	30
$90,000 to $99,999	814	4	97	226	253	157	76	49	26
$100,000 or more	3,091	19	371	820	949	639	292	176	117
Median income of women with income	$20,014	$8,653	$24,179	$26,368	$27,844	$24,186	$13,603	$14,079	$13,302
Median income of full-time workers	34,989	21,336	32,139	36,507	37,396	37,560	35,975	36,833	33,299
Percent working full-time	36.8%	16.3%	50.0%	52.1%	54.9%	40.7%	5.7%	9.6%	1.8%
TOTAL WOMEN	100.0%	100.0%	100.0%	100.0%	100.0%	100.0%	100.0%	100.0%	100.0%
Without income	13.9	35.4	13.6	11.0	9.2	9.8	4.1	4.7	3.5
With income	86.1	64.6	86.4	89.0	90.8	90.2	95.9	95.3	96.5
Under $10,000	23.1	35.1	17.9	17.9	15.9	20.5	31.5	31.9	31.1
$10,000 to $19,999	19.9	16.0	17.4	16.2	16.3	18.0	35.7	30.5	40.8
$20,000 to $29,999	13.9	7.4	17.3	14.7	15.5	14.7	13.6	13.8	13.4
$30,000 to $39,999	9.8	3.6	12.8	12.8	12.7	10.9	6.0	7.4	4.6
$40,000 to $49,999	6.4	1.4	8.5	8.9	9.0	7.4	2.9	3.6	2.2
$50,000 to $59,999	4.2	0.5	4.6	5.6	6.5	5.8	2.2	2.6	1.8
$60,000 to $69,999	2.7	0.2	3.1	3.5	4.8	3.7	1.2	1.9	0.4
$70,000 to $79,999	1.9	0.1	1.6	2.8	3.0	2.9	0.7	0.9	0.5
$80,000 to $89,999	1.1	0.0	1.0	1.6	1.8	1.5	0.4	0.6	0.3
$90,000 to $99,999	0.7	0.0	0.5	1.0	1.1	0.9	0.4	0.5	0.3
$100,000 or more	2.5	0.1	1.9	3.8	4.3	3.8	1.4	1.7	1.1

Source: Bureau of the Census, 2007 Current Population Survey, Internet site http://pubdb3.census.gov/macro/032007/perinc/ toc.htm; calculations by New Strategist

Table 6.6 Income of Women by Generation, 2006

(number and percent distribution of women aged 15 or older with income, by income and generation, 2006; women in thousands as of 2007)

	total	Millennial (15 to 30)	Generation X (31 to 42)	Baby Boom (43 to 61)	Swing (62 to 74)	World War II (75 or older)
TOTAL WOMEN	**121,443**	**32,696**	**24,846**	**38,887**	**14,682**	**10,334**
Without income	**16,861**	**8,937**	**2,961**	**3,745**	**861**	**359**
With income	**104,582**	**23,759**	**21,885**	**35,142**	**13,820**	**9,975**
Under $10,000	28,064	9,433	4,462	6,614	4,341	3,216
$10,000 to $19,999	24,194	5,474	4,035	6,414	4,056	4,216
$20,000 to $29,999	16,820	3,744	3,708	5,911	2,069	1,385
$30,000 to $39,999	11,911	2,303	3,153	4,779	1,195	479
$40,000 to $49,999	7,720	1,295	2,207	3,321	673	223
$50,000 to $59,999	5,081	596	1,361	2,472	467	184
$60,000 to $69,999	3,335	364	886	1,720	319	43
$70,000 to $79,999	2,262	181	634	1,213	185	52
$80,000 to $89,999	1,286	111	360	669	116	30
$90,000 to $99,999	814	52	229	425	86	26
$100,000 or more	3,091	209	852	1,600	314	117
Median income of women with income	$20,014	$15,099	$26,058	$27,095	$15,961	$13,302
TOTAL WOMEN	**100.0%**	**100.0%**	**100.0%**	**100.0%**	**100.0%**	**100.0%**
Without income	**13.9**	**27.3**	**11.9**	**9.6**	**5.9**	**3.5**
With income	**86.1**	**72.7**	**88.1**	**90.4**	**94.1**	**96.5**
Under $10,000	23.1	28.9	18.0	17.0	29.6	31.1
$10,000 to $19,999	19.9	16.7	16.2	16.5	27.6	40.8
$20,000 to $29,999	13.9	11.5	14.9	15.2	14.1	13.4
$30,000 to $39,999	9.8	7.0	12.7	12.3	8.1	4.6
$40,000 to $49,999	6.4	4.0	8.9	8.5	4.6	2.2
$50,000 to $59,999	4.2	1.8	5.5	6.4	3.2	1.8
$60,000 to $69,999	2.7	1.1	3.6	4.4	2.2	0.4
$70,000 to $79,999	1.9	0.6	2.6	3.1	1.3	0.5
$80,000 to $89,999	1.1	0.3	1.4	1.7	0.8	0.3
$90,000 to $99,999	0.7	0.2	0.9	1.1	0.6	0.3
$100,000 or more	2.5	0.6	3.4	4.1	2.1	1.1

Note: Number of women and median income by generation are estimates by New Strategist.
Source: Bureau of the Census, 2007 Current Population Survey, Internet site http://pubdb3.census.gov/macro/032007/perinc/toc.htm; calculations by New Strategist

The Incomes of Young Women Nearly Match Those of Young Men

A wide gap in the incomes of older women and men remains, however.

In 1960, women working full-time made about 60 cents for every dollar made by a man. Since then, the ratio of women's to men's incomes has increased to 78 cents for every dollar earned by a man.

The income gap between women and men varies by age. The median income of women aged 65 or older who work full-time is only 62 percent as high as that of their male counterparts. But among full-time workers aged 45 to 49, the median income of women is 72 percent as high as that of men. The youngest full-time workers come closest to income parity. Among full-time workers aged 25 to 29, women earn 90 percent as much as men.

Does this mean younger women are achieving income equality? Perhaps. With each generation, the educational level of women has increased, and women now spend more years in the labor force—two factors that contribute to the narrowing gap between men's and women's incomes. But the relatively low incomes of young workers may also play a role. The real test will be whether or not the gap narrows in the older age groups in the years ahead.

■ Well-educated younger women are now moving into jobs at the highest levels of business and government, positions previously held only by men. Their progress will help close the income gap.

The earnings gap is narrower among the young

(income of women working full-time as a percent of the income of men working full-time, by age, 2006)

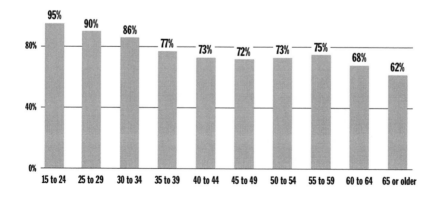

Table 6.7 Median Income of Full-Time Workers by Age and Sex, 2006

(median income of year-round, full-time workers by age and sex, and women's income as a percent of men's, 2006)

	men	women	women's income as a percent of men's
Total people	**$44,958**	**$34,989**	**77.8%**
Aged 15 to 24	22,434	21,336	95.1
Aged 25 to 29	34,167	30,719	89.9
Aged 30 to 34	41,093	35,404	86.2
Aged 35 to 39	47,094	36,218	76.9
Aged 40 to 44	50,117	36,758	73.3
Aged 45 to 49	51,202	37,006	72.3
Aged 50 to 54	52,362	38,096	72.8
Aged 55 to 59	52,432	39,211	74.8
Aged 60 to 64	53,045	36,103	68.1
Aged 65 or older	57,974	35,975	62.1
Aged 65 to 69	59,478	36,961	62.1
Aged 70 to 74	58,909	36,681	62.3
Aged 75 or older	50,783	33,299	65.6

Source: Bureau of the Census, 2007 Current Population Survey, Internet site http://pubdb3.census.gov/macro/032007/perinc/toc.htm; calculations by New Strategist

Since 1980, Older Householders Have Seen Biggest Gains

Householders aged 55 to 64 have made the biggest gains since 2000.

Between 1980 and 2006, the median income of households headed by people aged 65 or older rose from $20,457 to $27,798, an increase of 36 percent, after adjusting for inflation. Younger households also saw their incomes rise, but by much less. The median income of householders under age 25 rose only 4 percent between 1980 and 2006, in large part because a growing proportion are in school and not yet working full-time.

Since 2000, householders in almost every age group have seen their incomes decline. Householders under age 35 have been the biggest losers, with a 5 percent drop in median income. In contrast, householders aged 55 to 64 saw their median income rise 4 percent between 2000 and 2006. Behind the gains for 55-to-64-year-olds is their rising labor force participation as early retirement becomes less common.

■ The incomes of householders aged 55 or older should continue to grow as labor force participation in the older age groups increases.

Most households lost ground between 2000 and 2006

(percent change in median household income, by age of householder, 2000 to 2006)

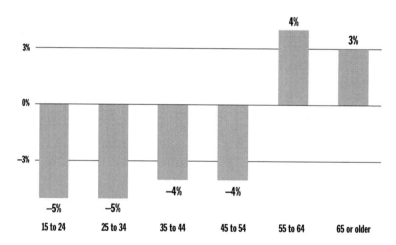

Table 6.8 Median Household Income by Age of Householder, 1980 to 2006

(median income of households by age of householder, 1980 to 2006; percent change for selected years; in 2006 dollars)

	total	15 to 24	25 to 34	35 to 44	45 to 54	55 to 64	65 or older
2006	$48,201	$30,937	$49,164	$60,405	$64,874	$54,592	$27,798
2005	47,845	29,713	48,932	59,988	64,471	53,973	26,890
2004	47,323	29,434	48,530	60,503	65,141	53,789	26,169
2003	47,488	29,657	49,089	60,343	66,041	53,952	26,077
2002	47,530	31,188	50,803	59,983	66,147	52,902	25,947
2001	48,091	32,111	51,339	60,723	66,104	52,232	26,328
2000	49,163	32,604	52,001	62,946	67,488	52,515	27,026
1999	49,244	30,430	50,931	61,482	68,853	54,046	27,586
1998	48,034	29,108	49,497	59,851	66,889	53,324	26,842
1997	46,350	28,286	47,814	58,066	64,975	51,800	26,004
1996	45,416	27,432	45,922	56,840	64,584	50,947	24,886
1995	44,764	27,559	45,585	57,098	63,132	50,020	25,086
1994	43,405	26,018	44,598	56,055	63,580	47,398	24,343
1993	42,926	26,564	42,981	56,145	63,489	45,994	24,390
1992	43,135	24,869	43,984	56,113	62,565	47,862	24,126
1991	43,492	26,438	44,526	56,808	63,163	48,081	24,507
1990	44,778	26,921	45,401	57,666	62,692	48,400	25,206
1989	45,382	29,301	46,822	59,087	65,191	48,386	24,760
1988	44,587	27,907	46,524	59,865	62,582	47,335	24,440
1987	44,247	27,924	45,783	59,738	63,167	46,792	24,522
1986	43,699	26,872	45,456	57,547	62,590	46,997	24,301
1985	42,205	26,892	44,826	55,514	59,368	45,669	23,684
1984	41,430	25,928	43,870	55,050	58,251	44,533	23,657
1983	40,182	25,785	41,839	53,254	58,397	43,824	22,545
1982	40,465	27,716	42,692	52,901	56,141	44,285	22,149
1981	40,573	28,168	43,634	53,996	57,527	44,757	21,065
1980	41,258	29,612	45,049	55,043	58,523	45,538	20,457

Percent change

	total	15 to 24	25 to 34	35 to 44	45 to 54	55 to 64	65 or older
2000 to 2006	−2.0%	−5.1%	−5.5%	−4.0%	−3.9%	4.0%	2.9%
1980 to 2006	16.8	4.5	9.1	9.7	10.9	19.9	35.9

Source: Bureau of the Census, Current Population Surveys, Internet site http://www.census.gov/hhes/www/income/histinc/inchhtoc.html; calculations by New Strategist

Americans Aged 45 to 54 Are Most Likely to Be Affluent

The age group accounts for nearly one-third of the richest 5 percent of households.

One way of examining the characteristics of households by income is to divide households into fifths, or quintiles, and examine the characteristics of households within each quintile. This exercise shows how the middle aged dominate the nation's affluent. Householders aged 45 to 54 account for the largest share of the most affluent households. Together with householders aged 35 to 44 and 55 to 64, the three age groups account for 81 percent of the richest 5 percent of households (with incomes of $174,000 or higher). Among householders aged 45 to 54, nearly 30 percent are in the top 20 percent of households, as are 26 percent of householders aged 35 to 44 and 25 percent of those aged 55 to 64.

At the other end of the income spectrum, householders aged 65 or older account for 36 percent of the poorest 20 percent of households, with incomes below $20,032. More than one-third of householders in the age group are in the bottom income quintile.

■ As Boomers fill the 55-to-64 age group and postpone retirement, the percentage of affluent households headed by 55-to-64-year-olds will grow.

Few of the affluent are aged 65 or older

(percent of households in the top income quintile, by age, 2006)

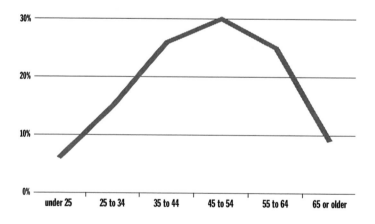

Table 6.9 Households by Age of Householder and Income Quintile, 2006

(number and percent distribution of households by age of householder, income quintile, and top 5 percent, 2006; households in thousands as of 2007)

	total number	total percent	bottom fifth	second fifth	middle fifth	fourth fifth	top fifth	top five percent
Total households	**116,011**	–	**23,202**	**23,202**	**23,202**	**23,202**	**23,202**	**5,803**
Lower income limit	–	100.0%	–	$20,032	$37,771	$60,000	$97,030	$174,000
Number of households								
Aged 15 to 24	6,662	5.7	2,242	1,774	1,453	795	399	75
Aged 25 to 34	19,435	16.8	3,139	4,146	4,624	4,557	2,970	517
Aged 35 to 44	22,779	19.6	2,938	3,720	4,772	5,507	5,841	1,467
Aged 45 to 54	24,140	20.8	3,184	3,408	4,545	5,835	7,169	1,883
Aged 55 to 64	19,266	16.6	3,378	3,257	3,875	3,988	4,768	1,357
Aged 65 or older	23,729	20.5	8,315	6,898	3,934	2,522	2,060	504
Aged 65 to 74	11,926	10.3	3,222	3,361	2,306	1,600	1,436	366
Aged 75 or older	11,803	10.2	5,093	3,537	1,627	922	624	138
Distribution by income quintile and top 5 percent								
Total households	**116,011**	**100.0%**	**20.0%**	**20.0%**	**20.0%**	**20.0%**	**20.0%**	**5.0%**
Aged 15 to 24	6,662	100.0	33.7	26.6	21.8	11.9	6.0	1.1
Aged 25 to 34	19,435	100.0	16.2	21.3	23.8	23.4	15.3	2.7
Aged 35 to 44	22,779	100.0	12.9	16.3	20.9	24.2	25.6	6.4
Aged 45 to 54	24,140	100.0	13.2	14.1	18.8	24.2	29.7	7.8
Aged 55 to 64	19,266	100.0	17.5	16.9	20.1	20.7	24.7	7.0
Aged 65 or older	23,729	100.0	35.0	29.1	16.6	10.6	8.7	2.1
Aged 65 to 74	11,926	100.0	27.0	28.2	19.3	13.4	12.0	3.1
Aged 75 or older	11,803	100.0	43.2	30.0	13.8	7.8	5.3	1.2
Distribution by age of householder								
Total households	**116,011**	**100.0%**	**100.0%**	**100.0%**	**100.0%**	**100.0%**	**100.0%**	**100.0%**
Aged 15 to 24	6,662	5.7	9.7	7.6	6.3	3.4	1.7	1.3
Aged 25 to 34	19,435	16.8	13.5	17.9	19.9	19.6	12.8	8.9
Aged 35 to 44	22,779	19.6	12.7	16.0	20.6	23.7	25.2	25.3
Aged 45 to 54	24,140	20.8	13.7	14.7	19.6	25.1	30.9	32.4
Aged 55 to 64	19,266	16.6	14.6	14.0	16.7	17.2	20.5	23.4
Aged 65 or older	23,729	20.5	35.8	29.7	17.0	10.9	8.9	8.7
Aged 65 to 74	11,926	10.3	13.9	14.5	9.9	6.9	6.2	6.3
Aged 75 or older	11,803	10.2	22.0	15.2	7.0	4.0	2.7	2.4

Note: "–" means not applicable.
Source: Bureau of the Census, 2007 Current Population Survey, Internet site http://pubdb3.census.gov/macro/032007/hhinc/toc .htm

The World War II Generation Has the Lowest Incomes

Boomers have the highest incomes.

The median income of World War II generation householders (aged 75 or older) was a modest $22,815 in 2006, well below the median income of the other generations because most are retired and many live alone. The median income of householders in the Baby-Boom generation was nearly three times as high, at $61,980—29 percent higher than the $48,201 median for all households. The incomes of Boomers are higher than those of the other generations because most of their households have at least two earners, and they are in their peak earning years.

Millennial householders had a median income of $37,674 in 2006, well below the median of $58,211 for Generation Xers. Millennial incomes are below average because many are still in school and not yet married. The median income of the Swing generation is also below average, at $38,478, because most are retired.

■ Boomer incomes are likely to remain high for several more years as two-income couples postpone retirement.

Boomer incomes are well above those of the other generations

(median income of households by generation of householder, 2006)

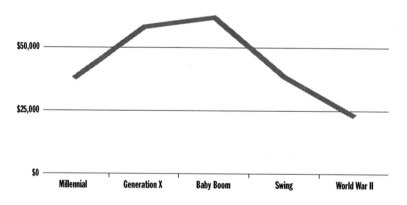

Table 6.10 Household Income by Age of Householder, 2006

(number and percent distribution of households by household income and age of householder, 2006; households in thousands as of 2007)

	total	15 to 24	25 to 34	35 to 44	45 to 54	55 to 64	aged 65 or older total	65 to 74	75 or older
Total households	116,011	6,662	19,435	22,779	24,140	19,266	23,729	11,926	11,803
Under $10,000	8,689	1,054	1,207	1,125	1,389	1,456	2,458	1,050	1,407
$10,000 to $19,999	13,726	1,094	1,717	1,641	1,633	1,812	5,827	2,157	3,671
$20,000 to $29,999	13,521	1,073	2,311	2,024	1,851	1,785	4,475	2,024	2,451
$30,000 to $39,999	12,698	937	2,414	2,241	2,104	1,968	3,034	1,678	1,355
$40,000 to $49,999	10,951	757	2,207	2,206	2,081	1,729	1,972	1,158	814
$50,000 to $59,999	9,530	518	1,914	2,049	1,983	1,703	1,362	803	559
$60,000 to $69,999	7,889	359	1,680	1,725	1,854	1,330	943	615	329
$70,000 to $79,999	6,904	248	1,297	1,685	1,697	1,167	811	516	295
$80,000 to $89,999	5,441	125	1,047	1,378	1,422	969	503	294	209
$90,000 to $99,999	4,510	111	827	1,115	1,276	787	395	261	135
$100,000 or more	22,151	385	2,814	5,588	6,852	4,565	1,948	1,369	579
Median income	$48,201	$30,937	$49,164	$60,405	$64,874	$54,592	$27,798	$33,953	$22,815

Percent distribution by income

	total	15 to 24	25 to 34	35 to 44	45 to 54	55 to 64	aged 65 or older total	65 to 74	75 or older
Total households	100.0%	100.0%	100.0%	100.0%	100.0%	100.0%	100.0%	100.0%	100.0%
Under $10,000	7.5	15.8	6.2	4.9	5.8	7.6	10.4	8.8	11.9
$10,000 to $19,999	11.8	16.4	8.8	7.2	6.8	9.4	24.6	18.1	31.1
$20,000 to $29,999	11.7	16.1	11.9	8.9	7.7	9.3	18.9	17.0	20.8
$30,000 to $39,999	10.9	14.1	12.4	9.8	8.7	10.2	12.8	14.1	11.5
$40,000 to $49,999	9.4	11.4	11.4	9.7	8.6	9.0	8.3	9.7	6.9
$50,000 to $59,999	8.2	7.8	9.8	9.0	8.2	8.8	5.7	6.7	4.7
$60,000 to $69,999	6.8	5.4	8.6	7.6	7.7	6.9	4.0	5.2	2.8
$70,000 to $79,999	6.0	3.7	6.7	7.4	7.0	6.1	3.4	4.3	2.5
$80,000 to $89,999	4.7	1.9	5.4	6.0	5.9	5.0	2.1	2.5	1.8
$90,000 to $99,999	3.9	1.7	4.3	4.9	5.3	4.1	1.7	2.2	1.1
$100,000 or more	19.1	5.8	14.5	24.5	28.4	23.7	8.2	11.5	4.9

Source: Bureau of the Census, 2007 Current Population Survey, Internet site http://pubdb3.census.gov/macro/032007/hhinc/toc .htm; calculations by New Strategist

Table 6.11 Household Income by Generation of Householder, 2006

(number and percent distribution of households by household income and generation of householder, 2006; households in thousands as of 2007)

	total	Millennial (15 to 30)	Generation X (31 to 42)	Baby Boom (43 to 61)	Swing (62 to 74)	World War II (75 or older)
Total households	**116,011**	**18,282**	**25,817**	**43,083**	**17,025**	**11,803**
Under $10,000	8,689	1,856	1,298	2,638	1,490	1,407
$10,000 to $19,999	13,726	2,195	1,936	3,192	2,731	3,671
$20,000 to $29,999	13,521	2,581	2,395	3,537	2,557	2,451
$30,000 to $39,999	12,698	2,454	2,682	3,960	2,246	1,355
$40,000 to $49,999	10,951	2,097	2,609	3,804	1,627	814
$50,000 to $59,999	9,530	1,683	2,357	3,672	1,261	559
$60,000 to $69,999	7,889	1,408	1,997	3,192	965	329
$70,000 to $79,999	6,904	956	1,927	2,942	785	295
$80,000 to $89,999	5,441	715	1,552	2,432	532	209
$90,000 to $99,999	4,510	538	1,277	2,134	428	135
$100,000 or more	22,151	1,801	5,790	11,578	2,403	579
Median income	$48,201	$37,674	$58,211	$61,980	$38,478	$22,815

Percent distribution by income

	total	Millennial (15 to 30)	Generation X (31 to 42)	Baby Boom (43 to 61)	Swing (62 to 74)	World War II (75 or older)
Total households	**100.0%**	**100.0%**	**100.0%**	**100.0%**	**100.0%**	**100.0%**
Under $10,000	7.5	10.2	5.0	6.1	8.8	11.9
$10,000 to $19,999	11.8	12.0	7.5	7.4	16.0	31.1
$20,000 to $29,999	11.7	14.1	9.3	8.2	15.0	20.8
$30,000 to $39,999	10.9	13.4	10.4	9.2	13.2	11.5
$40,000 to $49,999	9.4	11.5	10.1	8.8	9.6	6.9
$50,000 to $59,999	8.2	9.2	9.1	8.5	7.4	4.7
$60,000 to $69,999	6.8	7.7	7.7	7.4	5.7	2.8
$70,000 to $79,999	6.0	5.2	7.5	6.8	4.6	2.5
$80,000 to $89,999	4.7	3.9	6.0	5.6	3.1	1.8
$90,000 to $99,999	3.9	2.9	4.9	5.0	2.5	1.1
$100,000 or more	19.1	9.9	22.4	26.9	14.1	4.9

Note: Number of households and median income by generation are estimates by New Strategist.
Source: Bureau of the Census, 2007 Current Population Survey, Internet site http://pubdb3.census.gov/macro/032007/hhinc/toc .htm

Two Earners Means Higher Incomes

Middle-aged married couples have the highest incomes.

The key to economic security is two incomes. Married couples have far higher incomes than any other household type because most couples are dual earners.

In 2006, married couples had a median income of $69,716, 45 percent above the all-household median. Married couples with a householder aged 50 to 54 had the highest median income of all, at $89,186 in 2006.

In nearly every age group, the median income of married couples exceeds that of other household types. The only exceptions are among the youngest and oldest house-holders where the incomes of married couples are second to those of families headed by men. Behind this pattern is the greater number of earners in younger and older households headed by men.

Women living alone have the lowest incomes, with the median bottoming out at $15,235 among women aged 75 or older who live alone. Women aged 15 to 24 who live alone had a median income of only $16,203.

■ Because the early retirement trend has come to an end, the incomes of older couples will rise in the years ahead.

Among married couples, the oldest have the lowest incomes

(median income of married couples, by age of householder, 2006)

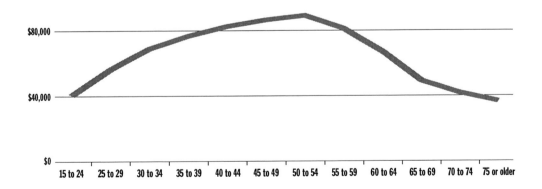

(median income of households by age of householder and type of household, and index of median to average, 2006)

| | | family households | | | | nonfamily households | | | | |
| | | | | | | | female householder | | male householder | |
	total	total	married couples	female hh, no spouse present	male hh, no spouse present	total	total	living alone	total	living alone
Total households	**$48,201**	**$59,894**	**$69,716**	**$31,818**	**$47,078**	**$29,083**	**$23,876**	**$21,346**	**$35,614**	**$31,268**
Aged 15 to 24	30,937	34,772	40,433	21,909	40,849	26,997	24,503	16,203	30,319	20,350
Aged 25 to 29	44,846	47,104	56,310	23,788	48,289	40,353	36,326	30,600	42,034	34,078
Aged 30 to 34	53,329	57,076	68,967	25,394	45,564	45,278	42,488	37,149	45,846	40,934
Aged 35 to 39	60,101	64,932	76,755	29,816	45,681	42,668	40,760	36,170	45,472	40,376
Aged 40 to 44	60,728	68,535	82,557	33,625	46,077	40,452	39,700	36,091	40,781	36,882
Aged 45 to 49	63,635	75,081	86,516	39,115	55,129	37,331	34,640	31,138	40,490	36,498
Aged 50 to 54	65,985	79,046	89,186	41,760	56,573	36,374	32,401	30,750	40,328	37,029
Aged 55 to 59	60,037	74,320	81,162	43,507	53,105	33,963	33,300	31,362	35,009	31,542
Aged 60 to 64	49,091	62,696	66,831	37,068	49,847	28,551	25,781	23,737	33,679	32,169
Aged 65 to 69	37,495	47,566	49,113	38,850	35,782	23,419	22,244	21,470	26,460	24,836
Aged 70 to 74	29,986	40,200	41,798	31,763	33,174	18,505	17,059	16,711	24,147	22,906
Aged 75 or older	22,815	34,900	34,642	32,883	44,333	16,439	15,401	15,235	21,444	20,629
Index of median income to average by age										
Total households	**100**	**124**	**145**	**66**	**98**	**60**	**50**	**44**	**74**	**65**
Aged 15 to 24	64	72	84	45	85	56	51	34	63	42
Aged 25 to 29	93	98	117	49	100	84	75	63	87	71
Aged 30 to 34	111	118	143	53	95	94	88	77	95	85
Aged 35 to 39	125	135	159	62	95	89	85	75	94	84
Aged 40 to 44	126	142	171	70	96	84	82	75	85	77
Aged 45 to 49	132	156	179	81	114	77	72	65	84	76
Aged 50 to 54	137	164	185	87	117	75	67	64	84	77
Aged 55 to 59	125	154	168	90	110	70	69	65	73	65
Aged 60 to 64	102	130	139	77	103	59	53	49	70	67
Aged 65 to 69	78	99	102	81	74	49	46	45	55	52
Aged 70 to 74	62	83	87	66	69	38	35	35	50	48
Aged 75 or older	47	72	72	68	92	34	32	32	44	43

Source: Bureau of the Census, 2007 Current Population Survey, Internet site http://pubdb3.census.gov/macro/032007/hhinc/toc .htm; calculations by New Strategist

Table 6.13 Household Income by Household Type, 2006: Householders Aged 15 to 24

(number and percent distribution of households headed by people aged 15 to 24, by household income and household type, 2006; households in thousands as of 2007)

| | | family households | | | | nonfamily households | | | | |
| | | | | | | | female householder | | male householder | |
	total	total	married couples	female hh, no spouse present	male hh, no spouse present	total	total	living alone	total	living alone
Total households	6,662	3,534	1,354	1,329	851	3,128	1,491	799	1,637	798
Under $25,000	2,703	1,268	323	716	230	1,435	755	558	678	487
$25,000 to $49,999	2,212	1,159	566	312	282	1,052	489	217	565	253
$50,000 to $74,999	1,003	641	320	140	183	359	166	22	195	33
$75,000 to $99,999	358	228	92	68	69	130	39	0	92	12
$100,000 or more	385	235	54	93	89	150	43	3	107	14
Median income	$30,937	$34,772	$40,433	$21,909	$40,849	$26,997	$24,503	$16,203	$30,319	$20,350
Percent distribution by income										
Total households	100.0%	100.0%	100.0%	100.0%	100.0%	100.0%	100.0%	100.0%	100.0%	100.0%
Under $25,000	40.6	35.9	23.9	53.9	27.0	45.9	50.6	69.8	41.4	61.0
$25,000 to $49,999	33.2	32.8	41.8	23.5	33.1	33.6	32.8	27.2	34.5	31.7
$50,000 to $74,999	15.1	18.1	23.6	10.5	21.5	11.5	11.1	2.8	11.9	4.1
$75,000 to $99,999	5.4	6.5	6.8	5.1	8.1	4.2	2.6	0.0	5.6	1.5
$100,000 or more	5.8	6.6	4.0	7.0	10.5	4.8	2.9	0.4	6.5	1.8

Source: Bureau of the Census, 2007 Current Population Survey, Internet site http://pubdb3.census.gov/macro/032007/hhinc/toc .htm; calculations by New Strategist

Table 6.14 Household Income by Household Type, 2006: Householders Aged 25 to 34

(number and percent distribution of households headed by people aged 25 to 34, by household income and household type, 2006; households in thousands as of 2007)

| | | family households | | | | nonfamily households | | | | |
| | | | | | | | female householder | | male householder | |
	total	total	married couples	female hh, no spouse present	male hh, no spouse present	total	total	living alone	total	living alone
Total households	19,435	13,668	9,381	3,143	1,144	5,767	2,168	1,580	3,599	2,350
Under $25,000	4,100	2,736	922	1,593	220	1,367	579	518	789	635
$25,000 to $49,999	5,756	3,719	2,402	932	382	2,037	747	634	1,291	1,012
$50,000 to $74,999	4,291	3,089	2,464	364	261	1,201	443	252	756	451
$75,000 to $99,999	2,474	1,945	1,694	142	110	529	165	71	364	134
$100,000 or more	2,814	2,184	1,902	113	169	630	231	105	399	119
Median income	$49,164	$52,016	$62,293	$24,605	$47,043	$42,053	$39,274	$32,463	$44,156	$36,344
Percent distribution by income										
Total households	100.0%	100.0%	100.0%	100.0%	100.0%	100.0%	100.0%	100.0%	100.0%	100.0%
Under $25,000	21.1	20.0	9.8	50.7	19.2	23.7	26.7	32.8	21.9	27.0
$25,000 to $49,999	29.6	27.2	25.6	29.7	33.4	35.3	34.5	40.1	35.9	43.1
$50,000 to $74,999	22.1	22.6	26.3	11.6	22.8	20.8	20.4	15.9	21.0	19.2
$75,000 to $99,999	12.7	14.2	18.1	4.5	9.6	9.2	7.6	4.5	10.1	5.7
$100,000 or more	14.5	16.0	20.3	3.6	14.8	10.9	10.7	6.6	11.1	5.1

Source: Bureau of the Census, 2007 Current Population Survey, Internet site http://pubdb3.census.gov/macro/032007/hhinc/toc .htm; calculations by New Strategist

Table 6.15 Household Income by Household Type, 2006: Householders Aged 35 to 44

(number and percent distribution of households headed by people aged 35 to 44, by household income and household type, 2006; households in thousands as of 2007)

| | | family households | | | | nonfamily households | | | | |
| | | | | | | | female householder | | male householder | |
	total	total	married couples	female hh, no spouse present	male hh, no spouse present	total	total	living alone	total	living alone
Total households	**22,779**	**18,053**	**13,371**	**3,650**	**1,031**	**4,726**	**1,733**	**1,360**	**2,993**	**2,366**
Under $25,000	3,720	2,434	851	1,389	192	1,286	522	448	764	684
$25,000 to $49,999	5,517	4,016	2,328	1,310	373	1,502	523	446	978	832
$50,000 to $74,999	4,700	3,720	2,925	541	253	983	354	261	624	467
$75,000 to $99,999	3,252	2,770	2,476	193	101	482	184	119	299	197
$100,000 or more	5,588	5,114	4,788	216	110	475	147	87	328	186
Median income	$60,405	$66,596	$80,212	$31,558	$45,875	$41,482	$40,282	$36,132	$42,117	$37,775
Percent distribution by income										
Total households	**100.0%**	**100.0%**	**100.0%**	**100.0%**	**100.0%**	**100.0%**	**100.0%**	**100.0%**	**100.0%**	**100.0%**
Under $25,000	16.3	13.5	6.4	38.1	18.6	27.2	30.1	32.9	25.5	28.9
$25,000 to $49,999	24.2	22.2	17.4	35.9	36.2	31.8	30.2	32.8	32.7	35.2
$50,000 to $74,999	20.6	20.6	21.9	14.8	24.5	20.8	20.4	19.2	20.8	19.7
$75,000 to $99,999	14.3	15.3	18.5	5.3	9.8	10.2	10.6	8.8	10.0	8.3
$100,000 or more	24.5	28.3	35.8	5.9	10.7	10.1	8.5	6.4	11.0	7.9

Source: Bureau of the Census, 2007 Current Population Survey, Internet site http://pubdb3.census.gov/macro/032007/hhinc/toc .htm; calculations by New Strategist

---

Table 6.16 Household Income by Household Type, 2006: Householders Aged 45 to 54

(number and percent distribution of households headed by people aged 45 to 54, by household income and household type, 2006; households in thousands as of 2007)

| | | family households | | | | nonfamily households | | | | |
| | | | | | | | female householder | | male householder | |
	total	total	married couples	female hh, no spouse present	male hh, no spouse present	total	total	living alone	total	living alone
Total households	**24,140**	**17,809**	**13,814**	**2,929**	**1,066**	**6,331**	**3,057**	**2,646**	**3,274**	**2,749**
Under $25,000	3,941	1,776	767	847	166	2,163	1,156	1,081	1,007	919
$25,000 to $49,999	5,117	3,222	2,013	907	299	1,899	927	820	970	867
$50,000 to $74,999	4,776	3,661	2,804	624	231	1,115	500	415	613	499
$75,000 to $99,999	3,456	2,945	2,478	292	174	509	200	133	309	227
$100,000 or more	6,852	6,204	5,753	256	195	648	271	198	376	235
Median income	$64,874	$76,697	$87,556	$40,264	$55,870	$36,832	$33,459	$30,877	$40,422	$36,763
Percent distribution by income										
Total households	**100.0%**	**100.0%**	**100.0%**	**100.0%**	**100.0%**	**100.0%**	**100.0%**	**100.0%**	**100.0%**	**100.0%**
Under $25,000	16.3	10.0	5.6	28.9	15.6	34.2	37.8	40.9	30.8	33.4
$25,000 to $49,999	21.2	18.1	14.6	31.0	28.0	30.0	30.3	31.0	29.6	31.5
$50,000 to $74,999	19.8	20.6	20.3	21.3	21.7	17.6	16.4	15.7	18.7	18.2
$75,000 to $99,999	14.3	16.5	17.9	10.0	16.3	8.0	6.5	5.0	9.4	8.3
$100,000 or more	28.4	34.8	41.6	8.7	18.3	10.2	8.9	7.5	11.5	8.5

Source: Bureau of the Census, 2007 Current Population Survey, Internet site http://pubdb3.census.gov/macro/032007/hhinc/toc .htm; calculations by New Strategist

Table 6.17 Household Income by Household Type, 2006: Householders Aged 55 to 64

(number and percent distribution of households headed by people aged 55 to 64, by household income and household type, 2006; households in thousands as of 2007)

| | | family households | | | | nonfamily households | | | | |
| | | | | | | | female householder | | male householder | |
	total	total	married couples	female hh, no spouse present	male hh, no spouse present	total	total	living alone	total	living alone
Total households	**19,266**	**12,976**	**10,910**	**1,530**	**535**	**6,291**	**3,636**	**3,287**	**2,654**	**2,331**
Under $25,000	4,196	1,623	1,091	425	108	2,575	1,562	1,507	1,009	955
$25,000 to $49,999	4,554	2,732	2,117	474	140	1,821	1,065	984	757	693
$50,000 to $74,999	3,652	2,694	2,278	307	110	956	538	453	416	352
$75,000 to $99,999	2,304	1,905	1,653	169	83	398	215	181	184	137
$100,000 or more	4,565	4,023	3,772	157	94	541	256	164	286	195
Median income	$54,592	$69,204	$74,582	$40,146	$52,244	$31,380	$29,702	$27,158	$34,318	$31,751
Percent distribution by income										
Total households	**100.0%**	**100.0%**	**100.0%**	**100.0%**	**100.0%**	**100.0%**	**100.0%**	**100.0%**	**100.0%**	**100.0%**
Under $25,000	21.8	12.5	10.0	27.8	20.2	40.9	43.0	45.8	38.0	41.0
$25,000 to $49,999	23.6	21.1	19.4	31.0	26.2	28.9	29.3	29.9	28.5	29.7
$50,000 to $74,999	19.0	20.8	20.9	20.1	20.6	15.2	14.8	13.8	15.7	15.1
$75,000 to $99,999	12.0	14.7	15.2	11.0	15.5	6.3	5.9	5.5	6.9	5.9
$100,000 or more	23.7	31.0	34.6	10.3	17.6	8.6	7.0	5.0	10.8	8.4

Source: Bureau of the Census, 2007 Current Population Survey, Internet site http://pubdb3.census.gov/macro/032007/hhinc/toc .htm; calculations by New Strategist

Table 6.18 Household Income by Household Type, 2006: Householders Aged 65 or Older

(number and percent distribution of households headed by people aged 65 or older, by household income and household type, 2006; households in thousands as of 2007)

| | | family households | | | | nonfamily households | | | | |
| | | | | | | | female householder | | male householder | |
	total	total	married couples	female hh, no spouse present	male hh, no spouse present	total	total	living alone	total	living alone
Total households	**23,729**	**12,385**	**10,115**	**1,834**	**436**	**11,344**	**8,164**	**7,932**	**3,180**	**2,934**
Under $25,000	10,642	3,034	2,248	663	124	7,609	5,887	5,831	1,719	1,662
$25,000 to $49,999	7,124	4,652	3,935	567	148	2,473	1,590	1,499	881	801
$50,000 to $74,999	2,730	2,051	1,663	311	79	680	393	358	289	246
$75,000 to $99,999	1,284	1,057	872	135	50	226	118	103	109	93
$100,000 or more	1,948	1,590	1,397	159	35	358	176	144	182	131
Median income	$27,798	$39,797	$40,813	$34,908	$39,101	$17,721	$16,424	$16,146	$22,831	$21,714
Percent distribution by income										
Total households	**100.0%**	**100.0%**	**100.0%**	**100.0%**	**100.0%**	**100.0%**	**100.0%**	**100.0%**	**100.0%**	**100.0%**
Under $25,000	44.8	24.5	22.2	36.2	28.4	67.1	72.1	73.5	54.1	56.6
$25,000 to $49,999	30.0	37.6	38.9	30.9	33.9	21.8	19.5	18.9	27.7	27.3
$50,000 to $74,999	11.5	16.6	16.4	17.0	18.1	6.0	4.8	4.5	9.1	8.4
$75,000 to $99,999	5.4	8.5	8.6	7.4	11.5	2.0	1.4	1.3	3.4	3.2
$100,000 or more	8.2	12.8	13.8	8.7	8.0	3.2	2.2	1.8	5.7	4.5

Source: Bureau of the Census, 2007 Current Population Survey, Internet site http://pubdb3.census.gov/macro/032007/hhinc/toc .htm; calculations by New Strategist

Table 6.19 Household Income by Household Type, 2006: Householders Aged 65 to 74

(number and percent distribution of households headed by people aged 65 to 74, by household income and household type, 2006; households in thousands as of 2007)

	total	family households				nonfamily households				
		total	married couples	female hh, no spouse present	male hh, no spouse present	total	female householder		male householder	
							total	living alone	total	living alone
Total households	**11,926**	**7,283**	**6,155**	**912**	**216**	**4,643**	**3,042**	**2,894**	**1,601**	**1,459**
Under $25,000	4,207	1,492	1,114	312	69	2,712	1,925	1,887	787	754
$25,000 to $49,999	3,860	2,634	2,260	294	79	1,228	765	702	465	422
$50,000 to $74,999	1,694	1,324	1,117	166	39	371	198	182	174	153
$75,000 to $99,999	795	670	603	52	17	126	58	52	66	55
$100,000 or more	1,369	1,162	1,060	88	13	207	95	72	112	75
Median income	$33,953	$44,372	$45,957	$35,990	$35,254	$20,719	$19,100	$18,468	$25,373	$23,861

Percent distribution by income

	total	family households				nonfamily households				
Total households	**100.0%**	**100.0%**	**100.0%**	**100.0%**	**100.0%**	**100.0%**	**100.0%**	**100.0%**	**100.0%**	**100.0%**
Under $25,000	35.3	20.5	18.1	34.2	31.9	58.4	63.3	65.2	49.2	51.7
$25,000 to $49,999	32.4	36.2	36.7	32.2	36.6	26.4	25.1	24.3	29.0	28.9
$50,000 to $74,999	14.2	18.2	18.1	18.2	18.1	8.0	6.5	6.3	10.9	10.5
$75,000 to $99,999	6.7	9.2	9.8	5.7	7.9	2.7	1.9	1.8	4.1	3.8
$100,000 or more	11.5	16.0	17.2	9.6	6.0	4.5	3.1	2.5	7.0	5.1

Source: Bureau of the Census, 2007 Current Population Survey, Internet site http://pubdb3.census.gov/macro/032007/hhinc/toc .htm; calculations by New Strategist

Table 6.20 Household Income by Household Type, 2006: Householders Aged 75 or Older

(number and percent distribution of households headed by people aged 75 or older, by household income and household type, 2006; households in thousands as of 2007)

	total	family households				nonfamily households				
		total	married couples	female hh, no spouse present	male hh, no spouse present	total	female householder		male householder	
							total	living alone	total	living alone
Total households	**11,803**	**5,102**	**3,960**	**922**	**220**	**6,701**	**5,121**	**5,038**	**1,580**	**1,475**
Under $25,000	6,435	1,540	1,134	351	55	4,896	3,963	3,946	934	909
$25,000 to $49,999	3,263	2,018	1,676	272	70	1,246	827	795	416	378
$50,000 to $74,999	1,037	727	547	144	39	309	192	175	115	94
$75,000 to $99,999	490	386	271	86	34	100	57	49	44	40
$100,000 or more	579	429	336	71	22	150	80	72	70	56
Median income	$22,815	$34,900	$34,642	$32,883	$44,333	$16,439	$15,401	$15,235	$21,444	$20,629

Percent distribution by income

	total	family households				nonfamily households				
Total households	**100.0%**	**100.0%**	**100.0%**	**100.0%**	**100.0%**	**100.0%**	**100.0%**	**100.0%**	**100.0%**	**100.0%**
Under $25,000	54.5	30.2	28.6	38.1	25.0	73.1	77.4	78.3	59.1	61.6
$25,000 to $49,999	27.6	39.6	42.3	29.5	31.8	18.6	16.1	15.8	26.3	25.6
$50,000 to $74,999	8.8	14.2	13.8	15.6	17.7	4.6	3.7	3.5	7.3	6.4
$75,000 to $99,999	4.2	7.6	6.8	9.3	15.5	1.5	1.1	1.0	2.8	2.7
$100,000 or more	4.9	8.4	8.5	7.7	10.0	2.2	1.6	1.4	4.4	3.8

Source: Bureau of the Census, 2007 Current Population Survey, Internet site http://pubdb3.census.gov/macro/032007/hhinc/toc .htm; calculations by New Strategist

Regardless of Race or Hispanic Origin, Incomes Peak in Middle Age

But the income peaks of black and Hispanic households are much lower than those of Asians and non-Hispanic whites.

Asians have the highest household incomes, a median of $63,900 in 2006. This figure is substantially higher than the $52,423 median of non-Hispanic whites and well above the $37,381 median of Hispanics and the $32,132 median of blacks.

Despite these differences, household income in every racial and ethnic group rises through adulthood, peaks in middle age, and then declines. This income trajectory follows a predictable life pattern: more years in the labor force translate into higher incomes. Once people reach their sixties, most retire. Health also begins to decline, forcing some people to leave the workforce because of disability. With fewer household members working, household income falls.

Among Asians, median household income peaks in the 45-to-49 age group, at $90,092, or 87 percent above the national median. Black and Hispanic median household incomes also peak in the 45-to-49 age group, but at much lower levels. For Hispanics, the income peak is $46,906, and for blacks an even lower $43,441. For non-Hispanic whites, householders aged 50 to 54 have the highest median income, at $73,079.

■ Black incomes are low because relatively few black households are headed by married couples. Hispanic incomes are low because many are recent immigrants with little education.

Asian households have the highest incomes

(median household income by race and Hispanic origin, 2006)

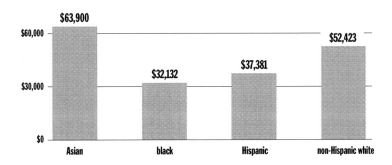

Table 6.21 Median Household Income by Age, Race, and Hispanic Origin of Householder, 2006

(median income of households by age, race, and Hispanic origin of householder, and index of median to average by age, 2006)

	total	Asian	black	Hispanic	non-Hispanic white
Total households	**$48,201**	**$63,900**	**$32,132**	**$37,381**	**$52,423**
Aged 15 to 24	30,937	40,322	21,140	30,213	33,272
Aged 25 to 29	44,846	51,602	28,586	37,896	50,827
Aged 30 to 34	53,329	70,044	35,694	41,307	61,172
Aged 35 to 39	60,101	75,357	39,979	41,075	68,119
Aged 40 to 44	60,728	72,355	41,385	44,661	70,076
Aged 45 to 49	63,635	90,092	43,441	46,906	70,881
Aged 50 to 54	65,985	79,719	38,423	45,745	73,079
Aged 55 to 59	60,037	78,786	38,353	36,061	66,195
Aged 60 to 64	49,091	63,974	27,688	35,154	52,497
Aged 65 to 69	37,495	44,517	27,352	24,412	39,409
Aged 70 to 74	29,986	27,519	19,800	21,524	31,801
Aged 75 or older	22,815	24,648	16,388	16,754	23,678

Index of median income by race and Hispanic origin to average by age

Total households	**100**	**133**	**67**	**78**	**109**
Aged 15 to 24	64	84	44	63	69
Aged 25 to 29	93	107	59	79	105
Aged 30 to 34	111	145	74	86	127
Aged 35 to 39	125	156	83	85	141
Aged 40 to 44	126	150	86	93	145
Aged 45 to 49	132	187	90	97	147
Aged 50 to 54	137	165	80	95	152
Aged 55 to 59	125	163	80	75	137
Aged 60 to 64	102	133	57	73	109
Aged 65 to 69	78	92	57	51	82
Aged 70 to 74	62	57	41	45	66
Aged 75 or older	47	51	34	35	49

Note: Data for Asians and blacks are for those who identify themselves as being of the race alone or in combination with other races. Data for non-Hispanic whites are for those who identify themselves as being white alone and not Hispanic. Hispanics may be of any race.
Source: Bureau of the Census, 2007 Current Population Survey, Internet site http://pubdb3.census.gov/macro/032007/hhinc/toc .htm; calculations by New Strategist

Table 6.22 Household Income by Age of Householder, 2006: Asians

(number and percent distribution of Asian households by household income and age of householder, 2006; households in thousands as of 2007)

	total	15 to 24	25 to 34	35 to 44	45 to 54	55 to 64	aged 65 or older total	65 to 74	75 or older
Asian households	**4,664**	**250**	**1,077**	**1,173**	**925**	**669**	**571**	**309**	**262**
Under $10,000	300	50	62	42	35	42	70	21	49
$10,000 to $19,999	353	16	71	55	48	34	130	64	64
$20,000 to $29,999	409	37	94	83	60	55	82	45	37
$30,000 to $39,999	358	20	99	88	52	48	52	27	25
$40,000 to $49,999	415	26	100	95	87	56	51	34	18
$50,000 to $59,999	324	21	92	95	40	45	30	20	10
$60,000 to $69,999	329	14	101	100	57	32	25	16	9
$70,000 to $79,999	294	13	61	79	68	42	29	12	18
$80,000 to $89,999	246	15	78	58	34	47	18	8	8
$90,000 to $99,999	210	14	43	48	61	35	10	3	6
$100,000 or more	1,427	24	276	432	385	233	77	58	19
Median income	$63,900	$40,322	$61,246	$74,561	$83,142	$75,118	$31,070	$39,310	$24,648

Percent distribution by income

Asian households	100.0%	100.0%	100.0%	100.0%	100.0%	100.0%	100.0%	100.0%	100.0%
Under $10,000	6.4	20.0	5.8	3.6	3.8	6.3	12.3	6.8	18.7
$10,000 to $19,999	7.6	6.4	6.6	4.7	5.2	5.1	22.8	20.7	24.4
$20,000 to $29,999	8.8	14.8	8.7	7.1	6.5	8.2	14.4	14.6	14.1
$30,000 to $39,999	7.7	8.0	9.2	7.5	5.6	7.2	9.1	8.7	9.5
$40,000 to $49,999	8.9	10.4	9.3	8.1	9.4	8.4	8.9	11.0	6.9
$50,000 to $59,999	6.9	8.4	8.5	8.1	4.3	6.7	5.3	6.5	3.8
$60,000 to $69,999	7.1	5.6	9.4	8.5	6.2	4.8	4.4	5.2	3.4
$70,000 to $79,999	6.3	5.2	5.7	6.7	7.4	6.3	5.1	3.9	6.9
$80,000 to $89,999	5.3	6.0	7.2	4.9	3.7	7.0	3.2	2.6	3.1
$90,000 to $99,999	4.5	5.6	4.0	4.1	6.6	5.2	1.8	1.0	2.3
$100,000 or more	30.6	9.6	25.6	36.8	41.6	34.8	13.5	18.8	7.3

Note: Asians are those who identify themselves as being of the race alone or in combination with other races.
Source: Bureau of the Census, 2007 Current Population Survey, Internet site http://pubdb3.census.gov/macro/032007/hhinc/toc.htm; calculations by New Strategist

Table 6.23 Household Income by Age of Householder, 2006: Blacks

(number and percent distribution of black households by household income and age of householder, 2006; households in thousands as of 2007)

	total	15 to 24	25 to 34	35 to 44	45 to 54	55 to 64	aged 65 or older total	65 to 74	75 or older
Black households	**14,709**	**1,145**	**2,927**	**3,150**	**3,163**	**2,113**	**2,210**	**1,299**	**911**
Under $10,000	2,306	299	432	352	385	331	511	260	249
$10,000 to $19,999	2,401	251	451	388	369	340	601	317	284
$20,000 to $29,999	2,041	157	499	365	403	262	356	201	153
$30,000 to $39,999	1,862	162	406	433	371	275	216	144	72
$40,000 to $49,999	1,343	87	268	364	325	169	132	96	36
$50,000 to $59,999	1,112	74	210	267	259	172	127	89	38
$60,000 to $69,999	813	34	197	190	208	109	74	55	20
$70,000 to $79,999	614	28	113	176	158	80	56	36	20
$80,000 to $89,999	507	15	78	150	149	83	31	24	7
$90,000 to $99,999	337	0	73	84	107	55	20	8	11
$100,000 or more	1,371	38	199	382	429	236	86	67	20
Median income	$32,132	$21,140	$31,253	$40,658	$41,184	$33,764	$19,856	$23,500	$16,388

Percent distribution by income

	total	15 to 24	25 to 34	35 to 44	45 to 54	55 to 64	aged 65 or older total	65 to 74	75 or older
Black households	**100.0%**	**100.0%**	**100.0%**	**100.0%**	**100.0%**	**100.0%**	**100.0%**	**100.0%**	**100.0%**
Under $10,000	15.7	26.1	14.8	11.2	12.2	15.7	23.1	20.0	27.3
$10,000 to $19,999	16.3	21.9	15.4	12.3	11.7	16.1	27.2	24.4	31.2
$20,000 to $29,999	13.9	13.7	17.0	11.6	12.7	12.4	16.1	15.5	16.8
$30,000 to $39,999	12.7	14.1	13.9	13.7	11.7	13.0	9.8	11.1	7.9
$40,000 to $49,999	9.1	7.6	9.2	11.6	10.3	8.0	6.0	7.4	4.0
$50,000 to $59,999	7.6	6.5	7.2	8.5	8.2	8.1	5.7	6.9	4.2
$60,000 to $69,999	5.5	3.0	6.7	6.0	6.6	5.2	3.3	4.2	2.2
$70,000 to $79,999	4.2	2.4	3.9	5.6	5.0	3.8	2.5	2.8	2.2
$80,000 to $89,999	3.4	1.3	2.7	4.8	4.7	3.9	1.4	1.8	0.8
$90,000 to $99,999	2.3	0.0	2.5	2.7	3.4	2.6	0.9	0.6	1.2
$100,000 or more	9.3	3.3	6.8	12.1	13.6	11.2	3.9	5.2	2.2

Note: Blacks are those who identify themselves as being of the race alone or in combination with other races.
Source: Bureau of the Census, 2007 Current Population Survey, Internet site http://pubdb3.census.gov/macro/032007/hhinc/toc .htm; calculations by New Strategist

Table 6.24 Household Income by Age of Householder, 2006: Hispanics

(number and percent distribution of Hispanic households by household income and age of householder, 2006; households in thousands as of 2007)

	total	15 to 24	25 to 34	35 to 44	45 to 54	55 to 64	aged 65 or older total	65 to 74	75 or older
Hispanic households	**12,973**	**1,143**	**3,483**	**3,235**	**2,347**	**1,454**	**1,311**	**785**	**526**
Under $10,000	1,195	145	205	190	184	186	287	152	135
$10,000 to $19,999	1,896	211	463	387	235	230	373	200	172
$20,000 to $29,999	1,884	212	553	441	282	193	202	127	75
$30,000 to $39,999	1,758	158	515	475	296	186	128	78	49
$40,000 to $49,999	1,478	121	479	386	252	155	83	59	23
$50,000 to $59,999	1,059	96	303	287	212	105	56	38	20
$60,000 to $69,999	822	61	212	224	190	96	40	27	12
$70,000 to $79,999	676	45	184	174	171	73	32	21	11
$80,000 to $89,999	452	27	144	136	83	41	22	20	1
$90,000 to $99,999	388	22	94	126	89	33	23	13	9
$100,000 or more	1,364	46	331	412	353	155	67	49	18
Median income	$37,781	$30,213	$40,095	$42,515	$46,458	$35,561	$19,925	$22,993	$16,754

Percent distribution by income

	total	15 to 24	25 to 34	35 to 44	45 to 54	55 to 64	aged 65 or older total	65 to 74	75 or older
Hispanic households	100.0%	100.0%	100.0%	100.0%	100.0%	100.0%	100.0%	100.0%	100.0%
Under $10,000	9.2	12.7	5.9	5.9	7.8	12.8	21.9	19.4	25.7
$10,000 to $19,999	14.6	18.5	13.3	12.0	10.0	15.8	28.5	25.5	32.7
$20,000 to $29,999	14.5	18.5	15.9	13.6	12.0	13.3	15.4	16.2	14.3
$30,000 to $39,999	13.6	13.8	14.8	14.7	12.6	12.8	9.8	9.9	9.3
$40,000 to $49,999	11.4	10.6	13.8	11.9	10.7	10.7	6.3	7.5	4.4
$50,000 to $59,999	8.2	8.4	8.7	8.9	9.0	7.2	4.3	4.8	3.8
$60,000 to $69,999	6.3	5.3	6.1	6.9	8.1	6.6	3.1	3.4	2.3
$70,000 to $79,999	5.2	3.9	5.3	5.4	7.3	5.0	2.4	2.7	2.1
$80,000 to $89,999	3.5	2.4	4.1	4.2	3.5	2.8	1.7	2.5	0.2
$90,000 to $99,999	3.0	1.9	2.7	3.9	3.8	2.3	1.8	1.7	1.7
$100,000 or more	10.5	4.0	9.5	12.7	15.0	10.7	5.1	6.2	3.4

Source: Bureau of the Census, 2007 Current Population Survey, Internet site http://pubdb3.census.gov/macro/032007/hhinc/toc .htm; calculations by New Strategist

Table 6.25 Household Income by Age of Householder, 2006: Non-Hispanic Whites

(number and percent distribution of non-Hispanic white households by household income and age of householder, 2006; households in thousands as of 2007)

	total	15 to 24	25 to 34	35 to 44	45 to 54	55 to 64	aged 65 or older total	65 to 74	75 or older
Non-Hispanic white households	**82,675**	**4,059**	**11,906**	**15,003**	**17,450**	**14,841**	**19,416**	**9,408**	**10,008**
Under $10,000	4,818	557	509	534	758	887	1,572	605	967
$10,000 to $19,999	8,951	608	741	797	955	1,176	4,672	1,554	3,119
$20,000 to $29,999	9,041	651	1,169	1,098	1,082	1,252	3,789	1,626	2,163
$30,000 to $39,999	8,613	591	1,388	1,212	1,368	1,438	2,618	1,416	1,201
$40,000 to $49,999	7,607	513	1,354	1,344	1,388	1,329	1,681	955	727
$50,000 to $59,999	6,943	321	1,284	1,386	1,456	1,368	1,129	646	484
$60,000 to $69,999	5,876	249	1,163	1,194	1,383	1,086	799	510	289
$70,000 to $79,999	5,248	159	933	1,235	1,281	961	681	438	243
$80,000 to $89,999	4,200	65	748	1,026	1,144	785	430	239	190
$90,000 to $99,999	3,534	74	618	850	999	654	339	232	108
$100,000 or more	17,844	269	1,999	4,323	5,640	3,907	1,707	1,188	519
Median income	$52,423	$33,272	$55,519	$69,252	$71,893	$59,727	$29,070	$36,047	$23,678

Percent distribution by income

	total	15 to 24	25 to 34	35 to 44	45 to 54	55 to 64	aged 65 or older total	65 to 74	75 or older
Non-Hispanic white households	**100.0%**	**100.0%**	**100.0%**	**100.0%**	**100.0%**	**100.0%**	**100.0%**	**100.0%**	**100.0%**
Under $10,000	5.8	13.7	4.3	3.6	4.3	6.0	8.1	6.4	9.7
$10,000 to $19,999	10.8	15.0	6.2	5.3	5.5	7.9	24.1	16.5	31.2
$20,000 to $29,999	10.9	16.0	9.8	7.3	6.2	8.4	19.5	17.3	21.6
$30,000 to $39,999	10.4	14.6	11.7	8.1	7.8	9.7	13.5	15.1	12.0
$40,000 to $49,999	9.2	12.6	11.4	9.0	8.0	9.0	8.7	10.2	7.3
$50,000 to $59,999	8.4	7.9	10.8	9.2	8.3	9.2	5.8	6.9	4.8
$60,000 to $69,999	7.1	6.1	9.8	8.0	7.9	7.3	4.1	5.4	2.9
$70,000 to $79,999	6.3	3.9	7.8	8.2	7.3	6.5	3.5	4.7	2.4
$80,000 to $89,999	5.1	1.6	6.3	6.8	6.6	5.3	2.2	2.5	1.9
$90,000 to $99,999	4.3	1.8	5.2	5.7	5.7	4.4	1.7	2.5	1.1
$100,000 or more	21.6	6.6	16.8	28.8	32.3	26.3	8.8	12.6	5.2

Note: Non-Hispanic whites are those who identify themselves as being white alone and not Hispanic.
Source: Bureau of the Census, 2007 Current Population Survey, Internet site http://pubdb3.census.gov/macro/032007/hhinc/toc .htm; calculations by New Strategist

Nearly One-Third of the Elderly Receive Pension Income

For younger Americans, most income is from wages or salaries.

The proportion of people with wage and salary income is as high as 89 percent in the 25-to-34 age group. It falls slowly with age to 66 percent in the 55-to-64 age group, then drops sharply to 16 percent among people aged 65 or older as labor force participation declines with retirement.

The proportion of Americans who receive property income (interest, dividends, rents, or royalties) rises with age to a peak of 58 percent in the 55-to-64 age group, reflecting the accumulation of assets. Thirty-one percent of people aged 65 or older receive pension income, and 89 percent receive Social Security.

Predictably, those aged 25 to 34 are more likely than older adults to receive education grants or scholarships—5 percent received this type of income in 2006. The youngest age group is also the one most likely to receive public assistance, but the proportion is less than 2 percent.

■ A growing share of the elderly will receive income from wages and salaries in the years ahead as labor force participation climbs in the older age groups.

The percentage of people who receive wage and salary income falls sharply in the oldest age group

(percent of people receiving wage and salary income, by age, 2006)

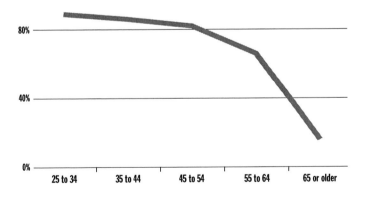

Table 6.26 Sources of Income by Age, 2006

(number and percent of total people aged 25 or older who receive income from specified source and median amount received, and percent receiving income by source and age, 2006; people in thousands as of 2007)

	total number receiving	total percent receiving	total median amount	percent receiving by age 25 to 34	percent receiving by age 35 to 44	percent receiving by age 45 to 54	percent receiving by age 55 to 64	percent receiving by age 65 or older
Total people	**181,131**	**100.0%**	**$29,297**	**100.0%**	**100.0%**	**100.0%**	**100.0%**	**100.0%**
Earnings	134,069	74.0	33,907	92.9	91.0	88.7	72.4	19.4
Wages and salary	124,793	68.9	34,628	89.3	85.6	82.1	65.6	16.1
Nonfarm self-employment	12,369	6.8	17,459	5.8	7.7	8.8	8.4	3.2
Farm self-employment	2,067	1.1	2,147	1.1	1.1	1.4	1.4	0.8
Social Security	40,418	22.3	11,146	1.7	2.8	5.0	18.4	89.4
SSI (Supplemental Security Income)	4,462	2.5	6,092	1.7	1.9	2.6	3.3	2.9
Public assistance	1,457	0.8	2,451	1.7	1.1	0.6	0.4	0.2
Veterans' benefits	2,375	1.3	7,900	0.4	0.5	0.9	2.4	2.8
Survivors' benefits	2,756	1.5	6,976	0.2	0.3	0.6	1.5	5.5
Disability benefits	1,730	1.0	9,054	0.3	0.6	1.3	2.1	0.5
Unemployment compensation	4,875	2.7	2,955	3.4	3.3	3.3	2.8	0.4
Workers' compensation	1,630	0.9	3,771	0.6	0.9	1.2	1.3	0.5
Property income	90,520	50.0	1,740	37.6	47.7	52.7	58.1	55.3
Interest	85,373	47.1	1,551	35.6	44.9	49.5	54.7	52.3
Dividends	31,962	17.6	1,722	9.3	16.5	20.0	23.6	19.8
Rents, royalties, estates, or trusts	10,359	5.7	2,203	2.4	4.6	6.3	8.4	7.5
Retirement income	19,543	10.8	11,065	0.5	1.1	3.3	16.7	36.1
Pension income	16,035	8.9	11,644	0.1	0.5	1.9	13.9	31.2
Alimony	395	0.2	6,616	0.1	0.2	0.3	0.4	0.1
Child support	4,635	2.6	3,707	4.5	5.0	2.3	0.4	0.0
Educational assistance	3,100	1.7	3,335	5.3	1.8	0.9	0.3	0.0
Financial assistance from other household	1,325	0.7	3,905	1.2	0.8	0.7	0.4	0.4
Other income	702	0.4	1,821	0.3	0.5	0.5	0.4	0.3

Source: Bureau of the Census, 2007 Current Population Survey, Internet site http://pubdb3.census.gov/macro/032007/perinc/toc.htm; calculations by New Strategist

Poverty Has Become More Prevalent among Working Age Adults

Children and older Americans are less likely to be poor.

Between 1980 and 2006, the percentage of people who live below the poverty level declined slightly, inching down from 13.0 to 12.3 percent. The poverty rate of 2006, however, was well above the low of 11.3 percent reached in 2000.

The proportion of children who live in poverty fell from 18.3 to 17.4 percent between 1980 and 2006. Among Americans aged 65 or older, the poverty rate dropped from 15.7 to 9.4 percent during those years. In contrast, the poverty rate among the working-age population, aged 18 to 64, climbed slightly from 10.1 to 10.8 percent.

Females are more likely to be poor than males. In 2006, 13.6 percent of the nation's females were poor versus 11.0 percent of males. Among females, those aged 18 to 24 are most likely to be poor (20.7 percent). Among males, children have the highest poverty rate (17.2 percent).

■ The overall poverty rate rises and falls with the economy, but poverty within age groups also depends on social conditions such as the prevalence of single-parent families.

Children are more likely than the elderly to be poor

(percent of people under age 18 and aged 65 or older living below poverty level, 2006)

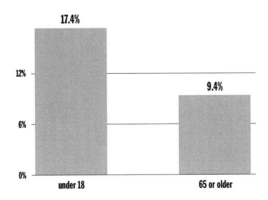

Table 6.27 People Living in Poverty by Age, 1980 to 2006

(percent of people living below poverty level by age, 1980 to 2006; percentage point change in poverty rate for selected years)

	total	under 18	18 to 64	65 or older
2006	12.3%	17.4%	10.8%	9.4%
2005	12.6	17.6	11.1	10.1
2004	12.7	17.8	11.3	9.8
2003	12.5	17.6	10.8	10.2
2002	12.1	16.7	10.6	10.4
2001	11.7	16.3	10.1	10.1
2000	11.3	16.2	9.6	9.9
1999	11.9	17.1	10.1	9.7
1998	12.7	18.9	10.5	10.5
1997	13.3	19.9	10.9	10.5
1996	13.7	20.5	11.4	10.8
1995	13.8	20.8	11.4	10.5
1994	14.5	21.8	11.9	11.7
1993	15.1	22.7	12.4	12.2
1992	14.8	22.3	11.9	12.9
1991	14.2	21.8	11.4	12.4
1990	13.5	20.6	10.7	12.2
1989	12.8	19.6	10.2	11.4
1988	13.0	19.5	10.5	12.0
1987	13.4	20.3	10.6	12.5
1986	13.6	20.5	10.8	12.4
1985	14.0	20.7	11.3	12.6
1984	14.4	21.5	11.7	12.4
1983	15.2	22.3	12.4	13.8
1982	15.0	21.9	12.0	14.6
1981	14.0	20.0	11.1	15.3
1980	13.0	18.3	10.1	15.7
Percentage point change in rate				
2000 to 2006	1.0	1.2	1.2	−0.5
1980 to 2006	−0.7	−0.9	0.7	−6.3

Source: Bureau of the Census, Current Population Surveys, Internet site http://www.census.gov/hhes/www/poverty/histpov/perindex.html; calculations by New Strategist

Table 6.28 People in Poverty by Sex and Age, 2006

(total number of people, number and percent living below poverty level, by sex and age, 2006; people in thousands as of 2007)

	total	below poverty level number	below poverty level percent
Total people	**296,450**	**36,460**	**12.3%**
Under age 18	73,727	12,827	17.4
Aged 18 to 24	28,405	5,047	17.8
Aged 25 to 34	39,868	4,920	12.3
Aged 35 to 44	42,762	4,049	9.5
Aged 45 to 54	43,461	3,399	7.8
Aged 55 to 59	18,221	1,468	8.1
Aged 60 to 64	13,970	1,357	9.7
Aged 65 or older	36,035	3,394	9.4
Aged 65 to 74	18,998	1,636	8.6
Aged 75 or older	17,037	1,757	10.3
Total females	**150,964**	**20,460**	**13.6**
Under age 18	36,085	6,335	17.6
Aged 18 to 24	13,982	2,896	20.7
Aged 25 to 34	19,843	2,969	15.0
Aged 35 to 44	21,582	2,390	11.1
Aged 45 to 54	22,166	1,881	8.5
Aged 55 to 59	9,342	845	9.0
Aged 60 to 64	7,371	770	10.4
Aged 65 or older	20,593	2,373	11.5
Aged 65 to 74	10,259	1,032	10.1
Aged 75 or older	10,334	1,342	13.0
Total males	**145,486**	**16,000**	**11.0**
Under age 18	37,643	6,491	17.2
Aged 18 to 24	14,422	2,151	14.9
Aged 25 to 34	20,024	1,951	9.7
Aged 35 to 44	21,181	1,659	7.8
Aged 45 to 54	21,296	1,518	7.1
Aged 55 to 59	8,879	623	7.0
Aged 60 to 64	6,599	587	8.9
Aged 65 or older	15,443	1,020	6.6
Aged 65 to 74	8,739	604	6.9
Aged 75 or older	6,703	416	6.2

Source: Bureau of the Census, 2007 Current Population Survey, Internet site http://pubdb3.census.gov/macro/032007/pov/toc .htm; calculations by New Strategist

Black and Hispanic Children Are Most Likely to Be Poor

The middle aged are least likely to be poor.

Social Security benefits have substantially reduced poverty among the elderly, but the nation's young have no similar program to improve their socioeconomic condition. Overall, 17.4 percent of the nation's children are poor. The figure ranges from a low of 10.0 percent among non-Hispanic white children to a high of 33.0 percent among black children. Hispanic children are slightly less likely than black children to be poor, with a poverty rate of 26.9 percent.

In nearly every age group, blacks and Hispanics are considerably more likely than Asians or non-Hispanic whites to be poor. Typically, females are more likely than males to be poor. Among Asians, however, male and female poverty rates are about the same and in some age groups the male poverty rate is higher than the female.

■ Lower educational attainment is one factor contributing to the higher poverty rates among blacks and Hispanics.

Poverty is higher for black and Hispanic children

(percent of people under age 18 who live below poverty level, by race and Hispanic origin, 2006)

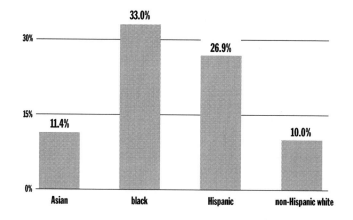

Table 6.29 People Living in Poverty by Sex, Age, Race, and Hispanic Origin, 2006

(percent of people who live below poverty level by sex, age, race, and Hispanic origin, 2006)

	total	Asian	black	Hispanic	non-Hispanic white
Total people	**12.3%**	**10.1%**	**24.2%**	**20.6%**	**8.2%**
Under age 18	17.4	11.4	33.0	26.9	10.0
Aged 18 to 24	17.8	16.7	27.0	21.0	14.6
Aged 25 to 34	12.3	8.3	22.6	17.9	8.5
Aged 35 to 44	9.5	7.9	16.2	16.8	6.5
Aged 45 to 54	7.8	8.2	16.0	12.9	5.6
Aged 55 to 59	8.1	8.0	15.7	16.1	6.1
Aged 60 to 64	9.7	8.8	20.2	17.8	7.6
Aged 65 or older	9.4	11.8	22.7	19.4	7.0
Aged 65 to 74	8.6	9.1	21.2	18.8	6.0
Aged 75 or older	10.3	15.1	24.9	20.4	8.1
Total females	**13.6**	**9.9**	**26.2**	**22.6**	**9.3**
Under age 18	17.6	11.1	32.9	27.2	10.2
Aged 18 to 24	20.7	16.3	31.3	23.6	17.6
Aged 25 to 34	15.0	7.2	28.5	22.1	10.3
Aged 35 to 44	11.1	8.3	19.6	20.0	7.5
Aged 45 to 54	8.5	8.2	16.6	14.3	6.1
Aged 55 to 59	9.0	7.6	17.2	19.1	6.8
Aged 60 to 64	10.4	11.6	21.0	18.8	7.9
Aged 65 or older	11.5	11.7	26.6	20.8	9.0
Aged 65 to 74	10.1	7.4	23.9	19.3	7.3
Aged 75 or older	13.0	16.9	30.1	23.1	10.6
Total males	**11.0**	**10.3**	**22.0**	**18.8**	**7.0**
Under age 18	17.2	11.7	33.1	26.6	9.8
Aged 18 to 24	14.9	17.1	22.4	18.7	11.6
Aged 25 to 34	9.7	9.6	15.7	14.5	6.7
Aged 35 to 44	7.8	7.4	12.1	14.0	5.5
Aged 45 to 54	7.1	8.3	15.3	11.5	5.0
Aged 55 to 59	7.0	8.3	14.0	13.1	5.4
Aged 60 to 64	8.9	5.7	19.0	16.7	7.2
Aged 65 or older	6.6	12.0	16.6	17.6	4.5
Aged 65 to 74	6.9	11.4	17.6	18.1	4.5
Aged 75 or older	6.2	12.7	14.5	16.7	4.4

Note: Data for Asians and blacks are for those who identify themselves as being of the race alone or in combination with other races. Data for non-Hispanic whites are for those who identify themselves as being white alone and not Hispanic. Hispanics may be of any race.
Source: Bureau of the Census, 2007 Current Population Survey, Internet site http://pubdb3.census.gov/macro/032007/pov/toc .htm; calculations by New Strategist

Many Workers Cannot Keep Their Family Out of Poverty

The proportion is highest among the youngest and the oldest workers.

Among all workers, 24 million—or 15 percent—do not earn enough to keep a family of four above the poverty level. The percentage of workers who earn wages below poverty level for a family of four is highest among young adults and the elderly. Twenty-seven percent of workers aged 18 to 24 do not earn enough to keep a family of four out of poverty. The figure bottoms out at 10 percent among workers aged 45 to 54, then rises to 39 percent among workers aged 65 or older.

Among full-time workers, more than 9 million do not earn enough to keep a family of four above poverty level. The proportion is highest among 18-to-24-year-olds at 21 per-cent. The figure falls to a low of 6 percent among 45-to-54-year-olds, then rises in the older age groups. Sixteen percent of full-time workers aged 65 or older have earnings below the poverty level for a family of four.

■ For many families, it takes more than one full-time worker to stay out of poverty.

Many full-time workers cannot support a family

(percent of full-time workers with earnings below poverty level for a family of four, by age, 2006)

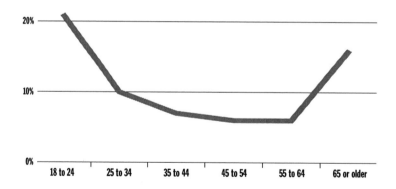

Table 6.30 Workers with Earnings below Poverty Level for Family of Four, 2006

(number and percent of employed people aged 18 or older with earnings below weighted average poverty threshold for four-person family, by sex, age, and work status, 2006; workers in thousands as of 2007)

	all workers			full-time, year-round workers		
		workers with earnings below poverty level for four-person family			workers with earnings below poverty level for four-person family	
	total	number	percent	total	number	percent
Total workers	**157,352**	**24,305**	**15.4%**	**107,734**	**9,189**	**8.5%**
Aged 18 to 24	20,386	5,516	27.1	8,186	1,731	21.1
Aged 25 to 34	33,647	5,289	15.7	24,530	2,374	9.7
Aged 35 to 44	36,033	3,999	11.1	27,966	1,959	7.0
Aged 45 to 54	36,006	3,572	9.9	28,304	1,674	5.9
Aged 55 to 64	21,716	2,936	13.5	15,640	972	6.2
Aged 65 or older	6,763	2,664	39.4	3,008	470	15.6

Source: Bureau of the Census, 2007 Current Population Survey, Internet site http://pubdb3.census.gov/macro/032007/pov/toc .htm; calculations by New Strategist

7

Labor Force

The labor force is changing rapidly as the Baby-Boom generation ages. The number of older workers will soar during the next decade, and the labor force participation rate among people aged 55 or older will continue to climb. As Boomers postpone retirement—thanks to the disappearance of defined-benefit pension plans—it will be harder for Gen Xers and Millennials to move up the corporate ladder.

The increased labor force participation of women, especially mothers with young children, defines the lifestyles of Boomers and younger generations of Americans. Businesses have adapted by offering their services 24/7, fast-food restaurants have proliferated, and Internet shopping has become a popular time saver. Although working mothers and dual-income couples are now the norm, conflicts between work and family have yet to be resolved.

What to expect in the future

■ The workforce will age rapidly during the next decade, creating competition between older and younger workers for the best jobs.

■ The bond between workers and employers will further erode as companies try to cut costs and workers look for jobs with better pay and benefits.

Men's Labor Force Participation Has Declined

Women's labor force participation rate has soared.

The percentage of men in the labor force has declined substantially in every age group since 1950. The largest drop has been among men aged 65 or older, falling from 46 percent in 1950 to a low of 16 percent in 1990. Since 1990, however, the labor force participation of men aged 65 or older has increased, rising to 21 percent in 2007. Among men aged 55 to 64, labor force participation climbed from 67 to 70 percent between 2000 and 2007 as early retirement became less common.

Women's labor force participation increased in every age group between 1950 and 2007. Women aged 25 to 54 saw their labor force participation rate rise by more than 30 percentage points between 1950 and 2007 as working wives (and mothers) became the norm. Since 2000, however, the percentage of women in the labor force has fallen among those younger than age 55. Rates are continuing to rise for older women, however.

■ The labor force participation rate of men and women aged 55 or older will continue to rise as Boomers postpone retirement.

The labor force participation rate of older men has risen

(percentage point change in labor force participation rate of men by age, 2000 to 2007)

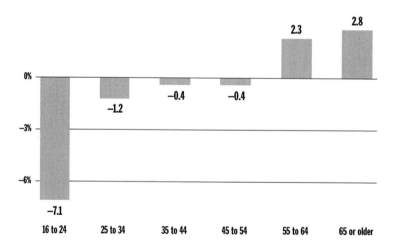

Table 7.1 Labor Force Participation Rate by Sex and Age, 1950 to 2007

(percent of people aged 16 or older in the civilian labor force by sex and age, and percentage point change, 1950–2007 and 2000–2007)

	2007	2000	1990	1980	1970	1960	1950	percentage point change 2000–07	percentage point change 1950–07
Total people	**66.0%**	**67.1%**	**66.4%**	**63.8%**	**60.4%**	**59.4%**	**59.2%**	**−1.1**	**6.8**
Aged 16 to 24	59.4	65.8	67.3	68.1	59.8	56.4	59.9	−6.4	−0.5
Aged 25 to 34	83.3	84.6	83.6	79.9	69.7	65.4	63.5	−1.3	19.8
Aged 35 to 44	83.8	84.8	85.2	80.0	73.1	69.4	67.5	−1.0	16.3
Aged 45 to 54	82.0	82.5	80.7	74.9	73.5	72.2	66.4	−0.5	15.6
Aged 55 to 64	63.8	59.2	55.9	55.7	61.8	60.9	56.7	4.6	7.1
Aged 65 or older	16.0	12.9	11.8	12.5	17.0	20.8	26.7	3.1	−10.7
Total men	**73.2**	**74.8**	**76.1**	**77.4**	**79.7**	**83.3**	**86.4**	**−1.6**	**−13.2**
Aged 16 to 24	61.5	68.6	71.5	74.4	69.4	71.7	77.3	−7.1	−15.8
Aged 25 to 34	92.2	93.4	94.2	95.2	96.4	97.5	96.0	−1.2	−3.8
Aged 35 to 44	92.3	92.7	94.4	95.5	96.8	97.7	97.6	−0.4	−5.3
Aged 45 to 54	88.2	88.6	90.7	91.2	94.3	95.7	95.8	−0.4	−7.6
Aged 55 to 64	69.6	67.3	67.7	72.1	83.0	87.3	86.9	2.3	−17.3
Aged 65 or older	20.5	17.7	16.4	19.0	26.8	33.1	45.8	2.8	−25.3
Total women	**59.3**	**59.9**	**57.5**	**51.5**	**43.3**	**37.7**	**33.9**	**−0.6**	**25.4**
Aged 16 to 24	57.2	63.0	63.1	61.9	51.3	42.8	43.9	−5.8	13.3
Aged 25 to 34	74.5	76.1	73.6	65.5	45.0	36.0	34.0	−1.6	40.5
Aged 35 to 44	75.5	77.2	76.5	65.5	51.1	43.4	39.1	−1.7	36.4
Aged 45 to 54	76.0	76.8	71.2	59.9	54.4	49.9	37.9	−0.8	38.1
Aged 55 to 64	58.3	51.9	45.3	41.3	43.0	37.2	27.0	6.4	31.3
Aged 65 or older	12.6	9.4	8.7	8.1	9.7	10.8	9.7	3.2	2.9

Source: Bureau of Labor Statistics, Public Query Data Tool, Internet site http://www.bls.gov/data; and Monthly Labor Review, December 1999; calculations by New Strategist

Men in Their Thirties Are Most Likely to Work

Among women, those in their forties have the highest labor force participation.

Between the ages of 25 and 44, more than 90 percent of men are in the labor force. Labor force participation peaks among men in their thirties at 93 percent. Labor force participation peaks among women in the 40-to-49 age group at 77 percent.

For men, labor force participation begins to fall rapidly after age 55. Many older men opt for early retirement if they can afford it, although some leave the labor force because they are disabled or were laid off. Only 78 percent of men aged 55 to 59 are working or looking for work—8 percentage points less than the rate among men aged 50 to 54. Among men aged 60 to 64, only 59 percent are still in the labor force.

Women's labor force participation also declines after age 55. Two-thirds of women aged 55 to 59 are in the labor force, a figure that drops to 48 percent among women aged 60 to 64.

■ Many Boomers will end up working longer than their parents because early retirement opportunities are becoming less common.

Women's labor force participation peaks among women in their forties

(labor force participation rate of women by age, 2007)

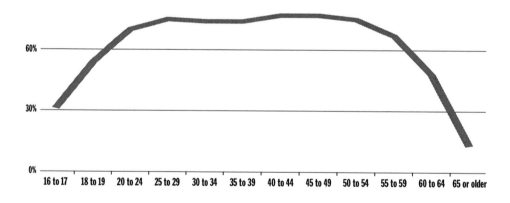

Table 7.2 Employment Status by Sex and Age, 2007

(number and percent of people aged 16 or older in the civilian labor force by sex, age, and employment status, 2007; numbers in thousands)

		civilian labor force				
					unemployed	
	civilian noninstitutional population	total	percent of population	employed	number	percent of labor force
Total people	**231,867**	**153,124**	**66.0%**	**146,047**	**7,078**	**4.6%**
Aged 16 to 17	9,222	2,771	30.0	2,286	485	17.5
Aged 18 to 19	7,760	4,242	54.7	3,625	616	14.5
Aged 20 to 24	20,427	15,205	74.4	13,964	1,241	8.2
Aged 25 to 29	20,607	17,130	83.1	16,247	883	5.2
Aged 30 to 34	19,144	16,000	83.6	15,339	661	4.1
Aged 35 to 39	20,738	17,292	83.4	16,677	615	3.6
Aged 40 to 44	21,664	18,235	84.2	17,625	610	3.3
Aged 45 to 49	22,661	18,903	83.4	18,285	618	3.3
Aged 50 to 54	20,882	16,795	80.4	16,278	517	3.1
Aged 55 to 59	18,194	13,104	72.0	12,691	413	3.1
Aged 60 to 64	14,339	7,646	53.3	7,417	229	3.0
Aged 65 or older	36,228	5,804	16.0	5,614	190	3.3
Aged 65 to 69	10,708	3,179	29.7	3,074	105	3.3
Aged 70 to 74	8,461	1,457	17.2	1,408	50	3.4
Aged 75 or older	17,059	1,167	6.8	1,132	35	3.0
Total men	**112,173**	**82,136**	**73.2**	**78,254**	**3,882**	**4.7**
Aged 16 to 17	4,658	1,354	29.1	1,091	263	19.4
Aged 18 to 19	3,960	2,187	55.2	1,827	360	16.5
Aged 20 to 24	10,291	8,095	78.7	7,374	721	8.9
Aged 25 to 29	10,336	9,441	91.3	8,943	498	5.3
Aged 30 to 34	9,523	8,867	93.1	8,509	358	4.0
Aged 35 to 39	10,247	9,531	93.0	9,221	311	3.3
Aged 40 to 44	10,663	9,768	91.6	9,445	323	3.3
Aged 45 to 49	11,125	9,995	89.8	9,677	318	3.2
Aged 50 to 54	10,187	8,806	86.4	8,533	273	3.1
Aged 55 to 59	8,807	6,848	77.8	6,628	219	3.2
Aged 60 to 64	6,851	4,057	59.2	3,927	129	3.2
Aged 65 or older	15,525	3,188	20.5	3,080	108	3.4
Aged 65 to 69	4,986	1,710	34.3	1,651	59	3.5
Aged 70 to 74	3,825	810	21.2	781	29	3.6
Aged 75 or older	6,714	668	10.0	648	20	3.1

(continued)

	civilian noninstitutional population	civilian labor force				
		total	percent of population	employed	unemployed	
					number	percent of labor force
Total women	**119,694**	**70,988**	**59.3%**	**67,792**	**3,196**	**4.5%**
Aged 16 to 17	4,564	1,417	31.0	1,195	222	15.7
Aged 18 to 19	3,800	2,055	54.1	1,798	256	12.5
Aged 20 to 24	10,137	7,110	70.1	6,590	520	7.3
Aged 25 to 29	10,271	7,689	74.9	7,304	385	5.0
Aged 30 to 34	9,622	7,132	74.1	6,829	303	4.2
Aged 35 to 39	10,491	7,761	74.0	7,456	304	3.9
Aged 40 to 44	11,000	8,467	77.0	8,180	287	3.4
Aged 45 to 49	11,536	8,908	77.2	8,608	300	3.4
Aged 50 to 54	10,695	7,988	74.7	7,745	244	3.0
Aged 55 to 59	9,388	6,257	66.6	6,063	193	3.1
Aged 60 to 64	7,488	3,589	47.9	3,489	100	2.8
Aged 65 or older	20,703	2,615	12.6	2,534	81	3.1
Aged 65 to 69	5,722	1,469	25.7	1,423	46	3.1
Aged 70 to 74	4,636	647	14.0	626	21	3.2
Aged 75 or older	10,345	499	4.8	484	15	2.9

Note: The civilian labor force equals the number of the employed plus the number of the unemployed. The civilian population equals the number in the labor force plus the number not in the labor force.
Source: Bureau of Labor Statistics, Current Population Survey, Internet site http://www.bls.gov/cps/home.htm

Boomers Are the Largest Share of the Workforce

But the dominance of Boomers is on the wane as they approach retirement age.

More than one-third of today's workers are Baby Boomers, aged 43 to 61 in 2007. Millennials (under age 30) make up 28 percent of the labor force and are the second largest generation at work. Generation X (aged 31 to 42) accounts for a slightly smaller 27 percent share of workers. Americans aged 62 or older (the Swing and World War II generations) make up only 7 percent of workers. The age distribution of men and women in the labor force is nearly identical.

The Baby Boom's share of workers is declining as the oldest members of the generation reach the age of early retirement. The Millennial generation's share of the workforce is rising rapidly and will surpass the Boomer share in a few years.

■ Generation X may find promotions more plentiful as Boomers retire.

The Swing and World War II generations account for few workers

(percent distribution of the labor force by generation, 2007)

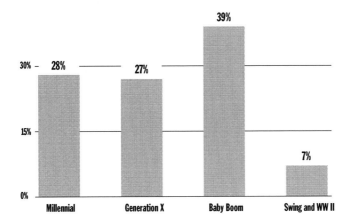

Table 7.3 Distribution of the Labor Force by Age, Generation, and Sex, 2007

(number and percent distribution of people aged 16 or older in the civilian labor force by age, generation, and sex, 2007; numbers in thousands)

	total in labor force		men in labor force		women in labor force	
	number	percent distribution	number	percent distribution	number	percent distribution
Total people	**153,124**	**100.0%**	**82,136**	**100.0%**	**70,988**	**100.0%**
Aged 16 to 17	2,771	1.8	1,354	1.6	1,417	2.0
Aged 18 to 19	4,242	2.8	2,187	2.7	2,055	2.9
Aged 20 to 24	15,205	9.9	8,095	9.9	7,110	10.0
Aged 25 to 29	17,130	11.2	9,441	11.5	7,689	10.8
Aged 30 to 34	16,000	10.4	8,867	10.8	7,132	10.0
Aged 35 to 39	17,292	11.3	9,531	11.6	7,761	10.9
Aged 40 to 44	18,235	11.9	9,768	11.9	8,467	11.9
Aged 45 to 49	18,903	12.3	9,995	12.2	8,908	12.5
Aged 50 to 54	16,795	11.0	8,806	10.7	7,988	11.3
Aged 55 to 59	13,104	8.6	6,848	8.3	6,257	8.8
Aged 60 to 64	7,646	5.0	4,057	4.9	3,589	5.1
Aged 65 or older	5,804	3.8	3,188	3.9	2,615	3.7
Labor force by generation						
Total people	**153,124**	**100.0**	**82,136**	**100.0**	**70,988**	**100.0**
Millennial (16–30)	42,548	27.8	22,850	27.8	19,697	27.7
Generation X (31–42)	41,033	26.8	22,485	27.4	18,547	26.1
Baby Boom (43–61)	59,154	38.6	31,179	38.0	27,975	39.4
Swing/World War II (62+)	10,392	6.8	5,622	6.8	4,768	6.7

Note: Labor force by generation is estimated by New Strategist.
Source: Bureau of Labor Statistics, Current Population Survey, Internet site http://www.bls.gov/cps/home.htm; calculations by New Strategist

Teenagers Are Most Likely to Be Unemployed

Unemployment rates are below average among people aged 30 or older.

Among all age groups, teenagers are most likely to be unemployed. More than 17 percent of teens aged 16 to 17 were looking for work in 2007, as were 15 percent of those aged 18 to 19. The unemployment rate of young adults is relatively high not only because they have more difficulty than older people finding work, but also because many are shopping around for the right job. If a job doesn't suit them, they are more likely than older workers to quit and look for something better.

The unemployment rate falls with age. By the 30-to-34 age group, the unemployment rate is below the overall average for both men and women.

■ The unemployment rate plays a big role in consumer confidence. When unemployment rises, consumers are more cautious.

Unemployment falls with increasing age

(percent unemployed by age, 2007)

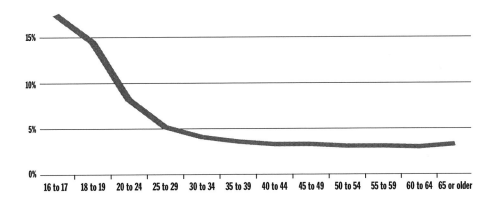

Table 7.4 Unemployed by Age and Sex, 2007

(number and percent unemployed and percent distribution of unemployed, by sex and age, 2007; numbers in thousands)

	number unemployed	percent unemployed	percent distribution
Total people	**7,078**	**4.6%**	**100.0%**
Aged 16 to 17	485	17.5	6.9
Aged 18 to 19	616	14.5	8.7
Aged 20 to 24	1,241	8.2	17.5
Aged 25 to 29	883	5.2	12.5
Aged 30 to 34	661	4.1	9.3
Aged 35 to 39	615	3.6	8.7
Aged 40 to 44	610	3.3	8.6
Aged 45 to 49	618	3.3	8.7
Aged 50 to 54	517	3.1	7.3
Aged 55 to 59	413	3.1	5.8
Aged 60 to 64	229	3.0	3.2
Aged 65 or older	190	3.3	2.7
Total men	**3,882**	**4.7**	**100.0**
Aged 16 to 17	263	19.4	6.8
Aged 18 to 19	360	16.5	9.3
Aged 20 to 24	721	8.9	18.6
Aged 25 to 29	498	5.3	12.8
Aged 30 to 34	358	4.0	9.2
Aged 35 to 39	311	3.3	8.0
Aged 40 to 44	323	3.3	8.3
Aged 45 to 49	318	3.2	8.2
Aged 50 to 54	273	3.1	7.0
Aged 55 to 59	219	3.2	5.6
Aged 60 to 64	129	3.2	3.3
Aged 65 or older	108	3.4	2.8
Total women	**3,196**	**4.5**	**100.0**
Aged 16 to 17	222	15.7	6.9
Aged 18 to 19	256	12.5	8.0
Aged 20 to 24	520	7.3	16.3
Aged 25 to 29	385	5.0	12.0
Aged 30 to 34	303	4.2	9.5
Aged 35 to 39	304	3.9	9.5
Aged 40 to 44	287	3.4	9.0
Aged 45 to 49	300	3.4	9.4
Aged 50 to 54	244	3.0	7.6
Aged 55 to 59	193	3.1	6.0
Aged 60 to 64	100	2.8	3.1
Aged 65 or older	81	3.1	2.5

Source: Bureau of Labor Statistics, Current Population Survey, Internet site http://www.bls.gov/cps/home.htm; calculations by New Strategist

Hispanic Women Are Least Likely to Work

Hispanic men have the highest labor force participation rate.

Women are less likely than men to be in the labor force, but the gap between men's and women's labor force participation rates varies by age, race, and Hispanic origin. The largest gap by gender is found between Hispanic men and women, with 81 percent of men and only 56 percent of women in the labor force.

Hispanic men have a higher overall labor force participation rate than Asian, black, or white men (81 percent versus 75, 67, and 74 percent, respectively). Hispanic men have a higher labor force participation rate than white men because the Hispanic population is younger and less likely to be retired. They have a higher participation rate than Asian men because young Hispanic men are much less likely to be in school.

Unemployment is highest among young black men, with 34 percent of those aged 16 to 19 looking for work. This compares with an unemployment rate of 20 percent among their Hispanic counterparts, 16 percent among whites in the age group, and 11 percent among Asians.

■ The lower labor force participation rate of Hispanic women—a group growing rapidly—explains why the overall labor force participation rate of American women has declined slightly since 2000.

Unemployment is highest for young black men

(percent of men aged 16 to 19 who are unemployed, by race and Hispanic origin, 2007)

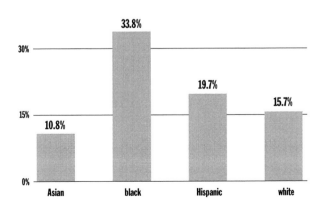

Table 7.5 Labor Force Participation Rate by Race, Hispanic Origin, Age, and Sex, 2007

(percent of people aged 16 or older in the civilian labor force, by race, Hispanic origin, age, and sex, 2007)

	percent in labor force		
	total	men	women
Total Asians	**66.5%**	**75.1%**	**58.6%**
Aged 16 to 19	24.5	24.7	24.4
Aged 20 to 24	59.7	59.3	60.1
Aged 25 to 34	77.6	89.3	66.6
Aged 35 to 44	82.8	93.6	72.8
Aged 45 to 54	82.0	90.2	74.7
Aged 55 to 64	65.6	76.0	56.6
Aged 65 or older	17.0	22.0	13.3
Total blacks	**63.7**	**66.8**	**61.1**
Aged 16 to 19	30.3	29.4	31.2
Aged 20 to 24	68.3	71.1	65.7
Aged 25 to 34	81.7	86.1	78.0
Aged 35 to 44	82.7	86.3	79.8
Aged 45 to 54	75.7	78.6	73.2
Aged 55 to 64	55.1	54.4	55.7
Aged 65 or older	14.0	17.3	12.0
Total Hispanics	**68.8**	**80.5**	**56.5**
Aged 16 to 19	37.1	40.0	34.0
Aged 20 to 24	74.8	85.3	62.9
Aged 25 to 34	80.7	94.1	64.6
Aged 35 to 44	81.8	93.9	68.4
Aged 45 to 54	78.6	88.3	68.7
Aged 55 to 64	58.5	70.3	47.6
Aged 65 or older	16.0	22.0	11.4
Total whites	**66.4**	**74.0**	**59.0**
Aged 16 to 19	44.4	44.3	44.6
Aged 20 to 24	76.4	80.9	71.6
Aged 25 to 34	84.1	93.4	74.5
Aged 35 to 44	84.1	93.1	75.0
Aged 45 to 54	83.1	89.6	76.6
Aged 55 to 64	64.9	71.2	58.9
Aged 65 or older	16.2	20.8	12.7

Source: Bureau of Labor Statistics, Current Population Survey, Internet site http://www.bls.gov/cps/home.htm

Table 7.6 Unemployment Rate by Race, Hispanic Origin, Age, and Sex, 2007

(percent of people aged 16 or older who are unemployed, by race, Hispanic origin, age, and sex, 2007)

	percent unemployed		
	total	men	women
Total Asians	**3.2%**	**3.1%**	**3.4%**
Aged 16 to 19	12.7	10.8	14.7
Aged 20 to 24	5.6	6.9	4.2
Aged 25 to 34	3.2	2.8	3.7
Aged 35 to 44	2.2	2.0	2.5
Aged 45 to 54	2.8	2.9	2.7
Aged 55 to 64	3.6	3.7	3.6
Aged 65 or older	1.5	2.2	0.6
Total blacks	**8.3**	**9.1**	**7.5**
Aged 16 to 19	29.4	33.8	25.3
Aged 20 to 24	15.2	16.9	13.6
Aged 25 to 34	8.6	9.1	8.1
Aged 35 to 44	5.4	5.6	5.3
Aged 45 to 54	5.4	5.8	5.0
Aged 55 to 64	4.3	5.2	3.7
Aged 65 or older	4.5	5.0	4.0
Total Hispanics	**5.6**	**5.3**	**6.1**
Aged 16 to 19	18.1	19.7	16.1
Aged 20 to 24	7.8	7.4	5.6
Aged 25 to 34	4.9	4.5	5.1
Aged 35 to 44	4.3	3.8	5.1
Aged 45 to 54	4.3	4.4	4.3
Aged 55 to 64	4.5	3.9	5.2
Aged 65 or older	4.9	5.5	4.0
Total whites	**4.1**	**4.2**	**4.0**
Aged 16 to 19	13.9	15.7	12.1
Aged 20 to 24	7.0	7.6	6.2
Aged 25 to 34	4.0	4.1	3.9
Aged 35 to 44	3.2	3.0	3.4
Aged 45 to 54	2.9	2.8	2.9
Aged 55 to 64	2.9	3.0	2.8
Aged 65 or older	3.2	3.3	3.1

Source: Bureau of Labor Statistics, Current Population Survey, Internet site http://www.bls.gov/cps/home.htm

The Middle Aged Are Professionals, Managers

Young workers are most often in sales or service jobs.

Thirty-five percent of American workers are in management or professional occupations. This category includes the highest-paying jobs in the country such as physician, lawyer, accountant, and corporate vice president.

Young adults start out in entry-level jobs—selling hamburgers at a fast-food restaurant or working at a construction site, for example. As they gain more experience with age, many move into professional or management positions. Among 16-to-19-year-olds in the labor force, fully 39 percent are employed in a service occupation, according to the Bureau of Labor Statistics. The proportion in service occupations falls with age to a low of 13 percent among 45-to-64-year-olds. Forty to 41 percent of workers aged 45 to 64 are employed as managers or professionals versus just 6 percent of 16-to-19-year-olds and 20 percent of 20-to-24-year-olds.

Although only 14 percent of the nation's workers are under age 25, more than 40 percent of food service workers are in the under-25 age group. Only 22 percent of food service workers are aged 45 or older.

■ Among workers employed in computer and mathematical jobs, a substantial 30 percent are in the youthful 25-to-34 age group.

Most managers and professionals are aged 35 to 54

(percent distribution of workers in management and professional occupations, by age, 2007)

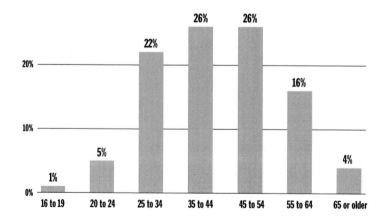

Table 7.7 Occupations by Age, 2007

(number of employed people aged 16 or older by occupation and age, 2007; numbers in thousands)

	total	16 to 19	20 to 24	25 to 34	35 to 44	45 to 54	55 to 64	65 or older
TOTAL EMPLOYED	**146,047**	**5,911**	**13,964**	**31,586**	**34,302**	**34,563**	**20,108**	**5,614**
Management, professional, related occupations	**51,788**	**359**	**2,763**	**11,428**	**13,272**	**13,659**	**8,304**	**2,003**
Management, business, and financial operations	21,577	73	813	4,126	5,751	6,146	3,694	976
Management	15,486	60	474	2,673	4,191	4,601	2,726	761
Business and financial operations	6,091	12	339	1,452	1,559	1,545	968	215
Professional and related occupations	30,210	286	1,950	7,303	7,521	7,513	4,610	1,027
Computer and mathematical	3,441	18	187	1,023	1,038	825	313	37
Architecture and engineering	2,932	12	159	681	732	800	441	106
Life, physical, and social sciences	1,382	8	115	363	345	316	189	46
Community and social services	2,265	20	132	472	520	574	428	119
Legal	1,668	5	72	365	427	439	275	85
Education, training, and library	8,485	106	641	1,995	1,988	2,009	1,466	281
Art, design, entertainment, sports, and media	2,789	77	265	735	612	579	401	120
Health care practitioner, technical occupations	7,248	40	380	1,668	1,859	1,971	1,098	232
Service occupations	**24,137**	**2,305**	**3,479**	**5,232**	**5,072**	**4,517**	**2,569**	**963**
Health care support	3,138	96	446	770	696	675	364	92
Protective service	3,071	98	270	739	867	653	329	116
Food preparation and serving related	7,699	1,509	1,632	1,665	1,212	976	513	192
Building and grounds cleaning and maintenance	5,469	240	478	1,077	1,308	1,284	792	290
Personal care and service	4,760	362	654	981	990	930	571	272
Sales and office occupations	**36,212**	**2,157**	**4,351**	**7,253**	**7,607**	**8,087**	**5,103**	**1,654**
Sales and related	16,698	1,378	2,098	3,293	3,423	3,423	2,243	840
Office and administrative support	19,513	779	2,253	3,959	4,184	4,664	2,860	815
Natural resources, construction, and maintenance occupations	**15,740**	**508**	**1,687**	**3,934**	**3,907**	**3,682**	**1,664**	**357**
Farming, fishing, and forestry	960	106	132	208	200	172	96	46
Construction and extraction	9,535	283	1,097	2,622	2,344	2,106	900	183
Installation, maintenance, and repair	5,245	119	459	1,103	1,363	1,405	668	127
Production, transportation, and material-moving occupations	**18,171**	**582**	**1,684**	**3,739**	**4,444**	**4,617**	**2,468**	**637**
Production	9,395	189	835	1,975	2,359	2,510	1,263	265
Transportation and material moving	8,776	394	849	1,764	2,085	2,107	1,205	372

Source: Bureau of Labor Statistics, unpublished data from the 2007 Current Population Survey

Table 7.8 Distribution of Workers by Occupation and Age, 2007

(percent distribution of employed people aged 16 or older by occupation, by age, 2007)

	total	16 to 19	20 to 24	25 to 34	35 to 44	45 to 54	55 to 64	65 or older
TOTAL EMPLOYED	100.0%	100.0%	100.0%	100.0%	100.0%	100.0%	100.0%	100.0%
Management, professional, related occupations	**35.5**	**6.1**	**19.8**	**36.2**	**38.7**	**39.5**	**41.3**	**35.7**
Management, business, and financial operations	14.8	1.2	5.8	13.1	16.8	17.8	18.4	17.4
Management	10.6	1.0	3.4	8.5	12.2	13.3	13.6	13.6
Business and financial operations	4.2	0.2	2.4	4.6	4.5	4.5	4.8	3.8
Professional and related occupations	20.7	4.8	14.0	23.1	21.9	21.7	22.9	18.3
Computer and mathematical	2.4	0.3	1.3	3.2	3.0	2.4	1.6	0.7
Architecture and engineering	2.0	0.2	1.1	2.2	2.1	2.3	2.2	1.9
Life, physical, and social sciences	0.9	0.1	0.8	1.1	1.0	0.9	0.9	0.8
Community and social services	1.6	0.3	0.9	1.5	1.5	1.7	2.1	2.1
Legal	1.1	0.1	0.5	1.2	1.2	1.3	1.4	1.5
Education, training, and library	5.8	1.8	4.6	6.3	5.8	5.8	7.3	5.0
Art, design, entertainment, sports, and media	1.9	1.3	1.9	2.3	1.8	1.7	2.0	2.1
Health care practitioner, technical occupations	5.0	0.7	2.7	5.3	5.4	5.7	5.5	4.1
Service occupations	**16.5**	**39.0**	**24.9**	**16.6**	**14.8**	**13.1**	**12.8**	**17.2**
Health care support	2.1	1.6	3.2	2.4	2.0	2.0	1.8	1.6
Protective service	2.1	1.7	1.9	2.3	2.5	1.9	1.6	2.1
Food preparation and serving related	5.3	25.5	11.7	5.3	3.5	2.8	2.6	3.4
Building and grounds cleaning and maintenance	3.7	4.1	3.4	3.4	3.8	3.7	3.9	5.2
Personal care and service	3.3	6.1	4.7	3.1	2.9	2.7	2.8	4.8
Sales and office occupations	**24.8**	**36.5**	**31.2**	**23.0**	**22.2**	**23.4**	**25.4**	**29.5**
Sales and related	11.4	23.3	15.0	10.4	10.0	9.9	11.2	15.0
Office and administrative support	13.4	13.2	16.1	12.5	12.2	13.5	14.2	14.5
Natural resources, construction, and maintenance occupations	**10.8**	**8.6**	**12.1**	**12.5**	**11.4**	**10.7**	**8.3**	**6.4**
Farming, fishing, and forestry	0.7	1.8	0.9	0.7	0.6	0.5	0.5	0.8
Construction and extraction	6.5	4.8	7.9	8.3	6.8	6.1	4.5	3.3
Installation, maintenance, and repair	3.6	2.0	3.3	3.5	4.0	4.1	3.3	2.3
Production, transportation, and material-moving occupations	**12.4**	**9.8**	**12.1**	**11.8**	**13.0**	**13.4**	**12.3**	**11.3**
Production	6.4	3.2	6.0	6.3	6.9	7.3	6.3	4.7
Transportation and material moving	6.0	6.7	6.1	5.6	6.1	6.1	6.0	6.6

Source: Bureau of Labor Statistics, unpublished data from the 2007 Current Population Survey; calculations by New Strategist

Table 7.9 Age Distribution of Workers by Occupation, 2007

(percent distribution of employed people aged 16 or older by age, by occupation, 2007)

	total	16 to 19	20 to 24	25 to 34	35 to 44	45 to 54	55 to 64	65 or older
TOTAL EMPLOYED	100.0%	4.0%	9.6%	21.6%	23.5%	23.7%	13.8%	3.8%
Management, professional, related occupations	100.0	0.7	5.3	22.1	25.6	26.4	16.0	3.9
Management, business, and financial operations	100.0	0.3	3.8	19.1	26.7	28.5	17.1	4.5
Management	100.0	0.4	3.1	17.3	27.1	29.7	17.6	4.9
Business and financial operations	100.0	0.2	5.6	23.8	25.6	25.4	15.9	3.5
Professional and related occupations	100.0	0.9	6.5	24.2	24.9	24.9	15.3	3.4
Computer and mathematical	100.0	0.5	5.4	29.7	30.2	24.0	9.1	1.1
Architecture and engineering	100.0	0.4	5.4	23.2	25.0	27.3	15.0	3.6
Life, physical, and social sciences	100.0	0.6	8.3	26.3	25.0	22.9	13.7	3.3
Community and social services	100.0	0.9	5.8	20.8	23.0	25.3	18.9	5.3
Legal	100.0	0.3	4.3	21.9	25.6	26.3	16.5	5.1
Education, training, and library	100.0	1.2	7.6	23.5	23.4	23.7	17.3	3.3
Art, design, entertainment, sports, and media	100.0	2.8	9.5	26.4	21.9	20.8	14.4	4.3
Health care practitioner, technical occupations	100.0	0.6	5.2	23.0	25.6	27.2	15.1	3.2
Service occupations	100.0	9.5	14.4	21.7	21.0	18.7	10.6	4.0
Health care support	100.0	3.1	14.2	24.5	22.2	21.5	11.6	2.9
Protective service	100.0	3.2	8.8	24.1	28.2	21.3	10.7	3.8
Food preparation and serving related	100.0	19.6	21.2	21.6	15.7	12.7	6.7	2.5
Building and grounds cleaning and maintenance	100.0	4.4	8.7	19.7	23.9	23.5	14.5	5.3
Personal care and service	100.0	7.6	13.7	20.6	20.8	19.5	12.0	5.7
Sales and office occupations	100.0	6.0	12.0	20.0	21.0	22.3	14.1	4.6
Sales and related	100.0	8.3	12.6	19.7	20.5	20.5	13.4	5.0
Office and administrative support	100.0	4.0	11.5	20.3	21.4	23.9	14.7	4.2
Natural resources, construction, and maintenance occupations	100.0	3.2	10.7	25.0	24.8	23.4	10.6	2.3
Farming, fishing, and forestry	100.0	11.0	13.8	21.7	20.8	17.9	10.0	4.8
Construction and extraction	100.0	3.0	11.5	27.5	24.6	22.1	9.4	1.9
Installation, maintenance, and repair	100.0	2.3	8.8	21.0	26.0	26.8	12.7	2.4
Production, transportation, and material-moving occupations	100.0	3.2	9.3	20.6	24.5	25.4	13.6	3.5
Production	100.0	2.0	8.9	21.0	25.1	26.7	13.4	2.8
Transportation and material moving	100.0	4.5	9.7	20.1	23.8	24.0	13.7	4.2

Source: Bureau of Labor Statistics, unpublished data from the 2007 Current Population Survey; calculations by New Strategist

The Middle Aged Work Full-Time

Part-time employment is more common among young and old.

There are sharp differences in who works part-time by age. While the majority of all workers have full-time schedules, 28 percent of workers in their early twenties and 22 percent of those aged 55 or older work part-time. The smallest share of part-time workers is found among 25-to-54-year-olds, only 11 percent of whom work part-time.

Reasons for working part-time vary by age. For those under age 25, school attendance and the fact that many still live at home with their parents influence their decision to take part-time jobs. For older Americans, part-time work provides a transition between full-time careers and full-time retirement.

Women of all ages are more likely than men to have part-time jobs. Two-thirds of the nation's part-time workers are women. But most women work full-time. Among women aged 25 to 54 who work, 81 percent have a full-time job.

■ Among the generations born after World War II, full-time work is the norm for both men and women. While this creates a time squeeze for most families, it also provides them with a middle-class lifestyle.

Teenagers are most likely to work part-time

(percent of employed people who work part-time, by age, 2007)

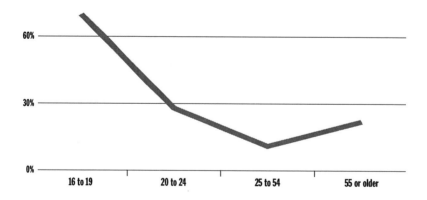

Table 7.10 Full-Time and Part-Time Workers by Age and Sex, 2007

(number and percent distribution of employed people aged 16 or older by age, employment status, and sex, 2007; numbers in thousands)

	total			men			women		
	total	full-time	part-time	total	full-time	part-time	total	full-time	part-time
Total employed	146,047	121,091	24,956	78,255	70,035	8,220	67,792	51,056	16,736
Aged 16 to 19	5,911	1,774	4,137	2,918	1,067	1,851	2,994	708	2,286
Aged 20 to 24	13,963	10,001	3,962	7,374	5,724	1,650	6,589	4,277	2,312
Aged 25 to 54	100,450	89,252	11,198	54,328	51,774	2,554	46,122	37,478	8,644
Aged 55 or older	25,722	20,063	5,659	13,635	11,470	2,165	12,087	8,593	3,494
Percent distribution by employment status									
Total employed	100.0%	82.9%	17.1%	100.0%	89.5%	10.5%	100.0%	75.3%	24.7%
Aged 16 to 19	100.0	30.0	70.0	100.0	36.6	63.4	100.0	23.6	76.4
Aged 20 to 24	100.0	71.6	28.4	100.0	77.6	22.4	100.0	64.9	35.1
Aged 25 to 54	100.0	88.9	11.1	100.0	95.3	4.7	100.0	81.3	18.7
Aged 55 or older	100.0	78.0	22.0	100.0	84.1	15.9	100.0	71.1	28.9
Percent distribution by age									
Total employed	100.0%	100.0%	100.0%	100.0%	100.0%	100.0%	100.0%	100.0%	100.0%
Aged 16 to 19	4.0	1.5	16.6	3.7	1.5	22.5	4.4	1.4	13.7
Aged 20 to 24	9.6	8.3	15.9	9.4	8.2	20.1	9.7	8.4	13.8
Aged 25 to 54	68.8	73.7	44.9	69.4	73.9	31.1	68.0	73.4	51.6
Aged 55 or older	17.6	16.6	22.7	17.4	16.4	26.3	17.8	16.8	20.9

Source: Bureau of Labor Statistics, Current Population Survey, Internet site http://www.bls.gov/cps/home.htm; calculations by New Strategist

Dual Earners Are the Norm

Working wives help families reach middle-class status.

The majority of married couples are dual earners. Both husband and wife were in the labor force in 54 percent of married couples in 2006. Only 22 percent of today's couples follow traditional sex roles in which only the husband works while the wife stays home.

The largest share of two-income couples is found among people aged 40 to 44—71 percent are dual earners. For the majority of couples aged 65 or older, both husband and wife no longer work. Married couples aged 55 to 64 are most likely to have a working wife and a nonworking husband. In most of these cases, a slightly younger wife is continuing to work after her husband has retired.

■ Two incomes are now needed to maintain a middle-class standard of living. But it comes at a cost—with both husband and wife in the workforce, families have much less time for other activities.

Most couples under age 55 are dual earners

(percent of married couples in which both husband and wife are in the labor force, by age, 2006)

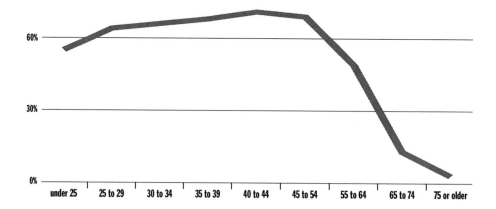

Table 7.11   Labor Force Status of Married-Couple Family Groups, 2006

(number and percent distribution of married-couple family groups aged 20 or older by age of householder and labor force status of husband and wife, 2006; numbers in thousands)

	total	husband and/or wife in labor force			neither husband nor wife in labor force
		husband and wife	husband only	wife only	
Married couples	**59,528**	**32,415**	**13,344**	**3,827**	**9,942**
Aged 20 to 24	1,589	873	610	65	43
Aged 25 to 29	4,092	2,627	1,286	94	85
Aged 30 to 34	5,595	3,710	1,650	158	78
Aged 35 to 39	6,467	4,398	1,782	176	111
Aged 40 to 44	7,123	5,083	1,654	269	118
Aged 45 to 54	13,886	9,634	2,939	795	518
Aged 55 to 64	10,639	5,185	2,248	1,405	1,802
Aged 65 to 74	6,116	776	919	684	3,738
Aged 75 or older	4,021	135	255	183	3,448
Married couples	**100.0%**	**54.5%**	**22.4%**	**6.4%**	**16.7%**
Aged 20 to 24	100.0	54.9	38.4	4.1	2.7
Aged 25 to 29	100.0	64.2	31.4	2.3	2.1
Aged 30 to 34	100.0	66.3	29.5	2.8	1.4
Aged 35 to 39	100.0	68.0	27.6	2.7	1.7
Aged 40 to 44	100.0	71.4	23.2	3.8	1.7
Aged 45 to 54	100.0	69.4	21.2	5.7	3.7
Aged 55 to 64	100.0	48.7	21.1	13.2	16.9
Aged 65 to 74	100.0	12.7	15.0	11.2	61.1
Aged 75 or older	100.0	3.4	6.3	4.6	85.7

Source: Bureau of the Census, America's Families and Living Arrangements: 2006, detailed tables, Internet site http://www .census.gov/population/www/socdemo/hh-fam/cps2006.html; calculations by New Strategist

Working Mothers Are the Norm

Single mothers are most likely to work.

The statistic that says the most about the revolutionary changes in sex roles over the past few decades is the labor force participation rate of mothers with young children. As younger generations of Americans have matured, new mothers have been increasingly likely to work. Fewer than one-third of mothers with children under age 1 were working in 1976, according to the Census Bureau. In 2006, 52 percent were in the labor force, most of them working full-time. Mothers with school-aged children are most likely to work, with a labor force participation rate of 74 percent in 2006.

Among married women with children under age 18, the 69 percent majority is in the labor force and 48 percent work full-time. Among single mothers, 77 percent are in the labor force and 58 percent work full-time.

■ The Millennial generation has grown up with working parents. As a result, many are developing independence and responsibility at a young age.

Most mothers with infants are in the labor force

(labor force status of mothers with children under age 1, 2006)

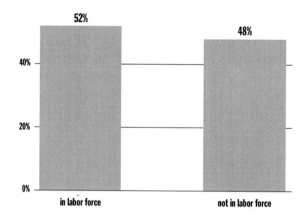

Table 7.12 Labor Force Status of Women by Presence of Children, 2006

(number and percent distribution of women by labor force status and presence and age of own children under age 18 at home, 2006; numbers in thousands)

| | civilian population | civilian labor force | | | |
| | | total | employed | | |
			total	full-time	part-time
TOTAL WOMEN	**118,210**	**70,173**	**66,926**	**50,381**	**16,545**
No children under age 18	**81,718**	**44,312**	**42,312**	**31,780**	**10,532**
With children under age 18	**36,492**	**25,861**	**24,614**	**18,601**	**6,013**
Children aged 6 to 17, none younger	20,318	15,585	14,952	11,629	3,323
Children under age 6	16,174	10,276	9,661	6,972	2,689
Children under age 3	9,431	5,675	5,315	3,751	1,564
Children under age 1	3,248	1,822	1,686	1,166	520
TOTAL WOMEN	**100.0%**	**59.4%**	**56.6%**	**42.6%**	**14.0%**
No children under age 18	**100.0**	**54.2**	**51.8**	**38.9**	**12.9**
With children under age 18	**100.0**	**70.9**	**67.5**	**51.0**	**16.5**
Children aged 6 to 17, none younger	100.0	76.7	73.6	57.2	16.4
Children under age 6	100.0	63.5	59.7	43.1	16.6
Children under age 3	100.0	60.2	56.4	39.8	16.6
Children under age 1	100.0	56.1	51.9	35.9	16.0

Source: Bureau of Labor Statistics, Employment Characteristics of Families, Internet site http://www.bls.gov/news.release/famee.toc.htm

Table 7.13   Employed Parents by Age of Child, 2006

(number and percent distribution of parents with own children under age 18 at home, and percent in the labor force by age of youngest child, marital status, and sex, 2006; numbers in thousands)

	number			percent distribution		
	total parents	fathers	mothers	total parents	fathers	mothers
WITH CHILDREN UNDER AGE 18						
Total	**64,680**	**28,188**	**36,492**	**100.0%**	**100.0%**	**100.0%**
In labor force	52,391	26,530	25,861	81.0	94.1	70.9
Employed full-time	43,485	24,884	18,601	67.2	88.3	51.0
Employed part-time	6,902	890	6,013	10.7	3.2	16.5
Unemployed	2,004	756	1,247	3.1	2.7	3.4
Married						
Total	**51,670**	**25,648**	**26,022**	**100.0**	**100.0**	**100.0**
In labor force	42,136	24,295	17,842	81.5	94.7	68.6
Employed full-time	35,500	22,925	12,575	68.7	89.4	48.3
Employed part-time	5,460	755	4,705	10.6	2.9	18.1
Unemployed	1,176	614	562	2.3	2.4	2.2
Not married						
Total	**13,010**	**2,541**	**10,470**	**100.0**	**100.0**	**100.0**
In labor force	10,255	2,236	8,019	78.8	88.0	76.6
Employed full-time	7,985	1,960	6,026	61.4	77.1	57.6
Employed part-time	1,442	134	1,308	11.1	5.3	12.5
Unemployed	827	142	686	6.4	5.6	6.6
WITH YOUNGEST CHILD AGED 6 TO 17						
Total	**35,912**	**15,594**	**20,318**	**100.0**	**100.0**	**100.0**
In labor force	30,100	14,515	15,585	83.8	93.1	76.7
Employed full-time	25,277	13,648	11,629	70.4	87.5	57.2
Employed part-time	3,799	476	3,323	10.6	3.1	16.4
Unemployed	1,024	392	632	2.9	2.5	3.1
WITH YOUNGEST CHILD UNDER AGE 6						
Total	**28,768**	**12,594**	**16,174**	**100.0**	**100.0**	**100.0**
In labor force	22,291	12,015	10,276	77.5	95.4	63.5
Employed full-time	18,208	11,236	6,972	63.3	89.2	43.1
Employed part-time	3,103	414	2,689	10.8	3.3	16.6
Unemployed	980	365	615	3.4	2.9	3.8

Note: "Not married" includes never married, divorced, separated, and widowed.
Source: Bureau of Labor Statistics, Employment Characteristics of Families, Internet site http://www.bls.gov/news.release/famee.toc.htm

Job Tenure Is Declining for the Middle Aged

Fewer workers have been with their current employer for 10 or more years.

The number of years workers have been with their current employer is falling in most age groups. The biggest drop has been among men aged 55 to 64. Median tenure for men in the age group fell from 10.5 years in 1996 to 9.5 years in 2006. Among women in the age group, median job tenure fell from 10.0 to 9.2 years.

Long-term employment is less common among both men and women. Layoffs, among other factors, have reduced the proportion of workers who have been with their current employer for at least 10 years. The biggest change has been among middle-aged men. In 1996, 51 percent of men aged 45 to 49 had been with their current employer for at least 10 years, but by 2006 the share had dropped to 43 percent. Long-term employment has fallen for men in every age group. Among women, it has declined in all but the oldest age group.

■ The decline in long-term employment could reduce retirement savings for many workers.

Long-term employment has fallen sharply among men aged 45 to 49

(percent of men aged 45 to 49 who have been with their current employer for ten or more years, 1996 and 2006)

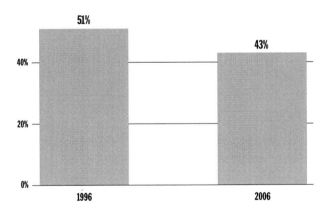

Table 7.14 Tenure with Current Employer by Sex and Age, 1996 to 2006

(median number of years workers aged 25 or older have been with their current employer by sex and age, and change in years, 1996 to 2006)

	2006	2000	1996	change in years 1996–2006
Total, aged 25 or older	**4.9**	**4.7**	**5.0**	**−0.1**
Aged 25 to 34	2.9	2.6	2.8	0.1
Aged 35 to 44	4.9	4.8	5.3	−0.4
Aged 45 to 54	7.3	8.2	8.3	−1.0
Aged 55 to 64	9.3	10.0	10.2	−0.9
Aged 65 or older	8.8	9.4	8.4	0.4
Men, aged 25 or older	**5.0**	**4.9**	**5.3**	**−0.3**
Aged 25 to 34	2.9	2.7	3.0	−0.1
Aged 35 to 44	5.1	5.3	6.1	−1.0
Aged 45 to 54	8.1	9.5	10.1	−2.0
Aged 55 to 64	9.5	10.2	10.5	−1.0
Aged 65 or older	8.3	9.0	8.3	0.0
Women, aged 25 or older	**4.7**	**4.4**	**4.7**	**0.0**
Aged 25 to 34	2.8	2.5	2.7	0.1
Aged 35 to 44	4.5	4.3	4.8	−0.3
Aged 45 to 54	6.4	7.3	7.0	−0.6
Aged 55 to 64	9.2	9.9	10.0	−0.8
Aged 65 or older	9.6	9.7	8.4	1.2

Source: Bureau of Labor Statistics, Employee Tenure, Internet site http://www.bls.gov/news.release/tenure.toc.htm; calculations by New Strategist

Table 7.15 Long-Term Employment by Sex and Age, 1996 to 2006

(percent of workers aged 25 or older who have worked for their current employer ten years or more by sex and age, and percentage point change, 1996 to 2006)

	2006	2000	1996	percentage point change 1996–2006
Total, aged 25 or older	**30.0%**	**31.5%**	**30.5%**	**–0.5**
Aged 25 to 29	2.4	2.5	2.8	–0.4
Aged 30 to 34	10.6	13.9	14.7	–4.1
Aged 35 to 39	22.8	26.1	26.9	–4.1
Aged 40 to 44	31.8	35.8	36.1	–4.3
Aged 45 to 49	39.9	45.2	44.5	–4.6
Aged 50 to 54	46.6	48.7	50.4	–3.8
Aged 55 to 59	50.1	53.1	54.0	–3.9
Aged 60 to 64	48.4	53.0	51.5	–3.1
Aged 65 or older	48.5	49.8	47.4	1.1
Men, aged 25 or older	**31.1**	**33.4**	**33.1**	**–2.0**
Aged 25 to 29	2.6	3.0	3.3	–0.7
Aged 30 to 34	11.6	15.1	15.6	–4.0
Aged 35 to 39	24.7	29.4	30.5	–5.8
Aged 40 to 44	34.8	40.2	41.7	–6.9
Aged 45 to 49	42.9	49.0	50.8	–7.9
Aged 50 to 54	49.7	51.6	54.9	–5.2
Aged 55 to 59	51.0	53.7	55.7	–4.7
Aged 60 to 64	48.1	52.4	50.4	–2.3
Aged 65 or older	47.2	48.6	47.6	–0.4
Women, aged 25 or older	**28.8**	**29.5**	**27.6**	**1.2**
Aged 25 to 29	2.1	1.9	2.2	–0.1
Aged 30 to 34	9.4	12.5	13.6	–4.2
Aged 35 to 39	20.5	22.3	22.9	–2.4
Aged 40 to 44	28.4	31.2	30.4	–2.0
Aged 45 to 49	36.9	41.4	38.1	–1.2
Aged 50 to 54	43.6	45.8	45.8	–2.2
Aged 55 to 59	49.1	52.5	52.1	–3.0
Aged 60 to 64	48.7	53.6	52.7	–4.0
Aged 65 or older	49.9	51.0	47.2	2.7

Source: Bureau of Labor Statistics, Employee Tenure, Internet site http://www.bls.gov/news.release/tenure.toc.htm; calculations by New Strategist

Union Representation Peaks among Workers Aged 55 to 64

Men are more likely than women to be represented by unions.

Union representation is lower in every age group today than it was 30 years ago. In 1970, 30 percent of nonagricultural workers were represented by labor unions. In 2007, the figure had fallen to just 13 percent.

Union representation peaks in the 55-to-64 age group at 18 percent. Representation is almost as high among workers aged 45 to 54, at 17 percent. Younger workers are considerably less likely to be represented by a union. Only 14 percent of workers aged 35 to 44 and just 11 percent of those aged 25 to 34 have union representation.

Men are more likely than women to be represented by a union, largely because they are more likely to work in jobs that are the traditional strongholds of labor unions. In fact, the decline of labor unions is partly the result of a shift in jobs from manufacturing to services. Among men, union representation peaks at 18 percent in the 45-to-64 age groups. Among women, representation peaks at 17 percent in the 55 to 64 age group.

■ Union representation is unlikely to rise unless unions focus more on service jobs and less on manufacturing.

Few workers are represented by unions

(percent of employed wage and salary workers who are represented by unions, by age, 2007)

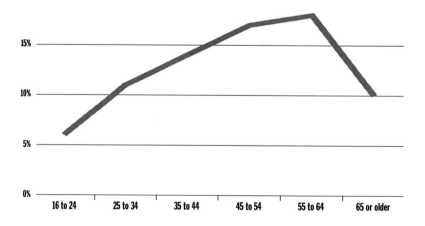

Table 7.16   Union Representation by Sex and Age, 2007

(number of employed wage and salary workers aged 16 or older, and number and percent who are represented by unions, by sex and age, 2007; numbers in thousands)

		represented by union	
	total employed	number	percent
Total people	**129,767**	**17,243**	**13.3%**
Aged 16 to 24	19,395	1,068	5.5
Aged 25 to 34	29,409	3,358	11.4
Aged 35 to 44	30,296	4,362	14.4
Aged 45 to 54	29,731	5,087	17.1
Aged 55 to 64	16,752	2,967	17.7
Aged 65 or older	4,183	402	9.6
Total men	**67,468**	**9,494**	**14.1**
Aged 16 to 24	9,959	627	6.3
Aged 25 to 34	15,994	1,884	11.8
Aged 35 to 44	16,070	2,501	15.6
Aged 45 to 54	15,040	2,745	18.3
Aged 55 to 64	8,286	1,532	18.5
Aged 65 or older	2,119	205	9.7
Total women	**62,299**	**7,749**	**12.4**
Aged 16 to 24	9,436	441	4.7
Aged 25 to 34	13,416	1,474	11.0
Aged 35 to 44	14,226	1,861	13.1
Aged 45 to 54	14,691	2,341	15.9
Aged 55 to 64	8,466	1,435	17.0
Aged 65 or older	2,065	197	9.5

Source: Bureau of Labor Statistics, Current Population Survey, Internet site http://www.bls.gov/cps/home.htm

One in Four Workers Has a Flexible Schedule

Flexible schedules are most common among older men.

American workers have long voiced a desire for more flexibility in their work schedules to make it easier to balance work and family. Today, more than one in four workers has a flexible work schedule, meaning they can vary the time they start or end their workday.

Surprisingly, the proportion of workers with flexible schedules varies little by age—despite the fact that home and family responsibilities peak in the 25-to-44 age group. Men aged 65 or older are the only ones significantly more likely than average to have a flexible work schedule, with 41 percent able to vary the beginning or end of their workday. Women are no more likely than men to have flexible work hours, despite their greater responsibility for home and family.

■ As older Americans increasingly postpone retirement, the proportion of workers aged 65 or older with flexible schedules should rise.

The oldest workers are most likely to have flexible schedules

(percent of workers with flexible work hours, by age, 2004)

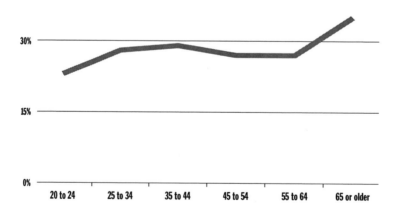

Table 7.17   Workers with Flexible Schedules, 2004

(number and percent of full-time wage and salary workers aged 20 or older with flexible work schedules, by age and sex, 2004; numbers in thousands)

	total		men		women	
	number	percent	number	percent	number	percent
Total workers	**27,075**	**27.5%**	**15,668**	**28.2%**	**11,406**	**26.6%**
Aged 20 to 24	2,058	22.9	1,065	20.7	993	25.8
Aged 25 to 34	6,902	28.0	4,051	28.2	2,851	27.7
Aged 35 to 44	7,807	29.2	4,605	29.9	3,202	28.2
Aged 45 to 54	6,651	26.8	3,769	28.0	2,882	25.2
Aged 55 to 64	3,181	27.1	1,865	29.2	1,316	24.5
Aged 65 or older	475	35.4	314	41.4	161	27.6

Note: Flexible work schedules are those that allow workers to vary the time they begin and end work.
Source: Bureau of Labor Statistics, Workers on Flexible and Shift Schedules in 2004, Internet site http://www.bls.gov/news
.release/flex.toc.htm

Older Workers Are Most Likely to Be Independent Contractors

Rather than retire, many older workers strike out on their own.

More than one in ten workers are employed in alternative work arrangements—independent contractors, on-call workers, workers for temporary-help agencies, or workers provided by contract firms. These types of work are considered alternative because workers are not employees of the organization for which they perform their services, nor do they necessarily work standard schedules. Most alternative workers are independent contractors—freelancers, consultants, real estate agents, and others who obtain their own customers. Many independent contractors are self-employed.

The proportion of workers who are independent contractors rises with age. Among workers aged 25 to 34, only 5 percent are independent contractors, but the figure rises to 18 percent among those aged 65 or older. Differences by age are less pronounced for other types of alternative workers.

■ Older workers have the freedom to be independent contractors because they are covered by Medicare, the government's universal health insurance program for people aged 65 or older.

Few young adults are independent contractors

(percent of the employed who are independent contractors, by age, 2005)

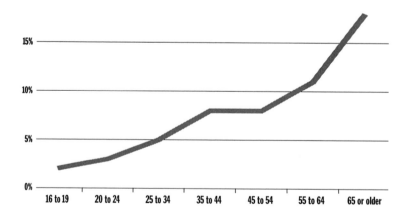

Table 7.18 Alternative Work Arrangements by Age, 2005

(number and percent distribution of employed workers aged 16 or older by alternative work arrangement and age, 2005; numbers in thousands)

	total workers	alternative workers				
		total	independent contractors	on-call workers	temporary help agency workers	workers provided by contract firms
Total people	138,952	14,826	10,342	2,454	1,217	813
Aged 16 to 19	5,510	262	89	133	33	7
Aged 20 to 24	13,114	1,000	356	355	202	87
Aged 25 to 34	30,103	2,622	1,520	535	362	205
Aged 35 to 44	34,481	3,774	2,754	571	253	196
Aged 45 to 54	32,947	3,602	2,799	417	200	186
Aged 55 to 64	17,980	2,459	1,943	267	135	114
Aged 65 or older	4,817	1,107	881	175	33	18
Percent distribution by age						
Total people	100.0%	100.0%	100.0%	100.0%	100.0%	100.0%
Aged 16 to 19	4.0	1.8	0.9	5.4	2.7	0.9
Aged 20 to 24	9.4	6.7	3.4	14.5	16.6	10.7
Aged 25 to 34	21.7	17.7	14.7	21.8	29.7	25.2
Aged 35 to 44	24.8	25.5	26.6	23.3	20.8	24.1
Aged 45 to 54	23.7	24.3	27.1	17.0	16.4	22.9
Aged 55 to 64	12.9	16.6	18.8	10.9	11.1	14.0
Aged 65 or older	3.5	7.5	8.5	7.1	2.7	2.2
Percent distribution by work status						
Total people	100.0%	10.7%	7.4%	1.8%	0.9%	0.6%
Aged 16 to 19	100.0	4.8	1.6	2.4	0.6	0.1
Aged 20 to 24	100.0	7.6	2.7	2.7	1.5	0.7
Aged 25 to 34	100.0	8.7	5.0	1.8	1.2	0.7
Aged 35 to 44	100.0	10.9	8.0	1.7	0.7	0.6
Aged 45 to 54	100.0	10.9	8.5	1.3	0.6	0.6
Aged 55 to 64	100.0	13.7	10.8	1.5	0.8	0.6
Aged 65 or older	100.0	23.0	18.3	3.6	0.7	0.4

Note: Numbers may not add to total because the total includes day laborers, an alternative arrangement not shown separately, and because a small number of workers were both on call and provided by contract firms. Independent contractors are self-employed (except incorporated) or wage and salary workers who obtain customers on their own to provide a product or service. On-call workers are in a pool of workers who are called to work only as needed, such as substitute teachers and construction workers supplied by a union hiring hall. Temporary help agency workers are those who said they are paid by a temporary help agency. Workers provided by contract firms are those employed by a company that provides employees or their services to others under contract, such as security, landscaping, and conputer programming.
Source: Bureau of Labor Statistics, Contingent and Alternative Employment Arrangements, February 2005, Internet site http:// www.bls.gov/news.release/conemp.toc.htm; calculations by New Strategist

Self-Employment Rises with Age

Few people under age 65 are self-employed.

Many Americans say they would like to be their own boss. But few people actually attain this goal—only 7 percent of workers are self-employed.

The self-employment rate rises with age. Only 1 to 3 percent of workers under age 25 are self-employed. Among workers aged 25 to 54, only 5 to 9 percent are self-employed. The rate rises slightly to 11 percent among workers aged 55 to 64 as people begin to make the transition from work to retirement. A much larger 18 percent of workers aged 65 or older are self-employed as the Medicare health insurance program frees them from the need to find a job with health insurance coverage.

Men are more likely than women to be self-employed, especially among older workers. Twenty percent of working men aged 65 or older are self-employed compared with 14 percent of their female counterparts.

■ The self-employment rate among older Americans is likely to grow as Boomers reach their 65th birthday and discover they cannot afford to retire.

Older workers are most likely to be self-employed

(percent of workers who are self-employed, by age, 2007)

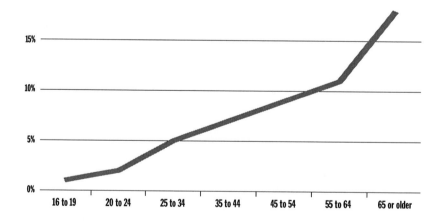

Table 7.19 Self-Employed Workers by Sex and Age, 2007

(number of people aged 16 or older in the labor force, number and percent who are self-employed, and percent distribution of self-employed, by sex and age, 2007; numbers in thousands)

		self-employed		
	total employed	number	percent of total	percent distribution
Total people	**146,047**	**10,413**	**7.1%**	**100.0%**
Aged 16 to 19	5,911	81	1.4	0.8
Aged 20 to 24	13,964	290	2.1	2.8
Aged 25 to 34	31,586	1,501	4.8	14.4
Aged 35 to 44	34,302	2,447	7.1	23.5
Aged 45 to 54	34,562	2,972	8.6	28.5
Aged 55 to 64	20,108	2,139	10.6	20.5
Aged 65 or older	5,613	985	17.5	9.5
Total men	**78,254**	**6,543**	**8.4**	**100.0**
Aged 16 to 19	2,917	55	1.9	0.8
Aged 20 to 24	7,373	201	2.7	3.1
Aged 25 to 34	17,452	961	5.5	14.7
Aged 35 to 44	18,666	1,498	8.0	22.9
Aged 45 to 54	18,210	1,834	10.1	28.0
Aged 55 to 64	10,556	1,370	13.0	20.9
Aged 65 or older	3,080	625	20.3	9.6
Total women	**67,792**	**3,870**	**5.7**	**100.0**
Aged 16 to 19	2,994	26	0.9	0.7
Aged 20 to 24	6,590	88	1.3	2.3
Aged 25 to 34	14,133	538	3.8	13.9
Aged 35 to 44	15,636	949	6.1	24.5
Aged 45 to 54	16,353	1,137	7.0	29.4
Aged 55 to 64	9,552	769	8.1	19.9
Aged 65 or older	2,534	362	14.3	9.4

Source: Bureau of Labor Statistics, Current Population Survey, Internet site http://www.bls.gov/cps/home.htm

Most Minimum-Wage Workers Are Teens or Young Adults

Even among teenagers, however, minimum-wage pay is uncommon.

Among the nation's 77 million workers who are paid hourly rates, fewer than 2 million (2 percent) made minimum wage or less in 2006, according to the Bureau of Labor Statistics. Of those minimum-wage workers, more than half (51 percent) are under age 25.

Among workers paid hourly rates in the 16-to-19 age group, just 8 percent earn minimum wage or less. Among those in the 20-to-24 age group, an even smaller 4 percent are minimum-wage workers. The proportion falls with age to just 0.9 percent of workers in the 55-to-64 age group. Among workers aged 65 or older, a larger 2 percent earn minimum wage or less.

■ The minimum wage is scheduled to increase over the next few years, but most employers had already boosted the wages of their employees.

Teens and young adults are most likely to be minimum wage workers

(percent of workers making minimum wage or less, by age, 2006)

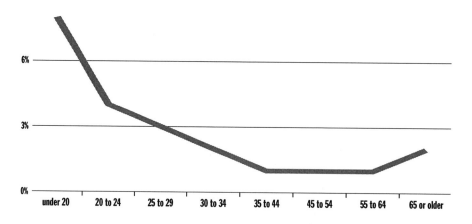

Table 7.20 Minimum Wage Workers, 2006

(number and percent distribution of total workers paid hourly rates and those paid at or below minimum wage, by age, 2006; numbers in thousands)

	total paid hourly rates	at or below minimum wage		
		total	at $5.15/hour	below $5.15/hour
Total aged 16 or older	**76,514**	**1,692**	**409**	**1,283**
Aged 16 to 19	5,687	436	165	271
Aged 20 to 24	10,962	430	82	348
Aged 25 to 29	9,187	241	36	205
Aged 30 to 34	7,833	117	15	102
Aged 35 to 44	16,396	191	32	159
Aged 45 to 54	15,672	150	31	119
Aged 55 to 64	8,402	72	24	48
Aged 65 or older	2,376	55	24	31
Percent distribution by age				
Total aged 16 or older	**100.0%**	**100.0%**	**100.0%**	**100.0%**
Aged 16 to 19	7.4	25.8	40.3	21.1
Aged 20 to 24	14.3	25.4	20.0	27.1
Aged 25 to 29	12.0	14.2	8.8	16.0
Aged 30 to 34	10.2	6.9	3.7	8.0
Aged 35 to 44	21.4	11.3	7.8	12.4
Aged 45 to 54	20.5	8.9	7.6	9.3
Aged 55 to 64	11.0	4.3	5.9	3.7
Aged 65 or older	3.1	3.3	5.9	2.4
Percent distribution by wage status				
Total aged 16 or older	**100.0%**	**2.2%**	**0.5%**	**1.7%**
Aged 16 to 19	100.0	7.7	2.9	4.8
Aged 20 to 24	100.0	3.9	0.7	3.2
Aged 25 to 29	100.0	2.6	0.4	2.2
Aged 30 to 34	100.0	1.5	0.2	1.3
Aged 35 to 44	100.0	1.2	0.2	1.0
Aged 45 to 54	100.0	1.0	0.2	0.8
Aged 55 to 64	100.0	0.9	0.3	0.6
Aged 65 or older	100.0	2.3	1.0	1.3

Source: Bureau of Labor Statistics, Characteristics of Minimum Wage Workers: 2006, Internet site http://www.bls.gov/cps/ minwage2006.htm; calculations by New Strategist

More Older Workers Will Be in the Labor Force

Participation rates are projected to climb in the older age groups.

The trend toward ever-earlier retirement has come to an end. Labor force participation rates among older men and women are projected to climb, according to the Bureau of Labor Statistics. Men's overall labor force participation rate should fall by 1 percentage point between 2006 and 2016, but only because of a decline in participation among younger men and the aging of the population. Labor force participation among men aged 65 or older is projected to climb by 7 percentage points between 2006 and 2016, to 27.1 percent. Women's labor force participation rate also will rise in the older age groups, with the biggest gain (6 percentage points) slotted for those aged 65 or older.

As Boomers age into their sixties, the number of older workers will soar. The number of workers aged 55 to 64 is projected to increase 51 percent between 2006 and 2016. The number of workers aged 65 or older should climb 43 percent.

■ Many Baby Boomers will have to stay in the labor force until they become eligible for Medicare at age 65.

The number of workers aged 55 or older will grow rapidly

(percent change in number of workers, by age, 2006 to 2016)

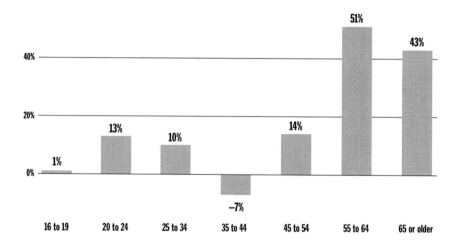

Table 7.21 Labor Force Projections by Sex and Age, 2006 and 2016

(number and percent of people aged 16 or older in the civilian labor force by sex and age, 2006 and 2016; percent change in number and percentage point change in rate 2006–16; numbers in thousands)

	number			participation rate		
	2006	2016	percent change 2006–16	2006	2016	percentage point change 2006–16
Total labor force	**151,428**	**164,232**	**8.5%**	**66.2%**	**65.5%**	**−0.7**
Aged 16 to 19	7,281	5,896	0.7	43.7	37.5	−6.2
Aged 20 to 24	15,113	14,955	13.3	74.6	71.8	−2.8
Aged 25 to 34	32,573	37,289	10.0	83.0	85.4	2.4
Aged 35 to 44	35,848	33,654	−6.8	83.8	83.3	−0.5
Aged 45 to 54	35,146	35,083	13.6	81.9	82.1	0.2
Aged 55 to 64	19,984	27,288	50.9	63.7	66.7	3.0
Aged 65 or older	5,484	10,066	43.4	15.4	21.7	6.3
Men in labor force	**81,255**	**87,781**	**10.0**	**73.5**	**72.3**	**−1.2**
Aged 16 to 19	3,693	2,923	−2.0	43.7	36.8	−6.9
Aged 20 to 24	8,116	7,992	11.6	79.6	76.4	−3.2
Aged 25 to 34	17,944	20,913	8.4	91.7	95.7	4.0
Aged 35 to 44	19,407	18,373	-8.0	92.1	91.7	−0.4
Aged 45 to 54	18,489	18,205	11.5	88.1	86.6	−1.5
Aged 55 to 64	10,509	13,865	45.3	69.6	70.1	0.5
Aged 65 or older	3,096	5,511	43.2	20.3	27.1	6.8
Women in labor force	**70,173**	**76,450**	**14.3**	**59.4**	**59.2**	**−0.2**
Aged 16 to 19	3,588	2,974	3.5	43.7	38.3	−5.4
Aged 20 to 24	6,997	6,963	15.1	69.5	67.2	−2.3
Aged 25 to 34	14,628	16,376	11.9	74.4	75.0	0.6
Aged 35 to 44	16,441	15,281	-5.3	75.9	75.1	−0.8
Aged 45 to 54	16,656	16,877	15.9	76.0	77.8	1.8
Aged 55 to 64	9,475	13,423	57.5	58.2	63.5	5.3
Aged 65 or older	2,388	4,556	43.7	11.7	17.5	5.8

Source: Bureau of Labor Statistics, Labor force projections to 2016: more workers in their golden years, Monthly Labor Review, November 2007, Internet site http://www.bls.gov/opub/mlr/2007/11/contents.htm; calculations by New Strategist

8

Living Arrangements

Baby Boomers and younger generations have changed American family life. As women delayed marriage and childbearing, the proportion of households with children has been shrinking, reaching a low of 32 percent in 2006. As Boomers and Generation Xers divorced, the nuclear family became less common. Mom, dad, and the kids are found in less than one-quarter of the nation's households today.

Among older Americans, rising affluence and improved health has allowed more people to live alone following the death of a spouse. Men and women who live alone now head 27 percent of the nation's households, outnumbering married couples with children under age 18.

What to expect in the future

■ The number of households headed by people aged 65 or older will grow rapidly as Boomers fill the age group.

■ Older married couples without children at home will become an increasingly important household segment as Boomers become empty-nesters.

■ As Millennials enter their thirties and have children, expect the number of households with preschoolers to expand.

Boomers Head the Largest Share of Households

Households headed by Generation Xers rank second in importance.

The middle aged dominate the nation's 116 million households because the large Baby-Boom generation is now in its forties, fifties, and sixties. Householders aged 43 to 61, the ages of the Baby-Boom in 2007, head 37 percent of households. The number of households headed by 55-to-64-year-olds grew by a substantial 42 percent between 2000 and 2007.

Generation Xers, aged 31 to 42 in 2007, account for 22 percent of households. As Generation X replaces the larger Baby-Boom generation in the 35-to-44 age group, the number of households headed by 35-to-44-year-olds fell 5 percent between 2000 and 2007.

The Millennial generation, the oldest of whom turned 30 in 2007, head 16 percent of households. Although the Millennial generation is second only to Boomers in population size, they head fewer households than Generation X because many still live with mom and dad. Soon, however, the number of households headed by Millennials will surpass the number headed by Generation Xers.

The Swing and World War II generations (people aged 62 or older) headed 25 percent of the nation's households in 2007. The percentage of households headed by the two older generations is shrinking.

■ The nation's households are dominated by older Americans, with people aged 50 or older heading nearly half (47 percent).

The Swing and WW II generations head the smallest share of households

(percent distribution of households by generation of householder, 2007)

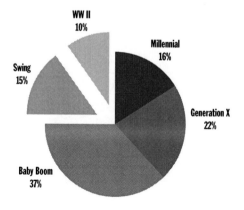

Table 8.1 Households by Age of Householder, 2000 and 2007

(number and percent distribution of households by age of householder, 2000 and 2007; percent change in number, 2000–07; numbers in thousands)

	2007		2000		percent change in number 2000–07
	number	percent distribution	number	percent distribution	
Total households	**116,011**	**100.0%**	**104,705**	**100.0%**	**10.8%**
Under age 25	6,662	5.7	5,860	5.6	13.7
Aged 25 to 34	19,435	16.8	18,627	17.8	4.3
Aged 35 to 44	22,779	19.6	23,955	22.9	–4.9
Aged 45 to 54	24,140	20.8	20,927	20.0	15.4
Aged 55 to 64	19,266	16.6	13,592	13.0	41.7
Aged 65 or older	23,729	20.5	21,745	20.8	9.1
Aged 65 to 74	11,926	10.3	11,325	10.8	5.3
Aged 75 or older	11,803	10.2	10,419	10.0	13.3

Source: Bureau of the Census, 2007 Current Population Survey Annual Social and Economic Supplement, Internet site http:// pubdb3.census.gov/macro/032007/hhinc/toc.htm; calculations by New Strategist

Table 8.2 Households by Age and Generation of Householder, 2007

(number and percent distribution of households by age and generation of householder, 2007; numbers in thousands)

	number	percent distribution
Total households	**116,011**	**100.0%**
Aged 15 to 24	6,662	5.7
Aged 25 to 29	9,667	8.3
Aged 30 to 34	9,767	8.4
Aged 35 to 39	10,841	9.3
Aged 40 to 44	11,938	10.3
Aged 45 to 49	12,604	10.9
Aged 50 to 54	11,537	9.9
Aged 55 to 59	10,767	9.3
Aged 60 to 64	8,499	7.3
Aged 65 to 69	6,642	5.7
Aged 70 to 74	5,284	4.6
Aged 75 or older	11,803	10.2
Households by generation		
Millennial (15 to 30)	18,282	15.8
Generation X (31 to 42)	25,817	22.3
Baby Boom (43 to 61)	43,083	37.1
Swing (62 to 74)	17,025	14.7
World War II (75 or older)	11,803	10.2

Note: Households by generation are estimates by New Strategist.
Source: Bureau of the Census, 2007 Current Population Survey Annual Social and Economic Supplement, Internet site http://pubdb3.census.gov/macro/032007/hhinc/toc.htm; calculations by New Strategist

Young and Old Have the Most Diverse Households

The majority of middle-aged households are married couples.

Households are most diverse among the youngest and the oldest adults. They are most alike among the middle-aged.

Many Millennials still live with their parents. Among Millennials who head their own household, only 35 percent are married couple householders. An even larger 39 percent are nonfamily householders, including 23 percent who live alone.

Married couples account for the 57 to 58 percent majority of households headed by Generation Xers and Boomers. The figure is a smaller 53 percent among the Swing generation and falls to just 34 percent for the World War II generation as widowhood becomes common.

Overall, people who live alone head 27 percent of the nation's households. The percentage is as low as 16 percent among Gen Xers and reaches the 55 percent majority among the World War II generation. Women who live alone account for 43 percent of households headed by the World War II generation, while men who live alone account for a smaller 12 percent.

■ Because the population is aging, the share of households headed by people who live alone will climb steadily in the years ahead.

The married-couple share of households peaks among Generation Xers

(percent of households headed by married couples, by generation, 2007)

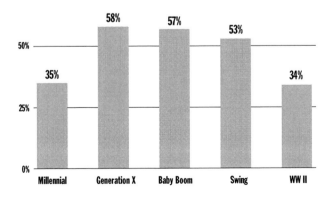

Table 8.3 Households by Age of Householder and Type of Household, 2007

(number and percent distribution of households by age of householder and type of household, 2007; numbers in thousands)

		family households				nonfamily households				
							female householder		male householder	
	total	total	married couples	female hh, no spouse present	male hh, no spouse present	total	total	living alone	total	living alone
Total households	**116,011**	**78,425**	**58,945**	**14,416**	**5,063**	**37,587**	**20,249**	**17,604**	**17,338**	**13,528**
Aged 15 to 24	6,662	3,534	1,354	1,329	851	3,128	1,491	799	1,637	798
Aged 25 to 29	9,667	6,214	3,920	1,629	665	3,453	1,305	915	2,148	1,350
Aged 30 to 34	9,767	7,454	5,461	1,514	479	2,313	863	664	1,451	1,001
Aged 35 to 39	10,841	8,700	6,492	1,742	465	2,141	741	569	1,401	1,078
Aged 40 to 44	11,938	9,353	6,879	1,909	565	2,585	992	791	1,593	1,288
Aged 45 to 49	12,604	9,432	7,169	1,662	601	3,171	1,480	1,249	1,692	1,429
Aged 50 to 54	11,537	8,377	6,644	1,267	465	3,160	1,578	1,397	1,582	1,319
Aged 55 to 59	10,767	7,457	6,192	917	348	3,310	1,832	1,644	1,478	1,279
Aged 60 to 64	8,499	5,519	4,718	613	187	2,981	1,805	1,644	1,176	1,051
Aged 65 to 69	6,642	4,264	3,610	523	130	2,379	1,526	1,435	853	765
Aged 70 to 74	5,284	3,019	2,545	389	85	2,264	1,516	1,459	748	694
Aged 75 or older	11,803	5,102	3,960	922	220	6,701	5,121	5,038	1,580	1,475

Percent distribution by age of householder

Total households	**100.0%**	**100.0%**	**100.0%**	**100.0%**	**100.0%**	**100.0%**	**100.0%**	**100.0%**	**100.0%**	**100.0%**
Aged 15 to 24	5.7	4.5	2.3	9.2	16.8	8.3	7.4	4.5	9.4	5.9
Aged 25 to 29	8.3	7.9	6.7	11.3	13.1	9.2	6.4	5.2	12.4	10.0
Aged 30 to 34	8.4	9.5	9.3	10.5	9.5	6.2	4.3	3.8	8.4	7.4
Aged 35 to 39	9.3	11.1	11.0	12.1	9.2	5.7	3.7	3.2	8.1	8.0
Aged 40 to 44	10.3	11.9	11.7	13.2	11.2	6.9	4.9	4.5	9.2	9.5
Aged 45 to 49	10.9	12.0	12.2	11.5	11.9	8.4	7.3	7.1	9.8	10.6
Aged 50 to 54	9.9	10.7	11.3	8.8	9.2	8.4	7.8	7.9	9.1	9.8
Aged 55 to 59	9.3	9.5	10.5	6.4	6.9	8.8	9.0	9.3	8.5	9.5
Aged 60 to 64	7.3	7.0	8.0	4.3	3.7	7.9	8.9	9.3	6.8	7.8
Aged 65 to 69	5.7	5.4	6.1	3.6	2.6	6.3	7.5	8.2	4.9	5.7
Aged 70 to 74	4.6	3.8	4.3	2.7	1.7	6.0	7.5	8.3	4.3	5.1
Aged 75 or older	10.2	6.5	6.7	6.4	4.3	17.8	25.3	28.6	9.1	10.9

Percent distribution by household type

Total households	**100.0%**	**67.6%**	**50.8%**	**12.4%**	**4.4%**	**32.4%**	**17.5%**	**15.2%**	**14.9%**	**11.7%**
Aged 15 to 24	100.0	53.0	20.3	19.9	12.8	47.0	22.4	12.0	24.6	12.0
Aged 25 to 29	100.0	64.3	40.6	16.9	6.9	35.7	13.5	9.5	22.2	14.0
Aged 30 to 34	100.0	76.3	55.9	15.5	4.9	23.7	8.8	6.8	14.9	10.2
Aged 35 to 39	100.0	80.3	59.9	16.1	4.3	19.7	6.8	5.2	12.9	9.9
Aged 40 to 44	100.0	78.3	57.6	16.0	4.7	21.7	8.3	6.6	13.3	10.8
Aged 45 to 49	100.0	74.8	56.9	13.2	4.8	25.2	11.7	9.9	13.4	11.3
Aged 50 to 54	100.0	72.6	57.6	11.0	4.0	27.4	13.7	12.1	13.7	11.4
Aged 55 to 59	100.0	69.3	57.5	8.5	3.2	30.7	17.0	15.3	13.7	11.9
Aged 60 to 64	100.0	64.9	55.5	7.2	2.2	35.1	21.2	19.3	13.8	12.4
Aged 65 to 69	100.0	64.2	54.4	7.9	2.0	35.8	23.0	21.6	12.8	11.5
Aged 70 to 74	100.0	57.1	48.2	7.4	1.6	42.8	28.7	27.6	14.2	13.1
Aged 75 or older	100.0	43.2	33.6	7.8	1.9	56.8	43.4	42.7	13.4	12.5

Source: Bureau of the Census, 2007 Current Population Survey Annual Social and Economic Supplement, Internet site http:// pubdb3.census.gov/macro/032007/hhinc/toc.htm; calculations by New Strategist

Table 8.4 Households by Type and Generation of Householder, 2007

(number and percent distribution of households by type and generation of householder, 2007; numbers in thousands)

	total	family households total	married couples	female hh, no spouse present	male hh, no spouse present	nonfamily households total	female householder total	female householder living alone	male householder total	male householder living alone
Total households	116,011	78,425	58,945	14,416	5,063	37,587	20,249	17,604	17,338	13,528
Millennial (15–30)	18,282	11,239	6,366	3,261	1,612	7,044	2,969	1,847	4,075	2,348
Generation X (31–42)	25,817	20,275	14,988	4,099	1,187	5,542	2,027	1,575	3,518	2,652
Baby Boom (43–61)	43,083	31,215	24,644	4,855	1,715	11,867	6,009	5,264	5,860	4,963
Swing (62–74)	17,025	10,594	8,986	1,280	327	6,432	4,125	3,880	2,307	2,090
World War II (75+)	11,803	5,102	3,960	922	220	6,701	5,121	5,038	1,580	1,475
Percent distribution by generation of householder										
Total households	100.0%	100.0%	100.0%	100.0%	100.0%	100.0%	100.0%	100.0%	100.0%	100.0%
Millennial (15–30)	15.8	14.3	10.8	22.6	31.8	18.7	14.7	10.5	23.5	17.4
Generation X (31–42)	22.3	25.9	25.4	28.4	23.4	14.7	10.0	8.9	20.3	19.6
Baby Boom (43–61)	37.1	39.8	41.8	33.7	33.9	31.6	29.7	29.9	33.8	36.7
Swing (62–74)	14.7	13.5	15.2	8.9	6.5	17.1	20.4	22.0	13.3	15.4
World War II (75+)	10.2	6.5	6.7	6.4	4.3	17.8	25.3	28.6	9.1	10.9
Percent distribution by household type										
Total households	100.0%	67.6%	50.8%	12.4%	4.4%	32.4%	17.5%	15.2%	14.9%	11.7%
Millennial (15–30)	100.0	61.5	34.8	17.8	8.8	38.5	16.2	10.1	22.3	12.8
Generation X (31–42)	100.0	78.5	58.1	15.9	4.6	21.5	7.8	6.1	13.6	10.3
Baby Boom (43–61)	100.0	72.5	57.2	11.3	4.0	27.5	13.9	12.2	13.6	11.5
Swing (62–74)	100.0	62.2	52.8	7.5	1.9	37.8	24.2	22.8	13.5	12.3
World War II (75+)	100.0	43.2	33.6	7.8	1.9	56.8	43.4	42.7	13.4	12.5

Note: Households by generation are estimates by New Strategist.
Source: Bureau of the Census, 2007 Current Population Survey Annual Social and Economic Supplement, Internet site http://pubdb3.census.gov/macro/032007/hhinc/toc.htm; calculations by New Strategist

Millennials Are Most Diverse

The World War II generation is the least diverse.

Non-Hispanic whites head 83 million of the nation's 116 million households. The proportion of households headed by non-Hispanic whites increases with each successively older generation. Among Millennials, non-Hispanic whites head only 62 percent of households. In the World War II generation, non-Hispanic whites head 85 percent of households.

The proportion of households headed by Asians is more than twice as great among Millennials than among the World War II generation (5 versus 2 percent). The same is true for households headed by blacks (16 versus 8 percent). Hispanics head nearly four times as many households in the Millennial generation as they do in the World War II generation (17 versus 4 percent).

The Baby-Boom generation accounts for the largest share of households among Asians, blacks, and non-Hispanic whites. Boomers especially dominate non-Hispanic white households. Among Hispanics, the proportion of households headed by Gen Xers equals the proportion headed by Boomers.

■ Among Millennials and Generation Xers, households headed by Hispanics outnumber households headed by blacks.

Older householders are more likely to be non-Hispanic white

(percent of households headed by non-Hispanic whites, by generation, 2007)

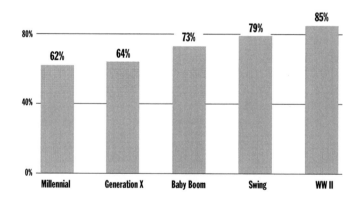

Table 8.5 Households by Age, Race, and Hispanic Origin of Householder, 2007

(number and percent distribution of households by age, race, and Hispanic origin of householder, 2007; numbers in thousands)

	total	Asian	black	Hispanic	non-Hispanic white
Total households	**116,011**	**4,664**	**14,709**	**12,973**	**82,675**
Aged 15 to 24	6,662	250	1,145	1,143	4,059
Aged 25 to 29	9,667	481	1,459	1,668	6,023
Aged 30 to 34	9,767	596	1,468	1,815	5,883
Aged 35 to 39	10,841	601	1,546	1,681	6,934
Aged 40 to 44	11,938	572	1,605	1,553	8,069
Aged 45 to 49	12,604	460	1,718	1,304	8,993
Aged 50 to 54	11,537	464	1,445	1,043	8,457
Aged 55 to 59	10,767	404	1,235	850	8,179
Aged 60 to 64	8,499	265	878	604	6,662
Aged 65 to 69	6,642	191	695	463	5,223
Aged 70 to 74	5,284	117	604	322	4,185
Aged 75 or older	11,803	262	911	526	10,008

Percent distribution by age of householder

	total	Asian	black	Hispanic	non-Hispanic white
Total households	**100.0%**	**100.0%**	**100.0%**	**100.0%**	**100.0%**
Aged 15 to 24	5.7	5.4	7.8	8.8	4.9
Aged 25 to 29	8.3	10.3	9.9	12.9	7.3
Aged 30 to 34	8.4	12.8	10.0	14.0	7.1
Aged 35 to 39	9.3	12.9	10.5	13.0	8.4
Aged 40 to 44	10.3	12.3	10.9	12.0	9.8
Aged 45 to 49	10.9	9.9	11.7	10.1	10.9
Aged 50 to 54	9.9	9.9	9.8	8.0	10.2
Aged 55 to 59	9.3	8.7	8.4	6.6	9.9
Aged 60 to 64	7.3	5.7	6.0	4.7	8.1
Aged 65 to 69	5.7	4.1	4.7	3.6	6.3
Aged 70 to 74	4.6	2.5	4.1	2.5	5.1
Aged 75 or older	10.2	5.6	6.2	4.1	12.1

Percent distribution by race and Hispanic origin

	total	Asian	black	Hispanic	non-Hispanic white
Total households	**100.0%**	**4.0%**	**12.7%**	**11.2%**	**71.3%**
Aged 15 to 24	100.0	3.8	17.2	17.2	60.9
Aged 25 to 29	100.0	5.0	15.1	17.3	62.3
Aged 30 to 34	100.0	6.1	15.0	18.6	60.2
Aged 35 to 39	100.0	5.5	14.3	15.5	64.0
Aged 40 to 44	100.0	4.8	13.4	13.0	67.6
Aged 45 to 49	100.0	3.6	13.6	10.3	71.4
Aged 50 to 54	100.0	4.0	12.5	9.0	73.3
Aged 55 to 59	100.0	3.8	11.5	7.9	76.0
Aged 60 to 64	100.0	3.1	10.3	7.1	78.4
Aged 65 to 69	100.0	2.9	10.5	7.0	78.6
Aged 70 to 74	100.0	2.2	11.4	6.1	79.2
Aged 75 or older	100.0	2.2	7.7	4.5	84.8

Note: Numbers by race and Hispanic origin will not sum to total because Asians and blacks include those who identify themselves as being of the race alone and those who identify themselves as being of the race in combination with other races, Hispanics may be of any race, and not all races are shown. Non-Hispanic whites are those who identify themselves as white alone and not Hispanic.
Source: Bureau of the Census, 2007 Current Population Survey Annual Social and Economic Supplement, Internet site http:// pubdb3.census.gov/macro/032007/hhinc/toc.htm; calculations by New Strategist

Table 8.6 Households by Generation, Race, and Hispanic Origin of Householder, 2007

(number and percent distribution of households by generation, race, and Hispanic origin of householder, 2007; numbers in thousands)

	total	Asian	black	Hispanic	non-Hispanic white
Total households	**116,011**	**4,664**	**14,709**	**12,973**	**82,675**
Millennial (15–30)	18,282	850	2,898	3,174	11,259
Generation X (31–42)	25,817	1,421	3,683	4,065	16,482
Baby Boom (43–61)	43,083	1,663	5,391	4,060	31,521
Swing (62–74)	17,025	467	1,826	1,147	13,405
World War II (75+)	11,803	262	911	526	10,008
Percent distribution by generation of householder					
Total households	**100.0%**	**100.0%**	**100.0%**	**100.0%**	**100.0%**
Millennial (15–30)	15.8	18.2	19.7	24.5	13.6
Generation X (31–42)	22.3	30.5	25.0	31.3	19.9
Baby Boom (43–61)	37.1	35.7	36.7	31.3	38.1
Swing (62–74)	14.7	10.0	12.4	8.8	16.2
World War II (75+)	10.2	5.6	6.2	4.1	12.1
Percent distribution by race and Hispanic origin					
Total households	**100.0%**	**4.0%**	**12.7%**	**11.2%**	**71.3%**
Millennial (15–30)	100.0	4.7	15.8	17.4	61.6
Generation X (31–42)	100.0	5.5	14.3	15.7	63.8
Baby Boom (43–61)	100.0	3.9	12.5	9.4	73.2
Swing (62–74)	100.0	2.7	10.7	6.7	78.7
World War II (75+)	100.0	2.2	7.7	4.5	84.8

Note: Households by generation are estimates by New Strategist. Numbers by race and Hispanic origin will not sum to total because Asians and blacks include those who identify themselves as being of the race alone and those who identify themselves as being of the race in combination with other races, Hispanics may be of any race, and not all races are shown. Non-Hispanic whites are those who identify themselves as white alone and not Hispanic.
Source: Bureau of the Census, 2007 Current Population Survey Annual Social and Economic Supplement, Internet site http:// pubdb3.census.gov/macro/032007/hhinc/toc.htm; calculations by New Strategist

Oldest Americans Have the Smallest Households

Many people aged 75 or older live alone.

The average American household is home to 2.57 people. Household size peaks among 35-to-39-year-olds, with an average of 3.28 people per household. Most people in the 35-to-39 age group have children at home. Households headed by the elderly are much smaller than average. Those headed by people aged 75 or older average only 1.6 people. Small households are the norm among older Americans because so many live alone.

Overall, more than 31 million Americans live by themselves—or 13 percent of the population aged 15 or older. Among men, 12 percent live alone, a figure that does not vary much by age except in the oldest age group, 22 percent of whom live by themselves. Among women, 14 percent live alone, a figure that rises to a high of 49 percent in the 75-or-older age group.

■ Older women are more likely than older men to live alone because of men's higher mortality rate, which leaves many women widowed in old age.

Women's chances of living alone rise steeply with age

(percent of women who live alone, by age, 2007)

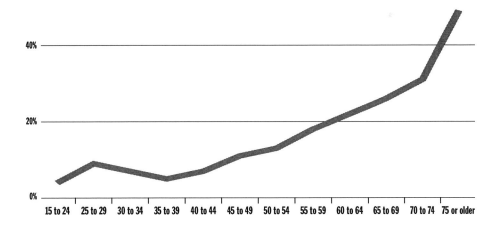

Table 8.7 Average Household Size by Age of Householder, 2006

(number of households and average number of persons per household, by age of householder, 2006; numbers in thousands)

	number of households	average number of persons per household
Total households	**114,384**	**2.57**
Under age 20	922	2.95
Aged 20 to 24	5,873	2.44
Aged 25 to 29	9,223	2.69
Aged 30 to 34	9,896	3.09
Aged 35 to 39	10,976	3.28
Aged 40 to 44	12,040	3.22
Aged 45 to 49	12,470	2.96
Aged 50 to 54	11,262	2.57
Aged 55 to 59	10,334	2.26
Aged 60 to 64	7,930	2.04
Aged 65 to 74	11,687	1.89
Aged 75 or older	11,772	1.60

Source: Bureau of the Census, America's Families and Living Arrangements: 2006, Internet site http://www.census.gov/ population/www/socdemo/hh-fam/cps2006.html; calculations by New Strategist

Table 8.8 People Living Alone by Sex and Age, 2007

(total number of people aged 15 or older, number and percent living alone, and percent distribution of people who live alone, by sex and age, 2007; numbers in thousands)

	total	living alone number	living alone percent	percent distribution
Total people	**236,020**	**31,132**	**13.2%**	**100.0%**
Aged 15 to 24	41,702	1,597	3.8	5.1
Aged 25 to 29	20,666	2,265	11.0	7.3
Aged 30 to 34	19,202	1,665	8.7	5.3
Aged 35 to 39	20,907	1,647	7.9	5.3
Aged 40 to 44	21,856	2,079	9.5	6.7
Aged 45 to 49	22,643	2,678	11.8	8.6
Aged 50 to 54	20,819	2,716	13.0	8.7
Aged 55 to 59	18,221	2,923	16.0	9.4
Aged 60 to 64	13,970	2,695	19.3	8.7
Aged 65 to 69	10,629	2,200	20.7	7.1
Aged 70 to 74	8,369	2,153	25.7	6.9
Aged 75 or older	17,037	6,513	38.2	20.9
Total men	**114,576**	**13,528**	**11.8**	**100.0**
Aged 15 to 24	21,156	798	3.8	5.9
Aged 25 to 29	10,440	1,350	12.9	10.0
Aged 30 to 34	9,584	1,001	10.4	7.4
Aged 35 to 39	10,402	1,078	10.4	8.0
Aged 40 to 44	10,779	1,288	11.9	9.5
Aged 45 to 49	11,100	1,429	12.9	10.6
Aged 50 to 54	10,195	1,319	12.9	9.8
Aged 55 to 59	8,879	1,279	14.4	9.5
Aged 60 to 64	6,599	1,051	15.9	7.8
Aged 65 to 69	5,013	765	15.3	5.7
Aged 70 to 74	3,726	694	18.6	5.1
Aged 75 or older	6,703	1,475	22.0	10.9
Total women	**121,443**	**17,604**	**14.5**	**100.0**
Aged 15 to 24	20,546	799	3.9	4.5
Aged 25 to 29	10,226	915	8.9	5.2
Aged 30 to 34	9,618	664	6.9	3.8
Aged 35 to 39	10,505	569	5.4	3.2
Aged 40 to 44	11,077	791	7.1	4.5
Aged 45 to 49	11,542	1,249	10.8	7.1
Aged 50 to 54	10,624	1,397	13.1	7.9
Aged 55 to 59	9,342	1,644	17.6	9.3
Aged 60 to 64	7,371	1,644	22.3	9.3
Aged 65 to 69	5,616	1,435	25.6	8.2
Aged 70 to 74	4,643	1,459	31.4	8.3
Aged 75 or older	10,334	5,038	48.8	28.6

Source: Bureau of the Census, 2007 Current Population Survey Annual Social and Economic Supplement, Internet sites http:// pubdb3.census.gov/macro/032007/hhinc/toc.htm and http://pubdb3.census.gov/macro/032007/perinc/toc.htm; calculations by New Strategist

Fewer than One-Third of Households include Children

Children can be found in most Gen X households, however.

Generation Xers, aged 30 to 41 in 2006, are busy raising children. Sixty-four percent of Gen X households include children under age 18. The percentage of households with children under age 18 peaks in the 35-to-39 age group at 67 percent. Generation X is the only generation in which the majority of households include children. Among households headed by Boomers, only 31 percent have children under age 18 at home. Among Millennials, the proportion is 39 percent.

Overall, 45 percent of the nation's married-couple households include children under age 18. The figure peaks at 84 percent among couples headed by 35-to-39-year-olds. Most Millennial and Gen X couples have children under age 18 at home. Among Boomer couples, the figure is just 42 percent.

Among female-headed families, most of those headed by Millennials and Gen Xers include children under age 18. Among male-headed families, only those headed by Gen Xers are likely to include children.

■ The Baby-Boom generation is rapidly entering the empty-nest lifestage as their children leave home.

Few older householders are caring for children under age 18

(percent of households that include children under age 18, by generation of householder, 2007)

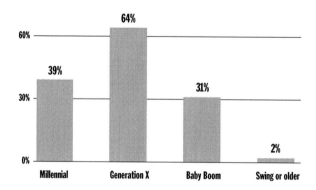

Table 8.9 Households by Age of Householder, Type of Household, and Presence of Children, 2006: Total Households

(number and percent distribution of households by age of householder, type of household, and presence of own children under age 18, and mean age of householder, 2006; numbers in thousands)

	all households		married couples		female-headed families		male-headed families	
	total	with children	total	with children	total	with children	total	with children
Total households	**114,384**	**36,466**	**58,179**	**25,982**	**14,093**	**8,389**	**5,130**	**2,095**
Under age 20	922	144	87	36	285	98	237	9
Aged 20 to 24	5,873	1,859	1,329	824	1,139	883	620	152
Aged 25 to 29	9,223	4,242	3,920	2,649	1,458	1,312	619	282
Aged 30 to 34	9,896	6,128	5,485	4,389	1,512	1,425	503	315
Aged 35 to 39	10,976	7,309	6,383	5,379	1,741	1,575	476	355
Aged 40 to 44	12,040	7,353	6,982	5,486	1,858	1,484	623	383
Aged 45 to 49	12,470	5,359	7,187	4,119	1,622	943	590	297
Aged 50 to 54	11,262	2,642	6,385	2,013	1,203	435	475	194
Aged 55 to 64	18,264	1,225	10,460	947	1,488	192	498	87
Aged 65 to 74	11,687	157	6,009	108	863	31	238	18
Aged 75 or older	11,772	48	3,953	33	924	12	251	3
Mean age (years)	49.2	38.6	49.1	39.4	44.0	36.2	41.4	38.7

Percent distribution by age of householder

Total households	**100.0%**	**100.0%**	**100.0%**	**100.0%**	**100.0%**	**100.0%**	**100.0%**	**100.0%**
Under age 20	0.8	0.4	0.1	0.1	2.0	1.2	4.6	0.4
Aged 20 to 24	5.1	5.1	2.3	3.2	8.1	10.5	12.1	7.3
Aged 25 to 29	8.1	11.6	6.7	10.2	10.3	15.6	12.1	13.5
Aged 30 to 34	8.7	16.8	9.4	16.9	10.7	17.0	9.8	15.0
Aged 35 to 39	9.6	20.0	11.0	20.7	12.4	18.8	9.3	16.9
Aged 40 to 44	10.5	20.2	12.0	21.1	13.2	17.7	12.1	18.3
Aged 45 to 49	10.9	14.7	12.4	15.9	11.5	11.2	11.5	14.2
Aged 50 to 54	9.8	7.2	11.0	7.7	8.5	5.2	9.3	9.3
Aged 55 to 64	16.0	3.4	18.0	3.6	10.6	2.3	9.7	4.2
Aged 65 to 74	10.2	0.4	10.3	0.4	6.1	0.4	4.6	0.9
Aged 75 or older	10.3	0.1	6.8	0.1	6.6	0.1	4.9	0.1

Percent of households with children by type

Total households	**100.0%**	**31.9%**	**100.0%**	**44.7%**	**100.0%**	**59.5%**	**100.0%**	**40.8%**
Under age 20	100.0	15.6	100.0	41.4	100.0	34.4	100.0	3.8
Aged 20 to 24	100.0	31.7	100.0	62.0	100.0	77.5	100.0	24.5
Aged 25 to 29	100.0	46.0	100.0	67.6	100.0	90.0	100.0	45.6
Aged 30 to 34	100.0	61.9	100.0	80.0	100.0	94.2	100.0	62.6
Aged 35 to 39	100.0	66.6	100.0	84.3	100.0	90.5	100.0	74.6
Aged 40 to 44	100.0	61.1	100.0	78.6	100.0	79.9	100.0	61.5
Aged 45 to 49	100.0	43.0	100.0	57.3	100.0	58.1	100.0	50.3
Aged 50 to 54	100.0	23.5	100.0	31.5	100.0	36.2	100.0	40.8
Aged 55 to 64	100.0	6.7	100.0	9.1	100.0	12.9	100.0	17.5
Aged 65 to 74	100.0	1.3	100.0	1.8	100.0	3.6	100.0	7.6
Aged 75 or older	100.0	0.4	100.0	0.8	100.0	1.3	100.0	1.2

Source: Bureau of the Census, America's Families and Living Arrangements: 2006, Internet site http://www.census.gov/population/www/socdemo/hh-fam/cps2006.html; calculations by New Strategist

Table 8.10 Households by Generation of Householder, Type of Household, and Presence of Children, 2006: Total Households

(number and percent distribution of households by generation of householder, type of household, and presence of own children under age 18, 2006; numbers in thousands)

	all households		married couples		female-headed families		male-headed families	
	total	with children	total	with children	total	with children	total	with children
Total households	**114,384**	**36,466**	**58,179**	**25,982**	**14,093**	**8,389**	**5,130**	**2,095**
Millennial (15–29)	16,018	6,245	5,336	3,509	2,882	2,293	1,476	443
Generation X (30–41)	25,688	16,378	14,661	11,962	3,996	3,594	1,228	823
Baby Boom (42–60)	41,914	13,148	24,037	9,992	4,833	2,384	1,738	773
Swing (61–73)	17,824	631	9,592	476	1,372	105	413	51
World War II (74+)	12,941	64	4,554	44	1,010	15	275	5

Percent distribution by generation of householder

Total households	**100.0%**	**100.0%**	**100.0%**	**100.0%**	**100.0%**	**100.0%**	**100.0%**	**100.0%**
Millennial (15–29)	14.0	17.1	9.2	13.5	20.4	27.3	28.8	21.1
Generation X (30–41)	22.5	44.9	25.2	46.0	28.4	42.8	23.9	39.3
Baby Boom (42–60)	36.6	36.1	41.3	38.5	34.3	28.4	33.9	36.9
Swing (61–73)	15.6	1.7	16.5	1.8	9.7	1.2	8.1	2.4
World War II (74+)	11.3	0.2	7.8	0.2	7.2	0.2	5.4	0.2

Percent of households with children by type

Total households	**100.0%**	**31.9%**	**100.0%**	**44.7%**	**100.0%**	**59.5%**	**100.0%**	**40.8%**
Millennial (15–29)	100.0	39.0	100.0	65.8	100.0	79.6	100.0	30.0
Generation X (30–41)	100.0	63.8	100.0	81.6	100.0	89.9	100.0	67.0
Baby Boom (42–60)	100.0	31.4	100.0	41.6	100.0	49.3	100.0	44.5
Swing (61–73)	100.0	3.5	100.0	5.0	100.0	7.6	100.0	12.3
World War II (74+)	100.0	0.5	100.0	1.0	100.0	1.5	100.0	1.7

Note: Households by generation are estimates by New Strategist.
Source: Bureau of the Census, America's Families and Living Arrangements: 2006, Internet site http://www.census.gov/population/www/socdemo/hh-fam/cps2006.html; calculations by New Strategist

Nearly Half of Hispanic Households include Children

Most Asian, black and non-Hispanic white households do not include children.

Forty-nine percent of Hispanic households include children under age 18. This compares with just 28 percent of non-Hispanic white households, 36 percent of black households, and 37 percent of Asian households.

Regardless of race or Hispanic origin, most households headed by people aged 35 to 44 include children under age 18. The proportion of households with children surpasses 50 percent beginning in the 25-to-29 age group for Hispanics and blacks, in the 30-to-34 age group for non-Hispanic whites, and in the 35-to-39 age group for Asians.

The lifestyles of Hispanics and Asians differ greatly. Among householders aged 25 to 29, for example, 62 percent of Hispanics have children at home. In contrast, only 21 percent of Asian householders in the age group are living with children.

■ Asians are the best educated Americans, which is why many postpone childbearing until they are in their thirties.

Non-Hispanic white households are least likely to include children

(percent of households that include children under age 18, by race and Hispanic origin of householder, 2006)

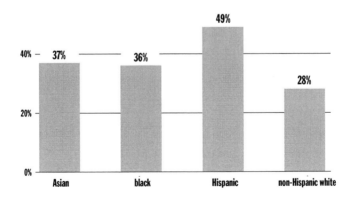

Table 8.11 Households by Age of Householder, Type of Household, and Presence of Children, 2006: Asian Households

(number and percent distribution of Asian households by age of householder, type of household, and presence of own children under age 18, and mean age of householder, 2006; numbers in thousands)

	all households		married couples		female-headed families		male-headed families	
	total	with children	total	with children	total	with children	total	with children
Total Asian households	**4,500**	**1,681**	**2,692**	**1,437**	**415**	**184**	**251**	**60**
Under age 20	47	2	5	2	6	0	21	0
Aged 20 to 24	264	41	33	17	41	19	39	4
Aged 25 to 29	459	95	148	69	44	20	41	7
Aged 30 to 34	586	276	362	233	46	36	28	7
Aged 35 to 39	566	388	435	350	35	30	17	9
Aged 40 to 44	543	375	409	340	36	24	21	12
Aged 45 to 49	461	252	312	221	47	20	28	10
Aged 50 to 54	395	160	270	135	48	17	19	9
Aged 55 to 64	644	80	422	61	69	17	18	3
Aged 65 to 74	303	8	180	7	27	2	12	0
Aged 75 or older	231	4	115	4	14	0	5	0
Mean age (years)	44.7	40.6	46.4	40.8	44.0	38.5	37.6	40.2

Percent distribution by age of householder

Total Asian households	**100.0%**	**100.0%**	**100.0%**	**100.0%**	**100.0%**	**100.0%**	**100.0%**	**100.0%**
Under age 20	1.0	0.1	0.2	0.1	1.4	0.0	8.4	0.0
Aged 20 to 24	5.9	2.4	1.2	1.2	9.9	10.3	15.5	6.7
Aged 25 to 29	10.2	5.7	5.5	4.8	10.6	10.9	16.3	11.7
Aged 30 to 34	13.0	16.4	13.4	16.2	11.1	19.6	11.2	11.7
Aged 35 to 39	12.6	23.1	16.2	24.4	8.4	16.3	6.8	15.0
Aged 40 to 44	12.1	22.3	15.2	23.7	8.7	13.0	8.4	20.0
Aged 45 to 49	10.2	15.0	11.6	15.4	11.3	10.9	11.2	16.7
Aged 50 to 54	8.8	9.5	10.0	9.4	11.6	9.2	7.6	15.0
Aged 55 to 64	14.3	4.8	15.7	4.2	16.6	9.2	7.2	5.0
Aged 65 to 74	6.7	0.5	6.7	0.5	6.5	1.1	4.8	0.0
Aged 75 or older	5.1	0.2	4.3	0.3	3.4	0.0	2.0	0.0

Percent of households with children by type

Total Asian households	**100.0%**	**37.4%**	**100.0%**	**53.4%**	**100.0%**	**44.3%**	**100.0%**	**23.9%**
Under age 20	100.0	4.3	100.0	40.0	100.0	0.0	100.0	0.0
Aged 20 to 24	100.0	15.5	100.0	51.5	100.0	46.3	100.0	10.3
Aged 25 to 29	100.0	20.7	100.0	46.6	100.0	45.5	100.0	17.1
Aged 30 to 34	100.0	47.1	100.0	64.4	100.0	78.3	100.0	25.0
Aged 35 to 39	100.0	68.6	100.0	80.5	100.0	85.7	100.0	52.9
Aged 40 to 44	100.0	69.1	100.0	83.1	100.0	66.7	100.0	57.1
Aged 45 to 49	100.0	54.7	100.0	70.8	100.0	42.6	100.0	35.7
Aged 50 to 54	100.0	40.5	100.0	50.0	100.0	35.4	100.0	47.4
Aged 55 to 64	100.0	12.4	100.0	14.5	100.0	24.6	100.0	16.7
Aged 65 to 74	100.0	2.6	100.0	3.9	100.0	7.4	100.0	0.0
Aged 75 or older	100.0	1.7	100.0	3.5	100.0	0.0	100.0	0.0

Note: Asians include those who identify themselves as being of the race alone or as being of the race in combination with other races.

Source: Bureau of the Census, America's Families and Living Arrangements: 2006, Internet site http://www.census.gov/population/www/socdemo/hh-fam/cps2006.html; calculations by New Strategist

Table 8.12 Households by Age of Householder, Type of Household, and Presence of Children, 2006: Black Households

(number and percent distribution of black households by age of householder, type of household, and presence of own children under age 18, and mean age of householder, 2006; numbers in thousands)

	all households		married couples		female-headed families		male-headed families	
	total	with children	total	with children	total	with children	total	with children
Total black households	**14,399**	**5,138**	**4,249**	**2,100**	**4,215**	**2,712**	**831**	**327**
Under age 20	228	40	5	3	96	34	50	3
Aged 20 to 24	978	410	109	80	352	302	95	28
Aged 25 to 29	1,372	757	266	206	530	487	121	64
Aged 30 to 34	1,481	929	431	325	568	544	81	60
Aged 35 to 39	1,497	982	489	413	564	517	74	51
Aged 40 to 44	1,632	909	575	424	548	436	94	48
Aged 45 to 49	1,677	605	623	345	447	223	95	38
Aged 50 to 54	1,350	294	468	182	317	91	58	20
Aged 55 to 64	2,049	173	742	100	397	67	82	7
Aged 65 to 74	1,198	33	374	17	213	10	50	6
Aged 75 or older	938	7	168	5	182	2	32	1
Mean age (years)	45.9	37.1	47.6	39.9	41.7	35.0	40.6	36.6

Percent distribution by age of householder

	all households		married couples		female-headed families		male-headed families	
Total black households	**100.0%**	**100.0%**	**100.0%**	**100.0%**	**100.0%**	**100.0%**	**100.0%**	**100.0%**
Under age 20	1.6	0.8	0.1	0.1	2.3	1.3	6.0	0.9
Aged 20 to 24	6.8	8.0	2.6	3.8	8.4	11.1	11.4	8.6
Aged 25 to 29	9.5	14.7	6.3	9.8	12.6	18.0	14.6	19.6
Aged 30 to 34	10.3	18.1	10.1	15.5	13.5	20.1	9.7	18.3
Aged 35 to 39	10.4	19.1	11.5	19.7	13.4	19.1	8.9	15.6
Aged 40 to 44	11.3	17.7	13.5	20.2	13.0	16.1	11.3	14.7
Aged 45 to 49	11.6	11.8	14.7	16.4	10.6	8.2	11.4	11.6
Aged 50 to 54	9.4	5.7	11.0	8.7	7.5	3.4	7.0	6.1
Aged 55 to 64	14.2	3.4	17.5	4.8	9.4	2.5	9.9	2.1
Aged 65 to 74	8.3	0.6	8.8	0.8	5.1	0.4	6.0	1.8
Aged 75 or older	6.5	0.1	4.0	0.2	4.3	0.1	3.9	0.3

Percent of households with children by type

	all households		married couples		female-headed families		male-headed families	
Total black households	**100.0%**	**35.7%**	**100.0%**	**49.4%**	**100.0%**	**64.3%**	**100.0%**	**39.4%**
Under age 20	100.0	17.5	100.0	60.0	100.0	35.4	100.0	6.0
Aged 20 to 24	100.0	41.9	100.0	73.4	100.0	85.8	100.0	29.5
Aged 25 to 29	100.0	55.2	100.0	77.4	100.0	91.9	100.0	52.9
Aged 30 to 34	100.0	62.7	100.0	75.4	100.0	95.8	100.0	74.1
Aged 35 to 39	100.0	65.6	100.0	84.5	100.0	91.7	100.0	68.9
Aged 40 to 44	100.0	55.7	100.0	73.7	100.0	79.6	100.0	51.1
Aged 45 to 49	100.0	36.1	100.0	55.4	100.0	49.9	100.0	40.0
Aged 50 to 54	100.0	21.8	100.0	38.9	100.0	28.7	100.0	34.5
Aged 55 to 64	100.0	8.4	100.0	13.5	100.0	16.9	100.0	8.5
Aged 65 to 74	100.0	2.8	100.0	4.5	100.0	4.7	100.0	12.0
Aged 75 or older	100.0	0.7	100.0	3.0	100.0	1.1	100.0	3.1

Note: Blacks include those who identify themselves as being of the race alone or as being of the race in combination with other races.
Source: Bureau of the Census, America's Families and Living Arrangements: 2006, Internet site http://www.census.gov/population/www/socdemo/hh-fam/cps2006.html; calculations by New Strategist

Table 8.13 Households by Age of Householder, Type of Household, and Presence of Children, 2006: Hispanic Households

(number and percent distribution of Hispanic households by age of householder, type of household, and presence of own children under age 18, and mean age of householder, 2006; numbers in thousands)

	all households		married couples		female-headed families		male-headed families	
	total	with children	total	with children	total	with children	total	with children
Total Hispanic households	**12,519**	**6,119**	**6,642**	**4,334**	**2,252**	**1,470**	**969**	**315**
Under age 20	206	45	36	16	75	26	63	3
Aged 20 to 24	1,008	402	327	230	204	146	189	27
Aged 25 to 29	1,612	996	845	679	279	253	160	64
Aged 30 to 34	1,715	1,237	1,047	916	282	259	125	62
Aged 35 to 39	1,636	1,205	969	865	325	294	102	46
Aged 40 to 44	1,530	1,053	903	765	312	242	110	46
Aged 45 to 49	1,293	667	754	488	229	149	72	30
Aged 50 to 54	981	319	570	238	174	58	52	23
Aged 55 to 64	1,253	170	635	117	204	42	52	11
Aged 65 to 74	728	20	352	16	89	0	18	3
Aged 75 or older	558	6	203	4	78	2	26	0
Mean age (years)	42.3	36.7	42.3	37.0	40.8	35.7	35.5	36.4

Percent distribution by age of householder

	all households		married couples		female-headed families		male-headed families	
Total Hispanic households	**100.0%**	**100.0%**	**100.0%**	**100.0%**	**100.0%**	**100.0%**	**100.0%**	**100.0%**
Under age 20	1.6	0.7	0.5	0.4	3.3	1.8	6.5	1.0
Aged 20 to 24	8.1	6.6	4.9	5.3	9.1	9.9	19.5	8.6
Aged 25 to 29	12.9	16.3	12.7	15.7	12.4	17.2	16.5	20.3
Aged 30 to 34	13.7	20.2	15.8	21.1	12.5	17.6	12.9	19.7
Aged 35 to 39	13.1	19.7	14.6	20.0	14.4	20.0	10.5	14.6
Aged 40 to 44	12.2	17.2	13.6	17.7	13.9	16.5	11.4	14.6
Aged 45 to 49	10.3	10.9	11.4	11.3	10.2	10.1	7.4	9.5
Aged 50 to 54	7.8	5.2	8.6	5.5	7.7	3.9	5.4	7.3
Aged 55 to 64	10.0	2.8	9.6	2.7	9.1	2.9	5.4	3.5
Aged 65 to 74	5.8	0.3	5.3	0.4	4.0	0.0	1.9	1.0
Aged 75 or older	4.5	0.1	3.1	0.1	3.5	0.1	2.7	0.0

Percent of households with children by type

	all households		married couples		female-headed families		male-headed families	
Total Hispanic households	**100.0%**	**48.9%**	**100.0%**	**65.3%**	**100.0%**	**65.3%**	**100.0%**	**32.5%**
Under age 20	100.0	21.8	100.0	44.4	100.0	34.7	100.0	4.8
Aged 20 to 24	100.0	39.9	100.0	70.3	100.0	71.6	100.0	14.3
Aged 25 to 29	100.0	61.8	100.0	80.4	100.0	90.7	100.0	40.0
Aged 30 to 34	100.0	72.1	100.0	87.5	100.0	91.8	100.0	49.6
Aged 35 to 39	100.0	73.7	100.0	89.3	100.0	90.5	100.0	45.1
Aged 40 to 44	100.0	68.8	100.0	84.7	100.0	77.6	100.0	41.8
Aged 45 to 49	100.0	51.6	100.0	64.7	100.0	65.1	100.0	41.7
Aged 50 to 54	100.0	32.5	100.0	41.8	100.0	33.3	100.0	44.2
Aged 55 to 64	100.0	13.6	100.0	18.4	100.0	20.6	100.0	21.2
Aged 65 to 74	100.0	2.7	100.0	4.5	100.0	0.0	100.0	16.7
Aged 75 or older	100.0	1.1	100.0	2.0	100.0	2.6	100.0	0.0

Source: Bureau of the Census, America's Families and Living Arrangements: 2006, Internet site http://www.census.gov/population/www/socdemo/hh-fam/cps2006.html; calculations by New Strategist

Table 8.14   Households by Age of Householder, Type of Household, and Presence of Children, 2006: Non-Hispanic White Households

(number and percent distribution of non-Hispanic white households by age of householder, type of household, and presence of own children under age 18, and mean age of householder, 2006; numbers in thousands)

	all households		married couples		female-headed families		male-headed families	
	total	with children	total	with children	total	with children	total	with children
Total non-Hispanic white households	**82,003**	**23,290**	**44,116**	**17,934**	**7,138**	**3,997**	**3,003**	**1,360**
Under age 20	440	58	42	15	111	39	103	4
Aged 20 to 24	3,601	990	859	493	531	407	292	90
Aged 25 to 29	5,719	2,362	2,617	1,666	602	551	290	145
Aged 30 to 34	6,057	3,660	3,611	2,893	610	583	260	183
Aged 35 to 39	7,217	4,704	4,478	3,739	811	727	271	237
Aged 40 to 44	8,212	4,949	5,018	3,897	960	783	389	268
Aged 45 to 49	8,897	3,780	5,418	3,030	882	535	386	215
Aged 50 to 54	8,427	1,858	5,019	1,447	663	270	341	141
Aged 55 to 64	14,137	805	8,571	663	818	76	341	65
Aged 65 to 74	9,342	94	5,047	68	520	17	148	9
Aged 75 or older	9,955	31	3,435	21	630	7	183	2
Mean age (years)	51.0	39.3	50.5	39.8	46.3	37.1	43.8	39.6

Percent distribution by age of householder

Total non-Hispanic white households	**100.0%**	**100.0%**	**100.0%**	**100.0%**	**100.0%**	**100.0%**	**100.0%**	**100.0%**
Under age 20	0.5	0.2	0.1	0.1	1.6	1.0	3.4	0.3
Aged 20 to 24	4.4	4.3	1.9	2.7	7.4	10.2	9.7	6.6
Aged 25 to 29	7.0	10.1	5.9	9.3	8.4	13.8	9.7	10.7
Aged 30 to 34	7.4	15.7	8.2	16.1	8.5	14.6	8.7	13.5
Aged 35 to 39	8.8	20.2	10.2	20.8	11.4	18.2	9.0	17.4
Aged 40 to 44	10.0	21.2	11.4	21.7	13.4	19.6	13.0	19.7
Aged 45 to 49	10.8	16.2	12.3	16.9	12.4	13.4	12.9	15.8
Aged 50 to 54	10.3	8.0	11.4	8.1	9.3	6.8	11.4	10.4
Aged 55 to 64	17.2	3.5	19.4	3.7	11.5	1.9	11.4	4.8
Aged 65 to 74	11.4	0.4	11.4	0.4	7.3	0.4	4.9	0.7
Aged 75 or older	12.1	0.1	7.8	0.1	8.8	0.2	6.1	0.1

Percent of households with children by type

Total non-Hispanic white households	**100.0%**	**28.4%**	**100.0%**	**40.7%**	**100.0%**	**56.0%**	**100.0%**	**45.3%**
Under age 20	100.0	13.2	100.0	35.7	100.0	35.1	100.0	3.9
Aged 20 to 24	100.0	27.5	100.0	57.4	100.0	76.6	100.0	30.8
Aged 25 to 29	100.0	41.3	100.0	63.7	100.0	91.5	100.0	50.0
Aged 30 to 34	100.0	60.4	100.0	80.1	100.0	95.6	100.0	70.4
Aged 35 to 39	100.0	65.2	100.0	83.5	100.0	89.6	100.0	87.5
Aged 40 to 44	100.0	60.3	100.0	77.7	100.0	81.6	100.0	68.9
Aged 45 to 49	100.0	42.5	100.0	55.9	100.0	60.7	100.0	55.7
Aged 50 to 54	100.0	22.0	100.0	28.8	100.0	40.7	100.0	41.3
Aged 55 to 64	100.0	5.7	100.0	7.7	100.0	9.3	100.0	19.1
Aged 65 to 74	100.0	1.0	100.0	1.3	100.0	3.3	100.0	6.1
Aged 75 or older	100.0	0.3	100.0	0.6	100.0	1.1	100.0	1.1

Note: Non-Hispanc whites are those who identify themselves as being white alone and not Hispanic.
Source: Bureau of the Census, America's Families and Living Arrangements: 2006, Internet site http://www.census.gov/population/www/socdemo/hh-fam/cps2006.html; calculations by New Strategist

Parents in Their Forties Have Teens

Younger parents have younger children.

Preschoolers are most likely to be found in households headed by people aged 30 to 34. Forty-two percent of households in the age group have preschoolers in their home, and 26 percent of the nation's households with preschoolers are headed by people in the 30-to-34 age group. Householders aged 35 to 39 are most likely to have children aged 6 to 11 at home, and householders aged 40 to 44 are most likely to have teenagers. Twenty-seven percent of the nation's households with teenagers are headed by 40-to-44-year olds, and 52 percent are headed by 40-to-49-year-olds.

Many households include children aged 18 or older. Among households headed by people aged 45 to 49, for example, a 43 percent minority include children under age 18, but the 58 percent majority include children of any age. The figure is 43 percent among householders aged 50 to 54 and a still substantial 24 percent among those aged 55 to 64. Even among the oldest householders, aged 75 or older, 11 percent have children in their home.

■ Although Boomers are rapidly becoming empty nesters, many still have children aged 18 or older at home.

Householders aged 30 to 34 are most likely to have preschoolers

(percent of households with children under age 6 at home, by age of householder, 2006)

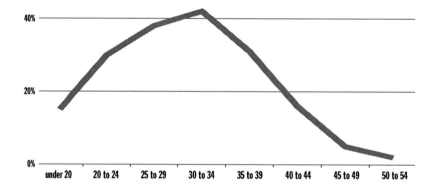

Table 8.15 Households by Age of Householder and Age of Children, 2006

(number and percent distribution of households by age of householder and age of own children living at home, and mean age of householder, 2006; numbers in thousands)

	total households	with children				
		any age	under 18	12 to 17	6 to 11	under 6
Total households	**114,384**	**47,201**	**36,466**	**17,323**	**16,713**	**16,002**
Under age 20	922	144	144	0	2	142
Aged 20 to 24	5,873	1,859	1,859	4	269	1,780
Aged 25 to 29	9,223	4,242	4,242	269	1,815	3,542
Aged 30 to 34	9,896	6,144	6,128	1,560	3,302	4,189
Aged 35 to 39	10,976	7,461	7,309	3,307	4,261	3,452
Aged 40 to 44	12,040	8,043	7,353	4,738	3,972	1,878
Aged 45 to 49	12,470	7,190	5,359	4,181	2,065	648
Aged 50 to 54	11,262	4,846	2,642	2,151	680	217
Aged 55 to 64	18,264	4,386	1,225	977	285	107
Aged 65 to 74	11,687	1,609	157	107	45	33
Aged 75 or older	11,772	1,277	48	28	17	15
Mean age (years)	49.2	43.0	38.6	43.5	38.2	33.1
Percent distribution by age of householder						
Total households	**100.0%**	**100.0%**	**100.0%**	**100.0%**	**100.0%**	**100.0%**
Under age 20	0.8	0.3	0.4	0.0	0.0	0.9
Aged 20 to 24	5.1	3.9	5.1	0.0	1.6	11.1
Aged 25 to 29	8.1	9.0	11.6	1.6	10.9	22.1
Aged 30 to 34	8.7	13.0	16.8	9.0	19.8	26.2
Aged 35 to 39	9.6	15.8	20.0	19.1	25.5	21.6
Aged 40 to 44	10.5	17.0	20.2	27.4	23.8	11.7
Aged 45 to 49	10.9	15.2	14.7	24.1	12.4	4.0
Aged 50 to 54	9.8	10.3	7.2	12.4	4.1	1.4
Aged 55 to 64	16.0	9.3	3.4	5.6	1.7	0.7
Aged 65 to 74	10.2	3.4	0.4	0.6	0.3	0.2
Aged 75 or older	10.3	2.7	0.1	0.2	0.1	0.1
Percent distribution by age of child						
Total households	**100.0%**	**41.3%**	**31.9%**	**15.1%**	**14.6%**	**14.0%**
Under age 20	100.0	15.6	15.6	0.0	0.2	15.4
Aged 20 to 24	100.0	31.7	31.7	0.1	4.6	30.3
Aged 25 to 29	100.0	46.0	46.0	2.9	19.7	38.4
Aged 30 to 34	100.0	62.1	61.9	15.8	33.4	42.3
Aged 35 to 39	100.0	68.0	66.6	30.1	38.8	31.5
Aged 40 to 44	100.0	66.8	61.1	39.4	33.0	15.6
Aged 45 to 49	100.0	57.7	43.0	33.5	16.6	5.2
Aged 50 to 54	100.0	43.0	23.5	19.1	6.0	1.9
Aged 55 to 64	100.0	24.0	6.7	5.3	1.6	0.6
Aged 65 to 74	100.0	13.8	1.3	0.9	0.4	0.3
Aged 75 or older	100.0	10.8	0.4	0.2	0.1	0.1

Note: Numbers will not add to total because many households have children in more than one age group.
Source: Bureau of the Census, America's Families and Living Arrangements: 2006, Internet site http://www.census.gov/ population/www/socdemo/hh-fam/cps2006.html; calculations by New Strategist

Householders in Their Thirties Have the Most Kids

Eighteen percent of householders aged 35 to 39 have three or more children.

Overall, only 32 percent of the nation's households include children under age 18. Fourteen percent of households have one child under age 18, 12 percent have two, 5 percent have three, and just 2 percent have four or more.

Householders aged 35 to 39 are most likely to have children under age 18 at home, and they also have the largest number of children in their households. Twenty percent of these householders have one child under age 18, 29 percent have two, and 18 percent have three or more.

The proportion of households with only one child under age 18 peaks in the older age groups as the nest begins to empty. Twenty-two percent of householders aged 40 to 49 have one child under age 18 at home—a larger proportion than in any other age group.

■ Although families have gotten smaller, housing and cars have gotten larger. Fewer children means parents have more resources to devote to each child—and to spend on themselves.

Many one-child families are the result of an emptying nest

(percent of households with one child under age 18 at home, by age of householder, 2006)

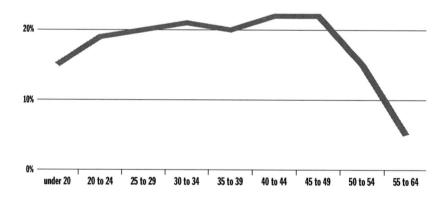

Table 8.16 Households by Age of Householder and Number of Children, 2006

(number and percent distribution of households by age of householder and number of children under age 18 living at home, 2006; numbers in thousands)

| | total | with one or more children under age 18 | | | | |
		total	one	two	three	four or more
Total households	**114,384**	**36,466**	**15,528**	**13,664**	**5,278**	**1,997**
Under age 20	922	144	136	8	0	0
Aged 20 to 24	5,873	1,859	1,114	575	139	31
Aged 25 to 29	9,223	4,242	1,883	1,497	632	231
Aged 30 to 34	9,896	6,128	2,101	2,450	1,075	503
Aged 35 to 39	10,976	7,309	2,200	3,177	1,399	534
Aged 40 to 44	12,040	7,353	2,683	3,059	1,171	440
Aged 45 to 49	12,470	5,359	2,689	1,892	593	185
Aged 50 to 54	11,262	2,642	1,700	703	191	49
Aged 55 to 64	18,264	1,225	887	255	63	21
Aged 65 to 74	11,687	157	101	41	12	2
Aged 75 or older	11,772	48	35	7	4	2

Percent distribution by age of householder

	total	total	one	two	three	four or more
Total households	**100.0%**	**100.0%**	**100.0%**	**100.0%**	**100.0%**	**100.0%**
Under age 20	0.8	0.4	0.9	0.1	0.0	0.0
Aged 20 to 24	5.1	5.1	7.2	4.2	2.6	1.6
Aged 25 to 29	8.1	11.6	12.1	11.0	12.0	11.6
Aged 30 to 34	8.7	16.8	13.5	17.9	20.4	25.2
Aged 35 to 39	9.6	20.0	14.2	23.3	26.5	26.7
Aged 40 to 44	10.5	20.2	17.3	22.4	22.2	22.0
Aged 45 to 49	10.9	14.7	17.3	13.8	11.2	9.3
Aged 50 to 54	9.8	7.2	10.9	5.1	3.6	2.5
Aged 55 to 64	16.0	3.4	5.7	1.9	1.2	1.1
Aged 65 to 74	10.2	0.4	0.7	0.3	0.2	0.1
Aged 75 or older	10.3	0.1	0.2	0.1	0.1	0.1

Percent distribution by number of children

	total	total	one	two	three	four or more
Total households	**100.0%**	**31.9%**	**13.6%**	**11.9%**	**4.6%**	**1.7%**
Under age 20	100.0	15.6	14.8	0.9	0.0	0.0
Aged 20 to 24	100.0	31.7	19.0	9.8	2.4	0.5
Aged 25 to 29	100.0	46.0	20.4	16.2	6.9	2.5
Aged 30 to 34	100.0	61.9	21.2	24.8	10.9	5.1
Aged 35 to 39	100.0	66.6	20.0	28.9	12.7	4.9
Aged 40 to 44	100.0	61.1	22.3	25.4	9.7	3.7
Aged 45 to 49	100.0	43.0	21.6	15.2	4.8	1.5
Aged 50 to 54	100.0	23.5	15.1	6.2	1.7	0.4
Aged 55 to 64	100.0	6.7	4.9	1.4	0.3	0.1
Aged 65 to 74	100.0	1.3	0.9	0.4	0.1	0.0
Aged 75 or older	100.0	0.4	0.3	0.1	0.0	0.0

Source: Bureau of the Census, America's Families and Living Arrangements: 2006, Internet site http://www.census.gov/population/www/socdemo/hh-fam/cps2006.html; calculations by New Strategist

Householders in the Northeast Are Older

The West has the youngest householders.

Because the South is the nation's most populous region, it is home to the largest share of households in each age group. But there are variations in the age composition of households by region, although the differences are not large.

The Northeast has the smallest share of young householders. Only 11 percent of householders in the Northeast are under age 30 compared with 15 percent in the South and West. Twenty-two percent of households in the Northeast are headed by people aged 65 or older, versus only 19 percent in the West.

By generation, Millennials are most prevalent in the South and West, where they account for 15 percent of households. Millennials' smallest share is in the Northeast, where they head just 11 percent of households. Households headed by Generation Xers are slightly more common in the West than in the Northeast (24 versus 22 percent). The Swing and World War II generations account for 25 percent of households in the West, but for a larger 29 percent of households in the Northeast.

■ Regional differences in households by age are small. Much larger differences by age can be found at the city level, especially in areas hosting universities, military bases, or retirement communities.

The Northeast has the largest share of older householders

(percent of households headed by people under age 30 and aged 65 or older, by region, 2006)

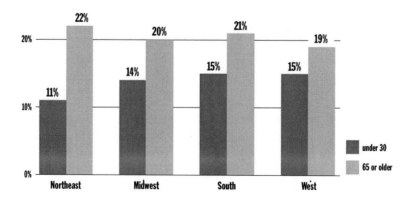

Table 8.17 Households by Age of Householder and Region of Residence, 2006

(number and percent distribution of households by age of householder and region of residence, and mean age, 2006; numbers in thousands)

	total	Northeast	Midwest	South	West
Total households	**114,384**	**21,054**	**26,351**	**41,805**	**25,174**
Under age 20	922	146	177	386	214
Aged 20 to 24	5,873	755	1,403	2,303	1,412
Aged 25 to 29	9,223	1,510	2,160	3,498	2,055
Aged 30 to 34	9,896	1,659	2,260	3,636	2,341
Aged 35 to 39	10,976	2,007	2,432	3,964	2,574
Aged 40 to 44	12,040	2,260	2,679	4,380	2,721
Aged 45 to 49	12,470	2,415	2,842	4,376	2,836
Aged 50 to 54	11,262	2,072	2,779	3,968	2,442
Aged 55 to 64	18,264	3,567	4,296	6,618	3,783
Aged 65 to 74	11,687	2,204	2,415	4,685	2,382
Aged 75 or older	11,772	2,458	2,908	3,991	2,415
Mean age (years)	49.2	50.5	49.3	49.0	48.3
Percent distribution by age					
Total households	**100.0%**	**100.0%**	**100.0%**	**100.0%**	**100.0%**
Under age 20	0.8	0.7	0.7	0.9	0.9
Aged 20 to 24	5.1	3.6	5.3	5.5	5.6
Aged 25 to 29	8.1	7.2	8.2	8.4	8.2
Aged 30 to 34	8.7	7.9	8.6	8.7	9.3
Aged 35 to 39	9.6	9.5	9.2	9.5	10.2
Aged 40 to 44	10.5	10.7	10.2	10.5	10.8
Aged 45 to 49	10.9	11.5	10.8	10.5	11.3
Aged 50 to 54	9.8	9.8	10.5	9.5	9.7
Aged 55 to 64	16.0	16.9	16.3	15.8	15.0
Aged 65 to 74	10.2	10.5	9.2	11.2	9.5
Aged 75 or older	10.3	11.7	11.0	9.5	9.6
Percent distribution by region					
Total households	**100.0%**	**18.4%**	**23.0%**	**36.5%**	**22.0%**
Under age 20	100.0	15.8	19.2	41.9	23.2
Aged 20 to 24	100.0	12.9	23.9	39.2	24.0
Aged 25 to 29	100.0	16.4	23.4	37.9	22.3
Aged 30 to 34	100.0	16.8	22.8	36.7	23.7
Aged 35 to 39	100.0	18.3	22.2	36.1	23.5
Aged 40 to 44	100.0	18.8	22.3	36.4	22.6
Aged 45 to 49	100.0	19.4	22.8	35.1	22.7
Aged 50 to 54	100.0	18.4	24.7	35.2	21.7
Aged 55 to 64	100.0	19.5	23.5	36.2	20.7
Aged 65 to 74	100.0	18.9	20.7	40.1	20.4
Aged 75 or older	100.0	20.9	24.7	33.9	20.5

Source: Bureau of the Census, America's Families and Living Arrangements: 2006, Internet site http://www.census.gov/ population/www/socdemo/hh-fam/cps2006.html; calculations by New Strategist

Table 8.18 Households by Generation of Householder and Region of Residence, 2006

(number and percent distribution of households by generation of householder and region of residence, 2006; numbers in thousands)

	total	Northeast	Midwest	South	West
Total households	**114,384**	**21,054**	**26,351**	**41,805**	**25,174**
Millennial (15–29)	16,018	2,411	3,740	6,187	3,681
Generation X (30–41)	25,688	4,570	5,764	9,352	6,003
Baby Boom (42–60)	41,914	7,983	9,806	14,943	9,180
Swing (61–73)	17,824	3,410	3,892	6,864	3,657
World War II (74+)	12,941	2,678	3,150	4,460	2,653
Percent distribution by generation of householder					
Total households	**100.0%**	**100.0%**	**100.0%**	**100.0%**	**100.0%**
Millennial (15–29)	14.0	11.5	14.2	14.8	14.6
Generation X (30–41)	22.5	21.7	21.9	22.4	23.8
Baby Boom (42–60)	36.6	37.9	37.2	35.7	36.5
Swing (61–73)	15.6	16.2	14.8	16.4	14.5
World War II (74+)	11.3	12.7	12.0	10.7	10.5
Percent distribution by region					
Total households	**100.0%**	**18.4%**	**23.0%**	**36.5%**	**22.0%**
Millennial (15–29)	100.0	15.1	23.3	38.6	23.0
Generation X (30–41)	100.0	17.8	22.4	36.4	23.4
Baby Boom (42–60)	100.0	19.0	23.4	35.7	21.9
Swing (61–73)	100.0	19.1	21.8	38.5	20.5
World War II (74+)	100.0	20.7	24.3	34.5	20.5

Note: Households by generation are estimates by New Strategist.
Source: Bureau of the Census, America's Families and Living Arrangements: 2006, Internet site http://www.census.gov/population/www/socdemo/hh-fam/cps2006.html; calculations by New Strategist

More Children Live with Single Parents

Only 67 percent live with both mom and dad.

In 1970, 85 percent of children under age 18 lived with both parents, but by 2006 only 67 percent lived in a nuclear family. The increase in single-parent families headed by women accounts for most of the change in children's living arrangements during those years. The proportion of children living only with their mother increased from 11 percent in 1970 to 23 percent in 2006. Although single-parent families headed by men are more common than they once were, only 5 percent of children live with their father only.

Black children have the most diverse living arrangements. Only 35 percent live with both parents, while 51 percent live with their mother only. Another 7 percent live with relatives other than their mother or father.

Most white or Hispanic children live with both parents, although the percentage of those who live with a single parent has grown over the past few decades. One-quarter of Hispanic children and 18 percent of white children live with their mother only.

■ The percentage of children who live in a single-parent family is climbing more slowly than in the past, but still inching upwards.

Fewer children today live with both parents

(percent of children who live with both parents, by race and Hispanic origin, 1970 and 2006)

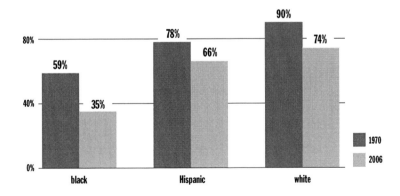

Table 8.19 Living Arrangements of Children by Race and Hispanic Origin, 1970 to 2006

(number and percent distribution of children under age 18 by race, Hispanic origin, and living arrangement, 1970 to 2006; numbers in thousands)

| | total | living with | | | | |
		both parents	mother only	father only	other relatives	nonrelatives only
Total children						
2006	73,664	67.4%	23.3%	4.7%	3.3%	1.3%
2005	73,494	67.3	23.4	4.8	3.4	1.0
2000	72,012	69.1	22.4	4.2	3.0	1.2
1995	70,254	68.7	23.5	3.5	3.3	1.0
1990	64,137	72.5	21.6	3.1	2.2	0.5
1985	62,475	73.9	20.9	2.5	2.1	0.6
1980	63,427	76.7	18.0	1.7	3.1	0.6
1975	66,087	80.3	15.5	1.5	2.1	0.5
1970	69,162	85.2	10.8	1.1	2.2	0.7
Black						
2006	12,261	35.4	50.6	5.0	7.1	1.9
2005	12,256	35.7	49.6	5.0	8.3	1.5
2000	11,412	37.6	49.0	4.2	7.7	1.5
1995	11,301	33.1	52.0	4.1	9.0	1.8
1990	10,018	37.7	51.2	3.5	6.5	1.0
1985	9,479	39.5	51.0	2.9	5.7	0.9
1980	9,375	42.2	43.9	1.9	10.7	1.3
1975	9,472	49.4	40.9	1.8	6.8	1.1
1970	9,422	58.5	29.5	2.3	8.7	1.0
Hispanic						
2006	14,697	65.9	25.0	4.1	3.6	1.4
2005	14,241	64.7	25.4	4.8	3.8	1.4
2000	11,613	65.1	25.1	4.4	3.7	1.7
1995	9,843	62.9	28.4	4.2	3.2	1.2
1990	7,174	66.8	27.1	2.9	2.5	0.8
1985	6,057	67.9	26.6	2.2	2.6	0.7
1980	5,459	75.4	19.6	1.5	3.4	0.1
1970	4,006	77.7	–	–	–	–
White						
2006	56,332	73.8	17.9	4.6	2.4	1.2
2005	56,234	73.5	18.4	4.7	2.4	1.0
2000	56,455	75.3	17.3	4.3	2.0	1.1
1995	55,327	75.8	17.8	3.4	2.2	0.8
1990	51,390	79.0	16.2	3.0	1.4	0.4
1985	50,836	80.0	15.6	2.4	1.5	0.5
1980	52,242	82.7	13.5	1.6	1.7	0.5
1975	55,500	85.4	11.3	1.5	1.3	0.4
1970	58,791	89.5	7.8	0.9	1.2	0.6

Note: "–" means data are not available.

Source: Bureau of the Census, Families and Living Arrangements, Historical Time Series, Internet site http://www.census .gov/population/www/socdemo/hh-fam.html; calculations by New Strategist

More than 3 Million Children Live with a Grandparent

Many also live with their mother.

The number of children living in the home of a grandparent grew between 1970 and 2006, rising from 2.2 million to 3.7 million. Five percent of children were living with a grandparent in 2006, up from 3 percent in 1970.

Most (60 percent) of the children living in the home of a grandparent also have a parent in the same household. But a substantial 40 percent—1.5 million children—live with only a grandparent. This proportion has declined from 43 percent in 1970, however.

■ Grandparents who are raising grandchildren on their own are especially likely to need assistance and advice.

The number of children who live with a grandparent fell slightly between 2000 and 2006

(number of children living in the home of a grandparent, 1970–2006; numbers in millions)

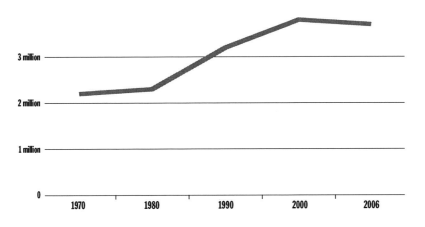

Table 8.20 Children Living with Grandparents, 1970 to 2006

(number and percent distribution of children who live in the home of a grandparent by presence of parent, 1970 to 2006; numbers in thousands)

| | total children | total | grandchildren living in grandparents' home | | | | |
| | | | with parents present | | | | without parents present |
			total	both parents	mother only	father only	
2006	73,664	3,731	2,246	412	1,650	184	1,484
2000	72,012	3,842	2,483	531	1,732	220	1,359
1990	64,137	3,155	2,221	467	1,563	191	935
1980	63,369	2,306	1,318	310	922	86	988
1970	69,276	2,214	1,258	363	817	78	957
Percent distribution by living arrangement							
2006	100.0%	5.1%	3.0%	0.6%	2.2%	0.2%	2.0%
2000	100.0	5.3	3.4	0.7	2.4	0.3	1.9
1990	100.0	4.9	3.5	0.7	2.4	0.3	1.5
1980	100.0	3.6	2.1	0.5	1.5	0.1	1.6
1970	100.0	3.2	1.8	0.5	1.2	0.1	1.4
Percent distribution of children living with a grandparent by presence of parent in the home							
2006	–	100.0%	60.2%	11.0%	44.2%	4.9%	39.8%
2000	–	100.0	64.6	13.8	45.1	5.7	35.4
1990	–	100.0	70.4	14.8	49.5	6.1	29.6
1980	–	100.0	57.2	13.4	40.0	3.7	42.8
1970	–	100.0	56.8	16.4	36.9	3.5	43.2

Note: "–" means not applicable.
Source: Bureau of the Census, Families and Living Arrangements, Historical Time Series, Internet site http://www.census .gov/population/www/socdemo/hh-fam.html; calculations by New Strategist

Living Arrangements Differ by Generation

Many Millennials aged 15 or older still live with mom and dad.

The generations are distinguished by their living arrangements. Among Millennials aged 15 or older, the largest share still live with their parents. Among Generation Xers, Boomers, and the Swing generation, most men and women are married couple householders or spouses. In the World War II generation, the largest share of women lives alone.

Women marry at a younger age than men, and they are more likely than men to be widowed and live alone in old age. In every age group under age 45, women are more likely than men to be a married-couple householder or spouse. From age 45 on, however, men are more likely than women to be married and living with a spouse. The majority of men are married and living with a spouse for the rest of their lives. But the percentage of women who live as a married-couple householder or spouse falls below 50 percent in the 75-to-84 age group as a growing share become widows. Fifty-six percent of women aged 85 or older live alone compared with only 29 percent of men.

■ The wants and needs of men and women diverge as lifestyle differences grow with age.

Women are much more likely than men to live alone in old age

(percent of people aged 85 or older who are living with a spouse or living alone, by sex, 2006)

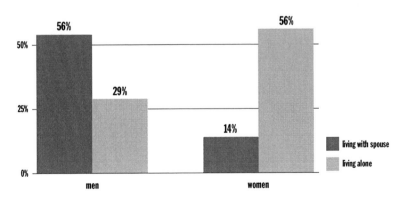

Table 8.21 Men by Living Arrangement and Age, 2006

(number and percent distribution of men aged 15 or older by living arrangement and age, 2006; numbers in thousands)

	total	15–17	18–19	20–24	25–29	30–34	35–39	40–44	45–49	50–54	55–64	65–74	75–84	85+
Total men	113,073	6,817	3,795	10,305	10,185	9,639	10,305	11,039	11,041	9,916	14,856	8,518	5,330	1,327
Married-couple householder or spouse	58,179	12	49	1,000	3,506	5,315	6,334	6,886	7,154	6,511	10,761	6,247	3,664	739
Married-couple householder	36,765	5	36	585	2,134	3,151	3,841	4,183	4,383	4,085	7,082	4,246	2,536	498
Spouse of householder	21,414	7	13	415	1,372	2,164	2,493	2,703	2,771	2,426	3,679	2,001	1,128	241
Other householder	21,883	102	272	2,097	2,547	1,957	1,932	2,158	2,282	2,007	2,859	1,808	1,383	477
Male family householder	5,130	100	137	620	620	503	476	623	589	475	498	237	170	81
Living alone	13,061	0	49	777	1,198	1,021	1,120	1,233	1,393	1,247	2,077	1,436	1,129	382
Living with nonrelatives	3,692	2	86	700	729	433	336	302	300	285	284	135	84	14
Other nonhouseholder	33,011	6,703	3,474	7,208	4,132	2,367	2,039	1,995	1,605	1,398	1,236	463	283	111
Child of householder	19,211	6,010	2,875	4,698	1,849	991	826	816	544	383	207	12	0	0
Other relative of householder	6,317	525	373	961	838	490	433	547	485	496	551	302	224	95
Living with nonrelatives	7,483	168	226	1,549	1,445	886	780	632	576	519	478	149	59	16
Total men	100.0%	100.0%	100.0%	100.0%	100.0%	100.0%	100.0%	100.0%	100.0%	100.0%	100.0%	100.0%	100.0%	100.0%
Married-couple householder or spouse	51.5	0.2	1.3	9.7	34.4	55.1	61.5	62.4	64.8	65.7	72.4	73.3	68.7	55.7
Married-couple householder	32.5	0.1	0.9	5.7	21.0	32.7	37.3	37.9	39.7	41.2	47.7	49.8	47.6	37.5
Spouse of householder	18.9	0.1	0.3	4.0	13.5	22.5	24.2	24.5	25.1	24.5	24.8	23.5	21.2	18.2
Other householder	19.4	1.5	7.2	20.3	25.0	20.3	18.7	19.5	20.7	20.2	19.2	21.2	25.9	35.9
Male family householder	4.5	1.5	3.6	6.0	6.1	5.2	4.6	5.6	5.3	4.8	3.4	2.8	3.2	6.1
Living alone	11.6	0.0	1.3	7.5	11.8	10.6	10.9	11.2	12.6	12.6	14.0	16.9	21.2	28.8
Living with nonrelatives	3.3	0.0	2.3	6.8	7.2	4.5	3.3	2.7	2.7	2.9	1.9	1.6	1.6	1.1
Other nonhouseholder	29.2	98.3	91.5	69.9	40.6	24.6	19.8	18.1	14.5	14.1	8.3	5.4	5.3	8.4
Child of householder	17.0	88.2	75.8	45.6	18.2	10.3	8.0	7.4	4.9	3.9	1.4	0.1	0.0	0.0
Other relative of householder	5.6	7.7	9.8	9.3	8.2	5.1	4.2	5.0	4.4	5.0	3.7	3.5	4.2	7.2
Living with nonrelatives	6.6	2.5	6.0	15.0	14.2	9.2	7.6	5.7	5.2	5.2	3.2	1.7	1.1	1.2

Source: Bureau of the Census, America's Families and Living Arrangements: 2006, Internet site http://www.census.gov/population/www/socdemo/hh-fam/cps2006.html; calculations by New Strategist

Table 8.22 Men by Living Arrangement and Generation, 2006

(number and percent distribution of men aged 15 or older by living arrangement and generation, 2006; numbers in thousands)

	total	Millennials (15 to 29)	Generation X (30 to 41)	Baby Boom (42 to 60)	Swing (61 to 73)	World War II (74 or older)
Total men	**113,073**	**31,102**	**24,360**	**36,494**	**13,609**	**7,509**
Married-couple householder or spouse	58,179	4,567	14,403	24,253	9,927	5,028
Married-couple householder	36,765	2,760	8,665	15,227	6,654	3,459
Spouse of householder	21,414	1,807	5,738	9,026	3,273	1,569
Other householder	21,883	5,018	4,752	7,299	2,771	2,041
Male family householder	5,130	1,477	1,228	1,737	413	275
Living alone	13,061	2,024	2,634	4,626	2,123	1,655
Living with nonrelatives	3,692	1,517	890	937	235	112
Other nonhouseholder	33,011	21,517	5,204	4,942	911	440
Child of householder	19,211	15,432	2,143	1,541	94	1
Other relative of householder	6,317	2,697	1,142	1,640	492	349
Living with nonrelatives	7,483	3,388	1,919	1,761	325	90
Total men	**100.0%**	**100.0%**	**100.0%**	**100.0%**	**100.0%**	**100.0%**
Married-couple householder or spouse	51.5	14.7	59.1	66.5	72.9	67.0
Married-couple householder	32.5	8.9	35.6	41.7	48.9	46.1
Spouse of householder	18.9	5.8	23.6	24.7	24.0	20.9
Other householder	19.4	16.1	19.5	20.0	20.4	27.2
Male family householder	4.5	4.7	5.0	4.8	3.0	3.7
Living alone	11.6	6.5	10.8	12.7	15.6	22.0
Living with nonrelatives	3.3	4.9	3.7	2.6	1.7	1.5
Other nonhouseholder	29.2	69.2	21.4	13.5	6.7	5.9
Child of householder	17.0	49.6	8.8	4.2	0.7	0.0
Other relative of householder	5.6	8.7	4.7	4.5	3.6	4.7
Living with nonrelatives	6.6	10.9	7.9	4.8	2.4	1.2

Note: Numbers of people by generation are estimates by New Strategist.
Source: Bureau of the Census, America's Families and Living Arrangements: 2006, Internet site http://www.census.gov/population/www/socdemo/hh-fam/cps2006.html; calculations by New Strategist

Table 8.23 Women by Living Arrangement and Age, 2006

(number and percent distribution of women aged 15 or older by living arrangement and age, 2006; numbers in thousands)

	total	15–17	18–19	20–24	25–29	30–34	35–39	40–44	45–49	50–54	55–64	65–74	75–84	85+
Total women	119,966	6,523	3,766	10,075	9,953	9,700	10,450	11,295	11,464	10,354	16,100	10,022	7,629	2,636
Married-couple householder or spouse	58,179	23	116	1,900	4,480	5,936	6,641	7,181	7,252	6,468	9,854	5,337	2,608	382
Married-couple householder	21,414	6	39	744	1,785	2,334	2,542	2,800	2,804	2,300	3,379	1,763	801	117
Spouse of householder	36,765	17	77	1,156	2,695	3,602	4,099	4,381	4,448	4,168	6,475	3,574	1,807	265
Other householder	34,323	108	354	2,447	2,757	2,454	2,660	2,900	3,000	2,870	4,945	3,870	4,235	1,725
Female family householder	14,093	102	183	1,139	1,458	1,511	1,741	1,858	1,622	1,203	1,488	863	697	227
Living alone	17,392	1	84	680	827	705	710	824	1,134	1,472	3,168	2,859	3,454	1,476
Living with nonrelatives	2,838	5	87	628	472	238	209	218	244	195	289	148	84	22
Other nonhouseholder	27,464	6,392	3,296	5,728	2,716	1,310	1,149	1,214	1,212	1,016	1,301	815	786	529
Child of householder	15,368	5,763	2,739	3,727	1,237	494	355	365	282	183	200	26	0	0
Other relative of householder	6,503	424	276	691	438	280	293	394	518	524	772	667	716	506
Living with nonrelatives	5,593	205	281	1,310	1,041	536	501	455	412	309	329	122	70	23
Total women	100.0%	100.0%	100.0%	100.0%	100.0%	100.0%	100.0%	100.0%	100.0%	100.0%	100.0%	100.0%	100.0%	100.0%
Married-couple householder or spouse	48.5	0.4	3.1	18.9	45.0	61.2	63.6	63.6	63.3	62.5	61.2	53.3	34.2	14.5
Married-couple householder	17.9	0.1	1.0	7.4	17.9	24.1	24.3	24.8	24.5	22.2	21.0	17.6	10.5	4.4
Spouse of householder	30.6	0.3	2.0	11.5	27.1	37.1	39.2	38.8	38.8	40.3	40.2	35.7	23.7	10.1
Other householder	28.6	1.7	9.4	24.3	27.7	25.3	25.5	25.7	26.2	27.7	30.7	38.6	55.5	65.4
Female family householder	11.7	1.6	4.9	11.3	14.6	15.6	16.7	16.4	14.1	11.6	9.2	8.6	9.1	8.6
Living alone	14.5	0.0	2.2	6.7	8.3	7.3	6.8	7.3	9.9	14.2	19.7	28.5	45.3	56.0
Living with nonrelatives	2.4	0.1	2.3	6.2	4.7	2.5	2.0	1.9	2.1	1.9	1.8	1.5	1.1	0.8
Other nonhouseholder	22.9	98.0	87.5	56.9	27.3	13.5	11.0	10.7	10.6	9.8	8.1	8.1	10.3	20.1
Child of householder	12.8	88.3	72.7	37.0	12.4	5.1	3.4	3.2	2.5	1.8	1.2	0.3	0.0	0.0
Other relative of householder	5.4	6.5	7.3	6.9	4.4	2.9	2.8	3.5	4.5	5.1	4.8	6.7	9.4	19.2
Living with nonrelatives	4.7	3.1	7.5	13.0	10.5	5.5	4.8	4.0	3.6	3.0	2.0	1.2	0.9	0.9

Source: Bureau of the Census, America's Families and Living Arrangements: 2006, Internet site http://www.census.gov/population/www/socdemo/hh-fam/cps2006.html; calculations by New Strategist

Table 8.24 Women by Living Arrangement and Generation, 2006

(number and percent distribution of women aged 15 or older by living arrangement and generation, 2006; numbers in thousands)

	total	Millennials (15 to 29)	Generation X (30 to 41)	Baby Boom (42 to 60)	Swing (61 to 73)	World War II (74 or older)
Total women	**119,966**	**30,317**	**24,668**	**38,255**	**15,460**	**11,267**
Married-couple householder or spouse	58,179	6,519	15,449	23,941	8,745	3,524
Married-couple householder	21,414	2,574	5,996	8,811	2,938	1,094
Spouse of householder	36,765	3,945	9,453	15,130	5,807	2,429
Other householder	34,323	5,666	6,274	10,577	5,461	6,347
Female family householder	14,093	2,882	3,995	4,833	1,372	1,010
Living alone	17,392	1,592	1,745	5,001	3,840	5,216
Living with nonrelatives	2,838	1,192	534	743	249	121
Other nonhouseholder	27,464	18,132	2,945	3,737	1,254	1,397
Child of householder	15,368	13,466	995	804	103	3
Other relative of householder	6,503	1,829	731	1,742	909	1,289
Living with nonrelatives	5,593	2,837	1,219	1,191	241	105
Total women	**100.0%**	**100.0%**	**100.0%**	**100.0%**	**100.0%**	**100.0%**
Married-couple householder or spouse	48.5	21.5	62.6	62.6	56.6	31.3
Married-couple householder	17.9	8.5	24.3	23.0	19.0	9.7
Spouse of householder	30.6	13.0	38.3	39.5	37.6	21.6
Other householder	28.6	18.7	25.4	27.6	35.3	56.3
Female family householder	11.7	9.5	16.2	12.6	8.9	9.0
Living alone	14.5	5.3	7.1	13.1	24.8	46.3
Living with nonrelatives	2.4	3.9	2.2	1.9	1.6	1.1
Other nonhouseholder	22.9	59.8	11.9	9.8	8.1	12.4
Child of householder	12.8	44.4	4.0	2.1	0.7	0.0
Other relative of householder	5.4	6.0	3.0	4.6	5.9	11.4
Living with nonrelatives	4.7	9.4	4.9	3.1	1.6	0.9

Note: Numbers of people by generation are estimates by New Strategist.
Source: Bureau of the Census, America's Families and Living Arrangements: 2006, Internet site http://www.census.gov/population/www/socdemo/hh-fam/cps2006.html; calculations by New Strategist

Most Americans Are Married

The divorced population peaks in middle age.

The proportion of people who are currently divorced peaks in midlife. Eighteen percent of women and 16 percent of men aged 50 to 54 are currently divorced—the highest proportions among all age groups. (The proportion of Americans who have ever been divorced is much higher, but many of the divorced have remarried.)

Older Americans are much less likely than the middle aged to be currently divorced, but they are far more likely to be widowed. Because women tend to marry older men, and because men tend to die at a younger age than women, widowhood is far more common for women than for men. Among women age 65 to 74, a substantial 26 percent are currently widowed. The share rises to an enormous 75 percent among women aged 85 or older. Only 7 percent of men aged 65 to 74 are widowers, a figure that climbs only to 32 percent among men aged 85 or older.

Most men aged 30 or older are married. Most women are married from age 30 to age 74. From age 75 on, most women are widows.

■ As the women of the Baby-Boom generation age, the number of widows in the population will surpass the number of divorcees.

The marital status of men and women differs greatly in old age

(percent of people aged 85 or older who are currently married or widowed, by sex, 2006)

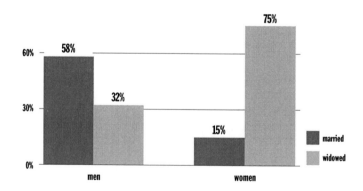

Table 8.25 Marital Status of Men by Age, 2006

(number and percent distribution of men aged 18 or older by age and marital status, 2006; numbers in thousands)

	total	never married	married, spouse present	married, spouse absent	separated	divorced	widowed
Total men	**106,256**	**30,345**	**59,514**	**2,085**	**2,034**	**9,654**	**2,623**
Aged 18 to 19	3,795	3,710	54	8	21	2	2
Aged 20 to 24	10,305	8,931	1,120	88	74	80	13
Aged 25 to 29	10,185	5,843	3,663	185	173	312	9
Aged 30 to 34	9,639	3,223	5,422	240	187	555	12
Aged 35 to 39	10,305	2,396	6,423	266	225	973	21
Aged 40 to 44	11,039	2,045	7,017	269	289	1,356	62
Aged 45 to 49	11,041	1,530	7,306	244	321	1,555	84
Aged 50 to 54	9,916	1,064	6,658	223	278	1,582	112
Aged 55 to 64	14,856	1,030	10,939	292	266	2,005	323
Aged 65 to 74	8,518	350	6,397	133	151	867	621
Aged 75 to 84	5,330	177	3,747	99	46	325	936
Aged 85 or older	1,327	46	767	37	4	43	429
Total men	**100.0%**	**28.6%**	**56.0%**	**2.0%**	**1.9%**	**9.1%**	**2.5%**
Aged 18 to 19	100.0	97.8	1.4	0.2	0.6	0.1	0.1
Aged 20 to 24	100.0	86.7	10.9	0.9	0.7	0.8	0.1
Aged 25 to 29	100.0	57.4	36.0	1.8	1.7	3.1	0.1
Aged 30 to 34	100.0	33.4	56.3	2.5	1.9	5.8	0.1
Aged 35 to 39	100.0	23.3	62.3	2.6	2.2	9.4	0.2
Aged 40 to 44	100.0	18.5	63.6	2.4	2.6	12.3	0.6
Aged 45 to 49	100.0	13.9	66.2	2.2	2.9	14.1	0.8
Aged 50 to 54	100.0	10.7	67.1	2.2	2.8	16.0	1.1
Aged 55 to 64	100.0	6.9	73.6	2.0	1.8	13.5	2.2
Aged 65 to 74	100.0	4.1	75.1	1.6	1.8	10.2	7.3
Aged 75 to 84	100.0	3.3	70.3	1.9	0.9	6.1	17.6
Aged 85 or older	100.0	3.5	57.8	2.8	0.3	3.2	32.3

*Source: Bureau of the Census, America's Families and Living Arrangements: 2006, Internet site http://www.census
.govpopulation/www/socdemo/hh-fam/cps2006.html; calculations by New Strategist*

Table 8.26 Marital Status of Women by Age, 2006

(number and percent distribution of women aged 18 or older by age and marital status, 2006; numbers in thousands)

	total	never married	married, spouse present	married, spouse absent	separated	divorced	widowed
Total women	**113,443**	**24,994**	**59,502**	**1,683**	**2,877**	**13,104**	**11,284**
Aged 18 to 19	3,766	3,565	143	17	24	13	5
Aged 20 to 24	10,075	7,589	2,044	127	146	152	17
Aged 25 to 29	9,953	4,289	4,654	166	276	526	43
Aged 30 to 34	9,700	2,327	6,042	164	337	778	52
Aged 35 to 39	10,450	1,741	6,731	146	384	1,334	114
Aged 40 to 44	11,295	1,476	7,292	145	418	1,764	201
Aged 45 to 49	11,464	1,299	7,432	163	371	1,916	281
Aged 50 to 54	10,354	947	6,620	142	323	1,901	421
Aged 55 to 64	16,100	1,041	10,039	225	387	2,868	1,540
Aged 65 to 74	10,022	391	5,445	178	142	1,235	2,631
Aged 75 to 84	7,629	247	2,661	146	56	531	3,989
Aged 85 or older	2,636	83	398	65	13	87	1,990
Total women	**100.0%**	**22.0%**	**52.5%**	**1.5%**	**2.5%**	**11.6%**	**9.9%**
Aged 18 to 19	100.0	94.7	3.8	0.5	0.6	0.3	0.1
Aged 20 to 24	100.0	75.3	20.3	1.3	1.4	1.5	0.2
Aged 25 to 29	100.0	43.1	46.8	1.7	2.8	5.3	0.4
Aged 30 to 34	100.0	24.0	62.3	1.7	3.5	8.0	0.5
Aged 35 to 39	100.0	16.7	64.4	1.4	3.7	12.8	1.1
Aged 40 to 44	100.0	13.1	64.6	1.3	3.7	15.6	1.8
Aged 45 to 49	100.0	11.3	64.8	1.4	3.2	16.7	2.5
Aged 50 to 54	100.0	9.1	63.9	1.4	3.1	18.4	4.1
Aged 55 to 64	100.0	6.5	62.4	1.4	2.4	17.8	9.6
Aged 65 to 74	100.0	3.9	54.3	1.8	1.4	12.3	26.3
Aged 75 to 84	100.0	3.2	34.9	1.9	0.7	7.0	52.3
Aged 85 or older	100.0	3.1	15.1	2.5	0.5	3.3	75.5

Source: Bureau of the Census, America's Families and Living Arrangements: 2006, Internet site http://www.census.gov/ population/www/socdemo/hh-fam/cps2006.html; calculations by New Strategist

Younger Generations Stay Single Longer

The World War II generation married early.

Perhaps no trend has so dramatically changed the lifestyle of young adults as the rise of singlehood over the past few decades. In 1970, only 36 percent of women aged 20 to 24 had never married. By 2006, the proportion had more than doubled, reaching 75 percent. Among men of the age group, the never-married proportion rose from 55 to 87 percent during those years. The rise in singlehood has not been confined to young adults. Since 1970, the never-married share has grown in every age group under age 55.

The World War II generation created the marriage boom of the 1950s and 1960s by marrying at a younger age and in greater proportions than their parents had. The share of Americans aged 55 or older who have never married is lower today than it was in 1970.

■ The growing importance of a college education has caused many young men and women to postpone marriage.

Young people today are more likely to be single

(percent of people aged 20 to 24 who have never been married, by sex, 1970 and 2006)

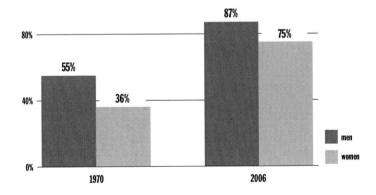

Table 8.27 Never-Married People by Sex and Age, 1970 to 2006

(percent of people who have never been married, by sex and age, 1970 to 2006; percentage point change 1970–2006)

	2006	2000	1990	1980	1970	percentage point change 1970–2006
Men						
Aged 20 to 24	86.7%	83.7%	79.3%	68.8%	54.7%	32.0
Aged 25 to 29	57.4	51.7	45.2	33.1	19.1	38.3
Aged 30 to 34	33.4	30.1	27.0	15.9	9.4	24.0
Aged 35 to 39	23.3	20.3	14.7	7.8	7.2	16.1
Aged 40 to 44	18.5	15.7	10.5	7.1	6.3	12.2
Aged 45 to 54	12.4	9.5	6.3	6.1	7.5	4.9
Aged 55 to 64	6.9	5.5	5.8	5.3	7.8	−0.9
Aged 65 or older	3.8	4.2	4.2	4.9	7.5	−3.7
Women						
Aged 20 to 24	75.3	72.8	62.8	50.2	35.8	39.5
Aged 25 to 29	43.1	38.9	31.1	20.9	10.5	32.6
Aged 30 to 34	24.0	21.9	16.4	9.5	6.2	17.8
Aged 35 to 39	16.7	14.3	10.4	6.2	5.4	11.3
Aged 40 to 44	13.1	11.8	8.0	4.8	4.9	8.2
Aged 45 to 54	10.3	8.6	5.0	4.7	4.9	5.4
Aged 55 to 64	6.5	4.9	3.9	4.5	6.8	−0.3
Aged 65 or older	3.6	3.6	4.9	5.9	7.7	−4.1

Source: Bureau of the Census, Families and Living Arrangements, Current Population Surveys, Internet site http://www.census .gov/population/www/socdemo/hh-fam.html; calculations by New Strategist

Most Cohabitors Are Young Adults

And most will eventually marry.

Among the nation's 114 million households in 2006, just over 5 million were headed by opposite-sex unmarried partners. Most of the men and women living as unmarried partners are relatively young. Fifty-three percent are under age 35.

Few older adults live together without marrying. The Swing and World War II generations combined account for only 7 percent of the nation's unmarried partner households. Millennials account for the largest share of unmarried couples, at 38 percent.

■ Most cohabiting couples are young and many will marry—although they may not marry the person with whom they are currently living.

Millennials account for the largest share of unmarried couples

(percent distribution of opposite-sex unmarried couples, by generation, 2006)

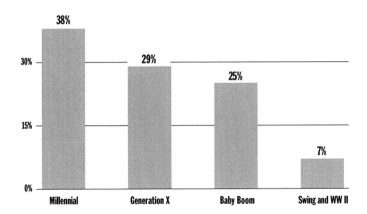

Table 8.28 Opposite-Sex Unmarried Couples by Age and Generation, 2006

(number and percent distribution of opposite-sex unmarried couples, by age of householder, 2006; numbers in thousands)

	number	percent distribution
Total couples	**5,012**	**100.0%**
Under age 20	97	1.9
Aged 20 to 24	874	17.4
Aged 25 to 29	955	19.1
Aged 30 to 34	706	14.1
Aged 35 to 39	570	11.4
Aged 40 to 44	488	9.7
Aged 45 to 49	439	8.8
Aged 50 to 54	335	6.7
Aged 55 to 64	334	6.7
Aged 65 or older	215	4.3
Total couples	**5,012**	**100.0**
Millennial (15–29)	1,926	38.4
Generation X (30–41)	1,471	29.4
Baby Boom (42–60)	1,267	25.3
Swing and World War II (61+)	349	7.0

Note: Numbers by generation are estimates by New Strategist.
Source: Bureau of the Census, America's Families and Living Arrangements: 2006, Internet site http://www.census.gov/ population/www/socdemo/hh-fam/cps2006.html; calculations by New Strategist

Divorce Is Highest among Men and Women in Their Fifties

At least half of men aged 30 or older are married and still living with their first wife.

Men and women aged 50 to 59 are most likely to have experienced a divorce, according to a Census Bureau study of marriage and divorce. Among women in the age group, 41 have been through a divorce. For their male counterparts, the figure is 37.5 percent.

Divorce is much less common for older men and women. Among those aged 70 or older, only 18 percent of women and 21 percent of men have ever divorced. Divorce is also less common among people under age 50, in part because they have not had as much time to get divorced.

Despite the frequency of divorce, more than half of men aged 30 or older have married only once and are still married to their first wife. Among women, most of those in their thirties have married only once and are still living with their first husband. After that, however, the proportion falls with age as women become widows.

■ Divorce is more common among Baby Boomers than older or younger generations for reasons not entirely understood by family experts.

More than one in five adults have experienced divorce

(percent of people aged 15 or older by selected marital history, by sex, 2004)

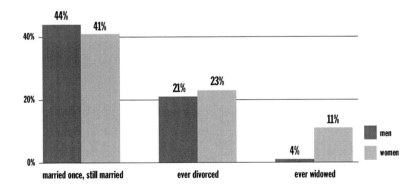

Table 8.29 Marital History of Men by Age, 2004

(number of men aged 15 or older and percent distribution by marital history and age, 2004; numbers in thousands)

	total	15–19	20–24	25–29	30–34	35–39	40–49	50–59	60–69	70+
TOTAL MEN, NUMBER	109,830	10,473	10,022	9,511	9,848	10,121	21,857	17,352	10,571	10,075
TOTAL MEN, PERCENT	100.0%	100.0%	100.0%	100.0%	100.0%	100.0%	100.0%	100.0%	100.0%	100.0%
Never married	31.2	98.1	84.0	53.6	30.3	20.2	14.1	8.7	4.8	3.2
Ever married	68.8	1.9	16.0	46.4	69.7	79.8	85.9	91.3	95.2	96.8
Married once	54.0	1.9	15.9	44.3	62.4	68.1	66.8	63.4	66.8	74.9
Still married	43.8	1.5	14.4	39.7	54.4	56.6	52.8	50.3	54.7	55.1
Married twice	11.8	0.0	0.1	2.0	6.7	10.3	15.7	21.3	20.6	17.0
Still married	9.2	0.0	0.1	1.9	6.0	8.5	12.5	16.1	16.1	12.6
Married three or more times	3.1	0.0	0.0	0.1	0.6	1.4	3.3	6.6	7.7	4.9
Still married	2.3	0.0	0.0	0.0	0.4	1.2	2.7	5.1	5.6	3.1
Ever divorced	20.7	0.1	0.8	5.1	13.1	20.7	30.3	37.5	34.1	20.6
Currently divorced	9.3	0.1	0.7	3.2	6.6	10.9	14.7	16.2	13.0	6.2
Ever widowed	3.6	0.2	0.0	0.1	0.1	0.6	1.1	2.8	7.1	23.8
Currently widowed	2.5	0.2	0.0	0.0	0.1	0.4	0.6	1.4	4.2	18.9

Source: Bureau of the Census, Number, Timing, and Duration of Marriages and Divorces: 2004, Detailed Tables, Internet site http://www.census.gov/population/www/socdemo/marr-div/2004detailed_tables.html

Table 8.30 Marital History of Women by Age, 2004

(number of women aged 15 or older and percent distribution by marital history and age, 2004; numbers in thousands)

	total	15–19	20–24	25–29	30–34	35–39	40–49	50–59	60–69	70+
TOTAL WOMEN, NUMBER	117,677	10,082	10,027	9,484	10,097	10,319	22,818	18,412	11,852	14,586
TOTAL WOMEN, PERCENT	100.0%	100.0%	100.0%	100.0%	100.0%	100.0%	100.0%	100.0%	100.0%	100.0%
Never married	25.8	97.3	73.3	41.3	22.3	16.2	11.9	7.6	4.3	4.9
Ever married	74.2	2.7	26.7	58.7	77.7	83.8	88.1	92.4	95.7	95.1
Married once	57.9	2.7	25.8	55.5	68.4	67.5	65.3	62.8	71.1	77.4
Still married	40.6	2.4	23.0	48.6	57.6	54.6	49.7	44.4	46.2	29.0
Married twice	13.2	0.1	0.8	3.1	8.2	14.1	18.9	22.6	18.7	14.9
Still married	8.8	0.0	0.7	2.8	6.6	11.3	14.0	15.5	11.3	5.3
Married three or more times	3.1	0.0	0.0	0.1	1.2	2.2	3.9	7.0	5.9	2.8
Still married	1.9	0.0	0.0	0.1	0.8	1.6	2.8	4.4	3.6	1.0
Ever divorced	22.9	0.2	2.5	7.0	17.1	25.6	33.9	40.7	32.3	17.8
Currently divorced	10.9	0.1	1.7	4.1	9.1	11.7	16.4	19.4	15.0	7.2
Ever widowed	10.8	0.1	0.1	0.3	0.7	1.1	2.5	7.8	21.2	54.5
Currently widowed	9.6	0.1	0.1	0.2	0.5	0.9	1.6	5.7	18.0	51.6

Source: Bureau of the Census, Number, Timing, and Duration of Marriages and Divorces: 2004, Detailed Tables, Internet site http://www.census.gov/population/www/socdemo/marr-div/2004detailed_tables.html

9

Population

For more than half a century, economic and cultural trends in the United States have been shaped by baby booms and baby busts. Today, the large Baby-Boom and Millennial generations are moving through the age structure, their size affecting not only the individual members of each generation, but also the nation as a whole. For decades, American society has had to cope with Boomer demands for education, housing, and jobs. Now Boomers are beginning to retire and their claim on Social Security benefits will grow each year. Today, the Millennial generation is crowding the nation's college campuses and entry-level workforce. Soon it will make itself felt in the housing market.

The small generations on either side of the Baby Boom—the Swing generation and Generation X—are frequently overlooked. The generation that follows Millennials is still forming and has yet to make its mark. These generations are also influencing the economy and culture and should not be overlooked. For example, Generation X now dominates the nation's parents.

Each generation is unique, with well-defined wants and needs. Some of those wants and needs depend upon lifestage, while others are created by the events that shape each generation as it ages.

What to expect in the future

■ Millennials are commanding attention as the nation's new young adults. Their numbers will give them confidence and a strong sense of their own importance.

■ Boomers will continue to exert more influence than other generations, especially now that they are in positions of corporate and political power.

■ The differing wants and needs of large and small generations will continue to create conflict. The biggest fight—how to distribute resources equitably among the generations—won't be easily resolved.

Social Trends Mirror Changing Age Structure

The age structure of the population determines what's hot and what's not.

The changing age structure of the population has greatly influenced American social and economic trends during the past century. It will continue to influence trends as long as there are sharp differences in the sizes of various age groups.

The youth movement of the late 1960s was a consequence of the age structure of the population. It is no coincidence that the youth movement arose just when the proportion of young people in the population expanded with the Baby-Boom generation. As Generation X moved into its teens and twenties, the youth population began to shrink to the consternation of businesses long accustomed to serving the young. Now the youth market has expanded again as another large generation occupies the under-30 age group. But the youthful share of the population will not reach the level seen when Boomers inhabited the age groups, limiting the youth market's influence.

The Baby Boom continues to exert a numerical influence on our culture and economy. Boomers have now swelled the ranks of people in their forties and fifties. This is why the concerns of the middle-aged—financial security, health care, and retirement—are getting so much attention.

In 1920, fewer than 5 percent of Americans were aged 65 or older. At that time, there were twice as many people under the age of 5 as aged 65 or older. In 2006, the oldest Americans outnumbered the youngest by nearly 17 million—a figure that will expand sharply as Boomers fill the age group.

■ The aging of the large Baby-Boom generation challenges Americans to come up with innovative ways to provide health care and retirement security.

Children and young adults shrink as a share of population

(percent of the population in selected age groups, 1920 and 2006)

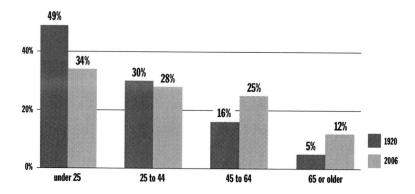

Table 9.1 Population by Age, 1920 to 2006

(number and percent distribution of people by age, and median age, 1920 to 2006; numbers in thousands)

	2006	2000	1990	1980	1970	1960	1950	1940	1930	1920
Total people	299,398	281,422	248,791	226,546	203,212	179,323	150,697	131,669	122,775	105,711
Under age 5	20,418	19,176	18,765	16,348	17,154	20,321	16,164	10,542	11,444	11,573
Aged 5 to 14	40,337	41,078	35,109	34,942	40,746	35,465	24,319	22,431	24,612	22,039
Aged 15 to 24	42,435	39,184	37,036	42,487	35,441	24,020	22,098	23,921	22,422	18,708
Aged 25 to 34	40,416	39,892	43,174	37,082	24,907	22,818	23,759	21,339	18,954	17,158
Aged 35 to 44	43,667	45,149	37,444	25,634	23,088	24,081	21,450	18,333	17,199	14,121
Aged 45 to 54	43,278	37,678	25,062	22,800	23,220	20,485	17,343	15,512	13,018	10,498
Aged 55 to 64	31,587	24,275	21,116	21,703	18,590	15,572	13,295	10,572	8,397	6,532
Aged 65 or older	37,260	34,992	31,084	25,550	20,066	16,560	12,270	9,019	6,634	4,933
Median age	36.4	35.3	32.9	30.0	28.1	29.5	30.2	29.0	26.5	25.3
Total people	100.0%	100.0%	100.0%	100.0%	100.0%	100.0%	100.0%	100.0%	100.0%	100.0%
Under age 5	6.8	6.8	7.5	7.2	8.4	11.3	10.7	8.0	9.3	10.9
Aged 5 to 14	13.5	14.6	14.1	15.4	20.1	19.8	16.1	17.0	20.0	20.8
Aged 15 to 24	14.2	13.9	14.9	18.8	17.4	13.4	14.7	18.2	18.3	17.7
Aged 25 to 34	13.5	14.2	17.4	16.4	12.3	12.7	15.8	16.2	15.4	16.2
Aged 35 to 44	14.6	16.0	15.1	11.3	11.4	13.4	14.2	13.9	14.0	13.4
Aged 45 to 54	14.5	13.4	10.1	10.1	11.4	11.4	11.5	11.8	10.6	9.9
Aged 55 to 64	10.6	8.6	8.5	9.6	9.1	8.7	8.8	8.0	6.8	6.2
Aged 65 or older	12.4	12.4	12.5	11.3	9.9	9.2	8.1	6.8	5.4	4.7

Note: Numbers by age in 1920 and 1930 will not add to total because "age not stated" is not shown.
Sources: Bureau of the Census, Historical Statistics of the United States, Colonial Times to 1970, Part 1, 1975; and Statistical Abstract of the United States: 2001; and Age: 2000, 2000 Census Brief, C2KBR/01-12, 2001; and Population Estimates, Internet site http://www.census.gov/popest/national/asrh/NC-EST2006-sa.html; calculations by New Strategist

Table 9.2 Population by Age and Generation, 2006

(number and percent distribution of people by age and generation, 2006; numbers in thousands)

	number	percent distribution
Total people	**299,398**	**100.0%**
Under age 5	20,418	6.8
Aged 5 to 9	19,710	6.6
Aged 10 to 14	20,627	6.9
Aged 15 to 19	21,324	7.1
Aged 20 to 24	21,111	7.1
Aged 25 to 29	20,709	6.9
Aged 30 to 34	19,706	6.6
Aged 35 to 39	21,186	7.1
Aged 40 to 44	22,481	7.5
Aged 45 to 49	22,798	7.6
Aged 50 to 54	20,481	6.8
Aged 55 to 59	18,224	6.1
Aged 60 to 64	13,362	4.5
Aged 65 to 69	10,376	3.5
Aged 70 to 74	8,541	2.9
Aged 75 to 79	7,381	2.5
Aged 80 to 84	5,666	1.9
Aged 85 or older	5,297	1.8
Total people	**299,398**	**100.0**
Post-Millennial (under age 12)	48,378	16.2
Millennial (12 to 29)	75,521	25.2
Generation X (30 to 41)	49,885	16.7
Baby Boom (42 to 60)	77,664	25.9
Swing (61 to 73)	27,898	9.3
World War II (74 or older)	20,052	6.7

Note: Numbers by generation are estimates by New Strategist.
Source: Bureau of the Census, Population Estimates, Internet site http://www.census.gov/popest/national/asrh/
NC-EST2006-sa.html; calculations by New Strategist

Sex Ratio Reverses with Age

Women dominate older Americans, while boys outnumber girls among the young.

In the beginning, boys have the upper hand, at least numerically. More boys than girls are born each year, although no one is quite sure why. By the later years of life, however, the ratio is reversed and women outnumber men. The reversal occurs because males have a higher death rate than females at every age.

Among Millennials, there are 2.3 million more males than females. Things equal out in Generation X, where men outnumber women by just 118,000. The Baby Boom is beginning to experience rising mortality rates, with a disproportionate impact on men. Boomer women outnumber Boomer men by 652,000.

In the Swing generation, the sex ratio changes more rapidly. There are 1.6 million more women than men. In the World War II generation, men account for only 39 percent of the population.

■ Because women greatly outnumber men among older Americans, women's needs dominate the industries that cater to the old, such as health care.

Males are scarce in the World War II generation

(number of males per 100 females, by generation, 2006)

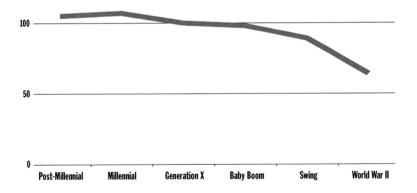

Table 9.3 Population by Age, Generation, and Sex, 2006

(number of people by age, generation, and sex, and sex ratio by age, 2006; numbers in thousands)

	total	female	male	sex ratio
Total people	**299,398**	**150,534**	**147,512**	**98**
Under age 5	20,418	9,928	10,442	105
Aged 5 to 9	19,710	9,555	10,077	105
Aged 10 to 14	20,627	10,186	10,563	104
Aged 15 to 19	21,324	10,260	10,935	107
Aged 20 to 24	21,111	10,195	10,910	107
Aged 25 to 29	20,709	9,815	10,584	108
Aged 30 to 34	19,706	9,943	9,980	100
Aged 35 to 39	21,186	10,452	10,650	102
Aged 40 to 44	22,481	11,493	11,200	97
Aged 45 to 49	22,798	11,384	11,262	99
Aged 50 to 54	20,481	10,213	10,028	98
Aged 55 to 59	18,224	8,930	8,845	99
Aged 60 to 64	13,362	6,801	6,379	94
Aged 65 to 69	10,376	5,411	4,839	89
Aged 70 to 74	8,541	4,705	3,831	81
Aged 75 to 79	7,381	4,298	3,119	73
Aged 80 to 84	5,666	3,481	2,179	63
Aged 85 or older	5,297	3,483	1,688	48
Total people	**299,398**	**150,534**	**147,512**	**98**
Post-Millennial (under age 12)	52,504	25,594	26,857	105
Millennial (12 to 29)	71,396	34,344	36,654	107
Generation X (30 to 41)	49,885	24,992	25,110	100
Baby Boom (42 to 60)	77,664	38,783	38,131	98
Swing (61 to 73)	27,898	14,616	13,007	89
World War II (74 or older)	20,052	12,203	7,753	64

Note: The sex ratio is the number of men per 100 women. Numbers by generation are estimates by New Strategist.
Source: Bureau of the Census, Population Estimates, Internet site http://www.census.gov/popest/national/asrh/ NC-EST2006-sa.html; calculations by New Strategist

Greater Diversity among the Young

Only 60 percent of Millennials are non-Hispanic white.

The United States is far more diverse today than it was half a century ago. Behind the growing diversity is generational replacement. Due to immigration and higher fertility rates among some racial and ethnic groups, each age group is more diverse than the one preceding it. Among the World War II generation, 83 percent are non-Hispanic white. Among Boomers, the proportion is 73 percent. A smaller 62 percent of Generation Xers are non-Hispanic white, as are only 60 percent of Millennials and just 57 percent of the post-Millennial generation.

The nation's racial and ethnic composition is also becoming more complex with many more Hispanics and Asians in the mix. Among Gen Xers and younger generations, Hispanics outnumber blacks. Among Boomers and older generations, blacks outnumber Hispanics.

Within racial and ethnic groups, the size of generations varies. Among Hispanics, for example, Boomers are outnumbered by both Generation Xers and Millennials. In contrast, Boomers account for 28 percent of non-Hispanic whites, while Millennials are a smaller 22 percent and Gen Xers just 16 percent.

■ Understanding the cultural diversity of younger generations is the key to reaching them.

Among the young, Hispanics are the largest minority

(Hispanics as a percentage of each generation, 2006)

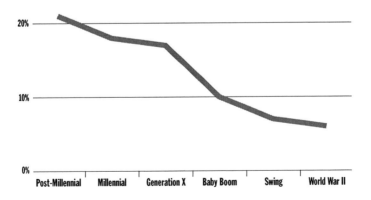

Table 9.4 Population by Age, Race, and Hispanic Origin, 2006

(number and percent distribution of people by age, race, and Hispanic origin, 2006; numbers in thousands)

	total	American Indian	Asian	black	Hispanic	non-Hispanic white
Total people	**299,398**	**4,498**	**14,907**	**40,241**	**44,321**	**198,744**
Under age 5	20,418	259	1,134	3,471	4,705	11,162
Aged 5 to 9	19,710	343	1,033	3,302	4,091	11,291
Aged 10 to 14	20,627	393	1,016	3,509	3,942	12,125
Aged 15 to 19	21,324	421	999	3,553	3,623	13,049
Aged 20 to 24	21,111	410	1,065	3,241	3,752	12,938
Aged 25 to 29	20,709	356	1,238	3,015	4,163	12,236
Aged 30 to 34	19,706	307	1,400	2,711	3,929	11,622
Aged 35 to 39	21,186	309	1,320	2,813	3,532	13,455
Aged 40 to 44	22,481	329	1,179	2,940	3,127	15,125
Aged 45 to 49	22,798	328	1,059	2,839	2,557	16,200
Aged 50 to 54	20,481	285	925	2,385	1,960	15,072
Aged 55 to 59	18,224	241	770	1,941	1,500	13,883
Aged 60 to 64	13,362	165	527	1,299	1,040	10,400
Aged 65 to 69	10,376	119	407	1,010	777	8,113
Aged 70 to 74	8,541	87	313	802	599	6,777
Aged 75 to 79	7,381	63	237	599	463	6,045
Aged 80 to 84	5,666	43	158	424	306	4,752
Aged 85 or older	5,297	40	128	388	256	4,501

Percent distribution by race and Hispanic origin

	total	American Indian	Asian	black	Hispanic	non-Hispanic white
Total people	**100.0%**	**1.5%**	**5.0%**	**13.4%**	**14.8%**	**66.4%**
Under age 5	100.0	1.3	5.6	17.0	23.0	54.7
Aged 5 to 9	100.0	1.7	5.2	16.8	20.8	57.3
Aged 10 to 14	100.0	1.9	4.9	17.0	19.1	58.8
Aged 15 to 19	100.0	2.0	4.7	16.7	17.0	61.2
Aged 20 to 24	100.0	1.9	5.0	15.4	17.8	61.3
Aged 25 to 29	100.0	1.7	6.0	14.6	20.1	59.1
Aged 30 to 34	100.0	1.6	7.1	13.8	19.9	59.0
Aged 35 to 39	100.0	1.5	6.2	13.3	16.7	63.5
Aged 40 to 44	100.0	1.5	5.2	13.1	13.9	67.3
Aged 45 to 49	100.0	1.4	4.6	12.5	11.2	71.1
Aged 50 to 54	100.0	1.4	4.5	11.6	9.6	73.6
Aged 55 to 59	100.0	1.3	4.2	10.6	8.2	76.2
Aged 60 to 64	100.0	1.2	3.9	9.7	7.8	77.8
Aged 65 to 69	100.0	1.1	3.9	9.7	7.5	78.2
Aged 70 to 74	100.0	1.0	3.7	9.4	7.0	79.3
Aged 75 to 79	100.0	0.9	3.2	8.1	6.3	81.9
Aged 80 to 84	100.0	0.8	2.8	7.5	5.4	83.9
Aged 85 or older	100.0	0.8	2.4	7.3	4.8	85.0

(continued)

	total	American Indian	Asian	black	Hispanic	non-Hispanic white
Percent distribution by age						
Total people	**100.0%**	**100.0%**	**100.0%**	**100.0%**	**100.0%**	**100.0%**
Under age 5	6.8	5.8	7.6	8.6	10.6	5.6
Aged 5 to 9	6.6	7.6	6.9	8.2	9.2	5.7
Aged 10 to 14	6.9	8.7	6.8	8.7	8.9	6.1
Aged 15 to 19	7.1	9.4	6.7	8.8	8.2	6.6
Aged 20 to 24	7.1	9.1	7.1	8.1	8.5	6.5
Aged 25 to 29	6.9	7.9	8.3	7.5	9.4	6.2
Aged 30 to 34	6.6	6.8	9.4	6.7	8.9	5.8
Aged 35 to 39	7.1	6.9	8.9	7.0	8.0	6.8
Aged 40 to 44	7.5	7.3	7.9	7.3	7.1	7.6
Aged 45 to 49	7.6	7.3	7.1	7.1	5.8	8.2
Aged 50 to 54	6.8	6.3	6.2	5.9	4.4	7.6
Aged 55 to 59	6.1	5.4	5.2	4.8	3.4	7.0
Aged 60 to 64	4.5	3.7	3.5	3.2	2.3	5.2
Aged 65 to 69	3.5	2.6	2.7	2.5	1.8	4.1
Aged 70 to 74	2.9	1.9	2.1	2.0	1.4	3.4
Aged 75 to 79	2.5	1.4	1.6	1.5	1.0	3.0
Aged 80 to 84	1.9	1.0	1.1	1.1	0.7	2.4
Aged 85 or older	1.8	0.9	0.9	1.0	0.6	2.3

Note: Numbers by race and Hispanic origin will not sum to total because American Indians, Asians, and blacks include those who identify themselves as being of the race alone and those who identify themselves as being of the race in combination with other races, Hispanics may be of any race, and not all races are shown. Non-Hispanic whites are those who identify themselves as being white alone and not Hispanic.
Source: Bureau of the Census, Population Estimates, Internet site http://www.census.gov/popest/national/asrh/ NC-EST2006-asrh.html; calculations by New Strategist

Table 9.5 Population by Generation, Race, and Hispanic Origin, 2006

(number and percent distribution of people by generation, race, and Hispanic origin, 2006; numbers in thousands)

	total	American Indian	Asian	black	Hispanic	non-Hispanic white
Total people	**299,398**	**4,498**	**14,907**	**40,241**	**44,321**	**198,744**
Post-Millennial (under 12)	52,504	838	2,777	8,878	11,161	29,728
Millennial (12 to 29)	71,396	1,345	3,708	11,212	13,114	43,072
Generation X (30 to 41)	49,885	747	3,191	6,700	8,712	31,127
Baby Boom (42 to 60)	77,664	1,084	3,567	9,188	8,102	56,310
Swing (61 to 73)	27,898	320	1,079	2,691	2,088	21,854
World War II (74 or older)	20,052	164	585	1,572	1,144	16,654
Percent distribution by race and Hispanic origin						
Total people	**100.0%**	**1.5%**	**5.0%**	**13.4%**	**14.8%**	**66.4%**
Post-Millennial (under age 12)	100.0	1.6	5.3	16.9	21.3	56.6
Millennial (12 to 29)	100.0	1.9	5.2	15.7	18.4	60.3
Generation X (30 to 41)	100.0	1.5	6.4	13.4	17.5	62.4
Baby Boom (42 to 60)	100.0	1.4	4.6	11.8	10.4	72.5
Swing (61 to 73)	100.0	1.1	3.9	9.6	7.5	78.3
World War II (74 or older)	100.0	0.8	2.9	7.8	5.7	83.1
Percent distribution by generation						
Total people	**100.0%**	**100.0%**	**100.0%**	**100.0%**	**100.0%**	**100.0%**
Post-Millennial (under 12)	17.5	18.6	18.6	22.1	25.2	15.0
Millennial (12 to 29)	23.8	29.9	24.9	27.9	29.6	21.7
Generation X (30 to 41)	16.7	16.6	21.4	16.6	19.7	15.7
Baby Boom (42 to 60)	25.9	24.1	23.9	22.8	18.3	28.3
Swing (61 to 73)	9.3	7.1	7.2	6.7	4.7	11.0
World War II (74 or older)	6.7	3.6	3.9	3.9	2.6	8.4

Note: Numbers by race and Hispanic origin will not sum to total because American Indians, Asians, and blacks include those who identify themselves as being of the race alone and those who identify themselves as being of the race in combination with other races, Hispanics may be of any race, and not all races are shown. Non-Hispanic whites are those who identify themselves as being white alone and not Hispanic.
Source: Bureau of the Census, Population Estimates, Internet site http://www.census.gov/popest/national/asrh/ NC-EST2006-asrh.html; calculations by New Strategist

Rapid Growth Is Projected for People in Their Sixties

Between 2010 and 2020, expect rapid growth in the number of people aged 65 to 74.

As large and small generations grow older, age groups expand and contract. During the remaining years of this decade, the largest expansion will be among 60-to-64-year-olds as the oldest Boomers enter their sixties. The age group is projected to expand by another 25 percent by 2010. During the 2010 to 2019 decade, the 70-to-74 age group will grow the fast-est—up by 56 percent—as the oldest Boomers enter their seventies.

Several age groups are shrinking as they fill with the small Generation X. The number of 35-to-44-year-olds is falling now, and between 2010 and 2020 the contraction will hit the 45-to-54 age group.

■ The generations that follow Generation X (Millennials and post-Millennials) do not vary as much in size, which will dampen future fluctuations in age groups.

Declines are projected for the 45-to-54 age group

(percent change in size of selected age groups, 2010 to 2020)

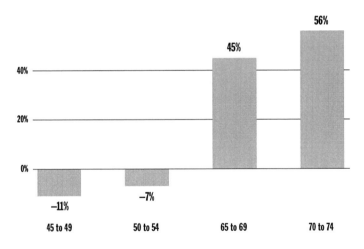

Table 9.6 Population by Age, 2006 to 2020

(number of people by age, 2006 to 2020; percent change, 2006–10 and 2010–20; numbers in thousands)

	2006	2010	2020	percent change 2006–10	percent change 2010–20
Total people	**299,398**	**308,936**	**335,805**	**3.2%**	**8.7%**
Under age 5	20,418	21,426	22,932	4.9	7.0
Aged 5 to 9	19,710	20,706	22,564	5.1	9.0
Aged 10 to 14	20,627	19,767	21,914	–4.2	10.9
Aged 15 to 19	21,324	21,336	21,478	0.1	0.7
Aged 20 to 24	21,111	21,676	20,751	2.7	–4.3
Aged 25 to 29	20,709	21,375	22,361	3.2	4.6
Aged 30 to 34	19,706	20,271	22,704	2.9	12.0
Aged 35 to 39	21,186	20,137	22,143	–5.0	10.0
Aged 40 to 44	22,481	20,984	20,673	–6.7	–1.5
Aged 45 to 49	22,798	22,654	20,219	–0.6	–10.7
Aged 50 to 54	20,481	22,173	20,702	8.3	–6.6
Aged 55 to 59	18,224	19,507	21,876	7.0	12.1
Aged 60 to 64	13,362	16,679	20,856	24.8	25.0
Aged 65 to 69	10,376	12,172	17,618	17.3	44.7
Aged 70 to 74	8,541	9,097	14,161	6.5	55.7
Aged 75 to 79	7,381	7,186	9,450	–2.6	31.5
Aged 80 to 84	5,666	5,665	6,134	0.0	8.3
Aged 85 or older	5,297	6,123	7,269	15.6	18.7

Source: Bureau of the Census, U.S. Interim Projections by Age, Sex, Race, and Hispanic Origin, Internet site http://www.census .gov/ipc/www/usinterimproj/; calculations by New Strategist

Immigration Contributes to Diversity

Twenty percent of 25-to-34-year-olds are immigrants.

Overall, 13 percent of Americans were born outside the United States, according to the 2006 American Community Survey. By age, the largest proportion of foreign-born is found among people aged 25 to 34. Twenty percent of the age group was born in another country. This compares with 12 percent of 18-to-24-year-olds and 10 percent of people aged 75 or older.

More than 1 million people legally immigrated to the United States in 2006. The number of immigrants coming to the United States is likely to reach a record high during this decade. Although people come to the U.S. for a variety of reasons, substantial numbers are looking for jobs. That explains why more than half of immigrants are of prime working age—between the ages of 25 and 54.

■ High levels of immigration, combined with the greater fertility of recent immigrants, means the U.S. population will become increasingly diverse.

Most Americans live in their state of birth

(percent distribution of population by place of birth, 2006)

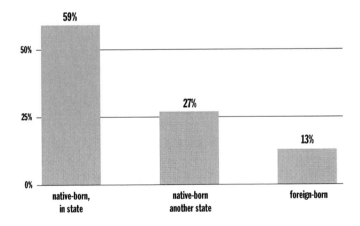

Table 9.7 Population by Age and Place of Birth, 2006

(number and percent distribution of population by age and place of birth, 2006; numbers in thousands)

| | | native-born | | |
	total	in state	in another state	foreign-born
Total people	**299,398**	**176,468**	**81,636**	**37,548**
Under age 5	20,386	18,107	1,859	318
Aged 5 to 17	53,379	41,345	8,787	2,727
Aged 18 to 24	29,701	18,716	6,993	3,593
Aged 25 to 34	39,906	20,717	10,482	8,099
Aged 35 to 44	43,893	21,613	13,285	8,301
Aged 45 to 54	43,325	22,077	14,385	6,215
Aged 55 to 59	18,049	9,036	6,505	2,273
Aged 60 to 61	5,616	2,659	2,126	753
Aged 62 to 64	7,953	3,861	3,061	942
Aged 65 to 74	18,937	9,184	7,095	2,444
Aged 75 or older	18,254	9,152	7,058	1,883
Percent distribution by place of birth				
Total people	**100.0%**	**58.9%**	**27.3%**	**12.5%**
Under age 5	100.0	88.8	9.1	1.6
Aged 5 to 17	100.0	77.5	16.5	5.1
Aged 18 to 24	100.0	63.0	23.5	12.1
Aged 25 to 34	100.0	51.9	26.3	20.3
Aged 35 to 44	100.0	49.2	30.3	18.9
Aged 45 to 54	100.0	51.0	33.2	14.3
Aged 55 to 59	100.0	50.1	36.0	12.6
Aged 60 to 61	100.0	47.4	37.9	13.4
Aged 62 to 64	100.0	48.6	38.5	11.8
Aged 65 to 74	100.0	48.5	37.5	12.9
Aged 75 or older	100.0	50.1	38.7	10.3
Percent distribution by age				
Total people	**100.0%**	**100.0%**	**100.0%**	**100.0%**
Under age 5	6.8	10.3	2.3	0.8
Aged 5 to 17	17.8	23.4	10.8	7.3
Aged 18 to 24	9.9	10.6	8.6	9.6
Aged 25 to 34	13.3	11.7	12.8	21.6
Aged 35 to 44	14.7	12.2	16.3	22.1
Aged 45 to 54	14.5	12.5	17.6	16.6
Aged 55 to 59	6.0	5.1	8.0	6.1
Aged 60 to 61	1.9	1.5	2.6	2.0
Aged 62 to 64	2.7	2.2	3.7	2.5
Aged 65 to 74	6.3	5.2	8.7	6.5
Aged 75 or older	6.1	5.2	8.6	5.0

Note: Numbers will not add to total because Americans born outside the United States are not shown.
Source: Bureau of the Census, 2006 American Community Survey, Internet site http://factfinder.census.gov/home/saff/main .html?_lang=en; calculations by New Strategist

Table 9.8 Legal Immigrants by Age, 2006

(number and percent distribution of immigrants admitted for legal permanent residence, by age, fiscal year 2006)

	number	percent distribution
Total legal immigrants	**1,266,264**	**100.0%**
Under age 5	45,570	3.6
Aged 5 to 9	62,918	5.0
Aged 10 to 14	83,182	6.6
Aged 15 to 19	111,132	8.8
Aged 20 to 24	121,845	9.6
Aged 25 to 29	146,551	11.6
Aged 30 to 34	164,751	13.0
Aged 35 to 39	138,033	10.9
Aged 40 to 44	106,542	8.4
Aged 45 to 49	79,089	6.2
Aged 50 to 54	59,405	4.7
Aged 55 to 59	46,642	3.7
Aged 60 to 64	35,435	2.8
Aged 65 to 74	48,429	3.8
Aged 75 or older	16,690	1.3

Note: Numbers will not add to total because immigrants of unknown age are not shown.
Source: Department of Homeland Security, 2006 Yearbook of Immigration Statistics, Internet site http://www.dhs.gov/ximgtn/ statistics/publications/LPR06.shtm; calculations by New Strategist

The West Is the Youngest Region

Millennials outnumber Boomers in the West.

Boomers and Millennials are the largest generations in every region, with Boomers outnumbering Millennials in all but the West. In the West, the Millennial share of the population exceeds the Boomer share (26 versus 25 percent).

There is little variation in the distribution of generations by region. The South, which is the most populous region, is home to more than one-third of each generation. The West is home to about one in four members of the younger generations and a slightly smaller share of the older generations. The Northeast has the smallest share of each generation, including only 17 percent of Millennials.

■ Most Americans live in the South or West.

The Northeast is the oldest region

(percent of population in selected generations, by region, 2006)

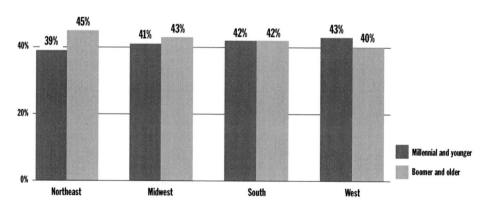

Table 9.9 Regional Populations by Age, 2006

(number and percent distribution of people by age and region, 2006; numbers in thousands)

	total	Northeast	Midwest	South	West
Total people	**299,398**	**54,741**	**66,218**	**109,084**	**69,356**
Under age 5	20,418	3,333	4,381	7,650	5,053
Aged 5 to 9	19,710	3,342	4,344	7,261	4,763
Aged 10 to 14	20,627	3,629	4,585	7,441	4,973
Aged 15 to 19	21,324	3,883	4,778	7,648	5,016
Aged 20 to 24	21,111	3,707	4,716	7,620	5,068
Aged 25 to 29	20,709	3,380	4,469	7,713	5,147
Aged 30 to 34	19,706	3,435	4,162	7,259	4,849
Aged 35 to 39	21,186	3,936	4,509	7,704	5,037
Aged 40 to 44	22,481	4,308	4,912	8,150	5,111
Aged 45 to 49	22,798	4,376	5,172	8,148	5,101
Aged 50 to 54	20,481	3,907	4,678	7,307	4,588
Aged 55 to 59	18,224	3,498	4,094	6,616	4,017
Aged 60 to 64	13,362	2,558	2,944	4,976	2,884
Aged 65 to 69	10,376	1,972	2,311	3,890	2,202
Aged 70 to 74	8,541	1,665	1,909	3,182	1,785
Aged 75 to 79	7,381	1,500	1,680	2,681	1,519
Aged 80 to 84	5,666	1,177	1,307	2,009	1,172
Aged 85 or older	5,297	1,133	1,266	1,827	1,070
Percent distribution by region					
Total people	**100.0%**	**18.3%**	**22.1%**	**36.4%**	**23.2%**
Under age 5	100.0	16.3	21.5	37.5	24.7
Aged 5 to 9	100.0	17.0	22.0	36.8	24.2
Aged 10 to 14	100.0	17.6	22.2	36.1	24.1
Aged 15 to 19	100.0	18.2	22.4	35.9	23.5
Aged 20 to 24	100.0	17.6	22.3	36.1	24.0
Aged 25 to 29	100.0	16.3	21.6	37.2	24.9
Aged 30 to 34	100.0	17.4	21.1	36.8	24.6
Aged 35 to 39	100.0	18.6	21.3	36.4	23.8
Aged 40 to 44	100.0	19.2	21.8	36.3	22.7
Aged 45 to 49	100.0	19.2	22.7	35.7	22.4
Aged 50 to 54	100.0	19.1	22.8	35.7	22.4
Aged 55 to 59	100.0	19.2	22.5	36.3	22.0
Aged 60 to 64	100.0	19.1	22.0	37.2	21.6
Aged 65 to 69	100.0	19.0	22.3	37.5	21.2
Aged 70 to 74	100.0	19.5	22.4	37.3	20.9
Aged 75 to 79	100.0	20.3	22.8	36.3	20.6
Aged 80 to 84	100.0	20.8	23.1	35.5	20.7
Aged 85 or older	100.0	21.4	23.9	34.5	20.2

(continued)

	total	Northeast	Midwest	South	West
Percent distribution by age					
Total people	**100.0%**	**100.0%**	**100.0%**	**100.0%**	**100.0%**
Under age 5	6.8	6.1	6.6	7.0	7.3
Aged 5 to 9	6.6	6.1	6.6	6.7	6.9
Aged 10 to 14	6.9	6.6	6.9	6.8	7.2
Aged 15 to 19	7.1	7.1	7.2	7.0	7.2
Aged 20 to 24	7.1	6.8	7.1	7.0	7.3
Aged 25 to 29	6.9	6.2	6.7	7.1	7.4
Aged 30 to 34	6.6	6.3	6.3	6.7	7.0
Aged 35 to 39	7.1	7.2	6.8	7.1	7.3
Aged 40 to 44	7.5	7.9	7.4	7.5	7.4
Aged 45 to 49	7.6	8.0	7.8	7.5	7.4
Aged 50 to 54	6.8	7.1	7.1	6.7	6.6
Aged 55 to 59	6.1	6.4	6.2	6.1	5.8
Aged 60 to 64	4.5	4.7	4.4	4.6	4.2
Aged 65 to 69	3.5	3.6	3.5	3.6	3.2
Aged 70 to 74	2.9	3.0	2.9	2.9	2.6
Aged 75 to 79	2.5	2.7	2.5	2.5	2.2
Aged 80 to 84	1.9	2.2	2.0	1.8	1.7
Aged 85 or older	1.8	2.1	1.9	1.7	1.5

Source: Bureau of the Census, Population Estimates, Internet site http://www.census.gov/popest/national/asrh/ NC-EST2006-sa.html; calculations by New Strategist

Table 9.10 Regional Populations by Generation, 2006

(number and percent distribution of people by generation and region, 2006; numbers in thousands)

	total	Northeast	Midwest	South	West
Total people	**299,398**	**54,741**	**66,218**	**109,084**	**69,356**
Post-Millennial (under age 12)	48,378	8,127	10,559	17,888	11,805
Millennial (12 to 29)	75,521	13,148	16,714	27,446	18,214
Generation X (30 to 41)	49,885	9,094	10,636	18,223	11,931
Baby Boom (42 to 60)	77,664	14,878	17,480	27,956	17,350
Swing (61 to 73)	27,898	5,351	6,194	10,417	5,937
World War II (74 or older)	20,052	4,144	4,635	7,154	4,118
Percent distribution by generation					
Total people	**100.0%**	**100.0%**	**100.0%**	**100.0%**	**100.0%**
Post-Millennial (under age 12)	16.2	14.8	15.9	16.4	17.0
Millennial (12 to 29)	25.2	24.0	25.2	25.2	26.3
Generation X (30 to 41)	16.7	16.6	16.1	16.7	17.2
Baby Boom (42 to 60)	25.9	27.2	26.4	25.6	25.0
Swing (61 to 73)	9.3	9.8	9.4	9.5	8.6
World War II (74 or older)	6.7	7.6	7.0	6.6	5.9
Percent distribution by region					
Total people	**100.0%**	**18.3%**	**22.1%**	**36.4%**	**23.2%**
Post-Millennial (under age 12)	100.0	16.8	21.8	37.0	24.4
Millennial (12 to 29)	100.0	17.4	22.1	36.3	24.1
Generation X (30 to 41)	100.0	18.2	21.3	36.5	23.9
Baby Boom (42 to 60)	100.0	19.2	22.5	36.0	22.3
Swing (61 to 73)	100.0	19.2	22.2	37.3	21.3
World War II (74 or older)	100.0	20.7	23.1	35.7	20.5

Note: Number of people by generation is estimated by New Strategist.
Source: Bureau of the Census, Population Estimates, Internet site http://www.census.gov/popest/national/asrh/
NC-EST2006-sa.html; calculations by New Strategist

Diversity Is Growing in Every Region

North, South, East, West—younger generations are more diverse.

Non-Hispanic whites dominate older generations of Americans, while they are in the minority among younger generations in some regions. In the Midwest, 91 percent of the World War II generation is non-Hispanic white, according to the 2006 American Community Survey. In other regions, the non-Hispanic white share of the older population ranges from 76 to 87 percent.

Non-Hispanic whites are a far smaller share of people under age 30—Millennials and post-Millennials. In the West, non-Hispanic whites account for only 48 percent of Millennials and an even smaller 43 percent of post-Millennials (under age 12). Hispanics account for 39 percent of post-Millennials in the West.

The Midwest is the least diverse region, with non-Hispanic whites dominating even the youngest residents of the region. Seventy-two percent of post-Millennials in the Midwest are non-Hispanic white. This compares with 63 percent of the youngest generation in the Northeast and 53 percent in the South.

■ The differences in racial and ethnic composition by region will persist, even as regions become more diverse, because immigrants settle in areas with large immigrant populations.

More diversity among the young in every region

(non-Hispanic white share of selected generations by region, 2006)

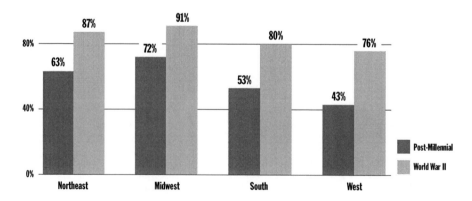

Table 9.11 Population of the Northeast by Age, Race, and Hispanic Origin, 2006

(number and percent distribution of people in the Northeast by age, race, and Hispanic origin, 2006; numbers in thousands)

	total	Asian	black	Hispanic	non-Hispanic white
Total, Northeast	**54,741**	**2,765**	**6,275**	**6,101**	**38,905**
Under age 5	3,334	183	472	551	2,030
Aged 5 to 9	3,362	180	460	496	2,148
Aged 10 to 14	3,616	157	521	504	2,362
Aged 15 to 17	2,316	97	339	299	1,547
Aged 18 to 19	1,603	77	219	202	1,078
Aged 20 to 24	3,688	198	492	514	2,428
Aged 25 to 29	3,343	230	431	547	2,083
Aged 30 to 34	3,419	286	409	523	2,161
Aged 35 to 44	8,266	513	959	978	5,731
Aged 45 to 54	8,291	391	840	691	6,297
Aged 55 to 64	6,062	246	552	424	4,797
Aged 65 to 74	3,645	133	333	228	2,928
Aged 75 to 84	2,707	58	184	109	2,343
Aged 85 or older	1,090	16	64	33	972
Total, Northeast	**100.0%**	**5.1%**	**11.5%**	**11.1%**	**71.1%**
Under age 5	100.0	5.5	14.1	16.5	60.9
Aged 5 to 9	100.0	5.4	13.7	14.8	63.9
Aged 10 to 14	100.0	4.3	14.4	13.9	65.3
Aged 15 to 17	100.0	4.2	14.6	12.9	66.8
Aged 18 to 19	100.0	4.8	13.6	12.6	67.2
Aged 20 to 24	100.0	5.4	13.3	13.9	65.8
Aged 25 to 29	100.0	6.9	12.9	16.4	62.3
Aged 30 to 34	100.0	8.4	12.0	15.3	63.2
Aged 35 to 44	100.0	6.2	11.6	11.8	69.3
Aged 45 to 54	100.0	4.7	10.1	8.3	75.9
Aged 55 to 64	100.0	4.1	9.1	7.0	79.1
Aged 65 to 74	100.0	3.6	9.1	6.2	80.3
Aged 75 to 84	100.0	2.1	6.8	4.0	86.6
Aged 85 or older	100.0	1.5	5.9	3.1	89.2

Note: Numbers will not add to total because each race includes only those who identified themselves as being of the race alone, not all races are shown, and Hispanics may be of any race. Non-Hispanic whites are those who identified themselves as being white alone and not Hispanic.
Source: Bureau of the Census, 2006 American Community Survey, Internet site http://factfinder.census.gov/home/saff/main .html?_lang=en; calculations by New Strategist

Table 9.12 Population of the Northeast by Generation, Race, and Hispanic Origin, 2006

(number and percent distribution of people in the Northeast by generation, race, and Hispanic origin, 2006; numbers in thousands)

	total	Asian	black	Hispanic	non-Hispanic white
Total, Northeast	**54,741**	**2,765**	**6,275**	**6,101**	**38,905**
Post-Millennial (under 12)	8,142	426	1,140	1,249	5,123
Millennial (12 to 29)	13,120	696	1,793	1,865	8,554
Generation X (30 to 41)	9,205	645	1,081	1,208	6,173
Baby Boom (42 to 60)	14,408	693	1,459	1,239	10,894
Swing (61 to 73)	5,705	218	520	375	4,554
World War II (74 or older)	4,161	88	282	165	3,608
Total, Northeast	**100.0%**	**5.1%**	**11.5%**	**11.1%**	**71.1%**
Post-Millennial (under 12)	100.0	5.2	14.0	15.3	62.9
Millennial (12 to 29)	100.0	5.3	13.7	14.2	65.2
Generation X (30 to 41)	100.0	7.0	11.7	13.1	67.1
Baby Boom (42 to 60)	100.0	4.8	10.1	8.6	75.6
Swing (61 to 73)	100.0	3.8	9.1	6.6	79.8
World War II (74 or older)	100.0	2.1	6.8	4.0	86.7

Note: Numbers will not add to total because each race includes only those who identified themselves as being of the race alone, not all races are shown, and Hispanics may be of any race. Non-Hispanic whites are those who identified themselves as being white alone and not Hispanic.
Source: Bureau of the Census, 2006 American Community Survey, Internet site http://factfinder.census.gov/home/saff/main .html?_lang=en; calculations by New Strategist

Table 9.13 Population of the Midwest by Age, Race, and Hispanic Origin, 2006

(number and percent distribution of people in the Midwest by age, race, and Hispanic origin, 2006; numbers in thousands)

	total	Asian	black	Hispanic	non-Hispanic white
Total, Midwest	**66,218**	**1,542**	**6,746**	**3,963**	**52,708**
Under age 5	4,395	110	551	454	3,097
Aged 5 to 9	4,356	112	549	407	3,131
Aged 10 to 14	4,584	98	612	358	3,377
Aged 15 to 17	2,899	61	381	193	2,186
Aged 18 to 19	1,946	49	231	140	1,475
Aged 20 to 24	4,666	123	506	346	3,589
Aged 25 to 29	4,393	139	495	400	3,284
Aged 30 to 34	4,140	172	452	381	3,067
Aged 35 to 44	9,459	272	947	584	7,514
Aged 45 to 54	9,872	186	894	364	8,300
Aged 55 to 64	7,049	126	558	192	6,098
Aged 65 to 74	4,220	58	318	86	3,719
Aged 75 to 84	3,022	28	187	46	2,743
Aged 85 or older	1,218	7	65	11	1,130
Total, Midwest	**100.0%**	**2.3%**	**10.2%**	**6.0%**	**79.6%**
Under age 5	100.0	2.5	12.5	10.3	70.5
Aged 5 to 9	100.0	2.6	12.6	9.3	71.9
Aged 10 to 14	100.0	2.1	13.4	7.8	73.7
Aged 15 to 17	100.0	2.1	13.2	6.7	75.4
Aged 18 to 19	100.0	2.5	11.9	7.2	75.8
Aged 20 to 24	100.0	2.6	10.8	7.4	76.9
Aged 25 to 29	100.0	3.2	11.3	9.1	74.8
Aged 30 to 34	100.0	4.2	10.9	9.2	74.1
Aged 35 to 44	100.0	2.9	10.0	6.2	79.4
Aged 45 to 54	100.0	1.9	9.1	3.7	84.1
Aged 55 to 64	100.0	1.8	7.9	2.7	86.5
Aged 65 to 74	100.0	1.4	7.5	2.0	88.1
Aged 75 to 84	100.0	0.9	6.2	1.5	90.8
Aged 85 or older	100.0	0.6	5.3	0.9	92.8

Note: Numbers will not add to total because each race includes only those who identified themselves as being of the race alone, not all races are shown, and Hispanics may be of any race. Non-Hispanic whites are those who identified themselves as being white alone and not Hispanic.
Source: Bureau of the Census, 2006 American Community Survey, Internet site http://factfinder.census.gov/home/saff/main .html?_lang=en; calculations by New Strategist

Table 9.14 Population of the Midwest by Generation, Race, and Hispanic Origin, 2006

(number and percent distribution of people in the Midwest by generation, race, and Hispanic origin, 2006; numbers in thousands)

	total	Asian	black	Hispanic	non-Hispanic white
Total, Midwest	**66,218**	**1,542**	**6,746**	**3,963**	**52,708**
Post-Millennial (under 12)	10,585	261	1,345	1,004	7,578
Millennial (12 to 29)	16,654	432	1,981	1,294	12,559
Generation X (30 to 41)	10,761	363	1,115	790	8,326
Baby Boom (42 to 60)	16,939	343	1,513	655	14,213
Swing (61 to 73)	6,617	103	509	154	5,786
World War II (74 or older)	4,662	41	283	65	4,246
Total, Midwest	**100.0%**	**2.3%**	**10.2%**	**6.0%**	**79.6%**
Post-Millennial (under 12)	100.0	2.5	12.7	9.5	71.6
Millennial (12 to 29)	100.0	2.6	11.9	7.8	75.4
Generation X (30 to 41)	100.0	3.4	10.4	7.3	77.4
Baby Boom (42 to 60)	100.0	2.0	8.9	3.9	83.9
Swing (61 to 73)	100.0	1.6	7.7	2.3	87.4
World War II (74 or older)	100.0	0.9	6.1	1.4	91.1

Note: Numbers will not add to total because each race includes only those who identified themselves as being of the race alone, not all races are shown, and Hispanics may be of any race. Non-Hispanic whites are those who identified themselves as being white alone and not Hispanic.
Source: Bureau of the Census, 2006 American Community Survey, Internet site http://factfinder.census.gov/home/saff/main .html?_lang=en; calculations by New Strategist

Table 9.15 Population of the South by Age, Race, and Hispanic Origin, 2006

(number and percent distribution of people in the South by age, race, and Hispanic origin, 2006; numbers in thousands)

	total	Asian	black	Hispanic	non-Hispanic white
Total, South	**109,084**	**2,669**	**20,777**	**15,328**	**68,300**
Under age 5	7,619	182	1,638	1,664	3,878
Aged 5 to 9	7,263	181	1,611	1,363	3,883
Aged 10 to 14	7,493	164	1,758	1,265	4,092
Aged 15 to 17	4,669	100	1,104	715	2,633
Aged 18 to 19	3,184	74	763	485	1,793
Aged 20 to 24	7,567	180	1,661	1,300	4,278
Aged 25 to 29	7,505	218	1,505	1,423	4,237
Aged 30 to 34	7,179	284	1,377	1,375	4,025
Aged 35 to 44	15,991	498	3,077	2,346	9,844
Aged 45 to 54	15,467	369	2,840	1,568	10,450
Aged 55 to 64	11,594	237	1,755	907	8,543
Aged 65 to 74	7,085	122	957	521	5,412
Aged 75 to 84	4,779	48	533	309	3,851
Aged 85 or older	1,691	11	198	89	1,380
Total, South	**100.0%**	**2.4%**	**19.0%**	**14.1%**	**62.6%**
Under age 5	100.0	2.4	21.5	21.8	50.9
Aged 5 to 9	100.0	2.5	22.2	18.8	53.5
Aged 10 to 14	100.0	2.2	23.5	16.9	54.6
Aged 15 to 17	100.0	2.1	23.6	15.3	56.4
Aged 18 to 19	100.0	2.3	24.0	15.2	56.3
Aged 20 to 24	100.0	2.4	22.0	17.2	56.5
Aged 25 to 29	100.0	2.9	20.1	19.0	56.5
Aged 30 to 34	100.0	4.0	19.2	19.1	56.1
Aged 35 to 44	100.0	3.1	19.2	14.7	61.6
Aged 45 to 54	100.0	2.4	18.4	10.1	67.6
Aged 55 to 64	100.0	2.0	15.1	7.8	73.7
Aged 65 to 74	100.0	1.7	13.5	7.3	76.4
Aged 75 to 84	100.0	1.0	11.1	6.5	80.6
Aged 85 or older	100.0	0.7	11.7	5.3	81.7

Note: Numbers will not add to total because each race includes only those who identified themselves as being of the race alone, not all races are shown, and Hispanics may be of any race. Non-Hispanic whites are those who identified themselves as being white alone and not Hispanic.
Source: Bureau of the Census, 2006 American Community Survey, Internet site http://factfinder.census.gov/home/saff/main .html?_lang=en; calculations by New Strategist

Table 9.16 Population of the South by Generation, Race, and Hispanic Origin, 2006

(number and percent distribution of people in the South by generation, race, and Hispanic origin, 2006; numbers in thousands)

	total	Asian	black	Hispanic	non-Hispanic white
Total, South	**109,084**	**2,669**	**20,777**	**15,328**	**68,300**
Post-Millennial (under 12)	17,879	429	3,952	3,533	9,398
Millennial (12 to 29)	27,420	671	6,089	4,682	15,397
Generation X (30 to 41)	18,372	633	3,531	3,017	10,916
Baby Boom (42 to 60)	27,220	661	4,816	2,816	18,529
Swing (61 to 73)	11,014	204	1,563	831	8,288
World War II (74 or older)	7,179	72	826	450	5,773
Total, South	**100.0%**	**2.4%**	**19.0%**	**14.1%**	**62.6%**
Post-Millennial (under 12)	100.0	2.4	22.1	19.8	52.6
Millennial (12 to 29)	100.0	2.4	22.2	17.1	56.2
Generation X (30 to 41)	100.0	3.4	19.2	16.4	59.4
Baby Boom (42 to 60)	100.0	2.4	17.7	10.3	68.1
Swing (61 to 73)	100.0	1.9	14.2	7.5	75.3
World War II (74 or older)	100.0	1.0	11.5	6.3	80.4

Note: Numbers will not add to total because each race includes only those who identified themselves as being of the race alone, not all races are shown, and Hispanics may be of any race. Non-Hispanic whites are those who identified themselves as being white alone and not Hispanic.
Source: Bureau of the Census, 2006 American Community Survey, Internet site http://factfinder.census.gov/home/saff/main .html?_lang=en; calculations by New Strategist

Table 9.17 Population of the West by Age, Race, and Hispanic Origin, 2006

(number and percent distribution of people in the West by age, race, and Hispanic origin, 2006; numbers in thousands)

	total	Asian	black	Hispanic	non-Hispanic white
Total, West	**69,356**	**6,107**	**3,223**	**18,860**	**38,264**
Under age 5	5,039	351	241	2,042	2,088
Aged 5 to 9	4,767	333	245	1,840	2,059
Aged 10 to 14	4,985	367	268	1,796	2,262
Aged 15 to 17	3,069	228	171	1,009	1,477
Aged 18 to 19	2,012	163	112	634	974
Aged 20 to 24	5,034	421	252	1,609	2,510
Aged 25 to 29	5,093	443	224	1,719	2,485
Aged 30 to 34	4,836	527	225	1,635	2,266
Aged 35 to 44	10,177	1,044	507	2,777	5,496
Aged 45 to 54	9,696	912	445	1,863	6,157
Aged 55 to 64	6,914	620	269	1,010	4,811
Aged 65 to 74	3,987	379	152	533	2,819
Aged 75 to 84	2,739	241	81	313	2,054
Aged 85 or older	1,008	78	30	80	805
Total, West	**100.0%**	**8.8%**	**4.6%**	**27.2%**	**55.2%**
Under age 5	100.0	7.0	4.8	40.5	41.4
Aged 5 to 9	100.0	7.0	5.1	38.6	43.2
Aged 10 to 14	100.0	7.4	5.4	36.0	45.4
Aged 15 to 17	100.0	7.4	5.6	32.9	48.1
Aged 18 to 19	100.0	8.1	5.6	31.5	48.4
Aged 20 to 24	100.0	8.4	5.0	32.0	49.9
Aged 25 to 29	100.0	8.7	4.4	33.8	48.8
Aged 30 to 34	100.0	10.9	4.7	33.8	46.9
Aged 35 to 44	100.0	10.3	5.0	27.3	54.0
Aged 45 to 54	100.0	9.4	4.6	19.2	63.5
Aged 55 to 64	100.0	9.0	3.9	14.6	69.6
Aged 65 to 74	100.0	9.5	3.8	13.4	70.7
Aged 75 to 84	100.0	8.8	3.0	11.4	75.0
Aged 85 or older	100.0	7.8	2.9	8.0	79.9

Note: Numbers will not add to total because each race includes only those who identified themselves as being of the race alone, not all races are shown, and Hispanics may be of any race. Non-Hispanic whites are those who identified themselves as being white alone and not Hispanic.
Source: Bureau of the Census, 2006 American Community Survey, Internet site http://factfinder.census.gov/home/saff/main .html?_lang=en; calculations by New Strategist

Table 9.18 Population of the West by Generation, Race, and Hispanic Origin, 2006

(number and percent distribution of people in the West by generation, race, and Hispanic origin, 2006; numbers in thousands)

	total	Asian	black	Hispanic	non-Hispanic white
Total, West	**69,356**	**6,107**	**3,223**	**18,860**	**38,264**
Post-Millennial (under 12)	11,800	831	594	4,601	5,052
Millennial (12 to 29)	18,199	1,475	921	6,048	8,803
Generation X (30 to 41)	11,960	1,257	580	3,579	6,114
Baby Boom (42 to 60)	16,897	1,597	759	3,302	10,693
Swing (61 to 73)	6,354	589	244	884	4,461
World War II (74 or older)	4,146	358	126	447	3,141
Total, West	**100.0%**	**8.8%**	**4.6%**	**27.2%**	**55.2%**
Post-Millennial (under 12)	100.0	7.0	5.0	39.0	42.8
Millennial (12 to 29)	100.0	8.1	5.1	33.2	48.4
Generation X (30 to 41)	100.0	10.5	4.8	29.9	51.1
Baby Boom (42 to 60)	100.0	9.5	4.5	19.5	63.3
Swing (61 to 73)	100.0	9.3	3.8	13.9	70.2
World War II (74 or older)	100.0	8.6	3.0	10.8	75.8

Note: Numbers will not add to total because each race includes only those who identified themselves as being of the race alone, not all races are shown, and Hispanics may be of any race. Non-Hispanic whites are those who identified themselves as being white alone and not Hispanic.
Source: Bureau of the Census, 2006 American Community Survey, Internet site http://factfinder.census.gov/home/saff/main .html?_lang=en; calculations by New Strategist

Young and Old Are Drawn to Different States

The middle aged are fairly evenly distributed across the states.

Alaska and Florida stand at opposite corners of the United States. Their differences extend beyond latitude and longitude, however. Alaska is one of the most youthful states in the nation, demographically speaking, while Florida is the oldest. Only 7 percent of Alaskans are aged 65 or older, while Florida's share is more than twice as great, at 17 percent.

Among all states, Utah has the largest proportion of people under age 25, accounting for 44 percent of the state's population in 2006. This share is nearly 10 percentage points above the national average. The reason for Utah's youthful population is the preponderance of the Mormon religion, which encourages large families. Alaska is youthful for a different reason. Its important industries, such as logging and oil extraction, attract working-age adults.

Florida's population is the oldest in the nation because the state attracts retirees with its warm winter climate. Other states with above average older populations are those in which older people have been left behind by young adults seeking opportunity elsewhere, such as Pennsylvania and West Virginia.

■ The elderly population will increase in every state as the large Baby-Boom generation ages.

Old and young are concentrated in different states

(percent of people under age 25 or aged 65 or older in selected states, 2006)

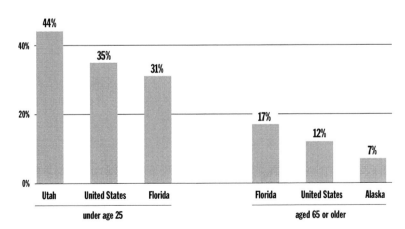

Table 9.19 State Populations by Age, 2006

(number of people by state and age, 2006; numbers in thousands)

	total	under 5	5 to 9	10 to 17	18 to 24	25 to 34	35 to 44	45 to 54	55 to 64	65 to 74	75 to 84	85+
United States	299,398	20,386	19,749	33,631	29,701	39,906	43,893	43,325	31,618	18,937	13,248	5,007
Alabama	4,599	294	305	516	460	582	650	663	518	326	210	74
Alaska	670	47	49	83	75	94	101	109	68	26	14	4
Arizona	6,166	479	444	704	586	900	858	787	619	405	292	93
Arkansas	2,811	195	195	303	271	366	384	391	317	203	135	50
California	36,458	2,673	2,515	4,344	3,793	5,232	5,525	5,018	3,430	2,003	1,400	524
Colorado	4,753	339	323	508	465	712	720	721	489	257	162	58
Connecticut	3,505	202	225	391	319	408	546	551	392	226	169	76
Delaware	853	57	56	90	83	110	125	122	95	61	40	14
Dist. of Columbia	582	35	29	51	71	105	85	75	60	36	26	9
Florida	18,090	1,118	1,056	1,845	1,611	2,247	2,603	2,534	2,042	1,452	1,172	410
Georgia	9,364	699	672	1,082	943	1,339	1,473	1,317	933	506	295	106
Hawaii	1,285	87	77	133	125	176	181	183	144	85	69	25
Idaho	1,466	112	108	174	153	200	192	205	153	89	56	24
Illinois	12,832	889	875	1,452	1,289	1,772	1,878	1,846	1,298	770	540	223
Indiana	6,314	434	429	717	623	836	896	927	671	397	276	108
Iowa	2,982	191	193	330	316	353	401	442	321	205	161	69
Kansas	2,764	195	189	311	298	344	385	401	285	170	128	57
Kentucky	4,206	277	269	454	393	573	613	619	473	286	183	67
Louisiana	4,288	301	295	493	464	554	584	616	457	279	182	62
Maine	1,322	70	72	140	116	152	194	218	167	98	68	26
Maryland	5,616	369	364	630	536	718	881	861	611	342	223	82
Massachusetts	6,437	388	386	675	643	817	993	973	706	412	309	135
Michigan	10,096	639	658	1,180	980	1,262	1,470	1,537	1,110	641	447	173
Minnesota	5,167	347	335	575	522	670	760	795	535	311	221	96
Mississippi	2,911	206	197	355	312	367	399	406	307	192	121	48
Missouri	5,843	391	384	648	571	758	815	863	633	396	276	108
Montana	945	58	59	102	96	112	120	152	115	68	47	17
Nebraska	1,768	128	120	197	187	230	234	256	183	113	84	37
Nevada	2,496	183	169	282	217	372	383	340	274	157	93	26
New Hampshire	1,315	73	79	145	120	154	208	218	155	83	55	23
New Jersey	8,725	560	566	964	764	1,083	1,393	1,325	944	560	402	164
New Mexico	1,955	142	135	233	205	257	260	271	210	128	85	29
New York	19,306	1,221	1,197	2,096	1,947	2,509	2,904	2,824	2,088	1,268	895	358
North Carolina	8,857	603	577	975	856	1,200	1,330	1,269	974	576	373	122
North Dakota	636	39	36	68	82	74	81	95	67	43	34	16
Ohio	11,478	736	742	1,295	1,103	1,445	1,628	1,739	1,263	764	556	208
Oklahoma	3,579	252	243	401	372	468	478	505	386	249	164	63
Oregon	3,701	230	231	396	342	514	512	560	438	240	167	70
Pennsylvania	12,441	724	743	1,340	1,201	1,439	1,778	1,918	1,414	887	724	272
Rhode Island	1,068	62	63	113	117	130	160	160	116	67	55	25
South Carolina	4,321	285	275	479	437	553	620	619	500	301	188	64
South Dakota	782	54	50	91	83	93	103	115	83	53	41	18
Tennessee	6,039	399	386	662	554	830	878	877	686	414	259	93
Texas	23,508	1,922	1,763	2,817	2,453	3,433	3,448	3,172	2,169	1,243	804	282
Utah	2,550	247	217	328	320	407	312	294	201	118	79	28

(continued)

	total	under 5	5 to 9	10 to 17	18 to 24	25 to 34	35 to 44	45 to 54	55 to 64	65 to 74	75 to 84	85+
Vermont	624	33	33	68	63	70	91	104	79	43	29	11
Virginia	7,643	503	479	823	768	1,014	1,192	1,141	835	475	301	109
Washington	6,396	407	409	712	614	889	948	971	709	380	254	103
West Virginia	1,818	104	102	184	165	224	250	280	231	144	102	33
Wisconsin	5,557	352	346	617	559	697	808	856	599	356	260	106
Wyoming	515	34	32	55	55	66	65	85	62	33	22	7

Source: Bureau of the Census, 2006 American Community Survey, Internet site http://factfinder.census.gov/home/saff/main .html?_lang=en; calculations by New Strategist

Table 9.20 Distribution of State Populations by Age, 2006

(distribution of state populations by age, 2006)

	total	under 5	5 to 9	10 to 17	18 to 24	25 to 34	35 to 44	45 to 54	55 to 64	65 to 74	75 to 84	85+
United States	**100.0%**	**6.8%**	**6.6%**	**11.2%**	**9.9%**	**13.3%**	**14.7%**	**14.5%**	**10.6%**	**6.3%**	**4.4%**	**1.7%**
Alabama	100.0	6.4	6.6	11.2	10.0	12.7	14.1	14.4	11.3	7.1	4.6	1.6
Alaska	100.0	7.1	7.4	12.4	11.2	14.0	15.0	16.3	10.1	3.9	2.1	0.6
Arizona	100.0	7.8	7.2	11.4	9.5	14.6	13.9	12.8	10.0	6.6	4.7	1.5
Arkansas	100.0	6.9	6.9	10.8	9.6	13.0	13.7	13.9	11.3	7.2	4.8	1.8
California	100.0	7.3	6.9	11.9	10.4	14.4	15.2	13.8	9.4	5.5	3.8	1.4
Colorado	100.0	7.1	6.8	10.7	9.8	15.0	15.1	15.2	10.3	5.4	3.4	1.2
Connecticut	100.0	5.8	6.4	11.2	9.1	11.6	15.6	15.7	11.2	6.4	4.8	2.2
Delaware	100.0	6.7	6.6	10.6	9.8	12.9	14.7	14.3	11.1	7.1	4.7	1.7
Dist. of Columbia	100.0	6.0	5.0	8.7	12.2	18.0	14.6	12.9	10.3	6.2	4.5	1.5
Florida	100.0	6.2	5.8	10.2	8.9	12.4	14.4	14.0	11.3	8.0	6.5	2.3
Georgia	100.0	7.5	7.2	11.6	10.1	14.3	15.7	14.1	10.0	5.4	3.1	1.1
Hawaii	100.0	6.8	6.0	10.4	9.7	13.7	14.1	14.2	11.2	6.6	5.4	2.0
Idaho	100.0	7.7	7.3	11.9	10.4	13.6	13.1	14.0	10.4	6.1	3.8	1.6
Illinois	100.0	6.9	6.8	11.3	10.0	13.8	14.6	14.4	10.1	6.0	4.2	1.7
Indiana	100.0	6.9	6.8	11.4	9.9	13.2	14.2	14.7	10.6	6.3	4.4	1.7
Iowa	100.0	6.4	6.5	11.1	10.6	11.8	13.5	14.8	10.8	6.9	5.4	2.3
Kansas	100.0	7.0	6.8	11.2	10.8	12.4	13.9	14.5	10.3	6.2	4.6	2.1
Kentucky	100.0	6.6	6.4	10.8	9.3	13.6	14.6	14.7	11.2	6.8	4.4	1.6
Louisiana	100.0	7.0	6.9	11.5	10.8	12.9	13.6	14.4	10.7	6.5	4.2	1.5
Maine	100.0	5.3	5.5	10.6	8.8	11.5	14.7	16.5	12.6	7.4	5.1	2.0
Maryland	100.0	6.6	6.5	11.2	9.5	12.8	15.7	15.3	10.9	6.1	4.0	1.5
Massachusetts	100.0	6.0	6.0	10.5	10.0	12.7	15.4	15.1	11.0	6.4	4.8	2.1
Michigan	100.0	6.3	6.5	11.7	9.7	12.5	14.6	15.2	11.0	6.3	4.4	1.7
Minnesota	100.0	6.7	6.5	11.1	10.1	13.0	14.7	15.4	10.4	6.0	4.3	1.9
Mississippi	100.0	7.1	6.8	12.2	10.7	12.6	13.7	13.9	10.6	6.6	4.2	1.6
Missouri	100.0	6.7	6.6	11.1	9.8	13.0	13.9	14.8	10.8	6.8	4.7	1.8
Montana	100.0	6.1	6.2	10.8	10.1	11.8	12.7	16.1	12.2	7.2	4.9	1.8
Nebraska	100.0	7.3	6.8	11.1	10.6	13.0	13.2	14.5	10.3	6.4	4.8	2.1
Nevada	100.0	7.4	6.8	11.3	8.7	14.9	15.3	13.6	11.0	6.3	3.7	1.0
New Hampshire	100.0	5.6	6.0	11.1	9.2	11.7	15.8	16.6	11.8	6.3	4.2	1.8
New Jersey	100.0	6.4	6.5	11.0	8.8	12.4	16.0	15.2	10.8	6.4	4.6	1.9
New Mexico	100.0	7.3	6.9	11.9	10.5	13.1	13.3	13.9	10.8	6.5	4.3	1.5
New York	100.0	6.3	6.2	10.9	10.1	13.0	15.0	14.6	10.8	6.6	4.6	1.9
North Carolina	100.0	6.8	6.5	11.0	9.7	13.5	15.0	14.3	11.0	6.5	4.2	1.4
North Dakota	100.0	6.1	5.7	10.8	13.0	11.7	12.8	14.9	10.5	6.8	5.3	2.5
Ohio	100.0	6.4	6.5	11.3	9.6	12.6	14.2	15.1	11.0	6.7	4.8	1.8
Oklahoma	100.0	7.0	6.8	11.2	10.4	13.1	13.4	14.1	10.8	6.9	4.6	1.8
Oregon	100.0	6.2	6.3	10.7	9.2	13.9	13.8	15.1	11.8	6.5	4.5	1.9
Pennsylvania	100.0	5.8	6.0	10.8	9.7	11.6	14.3	15.4	11.4	7.1	5.8	2.2
Rhode Island	100.0	5.8	5.9	10.6	11.0	12.2	15.0	15.0	10.9	6.3	5.1	2.4
South Carolina	100.0	6.6	6.4	11.1	10.1	12.8	14.3	14.3	11.6	7.0	4.4	1.5
South Dakota	100.0	6.9	6.4	11.6	10.6	11.9	13.1	14.7	10.6	6.8	5.2	2.3
Tennessee	100.0	6.6	6.4	11.0	9.2	13.7	14.5	14.5	11.4	6.9	4.3	1.5
Texas	100.0	8.2	7.5	12.0	10.4	14.6	14.7	13.5	9.2	5.3	3.4	1.2
Utah	100.0	9.7	8.5	12.9	12.6	15.9	12.2	11.5	7.9	4.6	3.1	1.1

(continued)

	total	under 5	5 to 9	10 to 17	18 to 24	25 to 34	35 to 44	45 to 54	55 to 64	65 to 74	75 to 84	85+
Vermont	100.0%	5.3%	5.3%	10.9%	10.1%	11.2%	14.5%	16.7%	12.7%	6.9%	4.7%	1.7%
Virginia	100.0	6.6	6.3	10.8	10.1	13.3	15.6	14.9	10.9	6.2	3.9	1.4
Washington	100.0	6.4	6.4	11.1	9.6	13.9	14.8	15.2	11.1	5.9	4.0	1.6
West Virginia	100.0	5.7	5.6	10.1	9.1	12.3	13.7	15.4	12.7	7.9	5.6	1.8
Wisconsin	100.0	6.3	6.2	11.1	10.1	12.6	14.5	15.4	10.8	6.4	4.7	1.9
Wyoming	100.0	6.6	6.1	10.7	10.6	12.7	12.7	16.4	12.0	6.3	4.2	1.4

Source: Bureau of the Census, 2006 American Community Survey, Internet site http://factfinder.census.gov/home/saff/main .html?_lang=en; calculations by New Strategist

Racial Diversity Differs by State

Hawaii, New Mexico, California, and Texas are the most diverse.

Although the nation as a whole is becoming more racially and ethnically diverse, there are large variations in the composition of the population by state. Racial and ethnic diversity not only vary by state, but they vary within states by generation. As a rule, younger generations of Americans are more diverse than their elders.

In the most populous state, California, fewer than half the population (43 percent) is non-Hispanic white. But the share varies substantially by age, from only 28 percent among children under age 5 to fully 74 percent among people aged 85 or older.

Mississippi has the largest share of blacks (37 percent). The black share of the state's population is likely to grow in the coming years since more than 40 percent of Mississippi's population under age 25 is black.

Some states have little racial diversity regardless of age. Non-Hispanic whites accounted for more than 95 percent of the population in Maine and Vermont in 2006. Even among the young in these states, more than 90 percent are non-Hispanic white—meaning racial and ethnic diversity is not likely to increase much in those states in the near future.

■ With diversity growing rapidly in many states, change lies ahead for the nation's governments and businesses.

The young are much more diverse in California than in Maine

(non-Hispanic white share of population under age 5 in selected states, 2006)

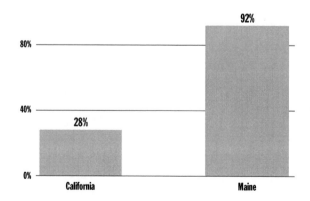

Table 9.21 Population by State, Age, Race, and Hispanic Origin, 2006

(number and percent distribution of people by state, age, race, and Hispanic origin, 2006)

	total	Asian	black	Hispanic	non-Hispanic white	total	Asian	black	Hispanic	non-Hispanic white
Alabama, total	**4,599,030**	**45,882**	**1,209,321**	**111,432**	**3,171,700**	**100.0%**	**1.0%**	**26.3%**	**2.4%**	**69.0%**
Under age 5	293,727	3,017	86,995	15,746	182,777	100.0	1.0	29.6	5.4	62.2
Aged 5 to 9	305,444	4,037	93,414	11,800	190,039	100.0	1.3	30.6	3.9	62.2
Aged 10 to 14	317,043	2,998	105,146	7,743	195,393	100.0	0.9	33.2	2.4	61.6
Aged 15 to 17	199,454	1,769	64,386	5,137	124,971	100.0	0.9	32.3	2.6	62.7
Aged 18 to 19	140,746	1,352	47,984	4,642	84,567	100.0	1.0	34.1	3.3	60.1
Aged 20 to 24	319,738	3,861	100,761	12,563	198,206	100.0	1.2	31.5	3.9	62.0
Aged 25 to 29	299,802	3,131	85,693	11,963	195,642	100.0	1.0	28.6	4.0	65.3
Aged 30 to 34	282,654	5,474	75,185	11,315	188,103	100.0	1.9	26.6	4.0	66.5
Aged 35 to 44	649,714	8,869	166,473	17,049	449,188	100.0	1.4	25.6	2.6	69.1
Aged 45 to 54	662,648	5,585	164,946	7,207	475,309	100.0	0.8	24.9	1.1	71.7
Aged 55 to 64	517,689	3,486	107,962	3,633	396,660	100.0	0.7	20.9	0.7	76.6
Aged 65 to 74	325,859	1,405	58,847	1,521	261,116	100.0	0.4	18.1	0.5	80.1
Aged 75 to 84	210,461	693	37,910	556	170,249	100.0	0.3	18.0	0.3	80.9
Aged 85 or older	74,051	205	13,619	557	59,480	100.0	0.3	18.4	0.8	80.3
Alaska, total	**670,053**	**30,151**	**21,476**	**37,498**	**443,944**	**100.0**	**4.5**	**3.2**	**5.6**	**66.3**
Under age 5	47,481	1,326	1,160	4,873	26,478	100.0	2.8	2.4	10.3	55.8
Aged 5 to 9	49,376	2,162	1,968	3,998	26,996	100.0	4.4	4.0	8.1	54.7
Aged 10 to 14	48,818	2,230	1,346	2,609	29,313	100.0	4.6	2.8	5.3	60.0
Aged 15 to 17	34,012	1,101	923	1,591	19,452	100.0	3.2	2.7	4.7	57.2
Aged 18 to 19	24,263	1,014	1,347	2,349	12,280	100.0	4.2	5.6	9.7	50.6
Aged 20 to 24	50,473	2,032	2,080	3,798	31,975	100.0	4.0	4.1	7.5	63.4
Aged 25 to 29	49,358	1,731	1,601	3,226	33,999	100.0	3.5	3.2	6.5	68.9
Aged 30 to 34	44,638	2,088	1,881	2,601	30,845	100.0	4.7	4.2	5.8	69.1
Aged 35 to 44	100,530	4,886	2,563	6,173	67,555	100.0	4.9	2.5	6.1	67.2
Aged 45 to 54	109,113	6,038	4,095	3,624	80,279	100.0	5.5	3.8	3.3	73.6
Aged 55 to 64	67,956	2,920	1,490	2,003	52,282	100.0	4.3	2.2	2.9	76.9
Aged 65 to 74	26,117	1,620	135	424	19,351	100.0	6.2	0.5	1.6	74.1
Aged 75 to 84	13,985	724	493	229	10,343	100.0	5.2	3.5	1.6	74.0
Aged 85 or older	3,933	279	394	0	2,796	100.0	7.1	10.0	0.0	71.1
Arizona, total	**6,166,318**	**144,858**	**207,837**	**1,803,377**	**3,668,571**	**100.0**	**2.3**	**3.4**	**29.2**	**59.5**
Under age 5	479,145	10,370	16,308	216,304	200,818	100.0	2.2	3.4	45.1	41.9
Aged 5 to 9	444,018	8,315	16,790	187,743	196,766	100.0	1.9	3.8	42.3	44.3
Aged 10 to 14	436,903	8,042	18,667	174,872	201,229	100.0	1.8	4.3	40.0	46.1
Aged 15 to 17	266,789	5,403	10,467	96,394	131,404	100.0	2.0	3.9	36.1	49.3
Aged 18 to 19	165,970	3,899	6,044	58,703	81,606	100.0	2.3	3.6	35.4	49.2
Aged 20 to 24	420,118	9,376	16,524	147,242	220,206	100.0	2.2	3.9	35.0	52.4
Aged 25 to 29	469,834	14,598	17,493	174,553	237,383	100.0	3.1	3.7	37.2	50.5
Aged 30 to 34	429,697	16,368	16,945	160,861	214,919	100.0	3.8	3.9	37.4	50.0
Aged 35 to 44	857,846	28,254	31,495	250,344	503,972	100.0	3.3	3.7	29.2	58.7
Aged 45 to 54	787,098	17,519	26,690	164,576	542,380	100.0	2.2	3.4	20.9	68.9
Aged 55 to 64	619,149	12,246	16,481	90,482	477,249	100.0	2.0	2.7	14.6	77.1
Aged 65 to 74	405,034	6,856	8,546	47,806	326,616	100.0	1.7	2.1	11.8	80.6
Aged 75 to 84	292,120	2,915	3,969	26,500	251,698	100.0	1.0	1.4	9.1	86.2
Aged 85 or older	92,597	697	1,418	6,997	82,325	100.0	0.8	1.5	7.6	88.9

(continued)

	total	Asian	black	Hispanic	non-Hispanic white	total	Asian	black	Hispanic	non-Hispanic white
Arkansas, total	**2,810,872**	**28,168**	**437,680**	**138,283**	**2,145,922**	**100.0%**	**1.0%**	**15.6%**	**4.9%**	**76.3%**
Under age 5	194,741	1,928	38,463	18,615	129,438	100.0	1.0	19.8	9.6	66.5
Aged 5 to 9	194,953	2,780	36,542	14,558	132,904	100.0	1.4	18.7	7.5	68.2
Aged 10 to 14	184,070	1,951	37,401	12,998	125,729	100.0	1.1	20.3	7.1	68.3
Aged 15 to 17	119,272	992	23,655	6,387	85,769	100.0	0.8	19.8	5.4	71.9
Aged 18 to 19	80,272	904	15,135	4,012	58,699	100.0	1.1	18.9	5.0	73.1
Aged 20 to 24	190,239	2,127	38,176	13,302	133,421	100.0	1.1	20.1	7.0	70.1
Aged 25 to 29	191,598	1,864	30,324	14,893	140,342	100.0	1.0	15.8	7.8	73.2
Aged 30 to 34	174,824	3,040	28,271	13,895	125,052	100.0	1.7	16.2	7.9	71.5
Aged 35 to 44	384,263	3,932	59,176	20,301	295,094	100.0	1.0	15.4	5.3	76.8
Aged 45 to 54	390,827	5,098	59,778	11,262	307,700	100.0	1.3	15.3	2.9	78.7
Aged 55 to 64	316,953	1,938	34,432	5,380	268,580	100.0	0.6	10.9	1.7	84.7
Aged 65 to 74	203,152	1,092	18,273	1,978	178,982	100.0	0.5	9.0	1.0	88.1
Aged 75 to 84	135,225	320	10,783	651	122,167	100.0	0.2	8.0	0.5	90.3
Aged 85 or older	50,483	202	7,271	51	42,045	100.0	0.4	14.4	0.1	83.3
California, total	**36,457,549**	**4,483,252**	**2,260,648**	**13,074,155**	**15,600,175**	**100.0**	**12.3**	**6.2**	**35.9**	**42.8**
Under age 5	2,672,666	257,728	162,948	1,384,142	754,798	100.0	9.6	6.1	51.8	28.2
Aged 5 to 9	2,514,639	245,864	166,414	1,249,117	750,500	100.0	9.8	6.6	49.7	29.8
Aged 10 to 14	2,700,465	274,347	188,616	1,257,439	874,102	100.0	10.2	7.0	46.6	32.4
Aged 15 to 17	1,643,276	172,275	122,169	708,005	575,313	100.0	10.5	7.4	43.1	35.0
Aged 18 to 19	1,095,451	122,796	80,652	446,122	398,710	100.0	11.2	7.4	40.7	36.4
Aged 20 to 24	2,697,878	315,259	174,253	1,128,042	993,863	100.0	11.7	6.5	41.8	36.8
Aged 25 to 29	2,629,253	320,755	148,735	1,165,257	911,850	100.0	12.2	5.7	44.3	34.7
Aged 30 to 34	2,603,007	384,458	152,292	1,113,940	887,934	100.0	14.8	5.9	42.8	34.1
Aged 35 to 44	5,525,036	770,694	356,328	1,955,045	2,315,882	100.0	13.9	6.4	35.4	41.9
Aged 45 to 54	5,017,599	672,491	314,648	1,313,579	2,604,336	100.0	13.4	6.3	26.2	51.9
Aged 55 to 64	3,430,449	450,162	194,212	701,219	2,011,964	100.0	13.1	5.7	20.4	58.7
Aged 65 to 74	2,002,937	275,350	114,530	370,561	1,206,165	100.0	13.7	5.7	18.5	60.2
Aged 75 to 84	1,400,449	167,110	62,830	224,401	929,079	100.0	11.9	4.5	16.0	66.3
Aged 85 or older	524,444	53,963	22,021	57,286	385,679	100.0	10.3	4.2	10.9	73.5
Colorado, total	**4,753,377**	**133,079**	**177,902**	**934,410**	**3,400,011**	**100.0**	**2.8**	**3.7**	**19.7**	**71.5**
Under age 5	338,995	9,559	13,757	104,950	198,153	100.0	2.8	4.1	31.0	58.5
Aged 5 to 9	322,980	9,294	14,049	92,991	194,715	100.0	2.9	4.3	28.8	60.3
Aged 10 to 14	313,386	8,657	13,678	81,380	198,702	100.0	2.8	4.4	26.0	63.4
Aged 15 to 17	194,282	3,539	8,573	45,085	130,607	100.0	1.8	4.4	23.2	67.2
Aged 18 to 19	127,504	2,975	5,739	27,516	86,248	100.0	2.3	4.5	21.6	67.6
Aged 20 to 24	337,730	11,107	14,023	76,751	225,409	100.0	3.3	4.2	22.7	66.7
Aged 25 to 29	365,092	11,614	13,424	92,383	239,960	100.0	3.2	3.7	25.3	65.7
Aged 30 to 34	346,409	14,916	13,349	88,745	222,794	100.0	4.3	3.9	25.6	64.3
Aged 35 to 44	720,020	24,217	29,505	134,207	521,978	100.0	3.4	4.1	18.6	72.5
Aged 45 to 54	720,742	18,222	26,594	92,266	570,776	100.0	2.5	3.7	12.8	79.2
Aged 55 to 64	489,352	9,890	13,863	51,414	406,513	100.0	2.0	2.8	10.5	83.1
Aged 65 to 74	256,742	5,286	7,079	28,341	212,660	100.0	2.1	2.8	11.0	82.8
Aged 75 to 84	161,816	2,944	2,682	15,166	139,429	100.0	1.8	1.7	9.4	86.2
Aged 85 or older	58,327	859	1,587	3,215	52,067	100.0	1.5	2.7	5.5	89.3

(continued)

	total	Asian	black	Hispanic	non-Hispanic white	total	Asian	black	Hispanic	non-Hispanic white
Connecticut, total	**3,504,809**	**117,054**	**332,711**	**391,935**	**2,610,863**	**100.0%**	**3.3%**	**9.5%**	**11.2%**	**74.5%**
Under age 5	202,071	8,502	24,153	35,667	128,094	100.0	4.2	12.0	17.7	63.4
Aged 5 to 9	224,594	9,685	24,166	37,614	148,311	100.0	4.3	10.8	16.7	66.0
Aged 10 to 14	239,033	5,963	31,422	33,398	162,775	100.0	2.5	13.1	14.0	68.1
Aged 15 to 17	152,168	3,786	19,331	20,887	105,299	100.0	2.5	12.7	13.7	69.2
Aged 18 to 19	97,951	2,708	10,409	13,068	69,687	100.0	2.8	10.6	13.3	71.1
Aged 20 to 24	221,481	9,100	26,609	32,370	148,571	100.0	4.1	12.0	14.6	67.1
Aged 25 to 29	198,582	10,445	23,475	37,881	122,065	100.0	5.3	11.8	19.1	61.5
Aged 30 to 34	209,348	13,133	23,007	35,619	134,915	100.0	6.3	11.0	17.0	64.4
Aged 35 to 44	545,542	22,787	52,362	63,614	400,261	100.0	4.2	9.6	11.7	73.4
Aged 45 to 54	551,480	15,322	43,995	41,400	444,927	100.0	2.8	8.0	7.5	80.7
Aged 55 to 64	392,094	8,905	27,456	22,788	329,185	100.0	2.3	7.0	5.8	84.0
Aged 65 to 74	225,872	4,773	15,916	11,469	192,489	100.0	2.1	7.0	5.1	85.2
Aged 75 to 84	169,048	1,316	7,729	4,880	153,739	100.0	0.8	4.6	2.9	90.9
Aged 85 or older	75,545	629	2,681	1,280	70,545	100.0	0.8	3.5	1.7	93.4
Delaware, total	**853,476**	**24,413**	**176,845**	**53,836**	**586,778**	**100.0**	**2.9**	**20.7**	**6.3**	**68.8**
Under age 5	57,091	2,310	13,844	7,223	30,955	100.0	4.0	24.2	12.7	54.2
Aged 5 to 9	56,193	2,058	13,981	5,570	33,252	100.0	3.7	24.9	9.9	59.2
Aged 10 to 14	54,623	1,290	14,333	4,505	33,136	100.0	2.4	26.2	8.2	60.7
Aged 15 to 17	35,829	697	9,499	2,744	22,491	100.0	1.9	26.5	7.7	62.8
Aged 18 to 19	25,541	202	6,554	2,064	16,582	100.0	0.8	25.7	8.1	64.9
Aged 20 to 24	57,887	1,411	13,703	4,356	37,541	100.0	2.4	23.7	7.5	64.9
Aged 25 to 29	56,637	2,643	12,789	5,527	35,177	100.0	4.7	22.6	9.8	62.1
Aged 30 to 34	53,050	3,123	11,798	5,576	31,802	100.0	5.9	22.2	10.5	59.9
Aged 35 to 44	125,406	4,583	27,584	8,610	83,569	100.0	3.7	22.0	6.9	66.6
Aged 45 to 54	122,004	2,591	23,911	3,886	90,610	100.0	2.1	19.6	3.2	74.3
Aged 55 to 64	94,661	1,680	15,214	2,091	75,286	100.0	1.8	16.1	2.2	79.5
Aged 65 to 74	60,623	1,380	8,134	1,272	49,205	100.0	2.3	13.4	2.1	81.2
Aged 75 to 84	39,772	445	4,206	244	34,476	100.0	1.1	10.6	0.6	86.7
Aged 85 or older	14,159	0	1,295	168	12,696	100.0	0.0	9.1	1.2	89.7
District of Columbia, total	**581,530**	**19,827**	**322,105**	**47,775**	**183,519**	**100.0**	**3.4**	**55.4**	**8.2**	**31.6**
Under age 5	34,980	872	21,811	3,672	7,602	100.0	2.5	62.4	10.5	21.7
Aged 5 to 9	29,331	603	20,425	3,176	4,727	100.0	2.1	69.6	10.8	16.1
Aged 10 to 14	31,081	386	23,958	2,677	3,484	100.0	1.2	77.1	8.6	11.2
Aged 15 to 17	19,438	399	14,590	1,547	2,195	100.0	2.1	75.1	8.0	11.3
Aged 18 to 19	19,797	827	9,630	2,028	6,751	100.0	4.2	48.6	10.2	34.1
Aged 20 to 24	51,273	1,867	21,958	3,898	23,177	100.0	3.6	42.8	7.6	45.2
Aged 25 to 29	56,455	3,784	21,150	6,431	24,008	100.0	6.7	37.5	11.4	42.5
Aged 30 to 34	48,063	2,939	18,828	5,381	20,440	100.0	6.1	39.2	11.2	42.5
Aged 35 to 44	84,648	3,139	42,312	8,091	29,926	100.0	3.7	50.0	9.6	35.4
Aged 45 to 54	75,160	2,185	46,212	5,192	20,403	100.0	2.9	61.5	6.9	27.1
Aged 55 to 64	59,849	1,254	34,689	3,117	20,394	100.0	2.1	58.0	5.2	34.1
Aged 65 to 74	36,338	944	23,260	1,731	10,308	100.0	2.6	64.0	4.8	28.4
Aged 75 to 84	26,199	548	17,489	795	7,258	100.0	2.1	66.8	3.0	27.7
Aged 85 or older	8,918	80	5,793	39	2,846	100.0	0.9	65.0	0.4	31.9

(continued)

	total	Asian	black	Hispanic	non-Hispanic white	total	Asian	black	Hispanic	non-Hispanic white
Florida, total	18,089,889	393,427	2,778,549	3,642,989	11,040,168	100.0%	2.2%	15.4%	20.1%	61.0%
Under age 5	1,117,630	24,761	240,906	299,598	516,674	100.0	2.2	21.6	26.8	46.2
Aged 5 to 9	1,055,789	26,302	214,495	249,221	541,544	100.0	2.5	20.3	23.6	51.3
Aged 10 to 14	1,127,349	21,189	242,818	257,658	574,509	100.0	1.9	21.5	22.9	51.0
Aged 15 to 17	717,876	14,693	154,065	150,660	384,874	100.0	2.0	21.5	21.0	53.6
Aged 18 to 19	456,718	12,122	99,761	103,838	232,786	100.0	2.7	21.8	22.7	51.0
Aged 20 to 24	1,154,089	24,779	235,548	274,698	605,823	100.0	2.1	20.4	23.8	52.5
Aged 25 to 29	1,147,634	26,479	212,815	292,278	602,873	100.0	2.3	18.5	25.5	52.5
Aged 30 to 34	1,099,501	38,202	183,318	300,793	563,684	100.0	3.5	16.7	27.4	51.3
Aged 35 to 44	2,602,876	73,572	406,145	611,059	1,486,998	100.0	2.8	15.6	23.5	57.1
Aged 45 to 54	2,534,472	59,503	356,615	446,009	1,644,811	100.0	2.3	14.1	17.6	64.9
Aged 55 to 64	2,041,838	40,414	213,551	288,595	1,479,865	100.0	2.0	10.5	14.1	72.5
Aged 65 to 74	1,452,008	19,915	128,252	200,747	1,096,977	100.0	1.4	8.8	13.8	75.5
Aged 75 to 84	1,171,721	9,122	69,524	126,634	963,787	100.0	0.8	5.9	10.8	82.3
Aged 85 or older	410,388	2,374	20,736	41,201	344,963	100.0	0.6	5.1	10.0	84.1
Georgia, total	9,363,941	254,899	2,794,300	696,146	5,501,019	100.0	2.7	29.8	7.4	58.7
Under age 5	698,935	16,900	224,302	98,184	341,555	100.0	2.4	32.1	14.0	48.9
Aged 5 to 9	671,546	16,540	230,558	70,607	338,465	100.0	2.5	34.3	10.5	50.4
Aged 10 to 14	668,385	16,751	239,442	51,066	348,198	100.0	2.5	35.8	7.6	52.1
Aged 15 to 17	413,359	10,332	150,071	27,522	219,625	100.0	2.5	36.3	6.7	53.1
Aged 18 to 19	291,744	7,828	100,131	19,889	157,686	100.0	2.7	34.3	6.8	54.0
Aged 20 to 24	651,722	15,104	217,085	63,094	347,374	100.0	2.3	33.3	9.7	53.3
Aged 25 to 29	665,568	21,715	207,301	83,843	346,625	100.0	3.3	31.1	12.6	52.1
Aged 30 to 34	673,099	29,587	205,606	80,965	349,814	100.0	4.4	30.5	12.0	52.0
Aged 35 to 44	1,472,645	49,699	439,918	115,107	855,207	100.0	3.4	29.9	7.8	58.1
Aged 45 to 54	1,316,787	35,734	376,904	51,009	839,934	100.0	2.7	28.6	3.9	63.8
Aged 55 to 64	933,272	20,581	218,562	21,124	666,269	100.0	2.2	23.4	2.3	71.4
Aged 65 to 74	505,861	9,028	108,725	9,107	376,528	100.0	1.8	21.5	1.8	74.4
Aged 75 to 84	294,712	4,185	54,199	3,735	231,264	100.0	1.4	18.4	1.3	78.5
Aged 85 or older	106,306	915	21,496	894	82,475	100.0	0.9	20.2	0.8	77.6
Hawaii, total	1,285,498	512,995	28,062	99,664	315,822	100.0	39.9	2.2	7.8	24.6
Under age 5	87,179	23,847	1,889	12,008	13,853	100.0	27.4	2.2	13.8	15.9
Aged 5 to 9	76,819	21,505	1,226	9,461	14,098	100.0	28.0	1.6	12.3	18.4
Aged 10 to 14	81,973	22,694	2,356	9,139	15,157	100.0	27.7	2.9	11.1	18.5
Aged 15 to 17	51,262	15,940	1,296	4,882	9,749	100.0	31.1	2.5	9.5	19.0
Aged 18 to 19	33,176	9,302	1,612	3,584	7,124	100.0	28.0	4.9	10.8	21.5
Aged 20 to 24	92,070	28,069	3,084	9,438	25,715	100.0	30.5	3.3	10.3	27.9
Aged 25 to 29	90,626	27,667	2,735	9,279	26,118	100.0	30.5	3.0	10.2	28.8
Aged 30 to 34	85,003	29,872	2,086	8,682	22,166	100.0	35.1	2.5	10.2	26.1
Aged 35 to 44	181,026	74,153	6,164	13,054	45,008	100.0	41.0	3.4	7.2	24.9
Aged 45 to 54	183,025	81,844	2,441	10,097	50,880	100.0	44.7	1.3	5.5	27.8
Aged 55 to 64	144,327	68,122	1,719	5,553	44,905	100.0	47.2	1.2	3.8	31.1
Aged 65 to 74	84,757	47,930	539	2,521	21,048	100.0	56.5	0.6	3.0	24.8
Aged 75 to 84	69,131	45,346	577	1,657	14,159	100.0	65.6	0.8	2.4	20.5
Aged 85 or older	25,124	16,704	338	309	5,842	100.0	66.5	1.3	1.2	23.3

(continued)

	total	Asian	black	Hispanic	non-Hispanic white	total	Asian	black	Hispanic	non-Hispanic white
Idaho, total	**1,466,465**	**15,335**	**–**	**138,871**	**1,265,241**	**100.0%**	**1.0%**	**–**	**9.5%**	**86.3%**
Under age 5	112,366	1,213	–	16,031	90,449	100.0	1.1	–	14.3	80.5
Aged 5 to 9	107,521	648	–	16,894	85,590	100.0	0.6	–	15.7	79.6
Aged 10 to 14	106,092	912	–	13,315	86,207	100.0	0.9	–	12.6	81.3
Aged 15 to 17	68,336	423	–	8,412	57,072	100.0	0.6	–	12.3	83.5
Aged 18 to 19	44,994	787	–	5,500	36,927	100.0	1.7	–	12.2	82.1
Aged 20 to 24	107,953	853	–	12,046	91,365	100.0	0.8	–	11.2	84.6
Aged 25 to 29	105,878	1,082	–	11,490	88,607	100.0	1.0	–	10.9	83.7
Aged 30 to 34	94,026	1,506	–	13,167	76,182	100.0	1.6	–	14.0	81.0
Aged 35 to 44	192,227	2,810	–	18,267	166,311	100.0	1.5	–	9.5	86.5
Aged 45 to 54	204,603	2,419	–	13,691	183,377	100.0	1.2	–	6.7	89.6
Aged 55 to 64	153,078	1,930	–	5,319	142,161	100.0	1.3	–	3.5	92.9
Aged 65 to 74	89,464	421	–	3,136	83,583	100.0	0.5	–	3.5	93.4
Aged 75 to 84	56,280	140	–	1,437	54,265	100.0	0.2	–	2.6	96.4
Aged 85 or older	23,647	191	–	166	23,145	100.0	0.8	–	0.7	97.9
Illinois, total	**12,831,970**	**536,992**	**1,898,346**	**1,888,439**	**8,357,564**	**100.0**	**4.2**	**14.8**	**14.7**	**65.1**
Under age 5	889,338	34,307	150,302	210,450	467,761	100.0	3.9	16.9	23.7	52.6
Aged 5 to 9	874,663	33,624	152,480	187,208	481,662	100.0	3.8	17.4	21.4	55.1
Aged 10 to 14	898,758	30,530	173,348	168,940	510,548	100.0	3.4	19.3	18.8	56.8
Aged 15 to 17	553,628	18,635	104,710	91,116	331,164	100.0	3.4	18.9	16.5	59.8
Aged 18 to 19	384,216	16,486	68,333	61,367	231,631	100.0	4.3	17.8	16.0	60.3
Aged 20 to 24	905,237	38,500	142,831	163,428	548,890	100.0	4.3	15.8	18.1	60.6
Aged 25 to 29	897,843	47,054	136,125	196,767	510,034	100.0	5.2	15.2	21.9	56.8
Aged 30 to 34	873,973	57,667	121,931	184,505	502,423	100.0	6.6	14.0	21.1	57.5
Aged 35 to 44	1,877,625	95,328	265,717	280,745	1,221,176	100.0	5.1	14.2	15.0	65.0
Aged 45 to 54	1,846,038	72,833	249,879	176,569	1,331,290	100.0	3.9	13.5	9.6	72.1
Aged 55 to 64	1,298,278	50,863	163,448	95,466	979,978	100.0	3.9	12.6	7.4	75.5
Aged 65 to 74	770,024	26,490	97,085	44,383	596,808	100.0	3.4	12.6	5.8	77.5
Aged 75 to 84	539,564	11,291	54,279	22,141	449,299	100.0	2.1	10.1	4.1	83.3
Aged 85 or older	222,785	3,384	17,878	5,354	194,900	100.0	1.5	8.0	2.4	87.5
Indiana, total	**6,313,520**	**81,054**	**551,864**	**299,398**	**5,291,080**	**100.0**	**1.3**	**8.7**	**4.7**	**83.8**
Under age 5	433,580	5,266	48,891	35,868	328,956	100.0	1.2	11.3	8.3	75.9
Aged 5 to 9	428,767	6,921	46,687	31,570	332,747	100.0	1.6	10.9	7.4	77.6
Aged 10 to 14	440,378	3,395	49,831	25,633	352,652	100.0	0.8	11.3	5.8	80.1
Aged 15 to 17	276,872	3,339	29,457	13,796	223,623	100.0	1.2	10.6	5.0	80.8
Aged 18 to 19	183,425	3,391	18,729	9,980	148,340	100.0	1.8	10.2	5.4	80.9
Aged 20 to 24	439,744	9,656	40,718	28,970	353,683	100.0	2.2	9.3	6.6	80.4
Aged 25 to 29	434,777	7,141	41,145	32,248	348,722	100.0	1.6	9.5	7.4	80.2
Aged 30 to 34	400,770	6,299	39,801	27,617	322,286	100.0	1.6	9.9	6.9	80.4
Aged 35 to 44	896,489	14,104	76,291	43,186	753,275	100.0	1.6	8.5	4.8	84.0
Aged 45 to 54	926,792	10,979	71,158	28,220	807,367	100.0	1.2	7.7	3.0	87.1
Aged 55 to 64	670,934	7,105	44,295	13,150	600,709	100.0	1.1	6.6	2.0	89.5
Aged 65 to 74	397,244	2,133	24,778	4,821	362,571	100.0	0.5	6.2	1.2	91.3
Aged 75 to 84	275,549	1,052	15,396	3,327	254,363	100.0	0.4	5.6	1.2	92.3
Aged 85 or older	108,199	273	4,687	1,012	101,786	100.0	0.3	4.3	0.9	94.1

(continued)

	total	Asian	black	Hispanic	non-Hispanic white	total	Asian	black	Hispanic	non-Hispanic white
Iowa, total	**2,982,085**	**45,647**	**67,297**	**112,987**	**2,714,414**	**100.0%**	**1.5%**	**2.3%**	**3.8%**	**91.0%**
Under age 5	191,127	3,082	5,842	13,087	161,035	100.0	1.6	3.1	6.8	84.3
Aged 5 to 9	192,953	3,684	7,512	13,569	160,824	100.0	1.9	3.9	7.0	83.3
Aged 10 to 14	200,655	2,210	6,577	11,211	175,881	100.0	1.1	3.3	5.6	87.7
Aged 15 to 17	129,785	2,276	3,495	6,863	114,410	100.0	1.8	2.7	5.3	88.2
Aged 18 to 19	93,887	1,399	2,506	5,556	83,081	100.0	1.5	2.7	5.9	88.5
Aged 20 to 24	221,652	5,229	5,931	9,798	197,417	100.0	2.4	2.7	4.4	89.1
Aged 25 to 29	179,340	4,312	4,730	10,387	158,187	100.0	2.4	2.6	5.8	88.2
Aged 30 to 34	173,492	5,297	6,021	11,218	149,660	100.0	3.1	3.5	6.5	86.3
Aged 35 to 44	401,183	8,362	9,320	15,379	363,891	100.0	2.1	2.3	3.8	90.7
Aged 45 to 54	441,849	4,874	6,730	9,329	417,092	100.0	1.1	1.5	2.1	94.4
Aged 55 to 64	320,789	2,525	4,342	3,600	308,525	100.0	0.8	1.4	1.1	96.2
Aged 65 to 74	205,409	1,365	2,590	1,635	198,728	100.0	0.7	1.3	0.8	96.7
Aged 75 to 84	161,333	969	1,429	936	157,806	100.0	0.6	0.9	0.6	97.8
Aged 85 or older	68,631	63	272	419	67,877	100.0	0.1	0.4	0.6	98.9
Kansas, total	**2,764,075**	**60,646**	**153,560**	**236,351**	**2,237,607**	**100.0**	**2.2**	**5.6**	**8.6**	**81.0**
Under age 5	194,702	4,349	11,296	28,351	139,048	100.0	2.2	5.8	14.6	71.4
Aged 5 to 9	189,279	4,119	11,777	25,602	139,136	100.0	2.2	6.2	13.5	73.5
Aged 10 to 14	189,718	3,974	12,290	22,834	143,389	100.0	2.1	6.5	12.0	75.6
Aged 15 to 17	120,968	1,613	9,491	11,636	93,835	100.0	1.3	7.8	9.6	77.6
Aged 18 to 19	85,492	2,028	6,089	8,976	64,675	100.0	2.4	7.1	10.5	75.7
Aged 20 to 24	212,731	5,138	14,155	21,490	164,622	100.0	2.4	6.7	10.1	77.4
Aged 25 to 29	179,361	5,651	11,051	22,104	136,738	100.0	3.2	6.2	12.3	76.2
Aged 30 to 34	164,645	7,044	8,468	21,519	124,375	100.0	4.3	5.1	13.1	75.5
Aged 35 to 44	385,320	12,665	23,146	36,910	303,688	100.0	3.3	6.0	9.6	78.8
Aged 45 to 54	401,047	5,709	22,046	18,975	346,532	100.0	1.4	5.5	4.7	86.4
Aged 55 to 64	285,148	5,430	12,774	10,193	252,044	100.0	1.9	4.5	3.6	88.4
Aged 65 to 74	170,065	1,700	5,956	4,039	156,083	100.0	1.0	3.5	2.4	91.8
Aged 75 to 84	128,393	994	3,534	2,917	119,140	100.0	0.8	2.8	2.3	92.8
Aged 85 or older	57,206	232	1,487	805	54,302	100.0	0.4	2.6	1.4	94.9
Kentucky, total	**4,206,074**	**38,835**	**310,146**	**83,015**	**3,715,900**	**100.0**	**0.9**	**7.4**	**2.0**	**88.3**
Under age 5	276,964	3,075	25,094	9,791	230,599	100.0	1.1	9.1	3.5	83.3
Aged 5 to 9	269,020	2,238	23,261	7,525	226,752	100.0	0.8	8.6	2.8	84.3
Aged 10 to 14	278,788	1,926	23,820	6,252	239,244	100.0	0.7	8.5	2.2	85.8
Aged 15 to 17	175,569	1,355	17,341	3,436	150,514	100.0	0.8	9.9	2.0	85.7
Aged 18 to 19	116,037	583	11,322	3,053	98,660	100.0	0.5	9.8	2.6	85.0
Aged 20 to 24	276,924	3,519	26,742	8,202	234,723	100.0	1.3	9.7	3.0	84.8
Aged 25 to 29	302,031	3,752	21,163	8,834	264,524	100.0	1.2	7.0	2.9	87.6
Aged 30 to 34	270,797	5,020	20,325	9,254	232,908	100.0	1.9	7.5	3.4	86.0
Aged 35 to 44	612,669	8,445	45,453	15,133	539,616	100.0	1.4	7.4	2.5	88.1
Aged 45 to 54	618,932	4,051	44,089	6,117	559,127	100.0	0.7	7.1	1.0	90.3
Aged 55 to 64	473,040	2,960	25,730	3,078	437,357	100.0	0.6	5.4	0.7	92.5
Aged 65 to 74	285,566	1,239	14,691	1,628	266,582	100.0	0.4	5.1	0.6	93.4
Aged 75 to 84	183,197	554	7,644	549	172,875	100.0	0.3	4.2	0.3	94.4
Aged 85 or older	66,540	118	3,471	163	62,419	100.0	0.2	5.2	0.2	93.8

(continued)

	total	Asian	black	Hispanic	non-Hispanic white	total	Asian	black	Hispanic	non-Hispanic white
Louisiana, total	4,287,768	57,084	1,356,981	123,281	2,689,206	100.0%	1.3%	31.6%	2.9%	62.7%
Under age 5	301,198	3,173	116,961	10,270	163,288	100.0	1.1	38.8	3.4	54.2
Aged 5 to 9	294,827	2,968	109,961	7,447	167,635	100.0	1.0	37.3	2.5	56.9
Aged 10 to 14	305,073	4,461	122,603	9,079	162,934	100.0	1.5	40.2	3.0	53.4
Aged 15 to 17	187,899	2,263	71,378	4,161	106,953	100.0	1.2	38.0	2.2	56.9
Aged 18 to 19	144,247	2,442	58,595	5,112	76,175	100.0	1.7	40.6	3.5	52.8
Aged 20 to 24	320,006	4,367	112,171	11,676	187,184	100.0	1.4	35.1	3.6	58.5
Aged 25 to 29	299,768	6,363	95,132	11,178	181,604	100.0	2.1	31.7	3.7	60.6
Aged 30 to 34	254,532	5,477	82,722	11,857	152,799	100.0	2.2	32.5	4.7	60.0
Aged 35 to 44	584,189	8,636	178,088	17,596	374,597	100.0	1.5	30.5	3.0	64.1
Aged 45 to 54	616,359	7,026	176,862	13,977	409,798	100.0	1.1	28.7	2.3	66.5
Aged 55 to 64	456,796	5,782	117,233	9,903	318,265	100.0	1.3	25.7	2.2	69.7
Aged 65 to 74	278,591	2,395	67,189	6,783	199,957	100.0	0.9	24.1	2.4	71.8
Aged 75 to 84	181,851	1,612	35,683	3,158	139,523	100.0	0.9	19.6	1.7	76.7
Aged 85 or older	62,432	119	12,403	1,084	48,494	100.0	0.2	19.9	1.7	77.7
Maine, total	1,321,574	12,004	13,669	12,622	1,259,089	100.0	0.9	1.0	1.0	95.3
Under age 5	70,227	1,386	1,679	1,469	64,418	100.0	2.0	2.4	2.1	91.7
Aged 5 to 9	72,033	702	1,587	1,461	65,940	100.0	1.0	2.2	2.0	91.5
Aged 10 to 14	83,029	662	1,702	846	77,450	100.0	0.8	2.0	1.0	93.3
Aged 15 to 17	56,583	890	1,151	528	52,168	100.0	1.6	2.0	0.9	92.2
Aged 18 to 19	34,386	371	935	594	31,476	100.0	1.1	2.7	1.7	91.5
Aged 20 to 24	81,988	528	1,330	1,550	76,491	100.0	0.6	1.6	1.9	93.3
Aged 25 to 29	75,710	1,070	641	1,075	71,291	100.0	1.4	0.8	1.4	94.2
Aged 30 to 34	76,282	1,623	954	1,112	70,626	100.0	2.1	1.3	1.5	92.6
Aged 35 to 44	194,089	1,562	1,828	1,224	185,864	100.0	0.8	0.9	0.6	95.8
Aged 45 to 54	217,754	1,718	971	1,308	210,913	100.0	0.8	0.4	0.6	96.9
Aged 55 to 64	167,059	740	745	857	163,276	100.0	0.4	0.4	0.5	97.7
Aged 65 to 74	98,317	440	99	457	96,157	100.0	0.4	0.1	0.5	97.8
Aged 75 to 84	68,040	243	47	141	67,143	100.0	0.4	0.1	0.2	98.7
Aged 85 or older	26,077	69	0	0	25,876	100.0	0.3	0.0	0.0	99.2
Maryland, total	5,615,727	276,362	1,624,858	336,390	3,275,198	100.0	4.9	28.9	6.0	58.3
Under age 5	368,501	17,848	119,421	35,328	179,043	100.0	4.8	32.4	9.6	48.6
Aged 5 to 9	363,536	17,506	117,110	28,468	185,780	100.0	4.8	32.2	7.8	51.1
Aged 10 to 14	382,153	15,408	126,476	26,657	202,645	100.0	4.0	33.1	7.0	53.0
Aged 15 to 17	247,942	9,788	83,212	15,228	133,956	100.0	3.9	33.6	6.1	54.0
Aged 18 to 19	164,785	7,497	54,248	9,680	90,347	100.0	4.5	32.9	5.9	54.8
Aged 20 to 24	371,298	16,883	118,396	29,062	199,307	100.0	4.5	31.9	7.8	53.7
Aged 25 to 29	363,534	20,744	113,834	35,160	188,607	100.0	5.7	31.3	9.7	51.9
Aged 30 to 34	354,344	26,794	106,025	33,413	181,751	100.0	7.6	29.9	9.4	51.3
Aged 35 to 44	880,892	52,626	266,697	58,357	492,578	100.0	6.0	30.3	6.6	55.9
Aged 45 to 54	860,739	40,821	235,941	34,888	538,328	100.0	4.7	27.4	4.1	62.5
Aged 55 to 64	610,671	27,445	150,943	16,925	409,167	100.0	4.5	24.7	2.8	67.0
Aged 65 to 74	341,696	15,162	79,574	7,472	236,431	100.0	4.4	23.3	2.2	69.2
Aged 75 to 84	223,325	5,756	38,329	4,963	172,979	100.0	2.6	17.2	2.2	77.5
Aged 85 or older	82,311	2,084	14,652	789	64,279	100.0	2.5	17.8	1.0	78.1

(continued)

	total	Asian	black	Hispanic	non-Hispanic white	total	Asian	black	Hispanic	non-Hispanic white
Massachusetts, total	**6,437,193**	**310,441**	**393,207**	**510,482**	**5,104,271**	**100.0%**	**4.8%**	**6.1%**	**7.9%**	**79.3%**
Under age 5	387,619	21,201	33,032	46,181	269,851	100.0	5.5	8.5	11.9	69.6
Aged 5 to 9	386,105	22,144	28,052	45,705	278,889	100.0	5.7	7.3	11.8	72.2
Aged 10 to 14	413,693	16,315	33,782	46,446	306,083	100.0	3.9	8.2	11.2	74.0
Aged 15 to 17	261,060	10,361	21,278	28,796	196,127	100.0	4.0	8.2	11.0	75.1
Aged 18 to 19	189,182	11,256	15,897	18,970	138,771	100.0	5.9	8.4	10.0	73.4
Aged 20 to 24	453,973	26,793	34,866	50,223	329,178	100.0	5.9	7.7	11.1	72.5
Aged 25 to 29	403,690	29,758	27,763	47,826	288,851	100.0	7.4	6.9	11.8	71.6
Aged 30 to 34	413,360	36,978	26,671	46,295	296,032	100.0	8.9	6.5	11.2	71.6
Aged 35 to 44	992,955	57,615	63,909	79,479	778,742	100.0	5.8	6.4	8.0	78.4
Aged 45 to 54	972,639	36,653	50,462	51,948	821,290	100.0	3.8	5.2	5.3	84.4
Aged 55 to 64	706,031	21,619	29,404	27,698	619,672	100.0	3.1	4.2	3.9	87.8
Aged 65 to 74	412,051	12,261	16,378	14,641	365,216	100.0	3.0	4.0	3.6	88.6
Aged 75 to 84	309,373	6,369	9,188	4,602	286,199	100.0	2.1	3.0	1.5	92.5
Aged 85 or older	135,462	1,118	2,525	1,672	129,370	100.0	0.8	1.9	1.2	95.5
Michigan, total	**10,095,643**	**236,972**	**1,426,809**	**392,770**	**7,836,885**	**100.0**	**2.3**	**14.1**	**3.9**	**77.6**
Under age 5	639,239	16,465	105,405	40,094	450,841	100.0	2.6	16.5	6.3	70.5
Aged 5 to 9	657,808	17,318	112,824	40,803	462,550	100.0	2.6	17.2	6.2	70.3
Aged 10 to 14	721,956	14,742	130,423	37,060	518,673	100.0	2.0	18.1	5.1	71.8
Aged 15 to 17	458,418	9,256	84,843	20,270	331,109	100.0	2.0	18.5	4.4	72.2
Aged 18 to 19	293,094	6,920	46,238	15,084	217,312	100.0	2.4	15.8	5.1	74.1
Aged 20 to 24	686,462	17,398	100,330	32,720	520,640	100.0	2.5	14.6	4.8	75.8
Aged 25 to 29	638,447	21,464	102,231	35,715	467,170	100.0	3.4	16.0	5.6	73.2
Aged 30 to 34	623,116	28,341	98,638	35,750	446,874	100.0	4.5	15.8	5.7	71.7
Aged 35 to 44	1,469,671	45,198	203,517	59,000	1,138,646	100.0	3.1	13.8	4.0	77.5
Aged 45 to 54	1,536,628	27,995	191,948	39,074	1,255,550	100.0	1.8	12.5	2.5	81.7
Aged 55 to 64	1,110,437	17,980	127,915	21,687	929,839	100.0	1.6	11.5	2.0	83.7
Aged 65 to 74	640,733	8,597	66,324	9,544	549,388	100.0	1.3	10.4	1.5	85.7
Aged 75 to 84	446,703	4,404	40,863	4,994	393,060	100.0	1.0	9.1	1.1	88.0
Aged 85 or older	172,931	894	15,310	975	155,233	100.0	0.5	8.9	0.6	89.8
Minnesota, total	**5,167,101**	**179,295**	**228,354**	**195,138**	**4,435,973**	**100.0**	**3.5**	**4.4**	**3.8**	**85.9**
Under age 5	347,404	15,587	27,238	26,825	260,131	100.0	4.5	7.8	7.7	74.9
Aged 5 to 9	335,072	16,204	21,159	20,126	260,866	100.0	4.8	6.3	6.0	77.9
Aged 10 to 14	350,245	15,234	20,659	17,500	280,927	100.0	4.3	5.9	5.0	80.2
Aged 15 to 17	225,209	9,599	13,276	8,643	185,134	100.0	4.3	5.9	3.8	82.2
Aged 18 to 19	150,314	5,969	9,740	6,568	123,473	100.0	4.0	6.5	4.4	82.1
Aged 20 to 24	371,409	13,512	18,231	17,714	311,210	100.0	3.6	4.9	4.8	83.8
Aged 25 to 29	342,899	16,012	19,862	21,185	277,843	100.0	4.7	5.8	6.2	81.0
Aged 30 to 34	326,607	20,683	19,108	20,314	258,190	100.0	6.3	5.9	6.2	79.1
Aged 35 to 44	759,760	29,839	35,573	28,598	652,316	100.0	3.9	4.7	3.8	85.9
Aged 45 to 54	795,187	18,510	25,398	15,931	722,435	100.0	2.3	3.2	2.0	90.9
Aged 55 to 64	534,890	9,980	10,283	6,467	501,653	100.0	1.9	1.9	1.2	93.8
Aged 65 to 74	311,051	4,913	4,902	3,795	294,227	100.0	1.6	1.6	1.2	94.6
Aged 75 to 84	220,590	2,207	2,345	1,243	213,417	100.0	1.0	1.1	0.6	96.7
Aged 85 or older	96,464	1,046	580	229	94,151	100.0	1.1	0.6	0.2	97.6

(continued)

	total	Asian	black	Hispanic	non-Hispanic white	total	Asian	black	Hispanic	non-Hispanic white
Mississippi, total	**2,910,540**	**22,116**	**1,087,114**	**46,348**	**1,724,848**	**100.0%**	**0.8%**	**37.4%**	**1.6%**	**59.3%**
Under age 5	206,089	1,045	90,923	5,538	104,726	100.0	0.5	44.1	2.7	50.8
Aged 5 to 9	197,451	1,008	87,203	2,750	102,322	100.0	0.5	44.2	1.4	51.8
Aged 10 to 14	222,284	1,589	104,015	3,570	110,535	100.0	0.7	46.8	1.6	49.7
Aged 15 to 17	133,103	841	59,543	2,084	68,544	100.0	0.6	44.7	1.6	51.5
Aged 18 to 19	96,932	427	42,788	1,832	50,916	100.0	0.4	44.1	1.9	52.5
Aged 20 to 24	214,999	2,624	93,188	6,263	109,774	100.0	1.2	43.3	2.9	51.1
Aged 25 to 29	195,506	2,029	78,269	6,675	107,155	100.0	1.0	40.0	3.4	54.8
Aged 30 to 34	171,768	2,290	64,737	4,316	99,771	100.0	1.3	37.7	2.5	58.1
Aged 35 to 44	398,694	4,251	146,823	4,907	240,024	100.0	1.1	36.8	1.2	60.2
Aged 45 to 54	405,857	2,371	143,360	4,948	251,229	100.0	0.6	35.3	1.2	61.9
Aged 55 to 64	307,164	1,546	89,003	1,752	212,557	100.0	0.5	29.0	0.6	69.2
Aged 65 to 74	192,151	1,239	48,951	1,165	139,553	100.0	0.6	25.5	0.6	72.6
Aged 75 to 84	120,948	666	25,681	233	93,628	100.0	0.6	21.2	0.2	77.4
Aged 85 or older	47,594	190	12,630	315	34,114	100.0	0.4	26.5	0.7	71.7
Missouri, total	**5,842,713**	**86,010**	**661,535**	**160,898**	**4,820,772**	**100.0**	**1.5**	**11.3**	**2.8**	**82.5**
Under age 5	390,715	6,407	54,353	22,015	292,014	100.0	1.6	13.9	5.6	74.7
Aged 5 to 9	383,940	6,096	53,565	16,406	293,301	100.0	1.6	14.0	4.3	76.4
Aged 10 to 14	393,812	6,042	57,339	12,216	305,807	100.0	1.5	14.6	3.1	77.7
Aged 15 to 17	253,962	3,201	37,208	7,327	200,357	100.0	1.3	14.7	2.9	78.9
Aged 18 to 19	165,621	2,209	21,778	6,893	131,103	100.0	1.3	13.1	4.2	79.2
Aged 20 to 24	405,388	7,308	50,749	14,475	325,522	100.0	1.8	12.5	3.6	80.3
Aged 25 to 29	400,567	8,000	49,051	15,389	321,915	100.0	2.0	12.2	3.8	80.4
Aged 30 to 34	357,364	9,953	44,372	14,086	282,192	100.0	2.8	12.4	3.9	79.0
Aged 35 to 44	815,052	13,685	91,708	21,712	675,139	100.0	1.7	11.3	2.7	82.8
Aged 45 to 54	863,408	11,301	90,927	14,985	732,525	100.0	1.3	10.5	1.7	84.8
Aged 55 to 64	633,279	7,321	52,963	7,752	557,997	100.0	1.2	8.4	1.2	88.1
Aged 65 to 74	395,919	2,809	32,250	3,926	352,686	100.0	0.7	8.1	1.0	89.1
Aged 75 to 84	275,684	1,542	18,579	3,101	250,187	100.0	0.6	6.7	1.1	90.8
Aged 85 or older	108,002	136	6,693	615	100,027	100.0	0.1	6.2	0.6	92.6
Montana, total	**944,632**	**5,525**	**–**	**20,513**	**836,541**	**100.0**	**0.6**	**–**	**2.2**	**88.6**
Under age 5	57,577	630	–	2,280	46,503	100.0	1.1	–	4.0	80.8
Aged 5 to 9	58,636	438	–	1,588	48,943	100.0	0.7	–	2.7	83.5
Aged 10 to 14	59,383	471	–	1,708	49,415	100.0	0.8	–	2.9	83.2
Aged 15 to 17	42,502	391	–	1,910	34,858	100.0	0.9	–	4.5	82.0
Aged 18 to 19	28,161	135	–	616	22,587	100.0	0.5	–	2.2	80.2
Aged 20 to 24	67,693	505	–	2,592	57,646	100.0	0.7	–	3.8	85.2
Aged 25 to 29	61,586	464	–	1,618	52,503	100.0	0.8	–	2.6	85.3
Aged 30 to 34	50,030	291	–	1,575	44,097	100.0	0.6	–	3.1	88.1
Aged 35 to 44	120,418	987	–	2,045	107,464	100.0	0.8	–	1.7	89.2
Aged 45 to 54	152,481	864	–	2,069	140,225	100.0	0.6	–	1.4	92.0
Aged 55 to 64	114,847	174	–	1,277	107,924	100.0	0.2	–	1.1	94.0
Aged 65 to 74	67,916	127	–	704	62,830	100.0	0.2	–	1.0	92.5
Aged 75 to 84	46,601	48	–	455	45,208	100.0	0.1	–	1.0	97.0
Aged 85 or older	16,801	0	–	76	16,338	100.0	0.0	–	0.5	97.2

(continued)

	total	Asian	black	Hispanic	non-Hispanic white	total	Asian	black	Hispanic	non-Hispanic white
Nebraska, total	**1,768,331**	**29,815**	**72,095**	**130,230**	**1,500,166**	**100.0%**	**1.7%**	**4.1%**	**7.4%**	**84.8%**
Under age 5	128,307	1,947	7,352	17,712	95,527	100.0	1.5	5.7	13.8	74.5
Aged 5 to 9	120,167	2,044	6,499	16,019	91,136	100.0	1.7	5.4	13.3	75.8
Aged 10 to 14	119,132	1,664	6,306	11,260	95,848	100.0	1.4	5.3	9.5	80.5
Aged 15 to 17	77,804	1,402	3,883	6,472	63,642	100.0	1.8	5.0	8.3	81.8
Aged 18 to 19	55,028	1,304	1,925	5,606	44,584	100.0	2.4	3.5	10.2	81.0
Aged 20 to 24	132,025	2,717	5,804	9,600	111,129	100.0	2.1	4.4	7.3	84.2
Aged 25 to 29	117,732	2,934	5,785	12,167	93,334	100.0	2.5	4.9	10.3	79.3
Aged 30 to 34	112,177	4,140	4,973	14,812	86,185	100.0	3.7	4.4	13.2	76.8
Aged 35 to 44	233,713	3,862	10,385	16,880	199,280	100.0	1.7	4.4	7.2	85.3
Aged 45 to 54	256,350	3,407	8,966	11,041	229,793	100.0	1.3	3.5	4.3	89.6
Aged 55 to 64	182,621	2,978	5,514	5,509	167,050	100.0	1.6	3.0	3.0	91.5
Aged 65 to 74	112,624	850	3,513	2,094	105,510	100.0	0.8	3.1	1.9	93.7
Aged 75 to 84	84,072	551	885	829	81,299	100.0	0.7	1.1	1.0	96.7
Aged 85 or older	36,579	15	305	229	35,849	100.0	0.0	0.8	0.6	98.0
Nevada, total	**2,495,529**	**147,363**	**183,064**	**610,051**	**1,463,452**	**100.0**	**5.9**	**7.3**	**24.4**	**58.6**
Under age 5	183,437	9,302	16,214	69,588	77,174	100.0	5.1	8.8	37.9	42.1
Aged 5 to 9	169,201	7,014	14,889	62,396	74,977	100.0	4.1	8.8	36.9	44.3
Aged 10 to 14	177,454	8,871	14,432	59,373	85,244	100.0	5.0	8.1	33.5	48.0
Aged 15 to 17	104,355	5,284	9,430	31,394	53,346	100.0	5.1	9.0	30.1	51.1
Aged 18 to 19	58,962	2,514	4,762	16,096	31,986	100.0	4.3	8.1	27.3	54.2
Aged 20 to 24	157,800	7,443	13,448	47,575	81,206	100.0	4.7	8.5	30.1	51.5
Aged 25 to 29	192,667	12,441	13,866	61,578	98,029	100.0	6.5	7.2	32.0	50.9
Aged 30 to 34	179,676	12,129	13,439	59,826	88,243	100.0	6.8	7.5	33.3	49.1
Aged 35 to 44	382,576	26,049	28,261	98,445	219,805	100.0	6.8	7.4	25.7	57.5
Aged 45 to 54	340,076	23,555	23,383	52,754	231,054	100.0	6.9	6.9	15.5	67.9
Aged 55 to 64	274,299	17,469	16,079	28,776	205,193	100.0	6.4	5.9	10.5	74.8
Aged 65 to 74	156,780	10,017	9,726	13,817	120,115	100.0	6.4	6.2	8.8	76.6
Aged 75 to 84	92,570	4,423	4,290	7,124	74,840	100.0	4.8	4.6	7.7	80.8
Aged 85 or older	25,676	852	845	1,309	22,240	100.0	3.3	3.3	5.1	86.6
New Hampshire, total	**1,314,895**	**26,136**	**13,842**	**29,721**	**1,230,377**	**100.0**	**2.0**	**1.1**	**2.3**	**93.6**
Under age 5	73,480	2,173	1,177	3,088	65,684	100.0	3.0	1.6	4.2	89.4
Aged 5 to 9	78,862	1,688	807	2,556	71,488	100.0	2.1	1.0	3.2	90.6
Aged 10 to 14	87,274	2,386	1,254	2,735	79,784	100.0	2.7	1.4	3.1	91.4
Aged 15 to 17	58,062	773	695	1,457	54,275	100.0	1.3	1.2	2.5	93.5
Aged 18 to 19	37,952	837	390	1,538	34,346	100.0	2.2	1.0	4.1	90.5
Aged 20 to 24	82,393	1,198	2,284	1,773	76,653	100.0	1.5	2.8	2.2	93.0
Aged 25 to 29	75,753	1,640	1,280	2,780	69,203	100.0	2.2	1.7	3.7	91.4
Aged 30 to 34	78,212	3,987	600	3,201	69,684	100.0	5.1	0.8	4.1	89.1
Aged 35 to 44	208,140	5,183	2,818	4,793	193,489	100.0	2.5	1.4	2.3	93.0
Aged 45 to 54	217,645	3,285	1,011	3,009	208,622	100.0	1.5	0.5	1.4	95.9
Aged 55 to 64	155,286	1,641	1,327	1,755	148,957	100.0	1.1	0.9	1.1	95.9
Aged 65 to 74	83,356	949	199	919	80,386	100.0	1.1	0.2	1.1	96.4
Aged 75 to 84	55,432	396	0	117	54,758	100.0	0.7	0.0	0.2	98.8
Aged 85 or older	23,048	0	0	0	23,048	100.0	0.0	0.0	0.0	100.0

(continued)

	total	Asian	black	Hispanic	non-Hispanic white	total	Asian	black	Hispanic	non-Hispanic white
New Jersey, total	**8,724,560**	**652,378**	**1,187,161**	**1,364,699**	**5,431,103**	**100.0%**	**7.5%**	**13.6%**	**15.6%**	**62.3%**
Under age 5	559,872	43,695	87,113	126,231	288,515	100.0	7.8	15.6	22.5	51.5
Aged 5 to 9	565,814	46,385	83,719	104,662	320,510	100.0	8.2	14.8	18.5	56.6
Aged 10 to 14	592,696	39,950	102,030	105,462	335,942	100.0	6.7	17.2	17.8	56.7
Aged 15 to 17	371,271	24,101	61,920	60,887	219,725	100.0	6.5	16.7	16.4	59.2
Aged 18 to 19	226,345	13,568	40,120	38,982	131,337	100.0	6.0	17.7	17.2	58.0
Aged 20 to 24	537,322	33,956	87,720	110,073	299,194	100.0	6.3	16.3	20.5	55.7
Aged 25 to 29	511,804	48,154	81,134	125,101	249,479	100.0	9.4	15.9	24.4	48.7
Aged 30 to 34	570,969	69,080	81,417	124,794	290,007	100.0	12.1	14.3	21.9	50.8
Aged 35 to 44	1,393,015	130,749	190,774	232,413	826,713	100.0	9.4	13.7	16.7	59.3
Aged 45 to 54	1,325,391	96,335	159,376	158,553	904,864	100.0	7.3	12.0	12.0	68.3
Aged 55 to 64	944,456	60,762	104,335	94,549	680,622	100.0	6.4	11.0	10.0	72.1
Aged 65 to 74	559,820	29,495	63,652	52,013	411,231	100.0	5.3	11.4	9.3	73.5
Aged 75 to 84	402,259	13,499	32,189	24,407	330,812	100.0	3.4	8.0	6.1	82.2
Aged 85 or older	163,526	2,649	11,662	6,572	142,152	100.0	1.6	7.1	4.0	86.9
New Mexico, total	**1,954,599**	**25,983**	**39,654**	**860,687**	**828,965**	**100.0**	**1.3**	**2.0**	**44.0**	**42.4**
Under age 5	141,732	1,846	2,487	77,735	41,517	100.0	1.3	1.8	54.8	29.3
Aged 5 to 9	135,446	1,524	4,097	73,868	39,043	100.0	1.1	3.0	54.5	28.8
Aged 10 to 14	144,396	1,315	4,108	72,831	47,006	100.0	0.9	2.8	50.4	32.6
Aged 15 to 17	88,776	872	2,262	44,993	27,760	100.0	1.0	2.5	50.7	31.3
Aged 18 to 19	58,823	721	1,467	31,035	17,630	100.0	1.2	2.5	52.8	30.0
Aged 20 to 24	145,993	1,418	3,872	71,908	50,950	100.0	1.0	2.7	49.3	34.9
Aged 25 to 29	133,813	2,871	2,700	65,133	47,767	100.0	2.1	2.0	48.7	35.7
Aged 30 to 34	123,019	2,718	3,085	62,183	43,336	100.0	2.2	2.5	50.5	35.2
Aged 35 to 44	260,001	4,292	5,560	115,017	108,161	100.0	1.7	2.1	44.2	41.6
Aged 45 to 54	270,937	3,360	4,349	102,690	137,076	100.0	1.2	1.6	37.9	50.6
Aged 55 to 64	210,384	3,209	3,162	67,738	121,522	100.0	1.5	1.5	32.2	57.8
Aged 65 to 74	127,571	1,159	1,029	42,362	75,474	100.0	0.9	0.8	33.2	59.2
Aged 75 to 84	85,009	579	738	25,454	53,885	100.0	0.7	0.9	29.9	63.4
Aged 85 or older	28,699	99	738	7,740	17,838	100.0	0.3	2.6	27.0	62.2
New York, total	**19,306,183**	**1,322,971**	**2,990,260**	**3,139,590**	**11,628,557**	**100.0**	**6.9**	**15.5**	**16.3**	**60.2**
Under age 5	1,221,010	82,878	219,626	267,862	620,397	100.0	6.8	18.0	21.9	50.8
Aged 5 to 9	1,196,762	78,001	220,693	240,829	634,056	100.0	6.5	18.4	20.1	53.0
Aged 10 to 14	1,281,783	73,075	235,169	253,683	698,199	100.0	5.7	18.3	19.8	54.5
Aged 15 to 17	813,934	45,796	159,013	150,972	451,046	100.0	5.6	19.5	18.5	55.4
Aged 18 to 19	580,825	35,477	99,177	102,457	335,340	100.0	6.1	17.1	17.6	57.7
Aged 20 to 24	1,365,987	97,648	238,646	263,567	748,643	100.0	7.1	17.5	19.3	54.8
Aged 25 to 29	1,253,355	110,862	207,621	275,457	644,894	100.0	8.8	16.6	22.0	51.5
Aged 30 to 34	1,255,764	128,512	191,462	258,550	663,000	100.0	10.2	15.2	20.6	52.8
Aged 35 to 44	2,903,901	236,192	450,295	497,419	1,687,580	100.0	8.1	15.5	17.1	58.1
Aged 45 to 54	2,823,776	197,342	404,513	369,534	1,826,401	100.0	7.0	14.3	13.1	64.7
Aged 55 to 64	2,088,198	126,237	273,893	238,920	1,431,706	100.0	6.0	13.1	11.4	68.6
Aged 65 to 74	1,268,161	70,459	167,792	132,272	889,989	100.0	5.6	13.2	10.4	70.2
Aged 75 to 84	894,543	29,487	90,218	66,834	704,895	100.0	3.3	10.1	7.5	78.8
Aged 85 or older	358,184	11,005	32,142	21,234	292,411	100.0	3.1	9.0	5.9	81.6

(continued)

	total	Asian	black	Hispanic	non-Hispanic white	total	Asian	black	Hispanic	non-Hispanic white
North Carolina, total	**8,856,505**	**162,578**	**1,892,469**	**597,382**	**5,999,236**	**100.0%**	**1.8%**	**21.4%**	**6.7%**	**67.7%**
Under age 5	602,733	11,107	134,839	83,871	345,904	100.0	1.8	22.4	13.9	57.4
Aged 5 to 9	576,895	12,284	144,715	59,871	338,882	100.0	2.1	25.1	10.4	58.7
Aged 10 to 14	604,628	11,171	157,882	46,629	368,250	100.0	1.8	26.1	7.7	60.9
Aged 15 to 17	370,763	7,864	98,272	24,422	227,221	100.0	2.1	26.5	6.6	61.3
Aged 18 to 19	255,023	4,517	70,030	19,606	155,220	100.0	1.8	27.5	7.7	60.9
Aged 20 to 24	601,228	12,764	141,383	57,988	368,952	100.0	2.1	23.5	9.6	61.4
Aged 25 to 29	588,088	13,503	125,932	72,679	363,621	100.0	2.3	21.4	12.4	61.8
Aged 30 to 34	611,849	17,779	126,125	73,999	381,567	100.0	2.9	20.6	12.1	62.4
Aged 35 to 44	1,330,032	29,736	283,604	90,860	903,034	100.0	2.2	21.3	6.8	67.9
Aged 45 to 54	1,269,316	20,260	269,879	41,911	913,869	100.0	1.6	21.3	3.3	72.0
Aged 55 to 64	974,151	12,752	173,738	15,812	758,370	100.0	1.3	17.8	1.6	77.8
Aged 65 to 74	576,276	6,060	92,925	6,773	462,927	100.0	1.1	16.1	1.2	80.3
Aged 75 to 84	373,398	1,958	52,931	2,335	312,066	100.0	0.5	14.2	0.6	83.6
Aged 85 or older	122,125	823	20,214	626	99,353	100.0	0.7	16.6	0.5	81.4
North Dakota, total	**635,867**	–	–	**9,332**	**575,108**	**100.0**	–	–	**1.5**	**90.4**
Under age 5	39,094	–	–	1,155	32,525	100.0	–	–	3.0	83.2
Aged 5 to 9	36,139	–	–	541	31,743	100.0	–	–	1.5	87.8
Aged 10 to 14	41,338	–	–	640	35,136	100.0	–	–	1.5	85.0
Aged 15 to 17	27,041	–	–	649	23,109	100.0	–	–	2.4	85.5
Aged 18 to 19	25,111	–	–	649	21,871	100.0	–	–	2.6	87.1
Aged 20 to 24	57,279	–	–	1,415	50,045	100.0	–	–	2.5	87.4
Aged 25 to 29	41,046	–	–	1,143	35,233	100.0	–	–	2.8	85.8
Aged 30 to 34	33,159	–	–	927	29,672	100.0	–	–	2.8	89.5
Aged 35 to 44	81,357	–	–	826	72,311	100.0	–	–	1.0	88.9
Aged 45 to 54	94,602	–	–	430	89,844	100.0	–	–	0.5	95.0
Aged 55 to 64	66,872	–	–	641	63,226	100.0	–	–	1.0	94.5
Aged 65 to 74	43,138	–	–	261	41,554	100.0	–	–	0.6	96.3
Aged 75 to 84	33,929	–	–	55	33,241	100.0	–	–	0.2	98.0
Aged 85 or older	15,762	–	–	0	15,598	100.0	–	–	0.0	99.0
Ohio, total	**11,478,006**	**175,000**	**1,357,343**	**265,762**	**9,506,469**	**100.0**	**1.5**	**11.8**	**2.3**	**82.8**
Under age 5	736,175	12,910	108,838	27,753	560,450	100.0	1.8	14.8	3.8	76.1
Aged 5 to 9	741,865	12,112	104,720	26,381	573,382	100.0	1.6	14.1	3.6	77.3
Aged 10 to 14	794,758	9,111	123,931	23,785	617,065	100.0	1.1	15.6	3.0	77.6
Aged 15 to 17	499,978	5,702	74,479	13,489	395,512	100.0	1.1	14.9	2.7	79.1
Aged 18 to 19	327,671	5,619	44,588	10,082	258,023	100.0	1.7	13.6	3.1	78.7
Aged 20 to 24	775,097	13,611	101,283	22,380	623,361	100.0	1.8	13.1	2.9	80.4
Aged 25 to 29	749,491	17,126	96,634	24,245	603,139	100.0	2.3	12.9	3.2	80.5
Aged 30 to 34	695,313	21,528	85,459	23,203	559,422	100.0	3.1	12.3	3.3	80.5
Aged 35 to 44	1,627,911	32,394	188,010	41,527	1,348,977	100.0	2.0	11.5	2.6	82.9
Aged 45 to 54	1,738,793	19,507	186,528	26,268	1,491,504	100.0	1.1	10.7	1.5	85.8
Aged 55 to 64	1,262,875	14,686	114,344	16,141	1,105,842	100.0	1.2	9.1	1.3	87.6
Aged 65 to 74	764,271	6,387	68,883	6,050	677,298	100.0	0.8	9.0	0.8	88.6
Aged 75 to 84	555,823	3,790	43,712	3,991	502,217	100.0	0.7	7.9	0.7	90.4
Aged 85 or older	207,985	517	15,934	467	190,277	100.0	0.2	7.7	0.2	91.5

(continued)

	total	Asian	black	Hispanic	non-Hispanic white	total	Asian	black	Hispanic	non-Hispanic white
Oklahoma, total	**3,579,212**	**59,164**	**263,271**	**244,822**	**2,577,447**	**100.0%**	**1.7%**	**7.4%**	**6.8%**	**72.0%**
Under age 5	252,053	4,562	21,793	31,318	153,454	100.0	1.8	8.6	12.4	60.9
Aged 5 to 9	242,570	4,014	22,517	27,052	148,612	100.0	1.7	9.3	11.2	61.3
Aged 10 to 14	245,332	2,936	19,856	21,989	157,655	100.0	1.2	8.1	9.0	64.3
Aged 15 to 17	155,231	2,604	14,901	12,867	100,335	100.0	1.7	9.6	8.3	64.6
Aged 18 to 19	104,007	2,186	10,290	7,811	68,638	100.0	2.1	9.9	7.5	66.0
Aged 20 to 24	267,898	5,048	22,567	24,411	177,651	100.0	1.9	8.4	9.1	66.3
Aged 25 to 29	250,164	6,011	21,383	24,487	169,750	100.0	2.4	8.5	9.8	67.9
Aged 30 to 34	217,397	4,865	17,209	22,533	146,656	100.0	2.2	7.9	10.4	67.5
Aged 35 to 44	477,860	8,929	34,025	35,356	344,195	100.0	1.9	7.1	7.4	72.0
Aged 45 to 54	505,295	9,090	36,024	19,639	389,715	100.0	1.8	7.1	3.9	77.1
Aged 55 to 64	385,768	4,548	21,026	10,247	314,683	100.0	1.2	5.5	2.7	81.6
Aged 65 to 74	248,712	3,262	12,118	4,063	207,292	100.0	1.3	4.9	1.6	83.3
Aged 75 to 84	164,101	1,109	6,828	2,476	143,148	100.0	0.7	4.2	1.5	87.2
Aged 85 or older	62,824	0	2,734	573	55,663	100.0	0.0	4.4	0.9	88.6
Oregon, total	**3,700,758**	**135,746**	**63,631**	**379,034**	**2,989,235**	**100.0**	**3.7**	**1.7**	**10.2**	**80.8**
Under age 5	229,956	7,727	6,466	43,990	156,392	100.0	3.4	2.8	19.1	68.0
Aged 5 to 9	231,329	9,409	4,419	41,839	162,279	100.0	4.1	1.9	18.1	70.2
Aged 10 to 14	240,957	10,214	5,243	37,555	176,881	100.0	4.2	2.2	15.6	73.4
Aged 15 to 17	155,375	5,057	3,655	19,110	118,579	100.0	3.3	2.4	12.3	76.3
Aged 18 to 19	95,513	3,362	2,400	11,491	72,830	100.0	3.5	2.5	12.0	76.3
Aged 20 to 24	246,256	10,771	4,648	32,483	187,438	100.0	4.4	1.9	13.2	76.1
Aged 25 to 29	268,023	11,124	4,029	41,972	202,620	100.0	4.2	1.5	15.7	75.6
Aged 30 to 34	245,978	13,537	3,689	40,396	179,554	100.0	5.5	1.5	16.4	73.0
Aged 35 to 44	512,348	24,469	9,898	54,295	408,254	100.0	4.8	1.9	10.6	79.7
Aged 45 to 54	560,444	18,056	9,551	30,408	485,094	100.0	3.2	1.7	5.4	86.6
Aged 55 to 64	437,714	11,423	4,786	15,728	394,683	100.0	2.6	1.1	3.6	90.2
Aged 65 to 74	239,586	6,025	2,742	6,068	220,580	100.0	2.5	1.1	2.5	92.1
Aged 75 to 84	166,829	3,624	965	2,831	157,229	100.0	2.2	0.6	1.7	94.2
Aged 85 or older	70,450	948	1,140	868	66,822	100.0	1.3	1.6	1.2	94.9
Pennsylvania, total	**12,440,621**	**289,289**	**1,289,799**	**527,142**	**10,201,475**	**100.0**	**2.3**	**10.4**	**4.2**	**82.0**
Under age 5	724,450	20,621	100,842	57,255	523,165	100.0	2.8	13.9	7.9	72.2
Aged 5 to 9	742,644	19,650	96,885	50,136	556,820	100.0	2.6	13.0	6.8	75.0
Aged 10 to 14	809,077	16,252	110,524	50,774	613,048	100.0	2.0	13.7	6.3	75.8
Aged 15 to 17	531,363	9,747	72,450	28,960	410,996	100.0	1.8	13.6	5.5	77.3
Aged 18 to 19	378,258	11,241	49,461	21,324	289,921	100.0	3.0	13.1	5.6	76.6
Aged 20 to 24	822,970	24,453	95,255	43,324	651,193	100.0	3.0	11.6	5.3	79.1
Aged 25 to 29	720,977	24,311	85,181	46,231	556,120	100.0	3.4	11.8	6.4	77.1
Aged 30 to 34	717,916	30,130	80,486	43,281	558,457	100.0	4.2	11.2	6.0	77.8
Aged 35 to 44	1,777,911	53,122	189,175	79,738	1,445,590	100.0	3.0	10.6	4.5	81.3
Aged 45 to 54	1,918,048	37,023	172,850	53,408	1,643,326	100.0	1.9	9.0	2.8	85.7
Aged 55 to 64	1,413,773	23,483	110,539	30,937	1,243,304	100.0	1.7	7.8	2.2	87.9
Aged 65 to 74	887,342	12,711	67,490	12,933	790,349	100.0	1.4	7.6	1.5	89.1
Aged 75 to 84	723,983	5,793	43,808	6,941	665,428	100.0	0.8	6.1	1.0	91.9
Aged 85 or older	271,909	752	14,853	1,900	253,758	100.0	0.3	5.5	0.7	93.3

(continued)

	total	Asian	black	Hispanic	non-Hispanic white	total	Asian	black	Hispanic	non-Hispanic white
Rhode Island, total	**1,067,610**	**29,406**	**54,396**	**117,708**	**842,726**	**100.0%**	**2.8%**	**5.1%**	**11.0%**	**78.9%**
Under age 5	61,798	2,249	4,029	12,382	39,161	100.0	3.6	6.5	20.0	63.4
Aged 5 to 9	62,571	1,599	4,124	12,930	40,835	100.0	2.6	6.6	20.7	65.3
Aged 10 to 14	69,382	2,059	5,091	10,289	50,302	100.0	3.0	7.3	14.8	72.5
Aged 15 to 17	43,696	1,307	3,294	6,540	31,822	100.0	3.0	7.5	15.0	72.8
Aged 18 to 19	37,453	1,640	2,346	4,341	27,751	100.0	4.4	6.3	11.6	74.1
Aged 20 to 24	79,726	3,491	4,965	10,408	59,092	100.0	4.4	6.2	13.1	74.1
Aged 25 to 29	66,345	3,014	4,129	10,267	47,335	100.0	4.5	6.2	15.5	71.3
Aged 30 to 34	63,506	2,028	4,571	9,847	46,271	100.0	3.2	7.2	15.5	72.9
Aged 35 to 44	159,682	4,509	7,952	18,631	125,822	100.0	2.8	5.0	11.7	78.8
Aged 45 to 54	159,950	3,181	7,169	11,569	135,453	100.0	2.0	4.5	7.2	84.7
Aged 55 to 64	116,057	1,928	3,832	5,919	102,883	100.0	1.7	3.3	5.1	88.6
Aged 65 to 74	67,112	1,362	1,453	2,838	60,512	100.0	2.0	2.2	4.2	90.2
Aged 75 to 84	54,909	989	1,199	1,201	51,337	100.0	1.8	2.2	2.2	93.5
Aged 85 or older	25,423	50	242	546	24,150	100.0	0.2	1.0	2.1	95.0
South Carolina, total	**4,321,249**	**46,939**	**1,237,900**	**148,632**	**2,823,274**	**100.0**	**1.1**	**28.6**	**3.4**	**65.3**
Under age 5	284,708	2,808	90,177	19,395	161,546	100.0	1.0	31.7	6.8	56.7
Aged 5 to 9	275,178	2,833	90,594	12,803	160,577	100.0	1.0	32.9	4.7	58.4
Aged 10 to 14	290,615	3,586	99,550	10,921	169,019	100.0	1.2	34.3	3.8	58.2
Aged 15 to 17	188,365	1,767	67,502	5,465	109,818	100.0	0.9	35.8	2.9	58.3
Aged 18 to 19	135,837	619	50,708	5,035	77,634	100.0	0.5	37.3	3.7	57.2
Aged 20 to 24	300,802	3,583	100,241	16,105	176,810	100.0	1.2	33.3	5.4	58.8
Aged 25 to 29	279,729	3,595	83,431	17,329	172,059	100.0	1.3	29.8	6.2	61.5
Aged 30 to 34	273,747	6,919	71,905	17,848	172,632	100.0	2.5	26.3	6.5	63.1
Aged 35 to 44	619,503	8,395	178,461	25,114	401,453	100.0	1.4	28.8	4.1	64.8
Aged 45 to 54	618,659	5,352	172,761	10,754	422,673	100.0	0.9	27.9	1.7	68.3
Aged 55 to 64	500,251	3,724	117,395	4,569	370,179	100.0	0.7	23.5	0.9	74.0
Aged 65 to 74	301,498	3,087	64,317	2,231	230,265	100.0	1.0	21.3	0.7	76.4
Aged 75 to 84	188,250	534	37,168	697	148,860	100.0	0.3	19.7	0.4	79.1
Aged 85 or older	64,107	137	13,690	366	49,749	100.0	0.2	21.4	0.6	77.6
South Dakota, total	**781,919**	**–**	**–**	**15,544**	**676,671**	**100.0**	**–**	**–**	**2.0**	**86.5**
Under age 5	53,701	–	–	1,601	41,554	100.0	–	–	3.0	77.4
Aged 5 to 9	49,689	–	–	1,644	38,470	100.0	–	–	3.3	77.4
Aged 10 to 14	56,911	–	–	2,031	43,379	100.0	–	–	3.6	76.2
Aged 15 to 17	33,676	–	–	528	27,966	100.0	–	–	1.6	83.0
Aged 18 to 19	23,228	–	–	335	18,795	100.0	–	–	1.4	80.9
Aged 20 to 24	59,477	–	–	1,751	50,241	100.0	–	–	2.9	84.5
Aged 25 to 29	50,687	–	–	1,502	43,145	100.0	–	–	3.0	85.1
Aged 30 to 34	42,053	–	–	1,191	35,250	100.0	–	–	2.8	83.8
Aged 35 to 44	102,730	–	–	1,976	89,354	100.0	–	–	1.9	87.0
Aged 45 to 54	114,930	–	–	1,643	104,130	100.0	–	–	1.4	90.6
Aged 55 to 64	83,198	–	–	630	77,975	100.0	–	–	0.8	93.7
Aged 65 to 74	53,237	–	–	421	49,789	100.0	–	–	0.8	93.5
Aged 75 to 84	40,502	–	–	224	39,495	100.0	–	–	0.6	97.5
Aged 85 or older	17,900	–	–	67	17,128	100.0	–	–	0.4	95.7

(continued)

	total	Asian	black	Hispanic	non-Hispanic white	total	Asian	black	Hispanic	non-Hispanic white
Tennessee, total	**6,038,803**	**76,208**	**1,011,726**	**187,747**	**4,677,757**	**100.0%**	**1.3%**	**16.8%**	**3.1%**	**77.5%**
Under age 5	399,006	6,335	80,376	27,264	273,256	100.0	1.6	20.1	6.8	68.5
Aged 5 to 9	386,039	6,430	77,626	17,189	273,522	100.0	1.7	20.1	4.5	70.9
Aged 10 to 14	406,769	5,074	89,533	15,986	287,458	100.0	1.2	22.0	3.9	70.7
Aged 15 to 17	255,236	2,525	56,470	6,798	184,198	100.0	1.0	22.1	2.7	72.2
Aged 18 to 19	162,348	2,131	35,995	4,962	117,219	100.0	1.3	22.2	3.1	72.2
Aged 20 to 24	391,579	4,271	78,794	18,249	285,884	100.0	1.1	20.1	4.7	73.0
Aged 25 to 29	432,397	7,007	79,656	24,995	316,960	100.0	1.6	18.4	5.8	73.3
Aged 30 to 34	397,266	8,630	69,777	20,740	293,918	100.0	2.2	17.6	5.2	74.0
Aged 35 to 44	877,946	14,089	146,608	25,828	681,174	100.0	1.6	16.7	2.9	77.6
Aged 45 to 54	877,038	9,649	135,559	13,875	706,016	100.0	1.1	15.5	1.6	80.5
Aged 55 to 64	686,086	6,095	82,611	6,709	584,044	100.0	0.9	12.0	1.0	85.1
Aged 65 to 74	414,416	2,534	43,845	2,735	361,979	100.0	0.6	10.6	0.7	87.3
Aged 75 to 84	259,230	1,179	23,915	1,893	230,836	100.0	0.5	9.2	0.7	89.0
Aged 85 or older	93,447	259	10,961	524	81,293	100.0	0.3	11.7	0.6	87.0
Texas, total	**23,507,783**	**787,208**	**2,718,515**	**8,385,118**	**11,309,011**	**100.0**	**3.3**	**11.6**	**35.7**	**48.1**
Under age 5	1,922,227	57,522	222,765	942,451	663,592	100.0	3.0	11.6	49.0	34.5
Aged 5 to 9	1,763,310	56,807	216,878	804,292	653,556	100.0	3.2	12.3	45.6	37.1
Aged 10 to 14	1,755,999	50,427	230,225	751,967	693,554	100.0	2.9	13.1	42.8	39.5
Aged 15 to 17	1,061,318	29,524	142,521	424,336	445,872	100.0	2.8	13.4	40.0	42.0
Aged 18 to 19	708,816	20,391	94,092	275,256	309,213	100.0	2.9	13.3	38.8	43.6
Aged 20 to 24	1,744,419	52,415	218,408	708,357	747,330	100.0	3.0	12.5	40.6	42.8
Aged 25 to 29	1,747,112	66,758	209,703	750,449	702,243	100.0	3.8	12.0	43.0	40.2
Aged 30 to 34	1,686,303	81,940	195,635	715,472	672,211	100.0	4.9	11.6	42.4	39.9
Aged 35 to 44	3,447,637	146,131	410,025	1,212,641	1,640,072	100.0	4.2	11.9	35.2	47.6
Aged 45 to 54	3,171,706	107,926	369,583	850,497	1,802,764	100.0	3.4	11.7	26.8	56.8
Aged 55 to 64	2,169,494	67,874	214,420	492,285	1,369,527	100.0	3.1	9.9	22.7	63.1
Aged 65 to 74	1,243,160	34,344	111,512	261,338	824,608	100.0	2.8	9.0	21.0	66.3
Aged 75 to 84	803,994	12,301	62,719	155,617	566,888	100.0	1.5	7.8	19.4	70.5
Aged 85 or older	282,288	2,848	20,029	40,160	217,581	100.0	1.0	7.1	14.2	77.1
Utah, total	**2,550,063**	**49,079**	**22,742**	**286,113**	**2,112,440**	**100.0**	**1.9**	**0.9**	**11.2**	**82.8**
Under age 5	247,167	3,126	2,681	36,140	194,537	100.0	1.3	1.1	14.6	78.7
Aged 5 to 9	216,550	3,262	2,173	31,490	169,719	100.0	1.5	1.0	14.5	78.4
Aged 10 to 14	205,303	3,345	2,305	27,497	162,988	100.0	1.6	1.1	13.4	79.4
Aged 15 to 17	123,152	1,909	1,167	14,515	99,734	100.0	1.6	0.9	11.8	81.0
Aged 18 to 19	83,962	1,984	713	9,574	67,678	100.0	2.4	0.8	11.4	80.6
Aged 20 to 24	236,368	4,090	2,379	25,507	197,865	100.0	1.7	1.0	10.8	83.7
Aged 25 to 29	232,726	3,679	1,758	30,017	190,389	100.0	1.6	0.8	12.9	81.8
Aged 30 to 34	173,977	5,804	2,075	26,767	133,179	100.0	3.3	1.2	15.4	76.5
Aged 35 to 44	311,641	8,554	2,716	40,540	251,496	100.0	2.7	0.9	13.0	80.7
Aged 45 to 54	294,153	5,848	2,664	23,472	255,819	100.0	2.0	0.9	8.0	87.0
Aged 55 to 64	201,104	3,536	1,271	12,527	180,349	100.0	1.8	0.6	6.2	89.7
Aged 65 to 74	117,551	1,919	433	4,976	108,659	100.0	1.6	0.4	4.2	92.4
Aged 75 to 84	78,755	1,835	308	2,269	73,611	100.0	2.3	0.4	2.9	93.5
Aged 85 or older	27,654	188	99	822	26,417	100.0	0.7	0.4	3.0	95.5

(continued)

	total	Asian	black	Hispanic	non-Hispanic white	total	Asian	black	Hispanic	non-Hispanic white
Vermont, total	623,908	5,693	–	6,644	596,638	100.0%	0.9%	–	1.1%	95.6%
Under age 5	33,014	691	–	582	30,796	100.0	2.1	–	1.8	93.3
Aged 5 to 9	32,899	353	–	283	31,177	100.0	1.1	–	0.9	94.8
Aged 10 to 14	40,434	205	–	710	38,197	100.0	0.5	–	1.8	94.5
Aged 15 to 17	27,557	366	–	403	25,656	100.0	1.3	–	1.5	93.1
Aged 18 to 19	20,564	197	–	467	18,907	100.0	1.0	–	2.3	91.9
Aged 20 to 24	42,510	622	–	703	39,389	100.0	1.5	–	1.7	92.7
Aged 25 to 29	36,529	661	–	736	34,156	100.0	1.8	–	2.0	93.5
Aged 30 to 34	33,473	372	–	271	32,269	100.0	1.1	–	0.8	96.4
Aged 35 to 44	90,578	1,009	–	981	86,871	100.0	1.1	–	1.1	95.9
Aged 45 to 54	104,478	589	–	723	100,967	100.0	0.6	–	0.7	96.6
Aged 55 to 64	78,927	431	–	384	77,044	100.0	0.5	–	0.5	97.6
Aged 65 to 74	42,743	147	–	215	41,591	100.0	0.3	–	0.5	97.3
Aged 75 to 84	29,416	0	–	121	28,947	100.0	0.0	–	0.4	98.4
Aged 85 or older	10,786	50	–	65	10,671	100.0	0.5	–	0.6	98.9
Virginia, total	7,642,884	365,515	1,496,076	470,871	5,167,028	100.0	4.8	19.6	6.2	67.6
Under age 5	503,491	24,542	106,707	53,824	296,576	100.0	4.9	21.2	10.7	58.9
Aged 5 to 9	479,241	21,553	107,880	39,192	291,563	100.0	4.5	22.5	8.2	60.8
Aged 10 to 14	506,389	22,293	117,395	33,952	316,396	100.0	4.4	23.2	6.7	62.5
Aged 15 to 17	316,432	12,266	74,234	20,531	199,341	100.0	3.9	23.5	6.5	63.0
Aged 18 to 19	231,887	10,110	54,113	15,134	147,068	100.0	4.4	23.3	6.5	63.4
Aged 20 to 24	536,451	24,504	117,487	47,432	336,736	100.0	4.6	21.9	8.8	62.8
Aged 25 to 29	510,868	28,016	102,734	55,224	315,386	100.0	5.5	20.1	10.8	61.7
Aged 30 to 34	503,234	41,272	94,790	46,712	312,325	100.0	8.2	18.8	9.3	62.1
Aged 35 to 44	1,192,313	71,443	237,358	77,368	791,899	100.0	6.0	19.9	6.5	66.4
Aged 45 to 54	1,141,333	50,769	217,423	46,292	812,810	100.0	4.4	19.0	4.1	71.2
Aged 55 to 64	835,231	33,032	132,152	20,582	641,780	100.0	4.0	15.8	2.5	76.8
Aged 65 to 74	475,451	17,834	73,751	9,305	370,622	100.0	3.8	15.5	2.0	78.0
Aged 75 to 84	301,207	6,814	44,932	4,078	243,156	100.0	2.3	14.9	1.4	80.7
Aged 85 or older	109,356	1,067	15,120	1,245	91,370	100.0	1.0	13.8	1.1	83.6
Washington, total	6,395,798	423,976	217,868	580,027	4,886,203	100.0	6.6	3.4	9.1	76.4
Under age 5	406,816	24,536	17,306	70,808	259,563	100.0	6.0	4.3	17.4	63.8
Aged 5 to 9	409,095	23,870	19,162	64,449	269,371	100.0	5.8	4.7	15.8	65.8
Aged 10 to 14	437,285	26,291	17,397	56,060	307,869	100.0	6.0	4.0	12.8	70.4
Aged 15 to 17	274,680	15,923	11,305	30,674	199,531	100.0	5.8	4.1	11.2	72.6
Aged 18 to 19	180,368	13,602	7,448	20,438	125,063	100.0	7.5	4.1	11.3	69.3
Aged 20 to 24	433,972	29,761	17,623	49,115	312,131	100.0	6.9	4.1	11.3	71.9
Aged 25 to 29	458,484	34,884	18,007	59,329	326,173	100.0	7.6	3.9	12.9	71.1
Aged 30 to 34	430,157	43,144	16,042	54,025	297,163	100.0	10.0	3.7	12.6	69.1
Aged 35 to 44	948,214	74,135	34,350	84,590	722,382	100.0	7.8	3.6	8.9	76.2
Aged 45 to 54	970,799	61,923	30,868	48,132	800,085	100.0	6.4	3.2	5.0	82.4
Aged 55 to 64	709,212	38,593	16,172	24,292	610,813	100.0	5.4	2.3	3.4	86.1
Aged 65 to 74	379,702	22,118	7,063	11,486	330,424	100.0	5.8	1.9	3.0	87.0
Aged 75 to 84	254,060	11,659	4,106	5,346	229,362	100.0	4.6	1.6	2.1	90.3
Aged 85 or older	102,954	3,537	1,019	1,283	96,273	100.0	3.4	1.0	1.2	93.5

(continued)

	total	Asian	black	Hispanic	non-Hispanic white	total	Asian	black	Hispanic	non-Hispanic white
West Virginia, total	1,818,470	10,479	58,693	14,383	1,711,605	100.0%	0.6%	3.2%	0.8%	94.1%
Under age 5	104,429	681	2,851	1,602	96,788	100.0	0.7	2.7	1.5	92.7
Aged 5 to 9	101,776	609	3,644	1,435	93,202	100.0	0.6	3.6	1.4	91.6
Aged 10 to 14	112,468	303	3,654	1,032	103,637	100.0	0.3	3.2	0.9	92.1
Aged 15 to 17	71,548	241	2,096	1,229	66,402	100.0	0.3	2.9	1.7	92.8
Aged 18 to 19	49,141	173	1,905	1,013	44,937	100.0	0.4	3.9	2.1	91.4
Aged 20 to 24	116,175	938	4,811	779	108,294	100.0	0.8	4.1	0.7	93.2
Aged 25 to 29	117,716	806	4,022	1,420	110,546	100.0	0.7	3.4	1.2	93.9
Aged 30 to 34	106,083	618	4,657	577	99,482	100.0	0.6	4.4	0.5	93.8
Aged 35 to 44	249,536	1,981	7,843	2,224	235,102	100.0	0.8	3.1	0.9	94.2
Aged 45 to 54	279,544	1,428	10,108	860	264,822	100.0	0.5	3.6	0.3	94.7
Aged 55 to 64	230,937	1,611	6,179	1,041	219,999	100.0	0.7	2.7	0.5	95.3
Aged 65 to 74	143,894	808	2,390	715	138,983	100.0	0.6	1.7	0.5	96.6
Aged 75 to 84	101,907	282	2,892	348	97,807	100.0	0.3	2.8	0.3	96.0
Aged 85 or older	33,316	0	1,641	108	31,604	100.0	0.0	4.9	0.3	94.9
Wisconsin, total	5,556,506	110,778	328,376	256,304	4,755,716	100.0	2.0	5.9	4.6	85.6
Under age 5	351,702	9,871	31,387	29,544	267,223	100.0	2.8	8.9	8.4	76.0
Aged 5 to 9	345,873	9,547	31,822	26,896	264,898	100.0	2.8	9.2	7.8	76.6
Aged 10 to 14	375,856	11,244	31,394	24,956	297,219	100.0	3.0	8.4	6.6	79.1
Aged 15 to 17	241,512	6,166	20,597	12,006	196,175	100.0	2.6	8.5	5.0	81.2
Aged 18 to 19	159,152	4,054	10,856	8,963	131,801	100.0	2.5	6.8	5.6	82.8
Aged 20 to 24	399,780	10,048	26,252	22,492	331,792	100.0	2.5	6.6	5.6	83.0
Aged 25 to 29	360,325	9,346	28,306	27,552	288,244	100.0	2.6	7.9	7.6	80.0
Aged 30 to 34	337,112	11,268	23,664	25,891	270,254	100.0	3.3	7.0	7.7	80.2
Aged 35 to 44	807,871	16,865	43,250	37,697	695,532	100.0	2.1	5.4	4.7	86.1
Aged 45 to 54	856,132	10,568	39,989	22,032	771,832	100.0	1.2	4.7	2.6	90.2
Aged 55 to 64	599,318	7,589	22,302	10,452	553,283	100.0	1.3	3.7	1.7	92.3
Aged 65 to 74	356,158	2,621	11,362	5,332	334,482	100.0	0.7	3.2	1.5	93.9
Aged 75 to 84	259,719	1,175	5,497	2,112	249,877	100.0	0.5	2.1	0.8	96.2
Aged 85 or older	105,996	416	1,698	379	103,104	100.0	0.4	1.6	0.4	97.3
Wyoming, total	515,004	–	–	35,732	453,251	100.0	–	–	6.9	88.0
Under age 5	34,128	–	–	3,632	27,701	100.0	–	–	10.6	81.2
Aged 5 to 9	31,557	–	–	3,711	26,419	100.0	–	–	11.8	83.7
Aged 10 to 14	32,883	–	–	2,469	28,048	100.0	–	–	7.5	85.3
Aged 15 to 17	22,362	–	–	1,726	19,531	100.0	–	–	7.7	87.3
Aged 18 to 19	14,802	–	–	828	12,870	100.0	–	–	5.6	86.9
Aged 20 to 24	39,874	–	–	2,651	34,263	100.0	–	–	6.6	85.9
Aged 25 to 29	35,505	–	–	3,214	29,832	100.0	–	–	9.1	84.0
Aged 30 to 34	30,148	–	–	2,319	25,924	100.0	–	–	7.7	86.0
Aged 35 to 44	65,430	–	–	4,620	57,979	100.0	–	–	7.1	88.6
Aged 45 to 54	84,698	–	–	5,457	75,902	100.0	–	–	6.4	89.6
Aged 55 to 64	61,987	–	–	3,571	55,813	100.0	–	–	5.8	90.0
Aged 65 to 74	32,630	–	–	793	31,124	100.0	–	–	2.4	95.4
Aged 75 to 84	21,573	–	–	535	20,837	100.0	–	–	2.5	96.6
Aged 85 or older	7,427	–	–	206	7,008	100.0	–	–	2.8	94.4

Note: Numbers will not add to total because each race includes only those who identified themselves as being of the race alone, not all races are shown, and Hispanics may be of any race. Non-Hispanic whites are those who identified themselves as being white alone and not Hispanic. "–" means sample is too small to make a reliable estimate.
Source: Bureau of the Census, 2006 American Community Survey, Internet site http://factfinder.census.gov/home/saff/main .html?_lang=en; calculations by New Strategist

10

Spending

Spending is directly linked to lifestage. Young adults are just starting out, and because their incomes are low, they have little to spend. The middle aged, on the other hand, have higher incomes and larger households, which means they spend more.

The spending of middle-aged householders has always been above average thanks to their higher incomes. Today, the Baby-Boom generation is beginning to exit the peak spending age groups (35 to 54), but Boomers still dominate spending on many products and services. In some categories, however, Boomers are less important than other generations. Older Americans dominate health care spending. Generation Xers are now the most important customers of products and services for children.

What to expect in the future

■ As Boomers age into their sixties, the average spending of households headed by 55-to-64-year-olds will grow along with labor force participation rates.

■ The Millennial generation, now filling the 25-to-34 age group, will have a harder time gaining a foothold in the middle class because of the high cost of college, housing, and health care.

■ The spending of older Americans is rising to meet the average. As Boomers fill the older age groups, expect the spending patterns and lifestyles of elderly Americans to become more like those of younger adults.

At All Ages, Housing Is the Largest Expense

Transportation ranks second in the household budget.

The average household spent $48,398 in 2006, but spending varies greatly by age. The biggest spenders, householders ranging in age from 35 to 54, average just over $57,000 in annual expenditures. Householders in this broad age group spend the most because they are in the crowded-nest and peak earning years. Householders under age 25 spend the least, just $28,181 in 2006.

Regardless of age, housing is the largest expenditure for the average household. Housing expenses absorb from 32 to 36 percent of total spending regardless of age. Spending on transportation is more variable, with the youngest householders devoting a larger share of spending to transportation than older householders. Transportation accounts for 20 percent of spending by householders under age 25. The figure bottoms out at 13 percent among householders aged 75 or older. The oldest householders spend more on health care (15 percent) than on transportation or food.

The youngest householders devote a larger share of their budget to food away from home than older households do. Seven percent of the budget of householders under age 25 is spent on food away from home compared with less than 5 percent for householders aged 75 or older.

■ Householders under age 25 devote almost as much of the household budget to education (4.5 percent) as to entertainment (4.8 percent) as they pursue the credentials they need to get ahead.

Health care spending rises sharply with age

(health care spending as a percent of total spending by the average household, by age of householder, 2006)

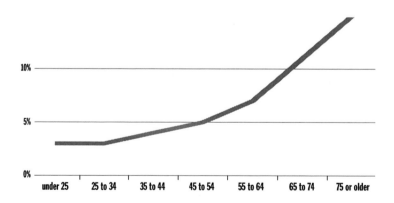

Table 10.1 Spending by Age of Householder, 2006

(average annual spending of consumer units (CU) by product and service category and age of consumer unit reference person, 2006)

	total consumer units	under 25	25 to 34	35 to 44	45 to 54	55 to 64	aged 65 or older total	65 to 74	75 or older
Number of consumer units (in 000s)	118,843	8,167	20,071	23,950	24,696	18,952	23,007	11,764	11,243
Average number of persons per CU	2.5	2.0	2.9	3.2	2.7	2.0	1.7	1.9	1.5
Average before-tax income	$60,533	$29,057	$57,208	$75,613	$77,043	$64,425	$37,982	$46,064	$29,525
Average annual spending	48,398	28,181	47,582	57,476	57,563	50,789	35,058	40,960	28,904
FOOD	**6,111**	**3,919**	**6,104**	**7,331**	**7,328**	**6,132**	**4,319**	**5,172**	**3,437**
Food at home	**3,417**	**1,946**	**3,186**	**4,128**	**4,036**	**3,518**	**2,659**	**3,062**	**2,244**
Cereals and bakery products	446	240	406	553	510	453	370	413	325
Cereals and cereal products	143	94	143	185	162	135	102	114	90
Bakery products	304	146	263	369	348	318	268	300	236
Meats, poultry, fish, and eggs	797	434	746	962	972	801	611	723	495
Beef	236	129	229	272	308	225	176	206	146
Pork	157	89	141	186	193	158	127	157	95
Other meats	105	59	92	131	132	100	80	91	70
Poultry	141	80	143	185	159	139	96	110	80
Fish and seafood	122	53	108	143	142	138	101	124	78
Eggs	37	23	34	45	39	40	30	34	26
Dairy products	368	219	352	452	420	370	293	330	256
Fresh milk and cream	140	92	142	179	151	128	113	120	105
Other dairy products	228	127	210	273	268	242	181	209	151
Fruits and vegetables	592	319	537	671	683	656	507	572	439
Fresh fruits	195	99	165	219	225	230	172	184	159
Fresh vegetables	193	99	178	207	234	219	162	192	131
Processed fruits	109	68	109	131	118	107	94	103	84
Processed vegetables	95	53	86	114	106	101	79	93	65
Other food at home	1,212	734	1,144	1,490	1,451	1,238	878	1,024	729
Sugar and other sweets	125	69	95	145	156	121	118	129	107
Fats and oils	86	47	76	97	97	99	73	89	57
Miscellaneous foods	627	401	623	793	731	621	430	488	371
Nonalcoholic beverages	332	200	315	409	413	342	222	266	176
Food prepared by household on trips	43	16	35	45	53	55	35	51	18
Food away from home	**2,694**	**1,973**	**2,918**	**3,203**	**3,292**	**2,613**	**1,659**	**2,110**	**1,193**
ALCOHOLIC BEVERAGES	**497**	**473**	**657**	**496**	**612**	**477**	**263**	**339**	**184**
HOUSING	**16,366**	**9,355**	**17,139**	**20,303**	**18,377**	**16,529**	**11,787**	**13,273**	**10,236**
Shelter	**9,673**	**5,923**	**10,725**	**12,445**	**10,896**	**9,199**	**6,281**	**6,934**	**5,597**
Owned dwellings*	6,516	1,405	6,132	8,965	8,024	6,866	4,210	5,151	3,224
Mortgage interest and charges	3,753	910	4,282	5,914	4,818	3,271	1,303	1,967	609
Property taxes	1,649	358	1,191	1,937	2,032	1,919	1,573	1,768	1,368
Maintenance, repairs, insurance, other expenses	1,115	137	660	1,114	1,175	1,676	1,334	1,416	1,247
Rented dwellings	2,590	4,315	4,286	2,938	2,064	1,460	1,630	1,191	2,090
Other lodging	567	203	307	541	807	873	441	592	284
Utilities, fuels, and public services	3,397	1,781	3,093	3,854	3,912	3,640	3,008	3,297	2,705
Natural gas	509	186	421	559	598	563	507	526	488
Electricity	1,266	693	1,133	1,419	1,445	1,362	1,154	1,275	1,028

	total consumer units	under 25	25 to 34	35 to 44	45 to 54	55 to 64	aged 65 or older total	65 to 74	75 or older
Fuel oil and other fuels	$138	$30	$73	$157	$150	$167	$176	$168	$185
Telephone services	1,087	722	1,129	1,271	1,269	1,115	770	889	645
Water and other public services	397	150	337	449	449	433	400	438	359
Household services	**948**	**374**	**1,130**	**1,380**	**793**	**934**	**720**	**718**	**722**
Personal services	393	213	706	811	192	221	105	–	157
Other household services	555	161	424	569	601	714	615	663	565
Housekeeping supplies	**640**	**295**	**531**	**761**	**727**	**739**	**554**	**660**	**445**
Laundry and cleaning supplies	151	83	155	189	160	165	112	132	91
Other household products	330	149	266	413	369	369	290	352	226
Postage and stationery	159	64	111	159	198	205	153	176	128
Household furnishings and equipment	**1,708**	**982**	**1,660**	**1,864**	**2,050**	**2,017**	**1,224**	**1,664**	**767**
Household textiles	154	56	124	140	175	207	163	239	85
Furniture	463	350	510	536	569	462	274	368	176
Floor coverings	48	24	35	40	48	80	47	52	41
Major appliances	241	104	194	272	285	295	208	258	156
Small appliances, miscellaneous housewares	109	52	109	113	149	111	79	98	58
Miscellaneous household equipment	693	396	687	762	824	862	454	649	251
APPAREL AND SERVICES	**1,874**	**1,464**	**2,152**	**2,368**	**2,176**	**1,892**	**930**	**1,212**	**639**
Men and boys	**444**	**294**	**544**	**575**	**538**	**400**	**207**	**282**	**129**
Men, aged 16 or older	353	273	409	403	439	354	187	252	119
Boys, aged 2 to 15	91	21	135	172	100	46	21	31	10
Women and girls	**751**	**554**	**737**	**922**	**913**	**835**	**416**	**538**	**290**
Women, aged 16 or older	629	520	579	671	782	773	386	490	279
Girls, aged 2 to 15	122	33	158	251	131	62	30	47	11
Children under age 2	**96**	**130**	**187**	**128**	**72**	**66**	**20**	**28**	**12**
Footwear	**304**	**251**	**371**	**404**	**343**	**288**	**133**	**160**	**106**
Other apparel products and services	**280**	**234**	**313**	**338**	**311**	**303**	**154**	**204**	**101**
TRANSPORTATION	**8,508**	**5,667**	**9,047**	**9,977**	**10,111**	**8,676**	**5,658**	**7,481**	**3,751**
Vehicle purchases	**3,421**	**2,396**	**3,912**	**4,057**	**3,983**	**3,165**	**2,301**	**3,273**	**1,284**
Cars and trucks, new	1,798	943	1,960	1,999	2,087	1,867	1,384	2,210	520
Cars and trucks, used	1,568	1,406	1,881	1,973	1,811	1,271	917	1,063	764
Gasoline and motor oil	**2,227**	**1,637**	**2,346**	**2,636**	**2,693**	**2,288**	**1,359**	**1,766**	**934**
Other vehicle expenses	**2,355**	**1,413**	**2,342**	**2,725**	**2,819**	**2,638**	**1,584**	**1,972**	**1,179**
Vehicle finance charges	298	199	401	374	334	299	123	190	53
Maintenance and repairs	688	400	624	744	866	799	508	640	371
Vehicle insurance	886	548	822	976	1,105	941	689	806	568
Vehicle rental, leases, licenses, other charges	482	266	495	631	514	599	264	336	188
Public transportation	**505**	**221**	**448**	**559**	**616**	**584**	**414**	**471**	**354**
HEALTH CARE	**2,766**	**706**	**1,652**	**2,284**	**2,757**	**3,556**	**4,331**	**4,379**	**4,282**
Health insurance	1,465	367	883	1,214	1,310	1,676	2,617	2,718	2,511
Medical services	670	193	469	634	798	978	663	636	692
Drugs	514	97	243	345	499	759	887	859	916
Medical supplies	117	49	58	90	151	143	164	166	163
ENTERTAINMENT	**2,376**	**1,348**	**2,237**	**2,966**	**2,770**	**2,666**	**1,584**	**2,049**	**1,099**
Fees and admissions	606	280	475	839	757	605	432	559	300
Audio and visual equipment and services	906	672	969	1,052	1,020	906	660	791	523
Pets, toys, hobbies, playground equipment	412	209	408	497	497	480	255	344	163
Other entertainment supplies, services	451	187	385	578	495	675	237	355	114

	total consumer units	under 25	25 to 34	35 to 44	45 to 54	55 to 64	aged 65 or older		
							total	65 to 74	75 or older
PERSONAL CARE PRODUCTS AND SERVICES	$585	$348	$547	$688	$696	$586	$475	$527	$421
READING	117	46	82	112	133	147	136	143	129
EDUCATION	888	1,259	710	857	1,736	662	219	274	162
TOBACCO PRODUCTS AND SMOKING SUPPLIES	327	286	318	354	433	370	171	241	97
MISCELLANEOUS	846	388	615	943	971	1,105	762	966	549
CASH CONTRIBUTIONS	1,869	632	1,070	1,707	2,118	2,266	2,579	2,121	3,058
PERSONAL INSURANCE AND PENSIONS	5,270	2,291	5,252	7,090	7,346	5,726	1,844	2,782	862
Life and other personal insurance	322	42	172	364	413	458	299	365	231
Pensions and Social Security	4,948	2,249	5,079	6,726	6,933	5,267	1,545	2,417	631
PERSONAL TAXES	2,432	522	1,532	3,167	3,360	3,531	1,230	1,759	675
Federal income taxes	1,711	332	990	2,245	2,396	2,604	804	1,236	352
State and local income taxes	519	165	443	727	728	657	157	209	102
Other taxes	202	25	99	195	236	270	269	315	221
GIFTS FOR PEOPLE IN OTHER HOUSEHOLDS**	1,154	393	929	775	1,814	1,522	1,004	1,219	781

* This figure does not include the amount paid for mortgage principal, which is considered an asset.
** Spending on gifts is also included in the preceding product and service categories. Food spending, for example, includes the amount spent on gifts of food.
Note: The Bureau of Labor Statistics uses consumer unit rather than household as the sampling unit in the Consumer Expenditure Survey. For the definition of consumer unit, see the glossary. "–" means sample is too small to make a reliable estimate.
Source: Bureau of Labor Statistics, 2006 Consumer Expenditure Survey, Internet site http://www.bls.gov/cex/home.htm

Table 10.2 Percent Distribution of Spending by Product Category and Age, 2006

(percent distribution of average annual spending of consumer units (CU) by product category and age of reference person, 2006)

Average annual spending	total consumer units 100.0%	under 25 100.0%	25 to 34 100.0%	35 to 44 100.0%	45 to 54 100.0%	55 to 64 100.0%	aged 65 or older		
							total 100.0%	65 to 74 100.0%	75 or older 100.0%
FOOD	**12.6**	**13.9**	**12.8**	**12.8**	**12.7**	**12.1**	**12.3**	**12.6**	**11.9**
Food at home	**7.1**	**6.9**	**6.7**	**7.2**	**7.0**	**6.9**	**7.6**	**7.5**	**7.8**
Cereals and bakery products	0.9	0.9	0.9	1.0	0.9	0.9	1.1	1.0	1.1
Cereals and cereal products	0.3	0.3	0.3	0.3	0.3	0.3	0.3	0.3	0.3
Bakery products	0.6	0.5	0.6	0.6	0.6	0.6	0.8	0.7	0.8
Meats, poultry, fish, and eggs	1.6	1.5	1.6	1.7	1.7	1.6	1.7	1.8	1.7
Beef	0.5	0.5	0.5	0.5	0.5	0.4	0.5	0.5	0.5
Pork	0.3	0.3	0.3	0.3	0.3	0.3	0.4	0.4	0.3
Other meats	0.2	0.2	0.2	0.2	0.2	0.2	0.2	0.2	0.2
Poultry	0.3	0.3	0.3	0.3	0.3	0.3	0.3	0.3	0.3
Fish and seafood	0.3	0.2	0.2	0.2	0.2	0.3	0.3	0.3	0.3
Eggs	0.1	0.1	0.1	0.1	0.1	0.1	0.1	0.1	0.1
Dairy products	0.8	0.8	0.7	0.8	0.7	0.7	0.8	0.8	0.9
Fresh milk and cream	0.3	0.3	0.3	0.3	0.3	0.3	0.3	0.3	0.4
Other dairy products	0.5	0.5	0.4	0.5	0.5	0.5	0.5	0.5	0.5
Fruits and vegetables	1.2	1.1	1.1	1.2	1.2	1.3	1.4	1.4	1.5
Fresh fruits	0.4	0.4	0.3	0.4	0.4	0.5	0.5	0.4	0.6
Fresh vegetables	0.4	0.4	0.4	0.4	0.4	0.4	0.5	0.5	0.5
Processed fruits	0.2	0.2	0.2	0.2	0.2	0.2	0.3	0.3	0.3
Processed vegetables	0.2	0.2	0.2	0.2	0.2	0.2	0.2	0.2	0.2
Other food at home	2.5	2.6	2.4	2.6	2.5	2.4	2.5	2.5	2.5
Sugar and other sweets	0.3	0.2	0.2	0.3	0.3	0.2	0.3	0.3	0.4
Fats and oils	0.2	0.2	0.2	0.2	0.2	0.2	0.2	0.2	0.2
Miscellaneous foods	1.3	1.4	1.3	1.4	1.3	1.2	1.2	1.2	1.3
Nonalcoholic beverages	0.7	0.7	0.7	0.7	0.7	0.7	0.6	0.6	0.6
Food prepared by CU on trips	0.1	0.1	0.1	0.1	0.1	0.1	0.1	0.1	0.1
Food away from home	**5.6**	**7.0**	**6.1**	**5.6**	**5.7**	**5.1**	**4.7**	**5.2**	**4.1**
ALCOHOLIC BEVERAGES	**1.0**	**1.7**	**1.4**	**0.9**	**1.1**	**0.9**	**0.8**	**0.8**	**0.6**
HOUSING	**33.8**	**33.2**	**36.0**	**35.3**	**31.9**	**32.5**	**33.6**	**32.4**	**35.4**
Shelter	**20.0**	**21.0**	**22.5**	**21.7**	**18.9**	**18.1**	**17.9**	**16.9**	**19.4**
Owned dwellings*	13.5	5.0	12.9	15.6	13.9	13.5	12.0	12.6	11.2
Mortgage interest and charges	7.8	3.2	9.0	10.3	8.4	6.4	3.7	4.8	2.1
Property taxes	3.4	1.3	2.5	3.4	3.5	3.8	4.5	4.3	4.7
Maintenance, repairs, insurance, other expenses	2.3	0.5	1.4	1.9	2.0	3.3	3.8	3.5	4.3
Rented dwellings	5.4	15.3	9.0	5.1	3.6	2.9	4.6	2.9	7.2
Other lodging	1.2	0.7	0.6	0.9	1.4	1.7	1.3	1.4	1.0
Utilities, fuels, public services	**7.0**	**6.3**	**6.5**	**6.7**	**6.8**	**7.2**	**8.6**	**8.0**	**9.4**
Natural gas	1.1	0.7	0.9	1.0	1.0	1.1	1.4	1.3	1.7
Electricity	2.6	2.5	2.4	2.5	2.5	2.7	3.3	3.1	3.6

	total consumer units	under 25	25 to 34	35 to 44	45 to 54	55 to 64	aged 65 or older total	65 to 74	75 or older
Fuel oil and other fuels	0.3%	0.1%	0.2%	0.3%	0.3%	0.3%	0.5%	0.4%	0.6%
Telephone	2.2	2.6	2.4	2.2	2.2	2.2	2.2	2.2	2.2
Water and other public services	0.8	0.5	0.7	0.8	0.8	0.9	1.1	1.1	1.2
Household services	**2.0**	**1.3**	**2.4**	**2.4**	**1.4**	**1.8**	**2.1**	**1.8**	**2.5**
Personal services	0.8	0.8	1.5	1.4	0.3	0.4	0.3	–	0.5
Other household services	1.1	0.6	0.9	1.0	1.0	1.4	1.8	1.6	2.0
Housekeeping supplies	**1.3**	**1.0**	**1.1**	**1.3**	**1.3**	**1.5**	**1.6**	**1.6**	**1.5**
Laundry and cleaning supplies	0.3	0.3	0.3	0.3	0.3	0.3	0.3	0.3	0.3
Other household products	0.7	0.5	0.6	0.7	0.6	0.7	0.8	0.9	0.8
Postage and stationery	0.3	0.2	0.2	0.3	0.3	0.4	0.4	0.4	0.4
Household furnishings and equipment	**3.5**	**3.5**	**3.5**	**3.2**	**3.6**	**4.0**	**3.5**	**4.1**	**2.7**
Household textiles	0.3	0.2	0.3	0.2	0.3	0.4	0.5	0.6	0.3
Furniture	1.0	1.2	1.1	0.9	1.0	0.9	0.8	0.9	0.6
Floor coverings	0.1	0.1	0.1	0.1	0.1	0.2	0.1	0.1	0.1
Major appliances	0.5	0.4	0.4	0.5	0.5	0.6	0.6	0.6	0.5
Small appliances, misc. houseware	0.2	0.2	0.2	0.2	0.3	0.2	0.2	0.2	0.2
Miscellaneous household equipment	1.4	1.4	1.4	1.3	1.4	1.7	1.3	1.6	0.9
APPAREL AND SERVICES	**3.9**	**5.2**	**4.5**	**4.1**	**3.8**	**3.7**	**2.7**	**3.0**	**2.2**
Men and boys	**0.9**	**1.0**	**1.1**	**1.0**	**0.9**	**0.8**	**0.6**	**0.7**	**0.4**
Men, aged 16 or older	0.7	1.0	0.9	0.7	0.8	0.7	0.5	0.6	0.4
Boys, aged 2 to 15	0.2	0.1	0.3	0.3	0.2	0.1	0.1	0.1	0.0
Women and girls	**1.6**	**2.0**	**1.5**	**1.6**	**1.6**	**1.6**	**1.2**	**1.3**	**1.0**
Women, aged 16 or older	1.3	1.8	1.2	1.2	1.4	1.5	1.1	1.2	1.0
Girls, aged 2 to 15	0.3	0.1	0.3	0.4	0.2	0.1	0.1	0.1	0.0
Children under age 2	**0.2**	**0.5**	**0.4**	**0.2**	**0.1**	**0.1**	**0.1**	**0.1**	**0.0**
Footwear	**0.6**	**0.9**	**0.8**	**0.7**	**0.6**	**0.6**	**0.4**	**0.4**	**0.4**
Other apparel products and services	**0.6**	**0.8**	**0.7**	**0.6**	**0.5**	**0.6**	**0.4**	**0.5**	**0.3**
TRANSPORTATION	**17.6**	**20.1**	**19.0**	**17.4**	**17.6**	**17.1**	**16.1**	**18.3**	**13.0**
Vehicle purchases	**7.1**	**8.5**	**8.2**	**7.1**	**6.9**	**6.2**	**6.6**	**8.0**	**4.4**
Cars and trucks, new	3.7	3.3	4.1	3.5	3.6	3.7	3.9	5.4	1.8
Cars and trucks, used	3.2	5.0	4.0	3.4	3.1	2.5	2.6	2.6	2.6
Gasoline and motor oil	**4.6**	**5.8**	**4.9**	**4.6**	**4.7**	**4.5**	**3.9**	**4.3**	**3.2**
Other vehicle expenses	**4.9**	**5.0**	**4.9**	**4.7**	**4.9**	**5.2**	**4.5**	**4.8**	**4.1**
Vehicle finance charges	0.6	0.7	0.8	0.7	0.6	0.6	0.4	0.5	0.2
Maintenance and repairs	1.4	1.4	1.3	1.3	1.5	1.6	1.4	1.6	1.3
Vehicle insurance	1.8	1.9	1.7	1.7	1.9	1.9	2.0	2.0	2.0
Vehicle rent, lease, license, other	1.0	0.9	1.0	1.1	0.9	1.2	0.8	0.8	0.7
Public transportation	**1.0**	**0.8**	**0.9**	**1.0**	**1.1**	**1.1**	**1.2**	**1.1**	**1.2**
HEALTH CARE	**5.7**	**2.5**	**3.5**	**4.0**	**4.8**	**7.0**	**12.4**	**10.7**	**14.8**
Health insurance	3.0	1.3	1.9	2.1	2.3	3.3	7.5	6.6	8.7
Medical services	1.4	0.7	1.0	1.1	1.4	1.9	1.9	1.6	2.4
Drugs	1.1	0.3	0.5	0.6	0.9	1.5	2.5	2.1	3.2
Medical supplies	0.2	0.2	0.1	0.2	0.3	0.3	0.5	0.4	0.6
ENTERTAINMENT	**4.9**	**4.8**	**4.7**	**5.2**	**4.8**	**5.2**	**4.5**	**5.0**	**3.8**
Fees and admissions	1.3	1.0	1.0	1.5	1.3	1.2	1.2	1.4	1.0
Audio and visual equipment and services	1.9	2.4	2.0	1.8	1.8	1.8	1.9	1.9	1.8
Pets, toys, hobbies, playground equipment	0.9	0.7	0.9	0.9	0.9	0.9	0.7	0.8	0.6
Other entertainment supplies, services	0.9	0.7	0.8	1.0	0.9	1.3	0.7	0.9	0.4

	total consumer units	under 25	25 to 34	35 to 44	45 to 54	55 to 64	aged 65 or older		
							total	65 to 74	75 or older
PERSONAL CARE PRODUCTS AND SERVICES	1.2%	1.2%	1.1%	1.2%	1.2%	1.2%	1.4%	1.3%	1.5%
READING	0.2	0.2	0.2	0.2	0.2	0.3	0.4	0.3	0.4
EDUCATION	1.8	4.5	1.5	1.5	3.0	1.3	0.6	0.7	0.6
TOBACCO PRODUCTS AND SMOKING SUPPLIES	0.7	1.0	0.7	0.6	0.8	0.7	0.5	0.6	0.3
MISCELLANEOUS	1.7	1.4	1.3	1.6	1.7	2.2	2.2	2.4	1.9
CASH CONTRIBUTIONS	3.9	2.2	2.2	3.0	3.7	4.5	7.4	5.2	10.6
PERSONAL INSURANCE AND PENSIONS	10.9	8.1	11.0	12.3	12.8	11.3	5.3	6.8	3.0
Life and other personal insurance	0.7	0.1	0.4	0.6	0.7	0.9	0.9	0.9	0.8
Pensions and Social Security	10.2	8.0	10.7	11.7	12.0	10.4	4.4	5.9	2.2
PERSONAL TAXES	5.0	1.9	3.2	5.5	5.8	7.0	3.5	4.3	2.3
Federal income taxes	3.5	1.2	2.1	3.9	4.2	5.1	2.3	3.0	1.2
State and local income taxes	1.1	0.6	0.9	1.3	1.3	1.3	0.4	0.5	0.4
Other taxes	0.4	0.1	0.2	0.3	0.4	0.5	0.8	0.8	0.8
GIFTS FOR PEOPLE IN OTHER HOUSEHOLDS**	2.4	1.4	2.0	1.3	3.2	3.0	2.9	3.0	2.7

* This figure does not include the amount paid for mortgage principal, which is considered an asset.
** Spending on gifts is also included in the preceding product and service categories. Food spending, for example, includes the amount spent on gifts of food.
Note: The Bureau of Labor Statistics uses consumer unit rather than household as the sampling unit in the Consumer Expenditure Survey. For the definition of consumer unit, see the glossary. "–" means sample is too small to make a reliable estimate.
Source: Calculations by New Strategist based on Bureau of Labor Statistics, 2006 Consumer Expenditure Survey, Internet site http://www.bls.gov/cex/home.htm

Under Age 30: Just the Basics

The low incomes of Millennial householders limit their spending.

The nation's householders under age 30 (members of the Millennial generation) accounted for 11 percent of total household spending in 2006. Consumer units headed by people under age 30 spend 25 percent less than the average household—$36,147 versus the $48,398 spent by the average household in 2006.

Householders under age 30 spend less than average in almost every category. There are exceptions, however. They spend 26 percent more than average on alcoholic beverages. They spend 83 percent more than average on rental housing and account for 27 percent of the rental market. They spend 12 percent more than the average household on education. They spend 71 percent more than average on clothes for children under age 2. The spending of this age group on used cars and trucks is 6 percent above average.

■ Because of the high cost of education and housing, young adults find it increasingly difficult to gain a foothold in the middle class.

Millennials are not big spenders on entertainment or clothes

(indexed spending of householders under age 30 on selected categories, 2006)

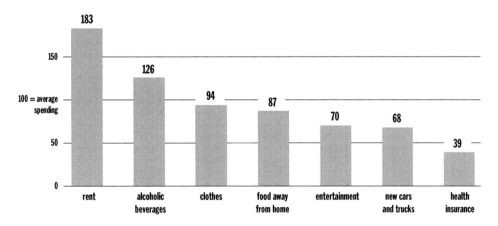

Table 10.3 Spending by Householders under Age 30, 2006

(average annual spending of total consumer units (CU) and those headed by people under age 30, indexed spending and share of total spending accounted for by consumer units under age 30; by product category, 2006)

	avg. spending of total consumer units	consumer units headed by people under age 30		
		average spending	indexed spending	market share
Number of consumer units (in 000s)	118,843	17,608	–	14.8%
Average annual spending	$48,398	$36,147	75	11.1
FOOD	**6,111**	**4,692**	**77**	**11.4**
Food at home	**3,417**	**2,344**	**69**	**10.2**
Cereals and bakery products	446	297	67	9.9
Cereals and cereal products	143	112	78	11.6
Bakery products	304	184	61	9.0
Meats, poultry, fish, and eggs	797	521	65	9.7
Beef	236	165	70	10.4
Pork	157	100	64	9.4
Other meats	105	65	62	9.2
Poultry	141	100	71	10.5
Fish and seafood	122	66	54	8.0
Eggs	37	25	68	10.0
Dairy products	368	267	73	10.7
Fresh milk and cream	140	106	76	11.2
Other dairy products	228	161	71	10.5
Fruits and vegetables	592	391	66	9.8
Fresh fruits	195	120	62	9.1
Fresh vegetables	193	124	64	9.5
Processed fruits	109	83	76	11.3
Processed vegetables	95	65	68	10.1
Other food at home	1,212	868	72	10.6
Sugar and other sweets	125	77	62	9.1
Fats and oils	86	53	62	9.1
Miscellaneous foods	627	478	76	11.3
Nonalcoholic beverages	332	236	71	10.5
Food prepared by CU on trips	43	24	56	8.3
Food away from home	**2,694**	**2,348**	**87**	**12.9**
ALCOHOLIC BEVERAGES	**497**	**624**	**126**	**18.6**
HOUSING	**16,366**	**12,772**	**78**	**11.6**
Shelter	**9,673**	**8,198**	**85**	**12.6**
Owned dwellings*	6,516	3,220	49	7.3
Mortgage interest and charges	3,753	2,153	57	8.5
Property taxes	1,649	659	40	5.9
Maintenance, repairs, insurance, other expenses	1,115	408	37	5.4
Rented dwellings	2,590	4,748	183	27.2
Other lodging	567	229	40	6.0
Utilities, fuels, public services	**3,397**	**2,322**	**68**	**10.1**
Natural gas	509	272	53	7.9
Electricity	1,266	863	68	10.1

	avg. spending of total consumer units	consumer units headed by people under age 30		
		average spending	indexed spending	market share
Fuel oil and other fuels	$138	$51	37	5.5%
Telephone	1,087	911	84	12.4
Water and other public services	397	226	57	8.4
Household services	**948**	**619**	**65**	**9.7**
Personal services	393	363	92	13.7
Other household services	555	256	46	6.8
Housekeeping supplies	**640**	**372**	**58**	**8.6**
Laundry and cleaning supplies	151	107	71	10.5
Other household products	330	184	56	8.3
Postage and stationery	159	81	51	7.5
Household furnishings, equipment	**1,708**	**1,261**	**74**	**10.9**
Household textiles	154	102	66	9.8
Furniture	463	391	84	12.5
Floor coverings	48	26	54	8.0
Major appliances	241	128	53	7.9
Small appliances, misc. houseware	109	91	83	12.4
Miscellaneous household equipment	693	523	75	11.2
APPAREL AND SERVICES	**1,874**	**1,767**	**94**	**14.0**
Men and boys	**444**	**400**	**90**	**13.3**
Men, aged 16 or older	353	342	97	14.4
Boys, aged 2 to 15	91	58	64	9.4
Women and girls	**751**	**625**	**83**	**12.3**
Women, aged 16 or older	629	553	88	13.0
Girls, aged 2 to 15	**122**	**72**	**59**	**8.7**
Children under age 2	**96**	**164**	**171**	**25.3**
Footwear	**304**	**292**	**96**	**14.2**
Other apparel products and services	**280**	**285**	**102**	**15.1**
TRANSPORTATION	**8,508**	**7,098**	**83**	**12.4**
Vehicle purchases	**3,421**	**2,958**	**86**	**12.8**
Cars and trucks, new	1,798	1,224	68	10.1
Cars and trucks, used	1,568	1,666	106	15.7
Gasoline and motor oil	**2,227**	**1,975**	**89**	**13.1**
Other vehicle expenses	**2,355**	**1,839**	**78**	**11.6**
Vehicle finance charges	298	288	97	14.3
Maintenance and repairs	688	506	74	10.9
Vehicle insurance	886	678	77	11.3
Vehicle rent, lease, license, other	482	367	76	11.3
Public transportation	**505**	**327**	**65**	**9.6**
HEALTH CARE	**2,766**	**1,092**	**39**	**5.8**
Health insurance	1,465	571	39	5.8
Medical services	670	312	47	6.9
Drugs	514	153	30	4.4
Medical supplies	117	56	48	7.1
ENTERTAINMENT	**2,376**	**1,669**	**70**	**10.4**
Fees and admissions	606	337	56	8.2
Audio and visual equipment and services	906	797	88	13.0
Pets, toys, hobbies, and playground equipment	412	281	68	10.1
Other entertainment supplies, services	451	254	56	8.3

	avg. spending of total consumer units	consumer units headed by people under age 30		
		average spending	indexed spending	market share
PERSONAL CARE PRODUCTS AND SERVICES	$585	$429	73	10.9%
READING	117	59	50	7.5
EDUCATION	888	992	112	16.6
TOBACCO PRODUCTS AND SMOKING SUPPLIES	327	299	91	13.5
MISCELLANEOUS	846	472	56	8.3
CASH CONTRIBUTIONS	1,869	797	43	6.3
PERSONAL INSURANCE AND PENSIONS	5,270	3,386	64	9.5
Life and other personal insurance	322	75	23	3.5
Pensions and Social Security	4,948	3,310	67	9.9
PERSONAL TAXES	2,432	954	39	5.8
Federal income taxes	1,711	616	36	5.3
State and local income taxes	519	291	56	8.3
Other taxes	202	48	24	3.5
GIFTS FOR PEOPLE IN OTHER HOUSEHOLDS**	1,154	849	74	10.9

This figure does not include the amount paid for mortgage principal, which is considered an asset.

** *Expenditures on gifts are also included in the preceding product and service categories.*

Note: Indexed spending is calculated by dividing the average spending of consumer units in the age group by the average spending of all consumer units and multiplying by 100; an index of 150 means the spending of consumer units in the age group is 50 percent above average; an index of 50 means spending by consumer units in the age group is 50 percent below average. The Bureau of Labor Statistics uses consumer unit rather than household as the sampling unit in the Consumer Expenditure Survey. For the definition of consumer unit, see the glossary. "–' means not applicable.

Source: Bureau of Labor Statistics, 2006 Consumer Expenditure Survey, Internet site http://www.bls.gov/cex/home.htm; calculations by New Strategist

25-to-34-Year-Olds: Spending on Children

Children determine the spending priorities of householders aged 25 to 34.

Households headed by people aged 25 to 34 controlled 20 percent of total household spending in 2006, more than their 17 percent share of households. Spending by households in the age group is close to the average in most categories. If their spending exceeds the average, it usually involves children.

Most households headed by people aged 25 to 34 include children. This is why they spend 80 percent more than the average household on personal services, primarily day care expenses. They spend nearly twice the average on clothing for children under age 2 and account for 34 percent of the market for this category.

In this age group, most people are not yet homeowners. This is why households headed by 25-to-34-year-olds spend 65 percent more than average on rent. They also spend more than average on alcoholic beverages and used cars and trucks. Surprisingly, they spend 6 percent less than the average household on entertainment.

■ Householders aged 25 to 34 are the primary market for goods and services for infants and young children.

Householders aged 25 to 34 spend more than average on clothes for infants

(indexed spending of householders aged 25 to 34 on selected categories, 2006)

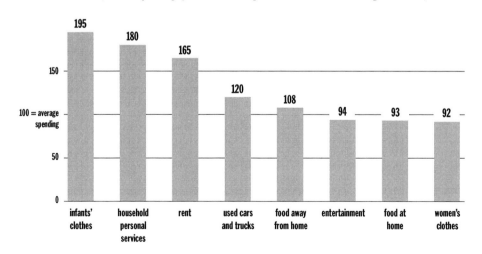

Table 10.4 Spending by Householders Aged 25 to 34, 2006

(average annual spending of total consumer units (CU) and those headed by people aged 25 to 34, indexed spending and share of total spending accounted for by consumer units aged 25 to 34; by category, 2006)

	avg. spending of total consumer units	consumer units headed by people aged 25 to 34		
		average spending	indexed spending	market share
Number of consumer units (in 000s)	115,356	20,071	–	17.4%
Average annual spending	$40,817	$47,582	117	20.3
FOOD	6,111	6,104	100	17.4
Food at home	3,417	3,186	93	16.2
Cereals and bakery products	446	406	91	15.8
Cereals and cereal products	143	143	100	17.4
Bakery products	304	263	87	15.1
Meats, poultry, fish, and eggs	797	746	94	16.3
Beef	236	229	97	16.9
Pork	157	141	90	15.6
Other meats	105	92	88	15.2
Poultry	141	143	101	17.6
Fish and seafood	122	108	89	15.4
Eggs	37	34	92	16.0
Dairy products	368	352	96	16.6
Fresh milk and cream	140	142	101	17.6
Other dairy products	228	210	92	16.0
Fruits and vegetables	592	537	91	15.8
Fresh fruits	195	165	85	14.7
Fresh vegetables	193	178	92	16.0
Processed fruits	109	109	100	17.4
Processed vegetables	95	86	91	15.8
Other food at home	1,212	1,144	94	16.4
Sugar and other sweets	125	95	76	13.2
Fats and oils	86	76	88	15.4
Miscellaneous foods	627	623	99	17.3
Nonalcoholic beverages	332	315	95	16.5
Food prepared by CU on trips	43	35	81	14.2
Food away from home	2,694	2,918	108	18.8
ALCOHOLIC BEVERAGES	497	657	132	23.0
HOUSING	16,366	17,139	105	18.2
Shelter	9,673	10,725	111	19.3
Owned dwellings*	6,516	6,132	94	16.4
Mortgage interest and charges	3,753	4,282	114	19.9
Property taxes	1,649	1,191	72	12.6
Maintenance, repairs, insurance, other expenses	1,115	660	59	10.3
Rented dwellings	2,590	4,286	165	28.8
Other lodging	567	307	54	9.4
Utilities, fuels, public services	3,397	3,093	91	15.8
Natural gas	509	421	83	14.4
Electricity	1,266	1,133	89	15.6

	avg. spending of total consumer units	consumer units headed by people aged 25 to 34		
		average spending	indexed spending	market share
Fuel oil and other fuels	$138	$73	53	9.2%
Telephone	1,087	1,129	104	18.1
Water and other public services	397	337	85	14.8
Household services	**948**	**1,130**	**119**	**20.7**
Personal services	393	706	180	31.3
Other household services	555	424	76	13.3
Housekeeping supplies	**640**	**531**	**83**	**14.4**
Laundry and cleaning supplies	151	155	103	17.9
Other household products	330	266	81	14.0
Postage and stationery	159	111	70	12.1
Household furnishings, equipment	**1,708**	**1,660**	**97**	**16.9**
Household textiles	154	124	81	14.0
Furniture	463	510	110	19.2
Floor coverings	48	35	73	12.7
Major appliances	241	194	80	14.0
Small appliances, misc. houseware	109	109	100	17.4
Miscellaneous household equipment	693	687	99	17.2
APPAREL AND SERVICES	**1,874**	**2,152**	**115**	**20.0**
Men and boys	**444**	**544**	**123**	**21.3**
Men, aged 16 or older	353	409	116	20.2
Boys, aged 2 to 15	91	135	148	25.8
Women and girls	**751**	**737**	**98**	**17.1**
Women, aged 16 or older	629	579	92	16.0
Girls, aged 2 to 15	122	158	130	22.5
Children under age 2	**96**	**187**	**195**	**33.9**
Footwear	**304**	**371**	**122**	**21.2**
Other apparel products and services	**280**	**313**	**112**	**19.4**
TRANSPORTATION	**8,508**	**9,047**	**106**	**18.5**
Vehicle purchases	**3,421**	**3,912**	**114**	**19.9**
Cars and trucks, new	1,798	1,960	109	19.0
Cars and trucks, used	1,568	1,881	120	20.9
Gasoline and motor oil	**2,227**	**2,346**	**105**	**18.3**
Other vehicle expenses	**2,355**	**2,342**	**99**	**17.3**
Vehicle finance charges	298	401	135	23.4
Maintenance and repairs	688	624	91	15.8
Vehicle insurance	886	822	93	16.1
Vehicle rent, lease, license, other	482	495	103	17.9
Public transportation	**505**	**448**	**89**	**15.4**
HEALTH CARE	**2,766**	**1,652**	**60**	**10.4**
Health insurance	1,465	883	60	10.5
Medical services	670	469	70	12.2
Drugs	514	243	47	8.2
Medical supplies	117	58	50	8.6
ENTERTAINMENT	**2,376**	**2,237**	**94**	**16.4**
Fees and admissions	606	475	78	13.6
Audio and visual equipment and services	906	969	107	18.6
Pets, toys, hobbies, and playground equipment	412	408	99	17.2
Other entertainment supplies, services	451	385	85	14.9

	avg. spending of total consumer units	consumer units headed by people aged 25 to 34		
		average spending	indexed spending	market share
PERSONAL CARE PRODUCTS AND SERVICES	**$585**	**$547**	**94**	**16.3%**
READING	**117**	**82**	**70**	**12.2**
EDUCATION	**888**	**710**	**80**	**13.9**
TOBACCO PRODUCTS AND SMOKING SUPPLIES	**327**	**318**	**97**	**16.9**
MISCELLANEOUS	**846**	**615**	**73**	**12.6**
CASH CONTRIBUTIONS	**1,869**	**1,070**	**57**	**10.0**
PERSONAL INSURANCE AND PENSIONS	**5,270**	**5,252**	**100**	**17.3**
Life and other personal insurance	322	172	53	9.3
Pensions and Social Security	4,948	5,079	103	17.9
PERSONAL TAXES	**2,432**	**1,532**	**63**	**11.0**
Federal income taxes	1,711	990	58	10.1
State and local income taxes	519	443	85	14.9
Other taxes	202	99	49	8.5
GIFTS FOR PEOPLE IN OTHER HOUSEHOLDS**	**1,154**	**929**	**81**	**14.0**

This figure does not include the amount paid for mortgage principal, which is considered an asset.
**Expenditures on gifts are also included in the preceding product and service categories.*
Note: Indexed spending is calculated by dividing the average spending of consumer units in the age group by the average spending of all consumer units and multiplying by 100; an index of 150 means the spending of consumer units in the age group is 50 percent above average; an index of 50 means spending by consumer units in the age group is 50 percent below average. The Bureau of Labor Statistics uses consumer unit rather than household as the sampling unit in the Consumer Expenditure Survey. For the definition of consumer unit, see the glossary. "–" means not applicable.
Source: Bureau of Labor Statistics, 2006 Consumer Expenditure Survey, Internet site http://www.bls.gov/cex/home.htm; calculations by New Strategist

35-to-44-Year-Olds: More Mouths to Feed

Households in the age group control a large share of spending.

Householders aged 35 to 44 spend almost the same amount as those aged 45 to 54—more than $57,000 in 2006. They account for a substantial 24 percent of total household spending, just a bit behind the 25 percent of spending controlled by householders aged 45 to 54. Behind the high level of spending by householders aged 35 to 44 is their household size. The average household headed by a 35-to-44-year-old includes 3.2 people, well above the 2.5 people in the average household.

Because householders aged 35 to 44 are in their childrearing years, their spending is above average on most categories of products and services. The age group spends much more than average on food—both at home (with an index of 121) and at restaurants (119). They spend 58 percent more than average on mortgage interest and 18 percent more on gasoline. Their spending on entertainment is 25 percent above average. They spend twice the average on girls' clothes and 89 percent more than average on boys' clothes. Householders aged 35 to 44 spend 18 percent more than average on personal care products and services.

■ Much of the spending of householders aged 35 to 44 is nondiscretionary, devoted to mortgages, car payments, food, and clothes.

Householders aged 35 to 44 spend more than average on most things

(indexed spending of householders aged 35 to 44 on selected categories, 2006)

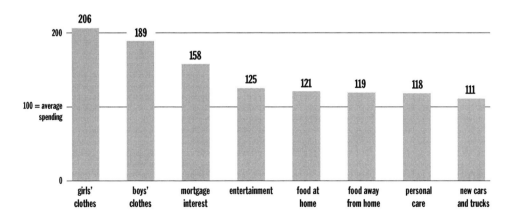

Table 10.5 Spending by Householders Aged 35 to 44, 2006

(average annual spending of total consumer units (CU) and those headed by people aged 35 to 44, indexed spending and share of total spending accounted for by consumer units aged 35 to 44; by category, 2006)

	avg. spending of total consumer units	consumer units headed by people aged 35 to 44		
		average spending	indexed spending	market share
Number of consumer units (in 000s)	118,843	23,950	–	20.2%
Average annual spending	$48,398	$57,476	119	23.9
FOOD	6,111	7,331	120	24.2
Food at home	3,417	4,128	121	24.3
Cereals and bakery products	446	553	124	25.0
Cereals and cereal products	143	185	129	26.1
Bakery products	304	369	121	24.5
Meats, poultry, fish, and eggs	797	962	121	24.3
Beef	236	272	115	23.2
Pork	157	186	118	23.9
Other meats	105	131	125	25.1
Poultry	141	185	131	26.4
Fish and seafood	122	143	117	23.6
Eggs	37	45	122	24.5
Dairy products	368	452	123	24.8
Fresh milk and cream	140	179	128	25.8
Other dairy products	228	273	120	24.1
Fruits and vegetables	592	671	113	22.8
Fresh fruits	195	219	112	22.6
Fresh vegetables	193	207	107	21.6
Processed fruits	109	131	120	24.2
Processed vegetables	95	114	120	24.2
Other food at home	1,212	1,490	123	24.8
Sugar and other sweets	125	145	116	23.4
Fats and oils	86	97	113	22.7
Miscellaneous foods	627	793	126	25.5
Nonalcoholic beverages	332	409	123	24.8
Food prepared by CU on trips	43	45	105	21.1
Food away from home	2,694	3,203	119	24.0
ALCOHOLIC BEVERAGES	497	496	100	20.1
HOUSING	16,366	20,303	124	25.0
Shelter	9,673	12,445	129	25.9
Owned dwellings*	6,516	8,965	138	27.7
Mortgage interest and charges	3,753	5,914	158	31.8
Property taxes	1,649	1,937	117	23.7
Maintenance, repairs, insurance, other expenses	1,115	1,114	100	20.1
Rented dwellings	2,590	2,938	113	22.9
Other lodging	567	541	95	19.2
Utilities, fuels, public services	3,397	3,854	113	22.9
Natural gas	509	559	110	22.1
Electricity	1,266	1,419	112	22.6

	avg. spending of total consumer units	consumer units headed by people aged 35 to 44		
		average spending	indexed spending	market share
Fuel oil and other fuels	$138	$157	114	22.9%
Telephone	1,087	1,271	117	23.6
Water and other public services	397	449	113	22.8
Household services	**948**	**1,380**	**146**	**29.3**
Personal services	393	811	206	41.6
Other household services	555	569	103	20.7
Housekeeping supplies	**640**	**761**	**119**	**24.0**
Laundry and cleaning supplies	151	189	125	25.2
Other household products	330	413	125	25.2
Postage and stationery	159	159	100	20.2
Household furnishings, equipment	**1,708**	**1,864**	**109**	**22.0**
Household textiles	154	140	91	18.3
Furniture	463	536	116	23.3
Floor coverings	48	40	83	16.8
Major appliances	241	272	113	22.7
Small appliances, misc. houseware	109	113	104	20.9
Miscellaneous household equipment	693	762	110	22.2
APPAREL AND SERVICES	**1,874**	**2,368**	**126**	**25.5**
Men and boys	**444**	**575**	**130**	**26.1**
Men, aged 16 or older	353	403	114	23.0
Boys, aged 2 to 15	91	172	189	38.1
Women and girls	**751**	**922**	**123**	**24.7**
Women, aged 16 or older	629	671	107	21.5
Girls, aged 2 to 15	122	251	206	41.5
Children under age 2	**96**	**128**	**133**	**26.9**
Footwear	**304**	**404**	**133**	**26.8**
Other apparel products and services	**280**	**338**	**121**	**24.3**
TRANSPORTATION	**8,508**	**9,977**	**117**	**23.6**
Vehicle purchases	**3,421**	**4,057**	**119**	**23.9**
Cars and trucks, new	1,798	1,999	111	22.4
Cars and trucks, used	1,568	1,973	126	25.4
Gasoline and motor oil	**2,227**	**2,636**	**118**	**23.9**
Other vehicle expenses	**2,355**	**2,725**	**116**	**23.3**
Vehicle finance charges	298	374	126	25.3
Maintenance and repairs	688	744	108	21.8
Vehicle insurance	886	976	110	22.2
Vehicle rent, lease, license, other	482	631	131	26.4
Public transportation	**505**	**559**	**111**	**22.3**
HEALTH CARE	**2,766**	**2,284**	**83**	**16.6**
Health insurance	1,465	1,214	83	16.7
Medical services	670	634	95	19.1
Drugs	514	345	67	13.5
Medical supplies	117	90	77	15.5
ENTERTAINMENT	**2,376**	**2,966**	**125**	**25.2**
Fees and admissions	606	839	138	27.9
Audio and visual equipment and services	906	1,052	116	23.4
Pets, toys, hobbies, and playground equipment	412	497	121	24.3
Other entertainment supplies, services	451	578	128	25.8

	avg. spending of total consumer units	consumer units headed by people aged 35 to 44		
		average spending	indexed spending	market share
PERSONAL CARE PRODUCTS AND SERVICES	**$585**	**$688**	**118**	**23.7%**
READING	**117**	**112**	**96**	**19.3**
EDUCATION	**888**	**857**	**97**	**19.4**
TOBACCO PRODUCTS AND SMOKING SUPPLIES	**327**	**354**	**108**	**21.8**
MISCELLANEOUS	**846**	**943**	**111**	**22.5**
CASH CONTRIBUTIONS	**1,869**	**1,707**	**91**	**18.4**
PERSONAL INSURANCE AND PENSIONS	**5,270**	**7,090**	**135**	**27.1**
Life and other personal insurance	322	364	113	22.8
Pensions and Social Security	4,948	6,726	136	27.4
PERSONAL TAXES	**2,432**	**3,167**	**130**	**26.2**
Federal income taxes	1,711	2,245	131	26.4
State and local income taxes	519	727	140	28.2
Other taxes	202	195	97	19.5
GIFTS FOR PEOPLE IN OTHER HOUSEHOLDS**	**1,154**	**775**	**67**	**13.5**

* This figure does not include the amount paid for mortgage principal, which is considered an asset.
** Expenditures on gifts are also included in the preceding product and service categories.
Note: Indexed spending is calculated by dividing the average spending of consumer units in the age group by the average spending of all consumer units and multiplying by 100; an index of 150 means the spending of consumer units in the age group is 50 percent above average; an index of 50 means spending by consumer units in the age group is 50 percent below average. The Bureau of Labor Statistics uses consumer unit rather than household as the sampling unit in the Consumer Expenditure Survey. For the definition of consumer unit, see the glossary. "–" means not applicable.
Source: Bureau of Labor Statistics, 2006 Consumer Expenditure Survey, Internet site http://www.bls.gov/cex/home.htm; calculations by New Strategist

45-to-54-Year-Olds: Big Spenders

They are in their peak earning—and spending—years.

Households headed by people aged 45 to 54 have the highest incomes and are also the biggest spenders. This age group accounts for 21 percent of households and 25 percent of household spending. Households headed by 45-to-54-year-olds spend 19 percent more than the average household.

Householders aged 45 to 54 spend more than average in almost every category. On some categories, spending by householders aged 45 to 54 is far above average. They spent 22 percent more than average on food away from home, 28 percent more than average on mortgage interest, and 17 percent more than average on entertainment.

Many 45-to-54-year-olds have teenagers and young adults in their household. Consequently, they spend 95 percent more than average on education. They spend 15 percent more than average on used cars and trucks, often buying vehicles for their children. They spend 25 percent more than average on fees and admission to entertainment events, such as movie tickets.

At this age, people are getting serious about saving for retirement. Householders aged 45 to 54 spend 40 percent more than average on pensions and Social Security.

■ As Boomers exit the 45-to-54 age group in the coming decade, the share of spending controlled by the age group will decline.

Householders aged 45 to 54 spend more than average on most items

(indexed spending of householders aged 45 to 54 on selected categories, 2006)

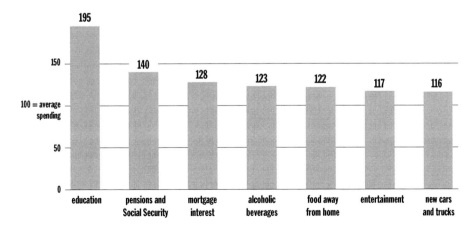

Table 10.6 Spending by Householders Aged 45 to 54, 2006

(average annual spending of total consumer units (CU) and those headed by people aged 45 to 54, indexed spending and share of total spending accounted for by consumer units aged 45 to 54; by category, 2006)

| | avg. spending of total consumer units | consumer units headed by people aged 45 to 54 | | |
		average spending	indexed spending	market share
Number of consumer units (in 000s)	118,843	24,696	–	20.8%
Average annual spending	$48,398	$57,563	119	24.7
FOOD	6,111	7,328	120	24.9
Food at home	3,417	4,036	118	24.5
Cereals and bakery products	446	510	114	23.8
Cereals and cereal products	143	162	113	23.5
Bakery products	304	348	114	23.8
Meats, poultry, fish, and eggs	797	972	122	25.3
Beef	236	308	131	27.1
Pork	157	193	123	25.5
Other meats	105	132	126	26.1
Poultry	141	159	113	23.4
Fish and seafood	122	142	116	24.2
Eggs	37	39	105	21.9
Dairy products	368	420	114	23.7
Fresh milk and cream	140	151	108	22.4
Other dairy products	228	268	118	24.4
Fruits and vegetables	592	683	115	24.0
Fresh fruits	195	225	115	24.0
Fresh vegetables	193	234	121	25.2
Processed fruits	109	118	108	22.5
Processed vegetables	95	106	112	23.2
Other food at home	1,212	1,451	120	24.9
Sugar and other sweets	125	156	125	25.9
Fats and oils	86	97	113	23.4
Miscellaneous foods	627	731	117	24.2
Nonalcoholic beverages	332	413	124	25.9
Food prepared by CU on trips	43	53	123	25.6
Food away from home	2,694	3,292	122	25.4
ALCOHOLIC BEVERAGES	497	612	123	25.6
HOUSING	16,366	18,377	112	23.3
Shelter	9,673	10,896	113	23.4
Owned dwellings*	6,516	8,024	123	25.6
Mortgage interest and charges	3,753	4,818	128	26.7
Property taxes	1,649	2,032	123	25.6
Maintenance, repairs, insurance, other expenses	1,115	1,175	105	21.9
Rented dwellings	2,590	2,064	80	16.6
Other lodging	567	807	142	29.6
Utilities, fuels, public services	3,397	3,912	115	23.9
Natural gas	509	598	117	24.4
Electricity	1,266	1,445	114	23.7

	avg. spending of total consumer units	consumer units headed by people aged 45 to 54		
		average spending	indexed spending	market share
Fuel oil and other fuels	$138	$150	109	22.6%
Telephone	1,087	1,269	117	24.3
Water and other public services	397	449	113	23.5
Household services	**948**	**793**	**84**	**17.4**
Personal services	393	192	49	10.2
Other household services	555	601	108	22.5
Housekeeping supplies	**640**	**727**	**114**	**23.6**
Laundry and cleaning supplies	151	160	106	22.0
Other household products	330	369	112	23.2
Postage and stationery	159	198	125	25.9
Household furnishings, equipment	**1,708**	**2,050**	**120**	**24.9**
Household textiles	154	175	114	23.6
Furniture	463	569	123	25.5
Floor coverings	48	48	100	20.8
Major appliances	241	285	118	24.6
Small appliances, misc. houseware	109	149	137	28.4
Miscellaneous household equipment	693	824	119	24.7
APPAREL AND SERVICES	**1,874**	**2,176**	**116**	**24.1**
Men and boys	**444**	**538**	**121**	**25.2**
Men, aged 16 or older	353	439	124	25.8
Boys, aged 2 to 15	91	100	110	22.8
Women and girls	**751**	**913**	**122**	**25.3**
Women, aged 16 or older	629	782	124	25.8
Girls, aged 2 to 15	122	131	107	22.3
Children under age 2	**96**	**72**	**75**	**15.6**
Footwear	**304**	**343**	**113**	**23.4**
Other apparel products and services	**280**	**311**	**111**	**23.1**
TRANSPORTATION	**8,508**	**10,111**	**119**	**24.7**
Vehicle purchases	**3,421**	**3,983**	**116**	**24.2**
Cars and trucks, new	1,798	2,087	116	24.1
Cars and trucks, used	1,568	1,811	115	24.0
Gasoline and motor oil	**2,227**	**2,693**	**121**	**25.1**
Other vehicle expenses	**2,355**	**2,819**	**120**	**24.9**
Vehicle finance charges	298	334	112	23.3
Maintenance and repairs	688	866	126	26.2
Vehicle insurance	886	1,105	125	25.9
Vehicle rent, lease, license, other	482	514	107	22.2
Public transportation	**505**	**616**	**122**	**25.3**
HEALTH CARE	**2,766**	**2,757**	**100**	**20.7**
Health insurance	1,465	1,310	89	18.6
Medical services	670	798	119	24.8
Drugs	514	499	97	20.2
Medical supplies	117	151	129	26.8
ENTERTAINMENT	**2,376**	**2,770**	**117**	**24.2**
Fees and admissions	606	757	125	26.0
Audio and visual equipment and services	906	1,020	113	23.4
Pets, toys, hobbies, and playground equipment	412	497	121	25.1
Other entertainment supplies, services	451	495	110	22.8

	avg. spending of total consumer units	consumer units headed by people aged 45 to 54		
		average spending	indexed spending	market share
PERSONAL CARE PRODUCTS AND SERVICES	$585	$696	119	24.7%
READING	117	133	114	23.6
EDUCATION	888	1,736	195	40.6
TOBACCO PRODUCTS AND SMOKING SUPPLIES	327	433	132	27.5
MISCELLANEOUS	846	971	115	23.9
CASH CONTRIBUTIONS	1,869	2,118	113	23.5
PERSONAL INSURANCE AND PENSIONS	5,270	7,346	139	29.0
Life and other personal insurance	322	413	128	26.7
Pensions and Social Security	4,948	6,933	140	29.1
PERSONAL TAXES	2,432	3,360	138	28.7
Federal income taxes	1,711	2,396	140	29.1
State and local income taxes	519	728	140	29.1
Other taxes	202	236	117	24.3
GIFTS FOR PEOPLE IN OTHER HOUSEHOLDS*	1,154	1,814	157	32.7

* This figure does not include the amount paid for mortgage principal, which is considered an asset.
** Expenditures on gifts are also included in the preceding product and service categories.
Note: Indexed spending is calculated by dividing the average spending of consumer units in the age group by the average spending of all consumer units and multiplying by 100; an index of 150 means the spending of consumer units in the age group is 50 percent above average; an index of 50 means spending by consumer units in the age group is 50 percent below average. The Bureau of Labor Statistics uses consumer unit rather than household as the sampling unit in the Consumer Expenditure Survey. For the definition of consumer unit, see the glossary. "–" means not applicable.
Source: Bureau of Labor Statistics, 2006 Consumer Expenditure Survey, Internet site http://www.bls.gov/cex/home.htm; calculations by New Strategist

55-to-64-Year-Olds: Spending More than Average

This age group spends more than average on many discretionary items, including entertainment.

Householders aged 55 to 64 spend less than those aged 45 to 54 for two reasons: One, their households are smaller because their children are grown; and two, many in the age group are retired. Consequently, the spending of households headed by people aged 55 to 64 is only slightly above average. In 2006, householders aged 55 to 64 spent only 5 percent more than the average household.

Although their overall spending is only slightly above average, households headed by 55-to-64-year-olds are big spenders on many discretionary items. They spend 54 percent more than average on other lodging (mostly hotel and motel expenses), 16 percent more on public transportation (mostly airline fares), and 12 percent more on entertainment.

Health care expenses increase in the 55-to-64 age group, which is why householders aged 55 to 64 spend 48 percent more than average on drugs and 46 percent more on medical services. Their homes are still a major expense, with spending on maintenance and repairs for owned homes 50 percent above average.

■ The spending of households headed by 55-to-64-year-olds will rise in the years ahead as early retirement becomes less common.

Householders aged 55 to 64 spend more than average on entertainment

(indexed spending of householders aged 55 to 64 on selected categories, 2006)

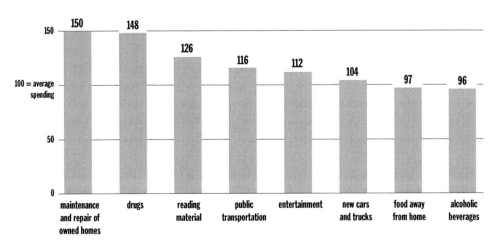

Table 10.7 Spending by Householders Aged 55 to 64, 2006

(average annual spending of total consumer units (CU) and those headed by people aged 55 to 64, indexed spending and share of total spending accounted for by consumer units aged 55 to 64; by category, 2006)

	avg. spending of total consumer units	consumer units headed by people aged 55 to 64		
		average spending	indexed spending	market share
Number of consumer units (in 000s)	**118,843**	**18,952**	**–**	**15.9%**
Average annual spending	**$48,398**	**$50,789**	**105**	**16.7**
FOOD	**6,111**	**6,132**	**100**	**16.0**
Food at home	**3,417**	**3,518**	**103**	**16.4**
Cereals and bakery products	446	453	102	16.2
Cereals and cereal products	143	135	94	15.1
Bakery products	304	318	105	16.7
Meats, poultry, fish, and eggs	797	801	101	16.0
Beef	236	225	95	15.2
Pork	157	158	101	16.0
Other meats	105	100	95	15.2
Poultry	141	139	99	15.7
Fish and seafood	122	138	113	18.0
Eggs	37	40	108	17.2
Dairy products	368	370	101	16.0
Fresh milk and cream	140	128	91	14.6
Other dairy products	228	242	106	16.9
Fruits and vegetables	592	656	111	17.7
Fresh fruits	195	230	118	18.8
Fresh vegetables	193	219	113	18.1
Processed fruits	109	107	98	15.7
Processed vegetables	95	101	106	17.0
Other food at home	1,212	1,238	102	16.3
Sugar and other sweets	125	121	97	15.4
Fats and oils	86	99	115	18.4
Miscellaneous foods	627	621	99	15.8
Nonalcoholic beverages	332	342	103	16.4
Food prepared by CU on trips	43	55	128	20.4
Food away from home	**2,694**	**2,613**	**97**	**15.5**
ALCOHOLIC BEVERAGES	**497**	**477**	**96**	**15.3**
HOUSING	**16,366**	**16,529**	**101**	**16.1**
Shelter	**9,673**	**9,199**	**95**	**15.2**
Owned dwellings*	6,516	6,866	105	16.8
Mortgage interest and charges	3,753	3,271	87	13.9
Property taxes	1,649	1,919	116	18.6
Maintenance, repairs, insurance, other expenses	1,115	1,676	150	24.0
Rented dwellings	2,590	1,460	56	9.0
Other lodging	567	873	154	24.6
Utilities, fuels, public services	**3,397**	**3,640**	**107**	**17.1**
Natural gas	509	563	111	17.6
Electricity	1,266	1,362	108	17.2

	avg. spending of total consumer units	consumer units headed by people aged 55 to 64		
		average spending	indexed spending	market share
Fuel oil and other fuels	$138	$167	121	19.3%
Telephone	1,087	1,115	103	16.4
Water and other public services	397	433	109	17.4
Household services	**948**	**934**	**99**	**15.7**
Personal services	393	221	56	9.0
Other household services	555	714	129	20.5
Housekeeping supplies	**640**	**739**	**115**	**18.4**
Laundry and cleaning supplies	151	165	109	17.4
Other household products	330	369	112	17.8
Postage and stationery	159	205	129	20.6
Household furnishings, equipment	**1,708**	**2,017**	**118**	**18.8**
Household textiles	154	207	134	21.4
Furniture	463	462	100	15.9
Floor coverings	48	80	167	26.6
Major appliances	241	295	122	19.5
Small appliances, misc. houseware	109	111	102	16.2
Miscellaneous household equipment	693	862	124	19.8
APPAREL AND SERVICES	**1,874**	**1,892**	**101**	**16.1**
Men and boys	**444**	**400**	**90**	**14.4**
Men, aged 16 or older	353	354	100	16.0
Boys, aged 2 to 15	91	46	51	8.1
Women and girls	**751**	**835**	**111**	**17.7**
Women, aged 16 or older	629	773	123	19.6
Girls, aged 2 to 15	122	62	51	8.1
Children under age 2	**96**	**66**	**69**	**11.0**
Footwear	**304**	**288**	**95**	**15.1**
Other apparel products and services	**280**	**303**	**108**	**17.3**
TRANSPORTATION	**8,508**	**8,676**	**102**	**16.3**
Vehicle purchases	**3,421**	**3,165**	**93**	**14.8**
Cars and trucks, new	1,798	1,867	104	16.6
Cars and trucks, used	1,568	1,271	81	12.9
Gasoline and motor oil	**2,227**	**2,288**	**103**	**16.4**
Other vehicle expenses	**2,355**	**2,638**	**112**	**17.9**
Vehicle finance charges	298	299	100	16.0
Maintenance and repairs	688	799	116	18.5
Vehicle insurance	886	941	106	16.9
Vehicle rent, lease, license, other	482	599	124	19.8
Public transportation	**505**	**584**	**116**	**18.4**
HEALTH CARE	**2,766**	**3,556**	**129**	**20.5**
Health insurance	1,465	1,676	114	18.2
Medical services	670	978	146	23.3
Drugs	514	759	148	23.5
Medical supplies	117	143	122	19.5
ENTERTAINMENT	**2,376**	**2,666**	**112**	**17.9**
Fees and admissions	606	605	100	15.9
Audio and visual equipment and services	906	906	100	15.9
Pets, toys, hobbies, and playground equipment	412	480	117	18.6
Other entertainment supplies, services	451	675	150	23.9

	avg. spending of total consumer units	consumer units headed by people aged 55 to 64		
		average spending	indexed spending	market share
PERSONAL CARE PRODUCTS AND SERVICES	**$585**	**$586**	**100**	**16.0%**
READING	**117**	**147**	**126**	**20.0**
EDUCATION	**888**	**662**	**75**	**11.9**
TOBACCO PRODUCTS AND SMOKING SUPPLIES	**327**	**370**	**113**	**18.0**
MISCELLANEOUS	**846**	**1,105**	**131**	**20.8**
CASH CONTRIBUTIONS	**1,869**	**2,266**	**121**	**19.3**
PERSONAL INSURANCE AND PENSIONS	**5,270**	**5,726**	**109**	**17.3**
Life and other personal insurance	322	458	142	22.7
Pensions and Social Security	4,948	5,267	106	17.0
PERSONAL TAXES	**2,432**	**3,531**	**145**	**23.2**
Federal income taxes	1,711	2,604	152	24.3
State and local income taxes	519	657	127	20.2
Other taxes	202	270	134	21.3
GIFTS FOR PEOPLE IN OTHER HOUSEHOLDS**	**1,154**	**1,522**	**132**	**21.0**

* This figure does not include the amount paid for mortgage principal, which is considered an asset.

** Expenditures on gifts are also included in the preceding product and service categories.

Note: Indexed spending is calculated by dividing the average spending of consumer units in the age group by the average spending of all consumer units and multiplying by 100; an index of 150 means the spending of consumer units in the age group is 50 percent above average; an index of 50 means spending by consumer units in the age group is 50 percent below average. The Bureau of Labor Statistics uses consumer unit rather than household as the sampling unit in the Consumer Expenditure Survey. For the definition of consumer unit, see the glossary. "–" means not applicable.

Source: Bureau of Labor Statistics, 2006 Consumer Expenditure Survey, Internet site http://www.bls.gov/cex/home.htm; calculations by New Strategist

65-to-74-Year-Olds: Average Spenders

Householders aged 65 to 74 spend less than average on many items, partly because their households are smaller.

Householders aged 65 to 74 spend 15 percent less than the average household. With only 1.9 people in their households compared with 2.5 people in the average household, householders aged 65 to 74 do not need to spend as much to live as well.

Many expenses are reduced for older householders. They spend far less than the average household on mortgage interest since most own their homes free and clear. But because their homes are older, they spend 27 percent more than average on maintenance and repair of owned homes.

Householders aged 65 to 74 spend more than the average household on many discretionary items such as household textiles (with an index of 155), new cars and trucks (123), and reading material (122).

Householders aged 65 to 74 spend considerably more than average on health care. They spend 58 percent more than average on health care overall and 67 percent more on drugs. They spend 13 percent more than average on cash contributions—a large portion of which is donated to religious institutions.

■ The spending of householders aged 65 to 74 is likely to rise as Boomers enter the age group and labor force participation rates rise.

Householders aged 65 to 75 are big spenders on maintenance and repairs for owned homes

(indexed spending of householders aged 65 to 74 on selected categories, 2006)

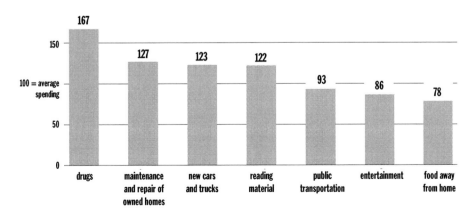

Table 10.8 Spending by Householders 65 to 74, 2006

(average annual spending of total consumer units (CU) and those headed by people aged 65 to 74, indexed spending and share of total spending accounted for by consumer units aged 65 to 74; by category, 2006)

	avg. spending of total consumer units	consumer units headed by people aged 65 to 74		
		average spending	indexed spending	market share
Number of consumer units (in 000s)	118,843	11,764	–	9.9%
Average annual spending	$48,398	$40,960	85	8.4
FOOD	6,111	5,172	85	8.4
Food at home	3,417	3,062	90	8.9
Cereals and bakery products	446	413	93	9.2
Cereals and cereal products	143	114	80	7.9
Bakery products	304	300	99	9.8
Meats, poultry, fish, and eggs	797	723	91	9.0
Beef	236	206	87	8.6
Pork	157	157	100	9.9
Other meats	105	91	87	8.6
Poultry	141	110	78	7.7
Fish and seafood	122	124	102	10.1
Eggs	37	34	92	9.1
Dairy products	368	330	90	8.9
Fresh milk and cream	140	120	86	8.5
Other dairy products	228	209	92	9.1
Fruits and vegetables	592	572	97	9.6
Fresh fruits	195	184	94	9.3
Fresh vegetables	193	192	99	9.8
Processed fruits	109	103	94	9.4
Processed vegetables	95	93	98	9.7
Other food at home	1,212	1,024	84	8.4
Sugar and other sweets	125	129	103	10.2
Fats and oils	86	89	103	10.2
Miscellaneous foods	627	488	78	7.7
Nonalcoholic beverages	332	266	80	7.9
Food prepared by CU on trips	43	51	119	11.7
Food away from home	2,694	2,110	78	7.8
ALCOHOLIC BEVERAGES	497	339	68	6.8
HOUSING	16,366	13,273	81	8.0
Shelter	9,673	6,934	72	7.1
Owned dwellings*	6,516	5,151	79	7.8
Mortgage interest and charges	3,753	1,967	52	5.2
Property taxes	1,649	1,768	107	10.6
Maintenance, repairs, insurance, other expenses	1,115	1,416	127	12.6
Rented dwellings	2,590	1,191	46	4.6
Other lodging	567	592	104	10.3
Utilities, fuels, public services	3,397	3,297	97	9.6
Natural gas	509	526	103	10.2
Electricity	1,266	1,275	101	10.0

	avg. spending of total consumer units	consumer units headed by people aged 65 to 74		
		average spending	indexed spending	market share
Fuel oil and other fuels	$138	$168	122	12.1%
Telephone	1,087	889	82	8.1
Water and other public services	397	438	110	10.9
Household services	**948**	**718**	**76**	**7.5**
Personal services	393	–	–	–
Other household services	555	663	119	11.8
Housekeeping supplies	**640**	**660**	**103**	**10.2**
Laundry and cleaning supplies	151	132	87	8.7
Other household products	330	352	107	10.6
Postage and stationery	159	176	111	11.0
Household furnishings, equipment	**1,708**	**1,664**	**97**	**9.6**
Household textiles	154	239	155	15.4
Furniture	463	368	79	7.9
Floor coverings	48	52	108	10.7
Major appliances	241	258	107	10.6
Small appliances, misc. houseware	109	98	90	8.9
Miscellaneous household equipment	693	649	94	9.3
APPAREL AND SERVICES	**1,874**	**1,212**	**65**	**6.4**
Men and boys	**444**	**282**	**64**	**6.3**
Men, aged 16 or older	353	252	71	7.1
Boys, aged 2 to 15	91	31	34	3.4
Women and girls	**751**	**538**	**72**	**7.1**
Women, aged 16 or older	629	490	78	7.7
Girls, aged 2 to 15	122	47	39	3.8
Children under age 2	**96**	**28**	**29**	**2.9**
Footwear	**304**	**160**	**53**	**5.2**
Other apparel products and services	**280**	**204**	**73**	**7.2**
TRANSPORTATION	**8,508**	**7,481**	**88**	**8.7**
Vehicle purchases	**3,421**	**3,273**	**96**	**9.5**
Cars and trucks, new	1,798	2,210	123	12.2
Cars and trucks, used	1,568	1,063	68	6.7
Gasoline and motor oil	**2,227**	**1,766**	**79**	**7.8**
Other vehicle expenses	**2,355**	**1,972**	**84**	**8.3**
Vehicle finance charges	298	190	64	6.3
Maintenance and repairs	688	640	93	9.2
Vehicle insurance	886	806	91	9.0
Vehicle rent, lease, license, other	482	336	70	6.9
Public transportation	**505**	**471**	**93**	**9.2**
HEALTH CARE	**2,766**	**4,379**	**158**	**15.7**
Health insurance	1,465	2,718	186	18.4
Medical services	670	636	95	9.4
Drugs	514	859	167	16.5
Medical supplies	117	166	142	14.0
ENTERTAINMENT	**2,376**	**2,049**	**86**	**8.5**
Fees and admissions	606	559	92	9.1
Audio and visual equipment and services	906	791	87	8.6
Pets, toys, hobbies, and playground equipment	412	344	83	8.3
Other entertainment supplies, services	451	355	79	7.8

	avg. spending of total consumer units	consumer units headed by people aged 65 to 74		
		average spending	indexed spending	market share
PERSONAL CARE PRODUCTS AND SERVICES	$585	$527	90	8.9%
READING	117	143	122	12.1
EDUCATION	888	274	31	3.1
TOBACCO PRODUCTS AND SMOKING SUPPLIES	327	241	74	7.3
MISCELLANEOUS	846	966	114	11.3
CASH CONTRIBUTIONS	1,869	2,121	113	11.2
PERSONAL INSURANCE AND PENSIONS	5,270	2,782	53	5.2
Life and other personal insurance	322	365	113	11.2
Pensions and Social Security	4,948	2,417	49	4.8
PERSONAL TAXES	2,432	1,759	72	7.2
Federal income taxes	1,711	1,236	72	7.2
State and local income taxes	519	209	40	4.0
Other taxes	202	315	156	15.4
GIFTS FOR PEOPLE IN OTHER HOUSEHOLDS**	1,154	1,219	106	10.5

* This figure does not include the amount paid for mortgage principal, which is considered an asset.
** Expenditures on gifts are also included in the preceding product and service categories.
Note: Indexed spending is calculated by dividing the average spending of consumer units in the age group by the average spending of all consumer units and multiplying by 100; an index of 150 means the spending of consumer units in the age group is 50 percent above average; an index of 50 means spending by consumer units in the age group is 50 percent below average. The Bureau of Labor Statistics uses consumer unit rather than household as the sampling unit in the Consumer Expenditure Survey. For the definition of consumer unit, see the glossary. "–" means not applicable or sample is too small to make a reliable estimate.
Source: Bureau of Labor Statistics, 2006 Consumer Expenditure Survey, Internet site http://www.bls.gov/cex/home.htm; calculations by New Strategist

75 or Older: Spending on Health Care

As people age, health care spending rises sharply.

Households headed by people aged 75 or older spent $4,282 on health care in 2006, much more than the $2,766 spent by the average household on this item. For the oldest households, health care accounts for a larger share of the budget than groceries.

The oldest householders spend far less than average on most items. They spend only 37 percent as much as the average household on alcoholic beverages, 34 percent as much as the average on clothing, and 46 percent as much as the average on entertainment. One factor behind the lower spending is the smaller size of the households headed by the oldest Americans.

Householders aged 75 or older spend 12 percent more than average on maintenance and repair of owned homes. They spend 10 percent more on reading material and 64 percent more on cash contributions.

■ Although their spending on entertainment is below average, households headed by people aged 75 or older spend almost as much on entertainment as householders under age 25.

The oldest householders are big spenders on health insurance

(indexed spending of householders aged 75 or older on selected categories, 2006)

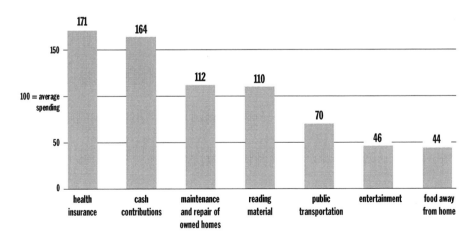

Table 10.9 Spending by Householders Aged 75 or Older, 2006

(average annual spending of total consumer units (CU) and those headed by people aged 75 or older, indexed spending and share of total spending accounted for by consumer units aged 75 or older, by category, 2006)

	avg. spending of total consumer units	consumer units headed by people aged 75 or older		
		average spending	indexed spending	market share
Number of consumer units (in 000s)	**118,843**	**11,243**	**–**	**9.5%**
Average annual spending	**$48,398**	**$28,904**	**60**	**5.6**
FOOD	**6,111**	**3,437**	**56**	**5.3**
Food at home	**3,417**	**2,244**	**66**	**6.2**
Cereals and bakery products	446	325	73	6.9
Cereals and cereal products	143	90	63	6.0
Bakery products	304	236	78	7.3
Meats, poultry, fish, and eggs	797	495	62	5.9
Beef	236	146	62	5.9
Pork	157	95	61	5.7
Other meats	105	70	67	6.3
Poultry	141	80	57	5.4
Fish and seafood	122	78	64	6.0
Eggs	37	26	70	6.6
Dairy products	368	256	70	6.6
Fresh milk and cream	140	105	75	7.1
Other dairy products	228	151	66	6.3
Fruits and vegetables	592	439	74	7.0
Fresh fruits	195	159	82	7.7
Fresh vegetables	193	131	68	6.4
Processed fruits	109	84	77	7.3
Processed vegetables	95	65	68	6.5
Other food at home	1,212	729	60	5.7
Sugar and other sweets	125	107	86	8.1
Fats and oils	86	57	66	6.3
Miscellaneous foods	627	371	59	5.6
Nonalcoholic beverages	332	176	53	5.0
Food prepared by CU on trips	43	18	42	4.0
Food away from home	**2,694**	**1,193**	**44**	**4.2**
ALCOHOLIC BEVERAGES	**497**	**184**	**37**	**3.5**
HOUSING	**16,366**	**10,236**	**63**	**5.9**
Shelter	**9,673**	**5,597**	**58**	**5.5**
Owned dwellings*	6,516	3,224	49	4.7
Mortgage interest and charges	3,753	609	16	1.5
Property taxes	1,649	1,368	83	7.8
Maintenance, repairs, insurance, other expenses	1,115	1,247	112	10.6
Rented dwellings	2,590	2,090	81	7.6
Other lodging	567	284	50	4.7
Utilities, fuels, public services	**3,397**	**2,705**	**80**	**7.5**
Natural gas	509	488	96	9.1
Electricity	1,266	1,028	81	7.7

	avg. spending of total consumer units	consumer units headed by people aged 75 or older		
		average spending	indexed spending	market share
Fuel oil and other fuels	$138	$185	134	12.7%
Telephone	1,087	645	59	5.6
Water and other public services	397	359	90	8.6
Household services	**948**	**722**	**76**	**7.2**
Personal services	393	157	40	3.8
Other household services	555	565	102	9.6
Housekeeping supplies	**640**	**445**	**70**	**6.6**
Laundry and cleaning supplies	151	91	60	5.7
Other household products	330	226	68	6.5
Postage and stationery	159	128	81	7.6
Household furnishings, equipment	**1,708**	**767**	**45**	**4.2**
Household textiles	154	85	55	5.2
Furniture	463	176	38	3.6
Floor coverings	48	41	85	8.1
Major appliances	241	156	65	6.1
Small appliances, misc. houseware	109	58	53	5.0
Miscellaneous household equipment	693	251	36	3.4
APPAREL AND SERVICES	**1,874**	**639**	**34**	**3.2**
Men and boys	**444**	**129**	**29**	**2.7**
Men, aged 16 or older	353	119	34	3.2
Boys, aged 2 to 15	91	10	11	1.0
Women and girls	**751**	**290**	**39**	**3.7**
Women, aged 16 or older	629	279	44	4.2
Girls, aged 2 to 15	122	11	9	0.9
Children under age 2	**96**	**12**	**13**	**1.2**
Footwear	**304**	**106**	**35**	**3.3**
Other apparel products and services	**280**	**101**	**36**	**3.4**
TRANSPORTATION	**8,508**	**3,751**	**44**	**4.2**
Vehicle purchases	**3,421**	**1,284**	**38**	**3.6**
Cars and trucks, new	1,798	520	29	2.7
Cars and trucks, used	1,568	764	49	4.6
Gasoline and motor oil	**2,227**	**934**	**42**	**4.0**
Other vehicle expenses	**2,355**	**1,179**	**50**	**4.7**
Vehicle finance charges	298	53	18	1.7
Maintenance and repairs	688	371	54	5.1
Vehicle insurance	886	568	64	6.1
Vehicle rent, lease, license, other	482	188	39	3.7
Public transportation	**505**	**354**	**70**	**6.6**
HEALTH CARE	**2,766**	**4,282**	**155**	**14.6**
Health insurance	1,465	2,511	171	16.2
Medical services	670	692	103	9.8
Drugs	514	916	178	16.9
Medical supplies	117	163	139	13.2
ENTERTAINMENT	**2,376**	**1,099**	**46**	**4.4**
Fees and admissions	606	300	50	4.7
Audio and visual equipment and services	906	523	58	5.5
Pets, toys, hobbies, and playground equipment	412	163	40	3.7
Other entertainment supplies, services	451	114	25	2.4

	avg. spending of total consumer units	consumer units headed by people aged 75 or older		
		average spending	indexed spending	market share
PERSONAL CARE PRODUCTS AND SERVICES	$585	$421	72	6.8%
READING	117	129	110	10.4
EDUCATION	888	162	18	1.7
TOBACCO PRODUCTS AND SMOKING SUPPLIES	327	97	30	2.8
MISCELLANEOUS	846	549	65	6.1
CASH CONTRIBUTIONS	1,869	3,058	164	15.5
PERSONAL INSURANCE AND PENSIONS	5,270	862	16	1.5
Life and other personal insurance	322	231	72	6.8
Pensions and Social Security	4,948	631	13	1.2
PERSONAL TAXES	2,432	675	28	2.6
Federal income taxes	1,711	352	21	1.9
State and local income taxes	519	102	20	1.9
Other taxes	202	221	109	10.4
GIFTS FOR PEOPLE IN OTHER HOUSEHOLDS**	1,154	781	68	6.4

* This figure does not include the amount paid for mortgage principal, which is considered an asset.
** Expenditures on gifts are also included in the preceding product and service categories.
Note: Indexed spending is calculated by dividing the average spending of consumer units in the age group by the average spending of all consumer units and multiplying by 100; an index of 150 means the spending of consumer units in the age group is 50 percent above average; an index of 50 means spending by consumer units in the age group is 50 percent below average. The Bureau of Labor Statistics uses consumer unit rather than household as the sampling unit in the Consumer Expenditure Survey. For the definition of consumer unit, see the glossary.
Source: Bureau of Labor Statistics, 2006 Consumer Expenditure Survey, Internet site http://www.bls.gov/cex/home.htm; calculations by New Strategist

11

Time Use

How people spend their time is determined by their life stage, attitudes, and values. Each generation of Americans is at a different life stage, and each has distinct attitudes and values. Consequently, the generations spend their time differently, as is revealed by the Bureau of Labor Statistics new American Time Use Survey. The survey indicates that young adults spend more time with computers, middle-aged adults are busy raising children, and older Americans spend the most time watching television.

The life stage demands confronting each age group, as well as generational preferences, determine how involved the generations are with technology, religion, politics, and community organizations. By knowing who is doing what, businesses and policy makers can hone their products and programs to best meet the wants and needs of the American public.

What to expect in the future

■ Gen X and Millennials devote more of their leisure time to computers than to reading. As they get older, electronic media will increasingly dominate print media as a source of entertainment and information.

■ Americans are busier than ever, and no one is busier juggling work and family than the middle aged. Boomers are now exiting the crowded-nest lifestage, but they will not have as much leisure time in the empty-nest phase as the Swing and World War II generations because many are postponing retirement.

Leisure Activities Rank Second in Time Use among Americans

Work ranks third in time use, behind leisure pursuits.

The American Time Use Survey asks a representative sample of Americans to detail their activities during the past 24 hours. These diary data are combined and analyzed by type of activity and demographic characteristic, revealing how much time people devote to eating, shopping, working, and playing.

The time use survey results show, not surprisingly, that people spend the most time on personal care activities, which include sleeping, bathing, and dressing—an average of 9.41 hours per day in 2006. Ranking second are leisure and sports activities, which absorb 5.09 hours per day on average. Work comes in third, at 3.75 hours per day (the figure is relatively low because it includes both workers and those not in the labor force). Housework, eating and drinking, and shopping are next in line.

The amount of time people spend doing activities varies by demographic characteristic. The youngest and oldest adults spend more time than the middle aged in personal care activities, in large part because they have more free time. Teenagers and young adults spend much more time than the average person engaged in educational activities. People aged 35 to 54 spend 32 to 35 percent more time than average working. Older Americans spend more time than the average person engaged in leisure and sports activities.

■ Researchers use the results of time use surveys to determine how people balance work and family issues.

Young adults devote the most time to personal care activities

(average number of hours per day spent sleeping, bathing, dressing, and doing other personal care activities, by age, 2006)

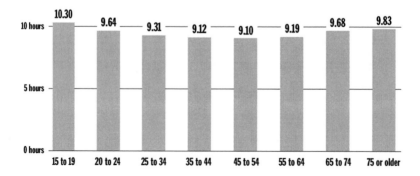

	15 to 19	20 to 24	25 to 34	35 to 44	45 to 54	55 to 64	65 to 74	75 or older
	10.30	9.64	9.31	9.12	9.10	9.19	9.68	9.83

Table 11.1 Time Use by Primary Activity and Age, 2006

(average number of hours and percent of day spent in primary activities, and index of time use by age to average, 2006)

	total people	15–19	20–24	25–34	35–44	45–54	55–64	65–74	75+
Total, all activities	**24.00**	**24.00**	**24.00**	**24.00**	**24.00**	**24.00**	**24.00**	**24.00**	**24.00**
Personal care activities	9.41	10.30	9.64	9.31	9.12	9.10	9.19	9.68	9.83
Eating and drinking	1.23	1.07	1.21	1.19	1.18	1.17	1.31	1.44	1.50
Household activities	1.79	0.76	1.05	1.55	1.87	1.97	2.11	2.64	2.32
Purchasing goods and services	0.81	0.56	0.67	0.81	0.87	0.82	0.91	0.93	0.80
Caring for and helping household members	0.53	0.15	0.51	1.07	0.98	0.36	0.16	0.13	0.12
Caring for and helping people in other households	0.21	0.21	0.20	0.12	0.19	0.24	0.28	0.30	0.21
Working and work-related activities	3.75	1.39	4.23	4.77	4.96	5.06	3.80	0.94	0.34
Educational activities	0.49	3.29	0.80	0.39	0.15	0.09	0.04	0.05	0.06
Organizational, civic, religious activities	0.30	0.34	0.21	0.16	0.30	0.29	0.39	0.38	0.43
Leisure and sports	5.09	5.40	5.03	4.30	4.09	4.52	5.41	6.97	7.82
Telephone calls, mail, and e-mail	0.19	0.33	0.19	0.14	0.13	0.17	0.18	0.24	0.30
Other activities, not elsewhere classified	0.21	0.22	0.24	0.17	0.16	0.20	0.20	0.29	0.27

Percent of day spent in activity

Total, all activities	**100.0%**	**100.0%**	**100.0%**	**100.0%**	**100.0%**	**100.0%**	**100.0%**	**100.0%**	**100.0%**
Personal care activities	39.2	42.9	40.2	38.8	38.0	37.9	38.3	40.3	41.0
Eating and drinking	5.1	4.5	5.0	5.0	4.9	4.9	5.5	6.0	6.3
Household activities	7.5	3.2	4.4	6.5	7.8	8.2	8.8	11.0	9.7
Purchasing goods and services	3.4	2.3	2.8	3.4	3.6	3.4	3.8	3.9	3.3
Caring for and helping household members	2.2	0.6	2.1	4.5	4.1	1.5	0.7	0.5	0.5
Caring for and helping people in other households	0.9	0.9	0.8	0.5	0.8	1.0	1.2	1.3	0.9
Working and work-related activities	15.6	5.8	17.6	19.9	20.7	21.1	15.8	3.9	1.4
Educational activities	2.0	13.7	3.3	1.6	0.6	0.4	0.2	0.2	0.3
Organizational, civic, religious activities	1.3	1.4	0.9	0.7	1.3	1.2	1.6	1.6	1.8
Leisure and sports	21.2	22.5	21.0	17.9	17.0	18.8	22.5	29.0	32.6
Telephone calls, mail, and e-mail	0.8	1.4	0.8	0.6	0.5	0.7	0.8	1.0	1.3
Other activities, not elsewhere classified	0.9	0.9	1.0	0.7	0.7	0.8	0.8	1.2	1.1

Indexed time use by age

Total, all activities	**100**	**100**	**100**	**100**	**100**	**100**	**100**	**100**	**100**
Personal care activities	100	109	102	99	97	97	98	103	104
Eating and drinking	100	87	98	97	96	95	107	117	122
Household activities	100	42	59	87	104	110	118	147	130
Purchasing goods and services	100	69	83	100	107	101	112	115	99
Caring for and helping household members	100	28	96	202	185	68	30	25	23
Caring for and helping people in other households	100	100	95	57	90	114	133	143	100
Working and work-related activities	100	37	113	127	132	135	101	25	9
Educational activities	100	671	163	80	31	18	8	10	12
Organizational, civic, religious activities	100	113	70	53	100	97	130	127	143
Leisure and sports	100	106	99	84	80	89	106	137	154
Telephone calls, mail, and e-mail	100	174	100	74	68	89	95	126	158
Other activities, not elsewhere classified	100	105	114	81	76	95	95	138	129

Note: Primary activities are those respondents identified as their main activity. Other activities done simultaneously, such as eating while watching TV, are not included. Travel time is included in the above figures.
Source: Bureau of Labor Statistics, 2006 American Time Use Survey, Internet site http://www.bls.gov/tus/home.htm; calculations by New Strategist

Table 11.2 Time Spent Sleeping by Age and Sex, 2006

(hours per day spent sleeping as a primary activity and index of time to average, by age and sex, 2006)

	total	men	women
Aged 15 or older	**8.63**	**8.56**	**8.69**
Aged 15 to 19	9.48	9.65	9.29
Aged 20 to 24	8.90	8.74	9.05
Aged 25 to 34	8.58	8.40	8.75
Aged 35 to 44	8.39	8.28	8.49
Aged 45 to 54	8.30	8.20	8.40
Aged 55 to 64	8.40	8.32	8.47
Aged 65 to 74	8.86	9.06	8.69
Aged 75 or older	8.97	9.00	8.95
Index of time to average			
Aged 15 or older	**100**	**99**	**101**
Aged 15 to 19	110	112	108
Aged 20 to 24	103	101	105
Aged 25 to 34	99	97	101
Aged 35 to 44	97	96	98
Aged 45 to 54	96	95	97
Aged 55 to 64	97	96	98
Aged 65 to 74	103	105	101
Aged 75 or older	104	104	104

Note: Primary activities are those respondents identified as their main activity. Other activities done simultaneously, such as eating while watching TV, are not included. Travel time is not included in the above figures.
Source: Bureau of Labor Statistics, 2006 American Time Use Survey, Internet site http://www.bls.gov/tus/home.htm; calculations by New Strategist

Older Adults Spend the Most Time in Leisure Pursuits

People aged 35 to 44 have the least amount of leisure time.

The average American spends 5.09 hours a day in leisure activities, half of it in front of a television set. After personal care activities (sleeping, bathing, dressing, etc.), leisure activities take up the largest share of the average person's day. Older men and women spend the most time watching TV, with men aged 65 or older spending more than four hours a day watching television as a primary activity.

Socializing and communicating is the second biggest leisure activity, but on average people spend only 0.67 hours socializing each day (or 40 minutes). Young adults spend the most time socializing, 19 percent more than the average person. Reading is the third-ranking leisure pursuit, but only for women. Men spend more time participating in sports than reading. Teenage boys aged 15 to 19 spend much more time than anyone else using a computer for leisure (except gaming) and playing games (a category that includes gaming on a computer as well as board and card games).

■ As young adults age, computer use may overtake reading as a leisure pursuit in the older age groups.

Young adults devote more time to computers than to reading

(average number of hours per day spent reading or using the computer for leisure, by age, 2006)

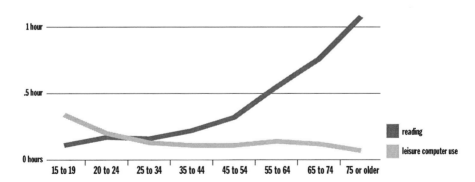

Table 11.3 Time Spent Watching Television by Age and Sex, 2006

(hours per day spent watching television as a primary activity and index of time to average, by age and sex, 2006)

	total	men	women
Aged 15 or older	**2.57**	**2.80**	**2.36**
Aged 15 to 19	2.11	2.19	2.02
Aged 20 to 24	2.16	2.27	2.05
Aged 25 to 34	2.20	2.41	1.98
Aged 35 to 44	2.11	2.29	1.95
Aged 45 to 54	2.38	2.67	2.11
Aged 55 to 64	2.88	3.35	2.45
Aged 65 to 74	3.83	4.22	3.51
Aged 75 or older	4.18	4.68	3.86
Index of time to average			
Aged 15 or older	**100**	**109**	**92**
Aged 15 to 19	82	85	79
Aged 20 to 24	84	88	80
Aged 25 to 34	86	94	77
Aged 35 to 44	82	89	76
Aged 45 to 54	93	104	82
Aged 55 to 64	112	130	95
Aged 65 to 74	149	164	137
Aged 75 or older	163	182	150

Note: Primary activities are those respondents identified as their main activity. Other activities done simultaneously, such as eating while watching TV, are not included. Travel time is not included in the above figures.
Source: Bureau of Labor Statistics, 2006 American Time Use Survey, Internet site http://www.bls.gov/tus/home.htm; calculations by New Strategist

Table 11.4 Time Spent Socializing and Communicating by Age and Sex, 2006

(hours per day spent socializing and communicating as a primary activity and index of time to average, by age and sex, 2006)

	total	men	women
Aged 15 or older	**0.67**	**0.62**	**0.71**
Aged 15 to 19	0.80	0.69	0.91
Aged 20 to 24	0.80	0.78	0.82
Aged 25 to 34	0.67	0.62	0.72
Aged 35 to 44	0.55	0.53	0.58
Aged 45 to 54	0.64	0.60	0.68
Aged 55 to 64	0.65	0.57	0.71
Aged 65 to 74	0.72	0.62	0.81
Aged 75 or older	0.69	0.79	0.63
Index of time to average			
Aged 15 or older	**100**	**93**	**106**
Aged 15 to 19	119	103	136
Aged 20 to 24	119	116	122
Aged 25 to 34	100	93	107
Aged 35 to 44	82	79	87
Aged 45 to 54	96	90	101
Aged 55 to 64	97	85	106
Aged 65 to 74	107	93	121
Aged 75 or older	103	118	94

Note: Primary activities are those respondents identified as their main activity. Other activities done simultaneously, such as eating while watching TV, are not included. Travel time is not included in the above figures.
Source: Bureau of Labor Statistics, 2006 American Time Use Survey, Internet site http://www.bls.gov/tus/home.htm; calculations by New Strategist

Table 11.5 Time Spent Reading by Age and Sex, 2006

(hours per day spent reading as a primary activity and index of time to average, by age and sex, 2006)

	total	men	women
Aged 15 or older	**0.36**	**0.31**	**0.42**
Aged 15 to 19	0.11	0.07	0.14
Aged 20 to 24	0.17	0.20	0.14
Aged 25 to 34	0.16	0.13	0.19
Aged 35 to 44	0.22	0.19	0.24
Aged 45 to 54	0.32	0.26	0.39
Aged 55 to 64	0.55	0.51	0.58
Aged 65 to 74	0.76	0.77	0.75
Aged 75 or older	1.08	0.88	1.22
Index of time to average			
Aged 15 or older	**100**	**86**	**117**
Aged 15 to 19	31	19	39
Aged 20 to 24	47	56	39
Aged 25 to 34	44	36	53
Aged 35 to 44	61	53	67
Aged 45 to 54	89	72	108
Aged 55 to 64	153	142	161
Aged 65 to 74	211	214	208
Aged 75 or older	300	244	339

Note: Primary activities are those respondents identified as their main activity. Other activities done simultaneously, such as eating while watching TV, are not included. Travel time is not included in the above figures.
Source: Bureau of Labor Statistics, 2006 American Time Use Survey, Internet site http://www.bls.gov/tus/home.htm; calculations by New Strategist

Table 11.6   Time Spent Relaxing and Thinking by Age and Sex, 2006

(hours per day spent relaxing and thinking as a primary activity and index of time to average, by age and sex, 2006)

	total	men	women
Aged 15 or older	**0.31**	**0.32**	**0.29**
Aged 15 to 19	0.14	0.16	0.13
Aged 20 to 24	0.19	0.22	0.16
Aged 25 to 34	0.18	0.17	0.19
Aged 35 to 44	0.26	0.27	0.25
Aged 45 to 54	0.26	0.26	0.25
Aged 55 to 64	0.36	0.38	0.34
Aged 65 to 74	0.52	0.56	0.49
Aged 75 or older	0.85	1.05	0.72
Index of time to average			
Aged 15 or older	**100**	**103**	**94**
Aged 15 to 19	45	52	42
Aged 20 to 24	61	71	52
Aged 25 to 34	58	55	61
Aged 35 to 44	84	87	81
Aged 45 to 54	84	84	81
Aged 55 to 64	116	123	110
Aged 65 to 74	168	181	158
Aged 75 or older	274	339	232

Note: Primary activities are those respondents identified as their main activity. Other activities done simultaneously, such as eating while watching TV, are not included. Travel time is not included in the above figures.
Source: Bureau of Labor Statistics, 2006 American Time Use Survey, Internet site http://www.bls.gov/tus/home.htm; calculations by New Strategist

Table 11.7 Time Spent Participating in Sports, Exercise, or Recreation by Age and Sex, 2006

(hours per day spent participating in sports, exercise, or recreation as a primary activity and index of time to average, by age and sex, 2006)

	total	men	women
Aged 15 or older	**0.28**	**0.38**	**0.18**
Aged 15 to 19	0.61	0.88	0.33
Aged 20 to 24	0.42	0.65	0.20
Aged 25 to 34	0.23	0.29	0.16
Aged 35 to 44	0.23	0.29	0.17
Aged 45 to 54	0.24	0.28	0.21
Aged 55 to 64	0.22	0.31	0.15
Aged 65 to 74	0.25	0.32	0.19
Aged 75 or older	0.18	0.31	0.09
Index of time to average			
Aged 15 or older	**100**	**136**	**64**
Aged 15 to 19	218	314	118
Aged 20 to 24	150	232	71
Aged 25 to 34	82	104	57
Aged 35 to 44	82	104	61
Aged 45 to 54	86	100	75
Aged 55 to 64	79	111	54
Aged 65 to 74	89	114	68
Aged 75 or older	64	111	32

Note: Primary activities are those respondents identified as their main activity. Other activities done simultaneously, such as eating while watching TV, are not included. Travel time is not included in the above figures.
Source: Bureau of Labor Statistics, 2006 American Time Use Survey, Internet site http://www.bls.gov/tus/home.htm; calculations by New Strategist

Table 11.8 Time Spent Playing Games and Using the Computer for Leisure by Age and Sex, 2006

(hours per day spent playing games and using the computer for leisure as primary activities and index of time to average, by age and sex, 2006)

	playing games			leisure computer use		
	total	men	women	total	men	women
Aged 15 or older	**0.18**	**0.24**	**0.13**	**0.14**	**0.18**	**0.10**
Aged 15 to 19	0.45	0.71	0.17	0.34	0.43	0.25
Aged 20 to 24	0.27	0.44	0.09	0.20	0.32	0.07
Aged 25 to 34	0.19	0.30	0.08	0.13	0.16	0.10
Aged 35 to 44	0.10	0.14	0.06	0.11	0.13	0.08
Aged 45 to 54	0.10	0.12	0.09	0.11	0.13	0.09
Aged 55 to 64	0.12	0.10	0.14	0.14	0.18	0.11
Aged 65 to 74	0.16	0.14	0.18	0.12	0.12	0.12
Aged 75 or older	0.28	0.18	0.34	0.07	0.09	0.05
Index of time to average						
Aged 15 or older	**100**	**133**	**72**	**100**	**129**	**71**
Aged 15 to 19	250	394	94	243	307	179
Aged 20 to 24	150	244	50	143	229	50
Aged 25 to 34	106	167	44	93	114	71
Aged 35 to 44	56	78	33	79	93	57
Aged 45 to 54	56	67	50	79	93	64
Aged 55 to 64	67	56	78	100	129	79
Aged 65 to 74	89	78	100	86	86	86
Aged 75 or older	156	100	189	50	64	36

Note: Leisure computer use does not include playing computer games. Playing games includes computer and video games, board games, and card games. Primary activities are those respondents identified as their main activity. Other activities done simultaneously, such as eating while watching TV, are not included. Travel time is not included in the above figures.
Source: Bureau of Labor Statistics, 2006 American Time Use Survey, Internet site http://www.bls.gov/tus/home.htm; calculations by New Strategist

Older Women Spend the Most Time Doing the Laundry

Older men devote the most time to their lawns.

Older Americans, both men and women, spend more time than younger adults doing housework. Women aged 65 to 74 spend the most time doing the laundry and preparing meals, while time spent cleaning the house peaks among women aged 75 or older. Men aged 55 or older spend more than twice as much time as the average person tending their lawns and gardens.

Older people spend more time than younger ones puttering around the house because younger adults are too busy working and raising children to have much time for domestic perfection. The time devoted to caring for household children is above average among women aged 20 to 44 and men aged 25 to 44. As the demands of children ease, pets take up the slack. The time people spend caring for pets rises above average among women aged 35 or older and among men aged 45 or older.

■ Although most women under age 65 are in the labor force, they still spend much more time than men doing housework. Men spend more time at work, however.

Older women spend the most time doing laundry

(indexed average number of hours per day women spend doing laundry as a primary activity, by age, 2006)

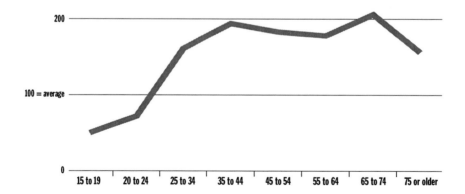

Table 11.9 Time Spent Housecleaning by Age and Sex, 2006

(hours per day spent housecleaning as the primary activity and index of time to average, by age and sex, 2006)

	total	men	women
Aged 15 or older	**0.38**	**0.17**	**0.58**
Aged 15 to 19	0.24	0.16	0.32
Aged 20 to 24	0.29	0.17	0.40
Aged 25 to 34	0.40	0.16	0.63
Aged 35 to 44	0.42	0.17	0.66
Aged 45 to 54	0.36	0.18	0.53
Aged 55 to 64	0.39	0.16	0.60
Aged 65 to 74	0.47	0.24	0.67
Aged 75 or older	0.47	0.14	0.69
Index of time to average			
Aged 15 or older	**100**	**45**	**153**
Aged 15 to 19	63	42	84
Aged 20 to 24	76	45	105
Aged 25 to 34	105	42	166
Aged 35 to 44	111	45	174
Aged 45 to 54	95	47	139
Aged 55 to 64	103	42	158
Aged 65 to 74	124	63	176
Aged 75 or older	124	37	182

Note: Primary activities are those respondents identified as their main activity. Other activities done simultaneously, such as eating while watching TV, are not included. Travel time is not included in the above figures.
Source: Bureau of Labor Statistics, 2006 American Time Use Survey, Internet site http://www.bls.gov/tus/home.htm; calculations by New Strategist

Table 11.10 Time Spent Doing the Laundry by Age and Sex, 2006

(hours per day spent doing the laundry as the primary activity and index of time to average, by age and sex, 2006)

	total	men	women
Aged 15 or older	**0.18**	**0.07**	**0.29**
Aged 15 to 19	0.06	0.03	0.09
Aged 20 to 24	0.09	0.04	0.13
Aged 25 to 34	0.19	0.09	0.29
Aged 35 to 44	0.22	0.07	0.35
Aged 45 to 54	0.20	0.07	0.33
Aged 55 to 64	0.20	0.06	0.32
Aged 65 to 74	0.24	0.10	0.37
Aged 75 or older	0.20	0.07	0.28
Index of time to average			
Aged 15 or older	**100**	**39**	**161**
Aged 15 to 19	33	17	50
Aged 20 to 24	50	22	72
Aged 25 to 34	106	50	161
Aged 35 to 44	122	39	194
Aged 45 to 54	111	39	183
Aged 55 to 64	111	33	178
Aged 65 to 74	133	56	206
Aged 75 or older	111	39	156

Note: Primary activities are those respondents identified as their main activity. Other activities done simultaneously, such as eating while watching TV, are not included. Travel time is not included in the above figures.
Source: Bureau of Labor Statistics, 2006 American Time Use Survey, Internet site http://www.bls.gov/tus/home.htm; calculations by New Strategist

Table 11.11 Time Spent Cooking by Age and Sex, 2006

(hours per day spent in food and drink preparation as the primary activity and index of time to average, by age and sex, 2006)

	total	men	women
Aged 15 or older	**0.40**	**0.23**	**0.55**
Aged 15 to 19	0.10	0.06	0.14
Aged 20 to 24	0.26	0.17	0.35
Aged 25 to 34	0.38	0.19	0.57
Aged 35 to 44	0.45	0.26	0.64
Aged 45 to 54	0.42	0.27	0.57
Aged 55 to 64	0.46	0.27	0.64
Aged 65 to 74	0.52	0.28	0.73
Aged 75 or older	0.51	0.34	0.62
Index of time to average			
Aged 15 or older	**100**	**58**	**138**
Aged 15 to 19	25	15	35
Aged 20 to 24	65	43	88
Aged 25 to 34	95	48	143
Aged 35 to 44	113	65	160
Aged 45 to 54	105	68	143
Aged 55 to 64	115	68	160
Aged 65 to 74	130	70	183
Aged 75 or older	128	85	155

Note: Primary activities are those respondents identified as their main activity. Other activities done simultaneously, such as eating while watching TV, are not included. Travel time is not included in the above figures.
Source: Bureau of Labor Statistics, 2006 American Time Use Survey, Internet site http://www.bls.gov/tus/home.htm; calculations by New Strategist

Table 11.12 Time Spent Cleaning Up in the Kitchen by Age and Sex, 2006

(hours per day spent cleaning up in the kitchen as the primary activity and index of time to average, by age and sex, 2006)

	total	men	women
Aged 15 or older	**0.13**	**0.06**	**0.19**
Aged 15 to 19	0.04	0.02	0.05
Aged 20 to 24	0.06	0.03	0.08
Aged 25 to 34	0.11	0.04	0.18
Aged 35 to 44	0.14	0.06	0.21
Aged 45 to 54	0.13	0.06	0.20
Aged 55 to 64	0.14	0.07	0.20
Aged 65 to 74	0.18	0.07	0.28
Aged 75 or older	0.23	0.15	0.28
Index of time to average			
Aged 15 or older	**100**	**46**	**146**
Aged 15 to 19	31	15	38
Aged 20 to 24	46	23	62
Aged 25 to 34	85	31	138
Aged 35 to 44	108	46	162
Aged 45 to 54	100	46	154
Aged 55 to 64	108	54	154
Aged 65 to 74	138	54	215
Aged 75 or older	177	115	215

Note: Primary activities are those respondents identified as their main activity. Other activities done simultaneously, such as eating while watching TV, are not included. Travel time is not included in the above figures.
Source: Bureau of Labor Statistics, 2006 American Time Use Survey, Internet site http://www.bls.gov/tus/home.htm; calculations by New Strategist

Table 11.13 Time Spent on Lawn, Garden, and Houseplant Care by Age and Sex, 2006

(hours per day spent in lawn, garden, and houseplant care as the primary activity and index of time to average, by age and sex, 2006)

	total	men	women
Aged 15 or older	**0.20**	**0.26**	**0.14**
Aged 15 to 19	0.06	0.11	0.02
Aged 20 to 24	0.03	0.01	0.05
Aged 25 to 34	0.12	0.15	0.09
Aged 35 to 44	0.17	0.22	0.12
Aged 45 to 54	0.22	0.29	0.15
Aged 55 to 64	0.32	0.43	0.21
Aged 65 to 74	0.37	0.52	0.23
Aged 75 or older	0.29	0.44	0.20
Index of time to average			
Aged 15 or older	**100**	**130**	**70**
Aged 15 to 19	30	55	10
Aged 20 to 24	15	5	25
Aged 25 to 34	60	75	45
Aged 35 to 44	85	110	60
Aged 45 to 54	110	145	75
Aged 55 to 64	160	215	105
Aged 65 to 74	185	260	115
Aged 75 or older	145	220	100

Note: Primary activities are those respondents identified as their main activity. Other activities done simultaneously, such as eating while watching TV, are not included. Travel time is not included in the above figures.
Source: Bureau of Labor Statistics, 2006 American Time Use Survey, Internet site http://www.bls.gov/tus/home.htm; calculations by New Strategist

Table 11.14 Time Spent Caring for Household Children by Age and Sex, 2006

(hours per day spent caring for household children as the primary activity and index of time to average, by age and sex, 2006)

	total	men	women
Aged 15 or older	**0.36**	**0.22**	**0.50**
Aged 15 to 19	0.10	0.06	0.13
Aged 20 to 24	0.42	0.09	0.75
Aged 25 to 34	0.87	0.41	1.32
Aged 35 to 44	0.67	0.47	0.87
Aged 45 to 54	0.20	0.19	0.22
Aged 55 to 64	0.06	0.04	0.07
Aged 65 to 74	0.02	0.02	0.02
Aged 75 or older	0.01	0.03	0.00
Index of time to average			
Aged 15 or older	**100**	**61**	**139**
Aged 15 to 19	28	17	36
Aged 20 to 24	117	25	208
Aged 25 to 34	242	114	367
Aged 35 to 44	186	131	242
Aged 45 to 54	56	53	61
Aged 55 to 64	17	11	19
Aged 65 to 74	6	6	6
Aged 75 or older	3	8	0

Note: Primary activities are those respondents identified as their main activity. Other activities done simultaneously, such as eating while watching TV, are not included. Travel time is not included in the above figures.
Source: Bureau of Labor Statistics, 2006 American Time Use Survey, Internet site http://www.bls.gov/tus/home.htm; calculations by New Strategist

Table 11.15 Time Spent on Pet Care by Age and Sex, 2006

(hours per day spent on pet care as the primary activity and index of time to average, by age and sex, 2006)

	total	men	women
Aged 15 or older	**0.09**	**0.07**	**0.10**
Aged 15 to 19	0.06	0.03	0.08
Aged 20 to 24	0.03	0.02	0.03
Aged 25 to 34	0.05	0.04	0.06
Aged 35 to 44	0.08	0.05	0.10
Aged 45 to 54	0.14	0.12	0.16
Aged 55 to 64	0.11	0.11	0.11
Aged 65 to 74	0.11	0.11	0.10
Aged 75 or older	0.11	0.09	0.11
Index of time to average			
Aged 15 or older	**100**	**78**	**111**
Aged 15 to 19	67	33	89
Aged 20 to 24	33	22	33
Aged 25 to 34	56	44	67
Aged 35 to 44	89	56	111
Aged 45 to 54	156	133	178
Aged 55 to 64	122	122	122
Aged 65 to 74	122	122	111
Aged 75 or older	122	100	122

Note: Primary activities are those respondents identified as their main activity. Other activities done simultaneously, such as eating while watching TV, are not included. Travel time is not included in the above figures.
Source: Bureau of Labor Statistics, 2006 American Time Use Survey, Internet site http://www.bls.gov/tus/home.htm; calculations by New Strategist

Young Adults Spend the Most Time on the Phone

The middle aged spend the most time traveling from one activity to another.

The average American travels more than one hour a day, making travel one of the most time-consuming daily activities. Travel time peaks among men aged 25 to 44 at 15 percent above average. Behind the peak traveling time for this group is the commute to work.

It is no surprise that teenagers spend the most time on the telephone as a primary activity. Teenage girls spend more than twice the average amount of time on the phone. Women aged 65 or older also spend more than twice as much time on the phone as the average person. People aged 65 or older spend the most time involved in religious activities.

Time spent grocery shopping peaks among people aged 65 to 74. This is the only age group in which men spend an above-average amount of time in the grocery store.

■ Time spent volunteering is lowest among people aged 25 to 34, when childrearing demands are at a peak.

People aged 65 or older spend the most time involved in religious activities

(indexed average hours per day people spend involved in religious activities as a primary activity, by age, 2006)

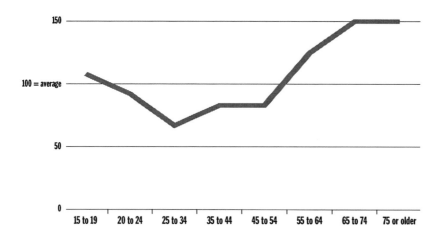

Table 11.16 Time Spent Shopping for Groceries by Age and Sex, 2006

(hours per day spent shopping for groceries as the primary activity and index of time to average, by age and sex, 2006)

	total	men	women
Aged 15 or older	**0.10**	**0.07**	**0.13**
Aged 15 to 19	0.05	0.06	0.05
Aged 20 to 24	0.03	0.02	0.04
Aged 25 to 34	0.10	0.07	0.14
Aged 35 to 44	0.13	0.08	0.17
Aged 45 to 54	0.10	0.05	0.14
Aged 55 to 64	0.10	0.09	0.12
Aged 65 to 74	0.14	0.12	0.16
Aged 75 or older	0.13	0.09	0.15
Index of time to average			
Aged 15 or older	**100**	**70**	**130**
Aged 15 to 19	50	60	50
Aged 20 to 24	30	20	40
Aged 25 to 34	100	70	140
Aged 35 to 44	130	80	170
Aged 45 to 54	100	50	140
Aged 55 to 64	100	90	120
Aged 65 to 74	140	120	160
Aged 75 or older	130	90	150

Note: Primary activities are those respondents identified as their main activity. Other activities done simultaneously, such as eating while watching TV, are not included. Travel time is not included in the above figures.
Source: Bureau of Labor Statistics, 2006 American Time Use Survey, Internet site http://www.bls.gov/tus/home.htm; calculations by New Strategist

Table 11.17 Time Spent Shopping (Except for Food or Gas) by Age and Sex, 2006

(hours per day spent shopping for consumer goods except food or gas as the primary activity and index of time to average, by age and sex, 2006)

	total	men	women
Aged 15 or older	**0.28**	**0.20**	**0.35**
Aged 15 to 19	0.24	0.15	0.33
Aged 20 to 24	0.29	0.14	0.44
Aged 25 to 34	0.29	0.22	0.37
Aged 35 to 44	0.31	0.23	0.39
Aged 45 to 54	0.28	0.18	0.37
Aged 55 to 64	0.28	0.20	0.36
Aged 65 to 74	0.29	0.24	0.33
Aged 75 or older	0.16	0.16	0.16
Index of time to average			
Aged 15 or older	**100**	**71**	**125**
Aged 15 to 19	86	54	118
Aged 20 to 24	104	50	157
Aged 25 to 34	104	79	132
Aged 35 to 44	111	82	139
Aged 45 to 54	100	64	132
Aged 55 to 64	100	71	129
Aged 65 to 74	104	86	118
Aged 75 or older	57	57	57

Note: Primary activities are those respondents identified as their main activity. Other activities done simultaneously, such as eating while watching TV, are not included. Travel time is not included in the above figures.
Source: Bureau of Labor Statistics, 2006 American Time Use Survey, Internet site http://www.bls.gov/tus/home.htm; calculations by New Strategist

Table 11.18 Time Spent Participating in Religious Activities by Age and Sex, 2006

(hours per day spent participating in religious activities as the primary activity and index of time to average, by age and sex, 2006)

	total	men	women
Aged 15 or older	**0.12**	**0.11**	**0.13**
Aged 15 to 19	0.13	0.14	0.13
Aged 20 to 24	0.11	0.13	0.09
Aged 25 to 34	0.08	0.07	0.10
Aged 35 to 44	0.10	0.09	0.12
Aged 45 to 54	0.10	0.08	0.12
Aged 55 to 64	0.15	0.12	0.18
Aged 65 to 74	0.18	0.17	0.19
Aged 75 or older	0.18	0.17	0.19
Index of time to average			
Aged 15 or older	**100**	**92**	**108**
Aged 15 to 19	108	117	108
Aged 20 to 24	92	108	75
Aged 25 to 34	67	58	83
Aged 35 to 44	83	75	100
Aged 45 to 54	83	67	100
Aged 55 to 64	125	100	150
Aged 65 to 74	150	142	158
Aged 75 or older	150	142	158

Note: Primary activities are those respondents identified as their main activity. Other activities done simultaneously, such as eating while watching TV, are not included. Travel time is not included in the above figures.
Source: Bureau of Labor Statistics, 2006 American Time Use Survey, Internet site http://www.bls.gov/tus/home.htm; calculations by New Strategist

Table 11.19 Time Spent Volunteering by Age and Sex, 2006

(hours per day spent volunteering as the primary activity and index of time to average, by age and sex, 2006)

	total	men	women
Aged 15 or older	**0.13**	**0.13**	**0.13**
Aged 15 to 19	0.15	0.18	0.13
Aged 20 to 24	0.06	0.06	0.06
Aged 25 to 34	0.05	0.05	0.06
Aged 35 to 44	0.14	0.12	0.15
Aged 45 to 54	0.16	0.17	0.14
Aged 55 to 64	0.16	0.17	0.16
Aged 65 to 74	0.14	0.12	0.16
Aged 75 or older	0.19	0.20	0.18
Index of time to average			
Aged 15 or older	**100**	**100**	**100**
Aged 15 to 19	115	138	100
Aged 20 to 24	46	46	46
Aged 25 to 34	38	38	46
Aged 35 to 44	108	92	115
Aged 45 to 54	123	131	108
Aged 55 to 64	123	131	123
Aged 65 to 74	108	92	123
Aged 75 or older	146	154	138

Note: Primary activities are those respondents identified as their main activity. Other activities done simultaneously, such as eating while watching TV, are not included. Travel time is not included in the above figures.
Source: Bureau of Labor Statistics, 2006 American Time Use Survey, Internet site http://www.bls.gov/tus/home.htm; calculations by New Strategist

Table 11.20 Time Spent on the Telephone by Age and Sex, 2006

(hours per day spent on the telephone as the primary activity and index of time to average, by age and sex, 2006)

	total	men	women
Aged 15 or older	**0.12**	**0.06**	**0.17**
Aged 15 to 19	0.22	0.15	0.30
Aged 20 to 24	0.12	0.10	0.14
Aged 25 to 34	0.09	0.04	0.13
Aged 35 to 44	0.07	0.03	0.11
Aged 45 to 54	0.10	0.04	0.17
Aged 55 to 64	0.10	0.03	0.17
Aged 65 to 74	0.16	0.05	0.25
Aged 75 or older	0.19	0.09	0.25
Index of time to average			
Aged 15 or older	**100**	**50**	**142**
Aged 15 to 19	183	125	250
Aged 20 to 24	100	83	117
Aged 25 to 34	75	33	108
Aged 35 to 44	58	25	92
Aged 45 to 54	83	33	142
Aged 55 to 64	83	25	142
Aged 65 to 74	133	42	208
Aged 75 or older	158	75	208

Note: Primary activities are those respondents identified as their main activity. Other activities done simultaneously, such as eating while watching TV, are not included.
Source: Bureau of Labor Statistics, 2006 American Time Use Survey, Internet site http://www.bls.gov/tus/home.htm; calculations by New Strategist

Table 11.21 Time Spent Traveling by Age and Sex, 2006

(hours per day spent traveling and index of time to average, by age and sex, 2006)

	total	men	women
Aged 15 or older	**1.24**	**1.28**	**1.21**
Aged 15 to 19	1.20	1.07	1.34
Aged 20 to 24	1.36	1.37	1.35
Aged 25 to 34	1.37	1.42	1.32
Aged 35 to 44	1.38	1.42	1.34
Aged 45 to 54	1.28	1.34	1.22
Aged 55 to 64	1.23	1.26	1.20
Aged 65 to 74	1.00	1.03	0.97
Aged 75 or older	0.73	0.80	0.68
Index of time to average			
Aged 15 or older	**100**	**103**	**98**
Aged 15 to 19	97	86	108
Aged 20 to 24	110	110	109
Aged 25 to 34	110	115	106
Aged 35 to 44	111	115	108
Aged 45 to 54	103	108	98
Aged 55 to 64	99	102	97
Aged 65 to 74	81	83	78
Aged 75 or older	59	65	55

Source: Bureau of Labor Statistics, 2006 American Time Use Survey, Internet site http://www.bls.gov/tus/home.htm; calculations by New Strategist

Older Americans Are Much Less Likely to Be Online

Nearly nine out of ten young adults are connected.

Seventy-one percent of Americans aged 18 or older were Internet users in 2007, up substantially from the 46 percent of 2000, according to surveys by the Pew Internet & American Life Project. Young adults are most likely to use the Internet, 87 percent doing so in 2007. Internet use falls with age. Only 32 percent of people aged 65 or older go online.

Between 2000 and 2007, the percentage of people who use the Internet grew the most—up 29 percentage points—among 50-to-64-year-olds as Boomers moved into the age group. The smallest gain was made by people aged 65 or older, the proportion of people who go online growing by 20 percentage points during those years.

Among people who use the Internet, the percentage who were online yesterday is highest among young adults (74 percent). It is lowest among those aged 65 or older (53 percent).

■ Computer use is now synonymous with going online. The percentage of people with a computer who go online increased from 74 percent in 2000 to 97 percent in 2007.

The oldest Americans are least likely to use the Internet

(percent of people who use the Internet, by age, 2007)

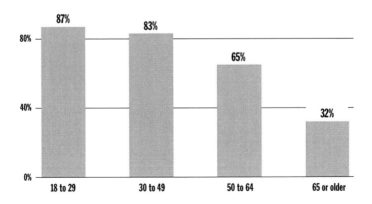

Table 11.22 Internet Use by Age, 2000 and 2007

(percent of people aged 18 or older who use a computer and the Internet, and who used the Internet yesterday, by age, 2000 and 2007; and percentage point change, 2000–07)

	2007	2000	percentage point change
Use a computer			
Total people	73%	62%	11
Aged 18 to 29	88	78	10
Aged 30 to 49	86	74	12
Aged 50 to 64	70	54	16
Aged 65 or older	33	20	13
Use the Internet			
Total people	71	46	25
Aged 18 to 29	87	64	23
Aged 30 to 49	83	56	27
Aged 50 to 64	65	36	29
Aged 65 or older	32	12	20
Were online yesterday			
(of those using the Internet)			
Total people	69	60	9
Aged 18 to 29	74	54	20
Aged 30 to 49	69	62	7
Aged 50 to 64	66	63	3
Aged 65 or older	53	67	–14

Source: Pew Internet & American Life Project, Latest Trends—Usage Over Time, Internet site http://www.pewinternet.org/trends.asp#demographics; calculations by New Strategist

Voting Is Down among All but the Oldest Americans

Older Americans have considerable influence because so many vote.

The older people are, the more likely they are to vote. This has long been true, but the gap between young and old has widened over the years. In the 1972 presidential election (the first in which 18-to-20-year-olds could vote), 63.5 percent of people aged 65 or older voted compared with 49.6 percent of those aged 18 to 24. In the 2004 election, 68.9 percent of people aged 65 or older voted versus only 41.9 percent of people aged 18 to 24—a 27 percentage point difference.

The largest percentage point decline in voting was among people aged 25 to 44. Voting by people in this age group fell 17 percentage points from 1964 to the 2004 elections. The voting rate climbed 3 percentage points among people aged 65 or older during those years.

■ The Swing and World War II generations dominated politics in the United States for decades. Now Boomers are becoming the most powerful generation in politics.

Few young adults vote

(percent of people who voted in the 2004 presidential election, by age)

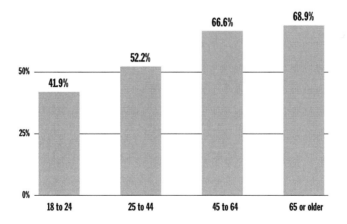

Table 11.23 Voting Rate in Presidential Elections by Age, 1964 to 2004

(percent of people of voting age who reported voting in presidential elections by age, 1964 to 2004; percentage point change for selected years)

	total people of voting age	18 to 24	25 to 44	45 to 64	65 or older
2004	58.3%	41.9%	52.2%	66.6%	68.9%
2000	54.7	32.3	49.8	64.1	67.6
1996	54.2	32.4	49.2	64.4	67.0
1992	61.3	42.8	58.3	70.0	70.1
1988	57.4	36.2	54.0	67.9	68.8
1984	59.9	40.8	58.4	69.8	67.7
1980	59.3	39.9	58.7	69.3	65.1
1976	59.2	42.2	58.7	68.7	62.2
1972	63.0	49.6	62.7	70.8	63.5
1968	67.8	50.4	66.6	74.9	65.8
1964	69.3	50.9	69.0	75.9	66.3
Percentage point change					
2000 to 2004	3.6	9.6	2.4	2.5	1.3
1964 to 2004	−11.0	−9.0	−16.8	−9.3	2.6

Note: Before 1972, data for 18-to-24-year-olds include only 21-to-24-year-olds.
Source: Bureau of the Census, Voting and Registration, Historical Time Series Tables, Internet site http://www.census.gov/population/www/socdemo/voting.html; calculations by New Strategist

Young Adults Dominate Some Religious Groups

Presbyterians and Methodists are much older than Catholics or Baptists.

The religious affiliations of Americans are changing, in large part because younger adults adhere to different religious groups than older adults. The American Religious Identification Survey, taken in 2001 through the efforts of Egon Mayer, Barry A. Kosmin, and Ariela Keysar and sponsored by the Graduate Center of the City University of New York, reveals the differing age distributions of religious groups. In the nationally representative survey, respondents were asked to identify the religious group to which they belonged.

Catholics are by far the most numerous, with an estimated 51 million American adults identifying themselves as belonging to the Catholic Church.

Twenty-four percent of Catholics are aged 18 to 29, 62 percent are aged 30 to 64, and only 14 percent are aged 65 or older. Many religious groups are much older. Fully 35 percent of people who identify themselves as Congregational/UCC are aged 65 or older, as are 30 percent of self-identified Protestants, 29 percent of Presbyterians, and 27 percent of Methodists. At the other extreme, more than half of Muslims and Buddhists are aged 18 to 29. Typically, younger denominations have a greater potential for growth.

■ Twenty-nine million Americans do not identify with any religious group. Among those with no religion, only 8 percent are aged 65 or older.

Mormons are much younger than Methodists

(percent distribution of self-identified Methodists and Mormons, by age, 2001)

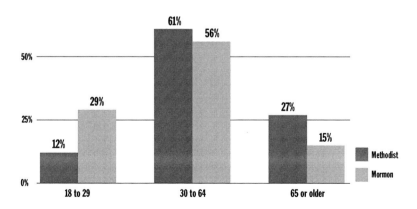

Table 11.24 Age Distribution of Religious Groups, 2001

(total number of adult members of selected religious groups and percent distribution by age, 2001; numbers in thousands)

	number	percent distribution			
		total	18 to 29	30 to 64	65 or older
Total U.S. adults	**208,000**	**100%**	**23%**	**61%**	**16%**
Catholic	50,873	100	24	62	14
Baptist	33,830	100	21	63	16
No religion	29,481	100	35	57	8
Christian	14,190	100	35	58	7
Methodist	14,140	100	12	61	27
Lutheran	9,580	100	15	63	22
Presbyterian	5,596	100	10	61	29
Protestant	4,647	100	13	57	30
Pentecostal	4,407	100	24	67	9
Episcopalian/Anglican	3,451	100	10	62	28
Jewish	2,831	100	14	58	28
Mormon	2,787	100	29	56	15
Churches of Christ	2,503	100	17	58	25
Nondenominational	2,489	100	23	65	12
Congregational/UCC	1,378	100	11	54	35
Jehovah's Witnesses	1,331	100	24	66	10
Assemblies of God	1,105	100	21	69	10
Muslim/Islamic	1,104	100	58	42	–
Buddhist	1,082	100	56	41	3
Evangelical/Born Again	1,032	100	19	72	9
Church of God	944	100	16	65	19
Seventh Day Adventist	724	100	10	64	26

Note: Religious group is self-identified; numbers will not add to total because not all groups are shown. "–" means sample is too small to make a reliable estimate.
Source: The Graduate Center of the City University of New York, American Religious Identification Survey 2001, Egon Mayer, Barry A. Kosmin, and Ariela Keysar, Internet site http://www.gc.cuny.edu/studies/aris_index.htm

12

Wealth

Every three years the federal government surveys the wealth of American households with its Survey of Consumer Finances. The most recent survey results, from 2004, provide a snapshot of household wealth following the dot-com boom, but before the slump in the housing market. That picture is presented in this chapter.

While the numbers will change when the 2007 survey results become available next year, the pattern of wealth accumulation will remain the same. Older householders are wealthier than younger householders, largely because they are more likely to own a home. Homes are the most important asset for the average American household. In 2004, median net worth peaked in the 55-to-64 age group at $248,700. In contrast, the net worth of householders under age 35 was just $14,200. Behind the difference is homeownership. Only 42 percent of householders under age 35 were homeowners in 2004 versus 79 percent of householders aged 55 to 64.

In retirement, older Americans must live off their accumulated wealth—either personal savings or retirement benefits earned through years of work. The disappearance of defined-benefit retirement plans has reduced the wealth of workers, and few are making up the difference through personal savings. Most workers have shockingly little savings. Only 41 percent of workers aged 55 or older have saved $100,000 or more.

What to expect in the future

■ The slump in the housing market, combined with greater mortgage debt, has probably lowered the net worth of Americans regardless of age.

■ With the cost of necessities rising, a shrinking share of workers are participating in employer-sponsored retirement plans. Expect Social Security to be the most important source of income for the largest share of Boomers in retirement.

Net Worth Climbed for 55-to-64-Year-Olds

It fell among householders aged 35 to 44.

Net worth, which is one of the most important measures of wealth, is what remains after a household's debts are subtracted from its assets. The median net worth of householders aged 35 to 44 (Boomers were aged 40 to 58 in 2004) fell a substantial 16 percent between 2001 and 2004, to $69,400. Among householders aged 45 to 54, net worth rose by a small 2 percent to $144,700. Householders aged 55 to 64 saw their net worth rise by a substantial 29 percent, to $248,700, during those years—the biggest gain among age groups.

One reason for the decline in the net worth of 35-to-44-year-olds and the relatively small gain for those aged 45 to 54 is their late arrival to homeownership. Many younger Boomers delayed buying homes as home values rose. When they jumped into the housing market, prices were relatively high, forcing them to take on bigger mortgages. Householders spanning the ages from 35 to 64 saw the median value of their primary residence grow substantially between 2001 and 2004, but the gain was twice as great for householders aged 55 to 64—up 44 percent to $200,000. Householders aged 35 to 54 saw their median home value rise by a smaller 18 to 20 percent. To make matters worse, the 35-to-54 age groups saw their financial assets plummet between 2001 and 2004 because of stock market losses. The 55-to-64 age group was the only one with growing financial assets during those years.

■ Behind the growing net worth of 55-to-64-year-olds is the postponement of retirement, allowing them to accumulate more wealth.

· Householders aged 55 to 64 made the biggest gains between 2001 and 2004

(percent change in net worth of households by age of householder, 2001 to 2004; in 2004 dollars)

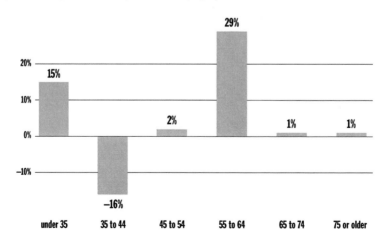

Table 12.1 Net Worth of Households by Age of Householder, 1995 to 2004

(median net worth of households by age of householder, 1995 to 2004; percent change, 1995–2004 and 2001–2004; in 2004 dollars)

	2004	2001	1998	1995	percent change 2001–04	percent change 1995–04
Total households	**$93,100**	**$91,700**	**$83,100**	**$70,800**	**1.5%**	**31.5%**
Under age 35	14,200	12,300	10,600	14,800	15.4	–4.1
Aged 35 to 44	69,400	82,600	73,500	64,200	–16.0	8.1
Aged 45 to 54	144,700	141,600	122,300	116,800	2.2	23.9
Aged 55 to 64	248,700	193,300	148,200	141,900	28.7	75.3
Aged 65 to 74	190,100	187,800	169,800	136,600	1.2	39.2
Aged 75 or older	163,100	161,200	145,600	114,500	1.2	42.4

Source: Federal Reserve Board, Recent Changes in U.S. Family Finances: Evidence from the 2001 and 2004 Survey of Consumer Finances, Federal Reserve Bulletin, February 23, 2006, Internet site http://www.federalreserve.gov/pubs/bulletin/default .htm; calculations by New Strategist

Fewer Boomers Own Stock

Most saw the value of their financial assets decline between 2001 and 2004.

Between 2001 and 2004, the financial assets of the average American household fell 23 percent after adjusting for inflation—to a median of $23,000, according to the Federal Reserve Board's Survey of Consumer Finances. The median financial assets of householders aged 35 to 44 fell 34 percent during those years (to $19,000), and the financial assets of 45-to-54-year-olds fell 20 percent (to $38,600). Householders aged 55 to 64 were the only ones to see their financial assets grow between 2001 and 2004, a 30 percent rise to $78,000. Householders aged 55 to 64 have more financial assets than any other age group.

Slightly fewer than half of households (48.6 percent) owned stock in 2004, down from the 51.9 percent majority in 2001. Stock ownership among householders aged 35 to 54 fell by 5 to 7 percentage points, while ownership among householders aged 55 to 64 climbed by 4.5 percentage points. Regardless of age, stock values fell and stock declined as a share of financial assets.

Only 49.7 percent of all households owned a retirement account in 2004, but among householders aged 35 to 64 the figures were a higher 56 to 63 percent. The median value of the retirement accounts owned by middle-aged householders is modest, ranging from $27,900 among householders aged 35 to 44 to $83,000 among those aged 55 to 64.

■ As stocks lost value, many households invested more in housing.

Financial assets are modest, regardless of age

(median value of financial assets of households by age of householder, 2004)

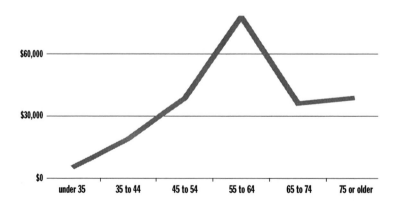

Table 12.2 Financial Assets of Households by Age of Householder, 2001 and 2004

(percentage of households that own financial assets and median value of assets for owners, by age of householder, 2001 and 2004; percentage point change in ownership and percent change in value of asset, 2001–04; in 2004 dollars)

	2004	2001	percentage point change, 2001–04
Percent owning any financial asset			
Total households	**93.8%**	**93.4%**	**0.4**
Under age 35	90.1	89.7	0.4
Aged 35 to 44	93.6	93.5	0.1
Aged 45 to 54	93.6	94.7	–1.1
Aged 55 to 64	95.2	95.0	0.2
Aged 65 to 74	96.5	94.6	1.9
Aged 75 or older	97.6	95.1	2.5

	2004	2001	percent change 2001–04
Median value of financial assets			
Total households	**$23,000**	**$29,800**	**–22.8%**
Under age 35	5,200	6,600	–21.2
Aged 35 to 44	19,000	28,600	–33.6
Aged 45 to 54	38,600	48,000	–19.6
Aged 55 to 64	78,000	59,800	30.4
Aged 65 to 74	36,100	54,700	–34.0
Aged 75 or older	38,800	42,600	–8.9

Source: Federal Reserve Board, Recent Changes in U.S. Family Finances: Evidence from the 2001 and 2004 Survey of Consumer Finances, Federal Reserve Bulletin, February 23, 2006, Internet site http://www.federalreserve.gov/pubs/bulletin/default .htm; calculations by New Strategist

Table 12.3 Financial Assets of Households by Type of Asset and Age of Householder, 2004

(percentage of households that own financial assets, and median value of asset for owners, by type of asset and age of householder, 2004)

	total	under 35	35 to 44	45 to 54	55 to 64	65 to 74	75 or older
Percent owning asset							
Any financial asset	**93.8%**	**90.1%**	**93.6%**	**93.6%**	**95.2%**	**96.5%**	**97.6%**
Transaction accounts	91.3	86.4	90.8	91.8	93.2	93.9	96.4
Certificates of deposit	12.7	5.6	6.7	11.9	18.1	19.9	25.7
Savings bonds	17.6	15.3	23.3	21.0	15.2	14.9	11.0
Bonds	1.8	–	0.6	1.8	3.3	4.3	3.0
Stocks	20.7	13.3	18.5	23.2	29.1	25.4	18.4
Pooled investment funds	15.0	8.3	12.3	18.2	20.6	18.6	16.6
Retirement accounts	49.7	40.2	55.9	57.7	62.9	43.2	29.2
Cash value life insurance	24.2	11.0	20.1	26.0	32.1	34.8	34.0
Other managed assets	7.3	2.9	3.7	6.2	9.4	12.8	16.7
Other financial assets	10.0	11.6	10.0	12.1	7.2	8.1	8.1
Median value of asset							
Any financial asset	**$23,000**	**$5,200**	**$19,000**	**$38,600**	**$78,000**	**$36,100**	**$38,800**
Transaction accounts	3,800	1,800	3,000	4,800	6,700	5,500	6,500
Certificates of deposit	15,000	4,000	10,000	11,000	29,000	20,000	22,000
Savings bonds	1,000	500	500	1,000	2,500	3,000	5,000
Bonds	65,000	–	10,000	30,000	80,000	40,000	295,000
Stocks	15,000	4,400	10,000	14,500	25,000	42,000	50,000
Pooled investment funds	40,400	8,000	15,900	50,000	75,000	60,000	60,000
Retirement accounts	35,200	11,000	27,900	55,500	83,000	80,000	30,000
Cash value life insurance	6,000	3,000	5,000	8,000	10,000	8,000	5,000
Other managed assets	45,000	5,000	18,300	43,000	65,000	60,000	50,000
Other financial assets	4,000	1,000	3,500	5,000	7,000	10,000	22,000

Note: "–" means sample is too small to make a reliable estimate.
Source: Federal Reserve Board, Recent Changes in U.S. Family Finances: Evidence from the 2001 and 2004 Survey of Consumer Finances, Federal Reserve Bulletin, February 23, 2006, Internet site http://www.federalreserve.gov/pubs/bulletin/default .htm; calculations by New Strategist

Table 12.4 Stock Ownership of Households by Age of Householder, 2001 and 2004

(percentage of householders that own stocks directly or indirectly, median value of stock for owners, and share of total household financial assets accounted for by stock holdings, by age of householder, 2001 and 2004; percent and percentage point change, 2001–04; in 2004 dollars)

	2004	2001	percentage point change, 2001–04
Percent owning stock			
Total households	**48.6%**	**51.9%**	**–3.3**
Under age 35	38.8	48.9	–10.1
Aged 35 to 44	52.3	59.5	–7.2
Aged 45 to 54	54.4	59.2	–4.8
Aged 55 to 64	61.6	57.1	4.5
Aged 65 to 74	45.8	39.2	6.6
Aged 75 or older	34.8	34.2	0.6

	2004	2001	percent change 2001–04
Median value of stock			
Total households	**$24,300**	**$36,700**	**–33.8%**
Under age 35	5,200	7,500	–30.7
Aged 35 to 44	12,700	29,300	–56.7
Aged 45 to 54	30,600	53,300	–42.6
Aged 55 to 64	59,500	86,500	–31.2
Aged 65 to 74	75,000	159,800	–53.1
Aged 75 or older	85,900	127,800	–32.8

	2004	2001	percentage point change, 2001–04
Stock as share of financial assets			
Total households	**47.4%**	**56.0%**	**–8.6**
Under age 35	30.0	52.5	–22.5
Aged 35 to 44	47.7	57.3	–9.6
Aged 45 to 54	46.8	59.1	–12.3
Aged 55 to 64	51.1	56.2	–5.1
Aged 65 to 74	51.1	55.2	–4.1
Aged 75 or older	39.1	51.4	–12.3

Source: Federal Reserve Board, Recent Changes in U.S. Family Finances: Evidence from the 2001 and 2004 Survey of Consumer Finances, Federal Reserve Bulletin, February 23, 2006, Internet site http://www.federalreserve.gov/pubs/bulletin/default .htm; calculations by New Strategist

The Nonfinancial Assets of Boomers Have Grown

The rise in housing prices added to the bottom line.

The median value of the nonfinancial assets owned by the average American household stood at $147,800 in 2004, a gain of 22 percent since 2001, after adjusting for inflation. The value of the nonfinancial assets owned by householders aged 35 to 54 rose an average amount—up by 21 to 22 percent during those years. The nonfinancial assets of householders aged 55 to 64 rose twice as fast as average, up 44 percent to $226,300. Householders aged 55 to 64 have more nonfinancial assets than any other age group.

Because housing equity accounts for the largest share of nonfinancial assets, the rise in home values between 2001 and 2004 was the biggest reason for the gains in this category. Among homeowners aged 35 to 64, median home value climbed from 18 to 44 percent between 2001 and 2004, after adjusting for inflation. The homes of householders aged 55 to 64 have the highest median value, at $200,000 in 2004. The value of home-secured debt also rose between 2001 and 2004, however, limiting gains in net worth.

■ The decline in home values in the past few years has probably reduced the net worth of millions of American households.

The nonfinancial assets of Boomers are above average

(median value of nonfinancial assets of households by age of householder, 2004)

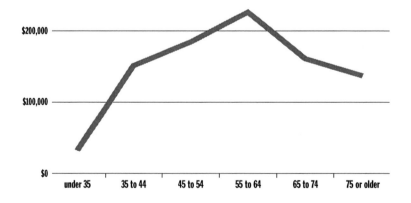

Table 12.5 Nonfinancial Assets of Households by Age of Householder, 2001 and 2004

(percentage of households that own nonfinancial assets and median value of assets for owners, by age of house-holder, 2001 and 2004; percentage point change in ownership and percent change in value of asset, 2001–04; in 2004 dollars)

	2004	2001	percentage point change, 2001–04
Percent owning any nonfinancial asset			
Total households	**92.5%**	**90.7%**	**1.8**
Under age 35	88.6	83.0	5.6
Aged 35 to 44	93.0	93.2	–0.2
Aged 45 to 54	94.7	95.2	–0.5
Aged 55 to 64	92.6	95.4	–2.8
Aged 65 to 74	95.6	91.6	4.0
Aged 75 or older	92.5	86.4	6.1

	2004	2001	percent change 2001–04
Median value of nonfinancial assets			
Total households	**$147,800**	**$120,900**	**22.2%**
Under age 35	32,300	31,700	1.9
Aged 35 to 44	151,300	125,500	20.6
Aged 45 to 54	184,500	150,800	22.3
Aged 55 to 64	226,300	157,500	43.7
Aged 65 to 74	161,100	158,900	1.4
Aged 75 or older	137,100	130,600	5.0

Source: Federal Reserve Board, Recent Changes in U.S. Family Finances: Evidence from the 2001 and 2004 Survey of Consumer Finances, Federal Reserve Bulletin, February 23, 2006, Internet site http://www.federalreserve.gov/pubs/bulletin/default.htm; calculations by New Strategist

Table 12.6 Nonfinancial Assets of Households by Type of Asset and Age of Householder, 2004

(percentage of households that own nonfinancial assets, and median value of asset for owners, by type of asset and age of householder, 2004)

	total	under 35	35 to 44	45 to 54	55 to 64	65 to 74	75 or older
Percent owning asset							
Any nonfinancial asset	**92.5%**	**88.6%**	**93.0%**	**94.7%**	**92.6%**	**95.6%**	**92.5%**
Vehicles	86.3	82.9	89.4	88.8	88.6	89.1	76.9
Primary residence	69.1	41.6	68.3	77.3	79.1	81.3	85.2
Other residential property	12.5	5.1	9.4	16.3	19.5	19.9	9.7
Equity in nonresidential property	8.3	3.3	6.4	11.4	12.8	10.6	7.7
Business equity	11.5	6.9	13.9	15.7	15.8	8.0	5.3
Other nonfinancial assets	7.8	5.5	6.0	9.7	9.2	9.0	8.5
Median value of asset							
Total nonfinancial assets	**$147,800**	**$32,300**	**$151,300**	**$184,500**	**$226,300**	**$161,100**	**$137,100**
Vehicles	14,200	11,300	15,600	18,800	18,600	12,400	8,400
Primary residence	160,000	135,000	160,000	170,000	200,000	150,000	125,000
Other residential property	100,000	82,500	80,000	90,000	135,000	80,000	150,000
Equity in nonresidential property	60,000	55,000	42,200	43,000	75,000	78,000	85,800
Business equity	100,000	50,000	100,000	144,000	190,900	100,000	80,300
Other nonfinancial assets	15,000	5,000	10,000	20,000	25,000	30,000	11,000

Source: Federal Reserve Board, Recent Changes in U.S. Family Finances: Evidence from the 2001 and 2004 Survey of Consumer Finances, Federal Reserve Bulletin, February 23, 2006, Internet site http://www.federalreserve.gov/pubs/bulletin/default .htm; calculations by New Strategist

Table 12.7 Household Ownership of Primary Residence by Age of Householder, 2001 and 2004

(percentage of households that own their primary residence, median value of asset for owners, and median value of home-secured debt for owners, by age of householder, 2001 and 2004; percentage point change in ownership and percent change in value of asset, 2001–04; in 2004 dollars)

	2004	2001	percentage point change, 2001–04
Percent owning primary residence			
Total households	**69.1%**	**67.7%**	**1.4**
Under age 35	41.6	39.9	1.7
Aged 35 to 44	68.3	67.8	0.5
Aged 45 to 54	77.3	76.2	1.1
Aged 55 to 64	79.1	83.2	–4.1
Aged 65 to 74	81.3	82.5	–1.2
Aged 75 or older	85.2	76.2	9.0

	2004	2001	percent change 2001–04
Median value of primary residence			
Total households	**$160,000**	**$131,000**	**22.1%**
Under age 35	135,000	101,200	33.4
Aged 35 to 44	160,000	133,100	20.2
Aged 45 to 54	170,000	143,800	18.2
Aged 55 to 64	200,000	138,500	44.4
Aged 65 to 74	150,000	137,400	9.2
Aged 75 or older	125,000	118,200	5.8

	2004	2001	percent change 2001–04
Median value of home-secured debt			
Total households	**$95,000**	**$74,600**	**27.3%**
Under age 35	107,000	82,000	30.5
Aged 35 to 44	110,000	85,200	29.1
Aged 45 to 54	97,000	79,900	21.4
Aged 55 to 64	83,000	58,600	41.6
Aged 65 to 74	51,000	41,500	22.9
Aged 75 or older	31,000	47,700	–35.0

Source: Federal Reserve Board, Recent Changes in U.S. Family Finances: Evidence from the 2001 and 2004 Survey of Consumer Finances, Federal Reserve Bulletin, February 23, 2006, Internet site http://www.federalreserve.gov/pubs/bulletin/default .htm; calculations by New Strategist

Debt Increased in Every Age Group

The biggest debtors are householders aged 35 to 44.

The debt of the average American household grew by a substantial 34 percent between 2001 and 2004—to $55,300—after adjusting for inflation. Among householders spanning the ages from 35 to 64, debt rose from 30 to 44 percent during those years. Householders aged 35 to 44 continue to be the biggest debtors, owing a median of $87,200 in 2004. Those aged 45 to 54 owe a median of $83,200.

Home-secured debt accounts for the largest share of debt by far. Forty-eight percent of households have home-secured debt, owing a median of $95,000. Householders aged 35 to 44 have the largest amount of home-secured debt ($110,000), while those aged 45 to 54 owe a slightly smaller $97,000, with the amount declining to $83,000 in the 55-to-64 age group. The majority of householders aged 35 to 54 carry a credit card balance, the amount ranging from $2,500 to $2,900. A 42 percent minority of householders aged 55 to 64 owe on their credit cards, with the median amount owed at $2,200.

■ Unless Boomers pay down their mortgage debt, they will not see much growth in their net worth.

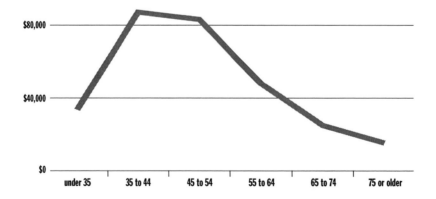

Debt declines with age

(median amount of debt owed by households by age of householder, 2004)

Table 12.8 Debt of Households by Age of Householder, 2001 and 2004

(percentage of households with debt and median amount of debt for debtors, by age of householder, 2001 and 2004; percentage point change in households with debt and percent change in amount of debt, 2001–04; in 2004 dollars)

	2004	2001	percentage point change, 2001-04
Percent with debt			
Total households	**76.4%**	**75.1%**	**1.3**
Under age 35	79.8	82.7	–2.9
Aged 35 to 44	88.6	88.6	0.0
Aged 45 to 54	88.4	84.6	3.8
Aged 55 to 64	76.3	75.4	0.9
Aged 65 to 74	58.8	56.8	2.0
Aged 75 or older	40.3	29.2	11.1

	2004	2001	percent change 2001–04
Median amount of debt			
Total households	**$55,300**	**$41,300**	**33.9%**
Under age 35	33,600	26,500	26.8
Aged 35 to 44	87,200	65,500	33.1
Aged 45 to 54	83,200	57,800	43.9
Aged 55 to 64	48,000	36,900	30.1
Aged 65 to 74	25,000	14,000	78.6
Aged 75 or older	15,400	5,300	190.6

Source: Federal Reserve Board, Recent Changes in U.S. Family Finances: Evidence from the 2001 and 2004 Survey of Consumer Finances, Federal Reserve Bulletin, February 23, 2006, Internet site http://www.federalreserve.gov/pubs/bulletin/default .htm; calculations by New Strategist

Table 12.9 Debt of Households by Type of Debt and Age of Householder, 2004

(percentage of householders with debt, and median value of debt for those with debt, by type of debt and age of householder, 2004)

	total	under 35	35 to 44	45 to 54	55 to 64	65 to 74	75 or older
Percent with debt							
Any debt	**76.4%**	**79.8%**	**88.6%**	**88.4%**	**76.3%**	**58.8%**	**40.3%**
Secured by residential property							
Primary residence	47.9	37.7	62.8	64.6	51.0	32.1	18.7
Other	4.0	2.1	4.0	6.3	5.9	3.2	1.5
Lines of credit not secured by residential property	1.6	2.2	1.5	2.9	0.7	0.4	–
Installment loans	46.0	59.4	55.7	50.2	42.8	27.5	13.9
Credit card balances	46.2	47.5	58.8	54.0	42.1	31.9	23.6
Other debt	7.6	6.2	11.3	9.4	8.4	4.0	2.5
Median amount of debt							
Any debt	**$55,300**	**$33,600**	**$87,200**	**$83,200**	**$48,000**	**$25,000**	**$15,400**
Secured by residential property							
Primary residence	95,000	107,000	110,000	97,000	83,000	51,000	31,000
Other	87,000	62,500	75,000	87,000	108,800	100,000	39,000
Lines of credit not secured by residential property	3,000	1,000	1,900	7,000	14,000	4,000	–
Installment loans	11,500	11,900	12,000	12,000	12,900	8,300	6,700
Credit card balances	2,200	1,500	2,500	2,900	2,200	2,200	1,000
Other debt	4,000	3,000	4,000	4,000	5,500	5,000	2,000

Note: "–" means sample is too small to make a reliable estimate.
Source: Federal Reserve Board, Recent Changes in U.S. Family Finances: Evidence from the 2001 and 2004 Survey of Consumer Finances, Federal Reserve Bulletin, February 23, 2006, Internet site http://www.federalreserve.gov/pubs/bulletin/default .htm; calculations by New Strategist

Retirement Plan Participation Peaks in the 45-to-54 Age Group

Many Americans are worried about economic security in retirement.

Only 40 percent of American workers participated in an employment-based retirement plan in 2006, according to an analysis of government statistics by the Employee Benefit Research Institute (EBRI). Retirement coverage peaks among workers aged 45 to 54, at 50 percent. Among wage and salary workers, those in the private sector are much less likely than public sector workers to participate in a retirement plan, 40 versus 73 percent.

Another EBRI study shows only 40 percent of workers owning either an IRA or participating in a 401(k)-type retirement plan. Even among older workers, the figure is less than 50 percent. With this low level of participation, the percentage of workers receiving pension or annuity income upon retirement may decline. Currently 45 percent of men and 28 percent of women aged 65 or older receive pension or annuity income.

With minimal savings, it is no surprise that many Americans are worried about retirement. Only 18 percent of workers are very confident they will have enough money to live comfortably throughout retirement. Even among workers aged 55 older—those closest to retirement—only 41 percent have saved $100,000 or more.

■ The substitution of defined-contribution for defined-benefit pension plans puts the burden of retirement savings on workers rather than employers. With so many finding it hard to save, millions will be forced to postpone retirement.

The percentage of workers who participate in an employment-based retirement plan peaks in the 45-to-54 age group

(percent of workers aged 25 to 64 who participate in an employer-sponsored retirement plan, by age, 2006)

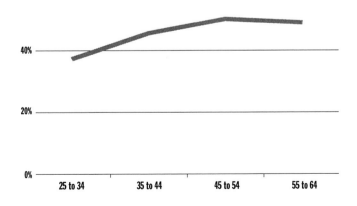

Table 12.10 Retirement Plan Coverage by Age, 2006

(total number of workers, percent whose employer offers a retirement plan, and percent participating in plan, by type of employment and age of worker, 2006; numbers in thousands)

	number of workers	percent with employer that sponsors a retirement plan	percentage of all workers participating in a plan
Total workers	**157,046**	**50.0%**	**39.7%**
Under age 21	10,622	24.6	5.3
Aged 21 to 24	12,810	37.6	19.5
Aged 25 to 34	33,410	49.3	37.3
Aged 35 to 44	35,794	53.6	45.6
Aged 45 to 54	35,939	57.3	50.2
Aged 55 to 64	21,708	56.2	49.0
Aged 65 or older	6,763	38.1	26.0
Private wage and salary workers aged 21 to 64			
Total workers	**109,553**	**50.6%**	**40.3%**
Aged 21 to 24	11,422	35.8	17.7
Aged 25 to 34	27,947	47.3	34.8
Aged 35 to 44	28,096	51.9	43.4
Aged 45 to 54	26,898	56.5	48.4
Aged 55 to 64	15,190	54.8	47.0
Public wage and salary workers aged 21 to 64			
Total workers	**20,784**	**81.8%**	**73.3%**
Aged 21 to 24	1,138	63.5	41.4
Aged 25 to 34	3,979	79.2	67.2
Aged 35 to 44	5,271	82.9	75.8
Aged 45 to 54	6,093	84.0	78.3
Aged 55 to 64	4,303	84.5	77.1

Source: Employee Benefit Research Institute, Employment-Based Retirement Plan Participation: Geographic Differences and Trends, 2006, Issue Brief, No. 311, November 2007; Internet site http://www.ebri.org/

Table 12.11 Ownership of IRAs and Participation in 401(k)s by Age, 2004

(percentage of workers aged 21 to 64 who own IRAs and/or participate in a 401(k)-type plan, by age, 2004)

	IRA and/or 401(k)-type plan	IRA only	401(k)-type plan only	both IRA and 401(k)-type plan	neither IRA nor 401(k)-type plan
Total workers	**40.4%**	**10.2%**	**19.0%**	**11.2%**	**59.6%**
Aged 21 to 24	13.0	3.3	7.9	1.8	87.0
Aged 25 to 34	32.7	6.1	18.8	7.8	67.3
Aged 35 to 44	43.8	9.9	22.1	11.8	56.2
Aged 45 to 54	48.1	12.4	21.0	14.7	51.9
Aged 55 to 64	49.8	18.1	16.7	15.0	50.2

Source: Employee Benefit Research Institute, 401(k)-Type Plans and Individual Retirement Accounts (IRAs), by Craig Copeland, Notes, Vol. 28, No. 10, October 2007; Internet site http://www.ebri.org/

Table 12.12 Pension and Annuity Income Received by People Aged 50 or Older, 2006

(percentage of people aged 50 or older who receive pension or annuity income, and median annual income from pensions and annuities, by sex and age, 2006)

	percentage receiving pensions or annuities	median annual income from pensions/ annuities
Men aged 50 or older	**25.1%**	**$14,280**
Aged 50 to 55	5.5	18,000
Aged 56 to 60	14.8	20,400
Aged 61 to 64	29.5	18,000
Aged 65 or older	44.6	12,108
Aged 65 to 67	37.6	14,400
Aged 68 to 70	41.3	13,200
Aged 71 to 75	47.0	13,020
Aged 76 to 79	46.6	12,000
Aged 80 or older	49.6	10,680
Women aged 50 or older	**17.8**	**7,848**
Aged 50 to 55	3.4	9,600
Aged 56 to 60	12.0	12,000
Aged 61 to 64	18.0	10,670
Aged 65 or older	28.4	7,092
Aged 65 to 67	22.9	9,000
Aged 68 to 70	25.6	9,096
Aged 71 to 75	29.7	6,400
Aged 76 to 79	29.8	6,468
Aged 80 or older	31.1	6,000

Source: Employee Benefit Research Institute, Retirement Annuity and Employment-Based Pension Income, Among Individuals Age 50 and Over: 2006, EBRI Notes, Vol. 29, No. 1, January 2008, Internet site http://www.ebri.org/

Table 12.13 Retirement Planning by Age, 2008

(percentage of workers aged 25 or older responding by age, 2008)

	total	25 to 34	35 to 44	45 to 54	55 or older
Percent very confident in having enough money to live comfortably throughout retirement	18%	18%	16%	21%	18%
Percent very confident in having enough money to take care of medical expenses in retirement	18	20	13	18	23
Worker and/or spouse have saved for retirement	72	60	75	76	79
Worker and/or spouse are currently saving for retirement	64	55	65	69	68
Contribute to a workplace retirement savings plan	61	59	61	65	59
Have an IRA that includes money saved outside of an employer's retirement plan	40	34	38	44	46
Expected retirement age					
Under age 60	11	19	10	10	2
Aged 60 to 64	21	21	18	24	22
Aged 65	24	25	29	23	18
Aged 66 or older	30	21	32	28	38
Never retire	6	6	6	7	8
Don't know/refused	7	6	5	7	11
Expected sources of income in retirement					
Money from a workplace retirement savings plan	74	76	78	74	64
Money from a traditional pension or cash balance plan	59	58	64	58	53
Total savings and investments (not including value of primary residence or defined benefit plans)					
Less than $10,000	36	49	33	29	28
$10,000 to $24,999	13	18	13	11	8
$25,000 to $49,999	12	14	12	13	7
$50,000 to $99,999	12	13	12	10	16
$100,000 to $249,999	15	4	21	18	18
$250,000 or more	12	2	8	20	23

Source: Employee Benefit Research Institute and Mathew Greenwald & Associates, 2008 Retirement Confidence Survey, Internet site http://www.ebri.org/surveys/rcs/2008/

Glossary

adjusted for inflation Income or a change in income that has been adjusted for the rise in the cost of living, or the consumer price index (CPI-U-RS).

American Community Survey The ACS is an on-going nationwide survey of 250,000 households per month, providing detailed demographic data at the community level. Designed to replace the census long-form questionnaire, the ACS includes more than 60 questions that formerly appeared on the long form, such as language spoken at home, income, and education. ACS data are available for areas as small as census tracts.

American Housing Survey The AHS collects national and metropolitan-level data on the nation's housing, including apartments, single-family homes, and mobile homes. The nationally representative survey, with a sample of 55,000 homes, is conducted by the Census Bureau for the Department of Housing and Urban Development every other year.

American Indians In this book, American Indians include Alaska Natives.

American Religious Identification Survey The 2001 ARIS, sponsored by the Graduate Center of the City University of New York, was based on a random telephone survey of 50,281 households in the continental U.S. Interviewers asked respondents aged 18 or older for their demographic characteristics and their religion. The 2001 ARIS updates the 1990 National Survey of Religious Identification.

American Time Use Survey Under contract with the Bureau of Labor Statistics, the Census Bureau collects ATUS information, revealing how people spend their time. The ATUS sample is drawn from U.S. households completing their final month of interviews for the Current Population Survey. One individual from each selected household is chosen to participate in ATUS. Respondents are interviewed by telephone about their time use during the previous 24 hours. About 26,300 households are included in the sample, with 13,300 completed interviews.

Asian The term "Asian" includes Native Hawaiians and other Pacific Islanders unless those groups are shown separately.

Baby Boom Americans born between 1946 and 1964.

Baby Bust Americans born between 1965 and 1976, also known as Generation X.

Behavioral Risk Factor Surveillance System The BRFSS is a collaborative project of the Centers for Disease Control and Prevention and U.S. states and territories. It is an ongoing data collection program designed to measure behavioral risk factors in the adult population aged 18 or older. All 50 states, three territories, and the District of Columbia take part in the survey, making the BRFSS the primary source of information on the health-related behaviors of Americans.

black The black racial category includes those who identified themselves as "black" or "African American."

Consumer Expenditure Survey The CEX is an ongoing study of the day-to-day spending of American households administered by the Bureau of Labor Statistics. The CEX includes an interview survey and a diary survey. The average spending figures shown in this book are the integrated data from both the diary and interview components of the survey. Two separate, nationally representative samples are used for the interview and diary surveys. For the interview survey, about 7,500 consumer units are interviewed on a rotating panel basis each quarter for five consecutive quarters. For the diary survey, 7,500 consumer units keep weekly diaries of spending for two consecutive weeks.

consumer unit *(on spending tables only)* For convenience, the term consumer unit and households are used interchangeably in the spending section of this book, although consumer units are somewhat different from the Census Bureau's households. Consumer units are all related members of a household, or financially independent members of a household. A household may include more than one consumer unit.

Current Population Survey The CPS is a nationally representative survey of the civilian noninstitutional population aged 15 or older. It is taken monthly by the Census Bureau for the Bureau of Labor Statistics, collecting information from more than 50,000 households on employment and unemployment. In March of each year, the survey includes the Annual Social and Economic Supplement (formerly called the Annual Demographic Survey), which is the source of most national data on the characteristics of Americans, such as educational attainment, living arrangements, and incomes.

disability The National Health Interview Survey estimates the number of people aged 18 or older who have difficulty in physical functioning, probing whether respondents could perform nine activities by themselves without using special equipment. The categories are walking a quarter mile; standing for two hours; sitting for two hours; walking up 10 steps without resting; stooping, bending, kneeling; reaching over one's head; grasping or handling small objects; carrying a 10-pound object; and pushing/pulling a large object. Adults who reported that any of these activities was very difficult or they could not do it at all were defined as having physical difficulties.

dual-earner couple A married couple in which both the householder and the householder's spouse are in the labor force.

earnings A type of income, earnings is the amount of money a person receives from his or her job. *See also* Income.

employed All civilians who did any work as a paid employee or farmer/self-employed worker, or who worked 15 hours or more as an unpaid farm worker or in a family-owned business, during the reference period. All those who have jobs but who are temporarily absent from their jobs due to illness, bad weather, vacation, labor management dispute, or personal reasons are considered employed.

expenditure The transaction cost including excise and sales taxes of goods and services acquired during the survey period. The full cost of each purchase is recorded even though full payment may not have been made at the date of purchase. Average expenditure figures may be artificially low for infrequently purchased items such as cars because figures are calculated using all consumer units within a demographic segment rather than just purchasers. Expenditure estimates include money spent on gifts for others.

family A group of two or more people (one of whom is the householder) related by birth, marriage, or adoption and living in the same household.

family household A household maintained by a householder who lives with one or more people related to him or her by blood, marriage, or adoption.

female/male householder A woman or man who maintains a household without a spouse present. May head family or nonfamily households.

foreign-born population People who are not U.S. citizens at birth.

full-time employment Full-time is 35 or more hours of work per week during a majority of the weeks worked.

full-time, year-round Indicates 50 or more weeks of full-time employment during the previous calendar year.

General Social Survey The GSS is a biennial survey of the attitudes of Americans taken by the University of Chicago's National Opinion Research Center (NORC). NORC conducts the GSS through face-to-face interviews with an independently drawn, representative sample of 3,000 to 4,000 noninstitutionalized people aged 18 or older who live in the United States.

Generation X Americans born between 1965 and 1976, also known as the baby-bust generation.

Hispanic Because Hispanic is an ethnic origin rather than a race, Hispanics may be of any race. While most Hispanics are white, there are black, Asian, American Indian, and even Native Hawaiian Hispanics.

household All the persons who occupy a housing unit. A household includes the related family members and all the unrelated persons, if any, such as lodgers, foster children, wards, or employees who share the housing unit. A person living alone is counted as a household. A group of unrelated people who share a housing unit as roommates or unmarried partners is also counted as a household. Households do not include group quarters such as college dormitories, prisons, or nursing homes.

household, race/ethnicity of Households are categorized according to the race or ethnicity of the householder only.

householder The householder is the person (or one of the persons) in whose name the housing unit is owned or rented or, if there is no such person, any adult member. With married couples, the householder may be either the husband or wife. The householder is the reference person for the household.

householder, age of The age of the householder is used to categorize households into age groups such as those used in this book. Married couples, for example, are classified according to the age of either the husband or wife, depending on which one identified him or herself as the householder.

housing unit A housing unit is a house, an apartment, a group of rooms, or a single room occupied or intended for occupancy as separate living quarters. Separate living quarters are those in which the occupants do not live and eat with any other persons in the structure and that have direct access from the outside of the building or through a common hall that is used or intended for use by the occupants of another unit or by the general public. The occupants may be a single family, one person living alone, two or more families living together, or any other group of related or unrelated persons who share living arrangements.

Housing Vacancy Survey The HVS is a supplement to the Current Population Survey, providing quarterly and annual data on rental and homeowner vacancy rates, characteristics of units available for occupancy, and homeownership rates by age, household type, region, state, and metropolitan area. The Current Population Survey sample includes 51,000 occupied housing units and 9,000 vacant units.

housing value The respondent's estimate of how much his or her house and lot would sell for if it were for sale.

immigration The relatively permanent movement (change of residence) of people into the country of reference.

income Money received in the preceding calendar year by each person aged 15 or older from each of the following sources: 1) earnings from longest job or self-employment), 2) earnings from jobs other than longest job, 3) unemployment compensation, 4) workers' compensation, 5) Social Security, 6) Supplemental Security income, 7) public assistance, 8) veterans' payments, 9) survivor benefits, 10) disability benefits, 11) retirement pensions, 12) interest, 13) dividends, 14) rents and royalties or estates and trusts, 15) educational assistance, 16) alimony, 17) child support, 18) financial assistance from outside the household, and other periodic income. Income is reported in several ways in this book. Household income is the combined income of all household members. Income of persons is all income accruing to a person from all sources. Earnings are the money a person receives from his or her job.

job tenure The length of time a person has been employed continuously by the same employer.

labor force The labor force tables in this book show the civilian labor force only. The labor force includes both the employed and the unemployed (people who are looking for work). People are counted as in the labor force if they were working or looking for work during the reference week in which the Census Bureau fields the Current Population Survey.

labor force participation rate The percent of the civilian noninstitutional population that is in the civilian labor force, which includes both the employed and the unemployed.

married couples with or without children under age 18 Refers to married couples with or without own children under age 18 living in the same household. Couples without children under age 18 may be parents of grown children who live elsewhere, or they could be childless couples.

median The median is the amount that divides the population or households into two equal portions: one below and one above the median. Medians can be calculated for income, age, and many other characteristics.

median income The amount that divides the income distribution into two equal groups, half having incomes above the median, half having incomes below the median. The medians for households or families are based on all households or families. The median for persons are based on all persons aged 15 or older with income.

Millennial generation Americans born between 1977 and 1994.

mobility status People are classified according to their mobility status on the basis of a comparison between their place of residence at the time of the March Current Population Survey and their place of residence in March of the previous year. Nonmovers are people living in the same house at the end of the period as at the beginning of the period. Movers are people living in a different house at the end of the period than at the beginning of the period. Movers from abroad are either citizens or aliens whose place of residence is outside the United States at the beginning of the period, that is, in an outlying area under the jurisdiction of the United States or in a foreign country. The mobility status for children is fully allocated from the mother if she is in the household; otherwise it is allocated from the householder.

National Ambulatory Medical Care Survey The NAMCS is an annual survey of visits to nonfederally employed office-based physicians who are primarily engaged in direct patient care. Data are collected from physicians rather than patients, with each physician assigned a one-week reporting period. During that week, a systematic random sample of visit characteristics are recorded by the physician or office staff.

National Health and Nutrition Examination Survey The NHANES is a continuous survey of a representative sample of the U.S. civilian noninstitutionalized population. Respondents are interviewed at home about their health and nutrition, and the interview is followed up by a physical examination that measures such things as height and weight in mobile examination centers.

National Health Interview Survey The NHIS is a continuing nationwide sample survey of the civilian noninstitutional population of the U.S. conducted by the Census Bureau for the National Center for

Statistics. In interviews each year, data are collected from more than 100,000 people about their illnesses, injuries, impairments, chronic and acute conditions, activity limitations, and use of health services.

National Hospital Ambulatory Medical Care Survey The NHAMCS, sponsored by the National Center for Health Statistics, is an annual national probability sample survey of visits to emergency departments and outpatient departments at non-Federal, short stay and general hospitals. Data are collected by hospital staff from patient records.

National Household Education Survey The NHES, sponsored by the National Center for Education Statistics, provides descriptive data on the educational activities of the U.S. population, including after-school care and adult education. The NHES is a system of telephone surveys of a representative sample of 45,000 to 60,000 households in the U.S conducted in 1991, 1993, 1995, 1996, 1999, 2001, 2003, and 2005.

National Survey of Family Growth The 2002 NSFG, sponsored by the National Center for Health Statistics, is a nationally representative survey of the civilian noninstitutionalized population aged 15 to 44. In-person interviews were completed with 12,571 men and women, collecting data on marriage, divorce, contraception, and infertility. The 2002 survey updates previous NSFG surveys taken in 1973, 1976, 1988, and 1995.

National Survey on Drug Use and Health The NS-DUH is an annual survey of a nationally representative sample of more than 68,000 people aged 12 or older living in households, noninstitutional group quarters (such as college dorms), and military bases in the United States. It is the primary source of information about illegal drug use in the United States and has been conducted since 1971. Interviews are held in person and incorporate procedures (such as anonymity and computer-assisted interviewing) that will increase respondents' cooperation and willingness to report honestly about their illicit drug use behavior.

Native Hawaiian and other Pacific Islander The 2000 census identified this group for the first time as a separate racial category from Asians. In most survey data, however, the population is included with Asians.

nonfamily household A household maintained by a householder who lives alone or who lives with people to whom he or she is not related.

nonfamily householder A householder who lives alone or with nonrelatives.

non-Hispanic People who do not identify themselves as Hispanic are classified as non-Hispanic. Non-Hispanics may be of any race.

non-Hispanic white People who identify their race as white and who do not indicate a Hispanic origin.

occupation Occupational classification is based on the kind of work a person did at his or her job during the previous calendar year. If a person changed jobs during the year, the data refer to the occupation of the job held the longest during that year.

occupied housing units A housing unit is classified as occupied if a person or group of people is living in it or if the occupants are only temporarily absent—on vacation, example. By definition, the count of occupied housing units is the same as the count of households.

own children Own children are sons and daughters, including stepchildren and adopted children, of the householder. The totals include never-married children living away from home in college dormitories.

owner occupied A housing unit is "owner occupied" if the owner lives in the unit, even if it is mortgaged or not fully paid for. A cooperative or condominium unit is "owner occupied" only if the owner lives in it. All other occupied units are classified as "renter occupied."

part-time employment Part-time is less than 35 hours of work per week in a majority of the weeks worked during the year.

percent change The change (either positive or negative) in a measure that is expressed as a proportion of the starting measure. When median income changes from $20,000 to $25,000, for example, this is a 25 percent increase.

percentage point change The change (either positive or negative) in a value which is already expressed as a percentage. When a labor force participation rate changes from 70 percent of 75 percent, for example, this is a 5 percentage point increase.

poverty level The official income threshold below which families and people are classified as living in poverty. The threshold rises each year with inflation and varies depending on family size and age of householder.

proportion or share The value of a part expressed as a percentage of the whole. If there are 4 million people aged 25 and 3 million of them are white, then the white proportion is 75 percent.

race Race is self-reported and can be defined in three ways. The "race alone" population comprises people who identify themselves as only one race. The "race in combination" population comprises people who identify themselves as more than one race, such as white and black. The "race, alone or in combination" population includes both those who identify themselves as one race and those who identify themselves as more than one race.

regions The four major regions and nine census divisions of the United States are the state groupings as shown below:

Northeast:
—*New England:* Connecticut, Maine, Massachusetts, New Hampshire, Rhode Island, and Vermont
—*Middle Atlantic:* New Jersey, New York, and Pennsylvania

Midwest:
—*East North Central:* Illinois, Indiana, Michigan, Ohio, and Wisconsin
—*West North Central:* Iowa, Kansas, Minnesota, Missouri, Nebraska, North Dakota, and South Dakota

South:
—*South Atlantic:* Delaware, District of Columbia, Florida, Georgia, Maryland, North Carolina, South Carolina, Virginia, and West Virginia
—*East South Central:* Alabama, Kentucky, Mississippi, and Tennessee
—*West South Central:* Arkansas, Louisiana, Oklahoma, and Texas

West:
—*Mountain:* Arizona, Colorado, Idaho, Montana, Nevada, New Mexico, Utah, and Wyoming
—*Pacific:* Alaska, California, Hawaii, Oregon, and Washington

renter occupied *See* Owner occupied.

Retirement Confidence Survey The RCS, sponsored by the Employee Benefit Research Institute and Mathew Greenwald & Associates, is an annual survey of a nationally representative sample of 1,000 people aged 25 or older. Respondents are asked a core set of questions that have been asked since 1996, measuring attitudes and behavior towards retirement. Additional questions are also asked about current retirement issues such as 401(k) participation.

rounding Percentages are rounded to the nearest tenth of a percent; therefore, the percentages in a distribution do not always add exactly to 100.0 percent. The totals, however, are always shown as 100.0. Moreover, individual figures are rounded to the nearest thousand without being adjusted to group totals, which are independently rounded; percentages are based on the unrounded numbers.

self-employment A person is categorized as self-employed if he or she was self-employed in the job held longest during the reference period. Persons who report self-employment from a second job are excluded, but those who report wage-and-salary income from a second job are included. Unpaid workers in family businesses are excluded. Self-employment statistics include only nonagricultural workers and exclude people who work for themselves in incorporated business.

sex ratio The number of men per 100 women.

Survey of Consumer Finances The Survey of Consumer Finances is a triennial survey taken by the Federal Reserve Board. It collects data on the assets, debts, and net worth of American households. For the 2004 survey, the Federal Reserve Board interviewed a representative sample of 4,522 households.

unemployed Unemployed people are those who, during the survey period, had no employment but were available and looking for work. Those who were laid off from their jobs and were waiting to be recalled are also classified as unemployed.

white The "white" racial category includes many Hispanics (who may be of any race) unless the term "non-Hispanic white" is used.

Youth Risk Behavior Surveillance System The YRBSS was created by the Centers for Disease Control to monitor health risks being taken by young people at the national, state, and local level. The national survey is taken every two years based on a nationally representative sample of 16,000 students in 9th through 12th grade in public and private schools.

Bibliography

Bureau of Labor Statistics
    Internet site http://www.bls.gov
    —2006 American Time Use Survey, Internet site http://www.bls.gov/tus/home.htm
    —2006 Consumer Expenditure Survey, Internet site http://www.bls.gov/cex/home.htm
    —2007 Current Population Survey, Internet site http://www.bls.gov/cps/home.htm
    —Characteristics of Minimum Wage Workers: 2006, Internet site http://www.bls.gov/cps/minwage2006.htm
    —Contingent and Alternative Employment Arrangements, February 2005, Internet site http://www.bls.gov/news.release/conemp.toc.htm
    —Employee Tenure, Internet site http://www.bls.gov/news.release/tenure.toc.htm
    —Employment Characteristics of Families, Internet site http://www.bls.gov/news.release/famee.toc.htm
    —"Labor force projections to 2016: more workers in their golden years," *Monthly Labor Review*, November 2007, Internet site http://www.bls.gov/opub/mlr/2007/11/contents.htm
    —Public Query Data Tool, Internet site http://www.bls.gov/data
    —Workers on Flexible and Shift Schedules, Internet site http://www.bls.gov/news.release/flex.toc.htm

Bureau of the Census
    Internet site http://www.census.gov/
    —2000 Census, American FactFinder, Internet site http://factfinder.census.gov/home/saff/main.html?_lang=en
    —2006 American Community Survey, Internet site http://factfinder.census.gov/home/saff/main.html?_lang=en
    —2007 Current Population Survey Annual Social and Economic Supplement, Detailed Income Tabulations from the CPS, Internet site http://www.census.gov/hhes/www/income/dinctabs.html
    —2007 Current Population Survey Annual Social and Economic Supplement, Detailed Poverty Tabulations from the CPS, Internet site http://www.census.gov/hhes/www/income/dinctabs.html
    —Age: 2000, *2000 Census Brief*, C2KBR/01-12, 2001
    —American Housing Survey for the United States: 2005, Internet site http://www.census.gov/hhes/www/housing/ahs/ahs05/ahs05.html
    —America's Families and Living Arrangements: 2006, Detailed Tables, Internet site http://www.census.gov/population/www/socdemo/hh-fam/cps2006.html

—America's Families and Living Arrangements, Historical Time Series, Internet site http://www.census.gov/population/www/socdemo/hh-fam.html
—Educational Attainment in the United States: 2006, detailed tables, Internet site http://www.census.gov/population/www/socdemo/education/cps2006.html
—Fertility of American Women, Historical Tables, Internet site http://www.census.gov/population/www/socdemo/fertility.html
— Geographic Mobility: 2005 to 2006, Detailed Tables, Internet site http://www.census.gov/population/www/socdemo/migrate/cps2006.html
—Health Insurance Tables, Internet site http://pubdb3.census.gov/macro/032007/health/toc.htm
—Historical income data, Current Population Survey Annual Demographic Supplements, Internet site http://www.census.gov/hhes/income/histinc/histinctb.html
—Historical poverty data, Current Population Survey Annual Demographic Supplements, Internet site http://www.census.gov/hhes/income/histinc/histpovtb.html
—*Historical Statistics of the United States, Colonial Times to 1970*, Part 1, 1975
—Housing Vacancy Surveys, Internet site http://www.census.gov/hhes/www/housing/hvs/hvs.html
—Number, Timing, and Duration of Marriages and Divorces: 2004, Detailed Tables, Internet site http://www.census.gov/population/www/socdemo/marr-div/2004detailed_tables.html
—Population Estimates, Internet site http://www.census.gov/popest/estimates.php
—School Enrollment, Historical Tables, Internet site http://www.census.gov/population/www/socdemo/school.html
—School Enrollment—Social and Economic Characteristics of Students: October 2005, detailed tables, Internet site http://www.census.gov/population/www/socdemo/school/cps2005.html
—*Statistical Abstract of the United States*, Internet site http://www.census.gov/compendia/statab/
—U.S. Interim Projections by Age, Sex, Race, and Hispanic Origin, Internet site http://www.census.gov/ipc/www/usinterimproj/
—Voting and Registration, Historical Time Series Tables, Internet site http://www.census.gov/population/www/socdemo/voting.html

Centers for Disease Control and Prevention
Internet site http://www.cdc.gov
—Behavioral Risk Factor Surveillance System, Prevalence Data, Internet site http://www.apps.nccd.cdc.gov/brfss/
—"Youth Risk Behavior Surveillance—United States, 2005," *Morbidity and Mortality Weekly Report*, Surveillance Summaries, Vol. 55/SS-5, June 9, 2006 Internet site http://www.cdc.gov/HealthyYouth/yrbs/index.htm

Department of Homeland Security

Internet site http://www.dhs.gov

— 2006 Yearbook of Immigration Statistics, Internet site http://www.dhs.gov/ximgtn/statistics/publications/LPR06.shtm

Employee Benefit Research Institute

Internet site http://www.ebri.org/

—"401(k)-Type Plan and Individual Retirement Accounts (IRAs)," Craig Copeland, *EBRI Notes*, Vol. 28, No. 10, October 2007, Internet site http://www.ebri.org/

— "Employment-Based Retirement Plan Participation: Geographic Differences and Trends, 2006," *Issue Brief*, No. 311, November 2007; Internet site http://www.ebri.org/

— "Retirement Annuity and Employment-Based Pension Income, Among Individuals Age 50 and Over: 2006," *EBRI Notes*, Vol. 29, No. 1, January 2008, Internet site http://www.ebri.org/

Employee Benefit Research Institute and Mathew Greenwald & Associates

Internet site http://www.ebri.org/

—2008 Retirement Confidence Survey, Internet site http://www.ebri.org/surveys/rcs/2008/

Federal Reserve Board

Internet site http://www.federalreserve.gov/pubs/oss/oss2/scfindex.html

—"Recent Changes in U.S. Family Finances: Evidence from the2001 and 2004 Survey of Consumer Finances," *Federal Reserve Bulletin*, February 23, 2006, Internet site http://www.federalreserve.gov/pubs/bulletin/default.htm

Graduate Center of the City University of New York

Internet site http://www.gc.cuny.edu/index.htm

—American Religious Identification Survey 2001, Internet site http://www.gc.cuny.edu/faculty/research_briefs/aris/aris_index.htm

National Center for Education Statistics

Internet site http://nces.ed.gov

—Adult Education and Lifelong Learning Survey of the National Household Education Surveys Program, Internet site http://nces.ed.gov/pubs2006/adulted/tables.asp

—Projections of Education Statistics to 2016, Internet site http://nces.ed.gov//programs/projections/

National Center for Health Statistics

Internet site http://www.cdc.gov/nchs

—*Ambulatory Medical Care Utilization Estimates for 2005*, Advance Data, No. 388, 2007, Internet site http://www.cdc.gov/nchs/about/major/ahcd/adata.htm#CombinedReports

—Births: Final Data for 2004, National Vital Statistics Reports, Vol. 55, No. 1, 2006, Internet site http://www.cdc.gov/nchs/births.htm

—Births: Preliminary Data for 2006, National Vital Statistics Reports, Vol. 56, No. 7, 2007, Internet site http://www.cdc.gov/nchs/births.htm

—Deaths: Final Data for 2004, National Vital Statistics Reports, Vol. 55, No. 19, 2007, Internet site http://www.cdc.gov/nchs/deaths.htm

— Deaths: Leading Causes for 2004, National Vital Statistics Reports, Vol. 56, No. 5, 2007, Internet site http://www.cdc.gov/nchs/deaths.htm

—Health, United States, 2007, Internet site http://www.cdc.gov/nchs/hus.htm

—Mean Body Weight, Height, and Body Mass Index, United States 1960–2002, Advance Data, No. 347, 2004, Internet site http://www.cdc.gov/nchs/pressroom/04news/americans.htm

—Summary Health Statistics for the U.S. Population: National Health Interview Survey, 2006, Series 10, No. 236, 2007, Internet site http://www.cdc.gov/nchs/nhis.htm

—Summary Health Statistics for U.S. Adults: National Health Interview Survey, 2006, Series 10, No. 235, 2007, Internet site http://www.cdc.gov/nchs/nhis.htm

—Summary Health Statistics for U.S. Children: National Health Interview Survey, 2006, Series 10, No. 234, 2007, Internet site http://www.cdc.gov/nchs/nhis.htm

—Use of Contraception and Use of Family Planning Services in the United States: 1982–2002, Advance Data, No. 350, 2004, Internet site http://www.cdc.gov/nchs/nsfg.htm

Pew Internet & American Life Project
Internet site http://www.pewinternet.org
—Latest Trends—Usage Over Time, Internet site http://www.pewinternet.org/trends.asp#demographics

Substance Abuse and Mental Health Services Administration
Internet site http://www.samhsa.gov
—National Survey on Drug Use and Health, 2006, Internet site http://oas.samhsa.gov/nsduh.htm

Survey Documentation and Analysis, University of California—Berkeley
Internet site http://sda.berkeley.edu
—General Social Surveys Cumulative Data File, 1972–2006, Internet site http://sda.berkeley.edu/cgi-bin32/hsda?harcsda+gss06

Index

obesity. *See* Weight.
occupation, 232–235
online, 419–420
overweight. *See* Weight.

Parkinson's disease, as cause of death, 141–142
pensions. *See also* Personal insurance and pensions,
      spending on.
    as source of income, 209–210
    expected in retirement, 442
    income from, 439, 441
people living alone
    by sex, 263–265, 269, 271, 291–295
    homeownership, 159–160
    housing costs, 175–176
    housing value, 173–174
    income of, 197–202
personal care activities, time spent, 394–395
personal care products and services, spending on,
    358–392
personal insurance and pensions, spending on,
    358–392
personal taxes, spending on, 358–392
pets, time spent caring for, 404, 411
physical activity, 96–97, 119
physician visits, 136–137
place of birth, 317–318
pneumonia and influenza, as cause of death,
    141–149
political leanings, 45–46
population
    by place of birth, 317–318
    by race and Hispanic origin, 311–314, 324–332,
        338–355
    by region, 320–332
    by sex, 309–310
    by state, 333–355
    historical, 306–307
    mobility of, 154–156
    projections, 315–316
poverty status
    by race and Hispanic origin, 214–215
    by sex, 211, 213
    historical, 211–212
    of workers, 216–217
premarital sex, attitude toward, 40–41
Presbyterian religion, 423–424
prescription medications. *See* Drugs, prescription.
projections
    of college enrollment, 73–74
    of labor force, 256–257
    of population, 315–316
public assistance, as source of income, 209–210

race. *See* individual race/Hispanic origin groups.
reading
    newspapers, 34–35
    spending on, 358–392
    time spent, 397, 400
recreational activities, time spent in, 394–395,
    397–403
region
    educational attainment by, 60–61
    homeownership, 166–168
    households, 284–286
    moving to different, 155–156
    population by, 320–332
relaxing, time spent, 401
religious activities, time spent in, 395, 412, 415
religious preferences, 423–424
renters. *See* Homeownership status.
rents, royalties, estates, trusts, as source of income,
    210
respiratory disease
    as cause of death, 141–145, 147–149
    as chronic condition, 123–125, 128–131
retirement
    accounts, as financial asset, 428, 430
    attitude toward, 439, 442
    expected age of, 439, 442
    plan coverage, 439–440

savings, 439, 442
savings, 439, 442
savings bonds, as financial asset, 430
school enrollment, 62–65. *See also* College
    enrollment and Educational attainment.
science, attitude toward, 36–37
self-employment, 250–253
septicemia, as cause of death, 141–144, 146–148
sex
    homosexuality, attitude toward, 40, 42
    ratio, 309–310
    roles, attitude toward, 40–41
    premarital, 40–41
shopping, time spent, 412–414
single-family detached homes, 169–172
single parents, 287–288. *See also* Households, family,
    female-headed and male-headed.
single-person households. *See* People living alone.
sinusitis, 123–125
sleeping, time spent, 396
smoking. *See* Cigarette smoking and Tobacco
    products.
Social Security, as source of income, 209–210
socializing, time spent, 397, 399
South. *See* Regions.
sports, time spent participating in, 397, 402